BELIEVING IN GLOUCESTER

The inside story of a city's regeneration

Paul James

To Caz,

Best wishes,

Paul James

Copyright © 2024 Paul James

All rights reserved

No part of this book may be reproduced, or stored in a retrieval system, or transmitted in any form or by any means, electronic, mechanical, photocopying, recording, or otherwise, without express written permission of the publisher.

Much of this book has been written on the basis of researching publicly-available information or by interviewing people directly involved in the events it covers. Some of it is based on the author's own experiences, memories and opinions. It is recognised that, in some cases, "recollections may vary".

Every effort has been made to trace copyright holders. If you are concerned that any image in this book has been used without permission, please contact the author on gloucesterpaul@gmail.com.

ISBN-13: 9798867681012

To Charlotte, Eirys and Tydwen, who have put up with me researching, writing and refining this book for well over three years.

Front cover photos (clockwise from top left): 1. Warehouses at Gloucester Docks and the new Merchants Quay building. 2. The opening of the new Gloucester Transport Hub. (Credit: Gloucester City Council) 3. Kings Square before refurbishment work. 4. The former E&J Printers building on the corner of Commercial Road and Ladybellegate Street. (Credit: Paul Dowle) 5. The outlet centre and Travelodge hotel at Gloucester Quays. 6. Gloucester Cathedral after phase one of Project Pilgrim has been completed. (Credit: Gloucester Cathedral)

The phrase 'Believe in Gloucester', which has been used for a promotional campaign and adopted for awards to celebrate all that is positive in the city, was coined by Peel Group Chairman, John Whittaker. He commented, when agreeing a huge new investment in the city, "I believe in Gloucester".

BELIEVING IN GLOUCESTER

1. Prologue
2. Introduction
3. Not Exactly Plain Sailing (Gloucester Docks)
4. University Challenge (The University of Gloucestershire)
5. Breaking the 'Curse of Blackfriars' (Blackfriars)
6. From BSE to B&Q (The Cattle Market/St Oswalds)
7. Repent at Leisure (Rebuilding Gloucester Leisure Centre)
8. Heartbreak Hotels
9. The GHURC Years
10. Determination, Persistence and Patience (The Story of Gloucester Quays)
11. Turning an Idea into Something Concrete (Kings Square/Kings Quarter)
12. Bringing History to Life
13. The Dirty Dozen
14. Water, Water Everywhere (The Floods of 2007)
15. Events, Dear Boy, Events
16. Sacred Space and Common Ground (Gloucester Cathedral)
17. Rugby and Regeneration
18. Football's Coming Home
19. Putting Gloucester on the Map
20. A Balanced Approach
21. Leadership and Delivery
22. Unfinished Business
23. A Tale of Two Cities
24. Personal Reflections
25. Regeneration Timeline

GLOSSARY

BT – Telecommunications company formerly known as British Telecom until 1991.

BID – Business Improvement District – a defined area, often a town or city centre, where a small levy is added to business rate bills to fund activities to support businesses in that area, following approval in a ballot of businesses eligible to pay the levy.

BWB – British Waterways Board – Often shortened to 'British Waterways'. The organisation responsible for maintaining the nation's canal network and a number of rivers and docks. Became the Canals and Rivers Trust in 2012.

CABE – The Commission for Architecture and the Built Environment – The successor to RFAC (see below), charged with promoting high standards of design and architecture.

CGCHE – The Cheltenham and Gloucester College of Higher Education – The predecessor to the University of Gloucestershire.

CPO – Compulsory Purchase Order - A legal function that allows certain bodies to obtain land or property without the consent of the owner.

CRT – The Canals and Rivers Trust – The successor to British Waterways (see above).

English Heritage – Originally a government body responsible for the national system of heritage protection which also managed a range of historic properties. In 2015, it was divided into two organisations – **Historic England**, which inherited the protection functions, and a new charity, English Heritage Trust, which manages the historic properties.

Full Planning Permission – When the full details of a development proposal are submitted for consideration and approved. The phrases 'planning permission' and 'planning consent' are used interchangeably.

GAMPA – Gloucestershire Academy for Music and the Performing Arts – A local music and performing arts group who were the driving force behind NYCPA (see next page).

GCH – Gloucester City Homes – Now a housing association, it was formed to manage the housing stock of Gloucester City Council. Ownership was transferred to GCH in 2015.

GHURC – Gloucester Heritage Urban Regeneration Company – An organisation set up with government support to bring about the regeneration of the city. It ran between 2004 and 2012. Sometimes this is abbreviated to simply 'the URC'.

GlosCAT – Gloucestershire College of Arts and Technology – The County's main further education college, later renamed Gloucestershire College (Gloscol).

GMA – Gloucester Market Auctioneers – A company jointly owned by local firms Bruton Knowles and Pearce Pope, which ran Gloucester's livestock market.

HCA – The Homes and Communities Agency – Formed from the merger of English Partnerships and the Housing Corporation, a government agency charged with delivering regeneration and new homes. Later renamed **Homes England**.

HEFCE – The Higher Education Funding Council for England – The body responsible for distributing funds to universities and higher education colleges.

HLF – Heritage Lottery Fund – The body responsible for distributing funds from the National Lottery relating to heritage projects. Later renamed the **National Lottery Heritage Fund (NLHF)**.

LEP – Local Enterprise Partnership – LEPs are voluntary partnerships between local authorities and businesses, set up in 2011 by the Government to help determine local economic priorities and lead economic growth and job creation within the local area. They carry out some of the functions previously held by the regional development agencies which were abolished in March 2012. Gloucestershire's LEP was known as GFirst.

LDO – Local Development Order – LDOs provide permitted development rights for specific types of development in defined locations. They are designed to help accelerate the delivery of appropriate development in those places.

LSC – Learning and Skills Council – A government agency responsible for planning and funding further education.

NYCPA – National Youth Centre for Performing Arts – A proposal for a new performing arts facility at Gloucester Docks in the 1990s.

Outline Planning Consent - A decision on the general principles of how a site can be developed. Outline planning permission is granted subject to conditions requiring the subsequent approval of one or more 'reserved matters'. Sometimes the approval of reserved matters is described as a 'detailed planning consent'.

Peel Group – A North West-based property company founded by John Whittaker, which developed Gloucester Quays. At other times referred to as Peel Holdings. The company operating the Gloucester Quays outlet centre was Peel Outlets, later known as Lifestyle Outlets.

RFAC – The Royal Fine Arts Commission – An organisation set up to promote excellence in design and architecture. Succeeded by CABE (see earlier in the Glossary).

Section 106 agreement – A legal agreement between a developer and a local planning authority designed to secure contributions to community infrastructure to mitigate the effects of a development.

SWRDA or RDA – South West Regional Development Agency – A government agency set up by the 1997-2010 Labour Government, designed to promote regional economic growth.

The Citizen – Gloucester's newspaper, which was published daily until 2016 when it was reduced to a single, weekly edition which runs alongside the *GloucestershireLive* website.

UWE – The University of the West of England – Previously Bristol Polytechnic.

University Title – Formal approval to use the word 'university', which is protected in law.

1. PROLOGUE

Some time ago, I decided that when I stood down from the City Council, and no longer had official duties filling up my diary, one of the tasks I would undertake was to write up an account of Gloucester's regeneration over the last 25 years or so. The first lockdown in Spring 2020 gave me an opportunity to start slightly earlier than I'd anticipated.

The reasons for wanting to do this were threefold. Firstly, for the sake of posterity – so others can look back in the future and understand what happened (and what didn't happen) and why. Secondly, so we can learn lessons from what those in positions of influence got right and, inevitably, what they could or should have done differently – me included. Hopefully this will spur on those in power today to finish the job. And, finally, because, with all the twists and turns, the colourful characters involved, the triumphs and the setbacks, I actually think it is a fascinating and compelling story. I hope that once you have finished reading this book you will share that view.

I believed that it was something worth researching and writing, for all of those reasons, and I concluded that if anyone was going to do it, it may as well be me. I was involved directly in a good deal of it – but by no means all of it. But I reckoned I knew enough of the people who were involved in those chapters and projects where I hadn't been, in order to be able to piece it together.

It hasn't been easy to put together the pieces of a complex jigsaw spanning an entire generation. In doing so, I have drawn on my own knowledge and my collection of documents retained from my 24 years on the City Council, as well as my lever arch files full of carefully-catalogued press cuttings from my time in local politics. I knew they'd come in handy one day!

I've spent numerous hours researching online – a process slightly hampered by the cyber-attack on the City Council's website in December 2021 which disabled access to both old committee reports and planning applications. Thankfully, I'd done most of my research before the hackers struck. I also spent many hours in the Gloucestershire Heritage Hub in Alvin Street, Gloucester, where the staff were patient and helpful. This involved leafing through old documents and scrolling through microfilm back copies of *The Citizen*.

I've also interviewed well over 100 people who were involved in one way or another - and some of these were on multiple occasions. The interviews were an enjoyable way of reconnecting with old friends and colleagues during some of the darker times of the Covid pandemic. I am grateful to everyone who gave their time so freely - and those who provided information in response to my emails.

Filling in some of the gaps has been tricky. Over time, memories fade and recollections vary. Most of the people I wanted to speak to, I've been able to. Some have long since left Gloucester and the positions they once held and, no doubt deliberately, have managed to evade the otherwise all-pervasive reach of Google. A few haven't wanted to speak, because the memories were painful for them of times when things went wrong or, in some instances, they had doubts about my motives. They really needn't have worried about the latter.

Lots of old documents which would have helped my research were no doubt shredded in the move to the much-vaunted 'paperless office' – something which is particularly unfortunate given the aforementioned cyber-attack. But we are where we are. Whenever I drew a blank on my research, the members of the Facebook groups 'Our History – Gloucester' and 'Gloucester: A Trip Back in Time' usually provided the answer – a great example of the positive power of social media. My thanks to them all.

I'd also like to thank my (small) army of fact-checkers for the particularly complex chapters and my team of proof-readers – made up of my good friend Mhairi Smith, my Mum Jackie Pritchard and my brother-in-law Lewis Cook. Thanks to my best friend Matt Cass for his expertise in uploading the text to the Amazon publishing platform. My wife Charlotte and daughters Eirys and Tydwen also deserve a mention for putting up with me spending numerous hours on my laptop writing this up, although it has to be said that most of it was done while all three were asleep! That said, Charlotte deserves credit for coming up with the title of this book and the girls had an influence on the choice of pink for the cover!

As these endeavours invariably do, this book has taken longer to complete than I envisaged at the start. I've taken a broad view of regeneration, covering not just buildings but events in the widest interpretation. The floods of 2007, of course, weren't regeneration in any sense – but they were a 'bump along the way' which could have knocked our ambitions off course but thankfully didn't.

The amount of time I have spent on this project could never be justified from a financial point of view. But that wasn't why I did it. In a way, it's part of me giving back to a city which, by and large, has been good to me.

My twin objectives when I set about writing this account were a) to get things right and b) to avoid upsetting anyone – at least not unnecessarily. That's a pretty tall order, but one I've worked carefully to the best of my ability to deliver. Only time will tell whether I've managed to achieve that successfully.

It's been a marathon to get to this point and I hope it will all have been worthwhile. I hope you enjoy reading it.

2. INTRODUCTION

This book isn't intended to be a history of Gloucester – there are plenty that already fulfil that function, including those written by my friends Philip Moss and Chris Witts, much more eloquently and comprehensively than I could. Nor is it intended to be my autobiography. I'm not immodest enough to believe, despite a quarter of a century in public life in Gloucester, I'm worthy of one. But I have been privileged to be involved in a momentous period in Gloucester's history which I believe will be judged to have been at least moderately successful, although not without its challenges. I believe this needs to be recorded for posterity and in order to learn lessons for the future. Having been in the thick of it for so long as well as being Gloucester born and bred, I am almost uniquely placed to do it. It isn't meant to be a book full of nostalgia, but you'll have to forgive me if occasionally I do lapse into that. It may also prompt questions of what might have been if all of those plans had gone ahead, all of those artists' impressions had turned into reality – which they never do. I hope it will be of interest not only to people in Gloucester and surrounding areas, but to those with an interest in regeneration and civic leadership.

To understand Gloucester's revival, it is important to set it in its historic context and also necessary to understand and track its decline. This is not intended to have the depth of an academic exercise but to enable readers, particularly those who haven't been in the city for that long, to see the wider picture.

Gloucester is one of the country's most important historic cities – on a par with London and Winchester. Its Roman origins, Queen Aethelflaed's burial at St Oswald's Priory, Henry III's Coronation, the Siege of Gloucester are just a few of the events in its history that should afford it a higher status than it has enjoyed in recent times. Perhaps the wealth of historical stories from which it can choose means that the message gets diluted. The Gloucester Miser Jemmy Wood being the inspiration for Scrooge, the evangelist George

Whitefield spreading the Great Awakening across America, Robert Raikes founding the Sunday School movement and W.E. Henley's Invictus poem being read daily by Nelson Mandela when incarcerated at Robben Island are all great stories, but almost get crowded out amongst the richness of heritage at our disposal. Until someone wrote to me asking why there was no statue of Gloucester's most famous son in the city, I hadn't even heard of Button Gwinnett. I soon discovered that he was the second signatory to the US Declaration of Independence, who was born at Down Hatherley and was believed to have attended the College (Cathedral) School.

So how did such an important and historic city decline to the extent that such a big regeneration programme was needed, that civic pride was almost non-existent, cynicism rife and aspiration sadly lacking? Probably the low point in the city's fortunes came with the discovery of bodies at 25 Cromwell Street and then 25 Midland Road, with Fred and Rose West arrested and charged. A number of books have been written on this subject and I don't propose to go into the detail that they have, but it would be wrong to ignore it completely.

The revelations about the Wests came as a huge blow to the city, not only because two of its long-term residents were exposed as serial killers but because their activities had gone undetected, right under the noses of the authorities, for so long. Both of the Wests' homes, in Cromwell Street and Midland Road, were close to Gloucester Park. Whereas most towns and cities' main parks are amongst the most desirable places to live (think Cheltenham's Imperial Square or Pittville Park or Bristol's Clifton Downs), the post-war flight of wealth from central Gloucester led to these large houses being carved up into low-value flats and bedsits, which to a large degree they still are today. This encouraged a transient population and a limited sense of community, allowing the comings and goings at the Wests' properties to go unnoticed or at least seem unremarkable.

My first inkling of the Cromwell Street murders was when, in 1994, Andrew Gravells – who was then a city councillor but I was not – called me to say, "The Police are digging up a garden in Cromwell Street. Do you know anything about it?" Of course, at that stage I didn't. When I was first elected in May 1996 and all the other Conservative councillors bar Pam Tracey lost their seats, I was elected

Group Leader and was immediately plunged into dealing with the aftermath of the case including what to do with 25 Cromwell Street.

A communications company, Robertson Bell, was brought in to carry out a consultation exercise. Options included a memorial garden, which wasn't favoured by the victims' families or the council for fear of attracting a ghoulish brand of tourism, a car park or a walkway between Cromwell Street and the adjacent St Michael's Square, as it ultimately became. Absurdly and in my view inappropriately it also suggested building a pub there! Naturally this wasn't a popular idea and I almost choked on my cornflakes when I read a headline a few days later in the Daily Express which said, "Cromwell Street pub bid blocked."

The Daily Express also angered city residents in November 1996 by describing Gloucester as a "den of iniquity" – saying, "No need to list the horrors of Cromwell Street. Most county folk wouldn't have been the least surprised to hear of such goings on in Gloucester: it is viewed as a den of iniquity with rough council estates." Turning one of our famous stories against us, they added, "Dr Foster isn't the only one who learned to stay shy of the place. Posh people live in Cheltenham."

It wasn't the first, or the only, time the city had received a bad press. In March 1993, the Sunday Times ran an article by journalist Jonathan Margolis headlined "Green, unpleasant land". He said there was "something ominous", "something dark beyond the obvious" in the city with "small town, shaven-headed ugliness", "lethargy and seedy crime", "a large drug underculture, a Saturday night tradition of fights and street robbery and acres of underclass housing and raw urban poverty". City MP Douglas French considered cancelling his subscription. Some residents wrote to *The Citizen* wondering why he hadn't just done it and demanded an apology while he was at it.

Theodore Dalrymple, a physician, psychiatrist and writer, contributing to the City Journal in Spring 1996, was equally damning. He said:

"Gloucester is a small cathedral city of about 100,000, where the city council has conclusively demonstrated that with the right combination of 1960s urban planning and an undiscriminating welfare policy, the degraded inner-city conditions of much larger conurbations may be successfully reproduced in small country towns. The ancient but decayed medieval city centre has been replaced almost in its entirety by concrete buildings that would have gladdened the hearts of another famous couple, the Ceausescus. As for Cromwell Street itself, once decent and even elegant nineteenth-century housing has degenerated into near-slum, where a shifting population of drifters rent dismal rooms by the week, and everything looks uncared for: the paint peels off the woodwork, the stucco crumbles, and litter - the packaging of junk food-flutters in the breeze. Next door to the Wests' house is a mean little Seventh-Day Adventist Church, whose noticeboard offers passers-by "peace and sanity in a mad, mad world."[1]

2019 marked the 25th anniversary of the West case arrests and, as Leader of the Council, I had some trepidation about what publicity this would attract. In the end, it didn't generate a great deal, other than a couple of documentaries. I was approached by one production company who were being blocked in their attempt to film on the walkway site. I took the view that they would do it with or without our co-operation anyway and, as long as it wasn't done in a sensationalist way, it was better to work with them. Sir Trevor McDonald, one of my wife's favourite men, hosted the programme and, as you would expect, dealt with it sensitively. I hung around in the Hampden Way car park like a groupie, waiting for the great man to arrive and to welcome him to Gloucester. He was charming as you would expect him to be. My message to Sir Trevor, and anyone else who asked, was that it was a very different city in 2019 to 1994 and Gloucester had "moved on".

I'm a huge supporter of town and city centres as places where people can come together and civic pride can be focussed. For as long as I can remember, people have complained about Gloucester city centre and its perceived weakness. But it wasn't always like that. In the late 1960s and 70s a huge swathe of development took place in the city centre, creating the Eastgate and Kings Walk shopping centres and three multi-storey car parks at the shopping centres and in Longsmith Street, which were joined by bridge links across the gate streets. Comments in the local media wondered whether Cheltenham would ever catch up again. How times change!

The development was inspired by the Jellicoe Plan, created by the eminent architect Sir Geoffrey Jellicoe. The Jellicoe Plan for

Gloucester (December, 1961) defined important central areas where development should not exceed a certain height and a number of important 'avenues of vision' based on the protection of the views towards the Cathedral. This plan was contained within a document titled 'A Comprehensive Plan for the Central Area of the City of Gloucester' which also proposed a comprehensive development plan for the city. Jellicoe is spoken about in largely negative terms these days, but it's important to note that his proposals were not followed completely by the City Council. The Council forecast a large increase in retail demand compared with the small increase in floorspace proposed by Jellicoe. A good analysis of Jellicoe's plans and the City Council's response to it can be found at www.gloucester500.co.uk/jellicoe-1961.

For example, Jellicoe's plans did not involve the loss of The Bell Hotel in Southgate Street, which was demolished in April 1968 to make way for the Eastgate Shopping Centre. It is recorded that the last drinks were served at 2.40pm on 29th September 1967! The demolition left only the narrow frontage of the Old Bell above Costa Coffee today, with Paddy Power and Poundland now occupying the shopping centre units, which have either concrete or brutalist cladding above. Darrel Kirby's "Gloucester Then and Now" contrasts the two images on its front cover. We look back on those decisions with horror and incredulity, but those were very different times. Those involved at the time say that many buildings within the city centre at the time were looking 'ragged'. The Bell Hotel was within the 'Comprehensive Development Area' (a designation created under the 1947 Town and Country Planning Act to redevelop urban areas) and as such was simply swept away. And that was that.

Jellicoe would also have kept 47-49 Eastgate Street (opposite where Boots is now) and the 18th century 'Duke of Norfolk's House' in Westgate Street, but did propose the loss of the Northend Vaults pub in Northgate Street and the 19th century terraces of Worcester Street which, in hindsight, we're pleased did not happen.

The loss of the Northgate Street Methodist Chapel to make way for Tesco (until recently Wilko) is looked upon today as a senseless destruction of our heritage, but finding uses for redundant church buildings is a challenge today as it was then. These days we are rather more creative about it, as the recent Discover DeCrypt project at St Mary de Crypt has shown. People often say Gloucester could have been another York or Chester if so much of our heritage hadn't been destroyed, not by bombs as in Coventry's case but by bulldozers. It wasn't a new phenomenon though – Charles II ordered the destruction of the city walls in revenge for the city's support of the Parliamentarian cause in the Siege of Gloucester. Imagine what an attraction they would have been if they were still here today.

To sustain town and city centres, you need to have people living and working there in decent numbers. As the residential suburbs were established in the early 20th century, the city centre depopulated, and was almost entirely commercial by 1914. Substandard housing in the centre was demolished to make way for The Oxebode, Bon Marche (which became Debenhams) and the Kings Square bus station and car park. This trend is something which the Council has been working slowly but surely to reverse for some years, but the process of repopulating a historic city centre is one that inevitably takes time.

People living in the city centre support the evening economy. Having people working in or close to the city centre is vital for the daytime economy. Over recent decades not only has there been a flight of residents from the city centre, but the number of people working there has declined. Business Parks on the edge of the city like Olympus Park and Waterwells in Quedgeley, Gloucester Business Park at Brockworth and Barnett Way in Barnwood became a more attractive destination for offices, with their free and plentiful parking. In the same way, supermarkets moved out to the suburbs (I remember the excitement when Tesco first opened in Quedgeley) and out of town retail parks, mostly allowed on appeal to a Government Inspector rather than by the City Council, became the places to go for bulky goods like furniture, electricals and DIY.

Brunswick Road and Spa Road used to be the hub for professional services in the city with the streets lined with solicitors, accountants, insurance brokers, surveyors and estate agents. Almost all have now left for the lure of purpose-built offices and easy parking. That trend has sadly continued with Ecclesiastical Insurance leaving the city centre in 2020 for new offices at Gloucester Business Park, despite huge efforts by the City Council over the years to get them to stay, initially at Southgate Moorings (see chapter on Gloucester Docks) and then at Kings Quarter.

They followed the direction set by fellow insurance company Northern Star/Fortis (now Ageas) who left their London Road offices to go to Gloucester Business Park as well, leaving a long-term empty office building still in search of a solution as I write.

As well as offices leaving the city centre, so too did more commercial and industrial uses on its fringes. The likes of famed engineering company Fielding and Platt reduced their presence and closed at the turn of the century. Serck (later Severn) Glocon made way for the Gloucester Quays development by relocating to Olympus Park. The lunchtime and after-work spending power of all of their workers went with them.

Later in this book, I'll describe how the closure of the Cattle Market at St Oswalds Road came about. That too had an impact on the city centre, both because the new development provided additional retail space which, arguably, competed with the centre but also because the loss of the livestock market removed another reason to come to the city. So the story goes, while the farmers would go to the Cattle Market on market days, their wives would head to the city centre for shopping and hospitality. When the market closed, they stopped coming.

The city didn't seem to get a great deal of support or recognition at a national level. That changed in the run-up to the 1997 General Election when the Labour Party identified Gloucester as the seat they needed to win in order to secure a majority in Parliament. Labour insiders tell me their chief spin doctor Peter (now Lord) Mandelson used an image of Gloucester Cathedral in his PowerPoint presentations to show what victory looked like.

All of these factors, and no doubt many more, combined with the lack of any substantial joined up plan to combat them contributed to the city's gradual decline and it was only in the early 2000s that the necessary resource or effort was put in place to hasten a revival. In the 2001 General Election, when I stood as the Conservative candidate, it was starting to become an issue. My Labour opponent Parmjit Dhanda, who won and served as Gloucester's MP for 9 years, pointed to the opening of the Oxstalls Tennis Centre and the laying of the foundation stone for the Oxstalls University Campus and promised £500 million of investment over the next

10 years. In addition to funding for regeneration in its traditional sense, public sector cash did pour into the city for a new women's unit at Gloucestershire Royal Hospital and a new County Police Headquarters at Waterwells, helped no doubt by its status as a marginal seat.

I said at the time, "Dirty streets, derelict buildings and a downmarket image are not what the people deserve. I want regeneration actually delivered. Promises about Blackfriars, the Docks and the Cattle Market have bred cynicism. I will work to make my home town of Gloucester something of which we can all be proud."[2] I didn't win the election but I like to think I kept my promise.

In the minds of most people, there was never any doubt about Gloucester's potential. Nick Alford of developers LXB described Gloucester as an "unpolished diamond". English Heritage's Urban Panel, in their report following their visit in 2003 called it "a truly great, historic Cathedral city whose heart is not beating as it should."

Others felt that, while in many ways it was an advantage, having a very active local newspaper could be counterproductive when it "latched onto any new vision even if it didn't have a cat in hell's chance of happening". The need to 'feed' a daily newspaper with stories created a sense of frustration when things didn't happen quickly enough. Over time I learnt that development, particularly good development, takes time and doesn't neatly fit in with the political cycle, let alone the news cycle.

In regeneration, as in life, not everything you try will succeed. As John Whittaker of the Peel Group - Gloucester's biggest investor - said, regeneration takes "determination, persistence and patience." Stewart Deering, Chief Executive of Reef Group, similarly quotes Samuel Beckett's "Ever tried. Ever failed. No matter. Try again. Fail again. Fail better." I would add that a slice of good fortune helps as well. In that sense, Gloucester hasn't always had the rub of the green but in recent years, it seems the city's luck might just have changed.

3. NOT EXACTLY PLAIN SAILING
The Regeneration of Gloucester Docks

History

Gloucester Docks is one of the city's greatest assets. The Docks are said to be the furthest inland port in the country, although that claim is also made by Goole in East Yorkshire. The inspector's report for the Gloucester Quays planning inquiry set out some useful and concise history about Gloucester Docks, saying:

The River Severn has always been an important trade route to Gloucester, and quays were established in the Roman, the Saxon and the medieval periods, around which suburbs were established extending south and west of the town. In 1580 Gloucester was granted the status of Port by Elizabeth 1. The port of Gloucester continued to grow during the 17th and 18th centuries and, in 1793, to facilitate further growth, both in capacity and trade potential, an Act of Parliament was passed for the establishment of a canal company, and the construction of a canal and basin on the south side of the city. This canal became the Gloucester and Sharpness Canal.

Excavation of the canal began in 1794 and by 1799, although the basin and locks had been completed, the work on the canal remained unfinished, and was halted due to a lack of funds. The basin was finally opened to vessels from the river in 1812, and the canal was finally completed in 1827. Construction of various warehouses and quays, along with other infrastructure in the area of the basin, now known as the Main Basin, and along the canal, commenced with the completion of the canal.

For completeness, I would add that The River Severn splits into three sections above Gloucester and re-joins further down river. The split in the river was the reason why the Romans built a fort here – it was the most southerly crossing point into Wales.

The smaller of the two dry docks, which today are operated by Tommi Neilsen's shipyard, was built in 1818 and enlarged in 1837. To accommodate larger ships, a second, bigger dry dock was built in 1853.

The Barge Arm, an extension of the basin, was added in 1824

before the canal was linked up in 1827, to allow smaller barges to keep out of the way of ships. In 1849 the Victoria Basin was opened as the port became busier. Warehouses continued to be built until the 1870's.

Corn from Ireland and Europe and timber from Scandinavia were main imports, and salt from Worcestershire was exported. In the 1900s petroleum products were an important commodity for the Docks.

Imagine dozens of tall ships, barges and other small craft manoeuvring around the docks. Warehouses being filled, ships loaded; trams, steam engines and horses vying for space among the barrels and boxes piled high. Imagine the dust from Corn Mills and timber yards, the smoke and soot from fires and engines mixing with the talk of labourers and seamen. That was 19th century Gloucester and helps to explain why Gloucester's Tall Ships Festival is both popular and authentic.

Decline and council intervention

During the 19th century, Gloucester flourished through the canal and railway ages and continued until the rise of motorways and container ships in the 1960's. The Docks declined because ships got bigger and couldn't get up the canal, losing business to Sharpness. Then Sharpness couldn't take even bigger ships and lost them to Avonmouth & Portishead. The prosperity created by the Docks was interrupted by three wars – the Crimean War 1854-56 and two World Wars. Overland pipelines killed off petroleum trade at the Docks.

As the Docks declined, it was reported that British Waterways was "alarmed at the prospect of having to repair an extensive number of vacant listed structures".[3]

In the 1970s, private companies showed interest in refurbishing the Docks warehouses but the costs were high and it was not commercially viable. In the mid-1980s the commercial market improved and the success of similar ventures in the US, such as Harbour Place, Baltimore and Fisherman's Wharf, San Francisco, provided inspiration. These were based on a 'Festival marketplace' shopping concept used to revitalise downtown areas. The Times published a four-page special report on Gloucester in May 1972 to mark the opening of Kings Square. On the subject of the Docks, it commented:

"Clearly a decision will have to be made at some time about the future of the Old Docks...These are early days and the debate has by no means reached the stage of controversy, although it must be said that some people think the situation would best be served by demolition of many of the old buildings and modern development on the site. There are others, though, who believe the Old Docks could, with thoughtful planning, be turned into one of Gloucester's attractive cultural, commercial and leisure areas. The ideas being discussed are varied. One group of people believes that a warehouse could be converted into an arts centre and theatre, while other buildings could be made into flats and offices. Although some doubt is expressed now about the readiness of people to move into dock building conversions, in the same way as trendy Londoners, the position may be changed within 10 years."

It would, in fact, take rather longer than a decade before the Docks warehouses were converted into 'trendy' apartments.

The Docks was also a popular film set with the 1970s BBC drama 'The Oneiden Line' being filmed in part there but that wasn't enough to give it a viable future. The buildings were in poor condition. The warehouses on West Quay were demolished in 1966 and in the late 1970s some of the smaller buildings around the Docks were being demolished and the Docks were increasingly used by pleasure craft.

North Warehouse, in particular, was in a very poor state and was being used for practice by the fire brigade, which meant gallons of water were being pumped in which made matters worse. The City Council had been pressing the British Waterways Board to refurbish it. Instead, they had applied for planning permission to demolish it in 1977, which the Council refused. British Waterways appealed the decision but it was dismissed by Environment Secretary Michael Heseltine in 1981.

City Council Chief Executive Richard Shackleton, along with Councillors Peter Robins (Chairman of Highways and Planning Committee) and Keith Fisher (Chairman of Planning Sub-Committee) went to meet BWB Chairman Sir Frank Price, a former Lord Mayor of Birmingham, at their offices in Marylebone, London. Price had been heavily involved in the creation of the Bullring Shopping Centre in Birmingham as council leader and was himself a property developer. They went for lunch on a canal barge and Sir Frank said, "I've had enough of your whingeing. Put your money where your mouth is. I'll give it to you for £1." Fisher gave him the pound there and then. Price undertook that if the Council restored North Warehouse, BWB would bring the National Waterways Museum to the Llanthony Warehouse at the other end of the Docks.

The existing Waterways Museum was at Stoke Bruerne in Northamptonshire and a bigger museum was needed. Curator Tony Conder had put together a paper outlining options for sites in Birmingham, Leeds and Gloucester. Price wouldn't have been able to take the decision on his own, but had the ability to carry others with him. Discussions were already taking place within British Waterways about the potential of Gloucester Docks and the Council's interest was probably seen as opportune. The Waterways Museum opened its doors in April 1988 before it was officially opened by Prince Charles on 5th August 1988. According to a Docks information pack for students, it initially attracted 70-100,000 visitors a year and sources at the Museum told me that at times it exceeded that number.

The Council had been considering bringing all their departments, which were then split between the Guildhall and the Treasury in separate buildings in Eastgate Street and the Planning and Technical Services department at Cedar House in Spa Road, together for some time. I'm told there had been an idea of building a new HQ at the bottom of Westgate Street where the flats are now. The Jellicoe plan had also proposed a new civic plaza opposite the Technical College in Brunswick Road (which would have obliterated St Michael's Square). Neither idea had come off so the Council took the opportunity to bring everything together at the Docks.

The Cheltenham & Gloucester Building Society was headquartered in Cheltenham's Clarence Street. They were looking to build a new HQ on the site of the former Cheltenham St James Station but the Borough Council had refused planning permission. They came to look at sites in the Docks and at Barnwood, thinking this would force the planners' hands in Cheltenham, but it didn't. So they ended up building their headquarters at Barnwood.

They still wanted bigger city centre premises to replace their small branch in Westgate Street and agreed to take the ground floor of the Guildhall for a premium of £3.1 million. The C&G paid for it by Banker's Draft. Richard Shackleton personally took it to the cashier's department to pay it in.

The merchant bank Morgan Grenfell became involved in a deal to ensure the capital receipt was used in the same year and didn't get clawed back by the Government. They took responsibility for the Docks project and paid the contractors.

The C&G were keen to move into the Guildhall as quickly as possible. The Council moved out in March 1985 and the new C&G branch opened in November 1986. The branch was due to be officially opened by television presenter Noel Edmonds on 20th November but he pulled out after the death of a contestant on his 'Late, Late Breakfast Show' in what was called the 'whirly wheel tragedy'.

In March 1985, the Council signed an agreement with British Waterways for the purchase of North Warehouse and lease of the Herbert, Kimberley and Phillpotts warehouses. North Warehouse was handed over to the Council by contractors in July 1986 and was officially opened by the then Mayor Councillor Tony Ayland on 1st May 1987. Contractor, The Britannia Group, handed over the Herbert, Kimberley and Phillpotts warehouses in October 1988, with council departments moving in the following month. The three warehouses were officially opened on 25th May 1989 by Princess Alexandra. The £3.1 million from the C&G went a long way towards paying the renovation costs.

The top floor of North Warehouse was originally occupied by the Council's Environmental Services team, with the Council Chamber still at the Guildhall. It was felt the Chamber too needed to be moved to the Docks, so Environmental Services reluctantly moved out to create the Civic Suite, which was completed in November 1989.

Councillor Andrew Gravells, one of the only current councillors who was on the authority in the late 1980s, tells how the then leader Keith Fisher asked members of the ruling Conservative Group to stay behind after a group meeting to tell them about the Docks plans. Fisher was a local businessman, owning the Gloucester Rope & Tackle Company as well as the Top Cue snooker club on Eastern Avenue. Although a meeting room at the Guildhall was named after him belatedly in 2013, some (including Gravells) felt that his contribution and vision were not sufficiently recognised.

The City Council's Local Plan, adopted in 1983, proposed a "retail-led (DIY store), comprehensive redevelopment, including offices, housing, tourist orientated uses and leisure uses". In December 1984, it was reported that the City Council were promoting sites in the Docks for retail stores selling furniture, electrical and DIY as an alternative to out-of-town sites, for which planning appeals were taking place. Possible sites included the former infirmary on Southgate Street and the corner of Llanthony Road and Severn Road. The Council was also considering a Compulsory Purchase Order for the Southgate Street premises of Jaco, Graham Reeves, The Barley Mow, Western Trading and the Southgate Congregational Church. [4]

By July 1986, Councillors were told that interest in the proposed shops at the Docks far exceeded expectations. It was described as a £30-50 million plan. Habitat reportedly wanted a 35,000 sq ft store on Southgate Street overlooking Victoria Basin, in what was to be called the Southgate Gallery, which would also have a multi-storey car park for 550 cars. The General Trading Company of Covent Garden, which sold upmarket gifts and homeware, were interested in taking two floors of the Double Reynolds warehouse. Alastair Cochrane of surveyors Lalonde Bros, who were acting for Pearce Developments, said. "We will not have a W H Smith or a Wimpey but we will have a Habitat and a Liberty perhaps." Hotel operators were also showing major interest in the site next to the Antiques Centre on the West Quay. A housing association was planning 86 new homes and an additional 50 if, as was believed likely, the Biddle & Shipton Warehouses had to be demolished. The architect for the scheme was Roger Dyer of Cheltenham. It was believed the development would take 3 or 4 years to complete. There was also the idea of an electric tram running from the Waterways Museum to North Warehouse, along The Quay, up Westgate Street, down Southgate Street and back to the Docks. [5]

A Planning Brief was drawn up in 1986 and Pearce Developments of Bristol, who were taken over by Crest Nicholson, were selected as the developer partner in 1987. In July 1987, an outline planning consent was granted to Pearce Developments for erection of new buildings for retail, residential, car parking, offices and workshops and the conversion of warehouses for the same mix of uses. The consent was amended in July 1992 and that year the company purchased a 200-year lease of the Docks. For those unfamiliar with property of this nature, the long lease gave Crest almost as much control as owning the freehold, but for certain things consent would need to be sought from the freeholder. For the Docks, this was British Waterways (now the Canal and Rivers Trust).

The recession of the late 1980s/early 90s put paid to the firm's original plans, causing a hiatus in the Docks regeneration. The scheme was refocused away from retail presumably because out of town retail parks were allowed on appeal, having been resisted by the City Council, in places like Eastern Avenue.

The City Council's move to the Docks and the opening of the National Waterways Museum was intended to act as a catalyst for the regeneration of the wider Docks area and to a large degree it was successful, but the initial phase of development was relatively modest. The Victoria Warehouse, which had been used as a flour store by Priday Metford, was converted for office use, with 100 staff from the Gloucestershire Health Authority and the Family Health Service Authority moving into the building in late 1992.[6]

Dr Fosters pub opened with Steamboat Willie's steak restaurant above and the Britannia Warehouse was rebuilt in 1990 in the same style after a fire on the 1st April 1987, which took 100 firefighters three hours to bring under control. The rebuilt Britannia Warehouse was officially opened by Mayor Eric Ede, who was piped ashore by the local Sea Cadets.[7] Barclays Bank were one of the tenants in the building and stayed until the building was sold for conversion to apartments in 2022.

Opposite the Docks, Southgate House was built for the Bank of England's Registrar's Department. A time capsule was planted on the site on 1st December 1989. The Bank operated from there between 1991-2004, when the function transferred to a private company, Computershare.

Also built in the late 1980s was the Merchants Quay shopping centre, which had a café and toilets as well as some interesting small shops, a Pizza Piazza Italian restaurant overlooking the water and an Edinburgh Woollen Mill store on the ground and first floor of Phillpotts Warehouse. The centre helped Gloucester Docks become a popular stop-off point for coaches passing through the area.

In late 1990, work started on an ornamental garden and sculpture park between the Victoria and Britannia Warehouses. There were plans for a Dockside restaurant overlooking the Victoria basin which didn't come to fruition. [8]

In 1995, the County Court relocated to the Kimbrose side of the Docks (fronting Commercial Road/Southgate Street), with associated offices. The two buildings, on either side of the Docks entrance, were an uninspiring design, and there was some comment that the development was a 'missed opportunity' to provide a more imposing gateway to the Docks. In fact, the £15 million court complex was voted the second worst building of 1995 by the Sunday Times. Shortly after it opened, the building was plunged into darkness because of issues with the electricity supply and hearings had to be moved to the Crown Court.

Gloucester Docks before the warehouses were converted and when much of the area was given over to car parking. Credit: Paul Dowle

Even at this stage there was frustration that the full-scale redevelopment plans hadn't yet been delivered. David Irwin of The

Galley Sandwich Bar at Merchants Quay said, "They need to do something about the Docks or it will die", with Tony Conder of the National Waterways Museum adding, "We have been waiting a long time for something to start moving." [9]

Cinema and Leisure Quarter proposals

Multiplex cinemas were flavour of the month with developers in the 1990s. In September 1998, Crest submitted an application to build a 10-screen, 2450-seat Odeon cinema on the Southgate Moorings site, east of the Victoria Basin, where the Docks car park is currently located. The Council, meanwhile, was working on plans for the Blackfriars area, and in January 1999 the Council's developer partner, Arrowcroft, submitted an application to build a cinema as a key element of the Blackfriars regeneration scheme. There was also an application to extend the existing Virgin cinema at the Peel Centre.

Both the Docks and Blackfriars sites were considered for planning purposes to be 'city centre'. A report by the Council's consultants GL Hearn had made clear there was "no pressing need" for a new multiplex in the Gloucester/Cheltenham area and there certainly wasn't room for two in the city centre. All three applications were considered at a meeting of the Full City Council in July 1999. The report by Council Officers recommended refusal of Peel Centre application but left councillors to consider which of the Docks and Blackfriars schemes to approve - it could have been one, both or neither.

I was in favour of the principle of a cinema at the Docks, which led to Labour councillor Nick Durrant, who could be quite excitable and prone to hyperbole, accusing me of "slitting the throat of the city centre".

Crest's cinema proposal was part of a planned Leisure Quarter, very much like that created at Gloucester Quays twenty years later. The cinema would be on the upper floor of a 45,000 sq ft contemporary building, with the lower floor used for restaurants and family leisure activities. To the north, there would be a family Mediterranean-themed restaurant, part of Surrey Free Inns, called Cafe Med. The application wasn't just for Southgate Moorings but for a 355-space car park north of Llanthony Road, 3 restaurant/retail units and the conversion/restoration of Albert Warehouse, Vinings, Double Reynolds, Biddle & Shipton and Weighbridge House. There was also a proposal for a 5-storey hotel at the end of the Barge Arm, where the new apartment block, commercial units and car park are today. Overall, it represented a potential £50 million investment which would create 500 full-time and 600 part-time jobs.

The report to the Council meeting described the plans as a "realistic, energetic attempt to bring about a comprehensive redevelopment in the Docks... creating a new leisure quarter". The Docks development was "no longer seen as retail-led", and this plan represented a "striking and innovative set of proposals", which was "eminently viable and would bring early major investment to Gloucester". It was noted that there was a "possible detrimental effect on the vitality of the city centre" as the Docks "could be perceived as a destination in its own right". The report noted that the "regeneration of the Docks would help to regenerate Bakers Quay as an urban village" but that "if the Docks were to proceed at the expense of Blackfriars, connections between city centre and Docks might not develop effectively".

Crest was proposing a cinema/leisure building that was 106m long by 55m deep. It had a flat roof supported on V shaped masts and cables – something the architects said was a structural requirement of a long roof span and provided "height and architectural presence". They added that its "lightweight filigree form reflects tall ship rigging and will act as a landmark." The materials were brick to the base with a glazed frontage, silver/grey aluminium cladding panels, painted steel masts (silver/grey/white) and metal tie rods.

It was a controversial design, which divided opinion. The Civic Trust said "our members like the scheme" and English Heritage said it was "appropriate". I didn't feel the ultra-modern design being proposed was right for the historic setting of the Docks, describing it as the "son of the Millennium Dome". There was strong opposition from the Royal Fine Arts Commission (RFAC), the predecessor body of the Commission for Architecture and the Built Environment (CABE). They said that "the multiplex building constitutes a significant mass in comparison with the warehouses and is consequently of a different and dominant form", it was "too large for the site" and "oppressive" by its height close to the water. Changes were made to meet the RFAC's concerns. The elevations were altered and the proposed car park near Llanthony Road - which was to be built with honeycomb brick panels, a profiled metal roof, powder coated aluminium glazing and timber infill panels - was reduced in size.

Crest proposed a phased approach to the redevelopment. Phase One would comprise the cinema/leisure building, multi-storey car park and restaurant units, alongside the conversion of Weighbridge House, at the Southgate Street entrance to the Docks, to retail. Later phases would include the conversion of the Albert and Vinings Warehouses with restaurant/retail uses on the ground floor and offices/residential above. There would be a new public space next to the Mariners' Church. Plans for a National Youth Centre for the Performing Arts (NYCPA), which are discussed later in this chapter, were incorporated into the masterplan and would proceed once funding had been secured. If they were not successful, the Double Reynolds and Biddle & Shipton warehouses would be converted in the same way as others and there would be a new building along the north side of the Barge Arm.

As you would expect, opinion from both the public and business was split. Many businesses, including bus operator Stagecoach, backed the Docks plans. Resident Barbara Keen of Southgate Street spoke against them at the Council meeting, presenting a petition of 534 names.

It was acknowledged that the Council's Blackfriars scheme did not have a cinema operator signed up (although it was later named in an appeal document as Virgin) nor did they control all of the land needed to deliver the development. In contrast, Crest had "unencumbered control" of the land in the Docks – due in part to the Council's use of its CPO powers in the 1980s – as well as an agreement with a cinema operator and interest from bar/restaurant companies.

External legal opinion from a barrister advised the Council that "it would be legitimate, and perhaps desirable, to grant permission for both and leave market forces to determine which went ahead." In any case the successful application would have to be referred to the Secretary of State before planning consent could be issued.

Although planning decisions are meant to be taken in a 'quasi-judicial' way the debate was divided on party political lines. Labour had the numbers in the Council Chamber, so got their way – the Blackfriars application was approved and the Docks plans were turned down. In January 2000, the Secretary of State decided not to intervene and authorised the Council to issue planning consent for the Blackfriars scheme.

Crest appealed against the decision, but was initially only partially successful. In February 2000, the appeal relating to the outline consent (confirming the principle of the development) for the Docks scheme was granted. The appeal Inspector noted that the Blackfriars scheme delivered a profit of 14.5% with its own cinema, but without a cinema the profit margin was just 10%. His conclusion was that without a cinema the Blackfriars scheme would not be able to proceed in its current form.

The Inspector was, however, critical of Crest's design for the cinema. He said the "narrow strip between the building and the dockside would offer little attraction for pedestrians", the building "would dominate the Dockside and existing buildings" and "would be of overwhelming scale and quite incongruous". Despite allowing Crest's development in principle, the detailed design was rejected, forcing Crest back to the drawing board.

While Crest wrestled with coming up with a new design, the Council lodged a High Court challenge against the Inspector's decision. This was heard in August 2000 and dismissed, at a cost to the city taxpayer reported to be £17,000. The overall cost of fighting the appeals and launching legal action was believed to top £100,000.

Crest submitted a new application for its detailed design (known as a 'reserved matters' application) in June 2000. When the Council failed to make a decision on this, Crest lodged an appeal for 'non-determination' to force the issue. Two alternative designs for the cinema/leisure building were put forward and Crest submitted duplicate applications to keep negotiations going at the same time as running their appeal. The appeal was initially for the whole leisure quarter scheme, for which top architects Hemingways had designed all but the cinema/leisure building. The rest of the scheme was subsequently removed from the appeal to concentrate on the cinema/leisure building.

The first design for the cinema/leisure building was by architects Arup, and had bars and restaurants running the full length of

Dockside elevation, a brick plinth to Southgate Street, silver/grey aluminium cladding, the steel masts removed and a reduced height and footprint. The second, by Damond Lock Grabowski (DLG), had glazing by the dockside, local brick to the main elements, hardwood panels and metal cladding in a curved form.

A Council-appointed assessor, the eminent architect Robert Adam, said the Arup scheme "does not demonstrate a satisfactory solution in relation to Southgate Street" and the Southgate Street elevations of the DLG scheme are "massive and imposing" and did not "create an acceptable entrance experience for Southgate Street". The Civic Trust liked the Arup scheme but considered the DLG scheme unacceptable. Carlton Broadcasting (formerly Central Television) objected to the loss of light from and rear access to their Commercial Road studios, commenting that the view was used as a backdrop for studio shots. The owner of Discovery House in Southgate Street objected to the loss of light and effect of the elevation facing the Docks.

The Citizen reported in October 2000 that councillors had refused the £30 million Docks leisure scheme and now face a second public inquiry. Crest's Lawrence Clark said: "The council don't want to see a leisure development in the Docks for their own reasons. This is very difficult to understand because a planning inspector and a High Court judge have told them it's quite acceptable." [10]

Jane Hirst from Nathaniel Lichfield and Partners, Crest's planning consultants, said the council had delayed and refused to negotiate. In correspondence published on the Council's website she claimed that "no round table meeting (was) ever held" and that the Company had written to every member of the Council but got no response. The duplicate application was submitted to enable negotiation, but there was no reaction to that either. David Scott, for the Council, said he had concerns over the design of the hotel, whether the conversion of Albert Warehouse paid sufficient regard to the historic fabric of the interior and the relationship of the restaurants to the Mariners Church. He felt that neither cinema design was satisfactory for the main entrance to the Docks from Southgate Street. Despite those concerns, there was a 1000-signature petition in support from traders.

The DLG design was withdrawn but the Arup scheme was approved on appeal in February 2001. I was critical of the Council's stance at the time, accusing them of being "little short of hostile" to the Docks regeneration plans. I told *The Citizen* that "because of its obsession with its own Blackfriars scheme, the council has failed to negotiate and positively influence this scheme so it has thrown good money after bad." [11] It was also reported around the same time that "Developers (Crest and Arrowcroft) to meet for talks". Council Leader Kevin Stephens was quoted as saying, "I am optimistic that both the Docks and Blackfriars schemes can go ahead. We have a unique opportunity to regenerate the city centre and we will not be forgiven if we fail." It did indeed turn out to be an optimistic thought.

The cinema market went 'off the boil' and commercially the scheme no longer worked. After all of the planning battles about which cinema-led plan should go ahead, neither the Docks nor Blackfriars got built. It would take two decades more before the city would get a new cinema – at Gloucester Quays, which was further away from the city centre than the site Crest had promoted.

It seems inconceivable that so many top architects couldn't come up with a design that would satisfy the Council, but David Scott insisted they were trying to "fit a pint into a half pint pot". Depending on your point of view, the Council were either protecting one of their most important heritage assets (the Docks) or being deliberately obstructive to favour their preferred, but ultimately doomed, scheme at Blackfriars.

National Youth Centre for the Performing Arts

Caroline Lumsden was running a successful music school at Beauchamp House in Churcham, which started in 1982. She had the idea of a 'smallish' project to turn the Biddle & Shipton warehouses into a music academy. It was estimated to be a £4 million project. City Council Chief Executive Graham Garbutt, whose children went there (his daughter was learning to play the cello), encouraged her to make it a bigger, more ambitious project – hence it expanded to include the Double Reynolds warehouse and a new auditorium at the Barge Arm. There was nothing at the time for elite music students in Bristol or Cardiff – they had to go to London – so the case for a new facility in Gloucester was attractive.

The Gloucestershire Academy of Music and Performing Arts (GAMPA) Trust was founded on National Music Day in June 1992, when plans for the National Youth Centre for Performing Arts (NYCPA) were launched. GAMPA ran music coaching activities for highly-talented young people, based at The Crypt School. The NYCPA plans had the support and encouragement of organisations including the National Youth Orchestra of Great Britain, the National Youth Music Theatre, the National Children's Orchestra and the National Youth Theatre. NYCPA was established as a company limited by guarantee and registered as a charity. The principal users would be GlosCAT, Gloucestershire Music Service, Gloucestershire Dance Project and Artshape. GlosCAT planned to transfer their performance-based courses to the centre and would expand their offer, teaching 200 students at the new facility.

Not everyone was taken with the idea. Members of the City Council's Leisure Services Committee were worried that NYCPA would put the Council's Guildhall Arts Centre out of business. Labour councillor Derek Dobbins said, "Will the Guildhall Arts Centre be swallowed up by NYCPA? I see something hidden here." Committee Chairman and fellow Labour councillor Bob Duncan added, "We have fought for our Guildhall and we do not want to see activities hived off to some independent organisation. There is something going on here we are not being kept aware of."

In January 1995, it was reported that the National Youth Music Theatre, whose supporters included Andrew Lloyd-Webber and Prince Edward, wanted to move out of London and join with GAMPA. They planned to use it for rehearsals and productions and would use the residential elements during the Christmas and Easter holidays and the February and October half terms. Mike Cogger, who went on to play a key role at the Oxstalls Campus, was seconded from the Cheltenham and Gloucester College of Higher Education to prepare a bid to the National Lottery, working alongside Chief Leisure Officer Philip Cooke and Head of Leisure Management Steve Elway – both of whom he had taught on a Public Administration course at Oxstalls. Richard Ascough, who worked for the Bank of England and had overseen the construction of their new Registrars' Department building at Southgate House, also offered his assistance.

In March 1995, the City Council and Crest put an application to the Lottery on the basis of a £12.37 million scheme. Mike Cogger put together the bid with help of the songwriter Richard Stilgoe and former BBC Director General Sir Michael Checkland. Crest were prepared to give the Double Reynolds and Biddle & Shipton warehouses, to which they had assigned a value of £1 million. [12]

A gala concert was held in Gloucester Cathedral in June 1995 to launch the project. Afterwards, a bid was prepared to the Arts Council Lottery Fund for a feasibility study, which was submitted in December 1995, with an announcement expected in June 1996. [13]

Philip Oakey, who had been brought in to lead the University for Gloucester project, was a Director of NYCPA. When he left for personal reasons, the Head of Museums and Cultural Services Amanda Wadsley became the lead officer from the City Council.

There was a national launch at St James's Palace in March 1995 with Prince Edward, who was said to be supportive, which was sponsored by Severn Trent Water. The Beauchamp String Quartet played reception music and GAMPA students performed music and dance. Some of the pupils had already played for Edward at his birthday party. He agreed to be Patron of the project. After the concert, Prince Edward was quoted as saying the Docks was "an ideal environment for such a centre", adding that "it will be of enormous value to national groups needing suitable venues to rehearse and perform". HRH said, "I applaud the vision."

The students also played for the 80th birthday of the violinist and conductor Sir Yehudi Menuhin (which would have been in April 1996) in the Council Chamber at North Warehouse. [14]

The Arts Council awarded £80,000 for the design study of what was to be a £14 million project. It was reported that NYCPA would run degree courses, which would have been validated through the Cheltenham and Gloucester College of Higher Education. [15]

A design competition was launched in the EU journal in August 1996. 152 architects requested information, 99 registered an interest and 10 were selected for interview. Five were chosen to submit designs which were assessed in February 1997. [16]

The winners of the architectural competition were announced as Rick Mather Associates. Mather was an American-born architect who had done a lot of work on cultural buildings, including the Ashmoleum Museum at Oxford and London's Southbank Centre. The project was planned to be done in phases. Early phases would have included the conversion of the Double Reynolds and Biddle & Shipton warehouses into teaching spaces and student accommodation, with the final phase being a new-build 450-seat auditorium at the Barge Arm. [17] The student accommodation would have been delivered in partnership with Gloucestershire Housing Association, being used by GlosCAT students during term time and by NYCPA students at other times. The Government's regeneration agency English Partnerships were approached for a grant. [18] There would be 7 large music and performing arts studios, along with recital and rehearsal rooms. In the Double Reynolds warehouse there were plans for 25 teaching rooms, practice cubicles, a library, audio rooms, offices and hostel accommodation. A stage two lottery bid was submitted In June 1997. They had hoped to hear the outcome and commence preparatory work in November 1997, starting on site in mid-1998 and completing the project by the end of 1999. In January 1998, there was a proposal for a 'Vinings Centre for Visual Arts', in the Vinings Warehouse, put to the City Council's Leisure Services Committee, which would have involved the creation of a Lynn Chadwick Sculpture Trust. It would have been 'conceptually linked' to the NYCPA proposals but not part of them. It was agreed to apply to the Arts Council to fund a feasibility study, but this seems to never have got off the ground.

Although the Docks was reportedly the most-visited tourist site in the county, attracting 1.5 million visitors a year, that picture was not recognised by the likes of Tony Conder of the National Waterways Museum or Sally Styles, Manager of the Edinburgh Woollen Mill. They were hoping that what they called the 'Fame school' would have evening performances to bring the Docks alive later in the day. [19]

Others were less than positive about the plans. The Glass Heritage attraction in the Double Reynolds warehouse run by Joe, Gillian and Richard Paxton had attracted 40,000 visitors a year to the Docks since it opened in 1995. They supplied and manufactured stained and brown glass products and ran glass-blowing sessions for the public and weekend classes. Their lease ran out and Crest refused to renew it. They accused the Council of being "starry-eyed" about NYCPA. They left to go to new premises in Burford, with Joe Paxton saying, "We are very sorry to go because we had a big tourist attraction and a commercially viable business." They had tried to buy the Vinings Warehouse but that didn't work out. Philip Cooke, the Council's Chief

Leisure Officer, said the Council had tried to find them new premises and was sorry they had left Gloucester. [20]

In February 1999, it was reported that the Lottery bid had not been approved. Major arts capital projects were faced with severe difficulties following changes to the structure, membership and funding regimes of Arts Council and Lottery Board. They were invited to resubmit in light of the new regional strategy put together by South West Arts. Graham Garbutt advised that the Arts Council "preferred to see projects led by substantive organisations" and the project needed to be "recast in view of Arts Council's reduction in funding" and they were "exploring a more broadly-based arts project combining visual arts with performing arts".[21] By October 1998, it had grown to be a £28 million project. [22]

Those involved with NYCPA had worked hard to win over influencers and decision-makers, but then within a short space of time they changed. The 1997 general election saw a change of local MP, with Douglas French losing his seat to Tess Kingham, and Tony Blair's New Labour government replacing John Major's Conservatives.

Businessman Gerry Robinson, the Chief Executive of the Broadcaster Granada, became Chairman of Arts Council England in 1998, replacing the Earl of Gowrie, who was Arts Minister under Margaret Thatcher.

The entire panel of drama advisers to the Arts Council, who would have had some input on the NYCPA proposal, resigned in May 1998, claiming that changes being introduced by Robinson would be unworkable. The 16-strong panel was made up of some of the biggest names in British theatre, including the West End producer Thelma Holt, playwright Sir Alan Ayckbourn and the directors Sam Mendes and Jude Kelly. Ms Holt said the changes, which would have seen the panel lose much of its influence were "all about finance and not artistic merit".

The NYCPA project had hoped to be awarded £22 million but were offered a lesser amount, believed to be around £11 million, and turned it down. They had been optimistic about the outcome - someone had bottles of champagne in their car boot in North Warehouse car park in the expectation of a positive announcement. The Lottery grant for the Leisure Centre was announced about the same time, which didn't help, and some felt it was too big a project for

Gloucester. Although the project was abandoned, some believe it was the starting point for the Performing Arts Centre at the University of Gloucestershire's Oxstalls Campus some years later.

The proposed National Youth Centre for the Performing Arts at the Docks.

Regeneration stalls, Regional Development Agency steps in

The City Council were considering a compulsory purchase order as the large-scale regeneration of the Docks seemed to have stalled. But before they needed to do that, another solution came along. Sir Michael Lickiss, Chair of the newly-established South West Regional Development Agency was putting a regional strategy together – with its priorities being Gloucester, Bristol & Plymouth. SWRDA purchased the headlease of the Docks from Crest in 2001.

I was sceptical about what I saw as the 'nationalisation' of the Docks, but kept my reservations private. In hindsight, because of the investment they were able to put in, it was a good thing for the city.

A new masterplan was devised by Gillespies which went to the City Council's Cabinet in November 2004. The masterplan included a 4-star hotel with conference facilities near the Barge Arm East, apartments, small business units and decked parking south of the Barge Arm. It also included bridges across the Barge Arm, from the Dry Dock across the main basin and from Castlemeads to south of

West Quay. There were 9 coach parking spaces within the Docks and the plan was it should stay at the same number. It proposed 'The Crafts Village' with new townhouses and live/work units on Llanthony Road/West Quay with a 'striking entry building' on the 'Western Gateway' site on the corner of Llanthony Road and Severn Road.

There was also a proposal for a 'Gloucester Arts & Technology Enterprise' building south of the Victoria Basin which would house the arts, exhibitions and visual arts technology. On Southgate Street it was proposed to restore the street frontage with shopping and residential buildings in contemporary design.

The County Council had plans for a Cultural Centre in the Docks, which would have included a relocated library and museum. Those plans collapsed when the Government refused to grant Private Finance Initiative credits to finance it in August 2005. The project was promoted by Liberal Democrat councillor Jeremy Hilton in his role as County Council Cabinet Member for Libraries. At the time he said, "It would have provided a cultural renaissance for the city." I commented that there were "a lot of unanswered questions such as the effect on the city's museums and the Guildhall." When the Conservatives took control of the County Council in May 2005, there wasn't the same political commitment to it and following the Government's decision it was shelved.

The Gloucester Heritage Urban Regeneration Company's (see Chapter 9) Prospectus 2006 proposed the development of land next to the Dry Dock on the West Quay to create an important maritime heritage attraction and major city gateway from the South West Bypass. A 2008 masterplan by New Masterplanning for British Waterways proposed a new multi-storey car park, restaurants and a hotel, with a landmark building by Llanthony Bridge. GHURC also proposed a sail training facility or floating restaurant in the Docks. At the time of writing none of these ideas had progressed.

Restoration and new build – creating a desirable place to live

The first warehouse to be converted to residential, although strictly speaking outside the Docks estate, was the City Flour Mill operated by Priday Metford & Co. The company was taken over by Spillers (a subsidiary of Dalgety) in 1993 and the Gloucester operation closed in

March 1994 with loss of 60 jobs after 100 years of flour production. Workers claimed Spillers bought a profitable and efficient mill and closed it down to eliminate competition.

The building is notable for the 1854 Hadley v Baxendale landmark legal case which established the foreseeability test for consequential damages for breach of contract, which is used internationally, particularly in the US. The case centred on a broken steam engine shaft at the mill. The shaft could only be repaired in Greenwich, some 125 miles away. The owners of the City Flour Mill, Joseph and Jonah Hadley, hired a moving company, Pickfords, which was operated by Baxendale. For an unexplained reason, the shaft went astray and ended up on a canal boat instead of a train and took several days to reach Greenwich, during which time the mill lay idle. They sued Pickfords for the money they lost while it sat idle. The Court ruled that Pickfords could not be held liable for that level of damages as they did not necessarily know that the mill could not function without it – hence the 'foreseeability' test for contract breaches: You cannot be held liable for losses you could not have reasonably anticipated.

The property was put up for sale in September 1994 for a modest price, believed to be £275,000 but it was not a development opportunity for the faint-hearted. I'm told viewers had to wear face masks because of the risk of leptospirosis from the accumulated bird droppings. As the first residential conversion within the Docks, it was something of an unknown quantity.

Dalgety Food Ingredients Ltd were granted permission for a casino, restaurant and offices in July 1996 in what was reported as being a £2.5 million scheme. The City Council had already given planning permission for a casino at the Peel Centre after Gloucester was included in a list of towns and cities where restrictions would be relaxed. The huge concrete wheat silo, which was built in 1964, would be demolished and replaced by a glass and steel building at ground and mezzanine level only. [23]

The Citizen reported in May 1998 that development at Pridays Mill was to get the go-ahead from the City Planners. According to the article, developer Martin Graham of the Longborough Construction Company had bought it the previous month. He said it had been a four-year battle, done as an act of good faith because he loved

Gloucester and wanted to help the conservation of the city. He also planned to demolish the concrete silo. The latest consent was for a pub on the ground floor and 24 flats above.[24] But it wasn't Longborough who eventually undertook the conversion. According to Land Registry records, Longborough sold the property to a Jersey-based company Millhouse Gloucester Limited in September 1999. Because of different rules on disclosure of information for Jersey-based companies, it's not possible to find out who Millhouse Gloucester were or the people behind the company.

In April 2001, consent was granted for the conversion, alteration and extension to the building to create a restaurant/public house on the ground and first floors with 30 apartments above.

This was amended in February 2002 to provide 38 flats to part of the 1st floor and above. The consent was granted to Thornton Baker Homes.[25] Those involved at the time tell me that Thornton Baker went bust part way through and work on site ground to a halt. Southplace Homes, part of the Edinburgh-based Miller Group, took over. Accounts filed at Companies House for Priday Mill Homes (Gloucester) Limited – the special purpose vehicle set up to deliver the development – for the year to 31/12/02 state the shareholding of Waterfront Enterprises (the joint venture partner) had been acquired by Miller Residential Development Services (part of the Miller Group) to take their shareholding to 100%. It also stated that they now anticipated the development would overall be loss-making but that Miller Group would support the completion of the development.

The first sales completed in December 2002, presumably 'off-plan'. Another planning permission was granted in February 2003 to convert part of the first floor previously granted for the public house to two more apartments. Despite several attempts to gain consent to convert the ground floor to more apartments, at the time of writing it remains empty.

Within the Docks estate, the Albert Warehouse was the first warehouse to be converted to residential. The Albert Warehouse was the home of the hugely popular Robert Opie 'Pack Age' Museum of old advertising and packaging, which had opened in 1984. It's true that the building wasn't in great condition, but other than a bit of dust it didn't affect the operation of the Museum. The public display was on the ground floor, with the upper floors given over to storage.

At one point it was supposed to move to the Vinings Warehouse with purpose-built exhibition space as part of redevelopment plans, but that didn't come about. Losing the attraction which, at its peak, brought in 50,000 visitors a year was, in my view, a retrograde step. I protested against it and urged the RDA to find them a new home in the city, but my pleas fell on deaf ears. It closed at the end of October 2001. If I had been part of the Council's Administration, I like to think I would have made a much greater effort to keep them in the city. The collection, which was so extensive it took 12 removal lorries to transport it, went into storage for a few years until the Museum found a new home in Notting Hill (and subsequently to bigger premises in Ladbroke Grove in 2015) and was later renamed the Museum of Brands. Although I made some approaches to them in future years, they never came back.

The conversion work at Albert Warehouse was undertaken by local firm Barnwood Construction. Prices were between £95,000-£130,000 for a 1 bed apartment and £150,000-£190,000 for a 2 bed. One penthouse went for £300,000 – a record for an apartment in Gloucester. Internally, the exposed brickwork was shotblasted and repointed. Those working on it told me that, 6-8 weeks before handover of the project, oil started oozing out of the walls. It turned out to be nut oil from when the warehouse was used to store nuts which had seeped into the brickwork over the years. The contractors had to apply an oil digesting microbe to deal with it.

Further conversions followed at the Double Reynolds, Vinings and Biddle & Shipton warehouses. For the conversion of the Double Reynolds warehouse, time-served skilled craftsmen had to use Piranha pine 16m long and 16" x 16" wide to replace the beams. In the Biddle & Shipton warehouse, there was Victorian machinery in the roof. The original winch was retained in the living area of the top floor apartment. Other bits of machinery were relocated to the ground floor lobby.

The corten steel extension to the Vinings Warehouse, designed by Hemingways architects, proved controversial and it became known locally as 'The Rusty Box' but that didn't stop it from winning awards. It stood vacant for some time before opening in April 2007 as The Vinings Restaurant – an 'all you can eat' buffet style Indian and Thai eatery run by Robin Chaudhury. He later rebranded it to 'The

Veranda Lounge', moving to more of a premium offering. That was short-lived until it changed again to a Mediterranean cuisine known simply as 'The Med', which closed in October 2022.

The first new build in a generation at the Docks took place with the construction of The Barge Arm, made up of 67 apartments and two retail units, and its sister building, The Barge Arm East, containing 17 apartments with four commercial units shielding a multi-storey car park. Crest engaged Manchester-based architect Ted Cullinan. He was a top architect, having been awarded both the CBE and the Royal Institute of British Architects 'Royal Gold Medal' for his work. He came up with a design which was unveiled in *The Citizen* on 10th September 2004. I'm told how Cullinan came up with his concept design using a whiteboard and pens at a meeting at Southgate House, with Crest, English Heritage and other interested parties. The previous designs for the site were described to me as 'terrible'.

It contained a host of environmental features, including water-conserving plumbing and effective insulation as well as a landscaped 'woodland' atrium, which ultimately didn't work. The design proved not to be to everyone's taste, as most designs aren't, but was described by GHURC's Peter Wynn at the time as being "precisely the kind of world-class brownfield development we want to see in Gloucester". I remember chairing a session when Ted presented to city councillors about the process he'd been through to formulate and refine the elevations. Nobody could say that the computer-generated images weren't accurate - that was exactly how it turned out! The scheme had support from English Heritage and the Commission for Architecture and the Built Environment. The construction had a negative effect on the nearby National Waterways Museum which, aside from the disruption caused by the building site, was now hidden from view for those coming from the north of the Docks. The Urban Regeneration Company made a financial contribution to the partial refurbishment of the museum, partly as an acknowledgement of the difficulties this regeneration had caused them. The Smiles convenience store (later McColls), nearest Southgate Street, opened in one of the ground floor commercial units in April 2007.

The commercial elements of the masterplan, on the whole, were slower to be delivered than the residential parts. This caused local people to worry that the Docks was turning into a 'private gated estate', which of course wasn't true. But the vision of a leisure destination full of bustling bars and restaurants seemed a long way off. Estate agents Naylor Powell (my employers for 19 years), who had taken a temporary office in Merchants Quay, opened a permanent branch in the Barge Arm East. Head Kandy Hairdressers run by Ryan Fortey took the unit at the other end of the building as a salon in 2007, with two Italian-style coffee shops – Tucci and Corretto – filling the units in-between in 2009.

It was announced that Merchants Quay would close because the building, which had only opened in 1989, had failed and was letting in water. Given its popularity with coach visitors and locals, this prompted an outcry. I took a lot of the flak personally, but defended it in an article in *The Citizen* on 21st October 2006 saying, "Housing creates the critical mass of people to support the shops, bars and restaurants", adding that the, "commercial elements arrive fashionably late for the party". There were numerous letters published in *The Citizen* and even a BBC television programme called 'Building Britain', featuring architect George Ferguson, who went on to be the first directly-elected Mayor of Bristol. George, who wore his trademark red trousers, commented that he found the "emptiness" of the Docks "a bit spooky". He later returned to the city and clarified that he thought Gloucester had "great potential" and his role was as a "critical friend".

I felt the right approach was to stick to our guns. I recall former Asda boss and Conservative MP Archie Norman saying that regeneration needs leadership and that meant holding firm in the face of criticism. Over the years it was interesting how the narrative changed from "You're ruining the Docks" to "Why does the Docks get everything at the expense of the city centre?"

Pizza Piazza and Maddison's Café at Merchants Quay closed at the end of October 2006, with the Edinburgh Woollen Mill shutting its doors for a final time on 29th December. In the New Year, Dug Out (a crystal shop) shut for good. The remaining tenants quickly followed, leaving what I described as a "big hole in the heart of the Docks". Crest lodged an application for its demolition in May 2009 which got underway a year later. Its replacement was a new apartment block of 40 flats with two commercial units on the ground floor. Its design went back and forth with the Urban Regeneration Company's Design

Review Panel for almost a year. It started off as an ultra-modern L-shaped building (which the architects said was "testing the water") inspired by shipping containers which created a new waterside public space, to a modern interpretation of a Docks warehouse. Along the way, the new design contained corten steel (like the Vinings restaurant unit) which was later replaced with stack-bonded brick, despite the Design Review Panel preferring the corten. This was not only due to cost but because of concerns that apartments in a corten steel building would be difficult to sell. Crest's Marketing Director was reported to have said to the architect, "You're expecting me to sell a rusty box!"

Members of the Design Review Panel told me the original design was a "monstrous carbuncle" but the end result was "immeasurably better" and it had been "quite a journey". The architect was Dominic Eaton of Stride Treglown who said, "The final design is a sensitive and valuable response to the location, whilst at the same time producing an exciting and contemporary building."[26] He told me that a proposed glazed atrium was "value engineered" out of the scheme but he was pleased the shutters had been kept. The Planning Committee report referenced concerns from Civic Trust, English Heritage and British Waterways about the design, particularly the stack-bonded brick.

The original design to replace the Merchants Quay shopping centre.

In May 2010, GHURC issued a press release entitled "Merchants

Quay saved from dismal development" which quoted Antonia Shield, Chair of its Design Review Panel, as saying, "The new building will have grown from the seed of an idea germinated within the existing architecture of the Docks rather than a design which did not bear any relationship to the rare character of the impressive warehouse buildings around it."

The ground floor commercial units proved difficult to let. Their boarded-up windows, despite being painted blue in May 2013 (in time for the Tall Ships Festival, following an email from me to Crest Nicholson's Chief Executive), were criticised by David Purchase (owner of On Toast and former Assistant to City MP Parmjit Dhanda), but his description of them as being like a "shanty town" prompted ridicule from some quarters. Perhaps it was understandable why they proved difficult to let when *The Citizen* reported that the glazing alone could cost £100,000. [27]

Eventually, in order to break the deadlock, one of the Merchants Quay units was bought by Dr Fosters owner and latterly City Councillor Dawn Melvin (who also bought the lease of the bottom two floors of the Phillpotts Warehouse). Dawn was going to buy both Merchants Quay units but the owners of what is now 'Greek on the Docks' came forward to buy the unit they now occupy and Dawn stepped back from buying that unit. 'Greek on the Docks' opened in the unit facing the main basin in June 2016 and quickly became one of the city's favourite restaurants. It was created by Yiannis Karayiannis, one of the nicest men you could meet. Californian eatery Grillshed opened in the other unit in August 2016. It was fronted by former Gloucester prop Paul Doran-Jones and backed by Gloucester Rugby stars Charlie Sharples, Henry Trinder and Jonny May. Despite its hype, particularly on social media, it didn't work out well – going bust to the tune of £400,000 in December 2017 but re-opening soon after. It closed at the start of 2019 for 'maintenance works' and never re-opened, presumably leaving its backers nursing losses. Italian restaurant Trattoria Settebello, run by the Bifulco family of Caffe Corretto, opened in 2019 after an extensive refit and soon became a popular destination.

Ownership of the Docks is made up of the headlease of the main Docks estate, which was owned by Crest, then acquired by SWRDA and then passed to the City Council in 2011. The West Quay and what we now know as Orchard Square was owned by British Waterways, now the Canal and River Trust. The West Quay also saw some new build in the early 2000s, with the construction of North and South Point – two apartment buildings with views over the main basin to one side and the River Severn and May Hill to the other. Work started in September 2004 and the project was completed in 2006, with prices ranging from £155,000-£295,000. These were built by Laing Construction and have proved popular, being away from the main hustle and bustle of the Docks. Some of the apartments are split level (duplex) and enjoy not one but two balconies. There appear to be more owner occupiers in these buildings and an active residents committee. At around the same time, the conversion of the Double Reynolds and Vinings Warehouses was also underway. In order to build North & South Point, it was necessary to divert Severn Road by 5-6m.

The remaining original warehouse on the West Quay was for many years occupied by the Gloucester Antiques Centre, which was the city's number one tourist attraction, attracting 400,000 visitors a year - more than Gloucester Cathedral. It was so popular that a weekend admission charge was introduced to restrict numbers for safety reasons. It housed over 40 traders and was owned by the Cook family. The building, however, was in poor condition by the time it was sold in 2005. It aroused suspicion that it was sold to a New Zealand-born property developer, Evan Maindonald, who was based in the Forest of Dean. However, he insisted that he intended to keep running the Antiques Centre.

He looked to relocate it, considering a number of locations including Merchants Quay, and managed to get planning consent to convert the current premises (known as Lock Warehouse) to 26 apartments with commercial space on the ground floor. The Antiques Centre was moved to the Matthews Warehouse, above TGI Fridays, at Gloucester Quays in June 2009 and work started on Lock Warehouse in October 2011. The lease at Gloucester Quays was abruptly ended in August 2013 amid stories of unpaid rent. Reports said that traders had been paying their rent but it hadn't been passed on to the landlord (The Peel Group). Staff turned up to find the doors locked. Centre Manager Richard Rawlings said, "Gloucester Quays have today effected the forfeiture of the lease," adding that, "Peel

Outlets are committed to an Antiques Centre remaining at Gloucester Quays." They did run the centre directly for a while, albeit reportedly at a loss, and gained planning consent to relocate it to the still unused first floor Upper Deck, just off the centre's car park. But the Peel board couldn't be persuaded to make the investment to enable this to happen. They issued notice for them to leave their premises and the race was on to find a new home for them.

We had long been searching for a solution for 26 Westgate Street, a 16th century Merchants house with an incredible but rarely-seen timber elevation along the Maverdine passage. It had been Winfields seed merchants for many years and was for a time a bookstore with an infamous erotic section. More recently it had been vacant for a number of years and had been sold by the Winfield family, who found maintaining it a drain on their resources, to veteran property developer Chance Malone. We had identified it as a potential location for the Tourist Information Centre but, in typical local government style, it wasn't going anywhere fast. I thought, as a heritage building, it could be an ideal location for the Antiques Centre and would bring another attraction to the city centre. I mentioned it to Marketing Gloucester Chief Executive Jason Smith at one of our weekly meetings and he liaised with Chance Malone and the Antiques Centre traders and made it happen. I had the privilege of officially opening it in December 2015 and it is still flourishing today. Comedian, television presenter and President of Civic Voice, Griff Rhys Jones, visited Gloucester in September 2016 and was particularly impressed with this building.

The other area owned by the Canal & Rivers Trust (CRT) is what would become Orchard Square. It ceased to be a car park in 2018 and a new public space was created (see chapter on Gloucester Quays). Adjacent to it was the former Coots café. When it closed, the CRT sought a new tenant and landed Wetherspoons. Peel had for years resisted Wetherspoons' approaches to open at Gloucester Quays, but they had no control when the deal was done with the CRT. To be fair, they did a good job on fitting out the pub, with some nice touches like part of the city crest on the doors. The pub was named 'The Lord High Constable of England', which is quite a mouthful! This was after Miles of Gloucester who founded the nearby Llanthony Secunda Priory and held the position of Lord High Constable. Somehow, they managed to get a late licence (until midnight Sunday-Thursday and 1am on Fridays and Saturdays). When they opened in July 2015, the mixture of cheap booze and a new setting caused some low-level disorder and a good deal of noise, upsetting the nearby residents in the Barge Arm and Barge Arm East. Efforts by the management, after lobbying by residents and councillors, seemed to have brought the problem under control.

Gloucester Brewery was founded by Jared Brown, who is still the Chairman, in September 2011. Jared, a former chef, had been a hobby brewer and prepared his first batch of their signature Gloucester Gold ale at home. He was introduced by Gloucester Heritage Urban Regeneration Company to the Canal & River Trust and they took space in a former store room used by the National Waterways Museum, accessed from the courtyard next to the then Coots café at the Docks.

When Coots closed, they wanted to take on their premises but, despite negotiating with the CRT for a number of months, were 'gazumped' by Wetherspoons. They relocated production to the other side of the Dock basin to Fox's Kiln, fittingly an old malthouse, and opened the 'Tank' bar next to Wetherspoons in May 2015. The next phase of their expansion was the Warehouse 4 venue combining a bar, shop and event venue, which opened in September 2021. Warehouse 4 was in the adjoining space to the brewery and was previously occupied by the Furniture Recycling Project. At around the same time they launched a crowdfunding campaign to raise £500,000 to fund their latest phase of expansion. They also signed a deal to supply Gloucester Rugby, whose Chairman Martin St Quinton, Chief Executive Lance Bradley and Head Coach George Skivington were all shareholders.

Public Realm

The Docks for many years was a sea of tarmac car parking. This seemed fine when it was a collection of slightly crumbling Victorian warehouses, but now it was a smart residential area and becoming part of a bustling leisure quarter as well as a link between the Quays and the city centre, the public realm needed to be something better. This is where SWRDA's ownership was helpful. They had the resources to pump in millions to replace the tarmac with quality paving. Trees were introduced, despite some initial reluctance from the planners, along the walkway by the Victoria basin – which we later renamed Paju Walk, after our friendship city in South Korea. New benches were introduced, along with public art which I described in the Gloucester Quays chapter of this book. One innovation which didn't stand the test of time were the 'infinity lights' by the Mariners Chapel, which were installed in February 2006. As the name suggests, these were designed to give the impression of a bottomless hole inside them. But water got in causing them to fail and eventually they were removed and filled in.

The public realm works were carried out by Barnwood Construction. Director Stuart Pearce recalls how they had to take GPS surveys and record each piece of the railway track, which had been used to bring stone down from Leckhampton Hill, as it was taken up so it was reinstated in exactly the same way.

Another story I was told was about a water diviner being brought in to find underground cables when ground penetrating radar wouldn't work. They came along with cans of different coloured paints and marked where railway tracks, gas mains etc were, along with the depth. Those involved were taken aback when the water diviner was absolutely correct. I don't think there is any truth in the suggestion that this story inspired the 2014 Russell Crowe film, 'The Water Diviner'.

New public squares were created within the Docks. Mariners Square was the name given to the area outside the Mariners Church and in between the Barge Arm apartment building and the Victoria basin. It is a well-used and valuable event space. Shipton Square was created in the space between the Barge Arm and the Shipton warehouse. Although it won a civic design prize, the space never seems to be particularly well-used, other than perhaps by customers of the adjacent Blue Bamboo bar. Shipton Square was completed in July 2008.

Back Badge Square was created in the area to the north of the Victoria basin, adjacent to the Soldiers of Gloucestershire Museum. It was named after the Gloucestershire Regiment's famous symbol but the brief for the floorscape was not tightly drawn and didn't specifically require anything related to the Soldiers of Gloucestershire Museum or even the military. The chosen design by artist Katayoun Dowlatshahi uses a series of curved timbers flush with the slate paving to represent boats entering the Docks. The timbers were fabricated by Tommi Neilsen's boat repair yard in the Docks. There is also a refurbished five-ton hand-operated crane which was used by the Midland Railway in the Docks around 1850. [28]

The works to Back Badge Square didn't finish the public realm at the north of the Victoria basin. That had to wait until 2017 when a new 'Grand Staircase' was created to the side of the Soldiers' Museum leading up to Ladybellegate Street and the remaining tarmac replaced with high quality paving. I commented at the time, "This is a really important project which is designed to draw people to the north end of the Docks and help the proposed Ladybellegate Quay restaurant development go ahead." [29] It did seem a lot of money when the city centre was desperate for improvements, but the funding came from the sale of 27-29 Commercial Road and there was an obligation which came with the transfer from the RDA to complete the public realm works.

The completion of public realm works within the Docks made a huge difference to the overall environment of the area and no doubt encouraged private investment by Crest Nicholson and others. In reality it would not have been possible without public sector support, principally from the South West Regional Development Agency. At times, SWRDA attracted criticism for elements of its spending. The millions of pounds spent on public realm in the Docks were, in my view, an entirely legitimate use of public money which attracted private investment on a much larger scale and helped to link Gloucester Quays and the city centre.

The Food Dock

27-29 Commercial Road was part of the package of assets the Council inherited from the RDA on its demise. It had been vacant for many years. There was a suggestion that it could become a museum dedicated to the Korean War.[30] That was a nice idea but would have taken a huge amount of money due to the condition of building and whether what is known as the 'forgotten war' would have attracted enough visitors to be sustainable we shall never know.

The building was put on the market in May 2015.[31] There was no shortage of interest and a number of bids were received. I was recommended by Council Officers to accept a bid from the L&R Group who had successfully developed and sold a scheme in Milsom Street, Bath. Their initial scheme for five restaurants looked good and gained planning consent in 2016. They boldly said their scheme would be about 'occasion dining' (going out for something special) rather than casual dining. Names like Carluccios, Cote and Wagamama (all of whom ended up at Gloucester Quays) were mentioned, along with Loch Fyne and Cau. L&R felt that, in order to have sufficient 'critical mass', they needed to include the adjacent 23-25 Commercial Road (occupied at the time by Davey Law and the ground floor was the Gloucester Yacht Club) and they negotiated to buy this from the City Council as well.

At the end of 2017 the restaurant market hit a downturn, with Jamie Oliver's Italian chain the first big name to enter a Company Voluntary Arrangement (CVA) and those that survived weren't taking on new leases. L&R revised their scheme to a 'Food Dock' concept based on 10-12 smaller independent food businesses. Although we were told there was quite a lot of operator interest, it was a struggle to keep the conversion costs within budget and therefore its viability was a challenge.

Work started in March 2021. Ken Elliott told me they were initially interested in The Fleece but didn't think it would work until the area between the Docks and the Cathedral was improved. Council Officers Anthony Hodge and Mark Dix introduced them to the Commercial Road site, which was about to be put on the market. They saw this site as a catalyst for getting The Fleece site to work, but gave up on The Fleece in late 2016 to concentrate on this site. Ken was very complimentary about the positive and proactive approach of the Council and its "strong team".

Work started on the Commercial Road property in March 2021. The opening date was put back a number of times due to delays with the construction project, caused by supply chain issues, for example with sourcing the steel frame. The first occupiers of the Food Dock were announced in March 2022, being the Sibling Distillery, Strip Steak Bar and Wholly Gelato ice cream. 'Smashing Plates', an 'unorthodox' Greek food business, and the Hop Kettle Brewing Company were added to the list in September 2022, which by that time also included Chuck brunch & burgers, Elote Mexican canteen and Bella Mia artisan pizzas. Hop Kettle opened their bar in October 2023, with several other businesses opening in November.

Still to do

The City Council kick-started the regeneration of the Docks by moving its offices there in the 1980s. But by the mid-2010s, it was starting to rattle around in its four warehouses. When I was first elected in 1996, the Council had around 1000 staff. By 2019 it would be down to a full-time equivalent of 180. This was due to a combination of factors – the transfer of the highways function back to the County Council, outsourcing of various functions like streetcare, leisure centres, IT and revenues and benefits and the sharing of other services like HR, legal and audit with other councils.

The first step in rationalising the Council's office accommodation was to consolidate in the Herbert, Kimberley and Phillpotts (HKP) Warehouses. North Warehouse, standing on its own, was easiest to deal with in terms of disposal, which was approved in June 2011. We considered creating a new council chamber in HKP but it was awkward in terms of creating a big enough space without pillars getting in the way. There was considerable councillor resistance to this, so we decided to keep the basement and third floor of North Warehouse and offer the ground, first and second to the market. In the end we did a deal with the global serviced office operator Regus, who carried out a major refurbishment of their parts while the council gave the top floor a much-needed revamp and reconfiguration. We had been accused by Liberal Democrat leader Jeremy Hilton of "flogging off North Warehouse". This wasn't true – Regus had a 10-year lease and the Council retained the freehold.

The deal, struck in difficult economic times, was based on a profit-share. The Council didn't initially see much from that after the refurbishment costs were taken out, but at least it lost the running costs of North Warehouse and secured substantial investment in the fabric of the building. As we consolidated in HKP, my office was moved from the first floor of North to the fourth floor of Phillpotts. Chief Executive Julian Wain bagged an enormous office for himself (which later would become mine) and I got lumbered with a very small one next door with no heating – which became known as 'The Fridge' because it was so cold in winter. I accepted it because we all had to make sacrifices in the face of austerity but, looking back, I shouldn't have done because it was seen by others as a diminution of my authority.

In February 2016, it was reported that the City Council could leave the Docks. I commented that: "We certainly do not need as much space as we used to. We have shrunk as an organisation." [32]

We decided to move in with the County Council at Shire Hall – the move took place in April 2019. I always thought the HKP Warehouses would make a stunning location for a good quality hotel – something which the city lacked. We marketed the buildings through agent Bruton Knowles and received several offers based on a conversion to a hotel. It was reported in January 2020 that Dowdeswell Estates, who were also the Council's preferred partner for the Fleece (see Chapter 22), had been selected for HKP too. Progress was slowed by the Coronavirus pandemic and legal issues related to the lease of Phillpotts Warehouse. It was reported in July 2022 that the Dowdeswell Estates Building Company Ltd had been put into liquidation but the Council insisted it was dealing with a separate company, the Dowdeswell Group. The Council had not entered into a contractual commitment with Dowdeswell and the Cabinet selected a new preferred bidder, believed to be for a residential and student accommodation scheme, in October 2023.

At the time of writing, the regeneration of the Docks is mature but not complete. One of the smaller sites to be developed within the Docks was some overgrown land next to the Tall Ship pub on Southgate Street. In 2016, The County to County Property Group from Cheltenham submitted a planning application for an apartment building on the site, which was approved in April 2017. They sold the site onto Cape Homes, part of the Mark Holland Group also from Cheltenham, who had refurbished Albion House over the road in Southgate Street. Cape Homes revised the planning consent, which was approved in September 2018, developing a three and a half storey building of 14 apartments with ground floor parking, as well as refurbishing four townhouses on Southgate Street. The project, which was described as 'challenging' started on site in 2018 and completed in spring 2019. The development was named Mariners Court after the nearby Mariners Church in the Docks.

Southgate Moorings car park, which in September 2008 had been earmarked as a new HQ for Ecclesiastical Insurance Group (EIG), is still a prime development site but until then remains a useful source of ongoing revenue, ringfenced to support the city's regeneration.

Ecclesiastical Insurance, who, in the early 1970's, had relocated their HQ from Aldwych, London to Gloucester, had outgrown their premises in Brunswick Road. As well as their main building at Beaufort House, they were also occupying several adjoining period properties on Spa Road and Fitzalan House on the corner of Park Road and Montpellier. Their lease on Beaufort House had a small number of years left to run and we were all keen to secure their future in the city. The Regional Development Agency identified the Southgate Moorings car park as a potential site for them.

Ecclesiastical proposed offices totalling 7250 sqm (78,000 sq ft). Sir Terry Farrell & Partners were appointed architects for the scheme by EIG following a design competition.[33] Farrells also designed the MI5 building and Embankment Place in London. The design was completed in January 2009.[34] A formal announcement was expected from the EIG Board in Spring 2010, but there was a hiatus as the economy recovered from the 2008 financial crash.

The Citizen reported in May 2011, "It's official, Ecclesiastical are moving to the Docks". It went on to describe how the company's 600 staff would move into a new purpose-built HQ by the water, following an agreement being signed with SWRDA, which was in the process of being wound up. Transformation Director of Ecclesiastical Graham Johnson sounded a note of caution, saying, "signing the agreement is only the beginning for some of the next crucial steps in the process."[35] Farrells were replaced as architects for the scheme by Stride Treglown following a procurement process. Stride Treglown had worked on a number of high-profile office schemes in the area, including the headquarters for St James's Place in Cirencester. At the time, initial design concepts for Ecclesiastical's new building were expected in April/May 2012, with the project due to be completed by late 2015. The new building was quite a challenge to design, with a constrained site required to accommodate 100,000 sq ft of offices, a 150-space multi-level car park and a desire for active uses on the ground floor by the Dockside.

Despite a lot of detailed work being done, Ecclesiastical pulled out of their Docks HQ move in 2013. Chief Executive Michael Tripp said he was "bitterly disappointed". Managing Director Steve Wood explained, "Unfortunately we have been defeated by the economic conditions and the challenging office construction market in the region. The funding options are simply not viable." It was reported to have cost the company in excess of £1 million.[36] They stayed put in their Brunswick Road offices until 2021, having signed an agreement for a new HQ on Gloucester Business Park in Brockworth, despite efforts by the City Council to keep them in the centre of Gloucester and a survey of staff preferences showing a majority in favour of staying in the city centre.

In January 2016, an image was revealed of what a new events venue on the Southgate Moorings car park could look like. The idea for the "development of a multi-purpose venue capable of use for theatre, concerts, exhibitions and conferences" was first mentioned in the City Council 1996 Draft Local Plan. The 2016 plan was said to have a capacity of 2500 and looked remarkably like the Sydney Opera House! In reality, its release into the public domain was premature as there was no detailed plan sitting behind the sketch, which was drawn up as a favour by a friendly local architect. The proposal wasn't progressed any further.

Conclusion

The Docks is Gloucester's most well-known and mature regeneration scheme. Like many others, it has been a long-time in the making, has changed over time from what was originally envisaged and still has some work to do before it can be truly described as complete.

4. UNIVERSITY CHALLENGE

The story of how the Oxstalls Campus came to be saved for higher education is a fascinating one and, like the best stories, it has a happy ending. The full tale includes a 'David and Goliath' battle of a residents' group versus a developer wanting to build a Tesco superstore, with public inquiries and court cases thrown in for good measure. It also provides an insight into the relationship between Cheltenham and Gloucester and between the City and County Councils at that time. The Oxstalls Campus was in the ward I represented for 24 years between 1996 and 2020, but it had been closed by the time I was elected. As an opposition member at the time, my involvement in the events leading up to its reopening was limited, but I was actively involved in the project two decades later to bring the University's Business School to Oxstalls.

The Closure of the Oxstalls Campus

The chain of events which led to the closure of Oxstalls is complex. A college (the College of Domestic Science) was first built on the site around 1955 and was expanded in the 1960s and 1980s.[37] The University of Gloucestershire itself can trace its roots back to the Mechanics Institutes in Cheltenham and Gloucester, established in 1834 and 1840 respectively.

In 1986, Janet Trotter arrived as Principal of the College of St Paul & St Mary, which were two Church of England colleges, predominantly providing teacher education, and based in Cheltenham. At that time, the County Council ran GlosCAT (the Gloucestershire College of Art and Technology), which provided post-16 further and higher education.

Government policy at the time was that there was no future for small teacher training colleges or for a 'mixed economy' of further and higher education institutions. So Janet Trotter was urged by the Department for Education and Science to work with the County Council and GlosCAT to establish a single college of higher education. She had just 18 months in which to do it. Discussions took place with the County Council and, in particular, with County Councillor Henry Elwes and Chief Education Officer Keith Anderson. There was considerable suspicion and hostility between the partners but they agreed to set aside their differences and set up a Working Party of both Governing Bodies and key staff to explore the options.

It wasn't a new idea. In the late 1960s and 70s, there had been some discussion that St Paul & St Mary plus the four County Council Colleges of Education could merge. Despite having appointed a Principal to take charge of the merged colleges, the deal fell through at the eleventh hour. Instead, GlosCAT was formed from the County Council colleges whilst the Colleges of St Paul and St Mary merged in 1979.

This time, the plan for a merger succeeded. In March 1990, the Higher Education section of GlosCAT merged with the College of St Paul & St Mary, Cheltenham to become the Cheltenham & Gloucester College of Higher Education. GlosCAT Principal, Derek Williams, had been in his role for some time and was heading towards retirement. Janet Trotter became the Principal of the merged college.

The conditions for acquiring what was known as University Title over this period changed as a result of government policy. In 1992, through the Further and Higher Education Act, all polytechnics were allowed to become universities without particular scrutiny, as part of Prime Minister John Major's vision of a 'Classless Society'. It was declared that no more universities would be created but in the mid-1990s criteria were set for the gaining of University Title. These included a minimum of 4000 students, a range of subjects, Taught Degree Awarding Powers (TDAP) and Research Degree Awarding Powers (RDAP). The latter was difficult to achieve and depended on the number of research degrees completed, staff ability to supervise higher degrees and scrutiny by the Quality Assurance Agency (QAA). The College received RDAP in the late 1990s and was the first college to meet these criteria. The way was then clear for it to apply to the Privy Council for University Title, which was finally granted in 2001.

In 1992, the new institution had eight separate sites including

Oxstalls, some with only a few dozen students, and it leased parts of the Park and Brunswick campuses from GlosCAT, making 10 sites in total. Some, including Oxstalls, were in poor condition and needed millions of pounds spent on them.

At its first meeting, the Governing Council of the College recognised it needed an accommodation strategy and appointed consultants to undertake a property review. The strategy adopted focused on the Park, Francis Close Hall and Pittville campuses and proposed disposing of Rosehill and Shaftesbury in Cheltenham, which was also very controversial, and Oxstalls in Gloucester. The College felt there was a logic in their campuses being close together and they could accommodate everything in Cheltenham.

The College insisted it remained committed to Gloucester and proposed "acquiring another piece of land for a small purpose-built higher education facility."[38] In August 1992, the County Council's Chief Education Officer Keith Anderson wrote to councillors saying, "the current thinking is that this might be in the form of a prestigious management centre offering post-experience, and post-graduate, particularly part-time, management programmes".

Although there was talk of a £4 million investment in partnership with the City Council, which could have been on the Cattle Market site or a business park on the fringes of the city, it was described as falling "well short of Council's ambitions for the city" in a report to councillors and dismissed as "a sop" by Liberal Democrat group leader Mary Gould.

The Oxstalls Campus closed in July 1993. It had been given top marks by a government inspector the previous November, who described it as a "pleasant and well-maintained site". A College spokesman at the time commented that a new purpose-built campus in Cheltenham would be better. Although superficially the campus buildings may have looked well-maintained, there was no doubt they required significant investment.

The closure raised fears the buildings would be demolished. City Council Leader Kevin Stephens said, "I have asked Principal Janet Trotter on several occasions to give a clear statement that the building will not be bulldozed while the future of higher education in the county is being considered." A College spokesman said there were no plans to demolish the buildings. [39]

The old Oxstalls college building. Credit: Paul Dowle

The University for Gloucester Project

The proposed closure of Oxstalls and the hole that would leave in terms of higher education in the city prompted thoughts about Gloucester trying to create its own university. Gloucester was one of just nine cities of its size not to have a university. The academic Sir Christopher Ball, who would act as a consultant for the project, had said: "A city without a university in the next century will be like a country without an airport."

In July 1992, Conservative group leader Councillor Mike Pullon put forward a motion to the City Council proposing the authority should start to look at such a move. It got unanimous backing and they agreed to investigate sites including the Oxstalls Campus and the Cattle Market at St Oswalds Road, which would have had to relocate. It was envisaged they could work with CGCHE or Bristol Polytechnic (which later became the University of the West of England or UWE). Although the motion was backed by the other parties, Liberal Democrat Mary Gould said, "I am slightly unhappy with a University of Gloucester – a broader-based county effort would be better."

In October 1992, City Council Chief Executive Graham Garbutt met Alf Morris, the new Vice Chancellor of UWE, saying, "My brief is to explore all options for higher education and I am doing this with the new University at the earliest opportunity." There was even a suggestion that UWE could buy the Oxstalls Campus.

The Council was also approached by Professor Frank Hartley of Cranfield University, based in Bedfordshire. Cranfield had wanted to diversify away from military physics and into medical physics in response to the end of the Cold War. The move was seen as part of the 'peace dividend'. Graham Garbutt, whose wife was a hospital consultant, held discussions with Lady Sonia Hornby, Chair of the Hospitals Trust, and Mariella Dexter, its Chief Executive. The hospital already had a medical physics research unit, so a partnership seemed logical. It was hoped it would grow into something substantial. Together they established the Cranfield University Institute of Medical Science and associated medical research at Gloucestershire Royal Hospital which was described as an "important part of the University's research and development project". The partnership with the hospital lasted a decade or more and produced a number of excellent graduates and research fellows, but ended when Cranfield moved away from offering health-related courses.

The City Council recruited Philip Oakley, the former Chief Executive of UCCA, the Universities Central Council on Admissions, to head up the university project. A report by Coopers & Lybrand, commissioned by the City Council, GlosCAT and UWE, showed that Gloucester and the Forest of Dean had the lowest proportion of 18–21-year-olds in Gloucestershire in higher education – hence the need for a significant HE presence in the west of the county. The difference was particularly pronounced in inner city Gloucester and some wards in the Forest of Dean where participation was less than 10%, compared with more than 80% in the more affluent areas of Cheltenham.

Partners in the university project included GlosCAT, Cranfield, UWE, Gloucestershire Royal Hospital NHS Trust, the County Council, the Open University and the Training & Enterprise Council. Some questioned whether, at a time of consolidation in the sector, the idea that Gloucester could have its own university was 'grounded in reality'.

In a letter to Gloucester MP Douglas French in March 1993, Janet Trotter, writing on behalf of her governors, said, "The present College's strategic plan is the only way to avoid having branches/outposts of neighbouring universities (e.g. Bristol, Bath, Birmingham) functioning in small and insignificant units within the county." She added, "The Government's current policy of consolidation would militate against any presence other than token."

Lord Lieutenant Henry Elwes, who had a long-standing interest in the issue as a former Vice Chair of the County Education Committee and Governor of a number of colleges, wrote in a letter to resident Ron Jones, "I don't find the current fragmented efforts to establish links with other universities very attractive when we already have our own college on the threshold of achieving all the criteria for university status." Elwes was Chairman of the County Council from 1983 to 1985 when the role was, in effect, the equivalent to being Leader of the Council today. He was an important and influential advocate for the College and its drive for university status. His contribution was acknowledged by being awarded the first Honorary Doctorate, having a building named after him on the Park Campus and later becoming the University's Pro-Chancellor.

In January 1995, the City Council bid £1.3 million for the Oxstalls site, but the offer was rejected by the College. In March 1996, the Council's Policy & Resources Committee authorised an increased offer. Council Leader Kevin Stephens said, "What we intend to do will complement what is provided at Cheltenham and Gloucester (College) not compete against it."

The Oxstalls Action Group

Prompted by the closure of the Oxstalls Campus and the threat of unwanted development of the site as a Tesco superstore, the 'Hands Off Oxstalls' group (which later became the Oxstalls Action Group), was set up in July 1992. An initial meeting was attended by 40 people. The Chairman was Dr Evelyn Christmas and the Vice Chairman Bryan Jerrard. Dr Christmas was a lecturer at the

Domestic Science College before being made redundant and Mr Jerrard lectured at Oxstalls for 16 years training teachers and for 8 years in the Department of Town and Country Planning. So, for them, the cause was not only about the community, it was personal.

Dr Christmas died in 2016 aged 91. Former Citizen journalist, Hugh Worsnip wrote an obituary of her describing how she entered this battle "armed with a push bike, a manual typewriter and three degrees in history". She was nominated for an honour but it was unsuccessful.

The Secretary for the majority of the time was Pauline Quinn, with Joan Jones taking over in later years. Mike Sargeant was Treasurer throughout. Bryan Jerrard, as Vice Chairman, provided support to Dr Christmas, but stepped down in May 1997 when he moved away for family reasons. Ron Pring, a churchwarden at the nearby Holy Trinity Church, organised the traffic surveys. Other committee members included residents Marion Pingriff, Linda Hillier, Daphne Poole, David Nicholls and Ann Veale. Resident, owner of Oxstalls Service Station and future councillor Jim Porter was an active member until resigning from the committee in May 1997. John Holman acted as the conduit between the group and the Civic Trust.

Public meetings held in August 1992 and January 1993 at Holy Trinity Church, Longlevens were attended by around 300 people. Two orderly protest marches around the perimeter of the campus were held in September 1992 and March 1993. *The Citizen* reported that the September march attracted 200 people holding a variety of banners. The group also arranged their own traffic surveys to challenge those produced by Tesco's consultants.

Membership of the group was at a minimum cost of £1 per family and there were almost 200 members as of October 1994. Fundraising was undertaken, which included quiz nights, barn dances, car boot sales and private donations, which raised over £10,000 in total. One barn dance featured the Green Willow Band. David Jones on the keyboard was a traffic consultant who appeared at both planning hearings on behalf of the Action Group. A concert at Holy Trinity Church included a gospel choir from the Church of God of Prophecy in Gloucester, Ukrainian singers and poetry for the princely sum of £2 per ticket. Car stickers were sold, alongside collecting signatures, in the city centre. The most important use of these funds was to pay for a barrister, William Upton, to represent the group at the planning inquiries and court cases.

The group organised two parliamentary petitions. The first, of over 7000 signatures, was presented to Gloucester MP Douglas French and his Cheltenham counterpart Nigel Jones in March 1993 and called for an "immediate independent appraisal of CGCHE's financial and educational strategy". The two MPs presented it to the House of Commons at 10.45pm on 29th March according to the Hansard record of proceedings. The second, with 3450 signatures, was presented to the House of Commons by Douglas French on 19th December 1995 and called for Government intervention to "ensure the College premises at Oxstalls are saved from demolition and reopened for the provision of vocational and technical courses."

The Action Group were prolific letter writers and garnered support for their cause from wherever they could. Letters of support were received from Hucclecote Community Association, Barton Residents Association, Gloucester Unemployed Community Resource Centre (headed by former councillor Dave Short), the Mothers' Union, Holy Trinity Whist Club, Holy Trinity Pram Club, Gloucestershire Chinese Community Association (chaired by Longlevens resident Mew Ning Chan) and the British Asian Ladies Association to name but a few.

Bryan Jerrard tried to involve the Bishop of Guildford, Rt Rev Michael Adie, as Chairman of the Church of England Board of Education. Sometime later, there is a suggestion that he wrote to the Sultan of Brunei to ask for a contribution towards the new facilities on the basis that there had been one or two students from Brunei at the College. There is no evidence that His Majesty put his hand in his very deep pockets on this occasion. Joan Jones wrote to the Archbishop of Canterbury. The group also wrote to MPs Frank Field, Michael Fallon and William Waldegrave. The letter to Waldegrave and a later one to Prime Minister John Major claimed the College's actions were a breach of the Government's 'Citizen's Charter' policy. Another to Michael Portillo, the Chief Secretary to the Treasury, focused on what they perceived as a waste of public money by the College. Dr Christmas had already written to Professor Graeme Davies, the Chief Executive of the

Higher Education Funding Council for England (HEFCE), who had allocated capital towards the building plan in Cheltenham, expressing concern about the "commitment of public money to a scheme which has been made highly questionable". In April 1993, City MP Douglas French wrote to Education Secretary John Patten urging him to intervene, but he refused to do so as the College was an independent body.

In December 1993, campaigners along with Douglas French and representatives from the City Council met with Tim Boswell, the Higher Education Minister. Douglas French said, "We want Oxstalls out of the clutches of the College in Cheltenham and this will be the first step in what will eventually become a new University of Gloucester." The Minister suggested early engagement with HEFCE.

In 1994, the College was continuing to work towards University Title. The Action Group asked people to write to Tony Newton MP, the 'Lord President' of the Privy Council, asking for it to be refused as it was not meeting regional needs. It also asked that if University Title were granted the institution should not be allowed to have Gloucester or Gloucestershire in its name. The latter would not have concerned some within the College who saw the 'University of Cheltenham' as a stronger marketing proposition. Others, including Mike Cogger and later Paul Drake (who had been a Labour County Councillor in the city), flew the flag for Gloucester within the College. Cogger would go on to become the Dean of the Faculty of Applied Sciences, playing a key role as the most senior person on site at the new Oxstalls Campus.

Relations between the College and the City Council were at this time exceptionally strained. The Oxstalls Action Group's campaign of letter writing did little to change what the College saw as its determination to create stronger higher education provision in the county.

In September 1996, the Oxstalls Action Group gave evidence to the Dearing Inquiry into access to higher education.

In May 1997, to mark the 150th anniversary of the founding of St Paul's College, one of the predecessors of CGCHE, a Cathedral service was held, attended by Archbishop of Canterbury George Carey. Protestors gathered in the Cathedral Close holding foot-high letters spelling out 'Gloucester Betrayed'. Although a deal between the City

Council and the College appeared to be in the offing at that time, there had been delays and it was not yet signed and sealed.

The Oxstalls Action Group closed in September 2001, once its work was done. Its remaining funds were given to a charity (the Edith Foster & Mary Playne Fund) to help students in the County who were "in need, hardship or distress", which was administered by the Chief Education Officer. £500 was given to the Parochial Church Council for Holy Trinity Church in Longlevens.

The Cheltenham/Gloucester and City/County dynamic

The battle over Oxstalls gives an insight into the relationship between Cheltenham and Gloucester at the time. There has long been a rivalry between 'town and city' but these days I like to think the relationship is more mature. The proposed concentration of higher education facilities in Cheltenham seemed to trigger a war of words between politicians, the newspapers serving the two places and the College.

In May 1992, when plans went on display for the £30 million Cheltenham scheme, Conservative city councillor Terry Wathen accused Cheltenham of "suffering delusions of grandeur". His colleague Mike Pullon, who was prone to hyperbole, added that "The College Board have shown all the subtlety of the classic unscrupulous asset stripper."

In November 1992, Janet Trotter wrote to councillors appealing for traditional rivalries to be put aside, saying, "There is little doubt that our aspirations will be jeopardised if rivalry between Cheltenham & Gloucester is allowed to override the needs of the County as a whole." In a letter to Douglas French in March 1993, she said, "the only consequences of thwarting the extremely far-sighted and imaginative plan of the College to consolidate at Cheltenham will be to deny the presence of a vigorous, modern university within the County."

While *The Citizen* was supportive of the campaign to save Oxstalls, its sister paper in Cheltenham, the Gloucestershire Echo, took a different view. Its comment piece on 27th September 1994 said, "The City Council is spending money on a study to discover whether a second university could be set up in Gloucester. That is money down the drain. If Gloucester councillors do not bury the hatchet and support the College, they will only have themselves to blame if the College chose to call the new institution the University of Cheltenham". On 12th December 1994 they added, "They may have good intentions but Gloucester City councillors are living in cloud cuckoo land if they think the Oxstalls site can remain an educational building. If councillors insist Oxstalls cannot be used for housing they will create a financial nightmare for CGCHE – and Oxstalls may be left to rot." The Oxstalls Action Group noted what they saw as The Echo's hostility to Gloucester's "laudable policy of restoring much-needed higher education in the city."

Even when the two sides had come together, The Echo was still pointing the finger at the city to blame for the years of stand-off. On 22nd July 1998 it added, "The College for its part has offered a succession of olive branches in the last five years which were roundly rejected."

The tension between the two layers of local government in Gloucester was also evident, perhaps fuelled by the City Council's aspirations at that time to acquire unitary authority status – which would have taken powers away from the County Council.

It is true that the County Council agreed to back the fight to save Oxstalls, but the drive seemed to come from councillors rather than council officers. Even after the County Education Committee had backed saving Oxstalls (led by Gloucester councillors Terry Wathen and Bob Wilton) in September 1992, Chief Education Officer Keith Anderson wrote to West Gloucestershire MP Paul Marland saying, "Everything possible must be done to ensure the Higher Education College can develop in the way proposed."

In October 1992, the issue was discussed by the County Council with a motion proposed by Di Phillips (Liberal Democrat) and seconded by Tony Ayland (Labour). It was passed by a large majority. The motion read:

"*That this Council:*

> *i. Views with considerable regret, and urges the Cheltenham & Gloucester College of Higher Education to reconsider, its decision to cease using Oxstalls Campus for Higher Education provision;*
>
> *ii. Expresses its concerns at the impending loss of Higher Education provision within the City of Gloucester and regrets*

> *the lack of strategic planning of Higher Education provision within the County;*
>
> *iii. Regrets, and urges the College to reconsider, its decision to dispose of the Oxstalls Campus;*
>
> *iv. In view of the proposals to develop the site, recognises the concerns of those residents living adjacent to the Oxstalls Campus and;*
>
> *v. Continues together with Gloucester City Council to seek a postponement of the planning inquiry into the development of the campus until after the Gloucester City Local Plan inquiry has been completed."*

In the middle of the Tesco planning inquiry, the County Council issued a press statement saying that its Chief Executive, Michael Honey, had been "misrepresented and his views completely misconstrued" during the inquiry. This came about after City Council Chief Executive Graham Garbutt proposed a study into having a University of the West of England presence in Gloucester. This led some to believe that the County Council also backed this idea. Whilst the County Council opposed the supermarket plans at the inquiry, Michael Honey said he wouldn't want to undermine the College or their bid for university status.

That wasn't enough to convince campaigners that the County Council was on their side. Dr Christmas wrote to Michael Honey in 1993 referring to the "County Council's prolonged silence and apparent failure to recognise the city has a legitimate interest… in higher education" and in October 1995 to County Councillors saying that she had "concluded officers are hostile to the city's endeavours".

As late as November 2000, *The Citizen* reported that Gloucester Mayor Terry Haines was disappointed not to be invited to photocall at the Campus. It involved the three parties' education spokespersons Terry Parker, Peter Clarke and Lady Mavis Dunrossil, who were photographed sitting on a JCB. College spokeswoman, Joanna Wynn, said the ceremony was to publicise the County Council's contribution of £500,000 to the new campus.

The Tesco planning battle

The Oxstalls site was marketed in 1991-92 by Bayleys,

Chartered Surveyors, of Cheltenham. Essex-based developer Carter Commercial Developments came forward with a scheme for a 55,000 sq ft Tesco superstore, complete with a filling station and hundreds of parking spaces, covering 15 acres of the 21-acre site. A complex planning battle then ensued. It has never been made public how much money the College would have received from the Tesco deal, but it is believed to have been £10 million – a sum which would have gone a long way towards financing its development plans.

Citizen reporter Hugh Worsnip wrote in his column on 22nd July 1992, that the Tesco store would have involved a dual carriageway from Estcourt Road to a new roundabout at the Oxstalls Lane junction, adding that, "We need a new supermarket at Oxstalls like a hole in the head."

Protestors were busy collecting signatures, citing the impact on the area and also its local traders, including the Co-op store on Cheltenham Road. A petition of 10,319 signatures was presented to Mayor Ben Richards, a Longlevens councillor and member of the planning committee, on 6th September 1992. The petitioners were "appalled by the iniquitous and unjustifiable determination of CGCHE to sell Oxstalls Campus for the sole purpose of investing the proceeds in its Cheltenham property."

The Oxstalls planning application was rejected by the Council's Planning Committee, with 222 objections received. The developers appealed against the decision and a public inquiry was held in April 1993. The atmosphere of the inquiry was described as 'difficult' and 'hostile'.

In May 1993, the supermarket appeal was dismissed by Inspector Michael Hurley on zoning, traffic and amenity grounds. He believed the supermarket should be at the Cattle Market as set out in the Council's Local Plan. In his decision notice, the Inspector put retention of educational use at Oxstalls top of his list of main issues, but noted that on its own it was not sufficient reason for refusal.

Vice Chairman of the Oxstalls Action Group, Bryan Jerrard, welcomed the news saying, "The inspector's decision is excellent news for the local community at Longlevens, for people who live near the College and local shopkeepers. We have won this battle but not the war. Now we have to make sure higher education is kept at Oxstalls and in Gloucester."

Within a matter of days, *The Citizen* reported a new plan for more than 250 homes for the Oxstalls site. Council Leader Kevin Stephens warned, "The College will be as unsuccessful in seeking permission for a housing estate as they were for a supermarket." [40] At that stage, the supermarket proposals hadn't been killed off completely as the applicants tried various routes through the planning system to get consent. But the College was clearly looking to keep their options open. A planning application was later lodged but was never decided.

A separate public inquiry was held in 1994 into the City Council's Local Plan, which had allocated the disused abattoir at the Cattle Market for the one additional supermarket which planning experts GL Hearn said the city needed. The freehold of that site was owned by the City Council, with a lease in place to Weddel Swift, part of Lord Vestey's empire, with 90 years remaining. Councillors had approved the principle of a new store at the Cattle Market in July 1993, which was likely to have the effect of both thwarting the College's plans and gaining a significant capital receipt for the Council.

Carter Commercial Developments and the College objected to that allocation, arguing that there was a weak relationship between the Cattle Market site and the city centre and that public transport to Oxstalls was better. They claimed the allocation of the Cattle Market site was "hasty, opportunistic and reactive".

Safeway had been expected to be the operator of the superstore on the Cattle Market site. On the eve of the first public inquiry, Tesco wrote to the City Council suggesting they might be interested in this site too. Safeway later bowed out of the Cattle Market site [41] leaving Tesco with a clear run to submit their own plans for a 51,000 sq ft store with 465 car parking spaces. [42] When it was announced that Tesco were in negotiations for the Cattle Market store, Evelyn Christmas said, with perhaps a hint of irony, "It is nice to know that Tesco has converted to our cause."

Campaigners thought they may have scented victory when Speyhawk, parent company of Carter Commercial, (owned by property tycoon Trevor Osborne) went into receivership owing

£350 million. But Carter kept trading as a going concern. [43]

Local Plan Inspector Peter Norman concluded that the land at Oxstalls was not suitable for a supermarket – but may be suitable for housing – noting that "highway works would be visually harmful to an attractive suburb." He ruled the Cattle Market site should be allocated instead. [44]

Carter appealed to the High Court to overturn the Inspector's decision on a technicality. They contended he had "misunderstood government policy on out-of-town supermarkets", "failed to reach a balanced judgement on traffic" and "failed to assess the financial benefits of the scheme". Mr Justice Latham threw out the appeal and ordered Carter to pay the Council's costs of between £10-15,000. He agreed with the Council that the Oxstalls application was 'premature' given the Cattle Market allocation.

Carter had planned to take their legal challenge to another level but in January 1995 they accepted defeat and withdrew their application to the Court of Appeal, agreeing to pay the Council's and the Secretary of State's costs – believed to run to tens of thousands of pounds. [45]

In June 1995, Oxstalls was advertised in the Estates Gazette magazine, but before any deal was concluded, events took another turn.

Peace Breaks Out

Vandalism of the site sparked renewed calls for Oxstalls to be sold to the City Council. The College had refused to accept an offer from the Council of over £1 million. [46] *The Citizen* reported in August 1996 that the College's adviser, Tim Griffin of Bayley Donaldson, recommended acceptance of the city's £1.3 million offer. The College's ruling Council refused, believing they could hold out for a higher bid. [47]

Lord Lieutenant Henry Elwes brought in Richard Payne, former Chief Executive of the Stroud & Swindon Building Society, to chair a high-powered working group, named the University for Gloucestershire Task Force, to break the deadlock. Also on the task force were Trevor Allen (boss of Ebley Tyres), Christine Megson of GlosCAT, Peter Easy from the College and Philip Oakley representing the City Council. Payne had also been Chief Executive of the Gloucestershire Development Agency and served on the board of Gloucestershire's Training and Enterprise Council. As a building society boss, he had overseen the takeover of several smaller building societies, so was a skilled negotiator. He told me he felt his independence was key and his aim was for everyone to feel they got something out of it.   Solicitor Jon Holmes was Leader of the City Council by that time and was a different character to his predecessor Kevin Stephens (to whom he would later hand back the leadership). The deal struck by Payne was that the City Council would buy the freehold of Oxstalls for £1.8 million (which later became £2 million) and lease it back to the College. Ironically this would be paid for from selling the Cattle Market site to Tesco. The Council would also back the College's bid for university status. [48]

Chair of the College's Council, Chris Callen, insisted this wasn't a U-turn, saying, "We always took the view that we should have a presence in Gloucester – not necessarily at the Oxstalls site." [49]

The election in May 1997 of Tony Blair's New Labour Government with its 'Education, Education, Education' mantra was also seen as timely by some, with its new drive to widen participation in higher education – something which had been recognised as an issue in the west of the County. The Government adopted a target of increasing participation in higher education to 50% of 18-year-olds. This opened up funding opportunities for the College to bid into.

The New Campus

The College started the process of designing a new campus and fundraising to build it. Peter Clegg of Bath-based firm Feilden Clegg was engaged as the lead architect. The practice had already worked with the College on one of its Cheltenham campuses.

There was debate about the nature of the campus and its design. An estimate of £5 million was set aside for building work, but a decision was taken to extend the campus to include student housing and a student union facility. There was a fear that if the campus did not match the award-winning Cheltenham campuses, students might migrate to Cheltenham, which would be counter-productive. It was decided that Oxstalls would be home to one of the College's strongest subject areas - Sport and Exercise Science.

It soon became apparent that the cost was going to be far more than originally envisaged. *The Citizen* reported on 5th March 1998 that the building would cost £10 million – twice the original estimate. The University's Annual Report 2002-3 referred to "the £19 million Oxstalls Campus".

The design went on view in July 1998. Janet Trotter was clear the College wanted to build an excellent building giving it 'parity of esteem' with Cheltenham. She said, "We really want to make a new statement for the new millennium in Gloucester." [50] It was well-received – of the 184 who filled in questionnaires, 180 backed the plans. [51]

The campus was made up of two main buildings. There was a Learning Centre with 200 workstations, library space and high-tech learning area, and a 200-seat lecture theatre. The Sports and Exercise Science building included a Sports Hall and adjacent research laboratories, with the latest biomechanical and physiological equipment. There was a state-of-the-art Environmental Chamber and Hydrostatic Tank, which were used by Olympic athletes to recreate the conditions in different locations where they would be competing. A floodlit all-weather synthetic pitch was proposed, which would be used for hockey, soccer and rugby. The Leisure and Sport Research Unit was able to access the new GL1 Leisure Centre, the nearby Oxstalls Tennis Centre and Plock Court playing fields and the sports injury clinic at the Winfield Hospital on Tewkesbury Road, where Olympic doctor Rod Jaques practised. There were also 175 units of student accommodation to supplement those on the corner of Westgate Street and Quay Street in the city centre. The initial estimate was that there would be 600 full-time and 300 part-time students at the campus.

The design had a strong environmental focus. The building became the first higher education institution to have solar panels and it won the 2002 Civic Award for 'outstanding building for the environment' as well as a Royal Institute of British Architecture (RIBA) award for outstanding architecture.

A planning application was submitted in August 1998 and seems to have had a fairly smooth passage through the system, being approved by the Council's Planning Committee in February 1999. There were 8 letters of objection from neighbouring properties in Oxstalls Lane and Oxstalls Way worried about lack of parking, siting of the artificial pitch close to houses and flooding from the Wotton Brook. There were also 13 letters which were supportive but also suggested a roundabout from Cheltenham Road and expressed concerns about parking and the siting of the artificial pitch. The Oxstalls Action Group also had worries about parking, which seem to have been well-founded as it has been an increasing issue since the opening of the new campus and was a point of contention for the Campus's expansion over a decade later.

The project was granted £4 million from the Higher Education Funding Council's 'Poor Estates Initiatives'. Other funding came from the County Council (£500,000), Allchurches Trust (owners of Ecclesiastical Insurance), Birds Eye Wall's, Cheltenham & Gloucester plc, CHK Charities and the Weston family (of Associated British Foods and Primark).

The College continued to work towards University Title. I put forward a motion to the Full City Council in July 1999 supporting their bid but stating that it "should not be granted until the College has entered into an irrevocable commitment to a major presence in Gloucester." The Chief Executive of the Council wrote to the Government to communicate this but Malcolm Wicks MP, Minister for Higher Education, responded that the status would be granted on academic merit not location. [52]

In July 2000, negotiations between the College and the City Council hit a stumbling block.[53] The protracted discussions meant the campus would not now be ready to use until September 2002 – a year later than planned.

The Council had given some ground in negotiations. It moved from asking for £60,000 per year rent (which was half the market rate) to a peppercorn rent and also offered the College a bursary of £30,000 a year. The deal foundered on the conditions attached to the option the College would have to buy the campus back from the Council. The main issue was what would happen to the profits if the College was to sell the campus in future, known as 'clawback'. The College was offering 20% for 20 years, reducing to 5% thereafter, whilst the Council wanted 50%.

Janet Trotter wrote to Honorary Fellows on the 19th June 2000 saying, "Having consulted the College's advisers we agreed we could not recommend this to the College's Council."

Council Leader Kevin Stephens told *The Citizen*, "Despite the best efforts of all sides, the original deal between the Council and the College fell through and the Council has withdrawn its offer of £2 million. But we are delighted that the College is able to proceed with demolition." [54] The College made up the shortfall by selling two of its properties in The Park area of Cheltenham.

Demolition started in November 2000 with construction following straight after. The contractors were HBG Construction. In May 2001, Sir Brian Fender, Chief Executive of HEFCE, was the guest of honour at a foundation stone laying ceremony.

The College was finally granted University Title in October 2001, after having first been granted Research Degree Awarding Powers. There was an initial intake of 350 Sports and Exercise Science students, plus 700 Level II and III students who transferred to Oxstalls from the Francis Close Hall and Hardwick campuses. Francis Close Hall had historically been the centre for sports and physical education, dating back to the days when the College of St Paul had been designated as a Secondary PE College after World War II. But its facilities were ageing and had been overtaken by others in the country.

The new Oxstalls campus was officially opened on 14th October 2002 by Gloucester MP Parmjit Dhanda, who stepped up when Minister of State for Lifelong Learning and Higher Education, Margaret Hodge (who is the sister of former City Council Officer Sue Oppenheimer) couldn't make it. Margaret Hodge did visit in January 2003.

The campus has been successful as a centre for sports development and associated research and, more recently, for nursing courses and, as described later, a new Business School.

A Triumph for the Awkward or for Common Sense?

Hugh Worsnip described the opening of the new campus at Oxstalls as a "Triumph for the Awkward" and nominated Evelyn Christmas as the "unlikely-to-become Vice Chancellor". Many would acknowledge that the Oxstalls Action Group, backed by the City Council, *The Citizen* newspaper, the Civic Trust and many others, had a significant influence on events.

Others argue that it was the election of the Blair Government in 1997, with their mantra of 'Education, Education, Education' and their focus on widening participation in higher education, which made funding available that otherwise would not have been there.

What we will never know is whether or how the result would have been different if the City Council had adopted a less confrontational approach to the College. Should they have embraced the College's offer of a Business School elsewhere in the city and used it as a starting point for negotiation, rather than pursuing their own ultimately unsuccessful university project?

But, most importantly, a significant higher education presence was maintained in the city and it would be the basis for future growth, both at Oxstalls and later elsewhere in the city. Janet Trotter can also look back on how things turned out with a good deal of pride. She secured University Title for the College, becoming its first Vice Chancellor, and built a state-of-the-art campus at Oxstalls. She later succeeded Henry Elwes as Lord Lieutenant for Gloucestershire and was a popular and highly-respected figure. Far from being hostile to Gloucester, which is how she was portrayed by some, in my experience as Lord Lieutenant she could not have been more helpful to the city. That was reflected by the award to her of Freedom of the City in 2018, when she became the first Honorary Freewoman of Gloucester. That is quite a turnaround by any standards.

Blackfriars

In January 2008, the University of Gloucestershire announced plans to relocate its Arts, Media and Communications faculty from Pittville to Blackfriars, bringing new programmes in dance, drama, fashion and creative industries. They also hoped to include student accommodation and a students' union.[55] It was due to cost at least £40 million and bring 2000 students to the city centre as part of plans to grow the University's overall numbers from 9500 to 15000 by 2012. Vice Chancellor Professor Patricia Broadfoot said at the time, "If we're to realise our ambitions for growth and for becoming embedded in the county, the university has to have a hard look at its estate and explore opportunities to work in partnership with others at its site in Blackfriars, Gloucester."

The proposal came about because GHURC's Chris Oldershaw had been searching for a way to increase the University's presence and impact in Gloucester. Oldershaw saw the important role that the University played in the local economy. Patricia Broadfoot came from Bristol University which had a city centre campus, bringing large economic benefits. The University had the Oxstalls Campus, but its impact was limited due to not being in the city centre. Universities generally were keen to partner with their host cities – both as a marketing tool but also as a broader partnership. The University had its roots in the Church and Patricia Broadfoot saw the links with Blackfriars Priory as both being a nod to its religious past and a unique opportunity to establish the University in a prestigious place with real gravitas. The University Council for its part recognised a 'strategic mistake' in the past of withdrawing from Gloucester and wanted to be a genuine University of Gloucestershire, not just of Cheltenham. They felt there was a sense of real vision and imagination for the city and wanted to be part of it.

City MP Parmjit Dhanda described it as "potentially one of the most exciting developments in Gloucester's long history."[56] The project was abandoned in October 2009, before it had a chance to gain any real momentum, when the University hit serious financial troubles. It had a £3 million deficit and was on the 'at risk list' of the Higher Education Funding Council. The University Council concluded the proposals were 'overambitious'. They felt they had overstretched themselves with a new campus in the East End of London to reach out to international students.

To ease its financial troubles, the University sold its London Campus for £9.7 million in April 2010 and later redeveloped its Pittville Campus in Cheltenham for student housing. Patricia Broadfoot retired as Vice Chancellor in July 2010.

Expansion at Oxstalls

Following the departure of Patricia Broadfoot, Deputy Vice Chancellor Dr Paul Hartley became interim Vice Chancellor for just over a year and steadied the ship.

In August 2011, Stephen Marston came into the role of Vice Chancellor, with this being his first job in a university. He took up the post after being a civil servant in the Department for Education for most of his career. His final role was as Director General (Universities & Skills) at the Department for Business, Industry and Skills - where Prime Minister Gordon Brown had moved responsibility for higher education and research. The role included advising former Secretary of State Vince Cable and Universities Minister David Willetts on student finance (which saw student fees increase from £3000 to £9000). Some would say he looked like a stereotypical civil servant – white haired with glasses, tall and slim and often wearing a grey suit. After spending a year renting in Cheltenham, he took on renovating a Georgian townhouse in the centre of Gloucester and had a great passion for the city, sitting on the boards of the Gloucester Culture Trust and the GFirst Local Enterprise Partnership.

He was attracted to Gloucestershire by his interest in widening participation and the fact that the University of Gloucestershire was the only university in the county at the time he joined – something he felt was a source of great strength in its relationship with the community.

Despite the efforts of Dr Hartley, Stephen Marston took on an institution still bruised by financial and personality issues, following a number of high-profile resignations, ultimately including the University's Chancellor, former Archbishop of Canterbury, Lord Carey. An employment tribunal brought by a former member of staff had led to some of the institution's dirty laundry being aired in public.

Marston's first project at Oxstalls was a £1.8 million performing arts centre including four performance spaces and drama rooms, which opened in September 2015. In some ways, as I reflect in chapter 3, this project can be seen as a legacy of the ultimately unsuccessful efforts to bring a National Youth Centre for the Performing Arts to the Docks.

Plans were unveiled in March 2015 to relocate the University's Business School from the Park Campus in Cheltenham to Oxstalls in my ward of Longlevens. Vice Chancellor Stephen Marston told me this was largely driven by space availability and where they were likely to get planning permission. The Growth Hub and GFirst LEP were already there so it gave an opportunity to integrate business services with a business school in a way which would be significant for the business community in Gloucester.

The University had never been the most popular of neighbours, largely due to student parking on the roads surrounding the campus. So I knew, as did my ward councillor colleagues Kathy Williams and Jim Porter, that their application wouldn't necessarily be plain sailing.

As Leader of the Council, I could see the benefits to the city of an increased University presence and, to be fair to them, so could Kathy and Jim. The proposal was for the Business School to be built on land at the rear of the campus site towards the Plock Court open space. The application was for up to 10,000 sq m of new educational space and 200 beds of student accommodation on the former Debenhams sports field off Estcourt Road which, at the time of writing, hasn't been built. In addition, there would be two 3G pitches, a cricket pavilion and sports hall. To put it into context, the existing campus facilities were 10,099 sqm. Most residents probably don't realise that only phase one of the development, of 5800 sqm, has been built to date. University bosses told me there could still be a later phase but it is not as urgent now they have bought the former Debenhams site in the city centre (see later in this chapter).

City MP Richard Graham supported the planning application citing Centre for Cities research which said "No city has been successfully regenerated without a key role played by its university/universities". The development represented an injection of £20 million to the local economy and was forecast to generate £77.5 million by 2020/21. A report by BiGGAR Economics estimated that the University contributed £151.2 million a year to the Gloucestershire economy and supported 2163 jobs locally.

As local councillors, we did press the University to look at alternative sites, including the now closed Bishop's College school – but the County Council had plans to sell that for housing and from a management point of view the University didn't want a split site.

To build the new Business School involved moving one artificial sports pitch but more crucially proposed moving the Estcourt Road allotments. In local politics, I learnt over the years not to mess with people's bins or their parking. I now learnt not to meddle with their allotments!

If the University bosses reckoned the allotment holders would be a pushover, they hadn't bargained on Julia Hurrell. Julia lived close by, was a magistrate and is the wife of former BBC Radio Gloucestershire boss Mark Hurrell. She was also Chair of the Friends of Hillfield Gardens, a small local park, and had done a sterling job in improving this open space including securing National Lottery funding. She was awarded the British Empire Medal for her efforts.

Julia and her fellow allotment holders weren't against the University's plans as a whole – they just wanted them to work around the allotments rather than move them. A huge effort was put into working up an alternative, including relocating them to the former Debenhams sports pitch off Estcourt Road, which the University had acquired. The allotment holders had come up with their wishlist, all of which they were likely to get. But they still didn't want to move after years of enriching their soil.

Moving the allotments would require a decision from the Council's Cabinet and a referral to the Secretary of State. I wasn't looking forward to that decision and, although my wife didn't believe me, I genuinely hadn't pre-judged the issue. Her uncle was one of the allotment holders and although it meant I could declare an interest and take no part in the decision-making, that felt like a cop-out. I never had to make that call, as the University dropped the plans to relocate the allotments. The reasoning behind that decision was that years of flooding had left residue and sediment on the soil and the ground would have had to be lowered because of its position in the flood zone. This would have meant 4000 lorry movements and £1 million of cost. The allotments were going to be landscaped rather than built on so it didn't turn out to be fundamental.

As local councillors, we submitted our representation on the planning application making a number of requests including a new junction onto Estcourt Road, a new access for the sports facilities onto Tewkesbury Road, to fund a 'controlled parking zone' for residents around the campus for 10 years, to move the proposed student accommodation away from existing houses and to put on a shuttle bus from the city centre student accommodation. The

University responded that they did not believe there was a case for an access via Estcourt Road, pointing out that in 1999 the planning committee accepted the cost would be prohibitive. Likewise, they countered that a new access onto Tewkesbury Road may be inappropriate in flood risk terms and involve the loss of playing field. They considered it was not necessary.

Parking was the main issue and the University had promised to implement a Controlled Parking Zone in the roads around the Oxstalls Campus and pay for its operation for 5 years. That later got watered down into a planning condition to carry out a study within three months of the Business School coming into use. The parking charges onsite (£1.50 a day at the time) were also a bone of contention as residents felt students parked in surrounding streets to avoid them. The University pointed out that students could buy an annual permit for £50 (at the time) and the revenue from parking charges subsidised the University's bus services.

The planning committee approved the plans in March 2016, despite 309 representations, (most of which were objections) and work started on site in Autumn 2016.

One major hiccup to the University's plans was the requirement to alter the junction of Oxstalls Lane and Cheltenham Road. For many years, we had campaigned for traffic lights at this junction but highways bosses had resisted, citing the importance of the Cheltenham to Gloucester bus corridor. But plans for new housing at Innsworth meant the cumulative impact would take the junction above its capacity – leading to tailbacks.

It wasn't just a matter of installing a few sets of traffic lights. The junction was home to a huge number of telephone wires, running from an innocuous-looking green cabinet next to the University's boundary railings, which complicated matters. It ended up costing the University £3 million (the original estimate was £500,000) and closing the junction for 10 months, which was a far-from-popular move with the local residents.

Duncan White, an architect by trade, managed the project for the University. Vice Chancellor Stephen Marston was full of praise for City Council planning officer Adam Smith, who was the go-to planner for large applications.

The relocation and expansion of the sporting facilities, with new 4G artificial pitches, sporting arena and cricket pavilion, more closely linked the Oxstalls Campus with the Tennis Centre at Plock Court (renamed the Oxstalls Sports Park), largely fulfilling the vision of Mike Cogger and Steve Elway of creating a sporting hub. The management of the University and City Council-owned facilities (run at the time by the Aspire Trust) was, to a large extent, joined up.

The Business School opened in September 2018 and an official ceremony was carried out by the then Chancellor of the Exchequer Philip Hammond in February 2019. Demographics led to lower numbers enrolling for business courses but nursing and allied health, which weren't part of the original vision for the business school, boomed and became the biggest school at Oxstalls.

A new City Campus

In March 2021, it was announced the University had bought the Debenhams building in Kings Square. When Debenhams went into administration, Vice Chancellor Stephen Marston asked his estates team to find out what was happening with the building. At the time, they were at the bottom of demographic dip, but the forecasts pointed to strong growth in the years ahead. The University's Governing Council had approved a plan for 65% growth over the next decade. Acquiring the 200,000 sq ft Debenhams building would enable the University to grow, especially in nursing and allied health and business. The University couldn't afford to build that much new space on an existing campus. Everything going on around the building – not just the refurbished Kings Square but also including the JOLT creative space in Kings House, which was initiated and sponsored by the University – made it an attractive proposition. There would be around 4000 students and staff. The subjects will be principally health and social care (working with public services), education and humanities (in partnership with schools in Gloucester). The County Council agreed to relocate the Gloucester Central Library from Brunswick Road to the ground floor of the new campus. A health and wellbeing facility was also proposed. Planning permission for the new city campus was granted in March 2022 and work was well-advanced at the time of writing.

A report by BiGGAR Economics, commissioned by the University, was published in June 2021 and forecast the operations of the City Campus would generate £750 million of economic activity across the UK and create over 7000 jobs. The University's aim was to start teaching at the new campus in September 2024.

5. BREAKING THE 'CURSE OF BLACKFRIARS'

History

The Blackfriars area is named after Blackfriars Priory, one of the city's four friaries and the most complete Dominican friary in the country, founded in c1239. Its structure includes timber taken from 200 oak trees from the Forest of Dean gifted by Henry III. There are a range of listed buildings dating from the 13th century, including the Grade 1 listed Blackfriars Church and the Scriptorium, which is the earliest surviving purpose-built library in England. The friary was sold at the Dissolution in 1539 and bought by Sir Thomas Bell, who turned it into his private house. Other parts of the site were Bell's cap factory, employing around 300 people. It continued as a private residence until the 20th century, with the rest of the buildings being used for industrial purposes. The Scriptorium was a mineral water bottling factory and part of the west range was a pub!

For all its magnificence and significance, Blackfriars Priory was surrounded by what looked like a bombsite – although its appearance couldn't be blamed on Hitler, it was self-inflicted. The area had become built up with commercial premises and houses, but much of it had been cleared in the 1970s. There was the City of Gloucester Electricity Works, which opened in 1900 but closed when a bigger power station opened at Castlemeads on the other side of the river. In recent times, much of the cleared space has been given over to car parking.

A large surface car park stands on what was the Priory's burial grounds. In his evidence to the Blackfriars Judicial Review, council officer David Scott described the area as having "a land use pattern dominated by vacant and underused sites combined with a poor visual appearance and a generally negative perception in the minds of businesses, residents and visitors alike."

On the corner of Commercial Road and Ladybellegate Street stood the former E&J Printers building (which had previously been Priestleys Studios), which displayed a sign saying 'Site acquired by Gloucester City Council for the Blackfriars redevelopment'. When the sign developed a weathered look, it became a symbol for the failure of regeneration in this part of the city. It was finally demolished along with the BT (formerly British Telecom) repeater station further along Ladybellegate Street in 2011 when both were under the ownership of SWRDA. The Longsmith Street multi-storey car park, which was opened in April 1972, has long been past its best but has somehow managed to limp on until this day, although it was scheduled for redevelopment as part of The Fleece scheme but was closed due to safety concerns in September 2023 and remains closed at the time of going to print.

The cleared Barbican site in Ladybellegate Street. Credit: Paul Dowle

It certainly wasn't the case that there was no effort put in to trying to regenerate the city. Some might say that the effort was badly-executed and, in some cases, misguided and the resource inadequate. Others would contend that the project failures were down to the actions of third parties, the complexities of trying to regenerate a historic city centre and simply some bad luck. As we would later find out, delivering large scale regeneration needed a dedicated team with the right skills. Council officers trying to do it in their spare time, on top of their other duties, was never likely to end well.

There were the bones of a vision. In January 2001, Head of Planning Services Jerry Spencer put together an Urban Design Strategy with the vision of linking the city's 'constellation of stars' – the collection of attractions in the city, ranging from the Cathedral to Blackfriars Priory to the House of the Tailor of Gloucester – into a cohesive whole. In Spencer's document they would be weaved together in the same way as the Tailor of Gloucester's waistcoat (but presumably this time he wasn't relying on it being magically done by fairies or mice!) Spencer also invented the 'Western Waterfront' label which, although it didn't survive as a phrase, has largely been implemented. It envisaged making the most of the Western edge of the city, from the Cattle Market to Westgate Quay, to the Docks and south along the canal. *The Citizen* on 26th September 2000 referred to a plan for 2620 homes and the Cabinet meeting in October 2000 referred to it being a 15-year strategy.

The city's flagship scheme was for decades the Blackfriars redevelopment, taking in the area between Southgate Street, Westgate Street, the Docks and the Quay. The project was led by David Scott, the Council's Director of Environment, and Richard Cook, its 'Director of Corporate Development'. Cook was in fact a solicitor and had been the City Secretary & Solicitor. His title should not be taken to mean he was an expert in property development. He should also not be confused with my successor as Leader of the Council, almost twenty years later, of the same name.

The Arrowcroft Scheme

The City Council was approached by Arrowcroft plc, a London-based development company founded by Leonard Eppel which had restored Liverpool's Albert Docks, in 1987 regarding a potential development of this part of the city. Discussions continued and Arrowcroft submitted a planning application in December 1988. It was reportedly an £80 million, 180,000 sq ft scheme, to be called The Blackfriars Centre.[57] The scheme was submitted jointly by Arrowcroft and local construction group Britannia. The two companies were working together to develop the Beechwood Place Shopping Centre in Cheltenham's High Street (now John Lewis) and were hoping for a similar arrangement for Blackfriars. The application included a shopping complex with an underground servicing tunnel under Ladybellegate Street. The Longsmith Street multi-storey car park would be demolished and replaced with a new one on the corner of Commercial Road and Ladybellegate Street. The bridge over Southgate Street linking the Longsmith Street multi-storey car park with the Eastgate rooftop car park would be demolished, which it later was.[58] The application was considered in March 1990 and the Council indicated that it was "favourably inclined to the proposals".[59]

In the interests of transparency, the Council decided it needed to go out to an open procurement process to select a developer partner at the end of November 1990. Arrowcroft-Britannia had already drawn up a revised 150,000 sq ft scheme anchored by a department store. *The Citizen* reported optimistically that "Poll tax payers (were) set to cash in on the development".[60]

The slump of the late 1980s/early 1990s saw interest rates hit a peak of 15% and a house price crash meant many households experienced negative equity – where the value of the home is less than what they owed on it. This hit the retail sector hard and affected market sentiment towards the development. The City Council's response was proactive – it promoted pedestrianisation of the city centre 'gate streets' and it continued to assemble land when opportunities arose. Council officers continued to court potential occupiers like Cineworld and Marks & Spencer and established a dedicated city centre management function.

The Council also sent letters going out to leading architectural practices asking them for ideas to attract developers[61] and in July 1994 ideas from architects RHWL, Corstorphine & Wright and Tibbalds Monro went on display.[62]

In September 1994, *The Citizen* reported that 22 developers were interested in Blackfriars.[63] Arrowcroft was chosen from a shortlist, which also included Boots Properties (a development offshoot of Boots the Chemist which had developed the Priory Meadow shopping centre in Hastings) and Crest Nicholson in April 1995. A development agreement between the City Council and Arrowcroft wasn't signed until November 1999.

Arrowcroft's new scheme was a £50 million, 150,000 sq ft development with a 50-unit mall using the Mercers Hall as centrepiece market building. The original 16th century Mercers Hall is hidden behind 20th century additions. The plan was that, once exposed, it would make a feature along with the Cross Keys Inn.[64] An article in *The Citizen* by journalist George Henderson article said, "Strip away the brick and rendering and you would find the heavy timbers of a 17th century guildhall that once formed a focus for the city's mercers – drapers, grocers, chandlers and apothecaries."[65] City Council Planning Officer Peter Wynn said it was a key point of the Blackfriars redevelopment, commenting, "At the moment the outside looks pretty terrible but we see its restoration along the lines of a traditional market hall with an open plan ground floor as a priority." They hoped, again very optimistically, that work would start in 1997, with the new centre up and running in Autumn

1999.[66]

Marks & Spencer were announced by Arrowcroft as the 'anchor store' for the development, to replace their rather dated premises in the city, and initially proposed a new 60,000 sq ft store, later increasing it to 75,000 sq ft – 20% bigger than their existing stores in Northgate and Southgate Street combined.[67] The frontage of the New County Hotel would have been the entrance to the new M&S store, with the rest of the store built behind.

A planning application was submitted in December 1995, which included 50 shops and 21,000 sq ft of offices. The new arcade would emerge on to Southgate Street, following the line of Ladybellegate Street, but also through the sites of TSB and BeWise (now Ladbrokes and Bargain Buys), which would be demolished.[68]

Other landmarks earmarked to go as part of the scheme were the Famous Army Stores (now David Christopher jewellers), Deep Pan Pizza (on the corner of Southgate Street and the Blackfriars Via Sacra), parts of the New County Hotel, the Longsmith Street car park, the Malt & Hops pub, Severn Motors and JJB Sports (now part of Kara's hair salon). Parts of The Fleece Hotel would also be demolished.[69]

In March 1997, the City Council's Planning Sub-Committee decided that it was 'minded to grant' consent for the redevelopment, which included the relocation of the magistrates' courts, 47 retail units including an 8000 sqm anchor store, an 800-space multi-storey car park and a small amount of residential accommodation overlooking the Priory and the proposed Mercers Square. The decision was subject to a number of issues being addressed including the visual impact of the multi-storey car park and the absence of shops and town centre uses on Ladybellegate Street itself.[70]

In June 1998, it was reported that the absence of a firm commitment from M&S was holding up the plans. Their commitment would have enabled a development agreement to be signed. Planning Officer Peter Wynn was still optimistic that the scheme could be completed within 4 years.[71] By October 1998 the reports stated that "councillors (were) waiting anxiously for the outcome of the M&S board meeting". In January 1999, "struggling" M&S pulled out, ending months of speculation. M&S said they had decided to concentrate on "improved values and better merchandise at its existing stores in Southgate Street and Northgate Street". Alan Cooke, Regional Manager for M&S, said, "Our decision has come about as a result of the general economic downturn, specifically in the retail sector."

Council Leader Jon Holmes said, "The scheme has been held up for a year by uncertainty about M&S. There is no doubt the scheme will go ahead."[72]

Arrowcroft made a number of revisions to the plans. As discussed later in this chapter, the proposal for a new magistrates' court building was abandoned in 1998, enabling Arrowcroft to amend their proposals. In January 1999, Arrowcroft submitted a revised scheme, extending the city's retail footprint with 40 new shops plus an anchor store. A cinema and a new 800 space multi-storey car park would be built on the Barbican site on the south side of Longsmith Street. In addition, there were pubs, restaurants, offices and flats proposed as part of the scheme, with 350,000 sq ft of new floorspace in total. The vision was along the lines of The Lanes in Carlisle, which had stopped the leakage of shoppers to nearby Newcastle. Cinemas at this time were very lucrative to develop and the profit from the first phase, which included the cinema, was to be used to implement the comprehensive development of the area.

Looking down Ladybellegate Street with the proposed cinema to the right and Blackfriars Priory to the left. Credit: Burrell Foley Fischer architects

The 9-screen multiplex cinema would have an oval shaped central lobby and natural stone elevations. Its auditoria would be roofed with terne-coated steel. A grass terrace over the car park would feature public works of art. The multiplex would help the "marginal viability" of the Blackfriars schemes.[73] The terrace would look out over the countryside to the west and the sunset in the Forest of Dean.

Architects Burrell Foley Fischer's design included a 'battered' (sloping) wall which enclosed the car park along Barbican Road and made reference to the former line of the Roman and Norman walls. It was architecturally attractive but costly. The Royal Fine Art Commission supported and liked "the use of the sloping site and battered wall" and the Civic Trust said it was "imaginative and sensitively designed".[74]

By this time, some real frustration locally was starting to build with *The Citizen*'s Comment column asking "How much longer are we going to have to wait for the fabled Blackfriars development?" and adding "The Romans probably constructed the whole of the city of Glevum quicker than we are managing to erect some shops and a cinema."[75]

Possible replacements for M&S as an anchor store were the House of Fraser, Beatties and Allders.[76] By June 1999, *The Citizen* reported that Wolverhampton-based James Beattie plc (Beatties) were set to be the new anchor store. Negotiations were, apparently, at an advanced stage to build a 100,000 sq ft store between Southgate Street and Ladybellegate Street. Beatties' Development Director Christine Levine said, "Talks are at an advanced stage and we hope to have a store in Gloucester in a couple of years." It would have been the 12th Beatties in England and one of the biggest. Their nearest other store was Worcester. Arrowcroft's Daniel Carter said, "Beatties is the frontrunner but they are not the only company in the race."[77] Beatties were later acquired by the House of Fraser.

As discussed in the chapter about the Docks, there was a competing proposal for a cinema on the Southgate Moorings site. Both applications were considered at Full Council meeting in July 1999 alongside a third application, for an extension to the existing cinema at Peel Centre. The Council expressed its preference for the Blackfriars site subject to referring it to the Government Office and was 'minded to refuse' the Docks scheme. In September 1999, *The Citizen* wrote a scathing 'Comment' column saying that the Blackfriars scheme was "no more than a fantasy land like the Emerald City in the Wizard of Oz". The article said that the threat to the Blackfriars development was "not a good enough reason to stop developers creating the leisure quarter at the Docks". In its view "the market should be left to decide" as the uncertainty over Blackfriars had been "keeping things in limbo and denying the city the chance to grow and evolve". If its view wasn't clear enough already, it concluded by saying, "We are sick of hearing about jam tomorrow, we are sick of hearing about the Blackfriars development."

The applicants for the Docks site, Crest Nicholson, appealed to a Government Planning Inspector against the City Council's decision to turn down the scheme. Outline planning permission was granted in February 2000 after an inquiry had taken place in November 1999. The Council also failed to make a decision on its subsequent application for detailed consent, so there was a second appeal and public inquiry in December 2000, with detailed consent granted for the Docks scheme on 5th February 2001.

The Government Office allowed the City Council to grant planning consent for the Blackfriars cinema as part of the first phase of development and the consent was issued in October 2000. An outline application for the comprehensive redevelopment of the area was considered by the Planning Committee in March 2001 and approved subject to consultation with the Government Office with the consent granted on 17th April 2001.

In July 1999, Crest Nicholson had promoted a residential scheme for Blackfriars which didn't rely on a cinema or retail – and would leave the way clear for their cinema scheme at the Docks. Their scheme would not have involved the loss of the New County or Fleece hotels.[78] Crest's scheme proposed 161 town houses, 36 shops, offices and a 500-space car park

Lawrence Clark, Crest Nicholson's Commercial Director said, "I don't believe a shopping development of the type suggested by Arrowcroft is a commercial proposition at the moment. It's been so long coming it is no longer commercially relevant."

Labour Councillor Nick Durrant, who chaired the Council's Highways & Planning Committee, responded, "We've been asking them for years to build some housing in the Docks, which is where people want to live, but they have failed to come up with any."

Magistrates' Court proposals

In the 1980s, at the same time as the City Council were trying to regenerate the Blackfriars area, the Magistrates' Court committee were looking for an alternative site for their ageing court building. A site for a new courthouse at Blackfriars was allocated in the City Council's Local Plan, so in that sense it ought to have been straightforward – but it was anything but. In echoes of what was happening in the dispute over the Oxstalls Campus, relationships between the City and County Councils were far from constructive – and the people of Gloucester were ultimately the losers.

As the Magistrates' Court function at the time came under the jurisdiction of the County Council, they were the planning authority who would decide the application. In April 1989, they granted outline consent for a new magistrates' court building on land at the Barbican.[79]

The first iteration of design came from Shire Hall's in-house architects' team and was described by some as a 'Grand Piano' design. In March 1989, it was reported that the Home Office had given the go-ahead for the new court complex after it had been submitted to Whitehall by the Magistrates Court committee. The building was estimated to cost £5 million and would have 60 parking spaces.[80]

In April 1989, it was reported that the County Council had agreed to buy a site at the Barbican from the Midlands Electricity Board (MEB) for £560,000. Further land was still needed from British Telecom (BT) and private householders and building wouldn't start until electricity cables had been diverted.[81] Records at Gloucestershire Archives show that land was bought from the MEB for £850,000 in 1991 and that the County Council bought land from BT for £655,000 in April 1990. The County Council had also gradually bought up and demolished a row of terraces on the site. Council officers told me that one house in the middle of the terrace remained, which was lived in by an eccentric couple. The wife had been born there and really did not want to sell. In the end, the County Council paid over the odds for the property to avoid having to issue a Compulsory Purchase Order.

In October 1990, detailed plans were unveiled for what was now estimated to be a £10 million court building. Demolition was to begin the next month, with construction getting underway the following year. The 3-storey building would have 8 courtrooms and was expected to be completed by March 1994. The existing courts were built for 5000 cases a year, but were now dealing with 30,000 a year.[82]

The plans were blasted by the City Council, English Heritage and the Civic Trust, who dubbed the design as unsuitable. The architects responded that it was the best use of a difficult site.[83]

The Gloucester New Magistrates' Courthouse Working Party – made up of the City and County Councils and the Magistrates' Court Committee – met in February 1991 and had a 'frank discussion'. The City Council agreed that the County's design team had done a great deal to accommodate their past criticisms.

However, they and others were still not happy with what was being proposed. English Heritage, the Royal Fine Art Commission (RFAC) and the City Council all criticised the £10 million plan.[84] The RFAC called for a 'fundamental rethink' of the scheme. The County Council responded that much of the criticism of the design was of a "highly subjective nature" and noted that it was "in vogue to criticise modern architecture."

The Magistrates' Court Committee warned that if agreement could not be reached, funding could be put in jeopardy and the project abandoned. They had to bring into service the redundant courthouse at Whitminster, which was 'inconvenient and expensive'.

The County Council revised the design again but the City Council's Planning Committee on 17th March 1992 was still not satisfied, saying the "scheme (was) not of sufficient quality" and asked the City Planning Officer to write to the Secretary of State to 'call in' the application to be taken to a public inquiry. On 21st April 1992, the Secretary of State for the Environment, Michael Howard, called in the planning application by County Council "in view of the importance of the site in the Conservation Area".

Despite this barrage of criticism, the County Council's Development Control sub-committee on 28th April 1992 determined that they would have granted consent, subject to a number of small amendments to the design, if the decision had been left in their hands. The Committee report described the design as an "innovative geometric form" which "resisted the simple solutions of mimicking the architecture of the past". The proposed building would be faced with handmade red brick, natural stone and rendered wall and would have a slate roof. There would be a cascade water feature in the front plaza. The report commented that "the scheme makes a brave and positive contribution to a largely degenerated part of the city which, at this time, has a very uncertain future." Demonstrating that government departments don't always agree with each other, the Home Office was supportive of the design but following the public inquiry, which took place in July 1992, the Secretary of State for the Environment refused planning permission and Conservation Area consent.

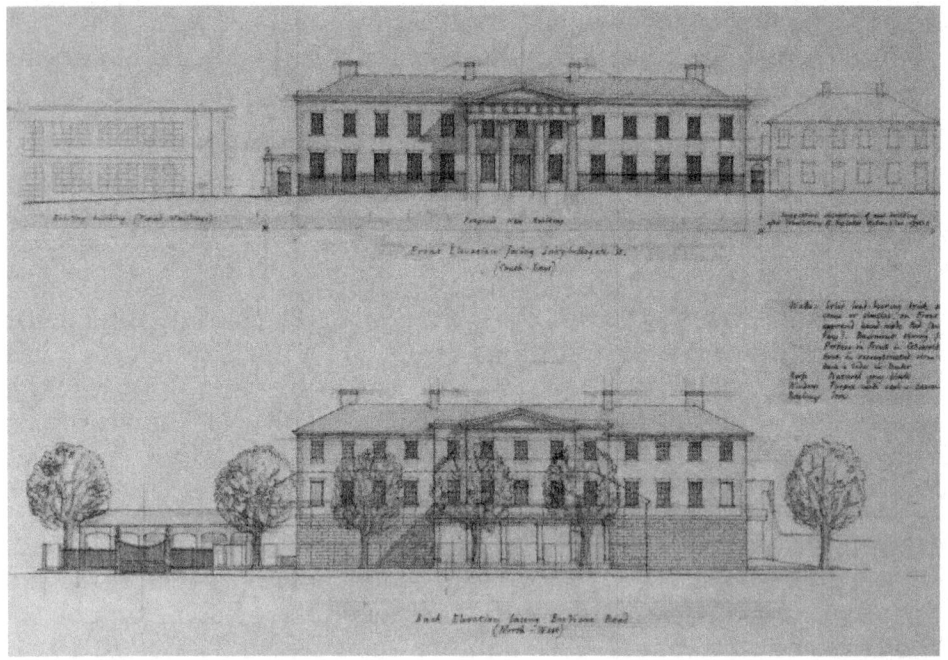

The Quinlan Terry design for a new magistrates' court. Credit: Quinlan Terry

In an attempt to build a consensus, the County Council then engaged two architects with sharply contrasting styles – Quinlan Terry and ABK (Ahrends, Burton and Koralek). The two very different approaches divided opinion. By this time, the proposal had been expanded to include the Crown Court and Family Courts. There hadn't been a great deal of work done on what would become of the existing Crown Court building, but ideas included a justice-themed museum or a restaurant along the lines of what Jamie Oliver would open in the Cheltenham courthouse some years later.

Quinlan Terry was known as Britain's 'high priest of classical architecture'. He was the then Prince Charles' favourite architect who helped to design Poundbury, the Prince's traditionalist village in Dorset, and remodelled 10 Downing Street for Margaret Thatcher.

Citizen reporter Hugh Worsnip wrote in his column that Quinlan Terry was "alleged to have said his style comes from God and modern architecture is the work of the devil" (something that Mr Terry denies). As Britain's foremost neo-classicist, he likes to make his buildings look like Greek temples – with columns, flights of steps and pediments. Experts Sir William Whitfield (Royal Fine Art Commission), Edward Booth (English Heritage), Rodney Purse (Civic Trust) and City Planning and Technical Services Officer David Scott all had misgivings. Worsnip preferred the modern style of Ahrends, Burton & Koralek, who had produced a design for an extension to the National Gallery which Prince Charles called a "monstrous carbuncle".[85]

In July 1993, *The Citizen* reported that, after a six-hour meeting, representatives of the Royal Fine Art Commission, English Heritage, the City Council and the Civic Trust had plumped unanimously for the ABK design. It is worth noting that opinion within these organisations wasn't necessarily unanimous, with many Civic Trust members apparently liking the Quinlan Terry design and the City Council's overall view being difficult to find conclusively in any documentation. A panel of County Councillors and magistrates ignored the meeting's conclusion and picked the Greek temple solution proposed by Quinlan Terry. Liberal Democrat councillor, Di Phillips, a member of the panel, said, "We chose the architect with the traditional approach because we thought he would produce the design most acceptable to this city."[86]

It was believed that County Councillors and magistrates did not want a modern building so near to the Cathedral, the Dominican Friary at Blackfriars and the Victorian Docks. The decision was now in the hands of the Lord Chancellor's office.[87]

The design was presented to the City Council's Planning Committee in June 1994. They asked the County Council to defer a decision to enable further discussions, but welcomed the general design and the use of Bath stone in the scheme.

In July 1994, County Councillors gave the scheme planning permission, but work couldn't start until the Secretary of State had given the go-ahead.[88] The City Council was still not happy about the detail, siting and archaeology. County Councillors expressed regret at the late response from the City Council and said deferral would be unsatisfactory. Labour councillor Maggie Levett commented that she was sorry they weren't considering a good modern building. Fellow Labour councillor Arthur Meredith, who also sat on the City Council, said, "Don't blame the City for being pernickety. If we get it wrong, we'll be blamed for 50 years."[89]

City Councillors asked for the proposed magistrates' court to be moved 20 yards to the right - nearer Longsmith Street - to enable a larger car park for the Blackfriars development. It would also have required the demolition of the ugly BT repeater station. BT had now decided that they no longer needed the repeater. Arrowcroft had considered bridging over the MEB's substation, but had decided that extending the frontage along Ladybellegate Street was preferable in financial and practical terms. Citizen columnist Hugh Worsnip said that after 6 years of argument over the design, it was 'perverse' of the City Council to make such a request at this point.[90]

In September 1994, the Secretary of State granted Conservation Area Consent to demolish the MEB building and the remnants of the power station and a year later gave consent to demolish the BT repeater station.

The stand-off between the two councils continued. In April 1995, the City Council threatened the County Council with Compulsory Purchase of the magistrates' court land because it would interfere with parking for the Blackfriars scheme.[91]

In May 1995, work started on a £100,000 contract to demolish the city's first power station at Blackfriars. Because of the historic importance of the site, archaeologists were watching every move. In July 1995, archaeologists unearthed Roman remains and the moat of the first castle. The ornate tiled interior of the 95-year-old power station was photographed by the Royal Commission on Historical Monuments. Again, City Council officers asked for the proposed courts to be moved to another site "to avoid a split car park" in the Blackfriars development. County Property Officer Norman Davis responded, "The courts are not moving."

In July 1995, it was reported that the Court building was expected to cost £8 million – made up of £6.7 million build costs and £1.2 million in fees for architects, engineers etc. It was expected to start in December 1995 and be completed in January 1998.

In October 1995, the building of the magistrates' court was called off by the Government Star Chamber on public spending. The Government was short of cash and falling rates of crime seemed a good excuse to argue that new courts were less of a priority. After 10 years of arguing and public inquiries, the Government announced a moratorium on all new court buildings. The magistrates were about to send out tender documents to build the new courts when a call from the Lord Chancellor's office came through to say it's off. Jeremy Dancey, Chairman-elect of the bench and member of the Magistrates' Court Committee (and also an architect in the city), said "The need for these courts has never been more urgent, so we were disappointed to say the least."

David Scott took a more optimistic view, seeing this as an opportunity to secure the City Council's objective of getting the proposed building moved. He said, "Moving the courts will enable us to reduce the bulk of the car park, have a much better entrance from Commercial Road and make better use of the key site on the corner with Ladybellegate Street."[92]

County Council Officers at the time tell me that the news came from the Lord Chancellor's Office as people involved were heading for a signing ceremony at Shire Hall, with Quinlan Terry on the train to the city from London.

The concept of a new court building stayed alive for some time, but little new work was done on it while the funding position remained uncertain. The Government's default method of financing was now through the Private Finance Initiative (PFI) – where private firms are contracted to complete, finance and manage public projects.

It was reported in August 1996 that the courts complex may never be built. Up to that point, it had cost council taxpayers nearly £3 million. Land acquisition, demolition and archaeology came to £1.7 million and the aborted design work had cost £950,000. Shortly after, a Labour government came to power. They wanted the PFI model to continue but Gloucester was not near top of the list. Labour County Councillor Paul Drake called it a "scandalous waste of money". He added, "The last government changed the rules of the game as we were about to take the final penalty kick."[93]

In March 1998, *The Citizen* reported that the Priestleys building would be demolished as a result of a land swap between the City and County Councils to accommodate the new magistrates' court. That didn't happen and, in 1998, the City Council made an approach to buy the Ladybellegate Street site from the County Council for the proposed Blackfriars scheme, at the same time as again threatening to use its Compulsory Purchase powers.

The County Council looked at alternative locations for the court building, including the Southgate Moorings site at the Docks and Roman Quay in Quay Street (which is now student accommodation). The City Council indicated they were prepared to make land at the Cattle Market site available but this wasn't the preference of the Magistrates Court Committee because of its distance from the police station.[94] They settled on land in their ownership at Quayside, next to Shire Hall, which they had been in discussions with developer Morrisons for (yet another) multiplex cinema proposal. In August 1999, the County Council lodged a planning application for the land on the corner of The Quay and Quay Street, including the former Ship Inn. The proposed building was much like the Quinlan Terry design. The orientation of the building, side on to The Quay, reportedly 'dismayed' city planning officials, who wanted it facing The Quay. The County Council said that the application was just establishing the principle and the detailed design would be dealt with later.[95] The Quayside site was eventually dismissed because of concerns over archaeology and a high water table, which would have required expensive piled foundations.

After some protracted negotiations, the land at Blackfriars was eventually sold by the County Council to the City Council in June 1999 for £1.1 million. Documents in the Gloucestershire Archives show that the abortive plans for the Magistrates' Court at Blackfriars ended up costing the County Council nearly £4 million – including £1.6 million for land assembly, £600,000 for diverting electricity cables (given the site's previous use as a power station), £180,000 on archaeology and a whopping £1.4 million on architects' and other professional fees! The failure to deliver the magistrates' court scheme arguably damaged confidence in the regeneration of the Blackfriars area generally and it was certainly seen as an unwanted complication by the City Council and Arrowcroft.

The County Council later acquired another piece of land in the city, the former BT Telephone House site in Great Western Road, for a new court building, using funding from the Department for Constitutional Affairs (DCA) (formerly the Lord Chancellor's Department) and would be built under the Government's Private Finance Initiative (PFI). This was planned to accommodate the magistrates' court and the Crown Court, which was (and still is) housed in a Grade II listed building dating back to 1815. The Crown Court fails to comply with disability legislation and has a host of other practical issues such as not being able to segregate victims, witnesses and defendants. The City Council issued a Design Brief for the site in July 2004. Legislation which took effect in 2005 meant the land transferred to the DCA (later the Ministry of Justice). It was later turned back into a car park to serve the railway station, by rail operator GWR, which opened in April 2018, following a campaign by City MP Richard Graham. (See Chapter 22)

The City Council's land holdings at the Barbican were later sold to the Regional Development Agency for a figure believed to be £2 million but later re-acquired by the City Council in 2011 (at a much lower cost), when SWRDA was wound up. It was announced in February 2016 that the magistrates court in Gloucester would close.

BT and the Battle of Barbican

BT objected to the Blackfriars planning application on the basis that they would lose their essential operational car parking – a small, private car park off Barbican Road. They contended they needed it for transit vans so engineers/contractors could undertake engineering works on the exchange. The City Council/Arrowcroft offered them space in the new multi-storey car park, but this was dismissed as being unsuitable because of height clearance issues. Council officers said there were increased heights for transits in the proposed multi-storey car park but that most BT vehicles were cars or small vans. *The Citizen* reported in April 2001 that City Highways chief David Greensweig had surveyed the use of the car park and only 33 of the 77 vehicles parked there were operational and the rest were BT employees who had parked there all day.[96]

BT had also claimed their car park was needed to set up a temporary exchange in the event of an emergency. To deal with this objection, the City Council employed a telecoms expert to draw up an alternative scheme for a temporary exchange, including blocking off roads. GPU Power, Midlands Electricity's parent company, also objected to the planning application on the basis it encroached on their operational area.

A Compulsory Purchase Order (CPO) was issued, prior to planning consent being granted, on 25th May 1999 for a number of properties that the City Council and Arrowcroft did not own. A second CPO, which included the Robert Raikes House on Southgate Street (now owned by Samuel Smith's Brewery – see Chapter 13) and the BT car park was issued on 16th August 2000. The CPOs were designed to bring landowners to the negotiating table, rather than necessarily result in a public inquiry.

The original Telephone Exchange from the 1930s which faces onto Berkeley Street is a fine-looking building with some attractive features, including a beautiful wooden staircase. But to describe the adjacent extension, built in the 1960s, as 'brutalist' would flatter it, particularly given its relationship to the listed Ladybellegate House – one-time home of the Raikes family, which was restored by the Civic Trust in 1978-9. I recall being told as the Blackfriars scheme went forward that, because of the evolution of technology, there was only equipment in the exchange 'the size of a shoebox'. I know from when I toured the facility probably twenty years later that it certainly wasn't the case. It's true that there is plenty of vacant space, particularly in the older building, which is difficult to fill because of security concerns, but there are telephone wires by the million in there!

BT would subsequently argue that the strategic importance of the exchange was why they were prepared to defend its car park with so much vigour – and cash. It's also true to say that the compensation BT would have received under a CPO would be limited to its existing use value, rather than any 'hope value'. The Council and Arrowcroft were under pressure from a weary and sceptical public to make progress with the development, so they may have hoped that delaying tactics would result in a higher offer for the land.

The Council had written to BT offering to buy the surface car park[97], but hadn't bargained on BT's reaction. Those involved at the time described some within BT's property team as "belligerent". Others suggest this may have been a response to a clash of personalities with key figures in Arrowcroft. It was believed they had a budget – understood to have been £2 million – to bring the legal challenge. There was reportedly unease within BT about this. One former BT employee described the property team as a "malign influence" and "a law unto themselves" and accused them of "playing hardball". The BT main board were said to be "fuming" about the level of costs incurred. These factors combined to work against the chances of a negotiated settlement being reached.

The CPO inquiry began on 24th April 2001. Both BT and MEB had objected to the CPO. The inspector for the inquiry was John Gray. An architect by trade, he also presided over the hearing for the Home Bargains inquiry (see Chapter 11) some years later. He suffered a mini stroke in the middle of the inquiry in another example of what became known as the 'Curse of Blackfriars'.

On 4th May 2001, BT and Bloomsbury Land, the owner of Robert Raikes House, notified the Council of their intention to seek a judicial review of the Council's decision to issue planning consent.

This was lodged on 18th May 2001. BT were the main protagonists, with Bloomsbury described as a 'passenger'. As is often the way with such cases, the claimants took a 'scattergun' approach, listing five grounds to challenge the consent, hoping one might stick – which it did. The rejected grounds were a) that the planning permission granted differed significantly from the original application b) the conservation and listed building issues were not properly taken into account c) there was a "misapprehension of material facts" – that profits from phase one would subsidise later phases and d) there was a breach of Article 6 of the European Convention on Human Rights.

The final, and ultimately successful, ground was based on the Council's failure to request an Environmental Statement, which "must be provided when a development would be likely to have significant effects on the environment by virtue of factors such as its nature, size and location."

At that time, the legislation was relatively new and councils were still getting to grips with how to apply it. It seems as though the Council's lawyers internally urged caution, but the external barrister they engaged 'sat on the fence'. The developer didn't want to spend the money (believed to be between £50-60,000) on it. The Council, which as ever was strapped for cash, didn't see it as their responsibility and believed if they had pushed Arrowcroft too hard for it they would walk. Council officers took the view that Arrowcroft had already submitted very detailed information on topics such as heritage, archaeology, traffic and retail impact, which they believed covered most of what an Environmental Statement would have included.

Arrowcroft's solicitors, Berwin Leighton, said in a letter dated 3rd October 2000 that they were surprised to receive a request for an Environmental Statement as the application had been lodged since January 1996. They argued that the relevant regulations were the 1988 not the 1999 regulations. The planning case officer was Mike Gethin, a long-serving and experienced officer. He responded to a Berwin Leighton, on 10th October 2000 saying he believed an Environmental Statement was required, mainly on grounds of archaeology, heritage and air pollution.

Berwin Leighton disputed that in a detailed legal analysis in their response of 13th October. After that, according to the court judgement, the trail runs cold. The decision not to require an Environmental Statement was taken by David Scott, who as Director of Environment had ultimate responsibility to determine how to apply the legislation, having taken legal advice. His decision was partly based on the fact that he felt the development overall would improve the environment in the area. But in his judgement, Mr Justice Maurice Kaye said, "Mr Scott took the view that considered overall the development would be beneficial. But that is not the point. There are features which can only be said to have an adverse effect on the environment. If Mr Scott considered there was no adverse effect on the environment, he erred in law and reached an irrational conclusion."

Legally, it was a battle of the big guns. BT's barrister was Matthew Horton QC who is described in an online profile as a "brilliant heavyweight advocate, who has a great presence and thinks outside the box". Guy Roots QC represented the Council. He went on to advise the London Development Agency on acquiring land for the London 2012 Olympics. The Judge was the Hon Mr Justice Elias.

The Judge ordered the Council to pick up 50% of the claimants' costs. Quashing the planning permission also caused the collapse of the CPO inquiry, leaving the Council to pick up BT's costs. They hadn't scrimped on their representation and the Council put aside a £2 million provision. In the end BT settled for £500,000 – bad enough but not as catastrophic as it could have been.

The Council's initial response was to keep on fighting. The Head of Legal Services was given authority to appeal the High Court judgement. Legal Counsel were to be instructed to apply to the Inspector to adjourn the CPO inquiry until Arrowcroft had provided an Environmental Statement and the Planning Committee had redetermined the application.[98]

That optimism soon petered out, with *The Citizen* headline describing the Judge's decision as a "Fatal Blow".[99] With both its funds and its confidence hit by the costs of the BT debacle, the Council ultimately didn't have the political appetite for 'one more push'. Arrowcroft's lack of willingness to meet the costs of the Environmental Statement appears not to have changed. Kevin Stephens told me that, because the Council had their fingers burnt, they wanted to concentrate on something "more deliverable". At around this time, the proposals for a Designer Outlet Centre at Gloucester Quays were emerging. This was a red flag for Beatties, who said they would withdraw if it went ahead. The Council were keen to grab onto something positive in regeneration terms in the aftermath of the Blackfriars debacle and Beatties and Arrowcroft both left the stage.

Council Leader Kevin Stephens declared the Blackfriars plan "Dead in the water", saying "The City Council will now look at all the options for the redevelopment of Blackfriars," adding that, "We will be trying to have more constructive dialogue with BT in the future." It felt a bit late. BT were unrepentant, commenting that, "BT is not to blame for the proposed abandonment of the redevelopment of Blackfriars. The reason is because the High Court has ruled that the City Council acted unlawfully in granting planning permission". I chipped in saying, "Taxpayers are going to have a shock when they realise how substantial the cost of this affair has been and they will have to pay for it. We need to find out who is responsible for this and ensure they are made accountable."[100]

In the Civic Trust's Annual Report of 2001, its Chairman Robin Morris, a well-known and respected local solicitor, said, "One is bound to feel concerned for council tax payers. In a sense, however, I feel much sadder for the people whose lives or businesses have been blighted by this longstanding saga... One cannot help thinking about the Fleece Hotel and the Rich family. I have not noticed a public expression of apology."

Citizen journalist Hugh Worsnip wrote, "The people of Gloucester are entitled to an explanation from BT but they won't get one. The company has refused all requests from *The Citizen* to provide a spokesman who could answer questions about the company's motives and reasons." He called it a "futile muscle flexing exercise".[101]

BT did comment publicly though. In January 2002, a letter was published in *The Citizen* from Eric Barr, BT's Head of Regional Media. He reminded readers that 26 organisations had objected to the Council's CPO and said that "this has never been an argument about a car park". He added, "Our primary reason for objecting... relates to the vital role it would play in the event of an emergency at the Gloucester exchange, which is one of the most important exchanges in this part of the UK." Mr Barr explained that it served up to 200,000 customers, meaning it was "absolutely critical" that "plans are in place in case of a major incident such as a fire" which would "necessitate the use of up to 28 mobile exchange units". This would require a "suitably-located secure site". He contended that the Council's proposed solution involved third party land and the third party "would not enter into a legal agreement ensuring its land would be available to BT". He concluded by saying that BT "remain willing to talk".

Council Officers told me that they believed the CPO would have been granted. Whether that really would have been the case we shall never know.

In December 2001, the Council's Cabinet asked for an investigation to be undertaken by the spending watchdog, the District Auditor, and the Council's own Internal Audit service into what happened. Their report, published in February 2002, questioned whether David Scott had a conflict of interest as both the officer leading the Blackfriars project and the City's Chief Planning Officer. It also highlighted the imbalance of risk between the City Council and Arrowcroft as its development partner. Arrowcroft had just acquired one property interest in the area (9 Westgate Street) and agreed to pay only £50,000 of the Council's costs. Another £150,000 was payable, but only once planning permission had been granted and the land transferred to Arrowcroft – which never happened. By contrast, the Council had spent £4 million on land acquisition and an unknown further sum on archaeology and other studies. The report also concluded that, in hindsight, the Council had "introduced an unnecessary risk" by issuing the CPO before planning consent had been granted.

An inquiry was set up by the Council's Executive Scrutiny Committee and chaired by the then Conservative Leader of the Opposition, Councillor Mark Hawthorne, along with Liberal Democrat councillor Bill Crowther and Labour councillor Mark Hobbs. They took evidence from Director of Environment David Scott, Director of Corporate Development Richard Cook, Head of Legal Services Gary Spencer and Council Leader Kevin Stephens. Their report, published in April 2002, made a number of recommendations including improving the Council's project management and risk management processes and reviewing the reporting structure between council officers and councillors.

What it taught me was that Compulsory Purchase Orders were more difficult than they sounded. You had to be sure of your ground. When you go up against someone with deeper pockets than you, who can employ the best legal firepower, it won't always end the way you want it to.

The Council did raise hopes of a 'Blackfriars Mark Two' in March 2002, after City MP Parmjit Dhanda brokered discussions with BT, who insisted they needed space to site an emergency exchange in the event of a fire or terrorist attack on their Bull Lane exchange.[102] It was portrayed publicly as a constructive meeting but some who were there described it as frustrating.

Leader of the Council at that time was Kevin Stephens and, probably unfairly, he took the blame for what happened. Stephens told me he wasn't aware of the Environmental Statement issue until the hearing (something the Blackfriars Inquiry accepted) and had he been he would have said "get it done". As I was later to find out with Marketing Gloucester, when you're Leader 'the buck stops here'. Stephens was big enough to admit that he would always be associated with the failure of regeneration at Blackfriars. He told the Blackfriars Inquiry, "I've never shirked my responsibilities and at the end of the day the buck stops with me." But, as I return to in Chapter 21, at least he had ambition and set about delivering it with energy, even if it didn't ultimately come off.

The other negative impact of the failed Blackfriars scheme was that it effectively blighted other city centre sites. Landowners were less likely to invest in their own assets if the centre of gravity for the city's retail offer was going to shift to the Blackfriars area. This, it could be argued, is why there was no major investment in the Kings Walk and Eastgate shopping centres for many years and led to the decline and ultimate closure of The Fleece Hotel – something the Council is still wrestling with at the time of writing.

Finding a new way forward

As the focus of regeneration in the city switched to St Oswalds Park and Gloucester Quays, responsibility for the Blackfriars project was handed over to the 'Shadow' Urban Regeneration Company, which was still awaiting Government approval. *The Citizen* reported that the City Council had taken a decision to hand over the project, the latest version of which included plans for a Cultural Centre opposite the Docks, with four developers interested.[103] However, by the time Chief Executive Chris Oldershaw was in place, those interests had withered.

Given the regeneration failures of the past, Blackfriars was certainly high on the list of priorities for the Gloucester Heritage Urban Regeneration Company (GHURC). The company took the symbolic step of locating its offices in the Blackfriars area, at 13-15 Ladybellegate Street, adjoining Blackfriars Priory. English Heritage Chief Executive Dr Simon Thurley performed the official opening ceremony.

Over the years, a number of different plans came forward. In July 2006, *The Citizen* reported on a new plan for a 4-star hotel, cultural buildings, housing, retail, bars and restaurants.[104]

The GHURC prospectus launched in 2006 set out a vision for the area, including a new public square (to be called Blackfriars Square) adjacent to Blackfriars Priory, surrounded by speciality shopping, bars and cafes. There would be a new flagship hotel, offices and apartments. A Sculpture Park at Alney Island would help the waterfront to be 'rediscovered'. Blackfriars would become a Creative Quarter, with creative and cultural industries, centred on Blackfriars Priory.

Later, in 2007, the plans had shifted to a civic focus, with a new hub for local government for the City and County Councils, a new magistrates court and police station. The proposals included narrowing The Quay to one lane and the innovative Eco Sculpture Park idea for Alney Island was gathering some momentum.[105] This was very much a project initiated by Chris Oldershaw, who told me that it was inspired by Charles Jencks' 'Northumberlandia' – a huge human landform sculpture. Gloucestershire Environmental Trust (which derived its income from landfill taxes) had agreed in principle to fund £250,000 for a new bridge over the River Severn by the Countrywide store (now Malvern Tyres) to open up the site. But there was concern from ecologists and for others the murder of council worker Anna McGurk in that area in the 1980s was still raw.

In January 2008, the University of Gloucestershire announced, with great fanfare, plans to have a major presence in the Blackfriars area. A press briefing was held and there was a good deal of excitement. An early version of the Greater Blackfriars masterplan was published in February 2008, refining the proposals set out by Terence O'Rourke in the GHURC Regeneration Framework. The University would occupy almost 18,000 sqm and there would be offices, almost 200 residential units, an 800-space multi-storey car park, a 180-bed hotel and a new small police station on the corner of Ladybellegate Street and Commercial Road. The University's financial problems at the time meant their proposals were withdrawn before they had progressed very far. I have covered this in more detail in Chapter 4.

In July 2009, the idea of Council offices was dismissed as "unrealistic and prohibitively expensive" by the City Council as it resolved to stay at the Docks for at least 8 years.[106] The County Council had never really been sold on the idea. Plenty of developers were keen to build a new civic HQ and rent it to the authorities at a healthy sum per square foot, but it was difficult to make this stack up financially when the Councils already owned their offices so were paying no rent at all.

Later that summer, a consultation was launched on the latest masterplan.[107] Sam Hoad and the late Martin Wallace from GHURC led on the public consultation. The final masterplan was approved by the GHURC board in October 2009, by which time the University plans had been dropped. It suggested a phased development – with The Fleece, East and West phases. The plans included a new Blackfriars Square, 40,000 sq m of commercial space, 6500 sq m of retail and leisure and 190 homes, including riverside residences. There would be a hotel with a multi-storey car park wrapped around it. The Longsmith Street multi-storey car park would be removed and the Prison relocated and re-used. By this time, the proposal was to relocate the Magistrates and Crown Courts to a site which had been purchased in Great Western Road. The idea of a sculpture park at Alney Island was very much still alive. The Shire Hall extensions would be demolished to make way for a cultural venue centred on the Crown Court building.

The objectives were to grow the city's knowledge economy, improve the pedestrian link between Docks and Cathedral and enhance the waterfront.

The big idea for Blackfriars Priory was to turn it into a centre for the Performing Arts on the lines of successful projects in cities such as Liverpool.[108]

At one time Blackfriars was to have involved a very large element of SWRDA financial assistance, potentially as much as £25-30 million in grant aid to deliver the masterplan scheme,[109] although in a speech in Parliament in May 2009 City MP Parmjit Dhanda made reference to a commitment of £8.865 million. When SWRDA's budget was curtailed in the run-up to the 2010 general election, the prospect of a big cash injection to make these ambitious plans a reality receded.

Blackfriars Priory

The Priory was acquired by the Ministry of Works in the 1950s. In November 1993, it was reported that the site may be ready to open to the public in 1995 following a 35-year restoration by English Heritage. Their South West Regional Director Beric Morley said, "We have had it a very long time and after completing the church in 1980 we had a bit of a lull due to funding problems."[110]

Environment Secretary John Gummer, whose Parliamentary Private Secretary was City MP Douglas French, visited Gloucester in the mid-1990s for a tour of the city centre. He was concerned to see parts of Blackfriars Priory being propped up by timber and asked City Planning Officer David Scott who owned them. When David Scott said that it was English Heritage, Gummer was shocked and took away an action to follow this up. It's not known exactly what happened after this, but Douglas French told me Gummer was assiduous about things like this. I'm told the wheels moved more quickly after that.

The Priory is a stark example of how Gloucester's heritage has been underplayed. Even after it did open to the public it was limited to tours on the odd Sunday, conducted mainly by local historian Philip Moss.

In 1998, the early 19th century houses on Ladybellegate Street, later to be the Urban Regeneration Company's offices, were subject to a plan for a 'house of care and prayer', combining a monastery with housing for the homeless. The plans were shelved when monks from Prinknash Abbey and the Jericho community in Scotland pulled out. In 1994, I'm told there had even been a suggestion that the houses could be demolished, which would have revealed the foundations of the Priory's west range.

In January 1996, the City Council's Leisure Services Committee and English Heritage agreed the Priory should be the subject of a major Heritage Lottery Fund bid, to provide a museum and heritage centre which would have become the major focus for the city's museum service, particularly medieval history, but would have involved the closure of the City Museum in Brunswick Road. It would have included exhibition space and a café.

The project was described as being valued at between £3-4.5 million. A bid to the Heritage Lottery Fund (HLF) for development funding was lodged in September 1998. The HLF granted £160,000 towards feasibility work. Architects Feilden Clegg Bradley did the work necessary for the bid for feasibility but Van Heyningen &

Haward, who had worked on Sutton Hoo Visitor Centre, worked up the detailed plans.[111] I'm told that the plan was for performance space in the North Range and to recreate the life of monks in the Scriptorium.

City Council Chief Executive Graham Garbutt met with the archivist of Dominican Order who expressed an interest in relocating their archives from Edinburgh, but in April 1999 Head of Museums and Cultural Services Amanda Wadsley informed the Order that 'the feasibility study has revealed there to be a lack of accommodation within the main body of the site suitable for this collection.' Funding was also lacking. She proposed it might be feasible as a 'Phase II' part of the project if funding became available to develop 'an area adjacent to the priory'.

City Council records show that in 2003 councillors were informed that the 'Stage Two' bid hadn't been successful. Council Officers involved at the time tell me that it was up against the Stonehenge visitor centre and the HLF wouldn't fund two big projects in the South West. It was also intimated that not all stakeholders were 100% committed.

So, it was back to the drawing board. The collapse of the Blackfriars development had also thrown into question the future of Blackfriars Priory. It was to have been "the centrepiece of the redevelopment". I demanded a "secure and viable future" for the building, saying "It should not be tucked away in an area that leaves a lot to be desired. People just don't know that it is there or that it has so much history. We need to change that and not let an asset like the Priory go to waste."[112]

In 2007, Gloucester Heritage Urban Regeneration commissioned architects Feilden Clegg Bradley to survey the historic fabric of the buildings in the Priory complex, to identify constraints and potential new uses. A Conservation Plan for the Priory complex was completed in October 2007. The plans for the Priory were intended to be the first phase of a phased approach to regenerating the wider Blackfriars area.

In April 2009, planning permission was granted for works to convert the Priory into a public venue. These works included new toilets in the East Range, new stairs and a lift in the North Range, heating, lighting and electrical works. The budget was £800,000 and the works, which were onsite in 2010, were seen as an "early and quick win".[113]

I was very proud to lead the City Council as we took it on in 2012 and developed it as an events venue, for weddings, parties (I held my

40th birthday party there), beer festivals and the Gloucester History Festival talks. I officially received the keys to Blackfriars from Sir Tim Laurence, husband of Princess Anne, in his role as an English Heritage Commissioner. At the time I said the city's "hidden gem" would now "be hidden a great deal less".[114]

The Gloucester Language Immersion Centre (GLIC)

Regeneration did finally come to Blackfriars, although in a different form from what was intended all those years ago. Immediately adjacent to the Priory, the Clutch Clinic car repair and sales business was demolished to make way for a new building to house the Gloucester (sometimes called the Global) Language Immersion Centre (GLIC). The Blackfriars Priory site was chosen over the Oxstalls Campus by the stakeholders in order to help contribute to the wider regeneration of Gloucester and the Greater Blackfriars area. Planning documents for the project stated that the "LIC will be an exemplary building which will act as a catalyst for further regeneration in the locality."

The idea behind this plan was for children to be able to be immersed in a language, like Russian or Arabic rather than the more mainstream languages taught in schools, making use of the latest technology. It was conceived and taken forward by a consortium of schools led by Chosen Hill in Churchdown. It was justified on the basis of language skills for GCHQ and language specialists from both the spy centre and the University of Gloucestershire gave their input.

The bid to the Department for Children, Schools and Families (DCSF) for funding for the Immersion Centre was made by G15, which is a consortium of all secondary school headteachers in the Gloucester area. Sue Turner, Headteacher of Chosen Hill School, fronted the bid for G15 as she took the lead on 14-18 education for G15 and had a lot of experience of 14-19 curriculum developments from her previous post in Leicestershire.

Documents submitted with the planning application explained the theory behind the project, saying: "Language immersion is a method of learning a second language. It uses the target language, in this case languages that are not widely taught in the UK such as Mandarin, Chinese, Arabic and Russian, as a learning tool. Students are surrounded or immersed in the second language during normal class activities, such as maths and history. Activities outside the class, including meals, are also conducted in the target language. The Language Immersion Centre (LIC) will use technology to recreate the experience of being in a foreign country and take students out of their everyday environment. The theory behind immersive learning is that once the students enter the centre they would speak no English and have no connection to the outside world in order to suspend the feeling of reality as much as possible. This aspect of the teaching method has effects on the building design as views out of the centre need to be reduced or restricted so that the students do not feel like they are in Gloucester. In order to create the suspension of reality, the building will make use of state-of-the-art computer-based projections as well as more traditional stage sets. Student numbers are expected to rise from an initial 190 a year up to 830 a year when fully operational. The courses will run for 5 days (Mon-Fri) and will repeat for potentially 20 weeks, before the language of study will change and the programme repeats. The centre will offer day visits for primary students during weekdays and the weekend users are more likely to be older students or private commercial users.

"The centre will be used by schoolchildren, mainly aged from 14 to 19. The centre provides accommodation for up to 22 people to stay overnight in ensuite twin rooms as part of the immersion experience. The centre will also be available for extra-curricular activities during weekends and school holidays. The funding for the centre is coming from £53 million allocated nationally by the Department for Children, Schools and Families (DCSF) to new facilities for learning foreign languages. Over 220 projects bid for this funding and 15 projects, including the Gloucestershire Language Immersion Project, were successful."

Sue Turner, Headteacher of Chosen Hill School, who led the project, said, "It is magnificent that a world class exemplar of learning, the Language Immersion Centre, is emerging alongside the medieval splendour of the Priory and the oldest known surviving library in England. The learning experience in these spaces is remarkable and represents the richest experience possible for those immersed within them. The power of extraordinarily different styles of communication across 800 years."

Few of us held out much hope of securing the £5 million needed for this scheme. Senior Officers from the County Council told me they were highly-sceptical and the proposal "came from left field". We were surprised when it got the thumbs up from the Department for Children, Schools and Families in November 2009 and then survived the new Coalition Government's spending cuts in 2010.

In addition to the £5 million from the DCSF, SWRDA contributed nearly £400,000 for site acquisition and another £400,000 for other capital works, including new toilets which would also serve the Priory, a new café for the Priory and a disability-compliant staircase for the East Range. English Heritage added another £200,000 for these works and the County Council made up the balance of £400,000. So, all in all, it was a £6 million building project excluding land acquisition costs.

The building needed to be sensitive due to its relationship with both the East Range of the Priory and the Scriptorium. The design incorporated the existing building at 4 Commercial Road into the centre. Feilden Clegg Bradley were the architects and local firm EG Carter were the contractors. The IT equipment alone is believed to have cost £2 million.

As it related to education, Gloucestershire County Council, rather than the City Council, was the planning authority for this scheme. In March 2010 a planning application for the LIC was submitted to the County Council. The City Council objected to the design of the Commercial Road elevation as did the Civic Trust. It should be noted that the City Council comments were from councillors not officers. The South West Design Review Panel and English Heritage didn't object. The Civic Trust commented: "The Trust has waited for 35 years to see a planning application which addresses the question of what to do with the setting of the most complete Dominican friary in England. The friary is second only to the cathedral in terms of the list of ancient ecclesiastical buildings in Gloucester. The panel supports the overall aim of providing a major new educational facility in Gloucester which will complement the unique setting of Blackfriars. But we had misgivings about several aspects of the design proposed. The drawings of the frontage to Commercial Road appeared at first viewing to show a huge slab of brickwork with a largely horizontal emphasis, completely at odds with the rest of the street. The panel regrets that the application is not being considered by the City Council under the normal planning procedure. The use of an arcane law has been invoked under which the Gloucestershire County Council will decide its own application. In the eyes of the public, this will be regarded as inherently suspicious."

The demolition of the Clutch Clinic building, which had a snooker club above it and was formerly the Talbot Mineral Water bottling plant (until 1954), took place between March and June 2010.

Construction began in September 2010 and the building was completed in October 2011, with the Language Immersion Centre opening for business in November 2011. The Centre was officially opened in May 2012 by David Willetts MP (now Lord Willetts) in his role as Minister of State for Education with responsibility for higher education and science.

13th century Medieval floor tiles were found under the Clutch Clinic building. They belonged to the Chapterhouse of Blackfriars Priory, where monks would meet every morning to 'hold chapter' i.e. to read from the Bible and the Priory's rule book and discuss monastery business.

The top floor of the Immersion Centre building was made up of overnight accommodation with furnished bedrooms and bathrooms. It was intended that students would stay for a few days as part of their 'immersion' in the target language, with a menu also appropriate to the language. It's not clear how many students actually stayed overnight. Sources tell me the vast majority of students were there during the daytime.

Unfortunately, the qualification for which the centre was established (the Languages and International Communications Diploma) was discontinued and the schools involved in the consortium felt the centre was too much of a distraction from their core purpose, so fell away one by one. There was no fanfare when this well-intentioned idea died in March 2015 and the County Council, as owners of the building, took advantage of the clause allowing it to be used for other purposes, filled it with their Adult Education Service and avoided paying back the £5 million to the government. The overnight accommodation was later removed and converted to offices for the County's Employment and Skills Hub.

A new masterplan

On the wider scheme, land assembly continued whenever there was an opportunity. In May 2010, the City Council acquired the BT car park (which had been the reason why the Blackfriars scheme of the 1990s had collapsed) and repeater station and the British Legion building on the corner of Ladybellegate Street and Commercial Road with £1.2million of RDA funding.[115] The Council had been using the former BT repeater station on Ladybellegate Street for museum storage. Repeater stations are used to amplify fading messages over copper cables. In times gone by, there needed to be lots of them but, as technology improved, they became redundant.

It's not clear why BT were willing to sell their car park less than a decade after they had been willing to spend £2 million in legal fees to defend it from compulsory purchase. Some suggested that the transition to digital made the visit of contractors less important. Others suggested that SWRDA paid a higher price than BT would have received through a compulsory purchase. Others thought it may simply be due to a change in personnel. Despite asking a number of people involved over the years I couldn't get a definitive answer, so the chances are we will never know.

In April 2014, City MP Richard Graham outlined in Parliament his vision of 2000 homes, 1500 jobs, joint council offices, a 5-star hotel and a justice centre to replace the city's crumbling magistrates and crown courts. Quite what detail lay behind the numbers of homes and jobs I don't know, but they seemed ambitious.[116]

He told Parliament: "We need to improve and regenerate the area that I call Greater Blackfriars, which stretches from the former prison to Shire Hall at Westgate Street and includes many buildings in between, which are ripe for regeneration, and a cleared site known as the Barbican outside the former prison, now in the ownership of the city council. This offers us a unique opportunity for a master plan of regeneration that will incorporate the prison, which is shortly to be sold, the buildings known as Quayside, which is surplus county council estate, the building in which the police currently have their city headquarters, which they will be leaving soon, and the city council site of the Barbican.

Regeneration enables us to offer a vision that includes new accommodation — new housing for perhaps 2,000 residents — new offices for perhaps 1,500 people, and a new justice centre which can incorporate all the current courts and tribunals, many of whose current premises have passed their sell-by date and need replacement. Perhaps in due course, if the proposal is right and properly costed, that vision could include a new civic centre which could house both the county and city councils, alongside a five-star hotel, perhaps close to Westgate, in which visitors can stay when they come to see our great rugby team."[117]

In May 2014, Mark Hawthorne and I signed a 'Memorandum of Understanding' between the City and County Councils to develop a masterplan for the area. Rather than a grand ceremony, we signed it on the bonnet of a car in Ladybellegate Street after a photo opportunity next to the then vacant Barbican site. I said at the time, "The Blackfriars area is a significant piece of city centre real estate which has enormous potential to enhance the city's economy. Almost all of the land in the area is in public ownership which gives us a head start."[118]

Paul James and County Council Leader Mark Hawthorne with Communities Secretary Sajid Javid, Richard Graham MP and University Vice Chancellor Stephen Marston at Blackfriars

Former Citizen journalist, Hugh Worsnip, who had spent decades covering previous attempts to regenerate Blackfriars and was now a leading member of the Civic Trust said, "Thank goodness something is happening. This is an area of Gloucester which has been growing increasingly derelict for far too long."

Richard Graham continued to pursue his idea of a new Justice Centre. In September 2014 he asked Justice Minister Shailesh Vara whether "a new justice centre in the city centre will be considered positively for all courts and tribunals once the justice review is finished?" All the Minister would say is that the decision would be taken as part of the court reform programme.[119]

In January 2015, Transport Secretary Patrick McLoughlin visited Gloucester to announce a £4.13 million government Growth Deal award for Blackfriars. This would be used to 'de-risk' the development by dealing with the archaeology on the Barbican site, creating a 'Local Development Order' which set the parameters for planning applications and contributed towards the re-cladding of Shire Hall.[120]

The new Blackfriars masterplan, which had been devised by local planning consultants Evans Jones, was launched in March 2015 at the Language Immersion Centre. Mark Hawthorne and I both spoke. The masterplan envisaged townhouses along The Quay and retirement and other housing elsewhere within site, plus 1100 student beds. Mark said, "Our ambition is to put Gloucester on the map as a vibrant city with opportunities to boost the local economy and attract more visitors. This masterplan marks the first step on that journey." I added, "The regeneration of this area has eluded the city for decades but now we have the best opportunity yet to make it happen."[121]

The Local Development Order for Blackfriars, which the committee report said made it "easier, less expensive and less risky for developers" was approved by the City Council's Planning Committee in March 2017 and got rubber-stamped by Communities Secretary Sajid Javid in May 2017. I commented at the time that "the transformation of Blackfriars has just jumped one more key hurdle".

Student Accommodation

The Barbican site ended up in the City Council's hands when the Regional Development Agency was wound up and, thanks in part to the grant from the government to help with archaeology and the like, was developed by CityHeart for student housing. The site was identified by the University of Gloucestershire when it went through a competitive process to find a developer of student accommodation in connection with its new Business School. Students from the expanding Hartpury University and College ended up occupying part of Phase One, which comprised 295 beds and was completed in September 2018.

The Phase One planning application was approved in February 2017, just before the LDO was given the thumbs-up but it took account of it as it evolved. The Barbican was a challenging site – which is why it had stood undeveloped for decades. Archaeology was a major issue because of the city's Roman origins, the Norman Castle on the adjacent Prison site and remains from nearby Blackfriars Priory. Some archaeological excavations were carried out by the City Council as part of the 'de-risking' works but CityHeart still had to do more. Glazed floor tiles were discovered, and the western wall of the city and a mound from Norman motte were found during the second phase of the development. It was possible to lift the development schemes to avoid the remains as the buildings were lightweight. They spent around £200,000 on archaeology but were relieved when what they uncovered was limited. It's worth pointing out that, while this sounds like a lot of money, it's a small percentage of the overall development cost and ensures what is underground in a historically very important part of Gloucester is dealt with sensitively.

Contractors also found an oval wall and tiled floor, believed to be a Roman bathhouse, on Commercial Road as they were connecting to the sewers. This was preserved in situ after the developer redesigned the scheme. There were also Scheduled Ancient Monuments, which made up an open area within the Roman walls, underground and CityHeart's contractors had to take great care not to damage them when they were piling the buildings' foundations.

The site was surrounded by 13 listed buildings, including the former Prison and Blackfriars Priory, as well as being in the shadow of the Cathedral, so the elevational treatments and roofscapes had to be sensitive and not dominate the existing buildings.

The timetable for Phase One was tight to get it ready for student occupation in September 2018. Legend has it that paint was still drying in some of the rooms as students moved in. One of the blocks didn't have a functioning lift, so two burly security guards could be seen helping students and their parents carry in their possessions. Move-in day in September 2018 was quite an operation, with the City Council and the nearby Brunswick Baptist Church making parking spaces available and the Church providing refreshments. The Phase One buildings are named after the Dymock Poets, an early 20th century literary community centred on the Gloucestershire village, whose original manuscripts and other documents are held in the University of Gloucestershire's archives.

Phase Two of the student accommodation (another 200 beds) was granted planning consent in November 2018. This phase was purely for Hartpury students. Work on site was due to start in May 2019 and be completed by September 2020, but was delayed by the pandemic. It was further delayed when the main contractor Midas went into administration in February 2022. Local firm Vitruvius Management Services, who had been involved in the project through their links with Hartpury, stepped in to manage the construction – achieving the quickest restart of any stalled Midas scheme. It was partially completed in time for the student intake of September 2022, with the remaining works, including landscaping, finished in December that year.

Shire Hall and Quayside

The County Council has played its part too. Quayside House was an eyesore County Council office building next to the Prison, designed as a 30-year lifespan building in the 1960s. County Council staff tell me it was claustrophobic to work in and a nightmare to maintain. It limped on until it was demolished, starting in April 2018. It was replaced by the new Quayside House health centre which is home to two GP surgeries serving around 18,000 patients, a pharmacy, office space and parking. The existing slab of the building was reused to avoid issues with archaeology The new centre opened in July 2021.

Councillor Tim Harman, the County Council's Cabinet Member for Public Health, said at the time, "The new health centre will be able to provide a high-quality service to the people in the city of Gloucester, and is part of the wider regeneration in the area. £16million of council funding has helped to make this project happen, and has been completed despite the difficulties posed by the COVID-19 pandemic."

The County Council had a decision to make on what to do with its main Shire Hall complex. The 1960s green panels on the Shire Hall extension were at risk of falling off. The windows leaked and were draughty, making heating costs very high. They were so bad that IT kit couldn't be positioned near windows. The Council wanted to invest in IT so needed to invest in its buildings. They considered three options – 1) demolition and rebuild onsite, 2) strip down and rebuild on the existing footprint or 3) relocate to an out of city site like Waterwells. Option 1 had high build costs, Option 2 was less expensive but still a significant investment. Option 3 was the cheapest but was politically unpalatable due to the economic impact on Gloucester city centre and the message it would send out.

When austerity hit, the County Council didn't want to be seen spending money on their own buildings, so put any plan on hold for five years, but returned to it as part of the wider Blackfriars and Quayside regeneration.

It was a disappointment to some that the 1970s Shire Hall extensions were not demolished but instead were reimagined in a design by the city's Quattro Design Architects, which included solar panels and insulated cladding systems. The project has been well-received and won a number of awards including three categories in the Constructing Excellence South West awards and Best Large Commercial Project in the LABC Building Excellence Awards 2020.

It is understood the cladding cost in excess of £11 million. Council Leader Mark Hawthorne and Chief Executive Peter Bungard are believed to have personally picked the colours for cladding and the copper-coloured feature after rejecting earlier designs they felt were inferior. Other organisations like the Police and NHS have moved into the remodelled Shire Hall and, between April 2019 and August 2022, the City Council moved its own offices onto the 5th Floor of the 'Bridge' across Longsmith Street. I had mixed feelings when it was announced that the City Council were moving out of Shire Hall to the former Severn Sound Radio Bridge Studios on Eastgate Street. I supported anything that brought more people into the heart of the city centre but I felt there were advantages to co-location for two organisations who work so closely together – and in the event of the Government imposing a unitary structure of local government for

Gloucestershire the City Council would already be there.

Still to do

At the time of writing, plans for the remainder of the County Council's site are unknown and the NCP 'bombsite' car park is still that, with no firm plans for it to change, but perhaps one day it will. It was put up for sale in November 2020 for just over £2.7 million, with 16 years remaining on the lease to NCP. It appears to have eventually been sold to a company connected to a New York-based private equity investor as part of a £300 million portfolio of 37 UK car parks in February 2023. Presumably, their interest is in the income from the site rather than any long-term development potential. In any case, developing the site would be a challenge. City Archaeologist Andrew Armstrong told me that a trench was dug at the car park in 1991 and it is believed to contain a large number of medieval burials (possibly as many as 2000), overlying Roman buildings, as it was the cemetery for Blackfriars. One discovery was a priest, who had been buried with an instrument used to administer the sacrament.

The student accommodation ended up being the largest single element of regeneration in the Blackfriars area and bringing in 500 new people to live in the city centre is welcome. But it didn't add up to the scale of transformation which had been envisaged and worked towards for so long.

6. FROM BSE TO B&Q
The development of the former Cattle Market at St Oswalds

History and the move to St Oswalds

The right to hold a market was conferred on the city in 1155 by Henry II after Gloucester was granted a general charter to become self-governing. In 1483, the rights were confirmed by a second charter including the instruction that they should be held within six and two third miles of The Cross.

For centuries the livestock and produce markets were held in the city's streets. In the mid-1780s a major reorganisation of the city's market facilities took the produce markets out of the streets.

The new cattle market south of lower Northgate Street was built under an Act of 1821 and opened in 1823. The leading promoter of the scheme was John Phillpotts, a land agent who lived at Bearland and went on to be Member of Parliament for Gloucester. The new market was extensively remodelled in 1862–3 and improvements were made several times in the late 19th and early 20th century as the volume of business showed a steady increase, encouraged by the easy access from the railway. In 1933, the market had accommodation for 5,000 sheep, 2,000 pigs and 1,000 cattle. The first cattle auctions were begun there in 1862 by the two founders of the firm of Bruton Knowles & Co. and came gradually to replace dealing by private treaty. General stock sales were being held twice a week by 1910, on Mondays and Saturdays, and on Saturdays there was also a horse market and private dealing in Irish cattle.

The new Cattle Market was sited where the bus station (and site of the Kings Quarter/The Forum development) is now. When the 'old' bus station was demolished, I ensured the plaque relating to the Livestock Market was retrieved and it was refurbished, with Bruton Knowles picking up the cost, and put in the new bus station.

According to the book 'Celebrating 150 Years of Bruton Knowles Heritage', produced to mark the firm's anniversary:

"It was becoming increasingly clear that Gloucester Market could no longer cope with the amount of stock that poured in every market day.

"The market needed a more up-to-date means of keeping the area free from contamination and the market office was old-fashioned and poky, meaning that the staff had to undertake extra work under difficult conditions. Worse still, accommodation, both for livestock and lorries, was insufficient.

"In 1951, Pat Lawrence read a paper to the City Corporation on the requirements of a new market. He had travelled as far as Edinburgh to see new markets and how they had adapted. A 35-acre site was chosen beside St Oswald's Road. The area had been subject to flooding by the River Severn, but it was reclaimed by tipping to a depth of 11 feet. The design by the city architect included facilities for offices, shops, banks and trade displays, a restaurant, snack bar, and lorry and car parks.

"The first stage for attested dairy cattle was opened by the Minister of Agriculture on 18th July 1955, almost exactly 100 years after the construction of its predecessor. Norman Bruton conducted the first sale but the new market opening did not go without the odd hitch!

"One cow, frightened by the clatter of the new gates, bolted through the sale ring and on to the roof. The cow ended up falling through a skylight onto Archie Workman, a local drover!

"Between 1955 and 1958, the cattle market was gradually moved completely over to the new 35-acre site and Cecil Bruton sold the last lot in the old market, where his grandfather had wielded the gavel nearly a century ago."

The new complex of buildings included traders' display units, shops, banks, a public house, and a restaurant, besides sale halls, covered accommodation for stock, an abattoir and meat market, and a large lorry park. Gloucester market had by then become one of the leading livestock markets in the country, known particularly for its pig and sheep sales, the latter attracting buyers from all over southern England. In 1980, when the firm of J. Pearce Pope & Sons shared the conduct of the market business with Bruton Knowles & Co, the stock sales were held on Mondays and Thursdays. The two firms, who jointly ran the market through Gloucester Market

Auctioneers, eventually merged.

Animal pens at the former Livestock Market in St Oswalds Road. Credit: Paul Dowle

At its peak, the market, which operated on Mondays, Thursdays and Saturdays, attracted custom from as far west as Aberystwyth and turned over £1 million a week. The facility was operating at its full capacity. Between 200 and 300 vendors attended the market on a Monday where animals traded included fat cattle, weaned and rearing calves, dairy cows, sheep, pigs, hay and straw. Thursdays saw the market selling store cattle – animals ready to be killed. It was estimated that the market brought £3 million a year of economic benefit to the city, although opinion on the scale of the economic benefits was split. Some said it brought hundreds of people into the city and while the farmers went to the market, their wives went shopping in the city centre. Others said this was a myth, that the economic benefit was very little and was to farmers who didn't even live in the city. It was also argued that it performed an important social role, bringing together rural communities who could otherwise suffer from social isolation. Citizen journalist Hugh Worsnip, in his column on 17th March 2000, argued that the "old-fashioned livestock market is now more of a farmers' day out" and a "social centre… where farmers meet to discuss their problems and compare notes."

On Wednesdays and Sundays, the land was turned over to an Outdoor Market and Car Boot sale. This was run by local businessman Chance Malone on behalf of the city and grew to be one of the biggest in the South West. The vast hardstanding space also made it a popular place to learn to drive.

Decline, closure and plans for redevelopment

By the 1990s, the St Oswald's site was starting to look tired. In addition to the market premises, the big four banks were still there – Barclays, Lloyds, Natwest and Midland (later HSBC). There were two pubs – the Bell & Gavel and Wheelwrights, although the latter was confusingly renamed the Baker Street Tavern for a short while before it closed. There was, and still is, a Baker Street pub in Southgate Street which has the stronger claim to the name as it is on the corner of what was Baker Street. The Charollais café and Yeung's Chinese restaurant catered for the hungry masses. I'm told the Chinese restaurant was originally called Ken's and then became Yeungs when the owner lost it in a card game. It stayed open very late and catered for people coming out of the nightclubs. John Stayte Services, who now operate from premises next to Kingsholm Rugby Stadium, had a prominent business there, as did the Hair of The Dog pet shop.

Gloucester Rugby legend Peter Ford's wholesale fruit and vegetable wholesale business operated from the rear of the site, as did Sommer Allibert, a plastics company. Another business situated there was 'The Private Shop' – the city's sex shop – run by Darker Enterprises. Its licence needed to be renewed every year by the Council's Licensing Committee. In July 1996, Councillor Pam Tracey suggested a site visit for members of the committee, which was widened to all councillors. Pam speculated that "it might be like Boots the Chemist in there". In the end, she was the only one to turn up! It may not have assisted the decision-making process a great deal, but it caused some amusement and even got a mention in The News of the World (under the headline "Burgher Sex Tour in Store" and the Daily Telegraph's 'Parish Pump' column! The Private Shop relocated to Barton Street ahead of the redevelopment.

Other businesses included Gloucester Building Supplies,

Gloucester Paving, the Tyre & Battery Centre (which moved to Hempsted) and the Driver Education Centre.

The BSE ('Mad Cow Disease') outbreak of the 1990s and the Foot and Mouth crisis of 2001 damaged the market and had a negative impact on the City Council's income from it. Use of the livestock market also declined because farmers started to deal directly with supermarkets. By the late 1990s, City Council Officers felt the Council needed to do something to gain extra revenue from the site. The Council was also seeking cash to finance its ambitious capital programme, including a rebuild of the Gloucester Leisure Centre. Gloucester-based Quantity Surveyor Steve Tandy, who was working on the leisure centre project, suggested to Chief Leisure Officer Philip Cooke that the Cattle Market might be a possible disposal to raise cash.

The market was ageing and needed an upgrade to comply with Government and EU regulations. *The Citizen* reported in October 1996 that the Council had lost £120,000 because of a decline in throughput of livestock due to BSE and the Government had turned down calls for compensation.[122]

In July 1996, the City Council's Policy & Resources Committee approved a phased approach to the redevelopment of the Cattle Market. The first phase was the new Tesco store on the old Weddel Swift abattoir site. As discussed in the 'University Challenge' chapter, the Council had granted planning consent for a superstore and filling station in August 1993 with the expectation it would be operated by Safeway. When they withdrew, Tesco stepped in.

Phase Two was the Livestock Market and area to the rear. This covered 17 acres at the Barratt Industrial Park, Spartans Rugby Club and the NCP Lorry Park. This phase was intended to be for retail, office, leisure, higher education and industrial use.

Phase Three, covering the remainder of the site, was due to be decided later but valuations indicated the land could be worth £9-10 million for non-food retail use but just over £4 million for an office-based Business Park.

GHK Economics and Management were commissioned to carry out a study on the market's economic impact. They advised that there was a trend towards fewer but bigger markets. Gloucester had increased its market share in the 1990s and there was farmer satisfaction with Gloucester Market Auctioneers (GMA), but livestock auctions were facing competition from other forms of marketing. They estimated that the Livestock Market contributed £2.5-3 million a year to the Council, GMA and local businesses and supported 22 full-time and 85 part-time jobs plus another 50 associated jobs onsite.

The cost of a full refurbishment was estimated at £2-3 million, whereas relocation would cost £4-5 million. The net income to the Council of a new market was forecast to be £250,000 a year. The option of closure was not recommended. It was felt that relocation offered the greatest potential to maximise the value of the land and improve the St Oswalds Road frontage.

Phase One went to plan with Tesco acquiring the Weddel Swift abattoir site. As an aside, Weddel Swift was a meat processing business which was part of the Vestey Group, owned by the family of Lord (Sam) Vestey. The abattoir no longer had the scale needed to compete. The Vestey family seat is at Stowell Park near Northleach and the family are amongst the wealthiest in the country, with a fortune estimated at £700 million. Lord Sam Vestey, who died in 2021, was for many years Chairman of Cheltenham Racecourse and was Master of the Horse to The Queen from 1999 to 2018.

A reserved matters planning consent for the food store, petrol filling station, car parking, a park and ride station and replacement toilets was granted in December 1996.

The freehold of the site was owned by the City Council, but it was subject to a lease in favour of Weddel Swift, so a deal was negotiated with the Vestey Group, with both parties sharing the spoils. Former Council Leader Kevin Stephens told me that Lord Vestey always teased him that the Council had out-negotiated him. I suspect that was just flattery.

In July 1996, *The Citizen* reported that the Council would get £3 million from the Tesco deal, which was due to be signed before the end of the month. In the end, the deal was between the City Council, Tesco and the receivers for Union International, part of the Vestey empire (which included the Dewhurst chain of butchers shops) which went into receivership in 1995.[123]

In November 1996, *The Citizen* reported that Tesco wanted to increase the size of the store from 53,000 sq ft to 60,000 sq ft. It added that, in some parts of the site, the methane concentration was 56%, meaning that special measures would be needed to alarm and vent the store. A report in December 1996 said that construction was due to start on site the next month. The store opened in 1997.

Phase Two

Surveyors Donaldsons put together a strategy for a leisure development as part of Phase II for the Cattle Market. Donaldsons' Peter Mawson, who had worked with Salisbury City Council on redevelopment of Cattle Market in Salisbury and the relocation of the facility to the edge of the city, led the project.

In March 1997, *The Citizen* reported that 500 jobs could be created according to Donaldsons. Their report suggested the development could include a 12-screen cinema, a casino, a 50-bed hotel, a nightclub, health and fitness and restaurants. As described in the Docks chapter, it was acknowledged that there was only room for one new cinema in the city in addition to the existing one at The Peel Centre.[124]

In August 1998, the City Council issued a development brief to shortlisted developers inviting proposals based on five key objectives. These were:
- Comprehensive redevelopment of undoubted architectural and urban design quality
- Mixed use development including a minimum 4-star hotel and conference centre
- Relocation of the cattle market
- Optimum financial return consistent with high quality development
- A deliverable scheme achievable in a rapid but realistic timeframe

It also outlined an acceptable range of uses, which comprised:
- Minimum 150 bed 4-star hotel (with a possible casino)
- Commercial leisure (health & fitness, bowling, nightclub, restaurant)
- 100-130,000 sq ft non-food retail
- Business Park

They were later amended to include a 3-star hotel, strong

pedestrian links and a residential element, at that time badged a 'Millennium Village'.

In October 1998, *The Citizen* reported that the Cattle Market was to be replaced by a 300-bedroom hotel and conference centre, with a "leading hotel chain ready to go". The Council's Strategy & Performance Committee met to examine bids by two rival developers on advice from Donaldsons' Peter Mawson and councillors had "secretly approved a £40 million proposal".

Rather optimistically, they hoped that a planning application would be made by Christmas. Chief Executive Graham Garbutt explained that the plan was to move the cattle market to the rear of the site near the railway line and create a multi-use market, not only for livestock but for car sales and antique sales. The move had the agreement of operators GMA. The article stated that "the City Council can expect a multi-million-pound receipt from the deal which can be invested in improvements elsewhere such as Kings Square, Blackfriars, The Docks and Greyfriars." Graham Garbutt added, "We expect the new market to be built, followed by a hotel at the end of 2000." Council Leader Jon Holmes said, "We are delighted that at last we are going to get the hotel and conference facilities that Gloucester deserves on a site so near to the city centre."

In November 1998, the spending watchdog District Audit was called in to check everything was above board following concerns raised by tenants at the site. Over a dozen of them said they wanted to stay and formed a group to buy land and build their own units. Chance Malone, who ran M&O Gates and operated the car boot sale, asked why 11 acres of land worth £5 million was being given to GMA. City Solicitor Richard Cook said the land had a negative value for use as a livestock market in the current circumstances. The Council promised to treat other tenants' interests in the same way as GMA.[125]

Malone had discovered, from a casual conversation at a reunion event, that GMA's lease had expired and their occupation was only on a monthly licence and had got indicative offers from three local developers to gain his valuation.

The Council's Strategy & Performance Committee in November 1998 agreed the principle that the Council would not finance the construction of a new market. It also endorsed the report's recommendation for use of the capital receipt, which stated "as a general principle, officers recommend that the central theme in this should be projects which will enhance the vitality and viability of the city centre. This is a very important strategic aim in itself, but would also help to allay any concerns that developments at the Cattle Market could adversely affect the city centre."

The committee meeting in January 1999 called the development 'St Oswald's Campus' and agreed to serve legal notices on tenants at the site and potentially use compulsory purchase powers. GMA produced data on animal throughput and asked for 14 acres of the site.

The meeting was informed that the developer's proposal comprised a 200 bed 4-star hotel and conference centre, a 100 bed 3-star hotel (Travelodge type), 130,000 sq ft of leisure space, 10,000 sq ft of fast food, 130,000 sq ft of non-food retail and a 100,000 sq ft business park. At this point, it was estimated work could start in late 1999/early 2000.

In March 1999, the committee agreed to grant a lease to GMA subject to it being not significantly less than the opportunity cost rent (i.e. what someone else would pay). They were also told that council officers were continuing to investigate the option of a casino.

The chosen developer was Grantchester, a retail parks specialist, who were floated on the Stock Exchange in 1996. Their business model was to build retail parks and sell them to pension funds. When the opportunity at St Oswalds was advertised in the property press, it was brought to the attention of Terry Webster of High Star Developments. Terry was a flamboyant character who fronted up the scheme, including speaking to farmers from the ring of the livestock market. Terry saw the potential of the site and worked up a scheme before bringing Grantchester on board. He told me that, with markets closing all over the country, the farmers "saw the writing on the wall".

Terry Webster lived in East Sussex but spent a lot of time in Gloucester as the scheme progressed, making The Greenway Hotel in Shurdington his second home. Some years later he took over the hotel to hold his son's wedding reception.

Grantchester strengthened their position by acquiring the lease of the Bell & Gavel pub before being formally chosen as the Council's developer partner.

Gloucester Market Auctioneers, headed by Richard Law, had put together an alternative proposal for the site to be redeveloped. It was based on a 'peppercorn' rent to the City Council and included residential, offices, retail and leisure uses as well as a new Cattle Market.

Grantchester was taken over by property giant Hammerson in October 2002 for £192 million. Director Nick Alford told me the company had 5 or 6 schemes in the pipeline and believed the market undervalued the company. The management team were going to launch a buyout, but Hammerson put in a higher bid because they wanted to move into the retail park business.

Spartans Rugby Club

At the back of the site was the Spartans Rugby Club. Spartans are a local Kingsholm Club and, as a Kingsholm councillor at the time, I was keen to look after their interests. I spent some great nights there, some of which I can't remember very well, with a wonderful bunch of friendly and genuine people like the late Colin Teague (uncle of rugby legend Mike), Rob Vallender, Dave Badhams and Aubrey Norton, father of England rugby sevens star Dan Norton. I managed to persuade the Council's Policy & Resources Committee in January 1997 to exclude them from the area of the development. They were grateful and their Honorary Secretary Dave Badhams wrote to me in February 1997 to express their thanks.

The Club struggled at the back of the site and looked for other options. Former Club Chairman Rob Vallender told me how he bumped into City Council surveyor, the late David Hook (son of former Gloucester Rugby player Bill Hook) and asked what was happening with the former YMCA building in Sebert Street. Spartans relocated their clubhouse to the YMCA in January 2010 and their pitch to the High School for Girls' playing field in nearby Lansdown Road. Council Officers were surprised by the willingness of the High School and their Headmistress Ewa Sawicka to allow Spartans to play on their school field. They asked for a new fence around the playing field as their price for the arrangement, which the Council were happy to provide. Sadly, David Hook passed away before the move took place.

The move took the club back to their Kingsholm roots, as they had been founded in the Mission Hall which is now the Sherborne Cinema. I helped to facilitate this as City Council Leader, but the project was driven by City Treasurer Keith Birtles who lived on the edge of the Kingsholm area. The Council bought out the Club's lease on their St Oswalds site, although the club didn't see any cash as that paid for the refurbishment of the new building. It came at a fairly substantial cost but cleared the area for future redevelopment, although at the time of writing that is still to take place.

The End of The Livestock Market

At a Special Council meeting in March 2000, it was decided that the Livestock Market would not continue to be on the St Oswalds site. Negotiations with Gloucester Market Auctioneers had gone on for nine months and the two sides were still miles apart. The City Council estimated that it was subsidising the market by £180,000 a year and claimed that GMA had missed the deadline for submitting its proposal. Council Leader Kevin Stephens said, "Although the Council is keen to see a new livestock market as part of the redevelopment it cannot be on any terms. This multi-million-pound development is vital to the city's long-term prosperity. GMA failed to meet a deadline set in January and the difference between us is so substantial that there is no realistic possibility of concluding the negotiations without jeopardising the whole development."[126]

Chief Executive Graham Garbutt added, "Reluctantly we have had to conclude negotiations. We wanted to include them and it is a matter of regret we cannot – the market is a significant part of the city's history."

I took a more supportive view of the market, saying, "We have no legal obligation to provide a livestock market but I believe we have an historic and moral obligation to retain a market with the substantial amount of money we will receive for the redevelopment of the land. We must make every effort to settle the negotiations or find an alternative site."[127]

Newent sheep farmer Roger Carter said, "Where would we go? We would have to travel much further to other cattle markets and the cost of fuel isn't cheap. People talk about the welfare of the animals but if we have to start travelling about, what will happen to them?"

Richard Crofton, Chief Executive of Bruton Knowles, "We are completely surprised and we still feel we are in discussion with the City Council. We have met all the deadlines we have been asked to meet as far as we are aware. The market is an essential part of Gloucester and we are happy to relocate because we could see the benefits the development plans would bring to the city."

The Citizen reported in September 2000 on plans for a new state-of-the-art livestock market on a 15-acre site at Drymeadow Farm, Innsworth. The £5.5 million scheme had been drawn up by consultants Hamiltons and would need a new roundabout off the Northern Bypass – something which has only just been built at the time of writing but, instead, to serve a new housing development at Innsworth. The new facility would include a farmers' produce market, rare breeds and machinery sales. Kevin Stephens said, "We recognise our obligations to the agricultural county and we are willing to make a substantial contribution to the cost of the roads necessary to build what I believe will be a centre of excellence for agriculture in Gloucester."[128] In the end that proposal didn't come about because Bruton Knowles saw it as too high a risk.

In October 2000, there were reports of "hordes of rats scurrying around" the St Oswalds site due to the neglected nature of the area, with the businesses left there demanding that action should be taken.[129]

In September 2001, *The Citizen* reported that the Livestock Market, which had closed since the outbreak of Foot and Mouth, would never re-open. Council Leader Kevin Stephens said, "We had been hoping that a new livestock market, possibly at Innsworth, might be opened before the existing market closed. But now, because of Foot and Mouth, that will not be possible."[130]

He added, "Historically this has benefitted the taxpayers of Gloucester substantially although in recent years there has been a loss on the operations of the market."

I'm told that some of the business went to slaughterhouses as deadweight while others went to markets in the Welsh marches, Tetbury, Cirencester and Ross-on-Wye.

At that time, the Bruton Knowles business had restructured. They had sold their estate agency business to the Cheltenham & Gloucester Building Society (although they didn't stay in the business for long) and had started managing property portfolios for big organisations like Buckinghamshire County Council and East Midlands Electricity. This was the start of their journey to becoming the national property advisers they are today and also led to them moving offices from Albion Chambers in Eastgate Street to an out-of-town business park in Quedgeley.

Planning application and delays

A planning application was lodged for the 21-hectare (53 acre) site in April 2000. *The Citizen* newspaper reported it as being a £100 million development. A supporting statement by planning consultants Littman & Robesen described the site, saying: "Constructed in the 1950s, the livestock market and associated industrial uses & retail service facilities are in a poor and rundown state. The buildings and external surfaces are of poor quality, both architecturally and in condition. Parts of the site are redundant and have in the past been used for tipping. Other areas accommodate a mixture of predominantly Class B8 uses (i.e. use for storage or distribution) in shed-style premises, all presenting a poor appearance at this predominant key site on the northern edge of the city centre." The architects were Lyons Sleeman Hoare, who designed the Bicester Village shopping outlet.

The application sought consent for a DIY store of 125,000 sq ft, other retail of 55,000 sq ft, leisure (Health & Fitness and bowling) of 60,000 sq ft and a 20,000 sq ft casino. The food and beverage element was split between fast food (4300 sq ft) and a restaurant of 5700 sq ft. In addition, it was envisaged there would be 86,000 sq ft of employment space and 650 residential units. At the time DIY store operators were fighting each other for space – with Homebase bidding against B&Q for sites across the country. Homebase were originally to be the tenants for the DIY store, but they started to retrench. B&Q had only wanted 100,000 sq ft but took 130,000 as that's what Homebase were going to have.

At this stage, an 80-bed 3-star budget hotel still formed part of the plans, but the site of the 4-star hotel had shifted to the Westgate Street car park as described in Chapter 8. There was also space for overflow parking and the open market (1.6 ha). The developer had offered £650,000 for linkages between the site and the city centre and a 300-space park and ride car park. The sum for the linkages to the city centre later seems to have been negotiated down to £450,000. This paid for improvements to St Oswald's Road, Priory Gardens, St Mary's Square and Three Cocks Lane, including cycleways, paths, new trees and lighting.

Head of Planning Jerry Spencer had a vision, inspired by the Italian village of Tosca of a 'castellated' development, as seen from the A40 bypass, achieved by buildings of different heights to frame views of the Cathedral. Whether that is what had been achieved is arguable.

He also envisaged linking the development to the city centre with a new pedestrian tunnel across St Oswald's Road under the railway line in the form of a pink brightly-lit tube, which he admitted made it slightly phallic. That didn't make it into the final plans, but there is a diagonal tree-lined walkway across the car park which was meant to encourage pedestrian links to the city centre but largely goes unnoticed.

The application went before the Council's Planning Committee in April 2001. It was an outline application with all matters reserved – basically approving the broad principle of the development. Councillors were told they must forget that the City Council owned the land. They were also told that, following the Barnwood hotel appeal, they did not need to apply the sequential test to the proposed 3-star hotel (i.e. demonstrate why it couldn't be anywhere closer to the city centre).

In his report to the Planning Committee, Development Control Manager Phil Staddon expressed concern that the "scheme philosophy and content is overwhelmingly a rather anonymous retail park" and the "St Oswalds Road frontage is extremely weak". The Civic Trust commented that there was "scant reference to the loss of the Cattle Market" and were worried about the impact on the city centre.

Allibert, who were based on the Barratt Industrial Estate at the back of the site, employed 66 people. They commented that, under the proposals, their factory would be demolished and replaced with a leisure development but no occupiers had been identified. Their observation turned out to be prescient as twenty years later that part of the site has still not been developed.

Contamination was also an issue and, prior to the planning application, the amount of material, depth and composition was not well recorded. An Environmental Statement by Hyder Consulting in February 2001 advised that the Cattle Market and its previous use as a landfill site had left a legacy of ground contamination. They advised that there was "virtually no organic material left of the type that produces landfill gas (methane & CO_2)". The accumulation of methane in unventilated spaces can cause explosions and the equivalent for CO_2 is asphyxiation – so getting this right was pretty crucial! The thin water table on top of the ground becomes leachate and because the drainage system had been damaged it allowed water run—off and cattle slurry to pollute the nearby River Twyver. There was also Japanese knotweed on site which had to be treated.

The developers proposed a purpose-built drainage system with a leachate interceptor/drain. A management company for the leachate drain was set up, involving the major players on the site (Persimmon, Hammerson, Tesco and the City Council) but even today it is not believed to be operational. It's unclear how much maintenance of the drainage system has taken place or how effective the system is. It is the role of the Environment Agency to monitor the water quality in the River Twyver and no doubt they have this on their radar.

There were also gas control and venting measures to remove the potential for landfill gas to impact future development. Grantchester's Nick Alford told me that during a public consultation event a member of the public referred to watching tanks being buried onsite after World War II. This turned out not to be correct.

The application was deferred by the Planning Committee in April 2001. The Committee strongly supported the scheme but needed reassurance on the risk from landfill gas, had concerns about the density of the residential development and wanted to wait for the results of a study into Gloucester's retail performance. The application came back to the Committee in July 2001 when councillors were 'minded to grant' planning permission. The application came infront of the Committee again in August 2001 after the developers of the former RAF Quedgeley site, Quedgeley Urban Village Limited (QUVL) launched a Judicial Review of the Council's decision in the High Court. This unwanted attention was more likely to have been a tactical move to bolster their case ahead of the Public Inquiry into their scheme rather than a principled objection to the plans for St Oswald's. The Committee was asked to reconsider its decision in the light of QUVL's actions. It resolved to grant outline planning permission in principle, subject to conditions and a referral to the Government Office for the South West. QUVL's High Court action was dropped in November 2001.

Call-In & Public Inquiry

Director of the Government Office for the South West (GOSW), Jane Henderson, said in April 2002 that a decision on whether to 'call in' the planning decision wouldn't be made until after May's elections. I commented, "The Government wants quicker planning decisions. Why don't they make one?". The decision was 'called in' by GOSW on 11th June 2002 and a public inquiry took place between 29th October and 5th November 2002. Nick Alford told me that their QC gave the longest closing speech ever at an inquiry as they needed to complete a legal agreement before it finished.

The matter was referred to Deputy Prime Minister John Prescott on 25th February 2003 for a decision. At around this time the Cattle Market part of the site was being bulldozed.

The City MP Parmjit Dhanda admitted to getting frustrated. He told me that he spoke in the Commons lobby with John Prescott and had 'stiff conversations' with Junior Ministers. He also told me he'd asked a question at Deputy Prime Minister's Questions saying that he'd learned this was the way it gets to the top of the Ministerial Red Box.

Cotswolds MP Geoffrey Clifton-Brown was at the time a Shadow Local Government Minister. At my request, he asked questions in Parliament about the delay, to increase pressure on ministers to make a decision.

I wrote to Prescott directly in August 2003. He'd been running the country while Tony Blair was on holiday at Sir Cliff Richard's villa in Barbados. On Blair's return, I suggested that now Prescott didn't have the weight of the whole country on his shoulders, he could perhaps make a decision on St Oswalds. I also encouraged others to write to him.

"All it needs is one minister to sign a piece of paper. As many people as possible should write to John Prescott – whatever pressure we can bring can only help to speed things up," I commented.[131]

The Citizen pointed out at the time that "Prescott can take as long as he likes", adding that "The Government is under no obligation to stick to its 13-week target of dealing with planning decisions." A spokesman added, "We work to that for making decisions because it's good housekeeping but if we don't it's not binding."[132]

The Secretary of State (John Prescott) finally issued his decision on 7th October 2003. In his decision letter, the Secretary of State expressed concerns that the 'sequential approach', which requires applicants to prove there are no sites in or nearer the city centre which could have accommodated the development or parts of it, hadn't been properly carried out. He also noted that the site was "partly derelict since the Cattle Market closed in Spring 2001" and that there is "soil contamination and landfill gas present". He also noted that the Inspector had described the appearance of the site as "grey, run down, neglected and depressing". He added that he "accepts that the regeneration aspect of the proposal requires a comprehensive and large-scale development to fund the high cost of decontamination and construction .... and any diminution of the commercial element of the proposal could jeopardise the viability of the whole development."

In short, Prescott (guided by his officials) had accepted that the regeneration benefits outweighed the rather technical policy concerns. It had taken a long time, but it was the right decision.

David Atkins, Hammerson's Retail Parks Director (who went on to be their Chief Executive for a decade) said, "It has been a long slog but we are delighted to be starting what we believe will be an excellent project for Gloucester."[133]

The City Council maintained freehold ownership of the site but granted a 150-year lease of Phase One on 31st March 2004.

Compulsory Purchase Order

The developers had bought in leases through negotiation where possible, conducted by well-known commercial property agent Tim Heal of Alder King, but the Council's compulsory purchase powers were there in the background should they be needed. A Compulsory Purchase Order was considered by the Council's Cabinet in May 2004 and served in October 2004, with Hammerson underwriting the Council's costs. Because of objections to it, an inquiry was held in October 2005.

In February 2006, the Compulsory Purchase Order was confirmed for the residential component of the development. The area occupied by Allibert Buckhorn UK Ltd (a plastic injection moulding company) was excluded by the Inspector as the plans for that part of the site were less developed. In any case, a deal was reached with the company for it to relocate and their premises were demolished in 2007 and used for County Council staff car parking. It was identified for leisure purposes with ancillary parking within the masterplan attached to the outline planning permission – which could have been a nightclub, casino or health & fitness. No reserved matters application was ever submitted within the required period, so the consent expired.

This part of the outline consent never got implemented and neither did the allocation of 2.25 hectares for employment land. This has been intended to be principally for existing businesses onsite who wished to relocate, but they all made their own arrangements and moved elsewhere, so it was no longer required.

The Development Phase

By the time of the Hammerson takeover in October 2002, the B&Q pre-let was already in place and 40% of the income for the retail park had been secured. Hammerson's David Atkins told me that the company enhanced the look of the scheme after inheriting the project. The reserved matters application for the first phase (the DIY store plus the retail and leisure units running at right angles) was approved on 4th May 2004.

As with many developments, what was proposed at the outset was not the same as what eventually got built. These things are generally driven by market demand. The 4-star hotel project was transferred to the Westgate Street car park with terrible, if unforeseen, consequences. At the outset it was intended the hotel would have links with the nearby University Campus and Gloucestershire Royal Hospital for conferencing purposes but the failure of the project meant those links were never developed. There was no demand for the other (3-star) hotel. Likewise, the casino idea didn't progress because no operator came forward who was prepared to navigate the regulatory hurdles – and it was seen not to sit well with the planned residential development.

The capital receipts started to flow when the development agreement went 'unconditional' in March 2004 – i.e. all conditions had been satisfied. The City Council no longer has a record of exactly how much was paid for the site, but it is believed to be between £11-£12 million, with a £2.65 million 'hotel subsidy' for the ill-fated 4-star hotel project. Council reports show £4.8 million was paid in the first tranche, with a further £4m due by the end of March 2005. Presumably the balance was paid in the 2005/6 financial year and records show that the additional £2.65 million was paid in 2006/7.

There was some debate on how the money would be used. Although the original intention was to use it on regeneration projects like Kings Square and the bus station, by the time it hit the Council's bank, repayment of debt had become a necessity. Council Leader Mary Smith said, "What we can do with regard to council tax is to reduce our debt. We would also want to look at our capital projects to see how we could use the money on those."

At the time I responded, "I think that a fair proportion of the money should be used to reduce debt because that will help to keep council tax down and give us money to support the services we supply for people in the city. When we first looked at what this money could go towards, we looked at both Kings Square and the bus station. Now that we look to have found a private investor interested in the Square, hopefully we can look at making the bus station a decent and welcoming facility."

As is set out in the chapter on Kings Square and Kings Quarter, the bus station took another 15 years before it was delivered and it was almost another four years on top of that before Kings Square was properly revamped.

The relocation of B&Q from Trier Way created the second largest of their stores worldwide – beaten only by one in China. It gave St Oswald's a strong anchor but left a gap when their old store closed. The prominent corner site on Trier Way/Barton Street stayed empty for quite some time. Various options were looked at including a retail scheme involving Next and TK Maxx, which was turned down, before the site was taken on by outdoor pursuits retailer Go Outdoors in 2010. The site was owned by New Star Asset Management. I managed to persuade its boss John Duffield to donate £2000 to the Barton Fayre to compensate the local community for the difficulties it had caused. In September 2007, it was described in *The Citizen* as a "dumping ground and squalid den" and in August 2009 its condition was condemned as an "insult" by local councillors.

Work started on the first phase of St Oswalds on 14th September 2004. By that time, 70% of the units had been let. In May that year, the Conservatives had formed a minority administration on the City Council. At the ground-breaking ceremony, I said: "I believe today marks a turning point in Gloucester's fortunes. We must ensure that the momentum created by this development is maintained. There will still be many difficulties we will have to face, but we can now say with confidence that the long-awaited new dawn for Gloucester is starting to become a reality."[134]

David Atkins of Hammerson said, "We are delighted that work has started on the St Oswalds development and look forward to working with the Council and the local community to create a retail destination of which Gloucester can be proud. The importance of Gloucester as a key location for economic growth and development is evidenced by the range of top retail names already attracted to come here."

Hammerson's Annual Review of 2004 reported: "Construction is underway at St Oswald's Retail Park in Gloucester. The first phase of the development is expected to be completed in June 2005 at a total cost of £44 million and leases in respect of 83% of the forecast rental income have been agreed." It was completed, only slightly behind schedule, in September 2005. Hammerson's Annual Review of 2006 lists St Oswalds as one of the company's top 40 properties.

In September 2004, Natwest confirmed they would be taking a unit – the only one of the four big banks who were previously on the Cattle Market site to retain a presence.

In December 2004, Phase Two, comprising three restaurants went before the Planning Committee and was approved. At the time, this was reported to be "a drive thru takeaway, a Pizza Hut and a Frankie and Benny's".[135] This consent was only partially implemented. Frankie & Benny's and a Harvester restaurant opened in September 2005.

In July 2005, Comet signed up for a store in the main terrace of units. The other occupiers of Phase One were JJB Sports, Argos and furniture retailer SCS, with Mothercare joining them in 2006. JJB, who proposed a ground floor health and fitness facility and first floor sports shop, had to submit a variation to the planning permission to take up occupancy as sports goods didn't fall within the 'bulky goods' classification of the consent. They already had an 'out of town' store at the Peel Centre and a city centre unit in Southgate Street (now occupied by Tesco Express). They managed to secure the consent by agreeing to a number of conditions, including keeping a city centre store for at least five years and not allowing the Peel Centre unit (which they would sublet, having 15 years left to run on the lease) and the St Oswalds unit to be used concurrently for the sale of sports goods for at least five years. The application was approved despite objections from the nearby Riverside Sports & Leisure Club and Hargreaves Sports, who had a shop in Westgate Street at the time.

Mothercare's occupation also needed a relaxation of the bulky goods planning condition, which was approved by the Planning Committee in November 2006. The company said they had been unable to find suitable city centre premises since BHS terminated their space in their Eastgate Street store. They gave a legal undertaking to search for a city centre store for 6 years – but never opened one.

Another controversial application was a new store for Borders, a bookstore with a difference. As well as selling books, DVDs, CDs and magazines it also included a coffee shop and put on children's clubs, book signings and even speed dating!

On 28th August 2007, Citizen journalist Lee Cain, who went on to be Prime Minister Boris Johnson's Downing Street communications chief, reported that Borders had pulled out of their plans to open a store. It was believed this was due to their national trading position.

In April 2008, it was announced that Homesense, part of the TK Maxx group, which was described as selling "unique finds at irresistible prices" was to open. The Homesense building was a one-off as the planners didn't want more terrace-style buildings. Natwest Bank, Costa Coffee and the Subway sandwich store all opened in spring 2008. The Natwest branch closed in September 2023.

In September 2010, *The Citizen* reported that Dominos Pizza was set to open, relocating from their premises at the top of Northgate Street now occupied by another pizza business, Roadrunner.

Comet closed in December 2012, when the chain went into administration. The unit was then split with kitchen company Wren opening a store in October 2013 and Tapi Carpets opening in June 2015.

The Planning Committee in August 2013 approved the building of another unit, to be occupied by McDonalds, on part of the car park. The report stated that it would create 65 new jobs (45 full-time equivalent). The restaurant and drive thru opened in September 2014.

Open Market & Car Boot Sale

Chance Malone had started a business making fencing and gates from the garage of his home in the early 1960s. When he was on holiday in Spain he bumped into City Council planning officer (and later councillor) David Evans. Evans said the Council didn't know what to do with some land at the Cattle Market. When Chance expressed an interest, David connected him with the right people and he took a 66-year lease at £200 a year. When the 1989 recession hit, he needed a way to make money and came up with the idea of a car boot sale. He met Markets Superintendent Ron Drysdale and offered him £10,000 a year up front. Drysdale thought he'd lose money so suggested £5,000 a year in arrears. The first week there were only 5 cars (4 of which belonged to Chance), but within a few weeks it had risen to 400. The Council's Wednesday market was declining to nothing. Chance took it over and built it up to be two thirds the size of the Sunday one, with people coming from all over the country and even the continent. Chance Malone ran the operation for around a decade and at one point was looking to start a car auction business on the site, although the idea was not popular with GMA who had similar aspirations.

Running the car boot sale was lucrative, although subsequent operators were unable to match Malone's success at it. In 2001, when he was on his boat in Monte Carlo, he received a call asking if he would like to come back to run the car boot sale. He managed to resist the temptation!

The City Council continued running the car boot sale beyond the start of the development. Within the St Oswalds site 3.78 acres had been allocated for 197 pitches and 242 parking spaces. At that time, it was earning the Council almost £300,000 a year. It hit the buffers because studies showed that when St Oswalds was fully developed it would have soaked up all the highway capacity. This was an issue because St Oswald's Road was already an 'Air Quality Management Area' – meaning it was already suffering from significant air pollution. In February 2004, the Council proposed moving the car boot sale to Westgate car park, which provoked outrage from residents of retirement complex Castlemeads Court opposite it and was a far cry from the 4-star hotel proposed for that site a few years earlier. As a temporary measure it moved to the Barbican car park in Ladybellegate Street, but that was a far from ideal location and the number of car booters declined from an average of 250 in 2001 to an average of 30 in 2007. A new £1.5 million purpose-built site at Hempsted Meadows opened in July 2008 following the completion of the South West bypass. The access road was named David Hook Way after the late City Council surveyor who had the vision for the site.

Residential Development

The first phase of residential development, which was 51 apartments at the front of the site, was undertaken by Charles Church, part of Persimmon Homes. The development was called The Marketplace in a nod to the site's history as the Livestock Market.

The Citizen reported in May 2008 that Persimmon had suspended work on The Marketplace because the housing market had slowed as the global financial crisis took hold.[136] Persimmon restarted just before Christmas 2008. The development was 450 homes overall, which was a mix of houses and apartments, with some affordable housing. It was a largely attractive development but was granted during the John Prescott era when maximum parking standards were in place. These were introduced with good intent – to reduce reliance on the private car for environmental reasons – but didn't really work and led to lots of cars being parked on the narrow estate roads. The street names of Dexter Way, Longhorn Avenue and Old Spot Walk were chosen to fit in with the site's livestock market history, being named after breeds of cattle. Perhaps one of the more quirky facts about this development was that there was a planning condition saying residents couldn't have "domestic outbuildings with foundations" to avoid "disruption to the approved ground contamination remediation measures" – i.e. no garden sheds because of worries about disturbing any methane in the ground.

In November 2008, *The Citizen* reported that a £21 million, 169 home development by the Rooftop Housing Group and Extracare was underway.[137] The Extracare Village. which opened in October 2010, has a restaurant, fitness gym, IT suite, craft room, woodwork shop and greenhouse.[138] An ExtraCare Village is described as an "inspirational retirement village for the over 55s" which "enables older people to enjoy healthy, active, and independent lifestyles in their later years."

Tesco Extra superstore plans

Not long after the Tesco store opened, they were looking to expand. A Cabinet report in October 2000 said Tesco had offered £2 million for the Park and Ride site or £3 million with planning permission. It was estimated that the Park and Ride would cost £500,000 to move to another part of the site. The Park and Ride service operated between St Oswalds and the city centre and had been running since 1997.

The sale didn't go ahead at that time and the St Oswalds development included 300 parking spaces for the Park and Ride service. Operated by local coach firm Bennetts, this had been popular, although a lot of people did 'Park and Walk' given the proximity to the city centre until the County Council changed the parking arrangement to paying for the parking as well as the bus. In August 2011 the County Council withdrew the Park and Ride service as part of its budget savings, meaning the parking spaces reverted to the developer and were available for general use. City Councillor Jim Porter fought to save the Park and Ride service, but the County Council stood firm. It was another move which some argued was detrimental to the city centre and to Westgate Street, which was on the bus route, particularly. The County Council contended that the £200,00 a year cost couldn't be justified for a service which was carrying an average of 2 people per trip.

It might seem hard to imagine now, given the difficulties they have experienced since, but there was a time that the march of Tesco was relentless and they appeared intent on global domination. They had plans to demolish their existing and very successful St Oswald's store and build a brand new one on land immediately behind. The new store would have been 113,000 sq ft (almost twice the size of the existing store) with 985 parking spaces and would represent a £25 million investment. The development also included new retail units totalling 40,000 sq ft and moving the petrol filling station to the front of the site. So keen were they to do this that they were prepared to pay top price for the land, which was part owned by the City Council and part by Hammerson. Negotiations were protracted between the two parties, but a deal was reached with the City Council's share being £6 million. I'm told that initially Tesco were going to lease the site but then Chief Executive Sir Terry Leahy said, "I want to buy it." The new store was forecast to create an extra 160 full and part-time jobs on top of the 340 existing jobs at the current store.

The City Council's Planning Committee approved the plans in December 2011 despite fears about the impact on the city centre. The committee reconvened after a week's interval to allow questions, including regarding trade diversion from the city centre, to be answered. The application was then referred to the National Planning Casework Unit and then granted in June 2012. It was opposed by the City Centre Community Partnership (CCCP), the

Civic Trust and the Federation of Small Businesses (FSB) who believed it would adversely affect city centre traders. A CCCP survey showed 85% of respondents were against the proposal, with only 10% in favour. The FSB's Mark Owen claimed the City Council had a conflict of interest, which was true but the Planning Committee took the independence of their quasi-judicial role very seriously. 94 letters of support were received, mostly believed to be from existing Tesco staff, along with 7 objections. A 283-name petition was submitted by Linden resident Phil de Soisson, who collected signatures by standing for an hour on The Cross every Saturday for several weeks. Longlevens councillor Jim Porter objected, referring to a 'Tescopoly', as did Aviva, owner of Kings Walk shopping centre at the time. Roger Price, a resident of Priory Road, spoke against the proposal at the Planning Committee, citing concerns about the impact of traffic, flood risk, noise and nuisance.

The Council's retail consultant said there was no evidence of significant harm to the city centre, which he said was performing relatively well. They estimated the proposal would cause a 'trade diversion' from the city centre of 5.4%, which seems significant but was not enough to justify refusal.

If it went ahead, the plans would have led to a bonanza under the s106 planning gain rules. The shopping list included £150,000 for bus services, £50,000 for a traffic light upgrade, £120,000 for improvements to Westgate Island or Park & Ride and £100,000 for public art or city centre linkages. The police chipped in with a request for a £2,000 plasma screen television. One letter asked for a minibus for the nearby St Oswalds Village and another wanted the St Oswalds Road railway bridge painted.

In a letter, David Bevan, Tesco Development Executive, called St Oswalds the "forgotten" regeneration project and said their proposal was a "vote of confidence in Gloucester". Sophie Akokhia, Tesco Corporate Affairs Manager, tried to allay concerns about the city centre impact by telling the committee that people could use their car park and head into the city centre.

The City Council had only budgeted for £4 million from the sale of the land, so I took the decision in January 2012 that £2 million should be set aside to support the city centre. We called it the 'City Centre Investment Fund' and it was used over a number of years for a variety of projects, from car park improvements to replacing the roof on the Museum of Gloucester in Brunswick Road to property grants for building improvements and new Christmas lights. In some ways, I wonder whether spending it on a single, high-profile project such as improving the paving in one of the gate streets would have had more impact but in reality the money wouldn't have gone very far.

The world changed in 2015 with Tesco struggling to compete with the discounters like Aldi and Lidl (who would later open a store right opposite Tesco at St Oswalds) and the discovery of a £250 million black hole in their books following an accounting fraud. Building an expensive new megastore no longer seemed a good idea and the plans were put on hold, alongside a number of other changes including ending 24-hour opening. Tesco Chief Executive Dave Lewis said, "It is with a heavy heart that I am announcing that we are unable to proceed with 49 planned new store developments across the UK, including our planned replacement store in St Oswald's Road, Gloucester. Our performance as a business has fallen significantly short of where we would want it to be. I am very aware of the importance of the site and we will work closely with Gloucester City Council to find the right solution for the community."

How the proposed Tesco Extra store at St Oswalds would have looked.

From the city centre's point of view, this was no bad thing – it had benefited from £2 million of investment but without the potential harm from the development for which the funding was meant to compensate. Other ideas came forward from time to time, like a new Dobbies Garden Centre (which was part of the Tesco empire) which was revealed in 2014, but none of these came to fruition and Tesco put the land up for sale – at what will inevitably be a huge loss.

City Council buys back the development

In July 2017, in the only Full Council meeting I ever missed in my 24 years (which was due to the birth of my youngest daughter Tydwen), the City Council approved an £80 million Property Investment Fund. It was, at the time, a controversial policy, with the Liberal Democrat leader Jeremy Hilton claiming it would "bankrupt the Council". The initiative for the policy came from officers and in particular the Managing Director Jon McGinty. It was designed to allow the Council to take advantage of cheap borrowing from the Public Works Loan Board (i.e. the Government) to buy commercial property and produce a net revenue stream for the Council to help replace cuts in government grant. There was some lively debate between Officers, who wanted to invest across the country to create a 'balanced portfolio' and the Cabinet, who wanted to invest in our own patch. The compromise we reached was that we would have a preference for investing in our own economic area (which broadened it slightly beyond our administrative area), but would leave open the option to invest elsewhere if the deal was good enough.

Other councils, including some locally, had invested in commercial property both in and out of their own area. Some had done so to a much larger extent, like Spelthorne and Woking in Surrey who had borrowed over £1 billion, dwarfing their annual revenue budget of around £11 million. I was nervous at the prospect of borrowing £80 million and wouldn't have been able to sleep at night if the Council under my leadership had £1 billion of liabilities. This would remain a controversial subject for years, with the Treasury tightening the rules and adding 1% to the cost of borrowing in order to bring it under control. The rules now made clear that Councils should not be borrowing just to create income and should not be investing outside their area.

It took almost two and a half years before the first purchases would be finalised. I discuss the purchase of the Eastgate Shopping Centre elsewhere in this book (see Chapter 22), but the possibility of buying St Oswald's was put to us. Hammerson had adopted a strategy of concentrating on major cities and was looking to exit the retail park sector, so put St Oswalds up for sale. The initial asking price, although not advertised, was £68 million. Initially, I felt this was too big a chunk of our £80 million fund and would expose us to too much retail but, as the price came down, I warmed to the idea – especially as it would help unlock the remaining land for housing by removing Hammerson's control (via an open-ended option) on part of the undeveloped land. The deal would create net income of around £1.5 million a year for the Council and, even allowing for some rents to fall, would still have a comfortable cushion. We agreed a purchase at £54 million, which was completed in November 2019. We couldn't announce it initially due to signing a non-disclosure agreement with Hammerson and then because of 'purdah' rules related to December's snap general election, but speculation was rife in any case.

When we were able to confirm the purchase, I commented that, "There is also the opportunity for regeneration and housing on land off Gavel Way. The land has been vacant for 15 years and will provide many benefits for Gloucester."[139] It's fair to say that the public reaction to the purchase wasn't entirely positive, with many asking why we couldn't spend the money fixing potholes instead – which aren't even a City Council responsibility. The concept of borrowing a huge amount of money to buy an asset in order to create revenue to support services on an ongoing basis is, to be fair, quite a difficult concept to understand for those who aren't exposed to the world of local government finance.

For most of its life, the retail park had been fully let and the rent roll peaked in 2018 at £4.9 million a year. In recent years, particularly since the pandemic, there have been some casualties. Mothercare closed in January 2020 after going into administration, despite the store being described as a 'good trader' for the retailer. DW Sports also went into administration in August 2020 but the store and gym were taken over by Mike Ashley's Sports Direct. The two restaurants - Frankie & Benny's and Harvester – both took advantage of leases ending to exit the Park in August 2020 after months of being closed through lockdown. When they were opened, they were two of very few family chain restaurants in the city, but the development of the Gloucester Quays leisure quarter changed all that. The sale brochure for the retail park in 2018 had said that Harvester "would like to remain in occupation" but was already anticipating that Frankie & Benny's would leave, saying there was an opportunity "to re-let to a more exciting restaurant operator".

Argos also closed their store in August 2021, following their takeover by Sainsburys and integration into their supermarkets at Barnwood and Gloucester Quays. When the retail park was being sold in 2018, it spoke positively about the St Oswalds store taking over from Cheltenham as the area's 'hub store'. On the positive side, Burger King opened in the former Harvester restaurant in September 2021 and Taco Bell announced plans for a restaurant with drive thru in the former Frankie & Benny's unit, which opened at the end of April 2022.

The first major development to get underway when I took on the regeneration portfolio, which was built on City Council land, would come back to our full ownership in my last major announcement in that portfolio almost 16 years later.

Future Plans

The City Council designated the remaining land at St Oswald's, of which ownership was split between the Council and Tesco, for housing in its City Plan. It is a challenging site due to issues with contamination, the leachate drain referred to earlier in this chapter and an oil pipeline running through the site.

As long ago as November 2017, *The Citizen* reported on "Secret talks about St Oswalds land". I was quoted as saying, "I'm very keen we should complete the regeneration of the site."[140]

Homes England had looked at the site, including a visit from their previous Chief Executive Nick Walkley, but were frightened off by the scale of the challenge. Numerous other housebuilders had also cast their eyes over it, but didn't get beyond that.

As with many of Gloucester's difficult sites, it was the Rooftop Housing Group, led by Chief Executive Boris Worrall and Development Director David Hannon, who had the boldness, confidence and ambition to take it on. As Rooftop had developed the ExtraCare Village and other social housing on the site, there was a strong logic to their involvement.

A bid to the Government's Brownfield Land Release Fund saw the St Oswalds Project awarded £2.2 million in December 2021. Councillor Andrew Gravells, Cabinet Member for Planning and Housing Strategy at Gloucester City Council who requested that the bid be submitted, said: "We have been working with Rooftop Housing Association for several years to unlock the redevelopment of our former Cattle Market site at St Oswalds.

"The award of £2.2m of Brownfield Land Release Fund is a huge piece in the jigsaw here and will hopefully allow the delivery of 180 new affordable homes that meet the needs of our residents in a low carbon, sustainable way."

At the time of writing, Rooftop and the Council are working to deliver the scheme. Contracts were exchanged for the sale of the land in July 2023 but, at the time of writing, no planning application has been lodged.

7. REPENT AT LEISURE
Rebuilding Gloucester Leisure Centre

Gloucester Leisure Centre has played an important part in my life. It's where I learnt to swim, with the legendary Chris Maloney, in the learner pool. Maloney founded the Special Olympics in the UK and was awarded the MBE. As a child, I held 5-a-side football parties in the Sports Hall for my birthday. I've watched some good shows there, including the comedian Jethro. His act was pretty close to the knuckle, as you'd expect. Staff tell me that he insisted on being given the previous month's local papers to read before the show. When he came to Gloucester in the wake of the Fred West murder investigations, he walked onto the stage, the lights went on, he looked out at the audience and said, "It's good to see so many of you above ground!"

I even appeared on stage at the Leisure Centre - in the Gloucester Gang Show, alongside Mark 'Pasty' Cornwell (who went on to play rugby for Gloucester and may not thank me for the reminder) and Marcus Rea, a Crypt School contemporary and now a high-flying partner in an accountancy firm. I also spent a few good nights in the old 'Cinderellas' nightclub, later known as 'Fifth Avenue' and 'The Avenue'.

After its rebuild, Pam Tracey and I officially reopened the building as Mayor and Sheriff in August 2002 and I joined the gym that very day and used it religiously until fitness took second place to parenting. Since having children, I've taken them swimming in the new Barton Pool.

The 1970s Build

The 'new' Leisure Centre of the 1970s, and the problems which soon became evident, became something of a talking point – perhaps even a joke – in the city. The public baths, where the Atik nightclub is now, opened in 1891. There were two identical pools, side by side – one for men and one for women, with a balcony and changing rooms. There were originally 'spittoons' around the pool but these would have been removed when spitting was identified as a way of transmitting the disease 'Consumption' (or Tuberculosis). In the 1970s build, this became the learner pool. There were 'slipper baths' (named because they were shaped like a slipper) which you would hire by the half hour, rent a towel and buy a bar of soap. Men working in the foundry would go there at the end of the day for a bath before going home.

The 'old' Leisure Centre, as we now call it, opened for business in 1973 and was officially opened by the Duke of Gloucester on 6th November 1974 with representatives of our twin cities, Trier, Metz and Gouda, present. It was built by construction firm Module 2 under a design and build contract which gave the Council little control. The 1970s leisure centre was championed for all the right reasons by Leisure Committee chairman, Councillor Norman Partridge.

The original Victorian building also housed the city's popular Turkish baths with two steam rooms and a cold plunge pool. There was a room of beds to lie in, with times set aside for male and female use. Patrons of the facility say it was one of the finest in the country. "Like stepping back in time to the days of Ancient Rome," was how one described it to me. Another said it was the "best private club in the world". It had an illustrious customer base, ranging from barristers who went there when their Crown Court sessions finished early, to local characters like Town Crier Alan Myatt, jockey Terry Biddlecombe, boxer Johnny Williamson, comedian Gerry Thomas, radio presenter Chris Musk and cobbler (and later city councillor) Gerry Colley. Reportedly, the management stayed out of the way and many customers stayed there for hours, if not the whole day. The rooms were given the Latin names Tepidarium (warm room), Caldarium (hot room) and Laconium (sweating room). Patrons would gradually build up towards the most sweltering heat, before jumping in the cold plunge pool.

The centre's Cambridge Theatre was a 500-seater facility and hosted many top acts. A full list of them appears at the end of this chapter. I was told that, at one point, the fire alarm code for the building was 'Mr Pastry', but this had to be changed when Richard Hearne, the actor and comedian who played the character Mr Pastry on television, was one of the acts! It became the city's premier theatre when The Regal in Kings Square (now a Wetherspoons pub) became a cinema. When the Cambridge Theatre closed for reasons set out later in this chapter, the Gloucester Operatic and Dramatic Society (GODS) moved from the Kings Theatre in Kingsbarton Street to the larger New Olympus Theatre (also known as the Picturedrome) in Barton Street in 1984. This later prompted an introduction to television star Anneka Rice, whose 'Challenge Anneka' programme was brought in to give it a makeover in 1991.

It wasn't long before defects in the Leisure Centre building became evident and attempts to improve things weren't always successful. *The Citizen* reported in January 1984 that a Heat Recovery Plant for the Barton Pool, which cost £120,000 and was expected to save £25,000 a year, only generated savings of £1400. Staff tell me that by the mid-1990s the plant that heated the swimming pools was "on its last legs". It was kept going with 'sticking plasters', largely due to the efforts of the Centre's Maintenance Manager, Alan 'Tug' Wilson.

In September 1985, *The Citizen* reported that, following the shock disclosure of major structural problems in the Cambridge Theatre, defects had been found in the main sports hall. As workers were preparing for a show by Norman Wisdom, bricks were seen to fall from a huge wall at the back of the hall, which ended up having to be dismantled and rebuilt. The Council put aside £200,000 into a special repairs fund.

The main Barton Pool was 30 yards long and 12'6" deep, with a high diving board. The Pools Manager was Henri Meinike – a German prisoner of war, who won Citizen of the Year award in the 1990s and was an iconic figure in the local swimming world. The event control area in the new Barton Pool is named the 'Henri Meinike Suite' in his memory. Two new slides (known as Turbo Twisters) were brought in to halt the decline in swimming numbers. They were named 'Dolphin' (which was 83m long) and 'Stingray' (which was 72m long). They were installed by contractors C H Pearce at a cost of £500,000 and were officially opened on 23rd May 1987.

Former Citizen journalist George Henderson, in an article in March 2000, described the building of the "old Leisure Centre" as a "tale of incompetence, jerry-building, bad judgement and appalling design". He went on:

"When it was built in 1974 it was hailed as the great white hope for

Gloucester's future. It would herald a brave new world of leisure and entertainment giving Gloucester folk a place where they could swim, exercise, enjoy a night out and watch entertainers all under one roof.

"The building itself was thrown together using sub-standard materials and specifications. And when it opened, the design gaffes quickly came to the fore. The Cambridge Theatre became virtually unusable on many evenings because of the racket filtering up from the disco romping along at full volume in the room below. They asked the nightclub not to turn music up until 10pm when shows would have finished, but they often did sound testing at 9.30pm.

"At one point a refined recital by a string quartet descended into chaos when pandemonium erupted from the disco below. The theatre finally had to be closed when an aerobics group almost brought the building crashing around their ears."

A former member of staff told me that the aerobics group jumping up and down together led to a mirror ball falling off the ceiling in the nightclub below. An investigation revealed that the steel joists on the theatre floor/nightclub ceiling were substandard. This prompted a review of the whole building which found that the cavity walls of the squash court weren't tied together and the entire side of the building could easily have fallen into Nettleton Road at any time. Scaffolding went up and stayed there until the building closed in 1998.

Such was the sensitivity caused by the catalogue of problems with the 1970s rebuild that the Leisure Centre Redevelopment Sub-Committee in September 1999 agreed to take out buildings defect insurance.

One of the lines used by local people is that a comedian must have worked on the old building. It could even be true – I'm told that local funnyman Gerry Thomas was part of the construction team. Others told me that parts of the old Leisure Centre were run like 'The Brittas Empire' – the 1990s BBC sitcom set in a fictional leisure centre, run by incompetent manager Gordon Brittas.

Planning for a new Leisure Centre

The problems with the building meant a new leisure centre, either on the existing site or at another location, became a priority for the City Council. There was talk of alternative locations, such as the Cattle Market in St Oswald's Road or the former Coney Hill Hospital site (since developed for housing). Former Chief Leisure Officer Philip Cooke and Council Leader at the time Kevin Stephens told me these alternatives were never seriously considered. The ability to apply to the National Lottery for significant funding was a big factor and both were adamant that if the Leisure Centre wasn't near disadvantaged communities and on public transport routes, the Council's application to the Lottery would not have been successful. Indeed, in June 1996, the Council's Leisure Services Committee was told that the Sports Lottery Board had recently announced that the Eastgate, Westgate and Barton wards were priority areas where sports projects could be eligible for up to 90% funding. So a decision was made to rebuild on the existing site.

The project was fronted up politically by Bob Duncan, a tough-talking Labour councillor who was Chair of the Leisure Services Committee and then Cabinet Member for Culture, Learning and Leisure. He was a woodwork teacher at the former Linden Secondary School and then headed up the Pupil Referral Unit at the Hatherley Centre in Hatherley Road, which probably accounted for why he didn't suffer fools gladly.

Consultants Strategic Leisure, headed up by Peter Mann, were appointed by the Leisure Services Committee to work on the lottery bid in 1995. *The Citizen* reported on 20th October 1995 that Strategic Leisure were told to press ahead with the bid. Their recommendations for the new centre included reducing the swimming pool to a competition size 25m, ripping out the flumes in favour of a children's water play and spa pool, revamping the health suite and building an aerobics gym. Public consultation on the plans was to take place.

Gloucester-based architects Stephen Limbrick Associates won the contract to design the centre through an EU-compliant competition. They had a 31-strong team at the Alexandra Warehouse in the Docks. Stephen Limbrick is an Old Cryptian (a former pupil of The Crypt School, Gloucester) and his first contract as a self-employed architect was an £800,000 refurbishment of the Cascades leisure centre in Tewkesbury. The firm had also worked on a £10 million sporting facility for the American University of Sharjah in the United Arab Emirates, the Oasis Lakeland Holiday Village near Penrith developed by the Rank Organisation, which we now know as Center Parcs, and a leisure development in Glasgow called 'The Quay'. Limbrick and Strategic Leisure worked together on a number of leisure centres across the country. Stephen went on to be a joint founder of the largest, award-winning architects practice in the region, Roberts Limbrick, based in Gloucester.

Another Old Cryptian, Steve Tandy was the Quantity Surveyor for the project. He had done work for holiday camp Butlins on behalf of their owner The Rank Organisation at their sites at Minehead, Bognor Regis and Skegness, also working with Stephen Limbrick. Tandy suggested the Council could sell off the Cattle Market site to help raise the match funding for the lottery bid.

There were calls for an Olympic-sized (50m length) swimming pool. The existing Barton Pool was 30 yards long, so was not a competition size. The Sports Council would not have supported an Olympic-sized pool. These facilities were provided on a regional basis, as they were driven by the pursuit of Olympic medals, and already existed at Millfield School in Somerset and the University of Bath. There also wasn't the space for a 50m pool and it would have had to go out into the road to accommodate it! So the Council opted for a 25m length which would enable it to attract competitions. There were also public representations about the loss of the high diving board, but this also would not have found favour with the grant-making bodies

Limbrick's design incorporated the Council's desire for a national short competition pool, which was 25m in length with 8 lanes and a seating area to accommodate 700 and a separate 25m training pool. The separate training pool was included because of use by naturists and Asian women – two groups who didn't want to be overlooked while swimming. The main pool had a moveable floor which could alter the pool's depth. The unique, double-hinged, moveable floor allowed the depth across the pool to be adjusted from 0.2m to 3.0m and enabled it to be used for school swimming lessons with large groups. It could also be set at the required 2.0m constant depth, enabling the centre to host high-level competitions, including the National Short Course Swimming Competition, the European Junior Synchronised Swimming Competition and the National Synchronised Swimming Competition.

The South West Regional Development Agency gave a grant of

£50,000 for Gloucester to host the European event in 2009 on the basis of the economic benefit it brought to the city. It had some success in that respect, with the Russians apparently spending big in the city's Primark store!

The old sports hall would be re-roofed and re-clad, although the original intention was to demolish it. The rest of the building would be new build.

The building was constructed using a brick plinth with aluminium cladding panels above. A zinc alloy cladding was used for the curved entrance façade. The roof was made of embossed natural aluminium sheets.

Improvements to the main hall included a new floor, 1000 retractable 'bleacher' seats and freestanding seats, improved lighting, ventilation and internal decoration. The roof was strengthened to support lighting rigs at a cost of £20,000, a portable stage was purchased for £25,000, along with lighting and PA equipment with a budget of £20,000. The roof structure was overstressed, which was addressed by replacing the existing roof finish with a lightweight covering.

The Council's Leisure Services Committee was recommended to approve the content and design of the new Leisure Centre in March 1998, with a planning application due to be submitted by 20th April 1998 and decided by the middle of June 1998. The Council was also due to submit an application to the Sports Lottery Fund in April 1998 to convert funding for the new centre from being 'In Principle' to being a 'Formal Award'.

Financing

The Council's Policy & Resources Committee approved the financing of the new centre at its meeting in April 1998.

Initially, the 'provisional' lottery award was for £9.54 million, which was approved in 1997. This was increased to £10.453 million in April 1998 – the biggest-ever lottery grant awarded to a non-Metropolitan Council – and converted to a 'full award' in July that year. The Council's own contribution was £5 million. The original estimated total cost for all phases of the development was £15,793,000. Sponsorship was meant to make up the difference of £340,000.

The Council's £5 million contribution was initially made up of a £2.88 million contribution from its revenue budget, £1.1 million from its capital reserve, £200,000 from the Government's Single Regeneration Budget (which was being used in the Barton and Tredworth area at the time), £50,000 from the controversial Safer City Project (which was about road safety, delivered largely through traffic calming measures) with capital receipts from selling off land making up the balance of £770,000.

Over time, the financing changed, with the capital reserve contributing £2,200,000 and capital receipts from asset sales budgeted to provide £2,600,000. Later, further asset sales were used to pick up the shortfall in sponsorship of £340,000 and the additional costs over and above what was budgeted of £967,000.[141] The contribution from the Safer City Project, which seemed to be a bit tenuous, appears to have been dropped.

At the time I expressed concern about the sale of assets to finance the project, saying, "It is now sad to see they are placing such a great reliance on asset sales to make up their £5 million share. The trouble with selling off the parcels of land is that they bring in a revenue and that is lost in the future. It also calls into question whether we are getting value for money.

"When word gets around that the council is desperate to sell land it becomes a buyer's market. I think they should have kept their commitment to pay from revenues and made savings elsewhere. They took the easy option to avoid making some tough decisions."

Bob Duncan responded, "As far as selling assets is concerned, many of these things I never knew existed until recently. They were certainly never targeted from the start. You must remember that when we started considering a new leisure centre we didn't even have the lottery fund."

The article commented that the "latest to go on the market is the car park at the bottom of Westgate Street", although as described elsewhere in this book, that was one asset that ultimately wasn't sold.

The rebuild

The Centre closed on 19th July 1998 with most staff made redundant or redeployed but a core of half a dozen relocated to the Council's Docks offices to oversee the project.

There was criticism, reported by *The Citizen*'s Hugh Worsnip, when nothing happened after the doors closed in July. The City Council apologised, saying that legal issues had caused delays with the relocation of the nightclub. In addition, fixtures and fittings had to be removed as did asbestos and chemical residues in the swimming pool chlorination plant before more general demolition could take place.

A report to the Leisure, Education & Tourism committee and the Strategy & Performance committee in October/November 1998 appointed Hall & Tawse as contractor for Phase 1 – which included the demolition of the Victorian baths (except the façade), construction of the nightclub 'shell', demolition of the Barton Pool and ground clearance. An auction of unwanted furniture and fittings from the centre raised £25,000. The Pineapple water slide ended up in the garden of a house in Whiteway in Miserden, near Stroud.

The completion of Phase 1 was marked at the end of May 1999 when exterior works were completed and the nightclub building was handed over to the operators for the fit-out. As soon as the nightclub had relocated, work would begin on diverting services such as mains electricity, water supply etc. Phase 2 of the redevelopment, including the rest of the demolition and the major construction work, would then take place.[142] Tilbury Douglas were appointed contractors for Phase 2. A 'letter of intent' to proceed with the works was issued to them in November 1999. They took over the site that month, with construction starting in January 2000 and contracts being completed in February 2000

Journalist George Henderson wrote in his article in *The Citizen* on 25th March 2000, "Since the old disaster of a leisure centre was demolished in 1998, the sins of the father seem to be being visited on the proposed £15.7 million successor. Gremlins in the works have included buttresses which contained the pressure on the sides of the old swimming pool were not marked on the plans so the council had to find another £75,000 for their removal. Other extra costs were incurred when more asbestos than had been anticipated was found in the former nightclub on the site. Underground phone cables had to be diverted at extra cost."

In George Henderson's article, I commented: "The scheme has stumbled from one disaster to another from the beginning. Right from the start there were delays with the demolition of the old building and it was closed with nothing happening for several months."

Bob Duncan responded, saying: "It is complete nonsense to say this project has been dogged by delays. It is on target and on budget and we are very pleased with the way it is going. Obviously on a scheme this size there will always be problems to sort out. But we took this into account and there was extra time built into the scheme to allow for unforeseen delays. We also have very tight quality control on site and we have meetings with the contractors every fortnight.

"This is going to be a quality asset for Gloucester. It is not like the last leisure centre that was designed as it went along. This one has been designed by an architect and it will show. I think when people see the building rising above the boarding they will start to be impressed. We are now moving into Phase II of the work and the building will start soon."

Separately, Barrie Aldridge, the Council's Head of Building and Design, who took over leading the project when Philip Cooke left, is quoted as saying, "We gave the contractor all the information we had about the old leisure centre, but obviously it was not complete."[143]

Running projects like this can be stressful for council officers and councillors alike. I'm told that Council Leader Kevin Stephens regularly called people involved in the project into his office to 'bang heads together' as the budget and programme overran. Consultants working on the project also reported being on the receiving end of the Leader's frustrations when things weren't happening in the way that he would have liked.

The Sports Hall had works to improve the acoustics removed as part of the 'value engineering' exercise to get the project within budget, but the works still included curtaining around sides and a lot of infrastructure for bands such as 3 phase power and heavy-duty sockets. In addition, the roof was strengthened for heavy duty lighting and sound equipment. The report on the first year of operation said that GL1 would target concert promoters in December 2003 to use the Glevum Hall. Gary Moore, Joan Armatrading and Sir James Galway (accompanied by the London Mozart Players) were early performers at GL1 but after that it seemed to peter out. The management from the time told me that the lack of acts performing in the new hall was due to changes in the music industry and a move to bigger venues in London, Birmingham and Bristol where the capacity was more like 20,000 than 2,000 – and promoters and acts could make more money. Up and coming bands would go to Guildhall instead.

The Citizen reported in February 2002 that the Leisure Centre could stage events from national swimming competitions (which indeed it has) to Shakespeare (which I'm not aware has ever been performed there).

GL1 Leisure Centre under construction. Credit: Stephen Limbrick

The Nightclub

The nightclub next to the Leisure Centre has been through a few different incarnations over the years. It started off as Tiffany's then Cinderella Rockerfellas, then Fifth Avenue, then The Avenue. When it moved to Eastgate Street it reopened as Liquid & Diva, subsequently changing to Atik. The club was run by nightclub giant Luminar Leisure. One of the name changes was prompted by a major flood in the Cambridge Theatre when a water tank burst. It damaged the teak sprung floor in the theatre and went through to the nightclub, destroying their furniture and carpets – resulting in an insurance-funded refurbishment and a re-opening under another name.

When the Leisure Centre was being rebuilt, the nightclub was relocated to enable it to continue trading while the rebuild was taking place. It also removed the conflict between the noise from the club and any performances in the main hall, as well as putting it in a better trading position on the main Eastgate Street nightlife 'strip'. The original proposal had been to completely demolish the Victorian baths, but Stephen Limbrick, who regularly swam at the Barton Pool as a teenager, encouraged the retention of the Victorian façade facing onto Eastgate Street and the balcony which used to overlook the swimming pool, which now looks down onto the nightclub's dance floor. The relocation of the nightclub caused significant delays. It was necessary to negotiate an agreement to surrender the existing lease and agree a new lease for the nightclub shell, as well as obtaining agreement regarding access for the fire escape.

The Council's magazine *The Gloucester Voice* reported in Summer 1999 that the new club had undergone an almost £1 million refit. A Luminar spokesman said, "The Liquid concept is a totally new clubbing experience. The feel of Liquid is light, bright and airy. You would expect to stumble into this kind of venue if you were out clubbing in Ibiza or Tenerife. It will cause a massive stir."

Failure to attract sponsorship

The budget for the rebuild included £340,000 from private sector sponsorship. The Council felt this was on the conservative side. In 1998, councillors were told that corporate sponsorship "could yield very substantial sums". Consultants, the Peter Mann Partnership (PMP) were appointed that year to secure private sector contributions. PMP initially advised that they expected to raise £500,000 sponsorship from a single sponsor for a 10-year period. In addition to naming rights, there were other sponsorship opportunities, supplier deals for catering and equipment, advertising and merchandising which could all bring in cash. However, it didn't work out that way.

In January 1999, the Council agreed to employ a Project Officer on a salary of £20,000 a year to assist with efforts to secure sponsorship to fill the hole in the leisure centre project budget. During the debate on the proposal at the Leisure Committee, Chairman Bob Duncan, in an exchange of banter with Councillor Pam Tracey, quipped, "I christen this ship Titanic." This led to a front-page headline in *The Citizen* of "Flagship Titanic", which didn't please the council's leadership.[144]

Labour councillor Terry Haines wrote to the newspaper to complain that Cllr Duncan's comments had been "mercilessly taken out of context by your reporter". The editor responded that they "thought our front page was also humorous and tongue in cheek". Liberal Democrat councillor Phil McLellan also wrote to the paper warning that "the captain went down with the sinking ship" but in a later letter said he was "pleased to hear the project was well and truly afloat and the captain is confident it will reach port on time". This led me to write my own letter pointing out that "this didn't happen in the original story" and to query whether Cllr McLellan had either "rewritten the script or simply lost the plot".

In June 1999, councillors discussed the efforts to find sponsorship. Bob Duncan, rounded on the "knockers and gripers" criticising the project, adding, "All people seem to want to do is knock it".[145]

Chief Leisure Officer, Philip Cooke, said, "We are very confident about sponsorship. We believe local companies will want to get involved."

The Citizen reported on its front-page headline on 23rd March 2000 that, 'Firms Snub Leisure Centre', noting that this would leave a £340,000 funding gap. Bob Duncan said, "We are confident that sponsors will come forward to fill this gap. It will present a striking image on a landmark site which companies will be proud to put their name to." Mayor Terry Haines was hopeful companies would come forward when the building project was further advanced, saying, "They will not sponsor a hole in the ground."

It was reported that efforts would switch to national and international companies in the sports and leisure field, including car manufacturers in motorsport. *The Citizen's* own comment piece was headlined, "Would you sponsor a hole?" and said it was "not surprising" that sponsors had not signed up at this stage and "no doubt once it begins to rise, the money will roll in."

The Council remained hopeful that sponsorship would generate significant cash, which was increasingly important as costs for the project were rising. A different company, BDS Sponsorship Consultants, was brought in to fill the budget gap, estimated at between £800,000 to £1 million, with private sector contributions. *The Citizen* newspaper reported in November 2000 that BDS had raised huge sums for big leisure venues like the London Eye and the Hampden Park stadium in Glasgow and were confident they could do the same for Gloucester's new leisure centre. Council leisure chief Steve Elway confirmed that potential sponsors "must not be anything connected with smoking or alcohol or other unhealthy pursuits".

An 82-page 'Sponsorship Strategy' report was presented to the Council's Cabinet in January 2001. BDS recommended that the shortfall could be generated from sponsorship. They believed that a title sponsor for the complex (naming it 'The Kelloggs Sports and Activities Complex' or similar) could command up to £1 million over 10 years plus sponsorship packages for the café, pool and other 'official sponsor' and 'official partner' opportunities. Papers show that their time didn't come cheaply, with their Chief Executive's time costing a cool £1155 a day! They charged a reduced rate for fees in return for a sliding scale of commission for any deals they signed up. In the end, the only sponsor who committed was the Cheltenham & Gloucester Building Society for £45,000. BDS's fees of £38,000 all but swallowed that up.

The minutes of the Cabinet meeting on 31st January 2001 records that Officers "confirmed there was no recommendation for Carlsberg's involvement despite *The Citizen* report". And that's probably the best council minute in the world!

City Council Leader Kevin Stephens dismissed my criticism of the failure to attract sponsorship by claiming the Full Council took the decision to appoint BDS.[146] That wasn't correct – the decision was taken by a Council Officer and reported to the Cabinet; something I pointed out in a letter to *The Citizen* published on 22nd January 2002. To be fair to Stephens, he did apologise publicly when I asked him a question on this subject at the next Full Council meeting.

A consultation exercise took place with local people about the name of the new centre and GL1 was selected rather than Gloucester Leisure Centre – with no commercial naming rights agreed.

Completion

The contractor initially gave a deadline of 12th November 2001 for completion of the building works but handover was delayed until 17th February 2002.[147] It was delayed again until May and again until July, with staff working long days to get the centre ready for opening.

Council Leader Kevin Stephens said, "In a building of this size and complexity there were bound to be delays. We are very disappointed with the overall progress and I can understand the frustration of people who want to get in and use its facilities. Given the history of the previous leisure centre we are insisting on the highest standards. If we have to wait a bit longer it will be better in the long run."

The centre was officially opened on 10th August 2002, with public use beginning on 12th August 2002. Mayor Pam Tracey cut the ribbon. 71-year-old Peter Lane from Matson, who had won a competition on local radio, pressed a button at the opening, releasing confetti into the crowds. Pam was quoted as saying, "It has wonderful facilities and is a major amenity for the area. It's well worth the wait."

Paul James with Mayor Pam Tracey and Sheriff's Lady Marie Journeaux at the opening of GL1 Leisure Centre in August 2002.

Cathy Daley, the Council's Recreational Facilities Manager, added, "It's the best facility without a doubt in the South West. It must be one of the top six in the country. It's not elite, it's for all sections of the community, whatever your ethnic background or if you are disabled or able-bodied."

The new facility had four swimming pools: the main Barton Pool with 8 lanes and spectator seating; the Tad Pool (for under 5s) with a slide, jets, geysers and bubble beds; the Twyver Pool for lane swimming and specialist sessions and the Elver Pool, a shallow learner pool for children. There was also a fitness arena, exercise studio, health suite with sauna, steam rooms and spa, gymnastics hall, martial arts room, bowls hall, living and learning centre, two licensed bars, a function room and café. The Living and Learning Centre, which promoted healthy lifestyles, was something of an innovation for a public leisure centre.

There was a dispute with the contractor Tilbury Douglas (who were renamed Interserve in 2001), as there often is with projects of this nature, with £153,000 being deducted from their £14.5 million bill for late completion. The dispute and final bill were eventually settled in July 2004.

The new leisure centre got off to a good start. Usage of the swimming pools was above expectation, with opening hours having to be divided into ninety-minute sessions, to cope with the demand during school holidays. The Horizons health and fitness area soon had over 1000 members, meeting the target set for its opening. The Living & Learning Centre, offered everything from support to stop smoking to stress awareness, stroke awareness and anti-drugs campaigns.[148] On a minor downside note, there were overspends on gas and electric costs as the estimates provided by the consultants when the centre was being built proved over-optimistic.

When the Amateur Swimming Association came to inspect the new pool, they sent their Facilities Officer Noel Winter, who had been an England water polo captain, to undertake the task. He knew Mike Cogger, from their days in the Manchester 'It's A Knockout' team, and Stephen Limbrick quite well. These relationships were no doubt helpful but, as a purpose-built national short course competition centre, GL1 was always likely to sail through the ASA's approval process.

Sport England visited GL1 in July 2003 to carry out their monitoring, to ensure that the Council were working to the aims and objectives specified in the Lottery submission. Their post-completion monitoring report said: "The centre has undoubtedly had a positive sporting impact providing a brand-new, large-scale leisure facility appealing to a wide cross section of the community but also to stage high level events in specific sports."

The management of the Centre was put out to tender because of the Government's 'Best Value' rules, which were designed to ensure councils could demonstrate value for money for council taxpayers. Although there was interest from the private sector, the Council's in-house bid was successful.

The Aspire Sports and Cultural Trust was created in July 2008 and started to run GL1 and the Oxstalls Tennis Centre (later rebranded the Oxstalls Sports Park) in September that year. This was both to reduce the business rates liability as it was a charitable trust but also to free it from the constraints of council decision-making. Steve Elway, Assistant Director for Culture, Learning and Leisure, at the City Council, transferred to Aspire as its first Chief Executive and stayed until his retirement at the end of 2015.

With councils facing reductions in their funding as austerity hit, Aspire's management charge to the City Council for running the facilities reduced from £1.5 million a year to zero over a seven-year period between 2011-12 and 2017-18. However, the Trust needed financial support from the Council in the wake of the Coronavirus pandemic and increased energy bills following Russia's invasion of Ukraine. Despite this financial support, the charity went into liquidation in September 2023, leading to the sudden closure of the GL1 facility and the Oxstalls Sports Park. The facilities reopened in November 2023 under interim operator Freedom Leisure.

ACTS WHO HAVE PERFORMED AT GLOUCESTER LEISURE CENTRE SINCE 1976

MUSIC

Andy Stewart
Barbara Dickson
The Beat
Big Country
Billie Joe Spears
Bonnie Tyler
Box Car Willie
Boys of the Lough
Bucks Fizz
Camel
Carter
Chas n Dave
Cliff Richard
Cockney Rebel
The Commitments
Culture Club
Daniel O'Donnell
David Essex
Deacon Blue
Depeche Mode
Don Williams
The Dooleys
Duran Duran
The Drifters
EMF
Echo & The Bunnymen
Elaine Paige
Elkie Brooks
Englebert Humperdinck
Everly Brothers
Fairport Convention
Foster and Allen
Frankie Vaughan
The Fureys
Gary Moore
Gary Newman
Gene Pitney
Gillan
Hank Marvin
Hawkwind
The Hollies
Howard Keel
James
Jerry Lee Lewis
Joan Armatrading
Joe Longthorne
Johnny Mathis
Judi Tzuke
Kim Wilde
Leo Sayer
Lindisfarne
Lloyd Cole
Madness
Marillion
Mike Oldfield
The Monkees
The Moody Blues
Morrissey
Nana Mouskouri
New Order
The Nolans
Oasis
The Pixies
Rick Wakeman
Rory Gallagher
The Shadows
Shakatak
Shakin Stevens
Sheena Easton
Showaddywaddy
Siouxsie and the Banshees
Sister Sledge
Slim Whitman
The Smiths
The Spinners
Status Quo
Steeleye Span
Steve Hackett
The Stranglers
The Style Council
T'Pau
Tears For Fears
Temptations
Thin Lizzie
Thomson Twins
Three Degrees
Tina Turner
UFO
Ultravox
Van Morrison
Vanilla Ice
Wonderstuff

COMEDY

Ben Elton
Bernard Manning
Billy Connelly
Cannon and Ball
Charley Pride
Danny La Rue
Duncan Norville
Freddie Starr
Jasper Carrott
Jethro
Jim Davidson
Lenny Henry
Little and Large
Max Boyce
Michael Barrymore
Mike Harding
Newman & Baddiel
Norman Wisdom
Phil Cool
Rab C. Nesbit
Richard Digence
Rik Mayall
Roy Chubby Brown
Russ Abbott
Smith & Jones
Victoria Wood

CLASSICAL EVENTS

Bournemouth Symphony Orchestra
Sir James Galway
Russian Ice Ballet (Swan Lake)
Glenn Miller Band
Marion Montgomery
The Syd Lawrence Orchestra

Thanks to Ken Meekings for providing this list.

8. HEARTBREAK HOTELS

Gloucester has for a long time suffered from a lack of city centre hotels. Over the years, it has lost some key ones – the Bell Hotel in Southgate Street had been demolished to make way for the Eastgate Shopping Centre, the Spread Eagle Hotel in Northgate Street was converted to offices as was the Royal Hotel in Bruton Way. A hotel was intended to be built above the Eastgate Shopping Centre and extra strong foundations were put in to enable this, but it didn't happen. In the South East corner of Kings Square, the Jellicoe plan envisaged an 84-room hotel of 10 storeys with underground car parking accessed from The Oxebode – but instead we ended up with the Golden Egg building!

This just left the New Inn, The New County and The Fleece in the heart of the city (plus the Station Hotel on Bruton Way). The New Inn is one of the finest medieval galleried courtyard inns in the country and in its day was the heartbeat of the city's night-time economy with 13 separate bars and restaurants – meaning it was possible to do a pub crawl without leaving the premises! In 1954 it was sold to Berni Inns and a small plaque on the Northgate Street frontage relating to Lady Jane Grey bears testament to this. The legend that Lady Jane Grey was proclaimed Queen from its steps is probably not true, according to many historians, but it's a great story. Over the years, it's had its problems, ranging from unauthorised works damaging its heritage carried out by one-time owners The Magic Pub Company, to closure in the late 1990s and a fire in May 2018, when 50 guests (including international Rotary Club members) had to be evacuated.

In the early 1990s, The Magic Pub Company, led by entrepreneur Michael Cannon, acquired the building. In 1995, they shocked planners by decimating the interior of the building, converting 15 bedrooms into offices, installing plastic trunking and carrying out unauthorised alterations to the historic wattle and daub walls.

In May 1996, the Council's Planning Committee considered

a retrospective application for the works and granted a 2-year temporary consent to The Magic Pub Company. Anthony Ault of the Civic Trust commented, "Changing the use of bedrooms without planning permission seems pretty outrageous." They also wanted to demolish the derelict Courtyard Bar and create a small car park accessed from Northgate Street – just as the Council were about to pedestrianise it. Mr Ault described the plans as "totally unacceptable" and Councillor Pam Tracey added, "It's crazy. What are they thinking about?"

The Magic Pub Company was taken over by brewing giants Greene King in 1996 who put the New Inn up for sale for £450,000 but had no serious offers. In February 1998, *The Citizen* reported that manager Mike Dee had been told that the building had become "uneconomical". Greene King's Property Manager, Richard Negus, said, "It's not viable for us to keep it operating. It's up for sale and we want to sell it quickly. We haven't been able to make it work and it needs something else."[149]

Bev Ward, Deputy Editor of *The Citizen* wrote, "Maybe it could be bought for the city and turned into a museum" but City Council Leader, Jon Holmes, said it was "highly unlikely" the Council would put in a bid for it. The hotel closed on the 18th February 1998.

The closure of the hotel coincided with a meeting of the City Council at which Councillor Pam Tracey was described as "fighting back tears" as she told of her sadness at its fate and recalled how it was "at the centre of social life for years" with 10 bars and 3 restaurants at its peak. The Council announced that Director of Marketing, Philip Cooke, would write to 100 hotel companies, looking for "a special type of operator which promotes and makes a commercial virtue out of its historical significance".[150] It's not known if the subsequent buyer was one of the companies written to by the Council.

The New Inn was bought by the Chapman Group of hotels from Sussex in March 1998. They spent £100,000 restoring the 15 bedrooms that had been converted into offices and refurbishing the buildings, bringing the number of rooms back to 34. The hotel reopened in May 1998. Landlord John Bagshaw, a Londoner, said, "The building has been badly neglected in recent years and we want to see it returned to its former glory." Richard Pope, Director of Operations at the Chapman Group, said, "We are working hand in hand with Gloucester City Council, English Heritage and the County Conservation Officer."[151] The hotel was officially re-opened by Mayor of Gloucester Councillor Arthur Meredith in May 1999.

A series of managers came and went. Some made a real effort and others less so. Mark and Sam Cooke ran the hotel between 2009 and 2012. They refurbished the restaurant and made improvements to the bar, as well as introducing tours of the building and new events like Shakespeare performances in the courtyard – which was a contrast to the more regular entertainment of karaoke in the main bar! They had Shaun Ryder of the Happy Mondays staying at the hotel and also served fish and chips to Robert Plant and his wife before he played the the Guildhall. Another two bedrooms were brought back into use, bringing the total to 36.

Former Policeman Mike Sage and his wife Marion ran the hotel from 2014-16 before retiring to Malta. They oversaw a steady rise in business, with the hotel taking an active part in events like the Blues Festival and Gloucester Day.

The New Inn is an important part of the city's heritage and nightlife offer but it doesn't have the scale, on its own, to meet the demand for hotel accommodation in a city the size of Gloucester. As an aside, it has played its part in recent political history. City MP Richard Graham used to stay there after he had been adopted as Conservative Parliamentary Candidate and before he had established a permanent base in Gloucester. As MP, he invited the then Home Secretary Theresa May for a breakfast meeting with local business people when they were both campaigning for 'Remain' in the EU referendum of June 2016 – something hardline Brexiteers take pleasure in reminding them about! Former Prime Minister Liz Truss, then Secretary of State for the Environment, Food and Rural Affairs, visited the New Inn as part of a walkabout in Gloucester following a visit to the Gloucester Services motorway service station. This came about after Mr Graham famously invited her in Parliament to sample some Gloucester Old Spot Sausage, something Miss Truss described as "one of the best offers I've had all year".

I touch upon the New County in Chapter 13, but it only had 40 rooms, had gone downhill over the years and at one point had closed. The New County was part of a small family-owned chain. The business failed in 1992 and the hotel was held by receivers on behalf of Lloyds Bank.

The Fleece, as covered in detail in Chapter 22, closed in 2002 after almost 500 years as an inn and never reopened. Both were threatened by the Council's proposed Blackfriars development in any case – which probably was indirectly responsible for The Fleece's eventual closure. The whole of The Fleece was to be acquired for the Blackfriars development, with the front of the hotel and façade to be retained and used as a pub/restaurant/wine bar. So there was, for many years, no hotel of any scale or of high quality in the city centre. The top-end hotels tended to be on the outskirts of the city, like the Country Club at Matson (later known as the Ramada, the Hallmark and, at the time of writing, The Robinswood), Bowden Hall and Hatton Court at Upton St Leonards and Hatherley Manor at Down Hatherley to the north of the city. Even the budget chains like Travelodge and Premier Inn opened on the fringes at places like Barnwood and Longford, although both would later be represented at Gloucester Quays.

Hugh Worsnip wrote in *The Citizen* that the "price of the latest Arrowcroft scheme for Blackfriars is the loss of two hotels, the New County and The Fleece. Hotels must be part of the development, not the price of a new Marks and Sparks."[152]

There has long been talk of a hotel in the Docks. In 1994, British Waterways were promoting a site on the corner of Severn Road and Llanthony Road for a hotel and had been attempting to attract hotel chains for around 18 months. At the time, the City Council's Chief Leisure and Tourism Officer Philip Cooke said that "the city's ambitions to become a major tourist destination are frustrated by the lack of a city centre hotel".[153]

A hotel study commissioned by the City Council in 1997 recommended promoting development of a hotel, with the Docks as the preferred location. It also referred to the site on the corner of Llanthony Road and Severn Road. Apparently, the Marriott group was interested but didn't raise the necessary funds so it didn't progress. There was also said to be interest from budget brands but Crest were hoping to land a 3-star operator and although Hilton, Copthorne and Stakis had all passed on the opportunity, Holiday

Inn, Ibis and Campanile were all still in the game. As described in the chapter on The Docks, a site at the Barge Arm was the location of a hotel in the later planning application. The completion of the South West bypass and the Inner Relief Road, which wouldn't happen for another decade, was seen as critical for access.

The Hotel Strategy report was presented to the Council's Highways & Planning Committee in June 1997 and stated that hotels in Gloucester did not cater for corporate business, including conferences and seminars. It noted that the Blackfriars development would have led to the "certain loss" of the New County Hotel and part, if not all, of The Fleece Hotel, involving a "loss of vitality to the city centre". It acknowledged that problems with city centre hotels included a lack of secure parking and difficult access onto the pedestrian area.

The masterplan for Gloucester Quays included a proposal for an 80-bed hotel next to Llanthony Priory. A scheme for a 120-bed Ramada Encore was presented to the Gloucester Heritage Urban Regeneration Company's Design Review Panel in 2008 and was slated as being more suited to a retail park than next to an important heritage asset. Unusually it was referred to the full Board of GHURC. Board members agonised over whether to endorse it on the basis of 'a bird in the hand' or urge the City Council to refuse it as an inappropriate design in a sensitive setting. In the end, the financial crisis of 2008 onwards took that decision out of their hands and the site was later given over to a retirement development by McCarthy & Stone.

A report to the Policy & Resources Committee in 1997 envisaged a budget hotel at the Cattle Market of up to 50 beds. The 1998 brief for the Cattle Market development included a requirement to provide a 150-bed hotel and conference centre. The initial proposal from Grantchester (the successful bidder) incorporated both a 200-room 4-star hotel with a conference centre and a 100-room 3-star hotel. It wasn't quite in the heart of the city centre, but it was pretty close and the site was big enough to do something on that scale. The Heads of Terms from Grantchester said the 4-star hotel needed a subsidy of £1.45 million (plus the land) but the 3-star could be delivered without subsidy.

The then Head of Planning Services, Jerry Spencer, made the

suggestion that it would be better to site the 4-star hotel on the Westgate car park owned by the City Council. He did so as he saw the Westgate approach as a key point of arrival into the city and the St Oswalds site as being disconnected from the core of the city centre. So the reasons were sound, but the decision was one that would trigger an episode that would cause "great cost and embarrassment" for the City Council.

Whether it was the right location was debatable – it was on a major route into the city, but it sat next to an unattractive block of council flats with their share of social problems and it was still something of a walk (uphill) to the heart of the city centre, although this hadn't prevented McCarthy & Stone successfully developing the Castlemeads Court retirement apartments directly opposite.

In April 2000, *The Citizen* reported that "Gloucester will have a four-star Holiday Inn and Conference Centre by October next year", with developers Grantchester planning to build a 120-bed hotel and 500-seater conference centre.[154]

Council Leader Kevin Stephens said, "Work will start in the summer. The four-star hotel is part of the same deal as the Cattle Market redevelopment." He paid tribute to Director of Corporate Development Richard Cook saying, "The effort that Mr Cook has put into this has been phenomenal. Hour upon hour of hard work, weekends and late nights. It would not have happened without him."

By September that year, the timetable had slipped but it was still hoped that work on the hotel would start in March 2001 and finish in Summer 2002.[155]

Negotiations led to the hotel not being part of the Grantchester scheme. The Council was introduced to Western Management Services by Grantchester who in turn introduced the Selsdon Group and Michael Jacquiss. The Council chose to conduct negotiations directly with Selsdon rather than through Grantchester and their agents. If they had stuck with Grantchester, the outcome would most likely have been different.

A report to the City Council Cabinet in October 2000 gave officers delegated powers to enter into an agreement with Selsdon Consultancy Limited and removed the link with the Grantchester/St Oswalds development. Grantchester agreed to pay £2.65 million towards the project if their scheme went ahead, which comprised the value of the Westgate car park, plus a £1.45 million subsidy to the developer. A Cabinet report in October 2000 said Selsdon would build the hotel and Holiday Inn would operate it. Holiday Inn wanted it operational by 1st July 2002 – ahead of the Grantchester scheme.

It seems that Selsdon and Jacquiss were taken at face value, without the Council undertaking the basic kind of due diligence checks that these days can be done in seconds online. Subsequent checks revealed a "lack of evidence of successful track record", "allegations of dishonesty", "inconsistency in names, addresses and dates of birth", "questions about professional memberships" and "creation and dissolution of companies".

Selsdon's proposal was for a 130-room 4-star, 5-storey hotel and 500-space conference centre. In addition, there would be a bar, swimming pool and gym and 120 car parking spaces. The building, which went through several iterations, was designed by top architects Broadway Malyan. There was an objection from the residents of Castlemeads Court who were concerned about the lack of parking for the anticipated 120 staff. The Civic Trust described the building as "mundane". The nearby Riverside Sports Centre supported a hotel with facilities for guests but didn't want them opened to the public, presumably for commercial reasons. The Council's Planning Committee were 'minded to grant' consent in March 2001, subject to approval by the Government Office for the South West.

In addition to the subsidy from the Council of £1.45 million and the value of the land, there was the matter of £140,000 a year of lost income from parking charges – although the total cost of the project to the Council never appears to have been stated in these terms, nor evaluated against the potential benefits.

The Council transferred the income from the car park to the Selsdon Group's nominated company in January 2001 and the land itself (for the sum of £1) in July 2001. There was never any justification found as to why the land was transferred before the hotel plans were more certain or why the income was transferred six months ahead of the land. The Council transferred the land without restrictive covenants which would have controlled its use.

The Scrutiny study says these were removed because of pressure from the developer. My sources tell me there was to be a clause that freehold wouldn't be transferred until the hotel was built and being operated but that was removed by the lawyers for Selsdon. When City Council solicitors queried this internally they were instructed to proceed with the document as it stood.

The Council's Director of Resources, Keith Birtles, did intervene and got agreement that the Council would get a share of the income up to October 2002 and all of the income after that date if the hotel project had not commenced, but that was rather like closing the stable door after the horse had bolted.

There were plenty of warning signs along the way. A hotel group wrote to the Council on 21st August 2001 to say it had been offered the Westgate site by Jacquiss. They wrote again on 3rd September 2001 to say that Selsdon had lost their funding for the project. On 14th September 2001, they copied a letter they had written to Jacquiss to Council Leader Kevin Stephens and Director of Corporate Development Richard Cook, setting out how they had made a formal offer to buy the land in June 2001. On 17th September 2001, the Council was made aware that NCP had been offered a long lease on the car park by Jacquiss. In January 2002, the Director of Finance raised concerns after being made aware that a contractor hadn't been paid by Selsdon Group.

All of these concerns were brushed away and the explanations given by Jacquiss were accepted. Richard Cook had refused to meet with the managing director of the hotel company who had rung the alarm bells. There was evidence that he had discussed these issues with Kevin Stephens but the concerns weren't taken any further.

I raised concerns publicly in February 2002, particularly in relation to the loss of income, saying, "The council failed to include in the original transfer a 'clawback' provision to recover car parking income in the event of a delay in construction of the hotel. To transfer the car park land without a clawback provision seems breathtakingly incompetent. It has cost city taxpayers a small fortune and the longer the delay in building the hotel, the more profits the developers rake in." Jacquiss was damning in his response, branding me a "nuisance" and promising work would start on site in March. He added, "If Marriot goes walk-about,

Gloucester won't get a hotel and I shall have a problem." He claimed to have spent £1 million on development costs. Kevin Stephens added for good measure, "Every time the Conservatives come near developers it frightens them away". In this case, it was a shame it didn't.

In April 2002, *The Citizen* reported that it would "almost certainly" now be Marriott (rather than Holiday Inn) who would operate the planned £15.2 million hotel and conference centre. The article advised that Marriott had signed a preliminary contract with the Selsdon Group and that their MD would be in Gloucester the next week for talks with the Council. Kevin Stephens believed he was meeting the head of Marriott, but looking back isn't so sure that's who it really was!

Marriott wanted 150 bedrooms rather than the 130 in the existing planning consent, so a new application for an additional (sixth) floor was submitted in April 2002 and granted in June 2002.

In July 2002, the City Council's Head of Legal Services, Gary Spencer, had a call from a hotelier who said they had an agreement with Jacquiss to buy the Westgate car park. Investigations revealed the paperwork passed to Selsdon by the prospective purchaser had been altered and signatures forged prior to forwarding to the Council. The hotel development under this agreement would have been a 3- star, not a 4-star, and other information wasn't correct – which would have made it a breach of the development agreement between Selsdon and the Council.[156]

The Council was alerted to potential fraud in Summer 2002 and informed the Police and the District Auditor (the Council's spending watchdog). Investigations revealed that suspected fraud had been committed to obtain the land and car park income. The Council believed that misrepresentation, both negligent and fraudulent, had occurred. It started proceedings for restitution of the money and return of the car park as they believed it had been fraudulently obtained.

Specialist advice was needed so the council engaged top solicitors Nabarro Nathanson to investigate action against the company and its directors and to protect the Council's position and landholdings. There was the threat of a £5 million counterclaim. The lawyers investigated UK and offshore bank accounts in an attempt to track down the car park income. There was concern that if the company went into liquidation or was wound up, the Council would lose the right to the land, the income and ultimately the development.

Jacquiss claimed to be ill and bedridden but the Council hired a private detective to follow him and caught him walking to a business meeting in Cardiff. Video evidence of this was eventually used in court. At one of the High Court cases, Jacquiss made an appearance with his head in his hands, surrounded by pills, giving the impression the Council was hounding a poor, seriously ill man.

There were a number of court hearings – some of which City Council lawyers say were only necessary due to the attitude and alleged illness of Jacquiss. The first court hearing in January 2003 was for a freezing injunction to protect the car park land and accumulated income. The second was to protect the assets of the company and individual. There was a separate application to the High Court for contempt with the threat of imprisonment if he didn't comply.

The work required to prepare for the civil court cases and to submit evidence to the Police for possible criminal charges was enormous. The information was in 14 files with thousands of pages of correspondence. Head of Legal Services Gary Spencer's statement to the Police was 138 pages long plus three lever arch files and 876 pages of exhibits.

The Council obtained a judgement in default against the company in which the High Court ordered the Land Registry to re-register the land in the City Council's name – only a week before the company was forced into liquidation by a creditor, which would have meant the land was lost to the Council.

The High Court advised that the accumulated income (which had been frozen since December 2002) and ongoing income should be released to the Council. The lawyers tried to track down where the earlier income had gone but despite finding various UK and offshore bank accounts, the whereabouts of the cash remained a mystery. The Council recovered the land in June 2003. The legal costs were just over £650,00[157] but the overall cost was closer to £1 million.[158]

The Council was advised in May 2004 that the Crown Prosecution Service (CPS) had decided it wasn't in the public interest to prosecute Jacquiss, primarily due to his ill health. He died in 2005.

The Scrutiny Inquiry

The decision of the CPS and the death of Michael Jacquiss cleared the way for a Scrutiny Panel study into what went wrong. It was undertaken by Liberal Democrat councillor Declan Wilson, an accountant in his day job, Conservative Sue Lewis, a Barclays Bank Corporate Manager, and Mark Hobbs, the Labour Group Leader. Their report was damning.

It recorded that there had been disagreements between Kevin Stephens and Council Officers as well as "poor segregation between Member and Officer roles" – code, in my view, for officers taking decisions without informing councillors and councillors getting involved in the detail that should properly be left to officers. There was "no evidence that Cabinet permission had been sought before the transfer of land or income".

The project was managed by one person (presumably Richard Cook), meaning "too much power was concentrated in too few people" with "no independent legal advice". The Head of Legal Services, Gary Spencer, had raised concerns but "felt that his contribution had been perceived to be negative".

There was a "huge amount of pressure delivered by the developer, including threats of project collapse" and a "propensity to bow to developer pressure" which "developed an environment for decision-making which was less than perfect."

The panel also asked the basic question, which has never been answered, that if there was a 127-bed hotel and a 500-capacity conference centre, where would the other 373 conference-goers stay?

Both Cook and Stephens attached conditions to their appearances in front of the Scrutiny Panel. Cook, who retired from the Council early in 2002, requested an assurance that no action would be taken against him. The panel declined and Cook "decided he was unable to assist". Stephens, who lost his Matson council seat to Conservative Stuart Wilson in 2003, sought an assurance that the session would be confidential and in private, stating that his new job with the Civil Service was "politically restricted". The panel was unable to agree and Stephens "decided not to attend".

This was in marked contrast to the hours of public questioning I went through at two Scrutiny meetings following the Marketing Gloucester saga 15 years later (see Chapter 19), although he did appear in front of the Blackfriars Inquiry which took place before he was subject to those restrictions.

I wrote in an article in *The Citizen* on 19th January 2006 that "even for those of us who were then in opposition on the Council the report makes uncomfortable reading," adding that, "The Westgate saga is a salutary reminder of what can happen when things go wrong. If we learn from this… we can spend less time picking over the bones of past failure and more time delivering the regeneration Gloucester needs and deserves."

The Barnwood Hotel

The Council had not only failed to deliver the Westgate Hotel project, but they had viewed other hotel schemes as competitors. In 2000, it had refused planning permission for a 3-star out of town hotel at Barnwood, claiming it would prejudice the Westgate project. Director of Corporate Development, Richard Cook, is said to have produced a last-minute email from the developer of the Westgate scheme saying if the Barnwood application was approved it would cause their scheme to fail. The City Council lost the subsequent appeal at a cost to the council taxpayer of £40,000.

The application was by brewers Scottish & Newcastle for an 83-bed Solus Lodge hotel (later renamed Premier Lodge) and Chef & Brewer pub. In 2003, the Spirit Pub Group bought Scottish & Newcastle's pub business, including Chef & Brewer and Premier Lodge. In 2004, Spirit sold the hotels to Whitbread who rebranded them to Premier Inn as they remain today. The hotel would have no catering facilities but would use the Chef & Brewer next door.

The Council's Development Control Manager at the time, Phil Staddon, was quoted in *The Citizen* saying, "Hotels are an incredibly fickle sector of the economy and this objection raises the whole question of priorities. We need to do more work on this and probe further the impact on the city centre."[159]

The developers of the proposed hotels in the Docks and at St Oswalds Park did not object. The County Council as highway authority opposed it as being against local and national policy. 77

local residents objected, citing concerns over traffic and noise.

Scottish & Newcastle appealed against the Council's failure to make a decision on the application and, at the same time, lodged a duplicate application. In October 2000, the Council's Planning Committee resolved to refuse the duplicate application, arguing that it could prejudice proposed hotel development in the city and in particular the 4-star at Westgate.

An inquiry took place in November 2000. During the inquiry, Michael Jacquiss advised that his company had entered into an agreement with the Council and was committed to the construction of the hotel. This pulled the rug from under the Council's feet as they could no longer argue that the Barnwood hotel would prejudice the development at Westgate. They had to rely upon a second reason for refusal stating the developer had failed to provide evidence the hotel was needed and that it met the 'sequential test' (i.e. to prove that there was no more central site available where the development could be located). However, the Council had not required this when they approved a budget hotel in Quedgeley in April 1999. The Inspector also noted in his report that "the majority of customers are likely to be engaged on business rather than leisure trips."

The appeal was allowed by Inspector Michael Hill in December 2000 and the hotel and pub were built and continue to trade today. Costs were awarded against the City Council.

Future Developments

The Westgate car park, at the time of writing, is still that – a car park - and looks likely to remain so for the foreseeable future.

There is now, however, genuine hotel operator interest in the city. I met bosses from the Hilton Hotel Group at the Local Government Association Conference in Bournemouth only a few years ago and invited them to Gloucester to look both at the former Council Offices at the Docks and the opportunity at Kings Quarter. Whether they will ultimately come to Gloucester is another matter, but having arguably the world's biggest hotel brand showing genuine interest in the city is a sign of how far it has come.

I cover in more detail in other chapters the hotel projects which have been proposed for the old Council Offices in the Docks, Kings

Quarter and The Fleece. Each is at a different stage at the time of writing, with the 4-star hotel at Kings Quarter/The Forum under construction and the other two projects either abandoned or stalled. It is to be hoped that after so many twists and turns and disappointments, the centre of Gloucester will finally get the stock of hotels of the quality and scale it needs and deserves.

9. THE GHURC YEARS

From an idea to inception

As I mentioned in the earlier chapter on the failures of regeneration at Blackfriars and Westgate, the revival of the city was never likely to happen when it was being overseen by council officers their alongside many other duties. So thoughts turned to how a dedicated resource could be created.

In 2002, the city's then Labour MP Parmjit Dhanda felt there was a need to get a single, cohesive, collective voice to take the politics out and bring the private sector on board. He had heard about Swindon's Urban Regeneration Company from Ian Knight of the South West Regional Development Agency (SWRDA). The other URC in the South West was in Camborne, Pool and Redruth.

Parmjit asked a question at Prime Minister's Question Time – his first at PMQs - on 17th July 2002 to PM Tony Blair about whether he would approve an Urban Regeneration Company for Gloucester. The exchange is recorded in Hansard as below. Parmjit told me that Tony Blair didn't know the question in advance.

Mr. Parmjit Dhanda (Gloucester): The Prime Minister will be aware of the success of URCs—urban regeneration companies—which have been set up in towns and cities throughout the land and are helping to encourage regeneration. Will he join me in calling for a URC to be set up in my constituency of Gloucester, where we are trying to push through £0.5 billion of regeneration and where a URC could make all the difference?

The Prime Minister: URCs have certainly been very successful, but I think I should take some advice before giving my hon. Friend the commitment that he seeks.

Organisations to drive regeneration come in many different shapes and sizes – like Urban Development Corporations, with full planning powers, which were used in places like Merseyside (famously championed by Michael Heseltine) and London Docklands. The URC model had no planning powers, no land of its own and no real money, other than to cover its annual running costs. Its £750,000 annual budget came from the Regional Development Agency and English Partnerships (£250,000 each) and the City and County Councils (£125,000 each). However, each of the four partners was expected to contribute their funding and landholdings in the city towards delivering the overall objectives.

SWRDA got involved in Gloucester at the City Council's invitation. SWRDA's Director at the time, Colin Molton, felt it needed "a firm hand on the tiller". The economic indicators showed a disparity between Gloucester and its neighbour Cheltenham, not just in terms of retail ranking but in the indices of multiple deprivation. Council planning officer Peter Wynn recalls being stood looking at the Bank of England building in Southgate Street with Colin Molton and explaining that the area behind that was one of the most deprived in the South West. Six out of the ten 'Super Output Areas' (council wards broken down into smaller areas) in the proposed URC area were in the top 25% most deprived in England. Three were in the top 10%. Gloucester had the second highest crime rate in the South West behind Bristol. Unemployment rates were higher and economic activity lower than the County average and 31% of residents in the URC area had no recognised skills or qualifications, 12% of residents considered themselves in poor health with 22% having a limiting long-term illness. There were twice as many vacant dwellings (4%) in the URC area than in Gloucester as a whole.[160]

Added to that, there was "enough to get stuck into" with the Docks and Blackfriars with a fair chunk of landholdings already in public ownership and others available to be acquired. The focus on heritage was as a result of the city's 10 Conservation Areas, 490 listed buildings, 35 Scheduled Ancient Monuments and nationally important heritage sites at the Docks and Blackfriars.

English Heritage's Urban Panel, which had visited recently (in May 2003), described the city as "awash with development potential", noting that the challenge was what to do with so much urban capacity. It also warned "the promise of the bypass threatened to suck most development pressure from the centre to the western sites" – something which "should be avoided at all costs". It described the decision of the RDA, URC and Councils to embrace characterisation as "inspiring". Characterisation is "a method of identification and interpretation of the varying historic character within an area that looks beyond individual heritage assets." That theme was later picked up in the Heritage Audit by Alan Baxter & Associates which said "GHURC continues to lead the way in the characterisation-based approach to heritage-led regeneration" and "has the potential to be a national exemplar of best practice."

During the visit, Peter Wynn had highlighted to the panel the monolithic Boots store in Eastgate Street as the last major retail investment in the city.

Approval was needed from the government, and in particular John Prescott's Office of the Deputy Prime Minister, to establish a URC. A submission was put together by Roger Tym & Partners in May 2003. In its summary, it told how "after years of various failed or only partially successful attempts at regeneration...the problems of key areas in Central Gloucester require a concerted, co-ordinated effort". It described a "run down, disjointed appearance which deters domestic interest and business investment." On the positive side it said there was "potential to lever in up to £400 million of private sector investment over 10 years" – something which turned out to be on the conservative side.

In January 2004, the Government warned that a decision would not be made until next month at least, citing concerns about the level of private sector representation on the Board. I was Chair of the Regeneration Scrutiny Committee at the time and commented, "The delay is no more than annoying at the moment but if it drags on much longer it will become more serious. Uncertainty is unsettling for investors and we want an answer quickly so we can get the URC up and running quickly. I hope John Prescott's New Year's resolution is not to take so long to make decisions."[161] Approval was finally granted in February 2004. At the time Peter Wynn commented, "There's 30 years of catching up for this city and big schemes will take a long time to deliver."[162]

GHURC's mission was "to bring life back to historic areas of

Gloucester, reflecting their special character, whilst creating a new, prosperous, attractive, safe and sustainable urban centre for the 21st century" and its objectives included 3000 new homes, 2000 new jobs, redeveloping 100 hectares of derelict land and securing the reuse of 80 historic buildings. The objectives became wrapped up in output targets set by the Government as a condition of continued funding and performance was reviewed annually.

It had got off to an inauspicious start. The 'Shadow Board' (before the URC was formally established) meetings were full of political game-playing. The then Leader of the County Council was Labour's Peter Clarke, a retired Education Officer with a long history of acerbic letters to the local paper and a habit of sending caustic late-night emails. The City Council's politics weren't much better, with a precarious Lib-Lab pact which changed its Leader every six months. County Council Deputy Leader Liz Boait (whose daughter Fran contested the Gloucester seat for Labour in the 2019 general election) also attended.

Members of the 'Shadow Board' included Colin Molton of SWRDA, Bill Crowther and Mary Smith (who shared the leadership of the City Council in the ill-fated one-year Lib-Lab pact), John Lancaster of British Waterways, Greg Smith (Principal of GlosCAT), Parmjit Dhanda MP, David Warburton (English Partnerships), Citizen Editor Ian Mean, Dr Kevin Brown (English Heritage) and Stan Jones (Chief Executive of economic development agency Gloucestershire First).

Some people apparently advised against Parmjit Dhanda sitting on the board as he "didn't always behave himself". Following the 2010 general election, his successor Richard Graham decided he would not take a place on the board, preferring to be able to hold the company to account.

One insider told me the meetings were "horrendous", describing how board members "all hated each other". One board member was labelled as "bonkers", another "difficult" and a third "incredibly rude".

The no-nonsense figure of Colin Molton of the RDA chaired the Shadow Board meetings, at times held in the splendour of the Cathedral's Parliament Rooms, at others on board a canal narrowboat or in the Coots café meeting room (now part of

Wetherspoons), and knocked things into shape. Ian Knight of the RDA and Duncan Innes of English Partnerships sat on either side of him like bouncers. Greg Smith did his best to maintain a sense of calm and keep people talking.

Molton reminded them that, "A lot of money is being brought to bear. Councils need to compromise on sovereignty and recognise it's a partnership approach." Insiders told me that the councillors involved in the early days couldn't understand why the English Partnerships and RDA funding couldn't just be given directly to the councils. Giving up some degree of control in exchange for the £50 million of public funding which came to the city during the GHURC years seems like a good deal to me!

The GHURC Board should under usual rules have been chaired by a private sector member, but there were no volunteers. Greg Smith, the Principal of GlosCAT, agreed to take it on after being asked by Ian Mean and Peter Wynn after "too many glasses of red wine".[163] His appointment was subject to Government approval, which was forthcoming. He told his governing body at the College that it would take half a day a month. At times, with evenings and weekends, it took as much time as his day job.

Smith had a vested interest in the city's regeneration. GlosCAT's Brunswick Campus was in poor repair and Smith had an ambition for a new city base for the College, as he had done in Cheltenham. English Partnerships bought the College's Brunswick Campus in 2004 and it was later developed by Linden Homes for new housing, as described in more detail later in this chapter. In his introduction in GHURC's final report, Smith said, "I suppose my initial involvement with regeneration began with my decision to build a new college campus in Gloucester Docks. Our rundown Gloucester campus, sad and dilapidated, seemed to mirror a large part of central Gloucester including King's Square, the Docks, Blackfriars, and the Railway Triangle. It was really apparent that nothing much had happened in Gloucester for a number of years and according to many Gloucester cynics, "nothing ever happens in Gloucester."

Ian Mean, the Editor of *The Citizen*, agreed to be Vice Chair.

He was a big character, with his heavily-pinstriped suits, loud ties and matching socks, and strong opinions. He wasn't publicity-shy and some commented that his photograph appeared in his newspaper more than anyone else's! Some people worried that he would have a conflict of interest, but in reality there were plenty of those in the room. Others were concerned with how he could hold the company to account as local editor if he was Vice Chair. His view was that he was for Gloucester and there was no conflict, saying in a comment piece, "I make no apology for being proud of being a board member. I have only been editor of *The Citizen* for two years and some may say that a new boy on the block must be here a bit longer before he voices opinions. Well, sorry, that is not what I'm about."[164] In the end it didn't prove to be an issue. Mean made a hugely valuable contribution and threw the weight of the local paper behind the regeneration effort.

He was scathing about the lack of vision for the city, saying, "Let's just concentrate on restoring the sense of pride in Gloucester that used to be part and parcel of this historic city and encourage a sense of real vision for the future. Frankly, I can't see that we have one."

In his comments in GHURC's final report, Mean continued that theme, saying, "Gloucester people have rightly tended to be cynical over the development of areas like King's Square" and "Gloucester has too often seen itself as second best". He noted that "it will never happen" was a cry often heard and written to him as editor of the local newspaper.

The only officer resource at the start was the City Council's Peter Wynn, a planner by background who went by the title of Strategic Development Officer. He was initially based at the former Bank of England building at Southgate House then moved to Albion Cottages in the Docks, which were owned by SWRDA.

Against the backdrop of political game-playing and scarce resources to do anything, it proved difficult to recruit potential board members, with even some of the 'usual suspects' not being keen to join. Later, Steve Simmonds, the ever-supportive Manager of the Kings Walk Shopping Centre, agreed to sit on the Board.

The situation started to change when control of the City Council shifted in 2004, with the Conservatives forming a minority administration under Mark Hawthorne's leadership.

The insistence of the City and County Councils of having two board members each meant, because of the '20% rule' (local authorities were limited to a maximum of 20% of the places on the board) that the board size had to be 21 – which could be rather unwieldy, especially when taking in the added number of 'observers' and advisers. When the idea began to gather some traction, the engagement of the private sector started to build. Over the life of the URC, there were numerous board members – Companies House lists 50. Aside from those representing the founding public sector partners, board members were chosen on the basis of their skills. Solicitor Antonia Shields, HSBC Bank Manager Alan Jarman, Mark Owen of the Federation of Small Businesses, Sally Pickering, Chief Executive of the Gloucester Centre for Voluntary Services, Bishop Michael Perham and Peter Foyle of Bruton Knowles are a few examples. They brought a great deal of expertise to the table, and a fresh, optimistic perspective, although some felt that there were too many people who didn't live, or even work, in Gloucester.

Political representation varied. Labour councillor Mary Smith took one of the City Council's places for a number of years, despite the authority being run by the Conservatives at the time, and made a valuable contribution. Julie Girling, who went on to be a Conservative MEP, represented the County Council between 2006-11. I sat on the board throughout the URC's formal existence.

Getting a team and a plan in place

With a Board in place the next job was to recruit an executive team, starting with a Chief Executive. I took part in the interviews with Pete Bungard, then Director of Environment at the County Council, Colin Molton and Greg Smith. We chose Chris Oldershaw, an experienced regeneration professional, who had been successful in delivering heritage-led regeneration in Grainger Town in Newcastle. He joined in 2005.

Oldershaw was a safe pair of hands. Under his leadership, the budgets came in on balance and reports for the board were comprehensive. He was respected by the Board and, crucially, the development industry. He was paid £100,000 a year plus benefits, which was a big pay cheque in Gloucester terms and higher than the City Council Chief Executive at the time – which did cause some 'salary envy', given the small team and budget he was responsible for managing.

He recruited a staff team, including Mike Tilt as Development Director. Tilt had headed up the Gloucester Quays development for British Waterways and was chosen after a nationwide recruitment campaign. Staff members included those who dealt with project management, community engagement and urban design.

A series of panels and forums were set up including a Residents and Community Forum, Business Forum, Design Review Panel, Marketing & Communications Panel and an Urban Youth Forum. There was an Employment and Skills Panel, which subsequently became the 'Gloucester Works' project. At times, it felt like an industry in itself, but was valuable in involving the wider community in the regeneration of the city and giving a sense of ownership. Members of the Youth Forum recorded a video diary of their perspective on the city's regeneration. GHURC also had the resources to communicate key messages about regeneration far more effectively than the City Council had done before or has since. This included regular newsletters, a mobile exhibition unit which went out to community events, two 'Future of the City' events attended by over 4000 people and even advertising hoardings – including several designs bearing the slogan 'The Best is Yet to Come', which was inspired by words from Bishop Michael Perham. It was Oldershaw's view, from his experience of working in places like Liverpool, Teesside and Newcastle, that proactive marketing was crucial in changing perceptions and creating investment confidence.

The Design Review Panel was set up to promote design excellence in GHURC's major schemes and included eminent architects like Professor Richard Silverman, who chaired the Cardiff Bay Design Review Panel, Geoff Rich from Feilden Clegg Bradley and Nick Childs from Childs Suzmann, as well as representatives from English Heritage, the City Council and the GHURC board.

GHURC commissioned many reports and masterplans and none was bigger than the 'Regeneration Framework' which set out detailed plans for the whole URC area and how the output targets would be delivered. Terence O'Rourke, a planning and design consultancy, were the successful bidders for the £250,000 commission. Their team included Alan Baxter Associates (transport & heritage), Roger Tym & Partners (town planners),

James Nisbet and Partners (quantity surveyors) and Paul Baker of King Sturge (property consultants). Andy Ward, one of the O'Rourke team, told me that market was still quite buoyant at that time before the financial crash hit, so it was a "bit rushed". Their impression of the city was that it was run-down and underinvested, and in the shadow of Cheltenham, but they were amazed by the potential. They liked the challenge and wanted to help make Gloucester better.

The Regeneration Framework led to an approach, endorsed by the Board, which was to concentrate on a number of major development sites rather than spread the jam too thinly. Oldershaw named these as the 'Magnificent Seven' projects – Gloucester Docks, Gloucester Quays, Greyfriars, Blackfriars, the Railway Triangle, Kings Quarter and the Canal Corridor. Some people commented that in the 1960s Western movie of the same name, not all seven survived...

The Regeneration Framework and the accompanying Investment Prospectus were launched in October 2006, in Gloucester and at the Palace of Westminster, with Greg Smith saying, "The launch of the regeneration framework sets the scene for what we hope will be one of the great decades in Gloucester's history. It's not a wish, it is not a dream, it is happening."[165] A series of Cabinet Ministers attended the Westminster launch including Alan Johnson, David Milliband and Alun Michael, along with over 70 developers and investors.

The Docks, Quays, Blackfriars and Kings Quarter projects, including GHURC's involvement, are each covered in their own chapters in this book. GHURC's role in each of these sites varied, depending on what stage plans had reached and who owned the land. Gloucester Docks had seen some progress, but a number of the warehouses were still derelict, some sites were undeveloped and the public realm was poor. The plans for Gloucester Quays were well-advanced, but GHURC threw its weight behind them and helped to secure some crucial infrastructure. Blackfriars was a blank sheet of paper following the collapse of the Arrowcroft retail scheme and the future of the Priory was still in doubt. Even when GHURC was created, Kings Square and the area around it was in a poor state and the Council was in discussions with Morley Fund Management (part of Norwich Union), owners of the Kings Walk shopping centre, about a potential development.

It is worth pointing out that responsibility for delivery of Kings Quarter returned to the City Council, as the principal landowner, in the light of the 'Roanne' ruling (which resulted in the need for a long-winded EU compliant procurement process), but which perhaps also reflected the difficult relationship between the two organisations. GHURC Chair Greg Smith says it was his greatest regret that this development didn't progress during the company's existence.

The company also backed the proposal for a Parkway railway station at Elmbridge, which was controversial in itself because of fears about the impact on the Gloucester and Cheltenham central stations, although this was never a focus of major activity for the Board or the executive team.

Although the Regeneration Framework was focused on the 'Magnificent Seven' projects, it also identified other issues it saw critical for success, including strengthening the Gate Streets, enhancing links between the Docks and the city centre, addressing insensitive development, protecting views of the Cathedral, enhancing use of the water and waterfront and increasing cycling, walking and public transport.

The Board adopted a vision statement saying, "To bring life back to historic areas of Gloucester, reflecting their special character while creating a new, prosperous, attractive, safe, sustainable urban centre for the 21st century."

Gloucester's Urban Regeneration Company was the only one in the country to put 'Heritage' in its title, demonstrating its commitment to heritage-led regeneration. But GHURC was a bit of a mouthful, so they appointed a local design agency, Litchfield Morris, to come up with a snappier version and a logo. They came up with 'Gloucester Renaissance'. Renaissance isn't really a word in the Gloucester vocabulary and it never caught on. The only other URCs that used it were Southend and West Lakes (which covered Barrow-in-Furness) and it was also used for the regeneration programme in Rotherham, where you suspect renaissance is used even less in conversation.

Some of the GHURC team, led by Chief Executive Chris Oldershaw (back row 1st left). Credit: Litchfield Morris/GHURC

Cabinet Minister David Milliband at the Parliamentary launch of GHURC's Regeneration Framework. Credit: Litchfield Morris/GHURC

Delivery

The success of the URC was mixed but, in my view, largely positive. It certainly helped to develop investor confidence in the city, which didn't exist before the URC was created. It brought together the major players around a common agenda and was able to draw down money from the RDA and English Partnerships (later the Homes and Communities Agency). In some people's eyes, it took the credit for Gloucester Quays – which was in some places described as its scheme - but, arguably, with Peel's determination and resources that would have happened anyway.

The completion of the £43 million South West Bypass (the final section of which was supported by the RDA) and the new £7.5 million 18m high, 400-ton High Orchard Bridge over the canal connecting the bypass to St Ann Way (which for so many years was known as the road to nowhere) paid for by English Partnerships were vital to Gloucester Quays going ahead. This investment in infrastructure was, in my view, a good use of public money, levering in hundreds of millions of private investment from Peel.

Docks Linkages

The URC can also justifiably lay claim to the success of the Gloucester Quays – Docks – city centre linkages, which were a £7 million investment paid for by the RDA after a good deal of lobbying. The scheme was designed by landscape architects LDA Design with the objective of encouraging as many of the forecast 3 million visitors a year to Gloucester Quays to make their way into the city centre. The sea of tarmac around the Docks was replaced by quality Forest of Dean stone. Inspired by GHURC's Public Art Strategy, 'A Place for Art', two major pieces of public art were added at either end of Kimbrose Steps. One, a 23m tall piece called 'The Candle' was a tribute to Ivor Gurney, with his words engraved on the base, and was installed in August 2010. The artist Wolfgang Buttress said, "My idea was to create a focal point within the scheme which lined up with prominent sightlines on various entrances and vistas. It seemed that a tall structure would be appropriate but I did not want it to dominate the space."

The other, 'St Kyneburgh's Tower' by Tom Price, told the story of what Price described as "one of the city's little known but most captivating legends". It told of a Saxon Princess who wished to devote herself to God and remain a virgin; to avoid an arranged marriage she fled to Gloucester and worked as a maid for a baker. The baker's wife, jealous of the young woman, killed her and threw her body into a well near the city's South Gate. Her body was recovered and buried nearby. Miracles began to be reported at her graveside, and when the relics were moved, the miracles followed them. The well became known as St Kyneburgh's Fountain, a place of pilgrimage famous for its supposed healing powers. St Kyneburgh's chapel was built there and later converted in the 16th Century into almshouses by Sir Thomas Bell, who ran a cap factory at the nearby Blackfriars Priory after its dissolution. The structure was designed to replicate the well and if you look up when you're at the bottom of it, that's what it feels like. There was also an accompanying 'art wall' in a similar style, running along the line of the city wall.

Tom Price said, "Depending on the position of the viewer, both works change dramatically in appearance, drawing people towards the square from the Docks and city centre."[166]

The two projects cost £200,000 and, as most pieces of public art do, attracted some controversy. I think both look pretty good. Some of the submissions I saw for the Kimbrose Square piece would have been far more controversial! That didn't stop The Candle being nicknamed 'The Kebab' or 'The Rusty Needle' and St Kyneburgh's Tower being known by the locals as 'The CD Rack'! I commented when the designs were revealed that "Public art is often subjective and can cause controversy and sometimes that is when it is best."[167] There are tacks on the lower levels of Tower – to discourage seagulls settling on it as well as daredevils and drunks from climbing it.

In total, four new routes to link the Quays, Docks and city centre were devised, but only route one through Kimbrose Triangle was ever implemented due to funding constraints. I always argued that we wanted Gloucester to be a "single cohesive destination" and saw the linkages project as being key to this. Route 1 of the linkages project was approved by the City Council's Planning Committee in July 2009, despite several objections and concerns, including about the loss of coach parking, introduction of 'pleached' trees and access to the Court building and the Soldiers of Gloucestershire Museum.

The plans involved the loss of 95 car parking spaces alongside the Victoria basin but it was felt there was sufficient parking capacity in the city centre. That same month, City MP Parmjit Dhanda told a Westminster debate that the linkages were "absolutely crucial". Business Minister Rosie Winterton responded that the Government needed to be sure of value for money. The Government gave the go-ahead in October 2009. Parmjit Dhanda thanked Peter (now Lord) Mandelson who had returned from being a Trade Commissioner in Brussels to become Business Secretary. It was getting close to what Dhanda acknowledged would be a difficult election for Labour and no doubt this helped him to secure the funding. Work got underway in April 2010. Traffic would no longer go around Kimbrose Triangle. Llanthony Bridge became closed to all bar buses, cycles and taxis, but old habits die hard (and satnavs take a while to update) and 16,000 drivers were fined for their transgression, providing a £500,000 windfall for the County Council but upsetting a lot of residents and visitors in the process.

County Council Leader Mark Hawthorne was successfully lobbied by fellow councillor Terry Hale, who represented Coleford, to use local Forest of Dean stone from the Bixslade Quarry in his electoral division on the highways section of the project. Previously materials had been shipped in from other parts of the UK and as far afield China. In all 4500 sqm of the stone was used.

County Councillors Terry Hale and Mark Hawthorne overseeing the use of Forest of Dean stone in the linkages project. Credit: Terry Hale

Greyfriars

The URC also deserves some credit for the eventual regeneration of the GlosCAT site at Greyfriars in Brunswick Road, which included the smaller media campus site opposite the library/museum. The site was acquired by the Government's regeneration agency English Partnerships in 2004 for a "very full" figure, believed to be in the order of £9 million. It was acquired both to enable the relocation of the campus to Llanthony Road as part of the Gloucester Quays development and to repopulate the city centre with a diverse and stable community in properties of a bigger size and higher specification than the market alone would have delivered. The original developers selected were Bristol-based Edward Ware Homes, who were appointed after a national marketing process which began in May 2007, but they couldn't agree final terms and their scheme didn't progress. The scheme would have included a host of low carbon measures including biomass combined heat and power, solar heating and water saving features.

They were replaced by Linden Homes, who were the 'underbidder', in January 2009. In January 2013, Linden applied to have the share of affordable housing reduced from 25% to 12.5% because of viability issues. GHURC supported the change and the City Centre Community Partnership (CCCP) "reluctantly" backed it. It was a challenging site with the city's Roman wall running along the front of the main campus and Roman burials uncovered on the media site.

Agreeing the design of the scheme wasn't straightforward. The original masterplan for English Partnerships was put together by John Thompson & Partners. English Partnerships had told Terence O'Rourke to 'keep off' Greyfriars when they drew up the Regeneration Framework, so the masterplan devised by John Thompson & Partners was used in the Framework document.

Linden brought in architects Stride Treglown to review the scheme. They came up with a diagonal route, which was counter to the orthogonal grid of Gloucester. New Masterplanning (a consultancy set up by Geraint Hughes and Andy Ward, formerly of Terence O'Rourke) were brought in to the review scheme with council officers Mick Thorpe and Matt Haslam. They felt there was not enough car parking. The idea of car parking under landscaped decked gardens, which was eventually used, came from Rotterdam.

The architecture for the scheme is, in my view, bland and uninspiring but it wasn't for the want of trying to get something better. As happens with such schemes, the design changed over time. It started off with a single building to the front to reflect the original college building. It ended up with three blocks to allow phasing (otherwise too many apartments would come to the market at the same time) and vehicle access between them. Stride Treglown had wanted to use Portland stone but this was dropped, presumably for reasons of cost, in favour of brick.

Keith Bradley and Mike Keyse of architects Feilden Clegg Bradley came in to design the detailed scheme. Their design principle was based on the villas around Gloucester Park and terraces from other parts of the city. The building on the corner of Parliament Street had to relate to the terraced houses there and turn the corner to the big blocks fronting Brunswick Road, which was a challenge, but which appears to have been addressed successfully. The project was shortlisted for the National Urban Design Award 2012.

The scheme had been looked at by the URC's Design Review Panel between April 2008 and February 2011. The Design Review Panel was chaired by Cheltenham solicitor and GHURC Board Member Antonia Shield who had studied for an MA in Architectural History at Edinburgh University before turning to law. In the end Linden lost patience and drew a line (which is what some people said the architects had done!) in February 2011, saying they were "not prepared to incur further fees" by amending the design. Whatever your views on the quality of the architecture, the development has helped to repopulate the city centre with a truly mixed community and provided a much better setting for the Greyfriars monument than the former GlosCAT Tower Block (remember that?). The nine-storey Tower was demolished in February 2011 as the site became increasingly derelict and its presence on the city centre skyline was not missed.[168]

The City Council's Greater Greyfriars Planning Brief had expressed a preference for retaining the main college building and for retaining trees wherever possible. There was a campaign to save the 1941 college frontage[169], with pressure on English Heritage to list it in 2006. English Heritage declined, with their evaluation of the building stating that it was a "relatively uninspired design" and "lacks architectural distinction". The Civic Trust called it a "missed opportunity" to create a "landmark development", describing the flat blocks as "too monolithic, repetitive and minimalist", urging that planning permission be refused because the "architecture is unworthy and pays no respect to its historic surroundings". The Linden Homes application was approved by the City Council's Planning Committee in November 2011. The developer had considered alternative uses for conversion – residential, office, hotel, restaurant, healthcare and manufacturing. Their analysis predicted a negative return on sales of between 10-40%. Linden's scheme delivered 254 homes – 183 on the main campus site at Greyfriars and 71 on the media campus site. Of these, 176 were apartments and 78 houses.

The Homes and Communities Agency's involvement meant there was a restriction of 25% on the number of units that could be 'bought to let'. Other developments, including the Docks, had seen huge numbers of properties bought for that purpose, crowding out owner occupiers with a strong stake in the community. Insiders tell me that English Partnerships (renamed the Homes and Communities Agency) didn't see any of its land acquisition money back, but delivering the regeneration made it a worthwhile investment.

The development on the main campus site was called Friars Orchard. This was previously the site of The Crypt School and I was pleased that Linden Homes, during its marketing, named some of the apartments 'Williams' (after The Crypt's former headmaster D. G. Williams) and 'Invictus' (after Old Cryptian W. E. Henley's most famous poem).

There was a planning condition that the college building's bronze doors should be retained and used within the new development, which they have been, plus the city coat of arms and planters if possible (which were put in storage at the Council's depot on Eastern Avenue). English Heritage said the demolition was justified. A survey by the City Centre Community Partnership showed that 79% supported demolition only if it was replaced by a high-quality design. Planning Officer Adam Smith described it as "an appropriate form, well designed but not overly elaborate" which would "defer to the attractive listed library building." The Council's Urban Design and Conservation Officers both judged that the positives of removing the Technical College building outweighed the negatives.

Another controversial element of the scheme was the proposed removal of a 60-year-old Dawn Redwood tree on site. A petition of 1239 signatures was organised by Janet Illingworth-Cooper, who was also one of the leading campaigners to save the bandstand in Gloucester Park. The petition was somewhat undermined by some of its signatories being from Stonehouse, Dursley, Cheltenham, Malvern, Bristol and even Cornwall. Retaining the tree was resisted because of the implications for the design and layout of the scheme, for insuring the buildings and the stability of the tree after removing the surrounding buildings. Additional planting around the site and a contribution of £12,471 for off-site planting was agreed as part of the planning conditions.

Both GlosCAT sites were sensitive from a historic point of view. The main campus site covered 10% of the walled city. The archaeology there had already been impacted by the construction of the existing college buildings, notably the tower and the basement of the technical college building and former air raid shelter where complete destruction is likely to have taken place.[170]

The media site included a large Roman cemetery and approximately 240 bodies were discovered in what was the biggest excavation in Gloucester for some decades. There was also evidence of a large medieval hall and of Roman light industry such as pottery, kilns etc (hence it was named Kiln Close). City Archaeologist Andrew Armstrong described it as "the most extreme excavation in a long time."

A new public square was created near Priory Place, improving the setting of the adjacent remains of Greyfriars Priory. Both the new square and the grassed area to the front of the site, which runs along the line of the city wall, included some new (and difficult to understand) public art.

The vacant media campus was set on fire in August 2011, as rioting which started in London spread to other parts of the country. The blaze was quickly extinguished and the building was soon to be demolished anyway.

The GlosCAT tower – a sight not missed from Gloucester city centre's skyline. Credit: Litchfield Morris/GHURC

One of the early designs for the Brunswick Road frontage of the Greyfriars development. Credit: Stride Treglown Architects

Simon Gait, Land Director at Linden Homes, was full of praise for GHURC's role in enabling the Greyfriars development, describing the company as being "instrumental in bringing to a conclusion" discussions and negotiations, adding that he believed "without them our project would not be going ahead."

The development was finished and all of the units sold in 2019.

The Four Gates Centre

The main community project from the GHURC days was the Westgate Neighbourhood Centre or the Four Gates Centre as it became known, which was to be built on the GlosCAT media campus site on Brunswick Road opposite the City Museum and Library. The City Council owned a small piece of land behind it known as the 'H Car Park' (presumably H for Hampden Way) and agreed to hand it over for the development.[171] SWRDA had agreed to contribute £2.5 million later but withdrew.

The plans included the relocation of the GP surgery from Rikenel as well as advice on jobs, education and training, access to computers, activities for young and old, meeting rooms, childcare and translation services. The Shopmobility service, which was based nearby, would also be incorporated. Barry Leach of the City Centre Community Partnership and Lizzie Abderrahim, who became Chair of the Westgate Community Trust, were among the community leaders behind the plan, supported by City Council Officer Andrew Maliphant.

Gloucester architects Quattro were appointed to come up with plans.[172] The feasibility study and business plan were completed in March 2009.[173] The scheme was reported to cost £5.7 million.[174]

SWRDA announced "revised investment priorities" in May 2009 and withdrew funding from the scheme. As a result, the City Council put the land deal on hold in July 2009 and sadly the project was abandoned. It was still hoped to relocate the doctors' surgery from Rikenel, but agreement couldn't be reached despite what Linden Homes described as "extensive but unsuccessful attempts".[175] In the end, a new block of apartments was built in its place, with commercial units on the ground floor and 200 sqm of community space, for which planning permission was approved in December 2016.

The Railway Triangle

The Railway Triangle was another long-term derelict site, which people thought would stay that way forever. It had been like this for so long, the reasons for its condition seem lost in the midst of time, but the GHURC Regeneration Framework provides a useful explanation, saying:

"The open, agricultural nature of the land in this area and its proximity to Gloucester made it an ideal place to build the first railway station in 1840, connecting Gloucester with Birmingham. Large sidings were constructed north and south of the main station and a rail link was built through Spa Field park to the Docks. Unfortunately, however, the original siting of the station meant that the lines from both Bristol and Birmingham entered the station from the same direction, so that trains had to wait in Gloucester while the locomotive was moved to the other end, before setting off again.

"The problem of the awkward siting of Gloucester station was partly overcome by the construction of a loop line, which joined the northern and southern railway lines some distance east of the station, missing the station out entirely. This allowed freight traffic and express trains to bypass Gloucester station and travel direct between Bristol and Birmingham. This loop line created a triangle of railway land, cut off from all directions, which became used for sidings.

"The decline in rail freight traffic in the 1950s and 1960s led to a decline in the use of the sidings, many of which were taken up. The considerable space they occupied to the north and south of the station has been used for commercial purposes and enabled the construction of Metz Way to relieve pressure on Barton Street."

The Railway Triangle was overgrown, contaminated, difficult to access and presented a poor image of the city for people arriving by train or heading in from Eastern Avenue. The land was owned by Network Rail (formerly Railtrack) and the County Council had a 'ransom strip' controlling access from Metz Way. Councillor Andrew Gravells wrote in a Council question that its appearance was like a 'time warp' and Citizen Editor Ian Mean had described it, perhaps in questionable taste, as being like Hiroshima. In April

2000, Citizen columnist Paula Smith suggested that it "looks as if it's waiting for someone to film an 'After Armageddon' epic on it". In a Youtube video in August 2012, Richard Graham MP likened it to "Yugoslavia during the civil war".

The northern part of the Railway Triangle had been allocated for industrial development in the Council's Local Plan since 1983. Like so many of the city's challenging development sites, the site has seen various schemes come and go. *The Citizen* published a timeline of previous schemes on 6th August 2010.

In 1996, owner Railtrack offered the site to developers for a business park. In 1997, there was a £16 million cinema-led leisure scheme with bars, restaurants and nightclubs. Jamie Noble, who was involved in the ultimately successful scheme with his company Tabacon, was at the time working for Morrison Developments, who were a leisure and retail developer. They were part of the same group as the utilities contractor rather than the supermarket giant of the same name. They won a tender with Railtrack for the leisure scheme, which was due to be anchored by an Odeon cinema and Hollywood Bowl tenpin bowling alley. Odeon 'switched horses' to back the Docks site referred to in Chapter 3. Without an anchor, the developer struggled to make it happen and then the leisure market took a downturn. Morrison had a draft contract with Railtrack but in the circumstances it lapsed.

In July 2000, there was the suggestion the site could be used for waste treatment. It was allocated in the County Council's Waste Local Plan 2002-12 (which was adopted in October 2004), which suggested it could be the site for a Waste to Energy facility i.e. an incinerator. City MP Parmjit Dhanda was pictured on the front page of *The Citizen* protesting against this and wrote to 2000 local residents as late as August 2009 to encourage them to sign a petition objecting. A row ensued between Dhanda and Mark Hawthorne, then the County Council's Cabinet Member for the Environment and later its Leader. Hawthorne complained that the MP had broken Commons rules on the use of prepaid postage and stationery. Dhanda stood by his claim that the County Council were considering the Triangle as the site for a ten-storey incinerator – which in the end went to Javelin Park near Junction 12 of the M5.

In January 2001, there were proposals for a new rail freight depot. In January 2002, there were rumours IKEA were eyeing up the site and, in February 2003, there were the first of many calls for a new mainline station.

In 2003, Jamie Noble's Tabacon teamed up with Nick Alford and his company LXB. LXB was formed by the management of Grantchester when their management buyout plans failed and the company was bought by Hammerson (see Chapter 6). LXB was backed by HBOS (Halifax Bank of Scotland), Sir Tom Hunter (at one time Scotland's richest man) and Baugur (an Icelandic company who owned Hamleys, Karen Millen and other retailers, which collapsed in wake of the 2008 financial crash).

In January 2005, Costco and Wickes were reported as potential tenants. Although there was strong interest from both, they couldn't get Costco over the line before their option with Network Rail expired. Planning policy made out of town retail more difficult too. They managed to persuade Network Rail to renew the option but Costco didn't sign up and the scheme took a different direction. Demonstrating how long it sometimes takes to land a new business, it wasn't until July 2023 that it was announced that Costco was coming to Gloucester, to the former Interbrew site on Eastern Avenue.

As well as challenges with contamination and access and the cost of putting services into the site, the viability of any scheme was made more difficult by Network Rail wanting a 'strong' price for the site, in the end believed to be £6.5 million. This was despite development of the site giving them the benefit of access to their remaining operational land.

In January 2006, the Urban Regeneration Company unveiled plans for a 20,000 seat multi-use community stadium, which would have been shared by Gloucester Rugby and Gloucester City Football Club. It would have included a new hotel, conference, educational and community facilities and 445 beds of student accommodation. Both Gloucester Rugby's Kingsholm Stadium and the Football Club's Meadow Park ground would be sold to help finance the project. Kingsholm was allocated for residential development in the draft of the City Plan at the time.

GHURC's funders, the Homes and Communities Agency and SWRDA, were expected to contribute to the cost. A report by surveyors Donaldsons endorsing the stadium proposal was approved by the GHURC Board in January 2007. The idea had some practical problems, not least of which was that Gloucester Rugby regularly sold out their 16,000-capacity stadium at Kingsholm whereas Gloucester City FC rattled around with a crowd of just a few hundred at Meadow Park. The stadium followed the City of Manchester Stadium model, whereby it would be owned by the Council and leased to the Clubs. I had my doubts whether Gloucester Rugby's then owner, Formula One tycoon Tom Walkinshaw, would really relocate to a stadium he didn't own. In the end, that's what broke the deal. I remember questioning Ken Nottage, the Club's long-serving MD, at a GHURC board meeting on that very point. GHURC Chair and Chief Executive, Greg Smith and Chris Oldershaw, arranged to have lunch with Nottage and Walkinshaw, who was due to fly in for the meeting, to agree a way forward. I'm told that Walkinshaw didn't show. Shortly after, in April 2007, the Club confirmed their intention to stay at their 'spiritual home' at Kingsholm.

So, it was back to the drawing board. In May 2007, the GHURC Board considered a report with a long list of ideas including a convention centre, a medical science and innovation park, a demonstration sustainable community project, eco excellent homes and even a snow dome!

The Citizen reported in September 2007 that the plan was now for 400 eco-homes, a medical-based science park, conference centre and urban park.[176] There would be an urban greenway linking Armscroft Park and Gloucester Railway Station.[177]

As ever, there was no shortage of consultants willing to give their opinion in exchange for a handsome fee. In February 2008, GVA Grimley were appointed to prepare a masterplan. In November 2008, it was 'peer reviewed' by another set of consultants, Aecom. A medi-science park and residential were still the favoured use but now 800 new homes and 6000 sqm of commercial space were proposed. This included the Great Western Road sidings and the land occupied by Allstone Sand & Gravel.

Allstone operates a waste and recycling business, including skip hire and a waste transfer station, as well as the supply of sand, gravel and aggregates. They are one of the most successful privately-owned businesses in the city. The Allstone landholdings were removed from the masterplan at the instruction of the company in April 2009. That year, Allstone also outsmarted other parties by acquiring a parcel of adjacent land from the British Rail Property Board that GHURC and its partners had hoped to buy. There have been complaints from some neighbours over the years about the impact of their operations, but the company would argue that they comply with all regulatory requirements and work with local residents to mitigate any issues. There has been talk about the business relocating for some years, but the scale, nature and success of their operation means it is difficult to find another suitable site. They were granted outline planning consent for 200 homes and 200 units of student accommodation on their site in April 2017, but the consent has not been implemented to date.

By the time the masterplan was approved by the URC Board in July 2010 and went public in August 2010, the figures had been revised to 360 homes, including 309 townhouses. The plans also included the health innovation centre, allotment space, tennis courts, retail areas and business premises. It totalled 30 acres and the plan was an estimated £65 million development. It was hoped the Homes and Communities Agency would fund the 'viability gap' for the housing element of the scheme.

GHURC Chief Executive Chris Oldershaw said, "This has always been a challenging site but now we have a scheme that makes sense for the city and for which there are already expressions of interest from the private sector." It was estimated that the scheme would take 5-7 years to deliver. City MP Richard Graham said, "This was one of the issues I campaigned on. The Triangle has stood untouched for the past 13 years. We need it to improve the city psychologically as much as anything." I added that this was "one of the city's biggest eyesores and has been for a long time. It is one of the main gateways into the city, so it is a symbolic piece of regeneration that we want to see happen as soon as possible."[178]

Richard Graham campaigned on regenerating the Railway Triangle prior to being elected as Gloucester's MP and LXB's Nick Alford said he was a good advocate for it. LXB weren't convinced that housing was the right answer for their site within the 'Greater Railway Triangle'. Alongside the railway isn't perhaps the best place to live, but plenty of people do. The City Council's Environmental Health team had concerns about the prospect, citing noise and pollution. A stand-off ensued but, in the end, the private sector delivered its own solution.

In February 2011, it was revealed that LXB had signed up Morrisons, the supermarket giant, to anchor a scheme which would be made up of a number of other commercial units. Alford told me that they landed Morrisons in a 'sweet spot', signing them up for a rent believed to be £1 million a year. It was suggested that even a year later they probably wouldn't have committed to the deal. Coming at a time when new supermarkets were springing up all over the city, it wasn't viewed as too exciting a prospect. But, crucially, it was deliverable. I defended the plan publicly, as did City MP Richard Graham, including one radio interview from a London hotel foyer when I was up in the Capital for an event the night before. The proposal gained support in varying degrees. Richard Graham said: "Some of the schemes proposed in the past have been too ambitious and too dependent on government funds." Chris Oldershaw appeared to be underwhelmed, saying it was "an interesting proposal" and the URC "would assess whether it can deliver the city's ambitions." I gave the proposal a cautious welcome as more suitable for the site than housing.

A determined and passionate band of people were publicly campaigning against the proposals and in favour of a new mainline railway station. I had some sympathy with this idea, but Network Rail weren't in favour "primarily because of the implications for the timetable" and were keen to get the receipt from selling the land. Nobody knew what the impact would be on the Gloucester Central station. Additional land in third party ownership would be needed. And there was no money available to build a new station. I said in *The Citizen* that it "just isn't going to happen".[179] The Office of the Rail Regulator said in a letter that there was "no evidence that the disposal would affect adversely existing or future railway operations." They added that "although Gloucester Chamber of Commerce suggested the land could site a new station, Network Rail considered it was not practical, the Department of Transport's preferred site is at Elmbridge and the train operators had no view."

A petition with 382 signatures was submitted. Former planning officer and Liberal Democrat councillor David Evans, representing the Gloucester Railway Action Group, spoke in favour of a new four platform station in the North East apex of the Railway Triangle. Gordon Doyle said there was a need to improve railway services. There were comments including "Gloucester does not need another supermarket", that it "will suck money out of the local economy" and "Gloucester needs a mainline station." It was presented as though it was a choice between a supermarket and a new railway station. But a new station wasn't on offer.

There were other concerns too. Elmbridge councillor Sue Witts was worried about flooding in the Armscroft area. The scheme included flood retention at Armscroft Park and bridge replacement at Blinkhorns Bridge Lane. Dr Colin Studholme, of Gloucestershire Wildlife Trust, wanted a better deal for wildlife as there were bats, badgers, common lizards and slow worms present on the site.

On the positive side, Nick Alford argued that the development would support 1000 jobs. The submission was a full application for the foodstore and an outline for the rest of development. It was argued that the foodstore supported the employment uses, which would be unable to meet the 'abnormal costs' (like decontamination and constructing an access) on their own. Planning Officers commented that an "innovative and interesting approach to buildings had not been achieved" but believed public art could deliver this. The developers were required to contribute £40,000 to public art, but the railway track themed piece of art which was installed adjacent to Morrisons largely goes unnoticed.

Despite the furious lobbying, the Planning Committee held their nerve and approved the plans, including the supermarket, meeting on 1st December 2011 and reconvening on 6th December before the application was referred to the National Planning Casework Unit. The application was considered alongside the plans for a much bigger Tesco store at St Oswalds (see Chapter 6).

A temporary access had to be built from Metz Way for construction traffic and tonnes of stone were imported for the foundations. Local firm Smiths undertook the site clearance and Gloucester's Barnwood Construction built the supermarket. Morrisons opened in November 2013 and although trade was slow at first, it built gradually. It was later joined by Rygor, a

Mercedes commercial vehicle dealer (for which work started in January 2016), a Costa Coffee drive-thru (inevitably!) a tanning salon and a gaudy bright orange Lok'n'Store self-storage building, which somehow made it through the Planning Committee without dissent.

In April 2013, when the application to name the new access road crossed my desk I dismissed the suggestion of Turntable Way (which I thought sounded like a record player). The public put forward ideas like Awdry Way (after the creator of Thomas the Tank Engine who lived near Stroud) and even Chugalong Way which were rejected. The safe option of Triangle Way was chosen.

The site is now largely completed. Plans for a pub to be built by the Spirit Pub Company came to nothing after the company got taken over by Greene King in 2015. After some legal wrangling, this part of the site was bought back by the developers and sold to the Bennetts coach company.

In 2018, developer Rockhaven started to build a speculative development of 22 industrial units on part of the site. Tenants included Bikini Bathrooms, who relocated from the City Business Centre opposite Llanthony Priory to enable the widening of the South West Bypass, and Gloucester Rugby legend Andy Hazell's Smart Home Sounds business, which opened a new showroom in April 2022.

On a lighter note, Nick Alford told me how he tries to keep a memento of each of the developments he has built. Amongst the rubbish dumped on the Railway Triangle over the years was a crushed car. Alford identified it as a Hillman Imp (his first car) from the gearstick knob – and kept it as his "special knob".

In December 2021, it was revealed that Eutopia Homes had bought the eight-acre Great Western Road sidings site for residential development and in May 2022 they held a public consultation on their proposals for 300 homes, which were a mix of terraced houses and apartments. The development is estimated to have a value of £70 million. Initial soundings appeared to indicate that city planners were more positive about residential development in this location than they had been when it was first proposed by GHURC. The proposals were approved by the Council's Planning Committee in February 2023.

The Railway Triangle in its derelict state before redevelopment.

Other projects

The Canal Corridor was perhaps the least high profile of the 'Magnificent Seven'. The GHURC prospectus of 2006 identifies it as a site for family and affordable housing. It also proposed that the canal should be upgraded as a competitive rowing venue.

The main focus for GHURC was a large former industrial site on Bristol Road and land at Monk Meadow, on the western side of the canal, which would both make a significant contribution to the company's target for delivering new homes.

The Contract Chemicals/St Gobain site, which also took in the former Simon Barron factory and the adjoining Van Moppes IDP site which was accessed from Tuffley Crescent, was known as the 'Three Factories' site. After protracted negotiations between the different landowners, an application for 340 homes was submitted in April 2007 and approved in January 2009. It was developed by Matthew Homes over a number of years. Mainly due to the costs of decontamination the scheme didn't provide any affordable housing.

The western side of the canal was successfully developed for housing, inbetween the canal and the south west bypass, although some of the planning applications for this development pre-dated the GHURC. The main developers were Bloor Homes, Linden Homes and Crest Nicholson. Plans for a Hungry Horse pub and eatery caused a storm amongst residents, who were concerned about noise and traffic generation, and were refused in January 2012.

The vision of a mirrored development on the eastern side (which would include parts of the Madleaze Trading Estate and the Mill Place Industrial Estate) has yet to be realised, although may still happen in the longer term.

The URC became involved in a proposal for a Business Improvement District (where businesses pay a levy on top of their business rates which is put into a pot to be used for specific projects in the area) along Bristol Road, which had been developed by Gloucestershire First and their 'Parklife' project on the Madleaze Trading Estate. The Canal Corridor Partnership was formed and supported by local businessmen including Dave Pedrette of Target Catering Equipment and Paul Ford of Peter Ford Transport. They pledged that a Canal Corridor BID would lobby for improvements, introduce a collective purchasing scheme, undertake marketing, cleaning, clearing of flytipping, landscaping improvements, security and crime prevention, such as CCTV and Automatic Number Plate Recognition. Former Gloucester rugby player Fred Reed was brought in as Project Manager.

Some businesspeople, including Westley Fry, who owned a number of properties in the area, were vehemently against the idea. A ballot was held on 6th August 2009. Only 28 (17%) voted in favour, with 137 (83%) against – one of the worst results for any BID proposal in the country.

Winding Down

The URC's job wasn't done by any means, but its future was under threat. The new Coalition Government elected in 2010 was determined to get the public sector budget deficit under control and both the RDA (who had been given advance notice of their impending demise as part of the Government's 'bonfire of the quangos') and the HCA both withdrew their funding. This just left the City and County Councils to pick up the tab to keep a slimmed-down company going. Staffing numbers were trimmed from 10 to 4 in October 2010.

There were fears that in the rush to 'pay down the deficit' there would be a 'fire sale' of RDA assets. I commented, "The assets acquired by SWRDA in Gloucester were bought for a good reason. They are important pieces of the regeneration jigsaw in the city. A fire sale would risk us having to buy them back at a greater cost in the future." I wrote to Business Secretary Greg Clark following a conversation I had with him at a Downing Street reception when my resolve had been stiffened by a couple of glasses of wine, calling for "clarity and urgency".

I told the BBC website in March 2011, "Despite the fact that times are difficult, we see the regeneration of the city as one of our top priorities. It is right that we should put the lion's share of our efforts and resources into what we feel is important - and the people in this city think is important too."

In April 2011, the City Council acquired the RDA's assets in Gloucester for a knock-down price which reflected the negative value of The Fleece hotel site. The package included the Docks headlease, Albion Cottages, the Southgate Moorings car park, 23-29 Commercial Road (all at the Docks) and The Fleece, with the deal being that all of the income would be 'ring-fenced' to support regeneration in the city.

The URC was eventually disbanded at the end of March 2013, despite a campaign to keep Chris Oldershaw employed. He continued as part-time Chief Executive of Marketing Gloucester for a few months but decided not to apply when it was advertised as a permanent appointment. He went off to work as a consultant for surveyors Bruton Knowles and did some consultancy work, including in the Forest of Dean, before quietly retiring. In his overview in the final GHURC report, he said the GHURC journey had seen high points but disappointments as well, noting that "as a regeneration professional you have to accept these knock backs." Duncan Innes of English Partnerships was Director of a number of URCs and said this was one of the better ones – with a "cohesive plan and some early wins". He felt it was a "well-run, well thought through operation."

Although the URC was wound up earlier than expected, it had made good progress in delivering the output targets agreed with the Government. Over £600 million had been invested in the URC area, with another £200 million in the pipeline. Collectively SWRDA and the HCA had invested over £50 million. Other key outputs included creating over 1000 jobs, nearly 80,000 sq ft of commercial floorspace, over 37 hectares of land reclaimed and nearly 1000 houses built.

The City Council created a 'Regeneration Advisory Board' chaired by the Very Reverend Stephen Lake, the Dean of Gloucester Cathedral. As a man of the cloth, Stephen could say things that other people couldn't – including politely telling councillors they had said enough!

When the Regeneration Advisory Board was formed Dean Stephen said, "This cathedral city is unique and can be more so. So much has been achieved and there is much to do. Acting as an advisory group to the Council, I hope we can help maintain momentum and provide honest-brokerage between all interested parties so that Gloucester can be great."[180]

URC Chair and Vice Chair Greg Smith and Ian Mean were awarded The Freedom of the City for their efforts. In my speech in the Council meeting when their award was approved, I described them as "The Laurel and Hardy of Gloucester's regeneration" with a "good cop, bad cop" approach but noted that "they hadn't got us into a fine mess, they'd got us out of one". I added, tongue firmly in cheek, that "We've never had a Citizen editor like Ian Mean before. In the past they would keep themselves to themselves, but Ian soon overcame his natural shyness."

Momentum from GHURC's work kept going for years. In its final report, former City MP Parmjit Dhanda said, "It raised the city's confidence and self-esteem". His successor Richard Graham added, "The crucial thing is for this period of GHURC not to be seen as some golden phase in the past – but a stimulus to great successes of the future."

Colin Haylock, President of the Royal Town Planning Institute, wrote, "What impressed me was the ambition and clarity of the strategy which you had been working with…which has literally and visibly linked the very varied aspects of the city."

Colin Molton, who had chaired those fractious early meetings, looked back and reflected, saying "The impressive results are there for all to see". My own reflection was as follows, "Perhaps the most valuable legacy that GHURC is leaving the Council is investor confidence in the city and it is this which has enabled regeneration to continue when in many other towns and cities it has stalled."

Chief Executive Chris Oldershaw commented that, "The path of regeneration is seldom straightforward and the last eight years has been a 'rollercoaster' ride of emotions." He told me that the lessons learned include:

- The importance of broad-based independent partnerships between public & private sectors
- The value of strong and visible leadership, particularly from the Chair and Vice Chair
- Coherent yet flexible regeneration strategies to help build up investor confidence
- The importance of a dedicated and multi-skilled project team
- The need to maintain momentum, even when faced with a major recession.

In many ways, we can look back on the GHURC period as some of the best years of Gloucester's regeneration and many felt that its time being cut short was to the detriment of the city. We will never know what else might have been achieved if the company had been allowed to see out its full term.

10. DETERMINATION, PERSEVERANCE AND PATIENCE

The Story of Gloucester Quays

It's easy to forget what the area south of Llanthony Road used to be like. The shiny and still relatively new outlet centre and leisure quarter that stands there today were preceded by low value and, in many cases, derelict buildings. Car repair businesses and other commercial and industrial uses were the norm, plus The Weavers Shop carpet warehouse, now located in Eastern Avenue, and Cooks Glass. West of the canal there was Hayes Metals and Keyway, Rutherford Skip Hire, Hobbs Oil, Hempsted Breakers and the Monk Meadow Trading Estate with a landmark seven storey grain silo. Numold, manufacturers of precast concrete moulds in Merchants Road, sits there today as an island amongst the chain restaurants and cinema and seems more than a bit out of place now. But prior to Gloucester Quays that's what it was all like – and nobody seemed too concerned about it. Numold supported the Gloucester Quays proposals but wanted to ensure that their site could be redeveloped for a mixture of uses to include retail, food and beverage, offices and residential, but, at the time of writing, no plans for that site had come forward – despite several approaches from Peel to acquire the buildings and a concept plan put together by architects Acanthus Ferguson Mann – the firm of former Mayor of Bristol, George Ferguson.

An arranged marriage?

Peel Holdings has been a landowner in the city for well over 30 years, at one point owning the Morelands Trading Estate on the former Match Factory in Bristol Road. It developed the Peel Centre retail park which was granted consent in April 1989, bringing Burger King, Toys R Us and a few other stores as well as housing the city's multiplex cinema when it relocated from The Regal in Kings Square (a move which was, in hindsight, to the detriment of the city centre).

Peel had been patiently assembling land in the area for years whilst simultaneously putting together a plan for how to develop it. The area to the east of the canal that we now know as Gloucester Quays was previously all known as Bakers Quay, whereas we now refer to Bakers Quay as the former West Midlands Farmers premises currently being developed by Rokeby Merchant. The major owner of land to the west of the canal was the British Waterways Board, who were also eyeing up plans for redevelopment.

The City Council put together a Planning Brief for Bakers Quay (Llanthony Road to St Ann Way) in 1990 and allocated it in the draft Local Plan for comprehensive development. The Local Plan allocation was for mixed use including offices, residential, leisure and car parking. The land in the area was largely owned by Peel, Carr-Speed Plastics and West Midlands Farmers. Peel put forward an office-based scheme but withdrew as others didn't want to sell. In 1997, they submitted an application for a Morrisons supermarket which wasn't decided but which would have been refused.

On the other side of the canal, British Waterways and developer Henry Boot lodged an application in 1997 for a mixed-use scheme on Monk Meadow and Llanthony Wharf including food and non-food retail, a petrol filling station, commercial and industrial accommodation, residential, a hotel and food and drink uses. This application was never determined before events moved on.

Peel and British Waterways came together because they realised the highways elements of their respective schemes wouldn't work without the completion of the South West bypass and a new bridge over the canal, where the infamous 'road to nowhere' was next to the Peel Centre. The Council wanted a comprehensive scheme for the area and encouraged the two parties to come together, which they agreed to do in 1998.

Peel were sceptical about whether it would ever happen with British Waterways. The original application was in joint names but they later created a limited liability partnership. They had to get approval from the BWB's sponsoring Government department (The Department for the Environment, Food and Rural Affairs or DEFRA) as well as the British Waterways Board themselves. It was unusual for them to put what were public assets into a joint venture. The British

Waterways land was deemed to be worth more than Peel's so the contributions were evened out with cash.

Peel's Development Director Lindsey Ashworth gave written evidence to the Environment, Food and Rural Affairs Select Committee, which scrutinised BWB's operations, in March 2008, saying: "Both our organisations in the nineties were struggling against an unwilling Council to develop our respective land holdings separately on opposite sides of this Canal. In 1999 we got together to form a partnership which initially was based on trust and latterly a Limited Liability Partnership.

"I cannot stress enough that 'Partnerships' is the only way forward to make things happen. Most of us are master of "something" but can't be master of "everything." We all have different skills and attributes to offer and the combination of these is the single ingredient that gives you the edge over others that you so much need in this highly competitive and complex world we live in."

I describe later in this chapter what has happened at what we now refer to as Bakers Quay. As mentioned above, the whole area between Llanthony Road and St Ann Way was known as Bakers Quay before the Gloucester Quays branding was created. The former West Midland Farmers buildings were included in the Peel/BWB planning application but were not developed by the partnership because of land ownership issues which I will cover later.

In 1994, there was a planning application for residential development of Provender Mill, Malthouse 2 and the former Dock workers' cottages in High Orchard Street (all part of what we now know as Bakers Quay). The application, which was approved, would deliver 51 two-bedroom and 67 one-bedroom flats and was lodged by Mill View Developments, a Liverpool-based company who specialised in the conversion of old mill buildings in the North West. It was a £5 million scheme and had the backing of English Heritage and the Civic Trust.

The Guinness Trust Housing Association were keen to be involved and the City Council was prepared to contribute £400,000 over two years. A bid for funding was submitted to the Government's Housing Corporation and Mill View met with English Partnerships to try to persuade them to offer a grant for the scheme. Before the plans were able to progress, West Midland Farmers instead sold the site to the local Bishop family in 1996.

I remember sitting in a meeting of City Council political group leaders, after the collapse of the Blackfriars scheme, and officers told us of the major Gloucester Quays proposal which was coming forward. When the planning application was submitted in March 2002, *The Citizen* broke the news with the front-page headline, "Britain's Biggest Factory Shops Village" and reported that the £200 million plan would bring 2000 jobs. Inevitably, the newspaper questioned whether these grand plans would be any different from the Blackfriars scheme, the new magistrates' court and the Docks leisure quarter, which had all come to nothing, but was optimistic that this time it would be different.

Decoupling the College

When Greg Smith arrived as Principal, the Gloucestershire College of Art & Technology (GlosCAT) was virtually bankrupt. It had been one of the biggest such colleges in the country. As described in the 'University Challenge' chapter, the higher education part split off from the College and merged with the Cheltenham and Gloucester College of Higher Education and, according to those involved, the majority of money went to the HE side. The remaining further education function of GlosCAT was made independent from the County Council. In advance of the handover, the County Council stopped spending money on the buildings.

The College's estate included around 50 wooden classrooms in the grounds. Space utilisation was calculated at 18%, well below the sector average. Smith told his governors that they had too many staff and too much space which was unfit for modern teaching. Because of differing levels disabled access was 'terrible' and IT 'in the dark ages'.

In order to start to get the finances back in order, Greg Smith had the unenviable task of making over 200 people redundant. They also needed to address the condition of their estate. They did consider one campus in Staverton to serve both Cheltenham and Gloucester but realised it was not doable because both the town and the city would want their own campus. In Cheltenham, they sold their valuable campus site in The Park area to Barratt Homes for what was described as a 'tidy sum' and built a new one at Princess Elizabeth Way, in one of the less upmarket areas of the town.

Gloucester was more difficult. The Brunswick Campus was life expired and far less valuable. The costs of demolishing the tower block would be substantial. The Governors warned Greg it wouldn't be easy and cautioned that "People will try to stop you". City Council Chief Executive Graham Garbutt asked to see Greg Smith and his Vice Principal for Estates, Jeremy Williamson, in his office at North Warehouse. An architect by background, as ever Garbutt had lots of drawings to hand. Garbutt took Smith and Williams to his large office window overlooking the Docks and said "This is where your new college will be".

GlosCAT started talking to British Waterways and Peel in 2000. In January 2001, *The Citizen* reported that "GlosCAT could be on the move" and looking for a new site in Gloucester.[181] A day later, a headline in the newspaper claimed that the Docks was "ideal for (the) new GlosCAT site". City Council Leader Kevin Stephens was quoted as saying, "We are aware of their aspirations and we have looked at several sites, particularly in and around the Docks".[182]

SWRDA had just become involved with the Docks and this provided an opportunity. They looked at a number of sites in the Docks, including Southgate Moorings. Greg Smith and Jeremy Williamson were summoned to a mysterious meeting with Peel's Lindsey Ashworth at a motorway service station. Peel had identified a 2.45-hectare site off Llanthony Road owned by British Waterways, known as Llanthony Wharf, which was within the red line of the Gloucester Quays plans. But British Waterways wanted residential value. The site was made up of a former tarpaulin works and a host of derelict asbestos-clad sheds. An explosion had blown asbestos all over the site, which later had to be hand-picked by demolition contractors, Smiths of Gloucester. The site was contaminated, but was big enough for GlosCAT's needs. Another potential obstacle was that the city planners wanted to list the former tarpaulin works close to Llanthony Priory, a late Victorian red brick building. However, English Heritage were comfortable with demolishing it. The site was heavily-used by drugtakers and before construction could begin, the first job was to remove hundreds of needles.

Having found a site, there was the small matter of securing the £38 million of funding needed for the project. Greg Smith and Jeremy Williamson, assisted by City MP Parmjit Dhanda, took a direct approach to lobbying ministers. Further Education Funding Council (FEFC) rules meant their contribution was limited to 35% of project costs, which often wasn't enough in less affluent areas. Williamson and Dhanda gave a presentation to Secretary of State for Education, Alan Johnson. This upset some within the FEFC who were quick to get on the phone to Smith, who had been on holiday when the meeting took place, afterwards. He recalls how he was "told off terribly" and was asked "What are you doing talking to Cabinet Members behind our backs?"

In June 2004, the Learning and Skills Council (LSC) agreed to award £15 million to the project. LSC Director Roger Crouch was a great champion for the project. The LSC required GlosCAT to take a £10.7m bank loan against future growth in student numbers. The rest of the money came from the sale of the Brunswick campus to the Government's regeneration agency, English Partnerships. The College leased back the Brunswick campus for a peppercorn until the new Llanthony campus was ready.

At the time, I commented, "This news is important for the regeneration of Gloucester on a number of levels. First of all, it will help create a much better environment for learning for students in the city who, after all, will provide us with the workforce of the future.

"Secondly, having a concentration of students in the Docks will help give the area a buzz and a vibrancy. It will also help us make the most of Llanthony Priory which has been under-used for years and is surrounded by poor quality buildings at the moment.

"Finally, this will free up the land where the college is currently situated on Brunswick Road. Whatever use that is put to, it will help gel the city centre together even more."[183]

The other major challenge was ensuring the project could move ahead within the timescale required by the funders, particularly given that it was tied to the larger Gloucester Quays regeneration scheme. Peel and British Waterways were keen to leverage the benefits of a new college campus in support of their wider development. Some even said the College was a 'bargaining chip'. It became clear that the two timescales would no longer match and the College needed to move ahead more quickly. Enabling this to happen became known as 'decoupling' the College project.

Efforts to find a solution to the 'decoupling' issue were not immediately successful. In his book 'My Political Race', Parmjit Dhanda accused the City Council of being "flaky", claimed that "the Council stalled" and said "I could see everything slipping away".

He went on to describe how he had been on the phone to DEFRA Secretary Alun Michael from his holiday in Spain, with his "toes in the swimming pool" in an effort to find a solution. On his return he met with the British Waterways Chairman and Chief Executive, describing the latter as "difficult".

Dhanda called a meeting in Parliament, inviting Alun Michael, the Leaders of City and County Councils, Greg Smith and Jeremy Williamson and representatives of British Waterways, the Regional Development Agency and English Partnerships. John Prescott's Private Secretary was there taking notes. To add to the sense of drama, what was described as a 'semi-riot' was taking place outside in response to the Hunting Bill which was making its way through Parliament.

After several hours of deliberation an agreement was reached. Peel Chairman, John Whittaker put his hand on the shoulder of his Development Director Lindsey Ashworth and whispered in his ear. On this occasion, Whittaker deferred to Ashworth as his 'man on the ground'. Ashworth, who had a reputation as a 'hard man' looked at his Chairman and said "Go on then, we'll take a punt". Apparently, the Chief Executive of British Waterways was furious – presumably because he felt 'bounced' into a decision and didn't get the inflated value for the site that he wanted.

The RDA would pay £2.5 million for the site. English Partnerships agreed to pay for the bridge over the canal. Peel and British Waterways agreed to 'decouple' the College application and the City Council would do its best to 'fast-track' it. GHURC, the College, the RDA and Parmjit Dhanda would all write in support of the wider Gloucester Quays application.

This was seen as a 'key moment' and it was generally acknowledged that Parmjit Dhanda had 'played a blinder'. To celebrate, Dhanda and Greg Smith sank a fair few glasses of wine in Parliament's opulent Pugin Room.

The planning application for the new campus was submitted in May 2004 and approved in September of that year. It was amended by a later application approved by the Planning Committee in August 2005, with some elements relocated or reduced in size and some reconfiguration to enable the project to stay within budget.

To give an idea of scale, the building was 20,000 sqm - roughly the same size as the outlet centre that would follow nearby. As with any project of this size, there were issues to overcome along the way. The owners of the adjacent 125 Business Park threatened to challenge the planning application as they had not been served notice, due to the British Waterways ownership pack being wrong. The College's solicitors Burgess Salmon found a right of way in favour of the College site running across the Business Park, meaning Jeremy Williamson was able to negotiate away their objection. The College later bought the Business Park.

Construction giant McAlpine were appointed under a pre-construction contract. They came in within £0.5 million of budget but said they hadn't priced in the risk of contamination and wanted another £5 million. The design team at McAlpine believed it could be delivered within budget and several senior members of the team, who had worked on the project for 6-9 months, walked out. They took the project, lock, stock and barrel to Bovis Lendlease who employed them and won the contract, and then went on to build the first phase of Gloucester Quays. English Partnerships helped out with the costs of dealing with the contamination which ended up being closer to £175,000 than £5 million! Local firm, Smiths of Gloucester, carried out the decontamination works. Work started onsite in October 2005.

The archaeology onsite was dealt with very sensitively and protected. The City Archaeologist told me that investigations showed that previous suppositions were wrong. Llanthony Priory's church and cloisters are likely to be beneath what are now the College buildings, but in an area that had previously been damaged. It is also likely that they were damaged by the construction of the canal. The archaeologists worked from south to north on the site, but found that the archaeology suddenly stopped. An A5 pencil drawing found in the British Waterways archive showed that there had been another Dock on the northern part of the site, which had been dug by hand and then backfilled when trains rather than boats were seen to be the future of transport. The pile grid for the new College was adjusted, necessitating all kinds of recalculations, to avoid disturbing the archaeology. This approach was very different to when the Brunswick campus was built, when piles for the tower block were drilled through a Roman villa 'like Swiss cheese'.

The new campus opened in June 2007 and was officially opened by Secretary of State for Innovation, Universities and Skills John Denham. The blue cladding on the building, which was apparently suggested by the city planners, was a bit of a shock to some, including College bosses themselves, although they said they "didn't get as much grief as expected". Apparently, the City's Labour MP Parmjit Dhanda, presumably as a joke, complained that it should have been red!

The influx of students making their way through the Docks to the new campus certainly helped bring a vibrancy to the area and apparently made the recently-opened Subway counter inside the Barge Arm convenience store one of the busiest in the country! It also strengthened the case for Llanthony Bridge to be closed to traffic due to the 7000 students crossing it.

College Principal Greg Smith moved his own office from Cheltenham to the new campus to show support for his Gloucester staff. His PA wasn't so keen on the idea and resigned! Smith's office overlooked Bakers Quay – giving him a daily reminder of the work still to do.

Gloucester's biggest ever planning application

The Peel Group had been patiently assembling land in the area we now know as Gloucester Quays for many years while they worked to come up with a viable plan for the area. Doing it before they achieved a high-profile planning consent avoided them paying over-inflated prices for the land, although some properties they acquired were above their normal market value. British Waterways' holdings were more a legacy from previous activities but the two were a good fit.

The idea for a Factory Outlet Centre (which then was badged as a Designer Outlet Centre and then simply an Outlet Centre) came after a RAM Euro Centre proposal for Tewkesbury, near Junction 9 of the M5, was refused by Environment Secretary John Gummer. Outlet Centres are a means by which retailers dispose of end of line stock or the last season's fashions at discounted prices, although these days some retailers have products, often of slightly lower quality, made specifically for outlet centre stores. Ironically, a 140,000 sq ft Outlet Centre, with a 70,000 sq ft garden centre alongside it, in a similar location in Tewkesbury (to be known as the Cotswold Designer Outlet), was granted outline consent by Tewkesbury Borough Council in 2018 and is due to open in Spring 2025.

Peel/BWB were approached by Freeport, an outlet operator, but already had the idea themselves. They held discussions with operators like McArthur Glen but decided to manage the centre themselves. At the time, outlets were an emerging market. Gloucester was an attractive location as it had a good catchment within an hour's drivetime.

There was internal opposition within Council including from some of the planners. Some wanted Kings Square to be done first. It's just as well that view didn't prevail as it would have involved a 20-year wait! The County Council were worried about the highway implications.

The proposals were fronted up for Peel by Lindsey Ashworth, a blunt-speaking Lancastrian, and Grenville Bird, his surveyor colleague. After working on Gloucester Quays, Ashworth returned north to progress the multi-billion pound Liverpool Waters scheme, something which was later blamed for the loss of Liverpool waterfront's World Heritage Status, until he retired in 2018.

Ashworth and Bird embarked on a campaign to get the public behind their plans and soon found an ally in Ian Mean, editor of the local newspaper, *The Citizen*, and Vice Chairman of the Gloucester Heritage Urban Regeneration Company. His editorials gave vocal support to the plans.

The Council's consultants Chase & Partners claimed a Factory Outlet Centre would be a "risky move" and would endanger the regeneration of Blackfriars. They suggested it could be looked at once Blackfriars was completed and let – that too would have been a long wait!

Savills were commissioned by the City Council and GHURC in 2004 to provide a report on the city's retail performance and prospects. The report recommended better parking, enhanced promotion and encouraging a café culture and warned that a major regeneration project was needed to deliver an "about turn" in the city's fortunes.

Council Officer Peter Wynn warned of a "short-term detrimental effect on the city centre" from the Gloucester Quays proposals. City Centre Manager Richard Dennery pointed to Braintree and Portsmouth where retailers who had stores at the Outlet Centre went on to open in the town/city centre. Lindsey Ashworth of Peel commented that the report "confirms our view that Gloucester Quays could act as the catalyst for the regeneration of the entire city centre. This totally independent report supports our own findings that the Outlet Centre will have no adverse impact on the city centre and will bring genuine benefits for the local economy. Visits to Designer Outlets are often combined with trips to other city centre attractions and will increase the number of overnight stays. The outward facing nature of the scheme will provide a seamless and integrated leisure and retail destination. It will mark the start of a new and very prosperous era for the people of Gloucester."[184]

In an article in response, I wrote, "The report confirms what we all knew – that Gloucester has been slipping down the league table of shopping destinations over the last couple of decades and will drop further unless action is taken.

"When the Blackfriars scheme foundered, I called for an action plan to revive the core shopping area. Although my motion was passed unanimously by the city council it was never implemented with the urgency I had hoped for. Many of the suggestions I made over two years ago now appear as recommendations in the consultant's report."[185]

The planning application was so big that it was felt the decision should be taken by the Full Council rather than its Planning Committee. In the run-up to the meeting, Ian Mean published a comment piece in *The Citizen* with a headline of "Our city's future is in THEIR hands"[186] with photos of all the then 36 city councillors, warning that "Peel Holdings say they will walk away if tomorrow's decision goes against their plans." Mean had consulted with veteran reporter Hugh Worsnip and was worried that councillors might reject it, that "we'd be back to square one" and it "could damage Gloucester's reputation irreparably".

Almost 500 questionnaires were completed in support of the scheme. Roger Crouch of the Learning and Skills Council ratcheted up the pressure by threatening that they may reconsider the grant for

GlosCAT's new campus if application was refused.

Phil Staddon, the Council's Regeneration Director, dealt with the planning application personally and irritated the likes of SWRDA by putting forward a 'neutral' recommendation, despite a huge amount of pressure from internal and external sources to recommend approval, leaving councillors to decide which way to jump. Phil told me the 'textbook planning recommendation' would have been a refusal because of the potential impact on the city centre, but the pragmatic conclusion was more finely-balanced. There was a wealth of information for councillors to digest in advance of the meeting, including Savills' very detailed retail study, which addressed concerns about the potential impact of the outlet centre on the historic city centre. In all, the report ran to 300 pages. Staddon "urged all stakeholders, including the media, to respect the decision, whatever it may be". Mean, in response, told him to stick to planning and "not tell me how to do my job".[187]

At the meeting itself on 23rd November 2004, the public and interested parties got the first chance to speak. The public gallery was packed. Ian Mean attended with his wife on what was perhaps an unusual date night! Lindsey Ashworth spoke on behalf of Peel and clearly had a lot to say in his allotted three minutes, coming across like Coronation Street's Les Battersby on speed! Former Chamber President Tom Taylor spoke against the application on behalf of the Chamber of Commerce. The Chamber was concerned that the projected 3 million visitors a year would bring the city to a standstill. Tom Taylor said, "If we are not careful, by the end of the decade Gloucester will be gridlocked. It would need five dual carriageways to take the traffic out of the city." I commented later, "I am glad we chose to try and alleviate traffic problems rather than have them as too great an obstacle to regeneration."[188] With the benefit of hindsight, ten years after the Outlet Centre opened, visitor numbers had reached almost 8 million without it having that effect – so I'm pleased we didn't accept that argument.

Local resident Francis Cutts, also a member of the Chamber of Commerce, undermined Taylor's case by weighing in with her support. Mrs Cutts, together with her husband Charles, ran a chiropractic clinic in the city. She told me that she was "gobsmacked" to read in *The Citizen* that the Chamber of Commerce were opposing the Gloucester Quays proposals, which she supported and felt would be good for the city, when it hadn't consulted its members – many of whom were supportive of the plans. She felt this was undemocratic. Although she didn't say it at the time, she felt that the Chamber was too heavily-influenced by Morley, as owners of Kings Walk, in whose offices they were based. The Chamber told the public inquiry into the application that they had circulated all of their members before their Executive signed off their submission and only received one negative reply.

From her own experience, customers who used to combine a visit to her clinic with shopping in the city centre were now just driving away. A chance meeting with representatives of Peel when they were exhibiting in the Eastgate Shopping Centre led to her speaking at the public meeting. Apparently, their faces "lit up" when she explained that she was a member of the Chamber of Commerce but was in favour of their plans.

She told the meeting that Gloucester was "bleeding" and in "dire need of regeneration". It "needed something to get the momentum going" and to "put Gloucester on the map again". It was a powerful contribution.

Steve Simmonds of Kings Walk Shopping Centre spoke on behalf of its owners Morley Fund Management. He said they were not against the whole Gloucester Quays plan, which included a hotel, restaurants, a supermarket and hundreds of new homes, but opposed the Outlet Centre. In his presentation Ashworth was clear that you couldn't have one without the other, saying, "With no factory outlet there can be no regeneration of Gloucester Quays". He said that there were £31 million of problems, like contamination, onsite; there would be a loss of £17 million if you replaced the outlet centre with housing; the scheme contributed £9 million to transport and traffic schemes and retained 14 listed buildings (six of which were Grade I).

It's worth noting that they would have been highly unlikely to have got consent to demolish any of the listed buildings even if they had wanted to. Phil Staddon's report noted that the application "does not secure the repair and reuse of the Priory as is anticipated by the Local Plan" and that "the future of ... Llanthony Priory and the listed West Midlands Farmers buildings appear to be uncertain and are not guaranteed by the application proposal."

Council Leader Mark Hawthorne opened the debate. I spoke in favour, saying the city centre would need to "raise its game". In the hours leading up to the meeting, there had been some last-minute horse-trading on the conditions that would apply if the Council were minded to grant permission. Liberal Democrat councillor, Chair of the Planning Committee and a self-confessed planning 'geek', Phil McLellan, proposed a number of restrictions designed to protect the interests of the city centre. These included a 'no poaching' condition, preventing any retailers closing in the city centre and opening up at Gloucester Quays for a period of years. Savills had proposed 2 years. McLellan suggested 10. Mark Hawthorne agreed to it being decided after consultation between the Chair, Vice Chair and group spokesperson of the Planning Committee. It ended up being 5 years. Another condition was proposed, giving the Council control of the Quays parking tariff to ensure it was broadly consistent with the city centre. A proportion of the car park's net revenue would also contribute to improving the linkages between the Quays and the city centre. Other conditions included that 85% of the outlet centre's retail area must be selling goods at least 30% below the recommended price and the remainder at least 20%.

Just before midnight we went to the vote, with a unanimous approval. The meeting, having started at 7.30pm, closed at 12.10am.

That was far from the end of the matter. There were fears that, as in the case of the St Oswalds development, the Government would take a long time to make the final planning decision. In this case, those fears proved unfounded. The application was 'called in' for a public inquiry by John Prescott in June 2005 because the "proposals may conflict with national policies in important matters". City MP Parmjit Dhanda and GHURC Chair Greg Smith jointly wrote to the Government urging a quick decision. The Government's response revealed that the public inquiry would take place in November 2005 with a decision within three months of the inquiry finishing. According to those who were there, it was the most one-sided inquiry they have ever been to. Apparently, most of the discussion was about technical issues regarding affordable housing. Dhanda and GHURC Chief Executive Chris Oldershaw were amongst those who gave evidence. According to one of those involved, it felt like a 'box-ticking exercise'.

Planning Committee Chair, Phil McLellan, also gave evidence. No-one appeared at the inquiry to object. The two main objectors – Morley and the Chamber of Commerce - provided written representations. The inspector said the representation by the Chamber "appears to be largely cancelled out by the full endorsement of the scheme by the Gloucester Federation of Small Businesses".

Gloucestershire College's Jeremy Williamson gave evidence to the inquiry and, unusually, asked for an adjournment to give the Inspector a tour of the new College site. By this point, the steels for the new College building were in place and Williamson took the Inspector to the top of the structure. The Inspector asked Williamson what would happen if he didn't support the Gloucester Quays application. Williamson responded that he'd probably lose his job and the College's governors would think they'd made a mistake – but they believed this was the right location for the new campus.

There was also a written representation from Maurice Critchley, boss of Severn Glocon who were based on part of the proposed site on Southgate Street. Severn Glocon design and manufacture control valves for oil, gas, petrochemical and power plants. Most of their customers are in the Middle and Far East and North and South America. He noted that the regeneration of Gloucester Quays had been discussed for 8-10 years, adding that "indecision and delay are destroying the value of existing assets and businesses in the area." He claimed that "much of the proposed Gloucester Quays area is already a no-go area", adding, "It is difficult to attract employees to this decrepit area.". He complained that his "Company cannot move because of a long lease and no-one is willing to make any decisions."

David Pedrette of Target Catering Equipment "apologised for the apathy of the people of Gloucester". The Pope family, Mr and Mrs Canning and Sue Llewellyn all supported the scheme, as did Francis Cutts. Communities Secretary Ruth Kelly approved the application in June 2006.

The grant of the outline consent was also not the end of the matter. Peel/BW had 8 years to submit their reserved matters (detailed) planning applications, of which there would be a number. The first was for the 17,825 sqm outlet centre and 1311 space car park, which was approved by the Planning Committee in September 2007. The 106-bed budget hotel (which became a Travelodge) was not included in outline consent so was part of this application.

CABE's Design Review Panel Chair Paul Finch (who had not visited the site) objected saying, "We feel the project does not do justice to the site, to Gloucester Quays as a whole and to the city itself", adding that the car park rotunda "will make a dispiriting contribution to Gloucester's townscape." The rotunda was Portland stone to the base and perforated green copper on the upper levels. The concerns were dismissed by Gloucester Quays' planning consultant saying there was no objection from the City Council or the Secretary of State and the rotunda had been set back from St Ann Way.

Architects Broadway Malyan objected on behalf of the Bishop family (owners of the adjacent Bakers Quay site), with their principal concern being about the junction capacity with St Ann Way and whether it would be sufficient to serve their development site too.

The outlet centre building along St Ann Way was over 130m in length. In his report, City Council Development Control Manager Steve Macpherson said: "The St Ann Way frontage will change the perception of this part of the city from what has become a rundown industrial wasteland to a vibrant commercial hub" and would "breathe new life into the city as a whole".

Any development on the scale of Gloucester Quays is bound to change over time. The original application included an 80-bed hotel with 40 parking spaces next to Llanthony Priory, which is discussed in Chapter 8, and a number of three storey office blocks on the corner of Hempsted Lane, adjacent to Llanthony Priory, where the High Orchard pub is now. There was interest from hotel operators and pre-application discussions, but the plans were sunk by the financial crash of 2008 before any planning application was made. Some years later the site was taken by retirement builder McCarthy & Stone. Those involved told me the offices didn't go ahead due to lack of demand.

It was originally expected that Morrisons would take the supermarket being planned as part of the development but in August 2007 it was announced that Sainsburys would be taking the 84,000 sq ft store with 450 car parking spaces. It would go on to include a host of environmental features, including a kinetic pad on the way into the car park which would generate energy every time a vehicle passed over it. The store opened in June 2009 and at the time was the most energy efficient in Sainsburys' portfolio.

The Regional Development Agency and English Partnerships (the Government's Regeneration Agency) were both firm supporters of the scheme and helped meet the costs of infrastructure improvements. The RDA had contributed to the completion of the South West Bypass, which was necessary for the outlet centre to open, while EP paid for the High Orchard Bridge over the canal (at a cost of £7.5 million), which was announced in April 2006, so the 'road to nowhere' by the Peel Centre actually became a road to somewhere.

County Council Chief Executive, Peter Bungard, told me that when he arrived as Director of Environment in 1998, the South West bypass route existed but it was based on £12 million of Government Local Transport Plan money and £5-6 million of developer contributions. By the summer of 2002, the projected cost had risen to over £35 million and there was still a shortfall in funding. In October 2002, City MP Parmjit Dhanda used a Westminster Hall debate to appeal to Transport Minister David Jamieson, who he described as "a good friend of Gloucester", for £18 million Government funding to complete the bypass and unlock regeneration at St Oswalds, Gloucester Quays and elsewhere. In his book, Dhanda described how he "cut a deal" with Jamieson for £12 million and the balance was met with £6 million from the developers of the Kingsway estate.

By the time the final 'Netheridge' section of the bypass was commissioned in 2005, the total cost of the bypass had reached £43 million. In the end it was financed by over £22 million of Government funding, nearly £17 million of developer contributions and smaller amounts from the County Council and SWRDA making up the balance.

The Llanthony section was scaled down to get the road completed. This was described as a 'fudge' by some who believed it should have been a dual carriageway all the way. Work finished on widening the Llanthony section in July 2023, thanks to £12.8 million awarded from the Government's 'Levelling Up Fund', meaning that construction of the bypass started in the mid-1990s and didn't finish until almost the mid-2020s.

Insiders tell me that English Partnerships weren't positive about the new bridge over the canal to start with and lobbying commenced, with Minister of State for Housing and Planning Yvette Cooper coming up with the money. The application for the bridge went to the Council's Planning Committee in June 2006. The Civic Trust called it a "well designed and elegant" bridge.

The Gloucester Quays development delivered a multi-million-pound package of transport improvements, including contributions to the Waterwells Park & Ride Service, Junction 12 of the M5 and bus shelters. Gloucester Quays themselves delivered the 'frankfurter' roundabout on Hempsted Lane. Initially the scheme was going to include a bus station within the development, but this changed because highways bosses wanted the buses to drop off on the main St Ann Way.

Construction of the outlet centre started in 2007 and almost ground to a halt in 2008 when the credit crunch hit. Legend has it that it was only because Peel's billionaire Chairman John Whittaker sent buckets of cash (not literally) from his base in the Isle of Man that building work continued. The truth is slightly different. The lenders for the scheme were the Royal Bank of Scotland and had agreed with Peel that a certain percentage of the units would be 'pre-let' prior to the centre's opening. When Muccini joined, he commented that this level had never been achieved before, let alone during a recession when retailers' credit ratings were bringing up red flags. The bank later revised it downwards following negotiations with Peel, but it was still only achieved the day before the centre opened!

Whittaker has a fierce reputation as a ruthless businessman and, in particular, his takeover battle for the Manchester Ship Canal is the stuff of corporate legend. But when I met him, he came across as a little shy, reluctant to speak in public and, with his hair now white, like a typical Grandad! I don't doubt for a moment his business acumen – you don't become a billionaire without it - and Gloucester has a lot to be grateful to him for. When he did speak to a gathered group of key stakeholders in the city, Whittaker spoke of the need for "Determination, Perseverance and Patience" to deliver developments. He told me that the Trafford Centre in Manchester, which really put Peel on the map, took 15 years to deliver from conception to completion. Gloucester Quays probably took something similar.

It was also Whittaker who coined the 'Believe in Gloucester' phrase, which went on to be used as a campaign to foster civic pride and an annual awards ceremony run by Gloucestershire Media to celebrate the best of the city. Thank goodness Whittaker did believe in Gloucester!

Franco Muccini, Centre Director of the McArthur Glen Designer Outlet Centre at Swindon, was recruited in January 2008 to run Gloucester Quays. He changed the branding from the orange colour used initially (which was felt to represent 'cheapness'- think EasyJet) to black and white, which was believed to be more upmarket – think Prada & Gucci. He faced an internal battle to get it changed as rumour has it that it had been designed by Lindsey Ashworth's son! It also meant the long stretches of orange hoardings around the site were rollered over, covering the orange colour with black paint. Later the corporate colour would be changed again to the current teal blue.

A computer-generated image of the hotel proposed for the site adjacent to Llanthony Priory.

I brokered a meeting between Muccini and Chris Paterson of Aviva, owners of the Kings Walk shopping centre at the time, to see if we could find common ground and a way of working together for the overall good of the city. GHURC Chief Executive Chris Oldershaw also travelled to London to meet Chris Paterson to try to find a way to overcome Aviva's objections. Despite all of our efforts we weren't able to find common ground and the stand-off between the two parties remained.

A watercolour of the High Orchard bridge, submitted with the planning application for the new structure.

Opening at a difficult time

The Outlet Centre and associated units reportedly cost £140 million to build. Some people said, in hindsight, that the building specification was too high - apparently higher than the upmarket Cheshire Oaks designer outlet. The floor was made of granite imported from China. It had a 'gull wing roof', which was ironic given that seagulls kept breaking it by dropping stones onto the glass! Plans for a 100ft piece of art on St Ann Way were dropped as part of keeping the project within budget.

Gloucester Quays Outlet Centre opened in May 2009 on the same day as the second Tall Ships Festival. TV style guru Gok Wan did the honours, speaking to a packed mall on a sunny Saturday. In the run-up to the opening, a steady stream of tenants was announced with M&S and Next anchoring the centre and other names like LK Bennett, The White Company, Austin Read, Hawes & Curtis, Jeff Banks and Calvin Klein joining them. By the time of opening the mall was half full (or half empty, depending on your point of view). The restaurant units were even more of a struggle, with only Pizza Express and Nandos opening before the end of 2009 – not quite the transformation of the city's eating offer that was promised, but it would come later.

In reality, Gloucester Quays had opened at almost the worst possible time. The credit crunch turned into a long and deep recession, making it difficult to attract tenants and with shoppers' spending power reduced. The predicted three million visitors a year was more like one and a half million and the centre, which was managed at arms' length through the joint venture with BWB, was haemorrhaging money. This rang alarm bells at Peel's head office. Muccini left in February 2010 to run outlet centres in China and the centre seemed rudderless. The cynics who claimed it would be a white elephant started to feel vindicated. Gloucester Quays was in breach of its banking facility covenants and was put under the control of Lloyds Bank's Business Support Unit – a polite way of describing what was effectively being in Administration.

It's easy to forget that Gloucester Quays was originally a joint venture between Peel and British Waterways. But when the scheme needed refinancing (i.e. another injection of cash), British Waterways didn't have the cash, so they quietly exited leaving Peel to lead and, perhaps more importantly, finance the later phases. At the time, British Waterways were moving to charitable status and the two partners agreed an amicable divorce. BW apparently didn't do well out of it financially but saw the value of its remaining assets in the area increase and had helped to achieve its wider objective of enlivening the waterside.

Peel's response to the difficulties Gloucester Quays encountered in the early days, thankfully, wasn't to retrench but to continue investing and a new troubleshooting boss, Jason Pullen, was brought in from Peel's Head Office in Manchester in 2010. Pullen, who started his career at business recovery consultancy Robson Rhodes, had previously worked on projects at John Lennon Airport in Liverpool and Peel's flagship Trafford Centre in Manchester. In their original business plan, Gloucester Quays had included a hefty sum, believed to be around £2.5 million a year, as car parking income but had only been achieving around a tenth of it. This raised red flags at Peel head office, who feared a fault with the system or, worse still, someone committing a fraud. Pullen was sent in to investigate and when he pulled into the shiny, new multi-storey car park, he immediately reported back the problem. "There's no bugger here," he said.

Initially he was denied access to the management suite as they didn't know who he was, but ended up staying far longer than originally anticipated. There were more deep-rooted problems than just the car park – the tenant mix was wrong, with an over-representation of outdoor-wear stores and not enough designer labels to justify the 'designer outlet centre' tag; footfall was barely half of the projected 3 million and sales were an average of £67 per square foot when it needed to be £200-225 per square foot, so it was barely covering the retailers' cost of stock and labour, meaning many of them wanted to leave. Pullen put together a turnaround plan for the centre and, having approved it, Lloyds insisted he stick around to implement it.

According to insiders, at the time the centre was a disappointment to those who visited. It took only 15 or 20 minutes to go round. People wouldn't travel far for that, so it had a limited catchment.

TV celebrity Gok Wan officially opens the Gloucester Quays outlet centre with a mall packed full of people. Credit: Litchfield Morris/GHURC

Pullen's strategy was to embrace the estate around it and to face outward to the water. He cancelled direct marketing and started to establish events – from markets to larger scale events like the Food Festival. The centre rebranded to a teal colour, influenced by the Docks, including repainting the car park and the 'designer' word was dropped from the outlet centre's title.

The Leisure Quarter and completing the masterplan

John Whittaker visited Gloucester Quays by helicopter and could still see the potential but believed it lacked the scale of somewhere like Gunwharf Quays in Portsmouth. Whittaker and Jason Pullen flew over Gunwharf in Whittaker's helicopter and decided they could do better. Another £60 million of investment was agreed to relocate the cinema from the Peel Centre to Merchants Road (meaning an expensive project to raise the roof by just a small amount), which triggered new sign-ups of restaurant tenants like TGI Fridays (apparently it took seven attempts to sign them up as they would only usually sign up for places with a 135,000 plus population), Carluccios and Bella Italia, and generous incentives were offered to attract new tenants for the Outlet Centre like White Stuff, Allsaints and Crew Clothing. Portivo Lounge was one of the first of the successful Loungers chain in the country. Jason Pullen recalls how he pursued Loungers' founder Alex Reilly at the British Open Golf tournament. Pullen estimated that the cinema alone would support 3 or 4 restaurants, but believed the Docks and city as a whole were 'undercatered'. His challenge was to convince operators to give the place a chance.

The cinema at the Peel Centre opened in 1991 and by the 2000s was looking very tired. Planning permission was granted in November 2008 to refurbish and extend the cinema, expanding it from six screens to nine and to add four restaurant units – as well as four wind turbines along the canal! But those plans were never implemented.

When plans for the new Leisure Quarter were announced, Jason Pullen said, "The changing economic times and markets have seen the scheme evolve and the latest phase of development would see the creation of a new leisure quarter for Gloucester. To invest a further

£60 million of privately funded money is a sign that we believe in the future of Gloucester."[189]

I responded, "Gloucester Quays opened at possibly the worst time in the economic cycle. The response of some organisations in these circumstances would be to retrench. Thankfully Peel takes a different approach. The announcement of further investment underlines its determination to make the scheme a success and shows that it believes in Gloucester."

At this point 50 out of the 70 units at the Outlet Centre had been leased. Footfall continued to rise and new tenants, both retail and restaurant, were added. Inevitably there were casualties along the way like the White Company, Ed's Diner and Cath Kidston. Events, like the Food Festival and Victorian Christmas Market, were used to bring in visitors from far and wide and to attract retail and restaurant tenants – with photos of busy spaces used in leasing material. There was also a major promotional campaign including television adverts. In 2013/14 footfall had reached 2.7 million a year, doubling to 5.5 million in 2014/15 and by 2018/19 the figure had grown to almost 7 million.

Of course, Gloucester Quays wasn't just about the outlet centre or indeed the Leisure Quarter. It was also intended to provide a significant number of new homes – but this was a challenge, as often was the case in Gloucester, because of a mixture of high decontamination costs and relatively low sales values. Jason Pullen took this on himself to deliver and managed to sign up retirement developer McCarthy & Stone for the land next to Llanthony Priory (which, as mentioned earlier, was initially earmarked for a hotel). City Archaeologist Andrew Armstrong told me they found the southern gatehouse for Llanthony Priory on site. The northern gatehouse was on the adjacent College site. I later became involved in naming the McCarthy & Stone development. The developer was, understandably, keen on naming one of the buildings 'Llanthony Place'. After some discussion, we settled on 'Scudamore Place' for the second building – named after the family who owned the Priory in the 17th century.

The site at Monk Meadow proved particularly challenging and negotiations with housebuilders took place over an extended period before a deal was struck with Crest Nicholson. They gained detailed planning consent for just over 400 homes which, ultimately, they split with Guinness Homes (a housing association) to help deliver affordable housing on site. Both sites were a real challenge. Peel took on the planning risk (including archaeology) and the clean-up costs of the contamination (believed to be around £4 million). Before they could do this, they had to relocate local business Hobbs Oil, who moved to nearby Spinnaker Park. De-risking the site was the only way development would happen.

There has always been some confusion where Gloucester Quays starts and the historic Docks ends. In my view the dividing line is Llanthony Road. That's where the land ownership changes at least. But from the visitor's point of view, it is all part of the same experience. Peel recognised this and took responsibility for the management of the Docks estate, now in the City Council's hands following the demise of the Regional Development Agency, and took a lease on the British Waterways (now renamed the Canal and River Trust) car park outside the National Waterways Museum and turned it into a public space called Orchard Square. Announcing the plans to create a new public space, Jason Pullen said, "At the moment it is just one big car park and I hope these plans will really transform the area and make it a real focal point."[190]

Many regretted the loss of car parking but with the pedestrian flows between the Docks and Quays rising, it was an uneasy mix of people and vehicles. Peel invested around £400,000 on an interim scheme in 2018 which is still there at the time of writing. Planning consent exists for a more permanent, attractive and expensive scheme but no date is scheduled for it to be implemented.

In June 2021, it was announced that the Gloucester Quays outlet centre and leisure quarter had been put up for sale for £105 million. Buyers could also have the Peel Centre (now renamed the Gloucester Quays Retail Park) over the road thrown in for another £20 million. Peel had already been looking to offload a minority stake in the scheme but were now seeking to dispose of it in its entirety.

Stephen Wild, Executive Director for Peel Land & Property said: "Gloucester Quays is a well-established place with an exceptionally diverse retail and leisure offering. We are currently looking for an investor to come on board and help take the centre to the next stage of its journey as a premier-choice, place-led destination in

Gloucester. Like any other retail and leisure offering in the UK, Gloucester Quays has faced challenges as a result of the pandemic and ensuing lockdowns, but it has weathered the storm well due to the quality and vibrancy of its customer proposition."[191]

Following the coronavirus pandemic, the outlet centre lost a number of its key tenants, including Gap, Nike and H&M.

At the time of writing no buyer had been announced and it was believed Peel had withdrawn the asset from sale – until it was reported in November 2023 that it was being marketed by agents Cushman & Wakefield for £85 million. The appointment of Paul Carter, previously of fellow property giant Hammerson, as Asset Director for Gloucester Quays in June 2022 seemed to give the centre new momentum with a number of new tenants signing up, including Timberland, The Real Greek and El Mexicana, as well as the return of Next and FatFace. This is important because in the 'easy in, easy out' world of outlet centres, standing still is, in effect, going backwards.

In October 2021, it was announced that Peel had sold the Madleaze Trading Estate on Bristol Road, immediately adjoining the Peel Centre, to property company Picton in a £13 million deal. The cash is believed to have been used to reduce bank debt. One of the consequences of the sale is that the opportunity for a comprehensive redevelopment of the Peel Centre and Madleaze Trading Estate, which could have created an attractive waterside mixed-use scheme, was lost – at least for the time being.

Bakers Quay

One piece of the jigsaw that remained was a 4.2-acre site at Bakers Quay. It was constructed in the 1830s with the widening of the canal. Downings Malthouse was built in 1893 with the Malthouse Extension following between 1899-1901. The Transit Shed was built in 1867 for the Midland Railway Company and has historic significance at the end of the rail lines into the site. Provender Mill was built in 1862 and extended between 1890-95. The four Malthouse Cottages were built in 1902. All of the buildings were on English Heritage's 'At Risk' register.

The former West Midlands Farmers premises had been vacant and increasingly derelict since the 1990s and were owned by a local family, the Bishops. They bought the land speculatively in 1996 after walking into it to price some demolition work. They say they saw the potential of the waterside location. Their style is to act quickly once they have made a decision to buy land and they completed the deal in two weeks – some say it was 'under the noses' of other interested parties. The Bishops had made their money through their demolition business, building it up to be one of the biggest in the UK and undertaking work all around the country. They also knocked down parts of central Gloucester in the redevelopment of the 1960s and 70s – a lot of which, looking back, we'd rather they hadn't! That, of course, wasn't their fault – they were acting on instructions and other people had made the decisions to demolish the buildings. They had a reputation, perhaps with some justification, of not being the easiest people to deal with.

Peel and British Waterways were understandably keen to include Bakers Quay within the Gloucester Quays development and indeed it was for planning purposes, being earmarked for housing and offices with leisure/restaurants at ground floor level. Peel did make an offer for the land. I wasn't party to those discussions, but what we do know is that the negotiations broke down and agreement on price wasn't reached – and relations between the Bishops and Peel never recovered.

If Peel had acquired Bakers Quay the site would have been fully developed by now – and probably in a different way to how it has been done by its subsequent developers. But the failure to agree a deal meant the buildings continued to deteriorate and a solution needed to be found. With a shiny new development next to it, Bakers Quay stood out like the proverbial sore thumb. Even Her Majesty The Queen commented on it on her visit in 2009, saying, "You've still got some work to do then!"

The Urban Regeneration Company looked at the options for a Compulsory Purchase Order, using the Regional Development Agency's CPO powers, but never actually pressed the button. The City Council debated a motion along the same lines in January 2015. CPOs aren't as easy as they sound. The process can be long, expensive and uncertain. And the Bishops were the type to relish a court battle rather than be intimidated by it.

Eventually the Bishops came up with their own masterplan in

December 2007, working with architects Broadway Malyan. Their masterplan included 257 residential units within the Downings Malthouse, Malthouse Extension and Provender Mill buildings with six new buildings. There would also be 215 car parking spaces, 7000 sqm of office, retail and leisure space, a possible new inlet from the canal and a new public square.[192]

In February 2008, Dick Bishop told *The Citizen*, "We want to build something special which puts Gloucester on the map".[193] He anticipated that work could start early in 2009 and would be completed in 2010. Mr Bishop pledged that at least 20% would be affordable homes. The Bishops insisted they had the funds available to complete the development.

But by July 2008, the Bishops had advised GHURC that they were "unwilling to progress at the current time".[194] They told *The Citizen* in December 2008 that the plan was "on hold for two years". As an aside, they said that the site was "not for sale but if anyone wants to buy it, the price is £12 million".[195]

Before that period was up, the Bishops lodged a planning application, assisted by Tewkesbury-based architect Bob Beswick in September 2009.[196] The four Maltsters Cottages in High Orchard Street were proposed for demolition. Two were saved in the negotiations and would have been put to leisure use. The application was for the conversion of Downings Malthouse plus new build for office and leisure use and a separate block of 12 residential units. English Heritage were supportive, including the demolition of the two cottages, as were the Ancient Monument Society, the City Centre Community Partnership and GHURC. The application was approved by the Planning Committee in February 2010. The same meeting approved a separate but related, and rather technical, planning application (known as a Section 73) to reallocate floorspace between buildings within the Gloucester Quays outline application, resulting in slightly less residential and slightly more office space. It ended up being academic as the scheme wasn't implemented.

In the end the site was put up for sale with BNP Paribas in May 2011. Dick Bishop told *The Citizen* there was "a hell of a lot of interest".[197] I would often bump into developers at one event or another who believed they had struck a deal with the Bishops. Eventually one did. Adrian Goodall, a Durham-based developer, knew

GHURC Chief Executive Chris Oldershaw from when they were both working on developments in Newcastle. Goodall was introduced to the site by Simon Horan, a property industry heavyweight who has worked for agents Savills and CBRE and is now with JLL, and Chris Oldershaw encouraged him. He teamed up with Michael Chicken of Merchant Place Corporate Finance to create a joint venture for Bakers Quay and took an option on the site.

Adrian Goodall presented his ideas to the GHURC Board in January 2013 – the final major development proposal to be presented to the Board before the company was wound up. The first major development to present to the Board when the company was created was for Gloucester Quays, so it seemed quite fitting that the company should start and finish with proposals for adjacent sites.

In March 2013, plans for a Premier Inn, Brewers Fayre and Costa Coffee drive thru (all Whitbread brands at the time) became public. I commented, "I'm not cracking out the champagne just yet. The owners of Bakers Quay aren't absentee landlords but a local family, who must feel embarrassed about the condition of their site every day of the week. During their talks with me they have assured me they have Gloucester's best interests at heart. Now is the time to prove it."[198]

The remainder of the site would be commercial units and around 160 apartments in a mixture of new build and conversion of the heritage buildings, despite the inevitable call for an ice rink to be sited there! Crest Nicholson, who had carried out the warehouse conversions in the Docks, were at one point interested in the residential elements but pulled out so Rokeby Merchant decided to do it themselves. In addition to the apartments, all four of the Maltsters Cottages in High Orchard Street were restored as part of the first phase and sold for good money – going on the market in 2017 for £295,000 each. In November 2017, GloucestershireLive reported on how 69-year-old Mary Kavanagh, who had lived in one of the cottages until she was 10, broke down in tears when she saw their restoration.

During the Rugby World Cup on 3rd October 2015, I had taken a few days away to my wife's former home in Little Haven, Pembrokeshire. Just as I was about to wander down to the local pub to watch the England v Australia match, my mobile phone started to go wild with texts, calls and pictures. The remains of the iconic

Provender Mill were alight in some spectacular fashion and those watching the match in the fanzone at Gloucester Docks were getting some warmth and light from an unexpected source. Arson attacks in this area weren't unusual. The Engine House, adjoining Provender, had been damaged in a previous attack and the adjacent Peel House office building had burned down as a result of arson some years earlier. Scott Parker, 19, of Southgate Street, and Martin Rodger, also 19, of Stroud Road, were arrested and ultimately convicted of arson but the fire was to prove fatal to the building, despite calls by some for it to be rebuilt 'brick by brick'. This was never a realistic prospect anyway, as the heat from the fire had destroyed many of the bricks.

The Council's Head of Regeneration, Anthony Hodge, felt that this site would need some public sector support and went about getting the Homes and Communities Agency (HCA), as it was then, on board. I took advantage of a visit by Greg Clark MP, then Secretary of State for Local Government, to show him the site and explain its significance. Anthony Hodge worked on Greg Clark's special adviser while he travelled in the car with him. Whether the then Secretary of State intervened at all is unknown, but the HCA made available funding to the council which was onward lent to the developer to buy the site and undertake initial works. The sale price was £4.5 million, which is seen as another 'very full market valuation' – more than the valuation when the URC had considered a compulsory purchase. This made it challenging to pass the 'state aid' tests and the proposal didn't get through the HCA Board at the first time of asking. Council and HCA officers had to work hard to come up with an acceptable arrangement for something I'm told was "on the edge of what was doable". Anthony Hodge told me they spent 12 hours in London with the HCA's lawyers trying to get a deal to work, particularly overcoming the concerns about state aid – which meant the deal had to be on a commercial basis. A loan of £4.8 million was agreed – which was £4.5 million for the land acquisition and £300,000 to tidy up and secure the site.

It was, without doubt, the right thing to do. The HCA got a profit share in return for its loan, but wouldn't receive any profit (and neither would the developers) until all phases of the development had been completed. I was able to announce to the Full Council in February 2015 that contracts had been exchanged. I approved the details of the legal agreement for completion the day before my brother-in-law's wedding on 1st April 2016, so there was reason for a double celebration.

Michael Chicken said, "We have already spent £1 million to date without a spade in the ground except for one archaeological trench and after almost pulling out of the development altogether after the fire last year. We have only persevered because of the huge support from the Council and Councillor Paul James. It is now down to us to build a scheme which Gloucester will be proud of for generations to come."[199]

The Bishops retained a narrow 'ransom strip' between Bakers Quay and the adjoining land owned by Peel (where Peel House had been). Peel were "genuinely supportive" of the proposals but noted that the "narrow strip effectively prevents future access to the Peel House plot", which they were concerned "sterilises" their land.

Historic England objected to the planning application for phase one (which was for a new-build Provender, the restoration of the Engine House to a Brewers Fayre, the new-build Premier Inn and the new-build Costa Coffee), saying it represented an unacceptable level of harm to the heritage. They objected to the lowering of the window cills in the Engine House, but agreed to reinstating the cills with a single glazed panel below. They also objected to the extension to the Transit Shed. For Provender, they wanted the hoist housing (the iconic blue part nearest the canal) revisited, the balconies omitted and a slate roof rather than the proposed metal one.

The Civic Trust welcomed the plans but regretted they did not include the Peel land fronting St Ann Way. They would like to have seen suitable pieces of redundant machinery from the mill used as external features. They felt the proposed rebuild of Provender was unacceptable, but would be acceptable without balconies. The Canals & Rivers Trust didn't like the projecting balconies either, saying they were "incongruous", or the "extensive surface parking". They felt that the Downings atrium with rooflights was an "admirable proposal". The Council's Conservation Officer said that balconies were "alien to the area". At the Planning Committee meeting in March 2016, former Mayor Chris Chatterton proposed, after a long debate, that the cladding, windows, balconies and hoist arrangements should be subject to approval by Historic England. I recall a phone conversation with a senior figure in Historic England following the Planning Committee, who assured me that a way through would be found – which, indeed, it was.

According to the Planning Committee report, the rebuild of the Provender gable walls to effectively what was like for like "serves to anchor the new scheme in its historic context". The red/orange cladding, which I'm told was chosen in a meeting in Historic England's offices in Queens Square, Bristol, "enlivens the appearance rather than dull grey and gives faithful reference to the brick finish of the original".

The "sea" of car parking across the middle part of the scheme was seen as "undesirable" but it was acknowledged that there were limited other options to "hide" it elsewhere.

Rokeby Merchant offered reasonable endeavours to address the remaining vacant and derelict listed buildings – not a guarantee that conversions would proceed following the new build.

The Planning Committee report said that the profit margin was 12.69% return on cost, arguing the scheme could not support any s106 contributions (community benefits). A 20% profit margin would normally be seen as reasonable for a project with this level of this risk. The Council's consultants said the scheme could afford £67,810 (£10,000 towards the play area at Gloucester Park, £5,000 for the library and £52,810 for housing in Westgate). Adrian Goodall told the committee that the project's viability was "very fragile".

The planning report described the scheme as a "sub optimal solution" in terms of the timing, security of delivery and the works themselves, but in a refreshing note of pragmatism, concluded that the "adverse impacts do not outweigh the benefits".

Phase One which was completed in July 2018. A little-known fact is that the development was financed in part by a fund looking after some of the wealth of a number of Liverpool football players.

In June 2016, local construction firm Barnwood were appointed for Phase One of the scheme. The Brexit vote later that month led to one of Rokeby Merchant's backers pulling out, but Savills & JLL secured £11.326 million of funding, for a private client advised by real estate consultancy Kimmre, and the City Council agreed £490,000 of funding on a commercial basis, enabling the scheme to get underway in December 2016.

At the time of writing, the later phases involving the Downings Malthouse and Malthouse Extension were still to be delivered. What the developers described as the "complete collapse" of the restaurant market meant they had to come up with another way of delivering a subsidy to fund the restoration of the heritage buildings. Since the completion of Phase One, the developers have worked on a number of iterations in order to find a solution for the remainder of the site.

In March 2020, dangerous sections of Downings Malthouse were demolished, leading some to believe that the second phase of the scheme was about to get underway, which unfortunately was not the case. Despite progress on the later phases being slow, the developers have undertaken a huge amount of preparatory work, including drilling every timber beam in the enormous Malthouse Extension building in order to establish its condition. A revised planning application for the Downings Malthouse phase of the development, including an "unapologetically tall" ten-storey 'Downings Tower', was submitted in Summer 2022. The plans were approved by the Council's Planning Committee in April 2023, despite concerns about the impact on the heritage in the area expressed by the Council's Conservation Officer and Archaeologist, the Civic Trust, Historic England and the Victorian Society. The votes were tied, with five in favour and five against, with Committee Chair Gordon Taylor using his casting vote to approve the plans.

The development became caught up in controversy in July 2020 when there were calls for it to be re-named in light of its alleged connections with the slave trade. The City Council had passed a motion proposing a review of statues and monuments linked to the slave trade in the light of the Black Lives Matters movement following the death of George Floyd in America and the toppling of the statue of slave trader Edward Colston in Bristol.

Samuel Baker and Thomas Phillpotts, who were the leading figures behind the development of Bakers Quay, had made money through owning property in Jamaica and through bringing the produce of the West Indies to London. When slavery was formally abolished in 1834, they were awarded £4283 compensation for 240 slaves. The counter argument is that they were not responsible for constructing the buildings on the site and simply sold plots for others to build. The developers also pointed out that the Bakers Quay name will not be part of the postal address for each of the buildings on site and they have agreed, through a planning condition, to install interpretation boards on site explaining the history of the area. By contrast, Baker's son Sir Samuel White Baker was a well-known abolitionist. Whatever happens, the Baker name is likely to live on through the Baker Street pub on Southgate Street, which still has a Baker Street sign on it from before that part of the highway was 'stopped up' as part of the Gloucester Quays development.

Another feature of Bakers Quay worthy of mention is the Sula Lightship. Sula is a nationally registered historic lightvessel commissioned by the Humber Conservancy Board in 1959. Originally named SPURN, she was stationed on the Humber Estuary to protect mariners for 26 years, until being decommissioned in 1985. Over the next 20 years, the vessel moved around from Southampton to Guernsey, Conwy, Milford Haven and Ireland before being restored for three years at Sharpness and being renamed Sula, which means 'peace'. She arrived at Llanthony Quay, alongside Llanthony Priory and Gloucestershire College, in October 2010. Sula became the base for Lightship Therapies, offering complementary healthcare and training.

Sula housed the Gloucester Buddhist Centre and owners Jan and Agnes van der Elsen lived on board. In February 2020, Sula was sold to new owners Colin and Vivienne Brooks. They have continued the restoration and converted her into luxury bed and breakfast accommodation, featuring on BBC's 'Mortimer & Whitehouse: Gone Fishing' in October 2021.

Provender Mill at Bakers Quay on fire due to an arson attack in October 2015.

Her Majesty Queen Elizabeth II on a visit to Gloucester Quays in October 2009. Credit: Gloucester City Council

The Peel Centre retail park

The Peel Centre, opposite Gloucester Quays on St Ann Way, had never really taken off in the way that Peel had hoped. Toys'R'Us, which closed in April 2018, had certainly been an attraction as had the cinema until it moved into Gloucester Quays in December 2013. The 'road to nowhere' across the canal hadn't helped for the first twenty years of the retail park's life and by the time the new bridge had been built, the centre was looking very tired.

There was an attempt to attract a full range John Lewis department store, including home and garden, to the Peel Centre. The retailer was looking for a store to serve the Cheltenham/Gloucester catchment and Peel came up with a multi-million-pound incentive package to lure them to this location. The new store would have been on the prominent Bristol Road/St Ann Way corner where Burger King is now and connected to the Gloucester Quays outlet centre by a bridge link. We pulled out all the stops to land them. City MP Richard Graham and I met Jeremy Collins, their then Property Director, at the House of Commons to put our case. In the end they couldn't get past Cheltenham's superior demographics (some called it 'postcode snobbery'!) and opened a store in the town's High Street in October 2018, despite their preference for a more 'accessible' (i.e. out of town) site.

When John Lewis were considering the Peel Centre option, they wanted reassurances they wouldn't be on their own and were particularly keen to be co-located with Next. Peel did secure Next as a tenant with a new 30,000 sq ft, £14 million store on the part of the site previously occupied by Pizza Hut and the Angel Chef Chinese restaurant. Peel also sought consent to build four other retail units adjacent to Next, including the conversion of the former cinema building, and to relax the 'bulky goods' condition on several existing units. This made the application controversial.

A campaign of sorts was put together to 'Save Our City Centre'. In reality, Next had made it crystal clear they would not move into a city centre store and, indeed, had not done so since they closed their Northgate Street unit (where Coffee#1 now is) around a decade earlier. And this proposal involved shutting their Quedgeley store – so it was, in fact, bringing it much closer to the city centre. When the management of the Eastgate Shopping Centre came to see me to oppose the plans, I gave them short shrift when they responded that they had no investment plans of their own.

The application for the new Next store at the Peel Centre only scraped through the planning committee on the casting vote of the Chair, Councillor Gordon Taylor, in September 2016. The new store opened in March 2019.

Conclusion

Gloucester Quays is the largest, the most high-profile, successful and arguably transformational of all Gloucester's regeneration schemes. Even twenty years after the masterplan for the area was first revealed, the development is still not the finished article. Debate still rages as to whether Gloucester Quays has been good for the city or otherwise, as I discuss in the chapter 'A Tale of Two Cities'. My strong view is that it has been positive for the city, transforming a run-down area, bringing in new brands that would otherwise have not come to Gloucester and helping to build investor confidence in the city. Despite its successes, Gloucester Quays still has some way to go before it has fulfilled its potential.

11. TURNING AN IDEA INTO SOMETHING CONCRETE
Kings Square and Kings Quarter

To say the Kings Square development plans have had a chequered history is putting it mildly. People in Gloucester have for many years believed it wouldn't ever happen. Citizen journalist Martin Kirby summed up the mood of the people in his 'Gloucester born and bred' column, after another announcement that the development was imminent, when he said something along the lines of, "It's good news that Kings Square is going to be done. But it was good news the last time, and the time before that and the time before that."

Until the 1960s, King Square was the bus station and a car park. The public space as we know it was created in the early 1970s as part of the Kings Walk development. The features I remember from my childhood – the fountains, the stepping stones, the bearpit toilets and the concrete structures – were typical of the design of that era. Indeed, the scheme was award-winning in its day, but it just didn't stand the test of time. One idea, however, that was never taken up was the tongue-in-cheek suggestion from Councillor Pam Tracey, before the 1996 council elections, that the city should put a bear in the bearpit!

The revamped Kings Square was opened in May 1972 by the then Environment Secretary Peter Walker. He was, like me, a former Chairman of Gloucester Young Conservatives. He started his career working at the General Accident insurance offices in Brunswick Road and went on to be one of the longest-serving Cabinet Ministers of the twentieth century.

The Citizen headline on that day read "Gloucester's example to the country". The new square, which cost £124,000, showed that, according to Peter Walker, "Gloucester, in environmental terms, has given a good lead to the rest of the country." The Mayor at the time, Harry Worrall, promised that "Funds would be made available to keep it in first class condition" – but he wasn't in office long enough to ensure that promise was honoured. Geoffrey Holmes, a vice president and director of Norwich Union, recalled a "major crisis" when contractors could not continue because of financial difficulties and Norwich Union had to take over. The Band of Royal Engineers from Aldershot, played 'Congratulations' to the crowd, which included visitors from our twin cities of Metz & Trier. The renowned architect and town planner Geoffrey Jellicoe, whose 1961 plan for the city centre had envisaged the new Kings Square, looked on. In a sign of what was to come, before the ceremony a workman with an elver net was fishing out soap suds from fountains!

Peter Walker presented me with a prize at the Crypt School's Speech Day in 1989, when the school was celebrating its 450th anniversary, and came back to visit with me during my 2005 general election campaign. His son Robin was also later to become MP for Worcester and a Government Minister. Robin came to see Kings Square, pretty much at its worst, as part of a House of Commons Select Committee delegation.

One of the pictures I had in my office as Leader of the Council was an advert from Norwich Union, owners of Kings Walk, showing an image of a newly-developed Kings Square with the slogan, "Turning an idea into something concrete". How true that was!

It's difficult to pinpoint exactly when Kings Square turned from being a nice place to meet, as I remember it as a child, to an embarrassment to the city. When I was first elected in 1996, it was firmly in the latter category. Council Officers from that time tell me it was starting to be a problem by the late 1980s. The focus at that time was the pedestrianisation of the gate streets, meaning there was not much money left for anything else like Kings Square. *The Citizen* on 1st April 2006 described how Kings Square in the 1980s started to "fall into disrepair" as the "fountains became too difficult and costly to maintain" and in the 1990s was "no longer a haven for shoppers" but instead was a "used as a dumping ground and gathering place for down and outs."

In June 1992, at a meeting of the City Council's Highways and Planning Committee, Councillor Pam Tracey branded Kings Square "a disgrace", adding, "Something needs to be done. I would like to see Kings Square buzzing again because it's a dead end at the moment."

The Citizen reported how Brian Jarlett, owner of greetings card shop Brandi was even more direct, saying, "Whoever built it should be shot". In December 1993, *The Citizen* ran a story of how the Square was "overrun" with rats. Martin Bingham, owner of the Health Food and Herbal Store, was quoted as saying, "It's always worse when the fountains are drained. The Square is so run down. What we need is a Pied Piper to get rid of them rather than a Mayor". Environmental Health Officer Derek Perry contended that "rats are part of life in any city."

A Planning Brief for the development of the area (the first of many) was adopted in 1994, with *The Citizen* reporting that the Council wanted to give the "timeworn" square a complete revamp, "getting rid of some of the obstructions". Cash was reported to be the biggest problem, with the Council looking for outside investment. Daniel Carter of Arrowcroft, who had been trying to regenerate the Blackfriars area of the city, wrote to City Planning Officer David Scott in April 1997 offering to pay £15,000 for architects BDP and surveyors Donaldsons to complete a design and financing study for Kings Walk and Square. BDP Chairman David Cash wrote to Carter in March 1997 and recalled visiting Gloucester in the mid-1970s and seeing "children and adults paddling in the sparkling waters and playing amid the stepping stones and fountains". He noted that "matters had certainly deteriorated dramatically by the time I revisited 18 months ago".

By 2001, the fountains had stopped working, following the odd report of washing up liquid being poured into them, in an echo of the soap suds incident at the opening in 1972.[200] There was a reported £150,000 bill to bring them back into use, which the Council couldn't stomach, and fears about legionnaires' disease after they had been unused for some time. The public toilets had become an unpleasant experience. The Golden Egg building (named after the restaurant chain from the 1960s and 70s which first occupied it) rapidly became an eyesore. The Burgerland café/restaurant had moved out and the only tenants interested in it were temporary, low value retailers. The Regal cinema moved from Kings Square to the Peel Centre in 1990 and was replaced by a Wetherspoons pub in 1996 which, although a novelty at first, attracted a certain kind of customer with its early opening times and cheap beer. A Citizen press cutting from October

1995 tells the story of how human remains were found on the site of The Regal. Although the Home Office pathologist was informed, it was found to be a several hundred-year-old jaw bone! This was perhaps not surprising as the site was once a cemetery. The article reported that Wetherspoons were investing £2 million and would be serving beer at 79p a pint.[201]

It's also difficult to track exactly when the first serious attempts to revamp the Square began. There have been a number of attempts over the years to redevelop the area, with all the twists and turns making it difficult to follow. Looking back, the number of reports that work "could start next year" are embarrassing. It should be noted that references to the development of Kings Square have been used interchangeably with Kings Quarter (the name given to the wider area including the 'old' bus station and Market Parade).

On 29th June 2002, *The Citizen* carried a front-page headline of "City Square Set for A New Look" which describes how the then Mayor Pam Tracey lobbied David Wise, property investment manager of Morley Fund Management (part of Norwich Union), at the Gloucester Cricket Festival. Pam is quoted as saying, "I want you to promise you will get rid of that dreadful building which used to be the Golden Egg restaurant and give us a square that would be a pleasure to look out on. What we want are some nice wine bars where people could go after a hard day at work and relax in a nice environment."

Wise responded, "We are not just looking at our side of the square, but the whole lot, in conjunction with other retailers and landowners. We don't have any specific plans or designs yet, but we are carrying out a complete audit with our partners, including the city council. We believe we can come up with a scheme which will provide more shops and still have plenty of space for an events area."

Those involved from Morley FM say that the response from the City Council to their efforts to bring forward a development scheme was lukewarm and obstacles seemed to be put in the way. The vision was then, as it is largely now, for a continental-style square with a café culture and a flexible space for events. It was potentially a big investment from Norwich Union, which at the time didn't feel the need to bring a developer partner on board.

It's also true to say that Norwich Union/Morley were nervous about the impact the proposed development at Gloucester Quays would have on the city centre. Their response could have been to raise their game and invest. Instead, they chose to retrench. I think events have shown they took the wrong path.

Kings Square and the Bus Station were the stated priorities for the capital receipt the Council would receive from the St Oswalds/Cattle Market development but when the cash arrived it was used, some would say squandered, in other ways.

An advert for Norwich Union featuring the 1970s design of Kings Square.

Interim Works

When the Conservatives formed the City Council's Administration in 2004, my predecessor as Leader Mark Hawthorne wanted to do something about Kings Square. The money wasn't there for a full-blown refurbishment, so in March 2006 some limited works costing £250,000 were undertaken, including removal of the remains of the fountains and replacement of the paving in the lower section with resin-bound tarmac. The proposed removal of some of the larger trees was controversial. Marnie Mitchell from Hartpury launched a petition to save the trees and was joined by Ros Lane from Maisemore.[202] After I had spent some time in the Square talking to members of the public, the loss of trees was scaled back a little. These interim works made the Square look a bit better, and made it a more usable space for events like the Christmas Ice Rink, but it was still a fairly bleak space. The photograph of Mark and me in hard hats, high viz jackets and holding sledgehammers would come back to haunt us later when the wider plans for the area didn't progress as we would have hoped.[203]

The Citizen's Hugh Worsnip wasn't impressed by the work, saying, "My fear is that political expediency to be seen as 'doing something' is prejudicing a long-term solution."[204]

When I became Leader I undertook my own set of interim works in 2011, principally filling in and grassing over the bearpit toilets and knocking down the small building which had housed the Pulp record shop. Citizen columnist Martin Kirby described it as a "free beer garden" for The Chambers pub, but it was never really misused in the way he had feared.

International Design Competition

There was some tension between those who wanted to ensure Kings Square was part of a wider masterplan for the area, which would have meant building over some of it and would have involved a delay, and those who just wanted it done. This mirrored the tension between the City Council and the GHURC.

In December 2007, the Urban Regeneration Company and the Royal Institute of British Architects launched an 'international design competition' to find a solution for Kings Square, with an indicative budget of £4 million. The Square had to be able to accommodate the Christmas ice rink and a 650 sqm pavilion building. I described it at the time as "a unique opportunity to help shape one of the most important areas of the city." A panel made up of key stakeholders was chaired by former CABE and English Heritage Commissioner Les Sparks OBE. The winning design by Nial McLaughlin Architects & Churchman Landscape Architects was based on a 'square within a square', with the smaller square flooding from time to time or, in their words, "A grid of slate paving platforms surrounded by trees and an elaborate water feature." Caireen O'Hagan, project architect at McLaughlin, said, "We feel that Gloucester hasn't got the recognition it deserves and Kings Square is being underused. The design is very modern and forward thinking. We wanted to encapsulate the history of Gloucester and its relationship with the River Severn." I had misgivings about this and feared it could be seen as an insult to people whose homes flooded in 2007. I wasn't that keen on the design generally and neither was the Council's Director of Regeneration at that time, Phil Staddon, who said it "would probably win awards but the people of Gloucester would hate it".

Work was expected to begin before Christmas 2008 following a public consultation and take two to three years to complete.

The winning design for Kings Square from the 2007 international design competition. Credit: Litchfield Morris/GHURC

Before the plan had a chance to go anywhere – either to be officially adopted by the Council, whose land it was, or to get planning permission – the money to fund it had vanished. The main public funders of regeneration, English Partnerships and the Regional Development Agency, had been given notice that their funding would be cut from 2011 and they, understandably, refused to make commitments beyond that. The fact that the City Council didn't control the whole Square and, in particular, the dreaded Golden Egg, also raised questions about its deliverability.

The Golden Egg

As mentioned earlier, this building was a former restaurant which bore this name before becoming a 'Burgerland' fast food joint. In the mid-1990s, Norwich Union had a £350,000 plan to turn it into an open-air café. It was met with scepticism by councillors. Councillor Pam Tracey said, "I thought it was a monstrosity before and I still think it's a monstrosity". Fellow Councillor Mike Pullon doubted it would work as a café as it was "perpetually in the shade" and accused Norwich Union of trying to trick the Council into the "wretched piecemeal development of Kings Square." The plans never came to pass and it was only ever brought into use as a short-term, low value retail unit.

By the 2000s, the Golden Egg was becoming infamous as an eyesore and stood as a symbol of the failure of regeneration.

In December 2009, it had been wrapped in Christmas vinyls in an attempt to make it the world's biggest advent calendar, but the vinyls were left in place thereafter, risking it becoming the world's longest-running advent calendar! It was owned by Aviva (the renamed Norwich Union) as part of Kings Walk Shopping Centre and hopes were raised when Aviva submitted their own application to demolish the Golden Egg in February 2011, which was approved in April 2011. Optimistically and perhaps even rashly, I said at the time that I "expect works to start in weeks not months." By February 2012 there was frustration as Aviva changed tack and said it would refurbish it instead.

I said, "I wish they would get on and demolish it." Westgate councillor Pam Tracey added, "I've had enough. I wash my hands of it."[205] City MP Richard Graham called it "the ugliest wart on the face of the city." Citizen columnist Martin Kirby pointed out, "There can't be many people who will be more pleased than I will to see the back of the decrepit Golden Egg that hangs over Kings Square like a concrete Grim Reaper. Although it is now considered ugly and looks older than Sir Bruce Forsyth, we shouldn't forget that it was once seen as modern and attractive."

To turn up the heat on Aviva, in November 2013 a demolition order was slapped on the Golden Egg.

In the end, towards the end of 2013, I lost patience and offered that the Council would buy the building and knock it down ourselves. Perhaps that was Aviva's game and I'd fallen for it, but I didn't mind as the £200,000 cost was probably the best £200,000 I'd ever spent. It was a popular move, although the then Labour Group Leader Mark Hobbs suggested moving the Tourist Information Centre to the Golden Egg.[206]

I'd never had so much pleasure swinging a sledgehammer as when this happened! Other councillors queued up to lend a hand and *The Citizen* ran a competition for a member of the public to join us. It was won by mother and son Rita and Joel Prystajeckyj-Townley from Hucclecote. Rita's Mum had worked at the Golden Egg in the 1970s.

The building was physically linked via a bridge to the Iceland building in Kings Walk and although it was in poor condition cosmetically it was still a solid structure and took quite some effort to demolish!

When the building was demolished in early 2014, the area was reinstated as an addition to the Square, albeit with a slight change of levels. It wasn't actively used other than for tables and chairs for the adjacent coffee shop, earning it the nickname 'Costa Square'. Aside from the symbolic nature of demolishing the infamous Golden Egg, we needed to acquire it and the two small kiosks alongside it, to be able to comprehensively refurbish the Square.

The former Golden Egg in Kings Square looking past its best.

Kings Quarter

As early as August 2005 it was reported that "work could start on Kings Square in less than a year", with the City Council about to enter into an 'Exclusivity Agreement' with Norwich Union. An agreement was signed in January 2007.

The GHURC Regeneration Framework referred to Kings Quarter being anchored by a major new department store, with Kings Square redesigned as a continental-style plaza and continuing as the city's principal outdoor events venue. It proposed 35,000 sqm of additional comparison retail. This was the starting point for the City Council/Norwich Union scheme.

Urban Initiatives were commissioned by Morley, GHURC and the City Council in February 2007 to come up with a masterplan for the area. Their plan was ambitious, with 300,000 sq ft of new retail/leisure space and 200,000 sq ft of refurbished space. In addition, they proposed 260 flats and envisaged a new bus station facing the Land Registry (where it ended up going), a pavilion building in Kings Square and the front of the Iceland building cut back to become level with the adjacent building (now Costa Coffee). There would be a new department store on the bus station site and new retail at Kings House (The Chambers pub) and the two Spread Eagle Road sites. Urban Initiatives didn't pull their punches, describing how "underperforming retail, empty buildings and tired public realm articulate a lack of civic pride" and pointing out that 20 years previously Gloucester had a retail ranking of 42nd in the country – and it was now in the high 80s. Their work also included coming up with a brief for an International Design Competition for Kings Square, which GHURC would run, as mentioned earlier.

The City Council and Aviva brought Thornfield Properties on board to progress a development. Their initial scheme was for an anchor store and 45 retail units, entailing building over much of Kings Square and creating a new, smaller square nearer the bus station.

Before the plans had progressed, the Council was given legal advice that it was necessary to go out to an EU-compliant procurement exercise, citing the 'Roanne case'. This was a landmark judgement in the case of 'Jean Auroux and others v the Commune de Roanne', where a public works contract had been awarded without a tender process and found to be unlawful. Roanne is a small town in the Loire area of France with a population of around 35,000. Such a tender process is lengthy, time-consuming and expensive. The end value of the proposed development, based on 28 acres (including parts of Northgate Street such as what was then the Wilkinsons, later Wilko, store), was estimated at £350 million, which dwarfed the £60 million scheme later suggested by Stanhope and the £100 million we talk about over a decade later.

As the procurement process was being taken forward, the credit crunch hit. The decision was taken, with external advice, to proceed with it – something which was seen as 'brave', to put it politely, at the time, with the Western Daily Press pointing out that big property companies like Hammerson and Land Securities were having to raise hundreds of millions of pounds to shore up their balance sheets. The logic was that by the time this lengthy process had come to a conclusion, the looming recession would have passed and the world would have returned to business as usual. It seemed logical advice at the time, but we didn't bank on the recession being the longest and deepest since the war. In hindsight it would have been better to have taken a different course.

The formal process got underway in February 2009 with the Council saying it "expected to have a developer in place by the year-end." I noted at the time that "People in Gloucester are understandably impatient for progress" but warned that "this is a complex project which will take time to deliver."[207]

Having come out of the other side of the procurement process, the only party still in the game was Thornfield – so, irritatingly, the lengthy and expensive process had achieved nothing other than confirming the developer who was already there at the start. Thornfield's Chief Executive Mike Capocci, a diminutive man of Italian descent, was described to me as a man who "never knew when to stop negotiating". Thornfield's other major scheme in gestation was in the city centre of Winchester – which was also later to come unstuck as a result of the Roanne ruling, with one of their own councillors taking the City Council to a judicial review.

In Gloucester's case, Thornfield's 300,000 sq ft scheme didn't have a chance to gather much of a head of steam before the company went into liquidation in March 2010. This cleared the way for the Council to talk to other parties without having to go through a tender process.

Terry Webster of High Star Developments (see chapter on St Oswalds Park) came up with a 'Gloucester Gateway' scheme, which took in Kings Square and the bus station and the then derelict former Dunelm and Courts Furnishings buildings on Bruton Way, which ended up being acquired by Aviva. Terry's approach was to work up a scheme, which he would then sign up a developer partner to deliver, as he had at St Oswald's with Grantchester/Hammerson.

Hammerson started to look at the scheme in April 2010. Their scheme had two anchor stores – a new Debenhams and a John Lewis at Home - and 52 retail units (including dividing up the existing Debenhams), a new Kings Square and a new bus station on the former Courts Furnishings site on the opposite side of Bruton Way (now the Railway House office building). In July 2010, Hammerson declared that the development was not viable, citing high costs, low rent levels and expensive incentives for tenants. They also believed the overall scheme was too big, and contained too much retail, for a city of Gloucester's size.

Peter Mawson of DTZ (the company which had taken over Donaldsons), who had advised the City Council on property matters previously, introduced the Council to Stanhope. His former colleague from Donaldsons, Martyn Chase, was now working at Stanhope, who were picking up development opportunities across the country in places like Salisbury, Truro and Crawley. They had just committed to delivering a scheme on the former Cattle Market at nearby Hereford, which ended up winning the 'New Centre of the Year' category at the British Council of Shopping Centres Awards in December 2014 – in fact it was the only major retail development to open that year!

The other interested party was a newer and much smaller outfit without Stanhope's standing and track record. Understandably, the Council's Cabinet chose Stanhope, initially entering into a six month 'exclusivity agreement' approved by Full Council in December 2011. Stanhope was founded by Sir Stuart Lipton, who was a legendary figure in the property world, and had completed £12 billion of developments. This included the former Regent Palace Hotel near Piccadilly Circus for office, retail and restaurant use. It was usually with other people's money, with Stanhope acting as development manager or partner and tended to be office developments in Central London rather than provincial retail developments. *The Citizen* described them as "a highly committed developer with an excellent pedigree"[208] and "a developer with a real feel for what needs to be done."[209] But to some it felt like this was the last chance saloon.

A development agreement was signed in September 2012. We staged a signing at a press ceremony in Kings Square itself and we were all optimistic about the prospects of finally delivering a solution. Martyn Chase said, "It shows investors it is real. It shows retailers it is real and it shows the people of Gloucester it is real."[210] The initial Stanhope scheme was not without its controversies though. It proposed building on much of Kings Square, leaving a much smaller public space near the Post Office building and another towards the bus station. We were told this was to continue the flow of retail units towards the north of the site at Market Parade, where the anchor store would be. Initially Stanhope proposed a supermarket anchor, which was believed to be Waitrose, but as with their sister store John Lewis they didn't feel Gloucester's demographics sufficiently matched their customer base. Later, Primark, whose Gloucester store was felt to be undersized, were touted as the anchor in an upsized and relocated store.

Stanhope's scheme went through several iterations over its time.

Their first scheme in 2011 was made up of 5 large stores and 21 smaller shops. In 2013 it was one anchor store, 35 smaller units and 6 restaurants and in 2014 it became one anchor store, 22 smaller units together with city centre living, restaurants and a cinema. In 2015 there was even talk of an ice rink at Kings Quarter, which delighted some locals who have regularly called for such a facility in the city.

Signing up tenants was also proving difficult. Without a planning consent and without even controlling all of the land required, most retailers would say "come back when you're a bit closer". In 2011, Stanhope claimed to be talking to John Lewis and House of Fraser. Various other brands were shown on plans, but without any form of commitment from them. Later it appeared the only tenants they seemed to be able to attract interest from were those already in the city centre – risking a game of musical chairs which would leave holes elsewhere.

Progress from Stanhope was slow – earning them the unwanted nickname from *The Citizen*'s Mike Wilkinson, a young journalist who gave the impression of being ambitious and ruthless in equal measure, of 'Stanhopeless'. Stanhope's apparent lack of confidence in the scheme, in themselves or both, was such that they were unwilling to spend the £500,000 or so a planning application would cost until tenants were signed up and the financial appraisal hit the magic 15% profit margin. Neither ever happened. Stanhope were pinning their hopes on Aviva funding the development – but Chris Paterson, their Fund Manager, was not persuaded, despite an offer to change (re-gear) Aviva's lease from the Council on the Kings Walk shopping centre to make it more favourable for them.

Stanhope missed their deadline to submit a planning application twice and were granted two extensions. The extensions had to be approved by the Full Council. The first time it was done there were a few grumbles, but it was fairly straightforward. The second occasion was one of my most uncomfortable times in a Full Council meeting with criticism from all sides, including my own, while I tried to defend the indefensible.

In June 2013, Stanhope claimed they had an anchor tenant but still wouldn't be submitting a planning application. White Young Green, who acted as planning consultants for Peel at Gloucester Quays, claimed "the proposals are in their infancy and are far from certain of being delivered" and disputed Stanhope's claim to have an anchor tenant. Martyn Chase said, "It's not true. They are trying to rubbish us but they are wrong."[211]

In March 2014, Pam Tracey, as ever, lightened the mood by setting out one of her aspirations for the Square, saying, "We might get one of those loos that looks like a Doctor Who tardis." In May 2014 two archaeological trenches were dug in Kings Square and in June, a further three were excavated at the bus station. City Archaeologist Andrew Armstrong said, "We are hoping to find Roman townhouses under the square and hopefully the remains of the Whitefriars Friary under the bus station".[212] As I record later in this chapter, Whitefriars wasn't found for another six years.

Under the original development agreement, the developer was to be responsible for land acquisition and building a new bus station as part of the scheme. Ultimately, the Council ended up doing both – buying Kings House (The Chambers pub building), Grosvenor House (next to the old bus station), Bentinck House (the old tax office) and the Bruton Way multi-storey car park from Aviva and securing £6.4 million of government grant for the bus station and financing the balance of the scheme.

The purchase from Aviva, in November 2014, at the time was the City's biggest property acquisition for many years and was described as a 'landmark deal'. We draped huge banners over Grosvenor House and Bentinck House to say they had been acquired by the City Council for the Kings Quarter development. Mindful of the signs that were fixed onto buildings in Blackfriars until they rotted, we didn't keep them there for long. In August 2015, *The Citizen* ran a story saying the City Council had spent £7 million on the Kings Quarter project. This didn't concern me as the vast majority of that sum was made up of property purchases which were generating an income.

Prior to the Council buying Grosvenor House, Aviva had granted a new 15-year lease to Tesco, inside the Landlord & Tenant Act, which meant they had renewal rights. This helped Aviva to maximise the value of the asset, but hamstrung the Kings Quarter development because without finding them a new site or paying Tesco huge compensation to break the lease, they would be there for the duration.

Patience with Stanhope was starting to wear thin by early 2015, with developer's claim that Kings Quarter would be up and running by December 2018 described on the front page of *The Citizen* as a "Christmas Miracle" with editor Jenny Eastwood adding "it has felt like pulling teeth."[213]

In July 2015, she added "Stanhope has continually put the dates back to the point where we really have to question if its plans will ever see the light of day."

Tension between Peel and Stanhope

The Council leading on land acquisition and taking on the bus station project stretched the credibility of the Development Agreement. Other landowners and developers with competing interests, notably Peel, reminded the Council of the Roanne judgement and shared the legal opinion they had obtained, suggesting the arrangement should be re-tendered in light of the changes.

There was a tension between Stanhope and Peel, as owners of Gloucester Quays and the Peel Centre retail park, when Peel was seeking a relaxation of planning restrictions which limited the type of goods that could be sold on their estate. This was demonstrated most clearly in 2014 by the application for Home Bargains, a discount retailer, to open at the Peel Centre. Stanhope objected and Chase, unwisely in my view, spoke against the application at the Planning Committee in February 2014 – despite admitting that Home Bargains wasn't the kind of retailer they wanted in Kings Quarter – calling it a "Trojan Horse". Councillor Lise Noakes (C, Barnwood) summed up the situation saying "…it (Home Bargains) is not the type of brand the city needed in Kings Quarter".

Peel and Home Bargains appealed and Peel's legal team set about taking apart the premise of Stanhope's objection. Their barrister apparently made mincemeat of Chase at the public inquiry. The Council's Head of Regeneration Anthony Hodge also took the witness stand and told me he was dismantled by Peel's barrister to the extent that he could barely remember his name! Apparently, the barrister afterwards pointed at the rope for the HMS Gloucester bell on the ceiling of the Council Chamber at North Warehouse, where the inquiry was being held, and said to him, "Mr Hodge, I thought you were going to hang yourself on that!"

The Planning Inquiry was held on 3-4 September 2014 and the appeal was granted on 27th October 2014. In written evidence from Robin Denness, a director of property advisers JLL on behalf of Peel, which I hadn't seen until researching this book, he gave a damning assessment of Kings Quarter, saying, "When considered against the aspirations for the regeneration of the Kings Square area it is neither transformational nor ambitious and will certainly not by any objective measure ultimately result in a noticeable step change in the performance and retail ranking of Gloucester City Centre."

He also produced emails from the potential tenants floated by Stanhope. Next said they were "not likely" to take a unit, Superdry said it was "not on our target list", Arcadia (owner of Burtons, Dorothy Perkins and Top Shop) said it had "no requirements at this time" and the House of Fraser "(didn't) currently have a requirement" either.

They also pointed to the failure, or at least the lack of progress, of Stanhope's other schemes. In Stevenage they were appointed by Stevenage Borough Council in a joint venture with ING in February 2004 and withdrew in May 2012. In Truro they were promoting a joint venture with LaSalle Investment Management in January 2011. The latest press comment in August 2013 stated that they were "...working behind the scenes to bring the proposal forward...".

In Salisbury, they were appointed by Wiltshire County Council and Salisbury Vision in February 2012. The original appointment envisaged a planning application would be submitted during 2013. The latest press comment in March 2014 stated they "...hope to submit a planning application towards the end of 2015...". And in Crawley they were appointed by Crawley Borough Council in July 2012 to work on a £200 million town centre regeneration scheme. A press comment in June 2014 stated that the "...£200 million plan to regenerate Crawley Town Centre is scrapped."

In his Appeal decision, Planning Inspector John Gray ruled, "Mr Chase, representing Stanhope, the Council's development partner, pointed out that his company is required to make a start on site by September 2017 and that he envisaged the development being open for business for Christmas 2018. That deadline could, however, be changed by agreement; and even a start by then leaves doubt about shops being open by Christmas 2018. There is no cogent reason to depart from the assessment above that the King's Quarter development is unlikely to open before Christmas 2019."

He added, "It is difficult to envisage a high-quality retailer with a similar business model that would fit with the intended retail style of the King's Quarter development."

When I brokered a meeting between Martyn Chase and Jason Pullen of Peel, the dynamics were fascinating. Pullen tried to reach out and be consensual. Chase acted as though he had the upper hand, despite what I saw as his weak position. Although Pullen was junior in years, in reality he was far more powerful as he had the ear and the trust of Peel Chairman John Whittaker who would make their multi-million-pound investment decisions.

In asset terms, the difference between the two companies was stark. In their accounts to 31st March 2014, Stanhope had net assets of just under £28 million. The accounts for Peel Land and Property (not the whole group) of the same date showed net assets of £667 million. You'd have thought from the body language that it was the other way round.

Stanhope wanted to restrict who Peel could sign up as tenants on the Peel Centre retail park as well as secure a hefty contribution from Peel, believed to be £1 million, towards their scheme. There was a difference in attitudes too. Peel saw the city centre as complementary to what they wanted to achieve at Gloucester Quays, Stanhope saw Peel as competition.

The Bus Station/Transport Hub

The 'old' bus station opened on 30th April 1962 and was given a Civic Trust award in December 1963.

By the time I became a councillor, and even more so by the time I became Leader, the bus station had become notorious in the city and beyond for all the wrong reasons and I was determined we would sort it out.

I hadn't realised until fairly recently that it had previously gained notoriety some years previously for an entirely different reason. Iconic sixties actor Peter Wyngarde, who played the on-screen detective and ladies' man Jason King, was fined £75 for 'gross indecency' relating to an incident at a Gloucester bus station toilets in 1975 which his defence in court tried to explain away as a "mental aberration". Wyngarde's flamboyant style is said to have inspired the Mike Myers spy spoof film character Austin Powers.

The City Council took on responsibility for delivering the bus station project from Stanhope in 2014 and it was led by Philip Ardley, the Council's regeneration consultant who was a former regional managing partner for GVA Grimley. We were lucky to have Philip – he didn't have to work and was further beyond normal retirement age than he looked. In property terms, he'd already been there and got the t-shirt. His skills and contacts over the years would prove invaluable.

I recall reading a cruel article about the city some years ago. It said that Gloucester Bus Station was reminiscent of a communist country and "told you all you needed to know about Gloucester". It's true that the old bus station wasn't the kind of first impression we wanted to give about the city, but it was unfair to suggest this was an accurate reflection of the city as a whole.

Grosvenor House, next to the bus station, had seen better days. I remember the school secretary when I was at The Crypt School, Gene Burgham, telling me that it had been designed by her late husband and whenever she went past it, it reminded her of him. I felt sorry for Mrs Burgham that it hadn't stood the test of time better, or been better maintained, and felt a little bit guilty that I was responsible for its demolition, at least in stages.

The old bus station wasn't a welcoming environment and didn't feel safe. It became a haven for beggars and rough sleepers and we desperately had to do something about it. Securing funding for it wasn't straightforward. In July 2013, our bid for £4.7 million to the Local Transport Body (which distributed Government transport funding) was turned down. After much lobbying, we secured £1.7 million from them and £4.7 million from the Government's Growth Deal (which was announced in July 2014), making a total of £6.4 million for the scheme, with the City Council picking up the rest of the £8.7 million cost. The brief to architects was to come up with a building which was "iconic yet affordable". BDP Architects of Bristol, led by Neil Sansum, were appointed to design it (beating 70 other bidders), based on their concept design, which was modelled on an aircraft wing as a nod to the city's aviation history, which was unveiled in May 2015. The public consultation we undertook was fairly positive, although some people asked, "Isn't it a bit nice for Gloucester?" Some locals described it as "the ironing board" or "the boomerang", but neither name seemed to stick.

Anthony Hodge, with my support, insisted on local stone being used on part of the building. This was expensive but worth it. There was some discussion about the roof material, with the initial suggestion being ETFE, a clear plastic polymer. There were concerns over seagull mess and whether local yobs would take pot-shots at it with an air rifle, so we settled on a solid roof.

After gaining planning permission in December 2015, work started in February 2016 to demolish the eastern end of Grosvenor House where the Furniture Recycling Project was based, along with the public toilets and the bus station café, which was something of an institution in the city. Many people will remember the FRP's unit as the House of Holland. The FRP moved to the other end of Grosvenor House, which had been vacated by a shop selling kitsch Italian furniture, which I'm surprised anyone in Gloucester bought!

In February 2016, I commented, "The existing one (bus station) has been a blot on Gloucester's landscape for far too long."[214]

Kier Construction were appointed contractors in May 2016. Demolition was completed In June 2016 with archaeological works beginning straight after. At the end of August 2016, a Roman building which may have been 35m long was found onsite which excited the archaeologists! Some believed that Roman flood defences had been uncovered but others were not convinced that was the case.

Once the archaeology was complete, HRH The Duke of Gloucester buried a time capsule under the site in September 2016. It contained various items including a Gloucester Rugby shirt, a Gloucester City football shirt, a bottle of Gloucester Brewery ale, a Scrumpty keyring, a Beatrix Potter mug and a letter from me, as Leader of the Council, to future generations.

Building a major piece of infrastructure within a confined and historic city centre is a complex project and takes time. There was archaeology, service diversions and changes to the road network around it, including opening up the junction of Station Road and Bruton Way opposite Asda, to deal with before anything could come out of the ground. Philip Ardley managed the project with remarkable skill and it was completed broadly on time and on budget.

Part way through we realised that the mains sewer wasn't quite in the place the maps said it was – which is not an entirely unusual occurrence. This meant the building had to be slightly redesigned as you can't build over the sewer, so a planning application for an amendment had to be submitted. I wrongly thought this wasn't particularly significant. It would reduce the building's footprint by a metre and would make it a metre higher, but perhaps more crucially would reduce the number of public toilets, in the end from ten to seven. There were also some minor changes like replacing some of the glazing on the north side with render on the Police's advice.

Planning applications are, of course, public and can be accessed online very easily by anyone. I recall when I was on paternity leave after the birth of my second daughter Tydwen getting a phone call from a Citizen journalist asking me about the planning application. I explained what it was all about and was then surprised to see a headline a day or two later claiming the bus station was being "quietly scaled back". This was probably the front-page headline that annoyed me most in my 24 years as a councillor. It wasn't "quietly" as it was in public and I didn't think a metre really amounted to it being "scaled back". In hindsight, I wished we'd taken a more proactive approach to communicating that.

I commented, "We've had to apply for a minor variation to the scheme because a sewer was in a different position to where we expected it to be". A spokesman for the Station Hotel described it as "a kick in the teeth", which I thought was rather over the top but I recognised that they had suffered inconvenience from the construction works. More importantly though, it fed the public's sense of cynicism that they weren't going to get something as good as they'd been promised.

The bus station opened on 27th October 2018, with a blessing from The Dean, and a cavalcade of vintage buses on its first public open day organised by Councillor Colin Organ, founder of the city's Retro Festival. It was well-received by the public. I'm proud to have an engraved foundation stone just by the entrance, which I unveiled in April 2018 – but it is deliberately faint to avoid drawing too much attention to it, particularly from those with cans of spray paint!

I was very pleased with how it turned out. Neil Sansum told me that, in hindsight, he wished that the column on the Bruton Way side of the building, which holds the roof cables, had been a couple of metres higher to make it even more striking. Even as it stands, it is a wonder of construction and had been calculated to within a millimetre by a highly-skilled structural engineer.

One of the conditions of the planning consent was for a piece of public art to be included. Anthony Hodge came up with the idea of 'The Gloucester Window' – a set of stained-glass panels with images depicting the city's history, which was inspired by the Burrell Collection of stained glass, based in Glasgow. I commented at the time "Gloucester needs its regeneration to be distinctive and of high quality. I'm sure it will be a stunning piece of work".[215] This was a controversial idea, largely because of the £100,000 budget.

It caused a split within Cabinet, with one member vehemently against it because of the cost, and another who he dragged along with him. The rest of us stood firm and the storm, if there really was one, soon passed. We had support from The Dean and, to be fair to them, the Liberal Democrats. It was hoped that Tom Denny, an internationally-renowned stained-glass artist who has windows in Gloucester Cathedral, would be able to do it. In the end he declined because the light wasn't right for his style of work, saying: "I made several designs in collaboration with my wife, the artist Benita Kevill Davies.

"We decided, however, when we saw the nearly completed building, that the available natural light was going to be inadequate for the sort of work that we were proposing.

"We both hope that the project thrives in other hands." He was also reportedly busy working on a Cathedral in Germany.

Daedalian Glass from Lancashire took on the project. We came up with a list of historical events and images to include in the panels. I vetoed the suggestion of a panel depicting the expulsion of the Jews from Gloucester in the 13th century. Coming at a time when the row about antisemitism in the Labour Party was at its peak, it seemed a little insensitive. I also replaced the fires and plagues with more positive and cheerful subjects. At the time of writing, we were still to see any of the panels but the City Council said that installation would take place early in 2024, attributing the delay to supply chain issues.

Bus operator Stagecoach initially declined to move its most popular service, the 94 which ran between Cheltenham and Gloucester, into the new Transport Hub, continuing to pick up and drop off on Market Parade. With the closure of Market Parade to enable the building of Phase Two of Kings Quarter in March 2022, their flagship service finally started to use the flagship Transport Hub.

Taking Back Control

The moment I decided the Stanhope scheme was going nowhere was in a meeting at the British Council of Shopping Centres Conference in Manchester – an annual get together of the retail and property industries where deals are done. Anthony Hodge, the Council's Head of Regeneration, and I met with Martyn Chase and the Head of Estates from a major target retailer. They were brutal in how they expressed that they were "not interested", saying it was "off pitch" and "not a retail site". In the end, that particular retailer went to an edge of centre retail park.

Once the conference proper was over and the beers started flowing, the three of us sketched out, literally, on the back of an envelope how a different scheme might look. The scheme we came up with – a strong route between the Railway Station and Kings Square, a replacement car park for the crumbling Bruton Way multi-storey, apartments, office space, a hotel and commercial units – is largely the one for which planning consent was granted in March 2020. Importantly for me, and for the city, it preserved Kings Square as a public space.

In March 2016, no doubt motivated by the forthcoming all-out elections that May, Labour and the Liberal Democrats combined to say it was "Time to scrap Kings Quarter." They demanded a 'Plan B'. In reality, we already had one. As I commented in the Gloucester Review, "Those who have been calling for us to look at an alternative approach should be reassured that we have been doing just that."[216] Our Plan B was unveiled – a replacement car park, hotel, some residential units, leisure and restaurants. I commented, "The world has moved on since our developer partner Stanhope unveiled their proposals some time ago. What may have been the right scheme four or five years ago isn't the right approach now. So we have taken the bold decision to refocus the scheme as a gateway to the city centre, not as a major retail-led development."[217]

Chair of the Regeneration Advisory Board, Dean Stephen Lake backed the move, saying, "It is time to move on as the influences on development have clearly changed and we are of the view that this is the right way forward for Gloucester."

In June 2016 we undertook public consultation on the revised Kings Quarter plans, with four options worked up by Robert Limbrick architects.

Negotiations then took place with Stanhope on their exit. The Council bought some of the technical reports that Stanhope had commissioned which would be of use as the development progressed and Stanhope quietly and amicably left the stage.

In November 2016 we appointed Jones Lang LaSalle and LDA Design to advise us commercially and work up a planning application – no small task and one which would cost upwards of £500,000. Working up the planning application took much longer than I had expected and it took longer to come out the other side than I had hoped. AHR Architects of Bristol were appointed to come up with the design. Esther Croft, who had worked in Gloucester for the Regional Development Agency, was now a Director of LDA and became the lead for the project.

Optimistically and perhaps with a sense of deja vu, it was claimed in September 2017 that Kings Quarter "could start in 12 months". JLL recommended splitting the site into 4 plots. I noted that "we are in charge of our destiny here"[218] but later added "we know people will be sceptical about it, they will believe it when they see it but we have to be persistent and determined to drive ahead with our plans".[219] I tried to show I understood how people felt about it, saying, "I completely understand why people haven't been dancing in the streets at the latest announcement that Kings Square is going to be sorted out. People feel let down and frustrated that it hasn't been done sooner."[220]

The planning application was finally submitted in December 2018, something which I described as "a huge milestone (to submit them), representing a significant investment of resources." Jason Smith of Marketing Gloucester wrote an article questioning whether the design was "distinctively Gloucester" – and asking "do they use materials and reference vernacular idioms", saying that the "designs need to evolve".[221] Cabinet Member for Housing and Planning, Colin Organ, and I spent several sessions with Karl Burford of AHR trying to address this and I felt we came out with a much better scheme.

Plans to demolish Kings House (home to The Chambers pub), which was now in the Council's ownership, were abandoned and the upper floors were put to cultural use. Other than a brief period in which they were used as Marketing Gloucester's offices, they had been empty for around 20 years when they were occupied by the Land Registry. Gloucester Culture Trust delivered the JOLT creative workspace for 'cultural entrepreneurs' on the first floor, managing to create a 'funky' environment on a shoestring. Work began in September 2019 but was delayed by the Covid pandemic and it finally opened in September 2021.

The Music Works took a lease on the second floor, spending £1.8 million to create studios, production and mixing suites, as well as a flexible events space, for their work with young people. They signed the lease in November 2019, work started in September 2020 and the facility fully opened in September 2021. Both leases were on favourable terms for the occupiers – something which some within the City Council queried. I took the view that the space had been empty for a long time and was in poor condition, so there wouldn't be a rush of people looking to rent it and if we could get someone else to spend money improving the condition of the building, everyone would be a winner.

There was also a suggestion of creating a lightweight structure on the roof, along with a roof garden. Not a lot of people know that the building was constructed to have a rooftop car park – but no access to it was ever built! There had also been suggestions that the building could be reclad and that a big screen could be mounted on it, but neither of these ideas had progressed at the time of writing. The Chambers pub closed during the pandemic and didn't reopen, with operator Greene King eventually surrendering the lease to enable the City Council to remarket the property to find a new, and hopefully higher quality, occupier, in January 2024.

In February 2019, archaeological works continued on-site, with seven trenches being dug at the old bus station in the hope of finding the 'long lost' Whitefriars Carmelite Friary, which was destroyed in 1567. A combination of the Dissolution, the Civil War and unsympathetic development in the 1960s and 70s meant that the only clue it had ever existed was a rather weathered small plaque on the side of the monstrous Bruton Way multi-storey car park. It wasn't found at this point but attracted interest from the Carmelite Order of Great Britain. City Archaeologist Andrew Armstrong told me that they found only poor-quality buildings. After the Bruton Way multi-storey car park came down in March 2020, more excavation was possible. Fieldwork took place in July 2000, finding substantial walls 1m thick in an East/West alignment, typical of ecclesiastical buildings.

Following evaluation, the finds were made public. In October 2020, City Archaeologist, Andrew Armstrong, said, "For around three hundred years, Whitefriars played an active part in Gloucester and produced some notable friars including Nicholas Cantelow (or Cantilupe) in the 15th century. It's very exciting to finally reveal the exact location of this 'long-lost' friary. Seeing and documenting this site will serve to underline, and recognise, the place of the friary in the city's history."

Gloucester's Whitefriars owned most of the land between what is now Station Road and Bruton Way, which is shown in some historic maps as 'Friars Ground'. Whilst a variety of sources suggest the Friary itself was located at the western end, next to Market Parade, historians had been unable to confirm the precise location of the friary until this point. The Friary's cemetery has yet to be located.

Further discoveries were unearthed onsite – a stone coffin and an 1800-year-old, 17cm figurine of Venus, the Roman goddess of love, in September 2021 and a medieval tiled floor in February 2022. A short video about "Whitefriars: The Lost Priory of Gloucester" shared on Twitter by television historian Dan Snow has been viewed more than 350,000 times.

Finally delivering a new Kings Square

In the aftermath of Stanhope's exit, the lack of progress in Kings Square was becoming an issue of confidence, just as the Golden Egg had been a number of years earlier. I decided we had to be bold and press on with it and told City Council finance chief Jon Topping that the £5 million cost had to be found. We certainly didn't have that much sitting in the bank and had to be creative in financing it. The funding, split over two years, was approved at the Council's budget meeting in February 2019.

I said in my speech at that meeting, "I would also draw Members' attention to the Capital Programme where we are making provision of £5 million over the next two years to deliver the regeneration of Kings Square, with our stated ambition to start on site in the Autumn. I do not doubt the importance of a rejuvenated Kings Square to civic pride in the city and we are going to deliver it."

I was determined to "bring back the fountains" in the way the public had demanded, but with a modern water feature which didn't compromise the Square as a flexible space for events. There would be a 'sculptured edge' around the Square designed by George King Architects and lighting by the Michael Grubb Studio. I also wanted to 'bring back' the stepping stones that I remember crossing the Square on as a child, or at least a representation of them. My suggestion was that each of them could have details inscribed of one of the Kings or Queens with a connection to Gloucester. I detected that Council Officers and the Council's development partner Reef weren't that keen, but they promised they would do it nonetheless. I wasn't entirely surprised when it was dropped from the project after I left the Council because it was 'too difficult'. I think if it had been included, it would have helped to combat comments from the public that the Square was not "distinctively Gloucester" and didn't make reference to the city's history.

New images for the Square were revealed in November 2019, with 'enabling works' to demolish, disconnect and remove items getting underway. This included the demolition of the kiosks occupied by Carol's Flowers and Westy's sandwich takeaway. I felt sad to be losing Carol's Flowers in particular as they had been in the Square for over 40 years and Carol was part of the Square's furniture. I wanted them to stay in some form. We genuinely tried hard to find a solution, but weren't able to come up with anything acceptable to them. We had a public falling out over that, which saddened me, but tough decisions like that are the stuff of leadership. I can't go into the detail of the arrangement, but I felt we were being more than fair to them.

In January 2020, Midas were appointed the preferred bidder for Kings Square on a 'design and build' basis, but their initial estimate which was within budget grew to be unaffordable and the job had to be re-tendered, with local firm EG Carter winning it second time round, which was a pleasing outcome. The retendering caused a hiatus onsite, coinciding with the Coronavirus pandemic, which provided some cover for the lack of action.

The Square was completed in April 2022 and was officially opened by Mayor Collette Finnegan on 30th April 2022 – almost 50 years to the day since the last time! It's fair to say that the public reaction to it was mixed. News website GloucestershireLive ran an article, which I felt was unfair, describing it as "the most boring skatepark in history" – despite it being designed to discourage skateboarders. Other social media commentators labelled it a "concrete jungle" – despite it being paved with Forest of Dean stone, not concrete! In an article published on their website to coincide with the official opening, I responded saying, "it may have (looked like a concrete jungle) done when it was a building site, but when the trees are in leaf, the planting in bloom, the high-tech lighting and water feature in use and it is filled with people and activity, it will feel a whole lot different!" Time alone will tell as to whether the new square gains more widespread public acceptance.

Debenhams

Debenhams had long been the premier store in Gloucester city centre, going back to the days when it was the Bon Marche, owned by the local Pope family. It opened in 1889 and had a purpose-built store constructed in the 1930s and an extension onto the Square in the 1960s. In more recent years it had declined, with the building providing an uninspiring frontage onto Kings Square with the upper floor windows painted over.

The Debenhams building was bought by Morley Fund Management (part of Aviva) in November 2004 for a figure well over £20 million,[222] reflecting the extraordinarily long 99-year lease to the department store. Chris Paterson, Head of Retail at Morley said, "We recognised it as a fantastic opportunity to secure a strategically important building immediately next door to King's Walk Shopping Centre, one of our funds' major assets." I commented, "It shows a big commitment from Morley to the city." I added optimistically, "I hope it will form the start of a real turnaround for the whole area." When Aviva bought the building, Debenhams was paying rent believed to be £2.4 million a year. Subsequent rent reviews saw this drop until it was just £400,000 and when Debenhams were struggling for survival, they weren't paying any rent at all!

It did get a mini-refurbishment in 2011, involving replacement escalators and new flooring, but even the reported £4 million cost could only provide superficial makeover for a store that size. As online shopping took hold and department stores went out of fashion, Debenhams struggled nationally. The Gloucester store started to cordon off areas as the 230,000 sq ft building became too much for their modern requirements, which were more like 70,000 sq ft. A lack of investment in the building started to show, with Heras fencing installed along The Oxebode to protect pedestrians from falling masonry.

The Coronavirus pandemic was the final straw for the whole Debenhams chain, which went into liquidation in December 2020. In March 2021 it was announced that the University of Gloucestershire had bought the building to convert into a City Campus to house 4500 health and social care students. The Debenhams store finally closed on 12th May 2021. The price the University paid has not been publicly disclosed but it is believed to be a mere fraction of what Aviva paid for it almost 20 years previously.

The project was awarded a share of Gloucester's successful £20 million Levelling Up Fund bid which was approved in October 2021. £10 million of the award was believed to have been initially set aside for the City Campus project, with more allocated when the regeneration of the Fleece Hotel site failed to progress. The University were in talks with Gloucestershire County Council about relocating the City Library to the ground floor alongside a new publicly-accessible café.

Images of how the building could look were published in February 2022 and the plans were approved unanimously by the City Council's Planning Committee the following month. The first students are expected to use the new City Campus at some point during 2024.

The University of Gloucestershire's City Campus under construction in the former Debenhams building.

Kings Walk

In 2016 the plans for Kings Quarter were progressing, albeit slowly, and the new bus station was getting built, but a question mark hung over Kings Walk Shopping Centre. Its owner Aviva, and its predecessor Norwich Union, hadn't put in any major investment for years and seemed unlikely to do so for the foreseeable future. It was looking tired and we were conscious that its condition could impact on the delivery of Kings Quarter. The key player at Aviva for many years had been Chris Paterson, their Head of Retail (not to be confused with the Scottish international full back who had a season at Kingsholm), who controlled billions of pounds of retail investment but as a stereotypical dour Scotsman, appeared not to like spending anything! Despite the billions in his funds, Paterson was a man of detail and had a hang-up about the mobile catering vans in the city centre. He had it in his power to invest in Kings Walk but clearly chose not to.

Aviva put the shopping centre up for sale. As the City Council still owned the freehold, any buyer would need our co-operation. The frontrunners were Vixcroft, who had been buying up shopping centres left, right and centre, including in Burton-upon-Trent, Londonderry, Maidenhead and Weston-super-Mare. They were headed up by Daniel Carter, former Chief Executive of Arrowcroft who were the developers of the aborted Blackfriars scheme (see Chapter 5). We were cautious given that his last foray into Gloucester hadn't ended well. In June 2016 it was announced that Kings Walk had been sold to Vixcroft. Daniel Carter said at the time: "We are making a significant investment in Gloucester because we have seen the progress made in recent years and we recognise the great potential the city has. We want to move on this project at pace."

The result of the EU referendum of June 2016 led to Vixcroft's financial backers withdrawing. Daniel Carter said, "Finance markets have gone through some turmoil but are showing signs of settling down." He said there was a "strong chance" the deal would still go through. After working to find an alternative backer, they came to the City Council asking us to finance the purchase. Again, this led to some tension within the Cabinet. I was willing to consider it as I knew we needed to find a solution. Others didn't like the idea at all. In the end, the deal we were offered by Vixcroft was, in our view, unbalanced in terms of risk and reward, so we couldn't support it. The centre included the BHS store in Eastgate Street, which closed in summer 2016 and knocked a big hole in the rent roll.

The Council's Cabinet formally decided not to proceed in January 2017. I explained, "We looked at it carefully and took expert advice and while the external assessment of the investment was positive, we felt that the proposal wasn't right for us at this time. We are committed to making a major investment in the Kings Quarter scheme and there are only so many things we can take on at any one time."

So, the centre went back on the market. This time the front-runners were Reef Estates, another London-based developer, who were financed by Alan English who sold his hotel and conference centre business, Hayley Conference Centres, to Principal Hotel Group for £358 million in May 2007. They came to present to Cabinet, with their joint Chief Executive Stewart Deering flying back from his family holiday in Portugal especially for the meeting. They proposed a partnership arrangement, based on an ambitious and optimistic plan for the centre. I questioned why they would want to share it if the prospects were so good. They convinced us that they wanted to work with us and it would be to our advantage if they did. Stewart Deering later told me that the opportunity for the wider Kings Quarter deal was what attracted them to look at acquiring Kings Walk.

Discussions continued, with Reef complaining (in a good-natured way) that every time they negotiated with Philip Ardley it cost them £1 million! The final package agreed earmarked £9 million for investment into regenerating the shopping centre. It passed through a closed session of Full Council in July 2017 with Labour Group Leader Kevin Stephens being particularly supportive. Reef were believed to have paid Aviva around £21 million for the shopping centre.

I commented at the time, "These improvements are not pie in the sky plans but work that can start quickly and for which funding already exists" but had to duck out of a Radio Gloucestershire interview on the subject at short notice when my wife went into labour!

Negotiations with Primark to take on the former BHS unit took some time to conclude and in January 2018 they denied, as they would, that there were any plans to relocate their Gloucester store. The cover was blown by a drawing submitted as part of a planning application showing a Primark sign. A later signage application confirmed this, although there was still no official word from Primark's head office. It became known as 'Gloucester's worst-kept secret'.

Despite a hugely difficult period in the world of retail, Reef signed up new tenants like Deichmann as well as Primark, refurbished the car park and started to build new public toilets, including the city centre's first Changing Places facility for the severely disabled. But there still remains a lot to do. The deal with Reef won recognition in the awards for The MJ, the local government journal, for 'Innovation in Property and Asset Management' in July 2019, which I described as "testament to the strong partnership we have with Reef".

The new, bigger Primark store in the former BHS unit opened in December 2021, with customers queuing out of the doors for several days after the store opened.

A planning application was lodged in December 2021 for the

recladding of the Eastgate Street frontage, which was approved in May 2022, but plans to demolish the bridge across Eastgate Street were abandoned. The cost of demolition alone was believed to be £800,000. Instead, the City Council announced plans in November 2021 to move their offices from Shire Hall to the former Heart Radio studios on the Eastgate bridge.

The final straight?

In early 2020, the Bruton Way multi-storey car park and the adjacent Bentinck House, the former tax office, were demolished.

On Gloucester Day in September 2020, it was announced by City MP Richard Graham, my successor as Council Leader Richard Cook and Reef's Esther Croft that there was a £100 million plan for Kings Quarter and that work would re-commence on Kings Square in October.

The proposals had been worked up during my time as Leader and Cabinet Member, with 'The Forum' being a hub for cyber and digital businesses. Reef felt The Forum would complement Cheltenham's plans for a cyber park adjacent to GCHQ. Reef owned a parcel of land along Market Parade, which would enable them to do a land deal with the Council and avoid a long and expensive procurement process.

In some ways it was an odd time to announce that it was planned to build 125,000 sq feet of offices (a figure which doesn't mean much to most people), when the pandemic had led to most office workers working at home and left a question mark over the future demand for offices. That point wasn't lost on some of the people watching the announcement on Facebook Live. I believe that there is still a place for offices, but developers will just have to work harder to attract tenants by offering a high-quality environment. In this sense, the works to Kings Square and the new bus station are crucial to the wider project's success. Reef are convinced that "the digital and cyber community is ever-growing and will need physical space to collaborate effectively and creatively as teams". The latest Kings Quarter/Forum scheme is still challenging in viability terms and has only got across the line with a big helping hand from the City Council, who agreed to fund the £107 million cost of the development. For a small council with a £14 million a year budget, this was a bold and brave decision – and something which Council Leader Richard Cook admitted gave him "sleepless nights".[223]

The first phase of Kings Quarter – a new 5000 sq ft store for Tesco with 19 apartments above, adjacent to Kings House on Market Parade - got underway in May 2021. Local firm EG Carter also won that contract. The new Tesco store opened on 3rd November 2022. Tesco relocated from Grosvenor House which allowed what remained of that particular eyesore to be demolished. The City Council secured £477,903 from the Government's Brownfield Land Fund in October 2023 to unlock the development of another 32 apartments on Market Parade.

The Forum development under construction.

The Forge, a "digital innovation hub for emerging cyber businesses and other fledgling companies to grow" as part of The Forum, was part of Gloucester's successful Levelling Up Fund bid which was approved in October 2021. £4 million of the £20 million award was initially earmarked for The Forge, but the figure increased when plans for The Fleece fell away.

Kier Construction, who were contractors for the Gloucester Transport Hub (bus station) and the refurbishment of Shire Hall, were announced as the main contractor for the Phase Two of the development in February 2022. Phase Two will see the main campus of The Forum delivered, including 125,000 sq ft of Grade A workspace, a 400-space car park, a 130-bedroom 4-star hotel, rooftop restaurant and bar, state-of-the-art digital conference facilities, a 9,000 sq ft wellness centre and a members' club on the site of the demolished Bruton Way car park and former bus station/Grosvenor House. Work started in March 2022 and is due to complete in Autumn 2024, bringing to fruition around 30 years of effort to regenerate this part of the city.

12. BRINGING OUR HISTORY TO LIFE

As I described in the introduction to this book, Gloucester is one of the most historic cities in this country, having played a huge part in shaping our nation's destiny. But until fairly recently we seemed fairly reluctant to shout about it. During my period in opposition on the Council, the ruling Labour Group were keen to talk up Gloucester as a 'modern city'. Of course, it's completely legitimate to want to move with the times and to ensure people in the city get the benefits of doing so, but it seemed wrong not to make more of the city's rich heritage.

City Archaeologist Andrew Armstrong told me that Gloucester is the most important archaeological site in the South West in terms of complexity with Roman, Anglo Saxon and Medieval remains. It is comparable with London and York but the investment returns are much lower here, making development of sensitive sites challenging. English Heritage's view when Gloucester Heritage Urban Regeneration Company was set up was that Gloucester had "an embarrassment of riches".

Gloucester Civic Trust was created in response to the city losing much of its heritage in the 1960s and 70s and it still has an important role today as the city's guardian of heritage matters, but I like to think that such considerations are more at the forefront of our mind today than they were 50 years ago.

If you rewind twenty years or so, Gloucester's heritage was in a poor state. Most of the Docks warehouses were still derelict. The heritage buildings in what we now know as the Quays area were run-down. Llanthony Priory was in serious disrepair. Blackfriars Priory only opened on the occasional Sunday. Those responsible for St Mary de Crypt were struggling to find a long-term solution for the building. St Michael's Tower was closed and the stonework was crumbling. The former Teapots building in Westgate Street was empty and propped up with scaffolding. There was no History Festival. The Folk Museum had been closed or at least mothballed.

The City Museum was pretty much unchanged from when I was a child, with a slightly random collection of objects on display including stuffed animals and a civic chain from another part of Gloucestershire. There was even a proposal from the City Council to close the City Museum in January 2002 as part of budget cut proposals. The Cathedral was our shining light, but even that had a car park to the front of it which detracted from the beauty of the building and, in some ways, seemed detached from the life of many in the city.

Prior to the creation of the GHURC, English Heritage's Urban Panel (now known as the Historic Places Panel) – made up of experts on regeneration, archaeology, estates etc – visited Gloucester but didn't stay overnight as there was no suitable hotel in the centre. The group went to the New Inn and saw an advertising board outside with the slogan "How low can we go?" That was referring to the price of a pint of lager, but the group felt it summed up where the city was. The panel thought the long-term solution was a merger with Cheltenham but felt they couldn't say it – other than that the relationship could be "positive and harmonious" again.

Gloucester has been a significant beneficiary of support from the Heritage Lottery Fund (HLF), now renamed the National Lottery Heritage Fund (NLHF). At one point, there were three major schemes running in the city with multi-million-pound support from the Fund – Project Pilgrim at the Cathedral (which, rightly, has its own chapter), Llanthony Secunda Priory and Discover De Crypt at St Mary de Crypt in Southgate Street. The HLF also supported a number of smaller projects in the city. The Gloucester Heritage Forum was set up, chaired by Anne Cranston from the Cathedral and Heather Forbes from the Gloucestershire Archives, which co-ordinated bids to avoid competition and shared best practice.

The stories of the Llanthony Priory and Discover De Crypt projects are included in this chapter.

Llanthony Secunda Priory

Llanthony Priory, alongside the canal, had been in the City Council's ownership since 1974 but, despite some restoration works, was in a poor state. The site was appropriated by Great Western Railways in 1906 and the Council purchased it from British Rail, who were responsible for introducing various industrial uses on and around the Priory site. The Council had planned to locate the City Archaeology Team (when there was one) there but it didn't happen, presumably because of cost. Its full name is Llanthony Secunda Priory, because of its connection with the original Llanthony Priory (known as 'Prima') in the Black Mountains in Wales. It was established by Miles of Gloucester to house Augustinian monks who fled from Llanthony Prima when the priory was attacked by the locals. Another interesting fact is that Eddie Fry, a local strongman known as 'Pocket Hercules' because of his diminutive size, lived in the Victorian farmhouse on the site in the 1960s.

The surviving buildings are of national significance and include the Grade I medieval two-storey roofed 'Range' between the Outer and Inner Courts. The building is known as the 'Priory Lodgings' and has an attached Grade II Listed Victorian farmhouse. This is the central focal heritage building in the site. In addition, there are five sets of Grade 1 listed remains, all protected as a scheduled ancient monument. All of the buildings were on the Historic England 'at risk' register at the time and they represented the single largest collection of 'at risk' buildings in the south west of England.

Such was the disregard for its historic importance in decades gone by, a waste disposal firm kept its skips leant up against the Priory boundary walls until it relocated in 2007. To be fair, the area around the Priory was made up of many more industrial uses at that time than it is now. A Council report 2013 noted that "For much of the time that the Council held the Priory, it was constrained by its context as it was surrounded by low grade and unsightly land uses which made it an unlikely site for heritage or amenity purposes." The site was within the 'red line' of the Gloucester Quays development, but the planning application didn't include proposals to secure its future. The Council's Local Plan had anticipated that development in that area would provide a solution for the Priory site.

Nonetheless, it can be argued Gloucester Quays and, in particular, the building of a new Gloucestershire College campus was the catalyst for the restoration of Llanthony. The new College building sensitively joined with the Priory remains and provided some natural surveillance, a custodian on hand, a future tenant and one Jeremy Williamson. Jem was Vice Principal of the College with responsibility for estates. He had overseen the building of a new campus at Princess Elizabeth Way in Cheltenham and would lead on the new Gloucester facility as well. Full of energy, Williamson would become the Chair of the Llanthony Secunda Priory Trust and also went on to be Managing Director of the Cheltenham Task Force, driving regeneration at the other end of the Golden Valley. Jem was, of course, supported in his endeavours during his time at the College by his boss, Principal Greg Smith, who was Chair of the Gloucester Heritage Urban Regeneration Company.

The legal agreement linked to the College's planning consent allowed their use of the Priory grounds and required them to work with the City Council to come up with a management plan for the site, ultimately leading to its restoration.

The Western Waterfront Steering Group commissioned architects Feilden Clegg Bradley to undertake a feasibility study, partly funded by the developers of Gloucester Quays. Their report, published in September 2004, led to interest from an English Heritage Commissioner Gilly Drummond, who convened and chaired the Llanthony Secunda Priory Steering Group to find a way forward for the Priory. The Feilden Clegg Bradley report advised that the 'do nothing' option would still involve finding £700,000 for essential repairs and it would cost another £1 million to make the buildings economically viable.

English Heritage were interested in buying Llanthony Secunda Priory from Gloucester City Council and would then establish a management trust to include the City Council. Such a move would reduce the Council's risk. The Council's Cabinet agreed in June 2006 to sell the Priory to English Heritage and report back in six months, but subsequently discovered that English Heritage would take at least 9 months to make a decision. Further discussions took place about selling directly to the management trust. It was noted that GlosCAT had a vision for the site. At this time, it was envisaged, as part of the Gloucester Quays masterplan, that a hotel would be built adjacent to the Priory.

At a Cabinet meeting in December 2006, Martyn White as Cabinet Member for Heritage and Leisure outlined the options appraisal for the future management of the site which were either a) to do nothing (which wasn't really an option), b) to sell to a management trust or c) to sell to a private individual for £100,000. The private individual was Tim Wiltshire, owner of Brockworth Court, which had once been owned by the Priory. He had restored the house and Tithe Barn at Brockworth and was promising to do the same for Llanthony, creating units to be occupied by businesses sympathetic to the Priory's heritage. It was estimated it would take 10-15 years. In a note to the Council, Tim Wiltshire described his vision, saying, "In essence the Priory will become a heritage site with a museum dedicated to the history of life as it once was in the C15th. There will be craft workshops, art galleries, indoor and outdoor exhibitions and space for a venue for a variety of activities and functions. Landscaped gardens will provide a peaceful haven for members of the public to enjoy." A complication of this option was that Gloucester Quays owner Peel Holdings had made clear that they would gift their land adjacent to the Priory to the Trust but not to a private individual.

Martyn explained that it was proposed to sell to the management trust within the current financial year to take advantage of English Heritage funding (£20,000). It was also proposed to maintain the Council's current budget for the Priory (£10,000) for the first three years (2007-2010) and to use it to sustain the management trust in its early stages.

The Council agreed in February 2007 to sell the Priory to a newly-established Trust to oversee the restoration of the Priory. The proposal was that the City Council would transfer it for £1 and provide two trustees, initially Councillor Martyn White and Regeneration Director Phil Staddon. The Trust was incorporated in February 2007 and the transfer took place later that year. The initial trustees included Jeremy Williamson from Gloucestershire College, Councillor Martyn White and Phil Staddon from the City Council and English Heritage nominees Regional Director Bob Bewley and South West Regional Commissioner Gilly Drummond OBE, a gardener and campaigner for the conservation of historic landscapes. Gilly is owner of the Cadland Estate near Southampton, with one of Capability Brown's smallest pleasure gardens. Former City Museum curator John Rhodes, who as a historian was something of an expert on Llanthony, gave the benefit of his knowledge to the Trust.

The Trust later appointed a number of other hugely capable and passionate trustees including former Lord Lieutenant Sir Henry

Elwes (whose Colesbourne Estate was owned by the Priory for 400 years before his family acquired it in 1789), former Barnwood Construction boss Graham Howell and Guildhall manager Sarah Gilbert. They, literally, rolled their sleeves up, spending many a weekend clearing overgrowth or doing other physical tasks, as well as putting together the plans to restore the buildings on site. Sir Henry told me that when the Trust was established, it didn't have any money – not even enough to put stamps on appeal letters.

Another trustee was Ledbury-based architect Ian Stainburn, whose firm Stainburn Taylor had done some of the plans for the site in the early days of the Trust on behalf of English Heritage. He had huge experience of working on historic buildings and in 2008 had helped to preserve the medieval canopied tomb of Edward II in Gloucester Cathedral by replacing wrought iron columns with carbon fibre columns, identical in appearance to the originals.

Bob Bewley's advice to his fellow trustees was "don't rush it". They put in early bids, mostly to English Heritage, to secure funding for investigative works, to commission an options appraisal and to undertake urgent repairs. The focus of the Trust in the following years was to achieve a greater understanding of the site and its significance, site stabilisation and emergency repair programmes to the standing structures, with associated activities as diverse as historic and archival research, grounds clearance, fundraising/grant applications and preparing for what was a complex restoration project. Trustees Liz Griffiths and Sarah Gilbert did the bulk of the work to put the initial bid into the Heritage Lottery Fund.

The project was nearly scuppered in 2013. The Trust sought to remove some of the restrictive covenants in the transfer document from the Council in order to meet the requirements of the Heritage Lottery Fund. These included the ability of the Council to buy back the Priory for £1 should the Trust fail and the right of the Council to hold events at the Priory for up to 20 days a year (which it had never exercised). It also prohibited the Trust entering into any lease agreements for the site, which would have prevented the proposed lease of the medieval range to Gloucestershire College. The Liberal Democrats opposed the move. I don't really know why, as the Council had for such a long time been a poor custodian of this hidden gem. In September 2013, they even went to the extent of calling in the decision to a special meeting of the Overview and Scrutiny Committee, which referred the matter to Full Council.

At the time, Trust Chairman Jeremy Williamson said, "The Trust has raised £300,000 for the Priory in six years and I can't see what the problem is." I added, "The Trust is made up of very capable people. We can do this transfer with a degree of confidence. I don't believe the Trust will fail." The Trustees threatened to hand the Priory back to the Council. They believed councillors wanted to take the glory after the hard work had been done.[224]

The Trust's own legal advice was that if the Trust failed the site would have to be sold for market value and the £1 buyback clause would be 'set aside'. The Trustees didn't mince their words. Their Position Statement for the meeting said, "The Trust wishes to record that it does not regard the recent events as helpful or positive to the prospects of the HLF bid or to the Trust itself. An unintended consequence of the public exposure to the 'call in' is that the Trust's credibility has been undermined. In particular, councillors have made references to liquidators and official receivers (including on BBC Radio Gloucestershire). The message received by many is that 'the Trust is not to be trusted'."

There were some further negotiations before going to Full Council, which resulted in a compromise that the buyback provision would be extinguished when the Trust secured its Heritage Lottery grant.

In the end, at a Full Council meeting in November, councillors unanimously backed plans to transfer ownership although some councillors "ended up in a spat". Councillor Pam Tracey got to the nub of the argument by asking, "If the council were to keep hold of the priory, just who is going to restore it and get it back to its former glory?" The meeting had to be brought forward two weeks as it was dangerously close to the bid announcement.[225] All involved breathed a heavy sigh of relief at the outcome.

Later that month, development funding of £311,400 was awarded to help the Trust to progress their plans to apply for a full grant at a later date. The Trust said the grant would go towards "bringing Llanthony back to life", noting that although the site was open, the buildings were "too fragile to enter". The plans were called the "Reformation Project" – a play on words based on the medieval Reformation and the need to reform the Priory for a new era.

Edwina Bell was appointed as Project Manager in April 2014 on a self-employed basis following an advert. She had been involved in lottery-funded projects as the Chapter Clerk at Rochester Cathedral. She had moved to the Forest of Dean and then this role came up.

In March 2016, the Trust's application to the Heritage Lottery Fund was approved and a grant of £3,194,400 was awarded. A spokesman for the Trust commented, "With this project Llanthony Secunda can finally put behind it the sad scrapyard years of the 1960s and 1970s".[226]

Jeremy Williamson said, "After eight years of dedication from trustees, friends and volunteers and with support from local businesses and other funders we are now one step closer to realising our ambition."

The Gloucestershire Environmental Trust awarded Llanthony a £250,000 Flagship Grant in March 2017. Its Chair of Trustees, Professor Stephen Owen said, "The project has taken a long time to reach fruition, and its implementation will now help to reverse decades of neglect that has blighted this part of Gloucester. The new vehicular and footpath access, the conservation of the buildings and provision of a quality landscaped setting for this important historic site, will provide the opportunity for bringing back new life into this part of the Docks and Gloucestershire College."

Other funds were secured, including from the Architectural Heritage Fund (£101,040), Gloucester City Council (£50,000), Gloucester Historic Building Trust (£25,000), the Garfield Weston Foundation (£650,000), the Pilgrim Trust (£25,000), Allchurches Trust (£20,000), the Wolfson Foundation (£20,000) and the Country Houses Foundation (£12,000).

Work on the delivery phase started in 2016 once official permission to start was granted. The Trust retained the design team and consultants from the development stage and set about finalising all the design and tender documentation for the capital works, gaining planning and scheduled monument consent. Croft Building and Conservation were appointed as the main contractor, but the full range of contractors included landscape architects, mechanical and electrical engineers and interpretation consultants. Trustee Liz Griffiths chaired the weekly Project Board, which brought them all together, during the restoration works.

The Trust appointed its first employee, Emma Davies, as Heritage Manager on 30th January 2017 to develop a programme of events and activities for when the site was fully open and engage with local communities and volunteers. There were two volunteer groups — one concentrating on the site and grounds and the other looking at interpretation, stories and the archive. The Heritage Lottery Fund would only pay for buildings that would be put to active use. Historic England supported works to the walls and other structures not included in the HLF grant, such as the Gatehouse and Tithe Barn. These works were completed at the end of February 2017.

With any project like this, you need to expect the unexpected. Anything below ground took longer than expected, with archaeologists having to attend pretty much every time a spade went in. However, there were no significant archaeological finds. Asbestos was discovered buried in the grounds between Llanthony Road and the medieval range. It cost £100,000 to encapsulate the material. This made it a very expensive lawn! The lime render had to be redone on the medieval range as it was falling off.

Trustees were rather bemused to be told by planners that they needed to commission a survey to look for unexploded ordnance, as various things had been dropped around the Docks during wartime. I'm told this was mostly done as a desk-based exercise by tracking the movement of planes but there was a site visit involving four men in orange jackets – with only one of them digging! Nothing was found but, in April 2018, the Sainsbury's superstore at Gloucester Quays (just over the road from the Priory) had to be evacuated as what was believed to be a World War II anti-aircraft shell was found on the Monk Meadow site being developed for housing, while groundworks were being undertaken. Soldiers from the Bomb Disposal Unit of the Royal Logistics Corps attended and removed the item in question. So the request to the Priory's trustees turned out not to be an unreasonable one at all.

Another issue which nearly scuppered the project was road access to the site. Highways bosses, understandably, wanted a separate entrance rather than one directly from Llanthony Road as the section next to the Priory was due to be widened to ease a bottleneck on the South West Bypass. They agreed that an undertaking to use 'all best efforts' to resolve the situation would suffice. The alternative entrance, next to the High Orchard pub, required consent from its operators, the Marstons Brewery and their landlords Legal & General. Marstons were concerned about users of the Priory taking up valuable customer spaces in their car park. Jeremy Williamson and I travelled to Wolverhampton to meet their Property Director. The Trust was able to demonstrate that events taking place at the Priory were actually good for their business, with many people who attended events at the Priory eating and drinking at the pub. Resolving the issue wasn't high on Marstons' list of priorities so it took a good deal of persistence from Williamson to get it over the line.

Despite the challenges faced along the way, the project was delivered on time and on budget. Trustees gained enormous satisfaction from seeing the fruits of their labour. The roof being put back on the Brick Range, which had previously been full of brambles, was a particular highlight.

The grand re-opening of Llanthony Priory was marked on August Bank Holiday Monday in 2018 with a stone carving festival.[227] The restored Priory was officially reopened by HRH The Duke of Gloucester in September 2019.

Since reopening, the Priory has been used for a variety of events, including music concerts, craft fairs and art installations. It is now the regular meeting place of the Rotary Club of Gloucester Quays and is a popular wedding venue.

The challenge for the trustees following the completion of the restoration works is to make the Trust financially sustainable and recruit trustees with the right skillset to take it on the next stage of its journey, while at the same time not compromising its important role as a heritage site. That is a delicate balance to strike. I joined as a trustee in 2021 and those challenges remain thanks to the unwelcome intervention of the Covid pandemic. Its success as a wedding venue seems to be key to its long-term financial sustainability.

Llanthony Secunda Priory with a waste transfer station next door. Not the best of settings for such a historic asset!

Discover DeCrypt

Another key restoration project was St Mary de Crypt and the Old Crypt Schoolroom in Southgate Street. The Schoolroom was the place where The Crypt School started in 1539. As an Old Cryptian this meant a lot to me. St Mary De Crypt was also the church where Robert Raikes was baptised, evangelist George Whitefield (also an Old Cryptian) preached his first sermon and Jemmy Wood (said to be the inspiration for Scrooge) is buried. It was seen as an important building historically, architecturally and because of its prominent location.

A dwindling city centre population had seen its congregation diminish in number, so a new use was needed. Sunday Services had stopped in 2009 and were replaced by a Friday lunchtime service which ran from April to September. It was too cold in the winter months! The Civic Trust had provided volunteers to open the building as a heritage attraction and it was used for a variety of events like concerts and art exhibitions from time to time.

There had been a proposal in the late 1990s for it to be a 'Centre for the Spoken Word', led by churchwarden and public relations consultant David Dorman, but its funding bid to the Heritage Lottery Fund had been turned down. A new rector, Canon Nikki Arthy, came in, charged with finding a new purpose for the building. It was in a desperate state. The floor in the Old Schoolroom was rotten. The electrics were condemned. Plaster was falling off the walls. The heating was ineffective, there was one inadequate toilet and there was asbestos in the Crypt.

After taking stock and consulting widely, a new plan was conceived. The church would become a heritage attraction, community space, educational resource and cultural space as well as a place of worship. The Discover DeCrypt project was launched on 28th September 2010. City MP Richard Graham, Lord Lieutenant Dame Janet Trotter and Bishop Michael Perham were the Project's Patrons. It came at a time when the Heritage Lottery Fund was treating Gloucester as a priority area and this led to a heritage theme for the proposals.

The parish backed the project financially in its early stages and Rachel Court was employed as Project Manager. A stage one pass from the Heritage Lottery Fund of £79,000 was awarded in September 2013. A number of other charitable trusts donated to the Project and Pam Tracey and I donated £3,000 from our 'Anniversary Charity Dinner' in 2017, but fundraising became more challenging when the Cathedral's Project Pilgrim started applying for funds at the same time as Discover DeCrypt.

The second stage bid to the HLF for £1.36 million was approved in December 2016. Nicola Dyer from the Prince's Foundation was appointed to project manage the work, with Croft Building and Conservation as the main contractor. As ever, with a project of this nature, issues arose along the way. In 2018, when I was travelling to the Local Government Association's Annual Conference in Birmingham, my phone started to buzz with texts and voicemails from Nikki Arthy and Paul Soden of the adjacent Café Rene pub. I phoned both parties back to find out what was happening.

The contractors had found an unknown underground vault with utility pipes (including gas) running through it, which undermined its stability, and were concerned that vibration could cause an explosion. Wales and West Utilities needed to attend to make it safe, but hadn't yet responded and the Marylone Passage, which led to Café Rene, would need to be closed until works were completed. As I sat on my hotel bed watching England's World Cup football match, I emailed the Chief Executive of Wales and West and, to my pleasant surprise, got a reply from their Operations Director before the match had finished.

Wales and West attended and the Marylone Passage had to stay closed for around 8 weeks while the vault was made safe, meaning disruption and loss of trade for Café Rene next door and much work and heartache for Discover DeCrypt. The works cost £70,000 and largely used up the project's contingency reserve. St Mary De Crypt re-opened in March 2019, with the first major event to take place there, fittingly, being the Old Cryptians' Club Dinner. Footfall to the building, with a diversity of uses, was running massively ahead of the project's Business Plan in its first year before coronavirus hit.

When a trench was being dug at the front of the church, in Southgate Street, to enable a waste connection to the sewer, two large pieces of stone were recovered. Upon examination, one was found to be a decorative structural cornice and the other was an upper part of an altar with burn marks to the top, indicating where sacrifices had been burnt. Both pieces were believed to date back to the last 1st or early 2nd century and are likely to have been part of a Roman temple of Jupiter.

Playing Statues

For many years, there was little in the way of statues or public art which told the story of the city - and that which did exist was not really understood or well-maintained. For example, few people realise the bollards in the gate streets are meant to represent pins and needles which were made in Gloucester and the stone bench on The Cross is based on the wave of the Severn Bore with various trades and industries associated with Gloucester featured on the base. When Northgate and Southgate Street were pedestrianised in the late 1990s, there were plans for three statues – the Bellmaker, the Bowmaker and the Aircraft Worker at a total cost of £75,000. These represented three of the city's main manufacturing industries. There was something of an outcry at the cost, as there almost always is with public art, but there weren't protests on the streets. In the end, only the Aircraft Worker survived. The statue, by artist Simon Stringer, proved controversial as former workers at the Gloster Aircraft Company, to whom it was supposed to be paying tribute, felt it wasn't an accurate or respectful portrayal of them. It was sited in Northgate Street by the Debenhams building and is not controversial, or even really noticed (other than when a seagull or traffic cone ends up on its head), any more.

The most recent statue to go up in the city was Emperor Nerva, who founded Glevum as a Roman colonia. This project was organised by the Civic Trust and the £80,000 cost paid for by public subscription, including a donation from Princess Anne and a £5000 contribution from the City Council. The horseback sculpture was cast by Anthony Stones. I was privileged to be there in my capacity as Sheriff of Gloucester, with Pam Tracey as Mayor, when the statue was lowered into place in October 2002. Prior to that, there was a wholly unnecessary public row between the Council and the Civic Trust about where exactly it should go. The Civic Trust wanted it to go as close as possible to the site of the original statue, of which bronze remains were found by archaeologist Henry Hurst when the Bell Hotel was demolished in 1969. The Council wanted it to be visible from the Blackfriars development. In the end it was the Blackfriars development that wasn't visible! After public consultation, and some pressure from me and others, the Council relented.

When the City Council embarked on the much-needed refurbishment of Gloucester Park in 2004 there was an opportunity to improve the appearance of the two statues within the Park – Robert Raikes, the Sunday School founder, and the lesser-known statue of Queen Anne. The Queen Anne statue was, and still is, in a secluded position on the edge of the Spa cricket ground and was in a poor state. It was made worse when vandals took her head off (and in the process won the Civic Trust's 'Off with their heads' award in their 34th Annual Report in 2005)! I took some stick for doing a television interview about the attack with the head under my arm in the style of Hamlet's 'Alas Poor Yorick!' Anyway, she got repaired and survives today, albeit in a heavily-weathered condition.

The bronze statue of Raikes, which is near the Park Road entrance to the Park and has been there since 1930, had turned quite green. Although I was keen to see this cleaned up, Council Officers told me the money for the Park's refurbishment had run out. When there was a £1.2 million budget for the Park, I thought this was a pretty poor show. The City Council did agree £2,000 towards the cost, as did the

Civic Trust. I wrote to Ecclesiastical Insurance, whose offices then bordered the Park and who had a good record of supporting local causes, to see if they would contribute to the £3,500 funding gap. I was delighted when in September 2005 they agreed to stump up for all of it, so Raikes got a well-deserved clean-up.

More recent attempts to add statues of historical features in the city have come to nothing. I had hoped we might get one of Colonel Massey to coincide with the 375th anniversary of the Siege of Gloucester in 2018, but despite the Civic Trust floating the idea in 2009 it never really gained any momentum. Similarly, ideas new pieces of public art of George Whitefield to mark the 300th anniversary of his birth in 2014 and Saxon warrior queen Aethelflaed to celebrate the 1100th anniversary of her death in 2018 didn't materialise. Someone wrote to me following an article I wrote in the free magazine 'The Local Answer' about statues, asking why we didn't have one for Gloucester's most famous son Button Gwinnett. At the time I didn't even know who he was but found out he was the second signatory to the US Declaration of Independence who was born at Down Hatherley. As someone who managed to go throughout his life without leaving too much of a trace, finding a site wouldn't be straightforward and the controversy over statues for those involved in the slave trade would be an added complication as Gwinnett owned a plantation after he moved to the US and would have owned slaves.

The Battle of the Bandstand

The funding for the Gloucester Park revamp, from 2004 onwards, came from the Government's 'Liveability Fund' which was a sweetener, counter-intuitively from a Labour Government, for councils to outsource their 'streetcare' services like waste collection, street cleaning and grounds maintenance.

One aspect of the 'Liveability' programme where I was accused of not respecting the city's history related to the Gloucester Park bandstand. Depending on your point of view, it was either an unattractive lump of concrete and brick and a poor example of municipal architecture or a rare example of a 1930s structure that needed to be preserved. Hugh Worsnip of Gloucester Civic Trust said, "We don't oppose knocking it down. It has no value."[228] The

Twentieth Century Society tried, but failed, to get it listed in 2005. What couldn't be argued was that it was in poor condition.

I will admit that we weren't as sure-footed on it as we should have been and kept shifting our position. The initial proposal from officers was a modern 'tensile' structure. That wasn't popular with the public, so we looked again at whether the existing bandstand could be restored and, in the end, put several options to a public vote, including the eventual winner which was a Victorian-style bandstand. The consultation, which took place towards the end of 2006, had over 1400 votes, with just under half of them opting for the Victorian option. It didn't please everyone, with Liberal Democrat Leader Jeremy Hilton describing it as "like something you'd buy from B&Q".[229] I was perplexed by this as I'd never seen a bandstand for sale in B&Q. It was true that it was an 'off the shelf' version, but coming up with something bespoke would have been far more expensive.

Bringing the matter to a conclusion was quite a battle, with opposition largely led by a small number of retired people who lived in flats in a converted period house in Spa Road, one of whom grandly badged himself as 'Gloucestershire Heritage & Conservation'. They were the same people who protested against the loss of the GlosCAT building in Brunswick Road (perhaps with more merit) and the Dawn Redwood tree on that site. At times it got personal, including a complaint against me to the now disbanded Standards Board for England, which dealt with (often vexatious) complaints against councillors. It was dismissed without me even needing to be questioned about it. Looking back, some of the twists and turns in the bandstand saga bordered on the bizarre.

In 2005, the Department of Culture, Media and Sport was asked to list the structure. It refused. An appeal against their decision also failed. An application to demolish the bandstand was deferred by the City Council's Planning Committee in January and February 2006, awaiting a decision on the application to list it. By the time of March's committee, the listing application had been turned down but the Planning Committee refused to grant consent for demolition as English Heritage had said the bandstand was of "local historic importance". Gloucestershire Heritage & Conservation claimed the application to demolish it breached Human Rights legislation. In January 2006, Rich Clifford and the Shadows and another brass band took to the streets to perform in protest against the proposed demolition. In 2007, Prime Minister Tony Blair was asked to intervene in response to a petition being collected. I commented at the time, "I think Mr Blair has more pressing issues to deal with" and noted that the petition was signed by councillors from Cam and Cinderford and people from Kingston-upon-Thames and the London Borough of Barnet.

When we resubmitted the planning application to demolish the bandstand in January 2007, I was asked by *The Citizen* to have my photograph taken with a musical instrument in-front of it. I duly obliged, borrowing my sister's saxophone. I should have declined as some of the genuine objectors saw this as me rubbing their noses in it, which wasn't the intention. You live and learn.

Demolition consent was granted by the Planning Committee by 5 votes to 4 and consent for the new bandstand was approved by 5 votes to 3 in May 2007. English Heritage commented that the Victorian design was "questionable" as it "removes a genuine aspect of the Park's development and replaces it with a fake design". The Civic Trust referred to it as "disappointingly dull". One of the objectors referred the Council to the Local Government Ombudsman for 'gross maladministration'. The complaint was dismissed.

There were further legal challenges, including to the High Court in 2009. When that was dismissed in October 2009, I gave an instruction, from a phonebox while on holiday in Mexico, that the bandstand should be demolished first thing in the morning to prevent any other challenge. That led to a front-page headline on *The Citizen* on 17th October 2009 saying, simply, "The End". I commented that I was "pleased to bring this long-running saga to an end".

The planning committee approved a slightly-revised application for a Victorian-style bandstand in February 2010 and it was in place in June 2010. It had only taken 6 years!

Museums

A city as historic as Gloucester ought to have a museum which really brings its story to life. Although they are much loved, I've felt for a long time that the two main city museums (as they were) haven't done that as well as they should have. The City Museum (now known as the Museum of Gloucester) has some great exhibits – like the

Birdlip Mirror, the largest prehistoric bronze mirror ever found, and the Gloucester Tables set - the oldest complete backgammon set in the world. But much of it, until the refurbishment of the ground floor in 2011, wasn't coherent and had been largely untouched for decades. At the time of writing, the first-floor display is still a slightly random collection of furniture and oddments.

The ground floor was refurbished in 2011 with support from the Heritage Lottery Fund at a cost of around £1 million and is now a much more coherent reflection of the city's history. My two regrets in this area from my time in office are firstly that we didn't manage to secure funding to refurbish the first floor and secondly that we introduced admission charges. This had the effect of suppressing visitor numbers and made it more difficult to secure grant funding. We removed them in April 2019 and the visitor numbers rocketed, but I wish we'd done it sooner.

The Folk Museum (for a while renamed the Gloucester Life Museum) has had a more complicated story. It was closed, or at least mothballed, by the Labour/Lib-Dem administration in 2003 and the Conservative Group made a manifesto pledge in 2004 to re-open it. This proved more difficult to deliver than originally anticipated and it took until early 2005 before that happened. Again, despite some really popular features, like the Victorian classroom, much of the displays were lacking in coherence (and still reflected the fact it used to be a county rather than a city museum) and had been unchanged for years. I worked with Museums Manager Angela Smith to refresh them in a low-cost way, but it wasn't transformational and didn't really have an impact on visitor numbers.

The Folk Museum's location at the bottom of Westgate Street meant it didn't get much in the way of passing trade and visitor numbers were stubbornly low. We introduced differentiated summer and winter opening hours, but the cost of heating, lighting and staffing the building were difficult to justify. Then the opportunity came to allow the Civic Trust to take on the management of the building, using it as a base for their activities, and for ownership to pass to Gloucester Historic Buildings (GHB) – a joint Civic Trust/City Council building preservation trust. I later learnt that the idea had come from a comment made by Labour councillor and former Mayor Neil Hampson. GHB hadn't taken on a new project for over twenty years, so this seemed an ideal opportunity, and it would allow them to lever in funding from elsewhere for conserve this important Grade II* listed building.

This proposal proved controversial both politically and publicly, despite the fact that public access would be maintained and actually enhanced and it would lead to improvements to the building. Some in the Civic Trust's ranks feared they were taking on too much. It took a long time to satisfy the Heritage Lottery Fund (who had paid to build the Education Building or Ed Shed, as it became known, in the museum garden) and, inevitably, the lawyers, but the transfer finally took place in March 2021.

The team from the Civic Trust worked hard to secure funding, bringing in grants from the Architectural Heritage Fund (£67,000) and the Cathedral Quarter Heritage Action Zone (£126,000) Funding was also provided by Enovert, the Landfill Tax body, and via a Disabled Facilities Grant, making around £300,000 in total. The building's façade was restored and limewashed in the bright colours that would have been used in the 16th & 17th century. While works were underway to improve access by installing a wheelchair lift, a 7m deep well was found, which was believed to be between 120 and 250 years old. When moving an old filing cabinet and other fixtures and fittings, volunteers also uncovered a range of rare Tudor wall paintings.

The city's other independently-run museums, the Soldiers of Gloucestershire Museum and the National Waterways Museum (both based at the Docks) both benefited from major Heritage Lottery Fund grants for refurbishments, but still struggled, as many museums do, to get sufficient visitor numbers to keep them going. In 2013, the Soldiers of Gloucestershire Museum, which had started out as a display at Folk Museum, got a £493,000 Heritage Lottery Grant. At the time it was getting 20,000 visitors a year. Former Mayor and Museum Curator Chris Chatterton told me that the award was about saving the building – without that funding the museum wouldn't have survived for a number of reasons including that their funding from the Ministry of Defence had changed. It paid for a new roof and other repairs and allowed them to retell the story in a more accessible and interactive way.

In 2015, the Waterways Museum got a £994,000 grant from

the Heritage Lottery Fund, as well as contributions from the Wolfson Museums and Galleries Improvement Fund and several local charitable trusts, to create a new, inviting entrance and refresh its galleries and displays.

Other historic buildings and monuments

In the early 2000s, many of the city's historic buildings and monuments were in a sorry state. St Michael's Tower on The Cross had been vacated by the Tourist Information Centre, which had been there since 1985, and stood empty for ten years, with the stonework crumbling internally. The nave of the church was demolished in the 1840s, leaving just the Tower standing. Marilyn Champion, who had been a driving force behind the revival of Brunswick Square, had joined the Civic Trust and turned her attention to finding a solution for the Tower. Marilyn, who sadly died in 2014, secured £300,000 from the Heritage Lottery Fund, turning St Michael's Tower into a heritage centre and starting point for the Civic Trust's city tours. The City Council's Cabinet approved the lease to the Civic Trust in March 2007. It opened in September 2009 with a service of dedication by Bishop Michael Perham. In October 2012, two treble bells which were cast in 1710 by Abraham Rudhall at his foundry in what is now Kings Square were returned from St Michael and St Wulfad's church in Stone, who had raised funds to refurbish their peal of bells and no longer needed them. The bells went on display from April 2013. I was also pleased to be able to approve major works (costing £100,000) to the external stonework in 2014 from the City Centre Investment Fund and climbed to the top of the scaffolding to inspect at the time. The Tower was lit in Marilyn's memory in December 2017. The City Council donated £10,000 to the lighting project.

The Eastgate Chamber which contained the remains of the city's East Gate opened on 13th April 1981. The structure around it wasn't in my view very attractive and at times I'd described it as a "concrete and glass monstrosity". Coming up with an alternative was difficult and complex. We looked at a glass floor, but didn't really want people walking over it and we had to be mindful of the heavy delivery lorries which used Eastgate Street, so we put a low rail around it. There was also the sensitive issue of people in the Chamber below being able to see up ladies' skirts!

We came up with a scheme which was granted planning consent In February 2010, with glass at a lower level than before with a rail around it. The original plans included a mirror and bench which weren't implemented for financial reasons. I noted at the time that "in engineering terms this is a really complex project"[230] and said the new viewing window would showcase the city's Roman remains in "a more effective and attractive way".[231] The work was completed by March 2012.

66 Westgate Street

The building at 66 Westgate Street dates back to 1460. Originally two dwellings, it was occupied by the 'Teapots' tea room until it closed in 1997. The City Council owned the building and carried out a partial (and superficial) restoration in 1975. In March 1997, the tenant asked for repairs to the fascia boards and shopfront. During the course of the inspection, it was noticed that timbers were deteriorating. Further investigations revealed severe structural problems with the timber frame caused by beetle infestation, woodworm and water penetration (believed to be as a result of valley gutters not being properly maintained). Due to deterioration of timbers, the front wall was inadequately tied into the flank walls and was effectively 'floating'. Shoring and scaffolding was erected to stabilise the front walls.

In 1997, £37,500 was allocated for repairs but got diverted to urgent health and safety works at the Guildhall. A report to the Council's Land and Property sub-committee in March 1998 said the Council was looking to commit £150,000 to the building and prepare a Heritage Lottery Fund bid. That didn't happen and the building continued to languish for a number of years. In 2003, when Her Majesty The Queen and Prince Philip visited Gloucester Cathedral for the Maundy Service, I took the Duke of Edinburgh on a walkabout in Westgate Street when he expressed concern that the building was going to fall on top of him!

Major structural works were required, estimated to cost £600,000 (compared with a value after the works were done of £265,000), which was beyond the Council's budget. The fact that the cost of works exceeds the end value of the building is known as a 'heritage deficit'. Gloucester Historic Buildings, a joint City Council and Civic

Trust building preservation trust, looked at taking on this project but I think were put off by the scale of it. Nick Joyce, a Conservation Architect, had produced a feasibility study for the building and had got so frustrated by the lack of a decision that he decided to take it on himself through his company Swan Developments. Nick had just finished a project in Tenbury Wells, so was in a position to take on something else. The City Council sold it for £5000 but gave a grant of £90,000 from its repairs budget. English Heritage initially placed a limit on their contribution of £25,000 but this didn't fill the gap. I spoke to their regional director on the fringes of a GHURC Board Meeting at the Cathedral's Parliament Room one day and managed to get that grant increased to £150,000.[232]

The upper floors were converted to a two-bedroom apartment, perhaps amongst the best ones in the city centre, and the ground floor reopened as a tea room operated by Hedleys who operated it until it closed in 2019 and was taken over and renamed as Brimbles. The one controversial part was replacing the half-timbered front elevation with render. This was historically more accurate, as the sash windows were Georgian and the building would have been rendered at that time, but black and white buildings always feel more historic. English Heritage supported this approach. Despite a Citizen headline describing it as "Desecration", and the Chair of the Planning Committee asking English Heritage to reconsider, the controversy soon died down. The keys were handed over to Swan Developments on 26th September 2006. Once the restoration was complete, I wrote to the Duke of Edinburgh to tell him the good news. His Private Secretary Brigadier Sir Miles Hunt-Davies replied to say that His Royal Highness was "most interested to hear the good news".

Saving the House of the Tailor

Just round the corner in College Court was the Beatrix Potter Museum and Shop, housed in the building which Potter had sketched in the Tailor of Gloucester book. The Tailor's real shop was in one part of what is now The Sword Inn (at one time The Tailor's House). The shop and museum was owned at the time by Frederick Warne's publishing house, part of the Penguin empire, and operated by Lakes Story Ltd. In August 2005, just two years after it had celebrated the 100th anniversary of the book's publication, they had decided to close the shop and sell the building due to falling sales and rising costs. This was bad news for the city. If it couldn't sustain the place representing its most famous story, what hope was there?

As Cabinet Member for Regeneration at the time, the media contacted me for comment and I expressed both my concern and my hope that someone would take it on. Ivan Taylor, owner of Truscott's Jewellers at the other end of College Court and Chairman of the Westgate Quarter group, came up with a plan to form a company, issuing shares to raise the money to buy the building and keep the business going, launching it in November 2005. People could buy up to £2500 of shares each. Ivan contacted me for support and I couldn't really do anything other than put my money where my mouth was. Former Civic Trust chairman Robin Morris, who was Ivan's lawyer, joined us in fronting the campaign and *The Citizen* enthusiastically backed the initiative. The response from the great Gloucester public was brilliant. We raised almost £200,000 and bought the building, reopening the shop and museum in February 2007. It was officially reopened by the actress Patricia Routledge, who is Patron of the Beatrix Potter Society. She is best known as Hyacinth Bucket, the social-climbing wife in the BBC sitcom 'Keeping Up Appearances'.

It is still running today, mostly staffed by volunteers to whom I'm very grateful. I still sit on the Board, but most of the work over the years has been done by Ivan, Jenny Norville (wife of Frank, former boss of the Norville Optical Company) and Chairman Chris Hill. I still hold the £2500 of shares today and, like everyone else, have only had a 10% dividend for the whole of that time, but we saved the attraction for the city, which is what really matters.

St Nicholas' Church

One historic building for which we didn't find a solution was St Nicholas' Church in Westgate Street. Its spire was damaged in the Siege of Gloucester during the Civil War and was later reduced to half its height. Samuel Gwinnett, father of Button Gwinnett (second signatory to the US Declaration of Independence) was curate there from 1735. These days it is in the ownership of the Churches Conservation Trust. In June 2015, I was informed their trustees were on a coach tour of some of their properties and would be stopping off at St Nicholas'. I agreed to meet them.

One of the trustees got off the phone and asked if I'd met their chairman. I said I didn't think so, but who was it? It turned out that the Chairman at the time was Loyd Grossman of Through the Keyhole and Masterchef fame. Later on, Pam Tracey, as one of the local councillors, joined us and introduced herself to him saying, "Hello Mr Grossman, I'm Pam Tracey. You can look through my keyhole anytime!" Visibly shocked, he replied, "I don't do that anymore" and got back on the coach. He resigned shortly afterwards, but I don't think it was connected!

St Nicholas' Church is used for occasional events, concerts and exhibitions and can be viewed using keys held by the Civic Trust over the road at The Folk of Gloucester.

Historic events

Buildings are only a part of history. As the title of this chapter suggests, you need to bring them, and the stories they hold, to life. Gloucester's history hadn't, in my view, been a big enough part of the city's events programme and we set about putting that right.

In April 2008, we successfully applied to the Heritage Lottery Fund to stage a 'Gloucester Through the Ages' parade through the city. It included 350 re-enactors, a parade featuring St George on horseback and Henry VIII with his wives. There were kings, medieval knights, English civil war scenes, boats and WWII vehicles. It was hugely popular.

City MP Richard Graham and Chris Oldershaw, who was at the time Chief Executive of Marketing Gloucester as well as the Urban Regeneration Company, came up with a proposal for a Gloucester History Festival. Richard Graham, a historian himself, became (and at the time of writing still is) the Festival's Chairman. Much of the early vision was around talks by leading 'celebrity' historians such as Simon Scharma and Michael Wood. I was keen that the festival should also be accessible and appealing to the masses with a living history element that brought the city centre to life.

It's fair to say that the talks have grown to be a huge success, focused on Blackfriars Priory, with names including Kate Adie, Earl (Charles) Spencer, Dan Snow, Tony Robinson, Max Hastings and Griff Rhys Jones appearing, some more than once. TV historian Janina Ramirez is the Festival's President. Although the living history element hasn't taken off in the same way, largely due to the cost and effort of staging it, there is a 'Voices Gloucester' programme of free events in communities.

Two living history events that were truly memorable were the recreation of the Coronation of Henry III in 2016 (marking the 800th anniversary) and the re-enactment of the funeral of Queen Aethelflaed, Lady of the Mercians (for the 1100th anniversary) in 2018. The Coronation of Henry III was the only one to take place outside London since 1066. Henry was the 'Boy King', who took the throne at age 9, following the death of his father King John. He was crowned at the then St Peter's Abbey. His father, the unpopular King John, had died and due to the uncertain situation at the time, with Prince Louis of France and rebels holding the south east, a coronation was hastily arranged with a simple gold circlet in place of a crown.

In June 2016, we set about recruiting a young boy to play the King. Dean Stephen Lake said, "It will be a huge honour and privilege for the young boy chosen to play the starring role and he will be blessed with life-long memories of his day spent in the Boy King's shoes." We held auditions and chose Fraser Martin, age 11, a pupil at The Crypt School. He was carried aloft from Blackfriars Priory along Southgate and Westgate Streets (by myself, Councillor Andy Lewis and others) to the Cathedral and was word perfect as the ceremony was recreated, with wafts of incense, with media coverage reaching Italy and China.

Fraser Martin presented The Duke of Gloucester with a framed print of King Henry III's Coronation Window at Gloucester Cathedral when HRH visited later in the year.

We went through a similar audition process to choose the lady to play Aethelflaed, but a different skillset was required. They had to appear motionless as they were carried off a ship at the Docks, through the city centre streets and onto St Oswald's Priory, which Aethelflaed founded and where she is buried, and to continue in the same way through the short funeral service conducted by Canon Nikki Arthy. We chose actress Samantha Swinford, 27, from Abbeymead, who performed the role admirably despite it being a pretty hot day. Work had been carried out at St Oswald's Priory to ensure it was restored in time for the re-enactment.[233]

Although the story of Aethelflaed is perhaps not as well-known as it should be in Gloucester and beyond, it has inspired Bernard

Cornwell's 'Saxon Stories' series of novels, a television documentary by historian Michael Wood, 'The Lady of the Mercians', and the drama series 'The Last Kingdom', based on Cornwell's novels, which aired on the BBC and Netflix. When former Mayor Chris Chatterton gave a talk on Aethelflaed as part of the 2014 History Festival it was so popular it had to be moved to a larger venue.

That same year was also the 375th anniversary of the Siege of Gloucester in the Civil War and a battle reenactment was staged in Gloucester Park, supported by the Gloucester BID.

Henry III, the Boy King played by Fraser Martin, carried through Gloucester city centre by Paul James and Andy Lewis as part of a re-enactment to mark the 800th anniversary of his coronation in 2016. Credit: Marketing Gloucester

Blue Plaques

Other small improvements have been made in telling Gloucester's story, such as new plaques for Colonel Massey and Jemmy Wood in

Westgate Street and refurbishment of the plaque for W E Henley at 5 Eastgate Street (now occupied by Card Factory). Even after leaving the Council, I worked with Martyn White of Gloucester Historic Buildings and the Gloucester BID to add a new plaque on the TK Maxx building in Northgate Street which, I discovered quite by chance, was the site of the first Bank of England branch outside London. A number of other blue plaques have been installed at various locations around the city.

There is always more that can be done, but the idea that Gloucester 'doesn't do anything to promote its history', which may have been true at one point, certainly isn't true any longer.

13. THE DIRTY DOZEN

Major projects are vitally important in delivering the regeneration of the city, but they are not the whole picture. Smaller sites and buildings, if neglected and allowed to become derelict, can have a disproportionately negative impact on the feel of a place and on civic pride. Getting them restored, demolished or replaced can be seen as positive, help to build confidence more broadly and can happen relatively quickly.

Sometimes all it takes is a bit of effort. It may be the threat of some kind of legal enforcement using the Council's powers, or some grant assistance or just a bit of encouragement! When properties are owned by absentee landlords they can be oblivious to the impact they can have on communities. When they are just a line on a balance sheet to an asset manager with the rest of their portfolio performing well, there is often no pressure for them to do very much. In places, like Gloucester, with relatively low property values, it doesn't take much before development schemes can struggle with viability. When properties have been bought at the top of the market, as happened with the former Kwik Save site in Northgate Street and the old Northern Star premises on London Road, companies are often reluctant to write down their value on the balance sheet and crystallise a loss.

Dealing with eyesore properties wasn't a particularly new idea. It had happened before, for example with the former Horton Road Hospital which in the Civic Trust's 30th Annual Report in 2001 won the 'Hapless Building Award II' as it "continues to languish". It was redeveloped by Redrow Homes into some very smart apartments renamed The Crescent, with the first sales completing in 2005. But taking a co-ordinated approach to addressing these problem sites was stepping it up a gear.

In 2005, we set about identifying a number of sites on which we could take action initially. Phil Staddon, the Council's Regeneration Director, advised that 12 was probably the right number at any one time and coined the phrase 'The Dirty Dozen'. As I said at the time, "We need to get these buildings back into use because regenerating the city is not just about multi-million-pound development schemes. If you improve these dilapidated individual properties then it can make a real difference to the street scene in a short period of time."[234]

The first ones we identified included The Raglan Arms, a former pub in Regent Street, Tredworth, which had become a hotspot for fly-tipping. This was redeveloped to provide housing association-owned apartments.

The 'Dirty Dozen' initiative lost some momentum when Phil Staddon left the City Council but was given fresh impetus when City MP Richard Graham and I relaunched it as the 'Regeneration Hitlist' on Gloucester Day in 2014. Richard liked to call it the 'Gloucester Old Spots', but I wasn't so keen on the idea of comparing our own very special brand of rare breed pig to a set of dilapidated buildings!

The following were some of the properties where action was taken.

Samsons Supplies, Southgate Street

Samsons Supplies was an Aladdin's Cave of a shop in Southgate Street, near Spa Road, which sold small toys, stationery and novelties. I remember it being open as a child, but when we became the Administration in 2004 it had been derelict and surrounded by scaffolding for around 15 years. The LVS (Licensed Victuallers Supplies) shop next door at 107 Southgate Street supplied 'crockery, cutlery, glassware, tableware and equipment' to the licensed trade. Rather randomly, I remember buying a bar towel from there as a child when such things were also used as break dancing accessories! Both were Grade II listed buildings. The two sites would later come together for redevelopment.

Taking the Samsons building first, in October 1990 planning permission was granted for demolition of some sections to the rear, but proposed to retain the remainder of the building and add an extension to the rear to create a wine bar with office accommodation above. The permission was never implemented and the building continued to deteriorate.

The Citizen reported in March 1997 that the structural damage to the Georgian buildings was so bad there was no hope of saving them. They had been propped up with scaffolding since a Dangerous Building Notice was served on them in October 1995. The front and back walls had become detached from the sides and were in imminent danger of collapse.[235] With "considerable reluctance", planning officers recommended the demolition of this listed building which councillors approved with "equal reluctance". This was following consultation with English Heritage who concluded the building was beyond economic repair. This is one of very few listed buildings in the city which have been demolished since Gloucester Civic Trust was established in 1972. The Planning Committee gave permission for offices and a wine bar in the replacement building. By this point, the scaffolding had been in place so long, the owner was finding it difficult to keep paying for it. This consent was also not implemented.

The Council's Planning Committee in May 2000 approved demolition of the buildings, with a restaurant/bar on the ground floor and 4 flats above, noting that they had been empty and derelict for 10 years by this point. Demolition was only allowed on the basis that construction of the new building started within a short period after.

Planning permission was granted in December 2005 (by planning officers using their 'delegated powers') for the demolition of the existing Samsons building and its replacement with a 3-storey block of 12 flats. This was a purely residential scheme with no active frontage to Southgate Street and, unfortunately in my view, turned its back on the street. The legal agreement required demolition work to start within 4 months and the subsequent new build to commence within 6 months of the demolition. It was reported in July 2006 that, while the building had been demolished, it appeared the site was now for sale.

In August 2004, the Planning Committee granted consent for a new shop front at 107 Southgate Street (the LVS building) and the creation of 17 flats, converting the upper floors and a warehouse building to the rear, linking to the main building and adding a new three storey block of flats to the rear of the site.

Ownership of the two sites was brought together. According to Land Registry records, a company called Southgate Street Developments Ltd of Bentham bought number 107 in September

2005 and an associated company, Southgate Street Construction Ltd, bought 109-111 in March 2006.

Cabinet Member for Planning, Steve Morgan, reported to a Full Council meeting in November 2006 that "reconstruction work has now begun on this site, the scaffolding has been improved, the walkway has been made safer and we have been assured by the developers that they are looking to complete their work on that site in the region of twelve to fifteen months."

The developer went bust part way through building the scheme and it ended up in the hands of receivers before being sold on their behalf by local agents Bruton Knowles. A Bristol-based developer took it on and completed it, holding the asset through a Channel Islands-based family trust, Cypress Investments Ltd, who rented out the flats for a number of years before selling them off one by one.

It turned out to be a fairly low-quality scheme – although far better than the derelict and dangerous structure which had blighted the street for so many years.

Robert Raikes's House

Still in Southgate Street, but further towards The Cross, was the former Golden Anchor Clothing Company building which had been occupied by JJB Sports. They moved over the road into the unit on the corner of the Eastgate Shopping Centre entrance which is now a Tesco Express. This was taken on by Kara's Hair and Beauty Salon, a locally-owned business run by the Ball family, in 2010, relocating from premises in The Oxebode and a smaller salon in Southgate Street above Caffe Nero.

Next door to this was the former Golden Cross pub, which linked with the Malt & Hops in Longsmith Street. This was owned by the Yorkshire-based Samuel Smith's Brewery who also had The Old Crown in Westgate Street. They had a passion for heritage buildings and had carried out some stunning restorations in other parts of the country. They took on The Golden Cross and The Malt & Hops in 2006 and transformed it into what we now know as Robert Raikes's House, named because it was where the founder of the Sunday School movement lived. They reportedly spent £4.5 million on it during a two-year refurbishment. After starting work, they found the building to be in poor structural condition. The planning permission included consent for 13 visitor rooms on the upper floors, which haven't been completed. The pub reopened in November 2008.

The Duke of Gloucester was so impressed with what they had done that he undertook a low-profile visit. Businessman and presenter of the BBC programme 'The Apprentice', Lord Alan Sugar stopped there for lunch while his plane was being repaired at Gloucestershire Airport at Staverton in 2013. Sam Smith's Brewery was a very private organisation and didn't respond well to any publicity or indeed contact from outsiders. When I wrote to them to chivvy them along with the project, they replied to say that "nothing the Council can do will make it happen any more quickly" and they turned down the opportunity of receiving a civic award for the project. I recall being told a story that when a journalist friend phoned them for a quote and asked who dealt with media enquiries, he was told "The Chairman deals with that himself". When he asked to speak to him, the response was, "Oh, he doesn't take phone calls!"

The New County Hotel

Just further down was the New County Hotel. Formerly the Ram Inn, it was rebuilt in 1840. In its day it was one of the city's best hotels with 37 bedrooms and an often-used function room which could seat 160. Over the years it had not received the investment it needed and had been poorly-managed. It closed in June 2008 when its then owner George of Colchester went into administration. Planning permission was granted in November 2008 for it to be converted to a restaurant on the ground floor and 10 flats above. The planners were persuaded that it didn't have a future as a hotel and there was, unfortunately, no planning policy to protect hotel uses. I had misgivings about this. At the time I said, "It's a great site for a hotel and the right investor could really make a success of it", later adding, "As we go through regeneration, we need to be increasing bed spaces not losing them and I hope there are solid grounds for refusing this application." *The Citizen's* own comment column agreed, with the headline stating "Hotel beds are needed in the heart of town".[236] The Civic Trust's Design Panel also questioned the loss of a city centre hotel.

The Citizen reported that work was set to start on the restaurant in June 2009.[237] Thankfully, the conversion to flats was never implemented.

Another use was on the cards. I recall walking from the Council Offices at the Docks over to an event at Gloucester Quays with the Director of Regeneration Phil Staddon, who had become aware of a proposal. I tried to coax out of him what it was and, eventually, he blurted out, "It's a f***ing swingers' club."

The proposal for a swingers' hotel, called 'Club Mystique', came from Gloucester resident Harry Sykes, father of pop star Nathan Sykes of boyband 'The Wanted'. Such an application was likely to attract publicity anyway, but the celebrity connection made that even more certain and one national tabloid ran a story about the connection. The Council's public line was that the application had to be decided on its planning merits and moral issues could not be taken into account. I was asked to do a radio interview for TalkSport. I had never listened to this station and thought it would just be like my usual interviews on Radio Gloucestershire. It wasn't. They were brutal. I tried to stick to the line, but they wanted to know how I was going to "control the spread of disease" and suggested I should resign because of it. I fought back and accused them of asking sensationalist questions but never did an interview with them again.

The application went to the Planning Committee in September 2009 but was refused by 6 votes to 5 with one member of the committee abstaining on the basis that it was an inappropriate location for the development. However, Sykes managed to get round the refusal by applying for a 'Certificate of Lawful Use', successfully arguing that a Private Members' Club didn't need planning permission.

After it opened, Harry Sykes offered me a tour around the building. At the front it looked fairly respectable but the further you went back, the seedier it became with erotic pictures on the walls and in the function room there was a naked male mannequin in a cage! Harry took pleasure in telling me that the Conservative Ladies Luncheon Club continued to hold their events in the function room. "Do they ask you to move the mannequin?" I enquired. "No, they insisted I keep it there," he replied.

The bedrooms were individually themed, such as the 'Roman Orgy

Room' and the 'Chinese Torture Room'. Each bed had a packet of tissues carefully placed on the corner. It was no doubt meant as a thoughtful touch but just seemed to me to make it seem even more tacky.

It didn't take off as Sykes had hoped. I recall an application form for support from the Council landing on my desk. One of the questions was, "What do you do to support minorities in the city?" Their answer was, "We cater for the Lesbian, Gay, Bisexual and Transgender communities and the Conservative Ladies' Luncheon Club".

Eventually the Club closed, with Club Mystique Limited going into liquidation in May 2020. The building reverted to a mainstream hotel, undergoing the kind of major renovation that 'Club Mystique' hadn't provided. It was reopened in November 2010 by Irish chain West Inns Ltd. A few years later it was sold to Antony Clark, who had built up an impressive property portfolio across the country after starting off by renting out his spare room when short of cash. His first foray into the city had been the Central Hotel in an empty office building on the corner of Clarence Street and Russell Street, which was approved in October 2013. Clark's business model didn't rely on food and drink. The Central Hotel had a microwave and fridge in each room but that was it. At The New County, the function room was turned into more accommodation and a new courtyard of rooms was created at the back, but the front bar stayed open. A long-term derelict building adjoining the NCP Blackfriars car park to the rear of the hotel was also acquired by Clark, restored and added to the hotel's footprint.

Southgate Street Townscape Heritage Initiative

Southgate Street got another big boost from the award of Townscape Heritage Initiative (THI) status by the Heritage Lottery Fund (HLF). First stage approval was granted in May 2012 and second stage approval in September 2013. This made £1.2 million available in grants (£900,000 from the HLF and £300,000 from the City Council) over 5 years. With contributions from property owners, the impact it made was far greater than that. The first property to get underway with grant assistance was 57 Southgate Street, just by Kimbrose Triangle, where work started in January 2015. Other sites it assisted included Albion House, the former Albion Hotel, opposite the Docks entrance. This was vacant for many years and becoming increasingly dilapidated in what *The Citizen* called "a decade of decay".[238] The doorway was also a favourite resting place for street drinkers. Cheltenham-based developer Mark Holland took on the project of converting it to apartments with mews-style houses to the rear. It was completed in November 2016 with the help of a £94,000 grant. Later, he would also restore numbers 136-142 Southgate Street to residential use.

The 'five ways' site on the corner of Southgate Street and Trier Way was taken on by the Markey Group, who built the Park View nursing home. Plans for the 80-bed care home in Southgate Street were unveiled in *The Citizen* in March 2013.[239] The THI contributed to improving the public realm in the area – or, in other words, better quality pavements.

The former Job Centre near St Mary de Crypt had also been empty for a number of years. It was in the 1970s brutalist style of architecture. It was bought by Roger Head, owner of Highnam Court and one-time High Sheriff of Gloucestershire. If anyone was a 'Gloucester boy done good' it was Roger. Born in a council house, he attended the Central School before getting an apprenticeship as a mechanic. He sold second-hand cars from a property in Southgate Street which he still owns, before turning to commercial property and telecommunications. He realised his boyhood ambition to buy Highnam Court, restoring the house and gardens from the wreck they had become. He allows the house and gardens to be used for charitable purposes numerous times each year, including for the Pied Piper Appeal which he chaired for 10 years. Despite his obvious success, he has never forgotten his roots.

Roger gained planning consent to turn the upper floors of the old Job Centre to 14 apartments and create a retail unit on the ground floor. There was also an issue in that the freehold of a small part of the site had been in the ownership of the 'The Corporation' (a forerunner of the City Council) in the 16th century when a 500-year lease was granted. I got involved in sorting this out, which brought a small windfall for the council taxpayer. The THI agreed to contribute towards recladding the front elevation with copper, which transformed the look of the building. It was unusual for a THI scheme to contribute to works to a modern building, but it was the right thing to do. In the end, Roger sold the building to his brother Colin, whose son Alex project-managed the build. A virtual reality experience took on the ground floor unit, which was a good addition to the city centre.

Colin Head also took on the derelict former Prince of Wales pub next to the GL1 Leisure Centre, which he demolished and built an apartment block of 14 units called 'Athelstan House' (after the first King of England who died at his Palace in Gloucester) which completed in 2016.

A number of Southgate Street properties benefitted from grants, including 174 (the former Spa Motor House) and 141, which was another long-term vacant property, having become over-run with Japanese knotweed.

Just round the corner in Spa Road, a number of properties saw improvement. The former Ribston Hall School (which won the 'Dying By Degrees Award' from the Civic Trust) which had become derelict was turned into apartments, with the first sales completing in 2004. Vacant land at number 4 Spa Road was sold, with a new modern apartment block built, which was approved by the Planning Committee in November 2005 – although Councillor Stuart Wilson told the planning committee that its design was better suited to Benidorm!

The former RAFA Club (short for Royal Air Force Association) next door was a more difficult problem. It closed in 2010 after 60 years of serving RAF veterans and others and its sign is now part of the vintage memorabilia on display in Portivo Lounge, a short walk away at Gloucester Quays. It had a sentimental connection for me as my Great Uncle Frank and Great Aunty Ivy were steward and stewardess of the club in its heyday. Uncle Frank (Stephens) was also a Conservative County Councillor for Podsmead between 1977-81 and stood, unsuccessfully, a number of times for the City Council. After it closed, the building was sold more than once, ending up in the hands of Gurjinder Dhaliwal, a developer from Leamington Spa, who made a start on creating 14 apartments, for which planning consent had been granted in July 2015. This was a mixture of conversion of the listed building at the front and a new extension to the rear. The development was very stop-start and took a number of years to complete, but had just been finished and was being marketed for sale at the time of writing.

Former Kwik Save, Northgate Street/Black Dog Way

Located in Northgate Street, the Kwik Save supermarket closed in August 2002. It offered "Top brands at rock bottom prices" but struggled to compete with the rise of the German discounters like Aldi & Lidl. Its site in Gloucester was sprawling, wrapping around Black Dog Way and Worcester Street. It was bought by Highland Developments who came up with a bold scheme for 84 apartments, later amended to 88, designed by well-known local architect Jeff Roberts of Roberts Gardner (later Roberts Limbrick)[240], which was approved in December 2005. It was sold on to locally-based housebuilder Newland Homes, who gained planning permission for a development of 98 apartments in July 2007. Half of the proposed parking capacity was to be made up of hydraulic car stackers operated by key or card control system. Soon after securing planning consent, the financial crisis and recession of 2008 onwards hit, meaning Newland struggled to make the scheme work commercially – having bought the site at the top of the market. They renewed their consent in May 2010 and came back to increase the number to 119 apartments in September 2010 in an attempt to make the scheme viable. The September 2010 scheme dropped the car stacker idea and in fact had no on-site parking provision. Despite maximising the number of units on the site, they still couldn't make it work financially. The Westgate ward councillors and I met with Newland on numerous occasions, trying to find a solution.

The Citizen reported in November 2015 that the site was to come forward with an, as yet, unnamed housing association.[241] It was later revealed as the Rooftop Housing Group, a Worcestershire-based housing association founded through the transfer of Wychavon Council's housing stock. They had previously developed properties at St Oswald's Park, including the Extra Care Village. Rooftop tell me that taking on this scheme was a difficult decision and their Board took a 'leap of faith' as it didn't meet their usual parameters – but it was about regeneration and 'doing the right thing'. You can get an idea of the complexity of the site by the fact the development required 18 different party wall agreements. Rooftop's scheme was for 95 apartments, with a mix of 21 shared ownership, 60 affordable rent and 14 for people with learning difficulties. A number of the apartments have stunning views of the Cathedral. It looks a million times better than it did before, but I must admit I'm not a huge fan of the Black Dog Way elevation – either the 'stick on' red brick or the green and yellow cladding, which seems rather incongruous set against the listed St Peter's Church on London Road. I'm told it was designed to replicate the railway bridge opposite. The building on the corner of Northgate Street and Black Dog Way, currently occupied by Roadrunner Pizza, sits slightly awkwardly amongst the scheme. Rooftop had wanted to include it in their development but at the time the owner didn't want to sell.

It was made possible by grants from the Homes and Communities Agency who were keen to support a brownfield development in Gloucester, the City Council (I signed off a £500,000 contribution on the recommendation of the Council's Housing Manager Helen Chard) and the County Council. It was a complex site to deal with. Work started in January 2017 but was halted on a couple of occasions – firstly because the River Twyver running through the site was in a marginally different position from what was expected. This caused a nine-month delay as the scheme was slightly redesigned. A further two-month delay happened in order to install a sprinkler system in the wake of the Grenfell Tower tragedy. The scheme has a strong environmental edge, with solar panels on the roof and a car sharing club for residents.

City MP Richard Graham had wanted a replica of the Black Dog, which used to sit on the pub of the same name before the road was built, to be displayed prominently on the building. But because of the link between 'The Black Dog' and mental health, this wasn't felt appropriate but Rooftop agreed to restore the feature which is kept in The Folk in Westgate Street.

I was delighted to be able to name the main building on the development Walkinshaw Court, after Tom Walkinshaw – the Formula One tycoon who owned Gloucester Rugby (fitting because the site was only a short distance from Kingsholm). The smaller block was named Carpenter Court after Alfred 'Bumps' Carpenter, who played rugby for Cinderford, Gloucester and England. Legend has it that he walked from Cinderford to Gloucester to catch the train to Twickenham to play for England.

Rooftop have made a remarkable investment in Gloucester of well over £70 million including some difficult sites like the former Norville factory in Hatherley Road and land by St Aldate's Church in Reservoir Road. In their biggest development in the city yet, they are working with the City Council to develop the remaining land behind Tesco at St Oswald's Road.

The original design for the former Kwik Save site in Black Dog Way. Credit: Roberts Limbrick Architects

Tanners Hall, Worcester Street

Opposite the Black Dog Way development of Rooftop's was a much smaller problem site of the Tanners Hall – or at least what remained of it. Tanners Hall was originally a medieval merchant's house built in the 13th century. It was taken over by tanners in 1540 and was used as a tannery until the 18th century. During the 12th and 13th centuries, most houses in Gloucester were built with timber-frames and as such were susceptible to damage by fire. However, Tanners Hall was one of the few structures at this time to be built entirely of stone, with parts of it having survived until the present day. Citizen columnist Martin Kirby quoted Pam Tracey as saying, "All it needs is a floodlight on it, a brass plaque put up and a wrought iron fence around it and it would look lovely"[242], but the reality was more complex than that. It was owned by Turnkey Construction Ltd from Woodchester and offered for sale by the Property Centre for £450,000. Planning permission had been granted to build a block of 14 apartments on the site, incorporating the remains of the building, but those plans were never implemented. Developer Mark Holland bought the site in partnership with Gloucester City Homes and increased the number of units to 24. The new building was completed in 2021. I agreed a grant of £10,000 towards conserving the remains and incorporating them into the new development, which seemed a price worth paying.

Former Marks & Spencer, Northgate Street

When Marks & Spencer relocated to their new Eastgate Street store in July 2012, in the former Woolworths premises, they left behind their previous two units in Southgate Street and Northgate Street. The Southgate Street unit was quickly let to discount retailer B&M (who closed in 2022), but the Northgate Street unit was more problematic. M&S owned the freehold and it had some challenges – mainly a huge amount of asbestos which was very expensive to remove. The store lay empty for a number of years, with the £300,000 a year rent being seen as an obstacle.

    I had regularly been in contact with TK Maxx to encourage them to come to Gloucester. They would have preferred an out-of-town store if we'd have allowed it, but we resisted it in order to protect the city centre. They initially looked at the Northgate Street store but were spooked by the amount of asbestos in the building – something M&S's property team described euphemistically as a "legacy issue" – and withdrew in April 2013. I said at the time, "I haven't given up hope".[243] Later, in November 2013, a proposal emerged to create a store for them on the site of the Indoor Market at the Eastgate Shopping Centre, with the market moving upstairs to the old Food Court on the first floor.[244] The proposal didn't go down well with traders and by December a 2000-signature petition had been gathered.[245] We looked at alternatives including, ironically, the former M&S store in Northgate Street, The Fleece and the furniture store in Kings Walk.[246] I gave an undertaking that the Market wouldn't be forced to move if traders didn't want to.

In June 2014, it was decided to leave the Market in place.[247] That month, I wrote to Marks & Spencers' Chief Executive Marc Bolland urging him to do more to let their vacant Northgate Street store.[248] In January 2015, it was announced that discount retailer Pure Bargains would open at the store. They only used the front 10m of the premises, selling electronic hamsters, shopping trolleys, pieces of luggage and £1 items. I told *The Citizen* that "I would hope for something more aspirational" and the newspaper's own comment column said "Gloucester deserves better". Later, the store had half empty shelves and seemed only to open when it felt like it. I regularly chased up M&S's property department for news of a more permanent occupier.

The planning inquiry into the Home Bargains proposal for the Peel Centre in September 2014 was told that TK Maxx had renewed their interest in the city.[249] The Northgate Street store was, ultimately, the perfect location for them. Eventually M&S sold the building in January 2016 to Northgate No.1 Securities Ltd, a London-based company run by financier Paul McGill, which managed to sign up TK Maxx as the tenant of the ground floor and the Snap Fitness gym above. It opened in March 2017 with Steve Wood, landlord of the Northend Vaults, who had regularly been quoted saying it was his favourite shop and he wanted it to come to the city centre, being first in the queue. He was clutching the press cutting from 2015 and claiming he was responsible for bringing TK Maxx to Gloucester. As they say, "Success has many fathers".

Northgate No.1 went into administration in June 2017, leaving creditors nursing some big losses, and the building was sold in September 2017. It is now owned by Atlantic Property Development of Cardiff, the property company of former Chairman of Cardiff Blues Rugby Peter Thomas, said to be one of Wales' richest men.

Recladding 'ugly' buildings

Getting the city to look its best for the Rugby World Cup was a key objective and in September 2013 we allocated £220,000 from the City Centre Investment Fund for property grants for the city centre and £150,000 for dealing with eyesore buildings, some of which were in the City Council's ownership. A good example of how an eyesore building can be transformed in this way is the former Duck Son & Pinker music shop in Southgate Street, which was redeveloped as student accommodation and a new retail unit and renamed Formal Place.

Sometimes you can try too hard and later wish you hadn't bothered and this was one of those occasions. We proposed recladding the Eastgate Street frontage of the Kings Walk car park and the Heart Radio bridge over the street. The plans got a good deal of media coverage, with the first images going public in April 2014. I wasn't sure about some of the computer-generated images and was nervous about spending large sums of money on something that people wouldn't like. Citizen editor Jenny Eastwood wasn't convinced either, saying, "Perhaps it will look better in the flesh".[250]

The projected costs started to get beyond the budget we had available and progress was slower than I would have liked, with the works missing the target of being done in time for the Rugby World Cup.[251] Predictably there was criticism from the Opposition, with Labour Group leader Kate Haigh accusing me of "misleading the public". I responded that, "I had the choice to press the button or take a more cautious approach. It is more important to get it right than regret it for years to come." This was reported in *The Citizen* on 27th July 2015 – the day my eldest daughter Eirys was born. I've kept a copy of that edition of the newspaper as a memento for her, so it's a shame my only mention in it is that story!

Citizen columnist Bob Newby defended me, saying it was a "sensible decision" and "rugby fans are not interested in cladding."[252] We scaled back our ambitions with *The Citizen* reporting that the "fancy cladding (has been) scrapped in favour of a cheaper paint job".[253] In the end it was just too difficult and too expensive, so the idea was scrapped but it is proposed to be done as part of the Kings Walk regeneration scheme.

Likewise, there was a suggestion that we could put solar panels and later a 'green wall' on the crumbling monolith that is the Longsmith Street multi-storey car park. It didn't proceed on the basis that the car park's shelf life was too short – but it is still standing, albeit closed due to safety concerns, more than eight years later!

The third proposal was for a 'Trompe L'Oeil' (a visual illusion in art, especially used to trick the eye into perceiving a painted detail as a three-dimensional object) of how the former Bell Hotel looked on the upper floors of what was B&M and bookmakers Paddy Power on Southgate Street, which are currently concrete and 1970s cladding. It would have had images of some of Gloucester's historical characters looking out of the windows. I liked the idea of this but others thought it would deteriorate quickly and soon look shoddy. With various leases and sub-leases in place, there were about five different parties who would need to agree to it – and that too became too difficult so the idea was dropped.

Former Jumpin' Jaks, Brunswick Road

Another long-term derelict property was the former 'Jumpin' Jaks' in Brunswick Road. It had opened as the 'Chicago Rock Café' in 1997, rebranding as Jumpin' Jaks in November 2000 after a £750,000 makeover. Some of us remember it as the 'Linbar' food store, owned by the Creed family who went on to create the Creed Food Service business. 'Jaks' as it was known locally was owned by Luminar Leisure who also operated the Liquid Nightclub in Eastgate Street (later known as 'Atik'). It was trading quite well, but in the boom years of 2006, a property developer, Duddingston House Properties Ltd, came along and offered them a huge amount of money to close it down to enable them to demolish it and create a new building with restaurants on the ground floor and apartments above.

Helen Bowyer, the general manager, said, "A property company came in, saw the size of the building and offered Luminar Leisure a substantial amount of money. I'm absolutely gutted, particularly for the middle-aged people who enjoy having a party here rather than discos. We have been doing extremely well. Since Christmas, we have been one of the top performing Jumpin' Jaks in the country." It was an offer they couldn't refuse, so Jaks closed on 27th August 2006 but the subsequent recession meant the plans never went ahead and the place lay empty. I have memories of many good nights there. Some of those memories are a bit hazy! The likes of Jason Donovan, Chesney 'The One and Only' Hawkes and Edwin Starr had all performed there. As I said in *The Citizen* at the time, "On a personal level, I'm sad to see it go because I have spent many a good night there. Jumpin' Jaks has always appealed to a slightly more mature age group and that market still needs to be catered for."

Luminar had shrewdly inserted a clause in the sale document to prevent it being used as a nightclub, so that put off a lot of the potential buyers when it was marketed by agents Bruton Knowles. It was in a very poor state as, inevitably, thieves stole the lead from the roof and the copper wiring for the electrics and vandals did their worst.

One Saturday in December 2014, I was at a Gloucester home match at Kingsholm and overheard someone talking about a friend of theirs having bought the site. I got in touch with Robert Smith at Bruton Knowles to try and find out who it was and offer my support. The buyer was Paul Williams and his brother Dave, a former doorman at KCs nightclub. They had managed to negotiate away the restrictive covenant and planned to re-open the place as a nightclub, but focusing on the older end of the market. The sale was completed in May 2015. After a lot of work to bring the building back into a usable condition, believed to cost about £1 million, and some arguments about licensing and opening hours, 'Jaks' reopened in December 2017 with a hair salon on the upper floors. The City Council gave a small grant of £10,000, stretching the boundaries of its City Centre building grant scheme for these exceptional circumstances.

Former KCs, Quay Street

Another former nightclub site that had become problematic was the former KCs in Quay Street. KCs stood for 'King of Clubs' or, as some of the locals cruelly joked, the 'Kennel Club'! It was founded by local boy Pete Holder in 1984 and was split over two floors, with more modern music downstairs and a 'cheesier' brand of pop for the older clubbers upstairs. It was famed, as many nightclubs are, for its sticky carpet, which added to the clubbing experience. A new bar called The Brewery was added in 1995 and the Club was renamed 'Envy & Lansons' in 2000 when it was taken over by Helena Leisure – but everyone still called it KCs! The company had commercial connections with Luminar Leisure, who owned both the Liquid and Jumpin' Jaks nightclubs, and between them seemed to have the city's nightlife neatly wrapped up. It closed in January 2009 in a blow for the city's night-time economy.

At the time I said, "It has been there a long time and no doubt many people in Gloucester have fond memories of time spent there. With so much of the city's night-time economy centred on Eastgate Street it was rather on a limb and, combined with the economic downturn, this must have made trade difficult."[254]

Aside from removing a clubbing option for revellers, it meant the pubs on Westgate Street no longer had the groups of people making their way down to Quay Street when KCs opened and instead activity was concentrated in Eastgate Street. This arguably made it easier to police by containing it in one area, but you could also contend that funnelling thousands of young people into the same confined area made trouble more likely to kick off.

It ended up in the hands of a Scandinavian bank, who seemed less than motivated to do anything about it, other than remove it from the business ratings list to free them of that liability. A consortium fronted by former Gloucester and England rugby prop forward Paul Doran-Jones came up with a plan for 115 beds of student accommodation which gained planning consent. The scheme also included the adjacent former 'Minx' lap dancing club, which opened in 2005 but seemed to go in and out of business with regularity. Apparently, the Council's licensing officers found a basement at the premises that they had previously been unaware of and it didn't take a genius to work out what it had been used for! At the time of writing, work hadn't started on the site and the Minx part of the site was put up for sale in late 2022.

67-69 London Road

As I mentioned in the introduction, the movement of office occupiers from the city centre to business parks on the fringe of Gloucester had led to a 'hollowing out' of the city. A case in point, albeit on the edge of the city centre, was the former Northern Star building on London Road. Northern Star changed their name, as seems to be the way of insurance companies, to Fortis and are now known as Ageas. They moved to new premises on the Gloucester Business Park. Their former building on London Road, on the corner of Heathville Road, has remained empty ever since – probably for 15 or more years. It is owned by Pall Mall Investments, an East London-based property company founded by Mathias Kraus. Their balance sheet shows net assets of around £500 million, so you imagine they're not under huge pressure to do anything with this building. I probably spent more time chasing up Pall Mall than any other owner of an empty property. Local councillor Jeremy Hilton even tabled a motion calling on the Council to compulsorily purchase the building. I agreed we would consider it but as I noted at the time, compulsory purchase orders (CPOs) are "time-consuming, expensive and the outcome is uncertain". I reminded them that taking CPO action against organisations with deeper pockets doesn't always end well – as the City Council found out against BT with the Blackfriars CPO.

I regarded this property as 'unfinished business' and even after standing down as a councillor, still tried to push for a solution behind the scenes. At the time of writing, nothing had been agreed, although in the City Plan it is earmarked for residential development with an indicative figure of 70 units.

100 Northgate Street

Other properties where we had put pressure on but progress was slow included 100 Northgate Street. The last time this was occupied it was the office of Remax Estate Agents. The owner bought it, probably imagining that Remax would be long-term tenants, but that's not how it worked out. This property had consent to convert the upper floors to residential, but that never happened and the consent lapsed. It was renewed after I continually badgered the owner who was a successful businessman from the Forest of Dean. Work finally started to restore the building in 2020, with a Czech supermarket occupying the ground floor from 2021 and the flats upstairs being completed in 2024.

Former Argos, Eastgate Street

The future was looking brighter for the former Argos building in Eastgate Street. Many will remember it as the Co-op Department Store. As a child I spent many a Thursday morning having a drink in the café with my grandparents on the weekly shopping trip before buying groceries from the Foodhall (which was later occupied by New Look) including tokens for the milkman! When it closed, it became 'InShops' for a while, which was a collection of 'shops within a shop'. That was controversial because some contended it was a market and therefore breached the City Council's Markets Charter. It was later hit by fire in 1994, making that argument academic.

Argos moved in during the mid-1990s but only occupied the ground floor. After opening a second store in the city at St Oswald's Park, this one always seemed vulnerable. The takeover by Sainsbury's, who created Argos collection points inside their supermarkets at Barnwood and Gloucester Quays, was the final straw, with the store closing in 2017. The Furniture Recycling Project moved in for a while before the property was sold, by London-based property company Burleigh Estates, to Cheltenham-based developer Michael Chittenden, who owns the Manor by the Lake venue at Arle Court. He hadn't set out his vision for the site in detail before the Coronavirus pandemic struck, other than talking of offices on the upper floors. He had, however, pledged to restore the Art Deco façade and fix the clock!

The Job Centre opened on the ground floor in April 2021 as one of 80 'temporary' job centres around the country, housing around 50 work coaches to support all seven of the county's Job Centres to help those affected by the pandemic back into work. It is believed that the Job Centre signed a 10-year lease. Chittenden also acquired the adjacent former New Look building which had been under different ownership. Other than a short stint as a Halloween experience, it has remained empty since New Look vacated. A plan for this site and the upper floors of the former Argos building is awaited.

Others

There were numerous other sites which received our attention and keeping on top of them is an ongoing battle. Of the others, perhaps the most memorable were a couple of sites in Wellington Street which were redeveloped for affordable housing. In 2014, I was pleased to name one 'Bagwell House' after Hal Bagwell, the late Gloucester boxer who lived for many years in Wellington Street.

14. WATER, WATER EVERYWHERE
The floods of 2007

A downfall of biblical proportions

It had been the wettest May to July period since national records began in 1766. 414.1mm of rain had fallen across England & Wales, which was double the average. It had been the wettest July over Central England since 1888 and rainfall in Gloucestershire in July was 197mm – 4.11 times the average.[255]

27.6mm of rain fell on July 19. During the day of 20th July, 100.2mm fell on Gloucestershire – three times the monthly average in just 17 hours. One county resident described it as being of "biblical proportions". What was to come became the "largest peacetime emergency to have affected this country in terms of complexity, duration and effects".[256]

For the residents of Cypress Gardens in my ward of Longlevens, the summer floods of 2007 started not on 20th July but on 25th June. There was some heavy rain, causing some limited flash flooding in Kingsholm, but what happened in Cypress Gardens was on a different scale. This development of 59 houses by Bellway Homes was tacked onto the end of Greyhound Gardens – the former Greyhound track. Cypress Gardens was on the site of the former Paygrove Farm, which had been the Ormond Eccles slaughterhouse before reportedly going out of business because of EU rules. Outline planning consent had been granted in 1999, with the detailed permission given in 2001. Some neighbours had warned that the site flooded, but there was no objection from the Environment Agency so the planning application was approved.

When Kathy Williams, my fellow Longlevens councillor, told me what had happened I was shocked – water had been up to waist height. By the time I had got round there it had receded and looked fairly normal. The Horsbere Brook, which ran alongside the estate, had always seemed pretty tame. What happened at Cypress Gardens was a taste of what was to come a few weeks later.

On Friday 20th July I was in the Council Offices early – by about 7am. Despite being the height of summer, it was dark due to the gloomy weather. I told my PA Sonia Tucker that I was looking forward to the Carnival the next day. She remarked that there was a severe weather warning in place.

I travelled to Coleford for a meeting at the Forest of Dean Council offices. While we were having lunch, we got a call saying that things weren't looking too good back home. I decided that I'd head back so I was closer at hand if needed. My next meeting was, perhaps ironically, of the Gloucester Partnership at the Oxstalls Tennis Centre. I didn't stay there long before getting a message that Cypress Gardens was in trouble again. I went straight there to find that the houses had flooded for the second time in a matter of weeks. Nathan Travis of the Fire Service (now the Chief Fire Officer for Hereford & Worcester) was also there and he would spend the rest of the day in Fire Control, liaising with the Police in what he described in an understated way as a "fairly intense" time.

Tally Giampa, Station Commander at Eastern Avenue at the time, explained to me that they didn't have data in the same way we do today and the network of warnings was not as sophisticated then as it is now. In fact, he was alerted by Gordon Macrae, a journalist from Severn Sound radio, a day before to warn that 4 inches of rain was going to fall in 24 hours. The Environment Agency's Anthony Perry told me that there was a lot of information from the Met Office but it was 24 hours out of date by the time they got it. They were told the storm was weakening, but revised reports came through which kept changing. Now they get reports with forecasts 5 days ahead. The Met Office issued a severe weather warning on 18th July followed by later flash warnings of heavy rain on 19th and 20th. This was not unusual – 465 warnings were issued in the year to October 2007. The Environment Agency issued a press release on 19th July warning of flooding but noting that it was "notoriously hard to predict". Chief Constable Tim Brain's post-event report noted that there was "no indication of the effects the rainfall would have on already fully saturated ground".

That afternoon, Gloucestershire Highways' phones started to ring off the hook and the emergency services were all overwhelmed with calls. At the City Council, custodian Bernie Sherratt was dispatched to the branch of Countrywide Stores on the Quay, which itself was vulnerable, to buy as many pairs of wellington boots as possible so staff could use them when they were out in the thick of the action. Sue on the City Council reception at North Warehouse had been at work taking calls without any idea that her own home had been flooded. Where she lived in Marlborough Crescent had seen water at levels of up to 5 feet in the properties.

In Longlevens, we did what we could – putting sandbags against doors, moving possessions and, in a couple of cases, vulnerable people – but it is difficult when you are fighting Mother Nature. As the water spread from Cypress Gardens into the Greyhound estate, I kept moving my car back a bit further – until I parked it in the Greyhound pub car park where it would stay overnight. I tried to keep in touch with what was going on elsewhere in the city, but my mobile phone charge was almost empty and my attempts to keep it topped up from my car charger were only having a limited effect. In addition to what happened in Cypress Gardens, in Longlevens the Big Normans Pumping Station failed, meaning the pumps were out of action and some houses in nearby Park Avenue flooded.

I did have one call, when I was literally up to my knees in water, asking if I was going to the Conservative barbecue in Quedgeley that night. "You are joking?" was my response. I don't think I could have got there even if I didn't have my hands full dealing with the situation. We, literally, lifted one vulnerable couple from a bungalow on the Cypress Gardens development to safety.

The conditions didn't discriminate. Gloucestershire's fire chief Terry Standing blew up the engine on his fire service BMW after going through a pool of water in Hempsted while taking a colleague to hospital.

The rain did stop eventually but it was clear that flooding throughout the city had been widespread. A car had become stranded under the Tredworth Road rail bridge and made the front page of the national papers when the driver seemed as concerned with retrieving his pack of cigarettes as he was with ensuring his own safety. Flooding along Eastern Avenue had made it difficult for the Fire Service to reach him. The mobile phone network had fallen over, hampering the wider rescue effort. It was, as one senior fire officer put it, "quite chaotic". All trains out of Gloucester had stopped running, meaning a group of around 500 passengers were stranded. The Council opened up the Sports Hall at the GL1 Leisure Centre as a rest centre for those affected. I walked from Greyhound Gardens, not even knowing whether my own home had been flooded (fortunately it hadn't been) and went to GL1. The Director of Resources, Keith Birtles, had gone to Asda and used his corporate credit card to buy up all of their bedding and sleeping bags to use at the rest centre. Once I'd done what I could, I headed home to my flat at Kingsholm. Thankfully the pizza takeaway on Worcester Street was still open so I could get something to eat on the way home.

A false sense of security

The next morning we woke up to bright sunshine. The water had disappeared and everything looked normal – other than, in some places, cars abandoned from the day before. It gave us a false sense of security and nobody imagined what was going to come down the River Severn that night. I headed back to GL1 early in the morning. We took an early, and easy, decision to postpone the Carnival. Carnival Organiser Mhairi Smith did a Radio Gloucestershire interview leaning against the glass front of GL1 in a hi-viz jacket, cigarette and can of Red Bull in hand, to communicate our decision. The Funfair in the Park also couldn't open – keen though they were to do so. It was a difficult balance between being sensitive to the flood victims and getting back to life as normal. I spent time talking to operators Willie and Emily Wilson over the coming days and we agreed, with Police support, that it would open a week and a half later.

I still had my other 'day job' to do and went into the office at letting agents Naylor Powell to take calls from tenants of our affected rental properties – of which there were quite a few. One of the impacts of the flooding was that the new flats at the Barge Arm in the Docks, which were proving a bit difficult to let, soon filled up with flood victims. Others decided to live in caravans on the driveway of their flooded homes and many were there into and through the cold winter months.

The focus soon switched elsewhere as the River Severn rose at The Quay. I headed to the Council Offices at North Warehouse. Spectators were gathering as it seemed inevitable the Quay would overtop.

Heading up the efforts to save it was Frank Heggs, an unassuming highway engineer from Abbeydale. That morning he'd been leading a church service at Christchurch Abbeydale when his mobile phone had been constantly vibrating against his hip. Frank recalled, "When I checked my messages they were all from the City Council. The next thing I knew, the person who had left the messages was standing in front of me so I dropped everything and went to the Docks." Over 100 prisoners had to be moved to other jails after water submerged the ground floor of the prison and interfered with its water supplies. There was concern that if the Quay wall was breached the city centre sewers would be overwhelmed. Frank directed operations as sandbags were placed strategically to shore up the Quay wall, which wasn't built to hold water like that, with water allowed to trickle through at selected points. Remarkably, and perhaps to the disappointment of some onlookers, the Quay was saved – and I put it down to Frank's expertise and oversight.

Flooding to the west of Gloucester with the Cathedral and Shire Hall extension in the background.

Alney Island, which regularly flooded, and which Prime Minister Tony Blair had visited during an earlier flood in 2000, found itself underwater again. The Environment Agency had erected flood walls in the aftermath of the 2000 floods but these weren't substantial enough to protect homes in the area in the face of the severity of the flood. Properties across the city were affected, largely along the routes of its main tributaries, the River Twyver, Daniels Brook, the Horsbere Brook and Wotton Brook. The University of Gloucestershire's lecture theatre at Oxstalls was flooded, as was Gloucester City Football Club's Meadow Park Stadium. Little did we know then that it would lead to a thirteen-year absence from the city for The Tigers.

I slept in my office at North Warehouse and Chief Executive Julian Wain set up a camp bed in his office so we were on hand to deal with any issues that arose. The two ground floor committee rooms in the Council HQ were set up as a control centre. Naturally, the eyes of the media were on us. Mayor Harjit Gill, who had recently suffered a heart attack 4 days after taking up office, fronted up the first few interviews, but I said that I felt it was important that I was visible too. I was literally only a few weeks into my leadership of the Council and wanted to lead from the front. Harjit himself was unable to get home to Birdwood and stayed overnight in Gloucester. When the floods had subsided, Harjit and I, who had always got on well despite our political differences, went on a city centre walkabout and knocked on doors to talk to flood victims to present a united front.

Infrastructure at risk

Over 1000 homes in the city were flooded and each one represented a traumatic experience for those individuals and families involved. But more was to come. The Castlemeads Power Station, next to the All Blues Rugby Club on the South West Bypass, flooded leaving 40,000 homes without electricity for up to 24 hours while the site was pumped out and temporary defences, which had come from Tamworth and Hull, were constructed.

The Severn Trent treatment plant at The Mythe in Tewkesbury was overwhelmed at 2.45am on Sunday 22nd July. Water supply to 140,000 homes (around 350,000 people), including most of the city, was cut off. The control room was in the basement, containing huge amounts of electrical switchgear and exposed buzzbars. Had it not been closed down before the waters overwhelmed it, it would have exploded and would have taken an indefinite time to bring back into use. So the decision by Tally Giampa to authorise its shutting down was a straightforward one, but a huge call nonetheless. When he communicated this to Chris Griffin, the Deputy Chief Fire Officer, at Gold Command the response was a simple, "Okay, thanks." The river levels were still rising, to a record peak, and work to bring Mythe back into use couldn't start until the water had receded. Tim Brain's report noted that– "at no point until 22nd July was Gold Command alerted to the extreme potential consequences at Mythe or Walham".

To the west of the city was Walham Power Station – a much bigger beast than Castlemeads. The waters were circling it. If that too was lost to the elements we had a problem - it supplied power to the majority of the County as well as large parts of Wales and Bristol. It if became overwhelmed it would have meant the loss of power to 450,000 homes in Gloucestershire. It was, as Tim Brain put it, "a critical infrastructure weakness waiting to be exploited" and a "single point of failure" and no contingency plan existed for its loss. We had all driven past it many times and seen water around it and thought those who had designed it must have done so with the elements in mind as it had never flooded. But that was wishful thinking. As well as the risk of water overtopping the temporary barriers, it was also coming up through the ground, so it had to be pumped at the same time as new defences were erected. Gloucestershire Highways supplied 15 immersible pumps and provided sandbags, taking a low loader to the nearby B&Q, which had been evacuated, to collect 60 dumpy bags of sand. The driveway to the power station had become impassable to normal vehicles so Gloucestershire Highways played a vital role in transporting plant, materials and labour onto the site.

Overnight on 23rd July around 250 people, led by Gloucestershire Fire & Rescue Service, with assistance from the Armed Forces (including 25 Gurkhas who arrived in a Chinook helicopter), the Environment Agency, other emergency services and National Grid, worked to protect Walham. Their heroic efforts saved the power station when the water was just two inches away from engulfing it. We are forever in their debt. In the Gloucestershire Media publication, 'The Great Gloucestershire Floods of 2007' Chief Fire Officer, Terry Standing, tells of 'The Battle for Walham. Our Trafalgar', explaining how Environment Agency flood defence equipment from Shropshire and Kidderminster was moved to Walham. Six huge pumps were installed along with nine smaller ones as the team set about building a barrier around the site. With an aluminium frame covered by huge lengths of plastic tarpaulin weighed down by sandbags and lengths of metal chain, the aim was to get more water out than was coming in. The pumps removed an amazing 20 million litres of water. Standing explained that it was getting dark, with floodwaters rising and "any work above head height could have been lethal as voltages of 400kv passed through a mass of wires, cables and transformers." High tide was expected at 3am and it was vital that flood defences were in place by that time. The job was done by 2.50am – 10 minutes before the peak was expected. As Standing put it, "they had kept the lights on for Gloucestershire." His Deputy, Chris Griffin, oversaw the operation. Standing "had his best man on the job." A letter published in a commemorative newspaper published by Gloucestershire Media said, "This surely was the second Siege of Gloucester". Just as it had 364 years earlier, the city prevailed.

Once the waters had subsided, a 1km protective ring of Hesco Bastions – wire cages filled with concrete, which were used in a variety of places including Camp Bastian in Afghanistan - was built before more permanent flood defences could be put in place as the authorities were concerned about another high tide on 28th July. Hesco Bastions were also put in place at Castlemeads.

Gold Command but no order to evacuate

Gold Command had been set up under the leadership of Chief Constable Tim Brain. He was born in the County and had been Chief Constable since 2001. Fortunately for the County, he had received specialist training in the management of major disasters and cut a reassuring figure on television. As the Pitt Report into the flooding, chaired by Sir Michael Pitt, noted, "The Gold Commander adopted a high profile, providing visible leadership at the local level." He was awarded the OBE for his role during the floods and some, including me, felt that he should have had a knighthood. Insiders tell me that the atmosphere at Gold Command was calm and businesslike. Gold Command was often referred to, but it was both the name for the group of senior officials which came to make decisions and the facility, made up of up to 25 partner agencies at its peak, including the military and the RSPCA. The Police named the response to the crisis 'Operation Outlook'.

The new Police HQ at Waterwells was only a couple of years old. It had a conference room with an oval-shaped table so everyone could see each other. The floors were open plan on a massive scale. It had been future-proofed from a technology point of view; it was designed with copper wire in mind but by the time of construction fibreoptics had arrived, meaning partner agencies could simply plug in their computers. Volunteers and partner agencies took over half a floor, with large signs hanging from the ceiling with the name of the organisation involved, making communication much easier. The benefits of the new Tri-Service control room would come into their own during this crisis, with the blue light services communicating from the moment rain started falling. Tim Brain's report said the Tri-Service centre "ensured an early, well-co-ordinated and true multi-agency response." In an ordinary flood, Monday morning would have seen the Police's role stepping back. That's what they were expecting, but the loss of water supply made this anything other than ordinary. Tim Brain described it as "the supreme test of (his) career". He recognised early on that the critical thing is public confidence. People needed to be reassured that there was a solution, a plan and that the people needed to deliver it were in place. In the end, handover to County Council as the lead local flood authority didn't take place until 15.15 on 6th August.

Media reports at the time suggested that contingency plans had been drawn up to evacuate the city, apparently to Birmingham and Bristol, if the electricity supply had been lost. But Tim Brain told me that this had never seriously been considered and was only "briefly" proposed. Not long before the Gloucestershire floods, there had been floods in Mississippi and an evacuation of New Orleans. Brain told colleagues, "We're not going to do a New Orleans on Gloucestershire." His assessment was that it would be easier to bring whatever people needed to them than evacuate 600,000 residents, which would have meant "people sleeping in aircraft hangars in Preston"; it would create massive security problems and some people wouldn't have left anyway. The Regional Civil Contingencies Committee (led by the Government Office for the South West) did consider evacuation of the County but did so "without reference to Gold" which "was not a fully helpful process" and "caused unnecessary confusion".[257]

Ensuring community spirit didn't run dry

With the Mythe water treatment plant out of action, a whole new operation had to be set up to distribute bottled water to residents from supermarket car parks and the old B&Q store on Trier Way. The Fire Service switched from rescue mode to community support, including knocking on doors to identify vulnerable people and delivering prescriptions. They knocked on the door of one elderly lady who was dehydrated after not having had anything to drink for two days. She had plenty of bottled water, but just didn't have the strength to open it and had suffered in silence.

Around 900 bowsers were despatched to the streets of the county, which rose to 1450 at the peak, for people to fill up with buckets to flush their toilets etc. Mayor Harjit Gill struggled a little with the word and confused people when he kept talking about "boozers"! In a Cathedral Service after the floods, Dean Nicholas Bury quipped in his sermon that "a new word has entered our vocabulary – bowsers!" There were stories of bowsers running dry across the city. Severn Trent were aiming to fill them 5 times a day but initially they were being emptied in 45 minutes. There were lots of calls to the City Council about this but staff could only pass on details to Severn Trent. Severn Trent couldn't cope and appealed to COBRA (the Government's Emergency Committee) for help. At the peak the bowsers were being filled an average of 3.7 times a day, with 53 large tankers deployed to keep bowsers and large tanks topped up.

One of the positives to come from this episode was the amazing community spirit that it fostered. But there was also a danger that, in some ways, the community could fracture. There were stories that some members of the Muslim community were stockpiling water while others struggled to get any. This was because some Muslims took large amounts of water to deliver to others in the community and bowsers were difficult to accommodate on the narrow streets of Barton, where most of the community lived. However, there were fears that the perception could damage community relations if it wasn't addressed. I gathered community leaders at the GL1 Leisure Centre, together with the Police, to discuss how we could keep the whole city together. Ismail Mehter, a senior figure in the Gloucester Muslim Welfare Association, led their response. They would go round taking water to vulnerable members of the community – and not just Muslims – who had been identified by the Police and the City Council. Many Muslims have 20 litre containers to store holy water from Mecca. The local community understandably wanted to keep their own containers, so a wider appeal was put out and within an hour around 500 had been donated. They were filled from a well on a farm in Newent and delivered to the most vulnerable in the city using a fleet of vans, which were accompanied by the Police. It was a major operation, all run from the Ryecroft Street mosque. At the peak they were delivering 6000 litres an hour with a volunteer force of up to 160 people and 30 vehicles, operating on a shift system. That effort, which we ensured was well-publicised, countered those who were painting a different picture about this section of the city community.

Help, in all its forms had come from far and wide – including hovercraft from the Italian Rescue Service. As a result, Gloucestershire's Fire and Rescue Service bought two of their own in 2008, paid for by Severn Trent's Community Rescue Fund.

All in all, water supply was lost for 17 days. As well as the impact on residents, it also impacted businesses like restaurants and hairdressers who couldn't open. Kara's hairdressing salon, in The Oxebode in Gloucester, put paddling pools on the roof of their building to collect rainwater, enabling them to stay open. The Mythe treatment plant was back operating on 30th July (after 8 days), with 100% of homes and businesses having mains water by 2nd August. Tap water was declared safe to drink on 7th August.

Gold Commander, Chief Constable Tim Brain, put together a 114-page report for the Police Authority after the event, including calling for the creation of "national strategic reserves of drinking water, food, fuel and temporary sanitation equipment". Getting through this crisis was a real team effort but particular praise is due to the Police who, under emergency planning arrangements, assumed responsibility for the overall co-ordination of the response. The Police were commended for "visible leadership at all levels" and "a number of exceptional acts... of selflessness and bravery".[258]

Severn Trent paid compensation for the loss of supply and rather than refund a few pounds to each billpayer, they sent a lump sum to the Council of over £400,000 which we were able to use to support a range of important community projects like the new athletics track at Blackbridge, the Al Ashraf Cultural Centre in Stratton Road and a new play area at Paygrove Lane (adjacent to the affected Cypress Gardens area).

High-profile visits

The events in the city attracted lots of media coverage and some high-profile visits. Prime Minister Gordon Brown, who had taken over from Tony Blair a few months earlier, helicoptered in to the Gold Command at Waterwells and later visited the Walham Power Station days after it had faced its most critical test. He also visited residents queuing for water at Quedgeley and the Mythe treatment works. Brown was at his best dealing with a crisis and was still basking in his honeymoon period. Tim Brain had kept the PM briefed through Downing Street's COBRA emergency operation. Opposition Leader David Cameron also came, visiting the water station at the old B&Q. By contrast, he was under fire for visiting Rwanda for a Conservative 'social action' project while his own constituency of Witney was under water. In his autobiography he admitted, "I knew it had been a mistake". He was an hour late arriving and I had to go and help a flood victim family find a temporary property, so I didn't get to meet him on this occasion. Princess Anne came to visit Cypress Gardens and I was given the task of showing her round. I recall her asking Kathy Williams and me, as local councillors, whether we lived here. When we explained that we didn't live here but weren't very far away she said, "Well I thought some councillors lived in their areas." Kathy did a sterling job during and after the floods, including returning from a caravan holiday in Wales as soon as the floods hit, and was widely-recognised as being a superb champion for her community.

The Princess Royal was introduced to residents, including Kelly Bartlett and Steve Byrne, who gave HRH a card for his cake business and offered to make Zara and Mike Tindall's wedding cake. Kelly was young, articulate and photogenic, so media attention often focused on her. She was a formidable and determined campaigner and became one of my closest friends even after she moved to South Africa in 2017. Steve and wife Louise's daughters Elysia and Sophia were *The Citizen*'s 'Face of the Floods'. As Princess Anne toured the flooded properties, I could feel that events were starting to take a physical toll on me and at times, very unusually for me, I thought that I might faint. That wouldn't have looked good on a Royal visit and I just about managed to hold it together. The Princess also visited Holy Trinity Church Hall in Longlevens, which had been set up as an emergency centre, and affected businesses in Hempsted. The Prince of Wales also visited the County.

Princess Anne visits Cypress Gardens in Longlevens after the floods of 2007.

Recovery and avoiding a recurrence

After the initial crisis came the recovery. Although I was no fan of the Labour government, I couldn't find fault with their response to this and I have a good deal of respect for how the Local Government Minister John Healey dealt with it. The 'Bellwin Formula' was triggered to help the Council meet its extraordinary costs. The formula kicks in when costs of such an event rise above 0.2% of the Council's budget. Ordinarily 85% of the costs are reimbursed but the Government raised it to 100%. We were also given a fairly generous 'Flood Recovery Grant'. Whereas some authorities simply divided it up between the victims, I felt it was more important to use it to try and ensure the same thing didn't happen again.

The Government invited City MP Parmjit Dhanda and me to nominate 'Flood Heroes' to attend a reception in London to mark their contribution. Rather than nominate independently, we pooled our nominations and put forward Kelly Bartlett, Frank Heggs, Stef Hopkins and Ismail Mehter. Stef Hopkins, is the founder of SARAID (Search and Rescue Assistance in Disaster) and the brother of former Housing Minister Kris Hopkins. He led a team of around 10 people working 18 hours a day for 15 days. His team rescued people trapped in their homes by boat and took supplies to those who didn't want to leave.

The reception took place at Lancaster House in the West End, near St James's Palace. It was hosted by Communities Secretary John Healey with Prime Minister Gordon Brown in attendance. The nominees attended with City Mayor Harjit Gill who afterwards took them on a tour of the capital's curry houses!

To help flood victims, particularly those without insurance, we set up the Gloucestershire Flood Relief Fund. Harjit Gill, Tewkesbury Mayor Phil Awford (a long-term family friend of mine who passed away in 2023) and I were the drivers behind this and we received enthusiastic backing from *The Citizen* and its editor Ian Mean. It was launched at a press conference on 27th July with Harjit, Phil, City MP Parmjit Dhanda and Bishop Michael Perham. Generous donations flowed in from county businesses, with Bristol Street Motors, Bottlegreen and Kraft Foods all being quick off the mark to donate £5,000 each. The Diocese of Gloucester donated £10,000, Unilever £20,000, Eon £25,000 and Severn Trent £50,000. Yusuf Islam, the singer formerly known as Cat Stevens, surprised Mayor Harjit Gill by sending a donation cheque for £20,000 to his home address.

Gloucester and Worcester Rugby Clubs jointly organised a festival of rugby, raising £70,000. Prince Charles also donated an undisclosed amount. Council officers had tried to persuade us to set up a Gloucester City fund (as happened after the 1947 floods) and when we resisted they suggested a Gloucester and Tewkesbury fund (as the two worst-hit areas in the county). We resisted this too and established the Gloucestershire fund which the whole county could get behind. In the end it raised over £2 million.

There were numerous events, including a sponsored walk from

Castlemeads Power Station to the Mythe Treatment works. Pam Tracey organised a meal at Angel Chef restaurant at the Peel Centre and I put on another at The Grill in Westgate Street (formerly The Lamprey). There was a charity City v County cricket match at the Spa Ground, which didn't attract much of a crowd despite an entirely false rumour that Liz Hurley was likely to attend! Most of the money raised by the event was from well-heeled county types who preferred to pay up rather than turn up! The Rotary Club gave £36,000 towards the £76,000 cost of a new play area at Paygrove Lane, adjacent to Cypress Gardens, including some cash given by supermodel Naomi Campbell from a London fashion show she organised. The balance came from Severn Trent's contribution.

The abandoned Carnival was rearranged for mid-September. The Royal Navy, RAF, SARAID, Police and Fire Service all took part and there was a flypast by a Sea King helicopter. I have on my office wall at home a picture from the procession showing Town Crier Alan Myatt walking ahead of an open-topped bus carrying Mayor Harjit Gill, Bishop Michael Perham, Chief Constable Tim Brain, Commodore Jamie Miller of the Royal Navy and me, holding 'Face of the Floods', Elysia Byrne, perilously close to the edge of the bus! The theme of the Carnival was the 'Spirit of Togetherness', which was intended to reflect the 50th anniversary of our twinning with Trier, 40th anniversary with Metz, 35th with Gouda and 20th with St Ann, but was also fitting as a nod to the community spirit shown during the floods. The twinning celebrations went ahead, with representatives of a number of our twin cities attending.

In hindsight, it's fair to say we had been complacent about the risk of flooding. Watercourses weren't cleared of blockages frequently enough and culverts had been blocked or, in some instances, had collapsed. One cul-de-sac had been flooded because of a wheelie bin blocking a stream! It could have been even worse. Extra culverts had been put in the Castlemeads section of the South West Bypass in response to concerns about flooding and material had been removed from the floodplain and used in the Gloucester Quays development. Despite what some critics say, the experts tell me that the amount of development in Gloucester's floodplain, most of which is historic, is much less compared with other cities. And I've never known the Council's Planning Committee go against the recommendations of the Environment Agency when it comes to flooding. That said, the development at Cypress Gardens had been granted without any objection from the Environment Agency despite warnings from neighbours that the land regularly flooded.

Over the coming years, we would carry out literally hundreds of schemes, large and small, to alleviate flooding, along with the County Council (who introduced a flood levy on council tax bills), Severn Trent and the Environment Agency. Anthony Perry of the Environment Agency was a strong ally. The one scheme I am most proud of is the £2 million Horsbere Flood Storage Area just off the Barnwood Bypass, which protects not only Cypress Gardens but other areas along the brook including Hucclecote and Elmbridge. In the interim before the new project was in place, there were several near misses, with the Fire Service regularly called to pump water from the brook into the adjacent field. Had it not been for this, houses in Cypress Gardens would have flooded 5 times in 12 months. Before the main scheme was in place, the Environment Agency removed a concrete footbridge which was seen as an obstruction and a gas pipe running along it was diverted in record time. The embankments around it, which had been lowered by the developers, were built back up.

The Horsbere Flood Alleviation Scheme was a challenge. As well as highly complicated flood modelling there was the small matter of purchasing the 50 acres needed for the scheme which was in private ownership. As ever, the landowner had ambitious expectations of its value but was eventually convinced it would never get developed. There was even a risk the scheme wouldn't happen. When future Government spending commitments were starting to be scaled back in 2009, those projects not under contract were frozen. EA officials quickly got the scheme committed, otherwise there could easily have been an extra 5-year wait.

The Horsbere scheme had its funding approved in June 2010 and was granted planning permission in November that year. Work started in February 2011 and it was officially opened by Environment Minister Richard Benyon, great-great grandson of former Prime Minister Lord Salisbury, in December 2011. This happened after determined and persistent lobbying by the residents, led by Kelly Bartlett and backed by local councillors and MPs Laurence Robertson and Richard Graham. The County Council also contributed to the scheme, which was able to store 3.7 million litres of water. In 2017, part of the adjacent nature reserve was named 'Jim's Orchard' in memory of Longlevens councillor Jim Porter, who died in August 2016 and had been a strong supporter of the project.

The city has a long and proud history of dealing with adversity and moving on. It did the same in 2007, although for many of the families affected it meant many months in temporary accommodation and it would be a mental scar for them for much longer. We marked the 10th anniversary of the floods with a Cathedral Service in 2017, but kept it appropriately sombre, respectful and low key.

15. EVENTS, DEAR BOY, EVENTS

Gloucester has for a long time held some good events – I remember in my childhood watching with excitement as the Carnival took place, or going to the Fireworks in Gloucester Park or the Barton Fayre on the Oxleaze. These were great events for local people but, on the whole, they weren't big enough draws to pull visitors to the city from far and wide.

When we became the Administration in 2004, the City Council had a decent-sized budget for events of around £160,000 a year. We then introduced a separate budget for Christmas events of around £100,000, principally to meet the cost of the ice rink in Kings Square. The Christmas budget got axed in 2010 and the events budget was halved in the 2011/12 financial year as austerity hit, but was reinstated the following year as the consequences of cutting popular events became clear and was judged not to be politically acceptable.

Events, in my view, are an important part of bringing people to the city and, in particular, the city centre. With competition for consumer spending as tough as it's ever been - from the internet, from other towns and cities, from supermarkets and out of town retail parks – it's increasingly important to give people more reasons to come into the city centre and to provide experiences that you can't get online or in those other places. It wasn't just the City Council that took this view – Gloucester's Business Improvement District, covering the city centre, spent a significant amount of its budget on events after it was formed in 2017.

Christmas

On becoming the Administration, I was keen to take things to another level. I thought that we should be doing more to promote the city at Christmas. The city's Christmas lights were tired, to put it politely, and were due for replacement. We inherited a project, funded by the Arts Council, working with artist Ron Haselden to make some new 'celebratory' lights designed by children. The Arts

Council had granted £30,000, with the City Council contributing £25,000. The theory was that these could be used at other times of the year and not just Christmas and the lights could stay in place permanently. It sounded like a nice idea but some of us in the Cabinet had misgivings.

We were offered a chance to see a sample 'catenary'. On a wet night we stood in Westgate Street looking up at a strip of rope lights hanging over the street. They weren't traditional Christmas images because of the wider potential use of the lights. This particular catenary included a cat. Just as we flicked the switch to illuminate this catenary, two things happened. The rain became torrential and Westgate councillor Pam Tracey walked up the street. As we sheltered in the doorway of the HSBC Bank, Pam, who was never backwards in sharing her opinions, backed Ron up against a wall saying, "I'm a traditionalist really, but I'm for the people. So if they want a f***ing cat they can have one!" Ron looked petrified.

We undertook some public consultation and the public seemed broadly in favour of the lights, so we put aside our reservations and went with it. When they were launched in 2005, we also had an ice rink in Kings Square for the first time, with a German market alongside it and machines from Stroud company Snow Business blowing fake snow off the roofs of buildings near The Cross. The evening would finish with a firework display at the Docks. Everyone was feeling optimistic, with Martyn White, Cabinet Member for Heritage and Leisure quoted as saying, "This is going to be the best Christmas Gloucester has ever seen."[259]

We promoted it heavily, including on Heart Radio at a time when it was in its heyday. The day of the switch-on and opening of the ice rink and market came and the city centre was hugely busy, at times almost dangerously so, with an estimated 15,000 people in attendance. The moment for the switch-on came and the Mayor, Councillor Lise Noakes, stood on the Guildhall balcony saying, "Isn't Gloucester great?" She flicked the switch, with the help of six-year-old Ewan Trehearne, who designed the centrepiece of the display. Where there should have been gasps of amazement there was stony silence, with people wondering, "Is that it?" Sparse was the adjective most commonly-used to describe the new lights. The local Civic Trust had been opposed to the project (their Civic Design group labelled them as "pathetic") and I had to go on Breakfast Television, even though it wasn't my portfolio, with the Trust's Marilyn Champion (who was a friend of mine) to be interviewed by presenter Fiona Phillips and defend a project I hadn't really believed in. I wasn't the first politician to do that and I won't be the last. Fiona Phillips commented that it was sad that the children's designs were getting so much scrutiny and all that was needed was more of them.[260]

A lesser-known fact is that when the centrepiece was being installed on The Cross, its fixing became loose and crashed through the contractor's van windscreen, impaling itself in the headrest! Thank goodness no-one was sitting in it.

2005 was a memorable Christmas, with Council Leader Mark Hawthorne and me sharing the part of Alderman Fitzwarren in the Gloucester Operatic and Dramatic Society's (GODs) production of Dick Whittington at the New Olympus Theatre in Barton Street. It was good fun but hard work. We got a laugh with the line, when responding to the Alderman's daughter Alice with the words, "Promised you? I'm a politician".

That year, we introduced a Christmas window display competition to reward those traders who put real effort and creativity into their displays. Westgate Street was always a hub for this, with cake decorating shop Sugar Celebrations (which has since closed) and the House of the Tailor of Gloucester always strong contenders.

In 2006, we had to decide what to do to avoid the controversy all over again and prevent the city being an object of Christmas ridicule each year. One suggestion was to concentrate the children's lights in one of the gate streets and buy new lights for the other three. But Ron Haselden had retained the intellectual property rights to his piece of art and, much to our frustration, said no! I commented at that time that, "It would be a terrible waste of money to only use them for one year and a terrible shame for the children who put so much effort into designing them. It is terrible that the intransigence of the artist will result in children being upset". *The Citizen* reported that tearful seven-year-old Ishaq Tily from Widden Primary was upset his lights might not be displayed, with him saying, "I worked very hard on my designs. I will be sad if my lights don't go up at Christmas."

We bought some new lights, this time playing safe and buying some 'off the shelf' – although the blue colour wasn't universally popular. Some people complained that they were 'cold' – although I'm not sure what they expected in November and December! Andrew Gravells, despite reluctance from Council Officers, insisted on a nativity scene on the College Street approach to the Cathedral, which still gets hung there each Christmas. The children's lights were kept in store until, sadly, they rusted and eventually ended up in a skip.

Although we thought we were playing safe, it didn't turn out that way. In early November when we would expect to see the lights already up in the streets, they weren't. Martyn White, boss of the McIntyre Caravans dealership and the Cabinet Member for Culture and Leisure, told us there was nothing to worry about. To be fair to Martyn, he was only repeating the reassurances he'd been given. It turned out that the lights, sourced through UK supplier MK Illuminations, were stuck on a lorry in Slovakia! Radio Gloucestershire made light of it by creating a fictional character 'Vaclav the lorry driver'. When Breakfast Show presenter Mark Cummings interviewed him, asking him where he would be delivering the lights to, he said, "To the house of Paul James". As I said, it wasn't even my portfolio!

Again, a Breakfast TV interview beckoned – this time Martyn White, as the Cabinet Member responsible, was on a Caribbean cruise and Steve Elway, the officer in charge, was having a knee operation.

The Citizen reported how "red-faced council officials vowed the show must go on".[261] The task fell to Mhairi Smith, the Council's Events Manager, to organise a switch-on event with no lights! Steve Simmonds, manager of Kings Walk shopping centre, generously chipped in some sponsorship and wise advice. Steve was the go-to man in a crisis and he and Mhairi hammered out the details over a pint or two in the Dick Whittington pub in Westgate Street. Real, live reindeer, a giant illuminated showman and a 'lighting extravaganza' were promised, accompanied by a procession with costumes by the people who worked on the Notting Hill Carnival. I commented in *The Citizen* that it was "a unique start to the seasonal festivities in the city". As a switch-on with no lights, it certainly was!

I like dressing up as much as anyone, so I was keen to take part. Mark Hawthorne, as my 'boss', told me, "Don't wear anything that makes you look stupid" as I had to do a live television interview on The Cross during the procession. When I went to get changed in St Nicholas' Church at the bottom of Westgate Street, I relayed the instruction to the people in charge of the costumes, Mahogany Carnival Arts, who had also worked on the Notting Hill Carnival. The costumes were largely white, in the style of snowflakes. The outfit they gave me had two enormous wings, which meant I could only just get up Westgate Street and, with the wind against me, it was quite a physical effort. I did the interview with my old schoolfriend, the BBC's Steve Knibbs. When it finished, he told me to rejoin the procession, so I turned to do so and almost took his head off with one of the wings, live on television! Still, I didn't fare as badly as the pair of dancing robins who we later had discovered had been locked in St Nicholas' Church while getting changed in the toilets!

We'd got away with it and I bought quite a few drinks afterwards at the Old Bell in Southgate Street for those who had been responsible for pulling it out of the bag. The real switch-on took place a couple of weeks later, with news presenter Lisa Aziz (formerly of TV AM) doing the honours live on the ITV Regional News. Even then, the timing was tight and the lights hadn't actually been tested before the switch was flicked. Thankfully they did work! These lights lasted a good while longer until they were replaced in 2018 by white lights. The old set went off to be re-used in Cinderford in the Forest of Dean.

We'd always struggled to settle on a fixed formula for the Christmas lights switch-on. For many years, the lights were switched on in Kings Square (although there weren't actually any Christmas lights in the Square!), before the event moved on to the Docks, with Father Christmas arriving by boat. Then there would be fireworks and Santa would move to a grotto in Merchants Quay shopping centre. The person switching them on often wasn't a household name. In 2002, Pam Tracey and I did it as part of our civic year. Previously, Terry Webster, the middleman behind the St Oswald's Park development, had done it and apologised that he wasn't one of the Spice Girls! He wondered how the switch worked when it wasn't connected to anything, but later realised someone inside the Guildhall was really pressing the button! I saw the big names who were doing the honours in other places and wanted a bit of that for ourselves. We did have the 'Fast Food Rockers' in 2003, who performed their 'Kentucky Fried Chicken and a Pizza Hut' song, but I wanted to raise the game. The only problem was that celebrities didn't come cheaply!

Ant & Dec apparently wanted £50,000 and our budget was a very small fraction of that. However, we managed to get Keith Chegwin (Cheggers) in 2007 for a very modest price and he went down well with the crowds. Cheggers said, "There has been a fantastic turnout. More people than I expected. I think there must have been 10,000."[262] As it was the year of the devastating floods, I wanted it to be special and a number of local celebrities joined us, including rugby players Ryan Lamb and James Simpson-Daniel, Stunt Driver Dick Sheppard, Miss Gloucester Dani Turner, flood campaigner Kelly Bartlett and *The Citizen*'s 'Face of the Floods' Elysia Byrne. Even 'Vaclav' the spoof lorry driver from 2006 made an appearance. The next year we struck lucky and secured Christopher Biggins for another knockdown fee and then he went on to become 'King of The Jungle' by winning 'I'm A Celebrity Get Me Out of Here' and his stock soared. We were listed in the top 10 celebrity switch-ons in the country, along with Witney whose local MP, a certain David Cameron, who was then the Leader of the Opposition, was flicking the switch.

Much as the celebrity switch-on excited me, I sensed it wasn't doing it for the rest of the population and cost was always an issue. In 2009, we changed to a procession led by Father Christmas. Mhairi Smith and Andrew Mitchell-Stead had previously come up with the idea of a lantern festival and, in 2010, we chose to do this at Christmas. Lanterns based on the '12 Days of Christmas, including French hens, turtle doves and a partridge in a pear tree,' were made by schoolchildren with the help of artists who were organised by the City Council's Pat Roberts. This gave it more of a community feel. Moving away from a single focal point also made it easier to manage the crowds.

The procession originally started at the Greyfriars Bowling Green but the starting point was switched to Blackfriars Priory as the event was drawing such a crowd that we needed to extend the route to enable everyone to see it safely. It headed up Southgate Street and turned into Westgate Street to end at the Cathedral for a short and informal service. It seemed right to do something centred on children – and it meant there was a good chance their families and friends would turn up to watch. It gave me a chance to dress up as part of the procession. The theme for the lanterns changed each year.

In 2014, we managed to source three real life camels, named Kazak, Bertie and Sophie, who were ridden through the streets by Delroy Ellis (of the Increase the Peace youth charity), scaffolding contractor Stuart McLain and me. *The Citizen*'s Martin Kirby wrote a satirical song in his column about the City Council, to the tune of 'The Old Bazaar in Cairo'. My Christmas card that year showed a picture of me riding the camel through the city streets with the caption 'O Camel Ye Faithful'. Some told me it wasn't appropriate but The Dean of Gloucester liked it and Gloucester Quays boss Jason Pullen kept it on his office wall for ages! The year after, we didn't manage to get real ones but used 'step in' camel costumes, which caused much hilarity! Martin Kirby also later suggested using a camel to replace the Civic Car!

In November 2016, I wore a costume which looked like a polar bear was carrying me. This prompted *Punchline* magazine to run a caption competition, with the winning entry saying, 'Police investigate as councillor is spotted walking through the city bear from the waist down.' The Christmas Lantern Procession has proved an enduring and popular Christmas event.

The ice rink in 2005 was provided by a private operator but they struggled to make it work financially. But it was popular with the public, so the City Council stepped in to fund and operate it, with the help of some sponsorship. The net cost was upwards of £100,000 but in those days we could do it. Events were organised, including (in 2007) an official opening with Mark Lester, a Cheltenham-based osteopath who had played Oliver Twist in the 1968 film and just as famously was a friend of the late pop star Michael Jackson, and ice dancers The Blackpool Twirlers. Just before the ceremony got underway, I went up to one of the dancers and thanked them for coming to perform at the event. In a broad northern accent they said to me, "Are you Oliver Twist?"

The ice rink stayed for a number of years until the cost became too much and we started to look for other ideas. Not having the ice rink wasn't popular with the public and traders protested too, despite previously telling us it didn't do anything for them! The alternative proposal in 2009 was to replace it with a 'Winter Wonderland', including a 'Spiegeltent' – an ornate Belgian travelling tent – and Santa's Post Office. Despite a range of activities, including performances by West Country legends 'The Wurzels' and punk rock band 'The Damned', this wasn't quite the attraction we hoped it would be. It may have worked as an add-on to other activities, but wasn't strong enough as the centrepiece, although it has since been used at Cheltenham's Literature Festival, at various festivals in Edinburgh and at the South Bank in London at Christmas.

It received mixed reviews, with Councillor Pam Tracey among the critics, branding it a "disgrace". Some letter writers to *The Citizen* agreed with her, others took a contrary view. We didn't do it again!

We were keen to better link Gloucester Quays and the city centre. Longstanding city trader Matthew Stevens ran a land train between the Quays and the city centre in 2009. This was something we repeated in August 2016, in partnership with Gloucester Quays, but we couldn't get it to work without subsidy and there wasn't the funding available to run it on a permanent basis.

Peter Rust, at the time the landlord of the Fountain Inn, brought the Dutch Victory organ, the world's biggest traditional fairground organ from The Netherlands, which played a huge repertoire from Christmas music to pop songs, into Kings Square in 2010. It wasn't everyone's cup of tea and didn't do my head much good when I was still suffering the effects of a Christmas party the night before.

In the early years after they opened, Gloucester Quays had their own Christmas switch-on event. In 2010 it starred Twist and Pulse, a street dance duo who were runners-up on 'Britain's Got Talent' that year and in 2011 it featured a performance from Stavros Flatley a British-Cypriot father-son dance duo who reached the final of the show in 2009.

A more enduring feature introduced for Christmas in the city is the Rotary Club's Tree of Light, which was introduced and is organised by Martyn White (formerly the Council's Cabinet Member for Heritage and Leisure) as a leading member of the Rotary Club of Gloucester. This is only one of many ways in which Martyn contributes to the life of the city. He is also Chairman of Gloucester Civic Trust, a trustee of Llanthony Secunda Priory Trust and sits on many trusts and boards.

The tree, placed outside the Guildhall for many years but now located in Kings Square, raises money for the Club's charities through sponsorship and donations. The tree switch-on has been performed by local Olympic gold medal-winning equestrian Charlotte Dujardin (in 2012) and Gloucester rugby star Ben Morgan amongst others.

Christmas Markets were a growing attraction in other places and were something we were keen to create in the city. The Kings Square German Market hadn't worked as well as we hoped and the operators weren't wanting to return. With Gloucester's Victorian Docks, a Victorian Christmas Market seemed a good idea. The opening of Gloucester Quays made it even more of an ideal location. In 2010, it was intended to be a joint event between the City Council and Gloucester Quays, but the Council had raided its Christmas budget to plug a funding gap at Marketing Gloucester meaning a difficult conversation with Alison Tennant, Gloucester Quays' Marketing Director, to say they would need to pick up the whole bill. They were disappointed but understanding.

The idea for the Victorian Christmas Market came initially from Marketing Gloucester's Mhairi Smith and Andrew Mitchell-Stead. Originally it was going to be on the Llanthony car park, which we now know as Orchard Square, but as Gloucester Quays were paying for it, they wanted it as close as possible to the Outlet Centre, so stalls were spread around Llanthony Road, High Orchard Street and Merchants Road. The Ragged Victorians living history group were brought in and Marketing Gloucester staff joined in by dressing in Victorian costume

Over the following years, the Quays Victorian Christmas Market grew to become the biggest in the South West, gradually increasing from one weekend to 11 days in total and adding an ice rink in later years. In 2019, the visitor numbers were estimated to reach almost half a million. Sadly, after the pandemic the Victorian Christmas Market didn't return in its previous format, although smaller Christmas markets were held each weekend from November and the ice rink at Gloucester Quays remained a popular feature.

The Tall Ships Festival

After the floods of 2007, we needed something to get the city economy going again and show the world we were open for business. Sometime before, GHURC Chairman Greg Smith and Chief Executive Chris Oldershaw had visited Charlestown Harbour in Cornwall and had tried to persuade the South West Regional Development

Agency to spend £3.5 million buying three tall ships, including the Kaskelot, to be a permanent presence in Gloucester Docks. The RDA couldn't be persuaded to stump up the cash as they didn't want to remove a tourist attraction from one part of their area to another. However, the visit provided the impetus for Oldershaw to take a report, by consultants The Leisure and Tourism Organisation (LTO), to the Urban Regeneration Company's Board Meeting suggesting Gloucester follow other places like Hartlepool, Sunderland, Liverpool and Greenwich in holding a Tall Ships Festival. The aftermath of the floods was an ideal time to put this into action. Funding was available from the City and County Councils and the Regional Development Agency, with a £70,000 government grant, and the date was set for 25th-28th October.

The Festival was a success, attracting 20,000 visitors and giving a £1 million estimated boost to the local economy, which was remarkable given that it had been organised in just eight weeks. I commented at the time that it was, "a truly outstanding achievement for all involved." The tall ships we brought in were The Ruth (a 90ft Baltic Trader), The Earl of Pembroke, The Phoenix, the Kathleen & May and the Johanna Lucretia.

Crowds gathered on the Friday to see the ships come in. At that time of year, it was dark by 4.30pm, so an added feature is that the ships were lit from then onwards. Saturday was planned to be the 'fun day' and on Saturday night two student string orchestras played on one of the ships, adding a cultural element. Sunday was planned to be a quieter day for photography, drawing etc. The BBC series 'The Oneiden Line', which was partly filmed in Gloucester, was shown in the Biddle & Shipton Warehouse. The Antiques Centre, then based in the Lock Warehouse, was very busy as it was the only place in the Docks with toilets. They later asked the Council to pay for their toilet rolls!

A decision was taken to hold the festival every two years, rather than annually, in order to keep it fresh, although a pirate-themed event took place in October 2008, which also served to mark the launch of Marketing Gloucester. A lookalike of Captain Jack Sparrow (played in 'Pirates of the Caribbean' by Johnny Depp) first appeared at the 2008 Pirates event. He kidnapped the then Mayor, Norman Ravenhill, at half-time during a Gloucester Rugby match at Kingsholm and then there was a Sunday afternoon battle in the Docks when he was rescued by the Redcoat soldiers.

The crowds were asked, "Do you want them to save the Mayor?" and the majority of them responded "No!" A little girl watching got very upset at this and said, "That's my Grandad!"

Sourcing enough tall ships was always something of a challenge, not only because you are competing against festivals elsewhere but because only so many can make it up the fairly narrow and relatively shallow Gloucester to Sharpness canal. The draft was even more of an issue when items, sometimes even including the odd car, had been dumped in the canal!

For this reason, making sure the Docks were properly dredged was important. At the 2011 event, some ships became stuck, so in November 2012, a new method of dredging was employed using a huge vacuum pump to suck up sediment and discharge it through a pipeline. It cost £80,000.[263] In May 2019, tall ship La Malouine 'touched bottom' in the main Dock basin as it tried to moor. Passengers, including former Mayor Councillor Steve Morgan, had to tug it to the shore.[264]

In 2009, the festival coincided with the opening of Gloucester Quays, who sponsored it to the tune of £40,000. This was probably one of the best, with beautiful sunshine, the added attraction of a Big Wheel at the Docks and some spectacular acrobatics from Cirque Bijou. The Mathew, the Johanna Lucretia, the Kaskelot, Phoenix and the Earl of Pembroke graced the Dock basin and living history events took place at Blackfriars, the Cathedral and at the Eastgate Chamber. An estimated 75,000 visitors attended.

The challenge was to keep the festival fresh, with new and different ships (which was difficult for the reasons set out earlier) and new land and water-based activities to complement live music and market stalls. In 2011, The Phoenix, the Kathleen & May and the Johanna Lucretia returned, with The Irene and the White Heather making their first appearance. Captain Jack Sparrow was again part of the land-based activity, wandering around the site having pictures taken with visitors and would be a regular feature of future events. Gloucester Quays maintained their headline sponsorship. An estimated 80,000 visitors were attracted and the whole city was busy according to Barry Leach of the City Centre Community Partnership.

In 2013, there were eight ships, including The Phoenix, The Amazon, The Ruth, The Matthew and La Belle Angele. Akwakats (bikes on water) were perhaps the most memorable addition to the activities. Wristbands, for which there was a modest charge, were introduced to try to control numbers wanting to go onboard the ships. The festival attracted an estimated 100,000 visitors. At the same time, there was a stonecarving festival at Llanthony Priory organised by Carrie Horwood of Cats Eye Carving, which raised money for the Priory's restoration project, including by auctioning off some of the works on display.

2015 was the festival debut for the brigantine Morganster and Baltic trawler Keewaydin. Atyla, a handmade schooner from Spain, suffered minor damage on the way and 15 volunteers were needed to help maintain it. Some spectacular flyboarding demonstrations took place in the main basin. A flyboard is a machine, attached to the feet, that propels a person through the air due to jets of water pumped through a hose attached to a Jet Ski. A Sea Shanty Festival took place in the city centre with the aim of spreading the economic benefit beyond the Docks and Quays. A new £2 entry fee was introduced without too much complaint from the 100,000 visitors. The stone carving festival took place at Llanthony Priory again.

For the 2017 festival there were seven ships including the Lady of Avenel, a 102ft Brigantine square rigger. The Newfoundland Rescue Dogs wowed the crowds by showing off their amazing water-rescue skills in the main basin. There was a Pro-wakeboarding championship, stand-up paddleboarding and sword fighting with Captain Jack Sparrow. Wakeboarding is a mix of water skiing, surfing and snowboarding where a board is strapped to your feet and you're towed at speed across the water. The Sea Shanty Festival again took place in the city centre and Café Rene organised their Pirate Walk to coincide with the festival. The food and drink stalls had an upmarket addition with a new Champagne and Oyster Bar. There is no evidence to show how well it traded, but suffice to say it never returned!

The 2017 festival coincided with the launch of Gloucester's latest sculpture trail – the Henson Pig trail, sponsored by the Three Counties Agricultural Society. The pig was based on the Gloucester Old Spot pig, known as the 'pig that saved the city' when, legend has it, it made so much noise during the Siege of Gloucester in the Civil War that the King's forces were convinced the city had plenty of food and could last for days. There was a competition on the Mark Cummings breakfast show on BBC Radio Gloucestershire to name the trail and listener Jennifer Richards suggested 'Henson' after Joe Henson, who founded Cotswold Farm Park and saved many rare breed animals. His son, television presenter, Adam Henson, attended the launch event. The names of the individual pig sculptures included 'Harry Trotter' (as a play on Harry Potter). This prompted me to suggest to Marketing Gloucester Chief Executive Jason Smith that we should name one 'Dame Janet Trotter' after the then Lord Lieutenant for Gloucestershire. His response was "we already have". A glamorous porcine tribute to Marilyn Monroe which was to have been called 'Norma Jean Porker' was rebadged 'Dame Janet Trotter'. She took it in good spirits.

At the start of the 2017 festival, despite my dislike of heights, I climbed the rigging of one of the ships with Citizen reporter Kim Horton, but to be fair, daredevil Kim went all the way to the top, while I was content with being about 80% of the way up.

For the 2019 festival, the Grayhound and the TS Royalist were new additions. A zipwire was installed across the Docks main basin, following a successful zipwire event in Northgate and Southgate Street in July 2018. Water City Music, led by Gloucestershire-based artistic director Michael Bochmann, which stages musical events at striking water-based venues across the UK, collaborated with the Gloucestershire Academy of Music and 15 local schools to provide a fresh musical angle. Not quite as melodic were the team from Gravity Industries, who flew around the Docks wearing some very impressive but rather noisy jet packs. The entry charge for the 2019 festival was £10 which some felt was too high. Nonetheless, Marketing Gloucester estimated that 200,000 people had been attracted to the city (although not 200,000 paying visitors to the festival) and that the economic benefit to the city was £11.2 million. The Wetherspoons pub 'The Lord High Constable', which had a good view of proceedings but was outside the charging zone, said they had their highest takings ever.

The festival didn't take place in 2021 because of ongoing concerns about the Coronavirus pandemic but did return in May

2022. Following the demise of Marketing Gloucester, the event organisation was outsourced to REM Events, organisers of the Bristol Harbour Festival. Gloucester BID and the City Council each contributed £50,000 but other sponsorship was thin compared with previous years – perhaps due to the state of the economy post-pandemic or the organisers' lack of local knowledge or both. The entrance charge was removed, although the paid-for wristband system for accessing the ships stayed. Although the organisers were able to reduce costs through economies of scale across all of their events, they were still believed to have lost a significant sum on the event. It followed a very similar format to other years but with a much-reduced marketing budget and a lack of innovations, it seemed to lack some of the buzz of previous festivals.

An aerial shot of the Tall Ships Festival in 2009. Credit: *The Citizen*/Paul Nicholls

Food Festival

Another festival taken on by Gloucester Quays which had its roots in something initiated by the City Council is the Food Festival. In 2008 the Council staged 'Taste' in Gloucester Docks, with local chef Rob Rees helping out. The idea was conceived by the City Council's Events Manager, Mhairi Smith, who is herself a keen cook. The event was sponsored by the Docks Trading Company and featured cooking demonstrations (but not celebrities). There was an Army/RAF/Navy cook-off and a 'Cooking Through the Ages' feature with re-enactors, including Romans. The clay ovens created a lot of smoke, which could be seen billowing out of the marquee! The event was a success but the £50,000 cost meant it was a one-off rather than a regular event.

Gloucester Quays took it on in 2011, but paid for Mhairi Smith and Andrew Mitchell-Stead to manage the festival. Town Crier Alan Myatt dressed as a chef to promote the event. The financial resources deployed by Gloucester Quays took the event to another level with celebrity chefs James Martin and Gino D'Acampo visiting to host demonstrations, although Gino's was as much about him charming the ladies present, with more than a little innuendo, as it was about the food!

Gino even suggested that he was seriously considering opening a restaurant in Gloucester – something which was reported by *The Citizen* in September 2011. He told the newspaper, "I think the people of Gloucester really rock and roll".[265] I followed up this interest, exchanging emails and speaking on the phone with Gino, but when he put me in touch with his business partner, the trail ran cold. Gino's 'My Pasta Bar' chain went into liquidation in January 2022, following losses incurred during the Covid pandemic, but he still has a portfolio of other restaurants, mainly in big cities like London, Manchester and Birmingham and upmarket locations like Alderley Edge in Cheshire.

Gino and James returned to the festival in 2012 and were joined by Gloucester's Phil Vickery, the rugby player turned Celebrity Masterchef winner, who also put on a show with local rugby legend Andy Deacon as his sidekick. Phil also took part in the festival in 2019.

Gino and James came back again in 2013 and shared the billing with Mary Berry of the Great British Bake Off. Her co-presenter Paul Hollywood headlined the Festival in 2014 and 2015 and Nadiya Hussain, the 2015 winner of GBBO, appeared at the Festival in 2016 along with Gloucester-born celebrity chef Tom Kerridge and 'Reggae Reggae Sauce' creator Levi Roots.

The Food Festival takes place annually but took a break in 2018 when Orchard Square, by the National Waterways Museum, was refurbished and in 2020 when the Coronavirus hit.

Paul James with celebrity chef Gino D'Acampo at the Gloucester Quays Food Festival.

Gloucester Goes Retro

The Docks is a natural event space, with plenty of open areas and lots of entrances/exits where crowds can be funnelled. But the number of successful events held at the Docks added to the perception that the city centre was 'missing out' because all of the focus was on the Docks and Quays.

Councillor Colin Organ, who represented Tuffley on the City Council and ran The Estate Agency in Clarence Street, sought to address that by creating the 'Gloucester Goes Retro' festival in the heart of the city centre. Colin was a classic car enthusiast and toured the country encouraging owners of vintage motors to bring them to Gloucester. But the festival was about more than classic cars, with each of the gate streets allocated to a certain decade and Kings Square used as a performance space.

It proved hugely popular and the best event of the year in the heart of the city centre. It won the 'Believe in Gloucester' best event award in 2015 and 2019. Colin secured the services of some of the cast of 'Allo, Allo', the hit 1980s sitcom set in wartime France. Vicki Michelle, who played Yvette, Richard Gibson (Herr Flick), Kim Hartman

(Helga), Guy Siner (Lieutenant Gruber) had all aged remarkably well and when they toured the city centre streets people would often say, "Oh you look just like the real ones!" They were happy to come back year after year and were joined in 2019 by Arthur Bostrum who played the English policeman, Officer Crabtree. The Retro event also fell victim to the Coronavirus in 2020, but came back strongly in 2021. That year, with works taking place to Kings Square, elements of the event were transferred to the Docks. The link with the Docks continued in 2022 with the introduction of 'Retro on the Water', showcasing some vintage boats.

Karen Pearson from the City Council's Events Team (and for a while Marketing Gloucester) has played a big role in organising and growing the event. Colin Organ sadly passed away in July 2022 following a battle with cancer. The 2022 event took place in his memory and the City Council gave a commitment to keep the event going, and indeed to keep growing and improving it, as part of Colin's legacy.

Stars from the 'Allo, Allo' TV sitcom with Colin Organ, founder of the Gloucester Goes Retro festival. Credit: Colin Organ

Gloucester Day

Former Mayor Gordon Williams wrote in *The Citizen* in August 2003 saying that we should be marking Gloucester Day, when the Civil War Siege in the city was lifted. His initial suggestion was that we should fly the Gloucester flag as had been done when he was Mayor in 1979. The theme was taken up by Radio Gloucestershire presenter Vernon Harwood in his column in *The Citizen*, suggesting a 'celebratory parade'.[266] I asked a question at the council meeting in November 2003 to then Leader Mary Smith, saying, "Will you join me in supporting the call by Vernon Harwood in *The Citizen* that we should have a Gloucester Day? We should undertake to investigate this proposal today." Mary Smith agreed to look into it.[267]

The first Gloucester Day was a re-enactment by the Marcher Stuarts at Llanthony Priory on the first weekend in September 2004, organised by the Council's Heritage Manager Malcolm Watkins. At the time, I commented: "This day is a great opportunity to learn about the city's history in an interactive way. It makes great use of the grounds of the historic priory, which is so often forgotten about. I would really like to see the celebrations extended in years to come."[268]

"I'm really pleased we have reintroduced Gloucester Day into the calendar. We should be proud of the fact that the city turned the tide in the Civil War and changed the course of English history. The fact that we are celebrating again shows that we are a city gaining in confidence. I hope we can expand the celebrations in the future to not just remember the past but celebrate our future as well."

Town Crier Alan Myatt had been helping to organise Barton Fayre for a number of years. He wanted to bring it into the heart of the city and combining it with Gloucester Day seemed an ideal opportunity. Alan's idea was to organise a big parade of different groups from the city. Council officers were initially against the idea of councillors taking part wearing their civic robes. Alan spoke to all councillors, who supported the idea, and officers relented. The day also incorporates the Mayor of Barton's procession in the morning, where the Mayor of Barton and his 'Court Leet' (a collection of largely self-appointed local characters) parade through the city centre to meet up with the Mayor of Gloucester. Each year the Mayor of Barton chooses an unusual form of transport, which over the years has ranged from a skip to a sedan chair to a Wall's 'Stop Me and Buy One' bike to an inflatable flamingo!

In 2011, construction giant Morgan Sindall sponsored the event after, earlier in the year, a moleing machine of theirs had cut through wires, pretty much knocking out the whole city's telephones, cash machines and card payment terminals. I emailed their then Chief Executive Paul Smith who was on holiday and was unaware of the incident and we agreed that something by way of compensation for the city was needed.

Music events

Gloucester has long had a strong music scene, with many top performers appearing over the years at the Leisure Centre and Guildhall. The Blues Festival has taken place around city centre pubs in the summer for many years and in more recent times the Folk Trail has been introduced.

Gloucester Rugby added to the events scene in the city by staging music concerts at the Kingsholm Stadium. The Wanted, including local boy Nathan Sykes, were the first to perform in 2011 to a less than capacity crowd. Tom Jones featured in 2012 and such was his popularity that he returned in 2017. Former Boyzone star Ronan Keating performed in 2013. Elton John was another big name to come to Kingsholm, in 2015. He later had to apologise after swearing at a female steward live on stage and reducing her to tears. Lionel Richie topped the bill in 2016 and Little Mix appeared in 2017. Little Mix were due to come back in 2020 but cancelled due to the pandemic. Concerts weren't reintroduced after the pandemic due to a new artificial pitch surface which risked being damaged if crowds were allowed on it.

Former GB Beach Volleyball player Jody Gooding (who went on to work for Marketing Gloucester) and former Gloucester Rugby player Jack Adams (who tragically died from cancer in 2021 aged just 34) introduced the Sportbeat Festival on Plock Court in 2013. Unusually, it combined music and sports, including netball, volleyball and rugby 7s. Not everyone was enamoured with it. Citizen columnist and latterly operator of the Hempsted Meadows car boot sale Bob Newby wrote in a letter to the newspaper, "I live a mile from Plock Court and I had to close my windows". He claimed that "this event was only condoned because the leader of the council 'thought it was a good idea'."

The festival attracted some big-name acts, including The Feeling in 2014 and De La Soul in 2015. Sportbeat never attracted the crowds it needed to make it financially sustainable and, following the loss of his father, Jody decided to pull the plug on it.

It hit the national headlines in 2014 when it was reported that the festival had 'snubbed' film star Kevin Costner's band. Former Mayor Chris Chatterton told me he was in the Northend Vaults pub having a pint with Jody Gooding after reopening it as Mayor. Chris used to DJ at Crackers nightclub and thus had knowledge of the music scene. Jody mentioned Kevin Costner's band as an option, but Chris said he had seen them before and didn't think they were very good. What they hadn't clocked was that Citizen journalist Nick Webster was sitting at the next table. Three weeks later the story appeared on *The Citizen*'s front page and then made the nationals. Chris Chatterton was on a civic trip to South Korea when the story broke and recalls how he woke up to 50 messages on his phone.

I certainly can't take credit for Gloucester's Cajun & Zydeco Festival, which takes place one weekend in late January at the Guildhall and has been running for around 30 years. It is a niche event but one which draws people not only from around the country but from abroad too and at a time of year when not that much is going on. But when it was struggling to break even, rather than pull the plug on it as some Council Officers had suggested, I ordered that it should continue – based on its wider value to the city's economic and cultural life. One of the leading lights behind the festival is former Labour councillor Terry Haines (my old school teacher). Terry was always very generous in pointing this out when I said a few words on stage each year on the Sunday night of the event and it was always something I enjoyed. I was presented with a bottle of Southern Comfort the final time I appeared on stage, as a thank you for my support over the years.

Other events

Sometimes we were fortunate and events came to us. In November 2004, former West Life band member Brian McFadden performed on a stage in the then Barbican car park in Ladybellegate Street for BBC Children in Need's 25th anniversary, along with pop group 'The Skandi Girls' and some local performers. Some complained that the bombsite of a car park wasn't the most picturesque backdrop for the concert, but on a dark November evening it didn't make any difference and people had come to see the performances rather than the surroundings.

In May 2012, the Olympic Torch came to the city. George Livingston-Thompson from Maisemore set off from Gloucester Docks, walking through an Honour Guard from the Allied Rapid Reaction Corps at Innsworth, before handing on to a series of other torchbearers. The route took in the city centre streets, including the Cathedral, before moving out to London Road and Estcourt Road and then heading out of the city. The 'Queen's Baton' for the Commonwealth Games also came to Gloucester in July 2022, arriving into the Docks by canoe and then making its way through the gate streets to the Cathedral. Founder of 'Gloucester Feed the Hungry', Hash Norat, was the first to carry the baton, coming in on a boat to the Docks.

In July 2012, I watched as celebrity chef and television presenter Heston Blumenthal created the world's largest 99 cone, complete with a flake, in front of crowds in Gloucester Park for his TV show 'Heston's Big Ideas'. It was 4m tall, using more than a tonne of ice cream (which was donated by the local Walls' Ice Cream factory) which took a month to freeze. Hundreds and thousands and strawberry sauce were scattered on top using a catapult – although most of it failed to stick. A local street artist added an image of Heston in the shape of an ice cream to the outside of a nearby accountant's office to mark the occasion.

The annual fireworks event at the Docks, organised by the Gloucester Round Table, was described as one of the best settings in the country for such an event and attracted around 10,000 people, but as more and more of its buildings got developed it became increasingly difficult to manage and was ultimately, and regrettably, stopped. Now fireworks events tend to take place in the suburbs at places like the Wall's Club and Longlevens Rugby Club. The fireworks event in Gloucester Park at the end of the Carnival fortnight was also very popular and drew a similar-size crowd. Apart from getting their bins emptied, many people saw this as the one tangible thing they got for their council tax! We tried to push the boundaries with the quality of the display, using top suppliers Kimbolton and

Titanium, who also put on the displays for New Year's Eve in London and Edinburgh and the 2012 London Olympics. The display never returned after the Covid pandemic as the Council were concerned about the environmental consequences of fireworks.

As Gloucester sought to become a more 'cultural' city, the balance of events changed, with events like the Rooftop Festival, which took place on top of the Eastgate Shopping Centre's rooftop car park, which was introduced in 2018. This was organised by Strike A Light, with support from Gloucester Culture Trust, the Music Works and Gloucester Guildhall and featured dance, music, film and theatre. This brought something new to the city, but by its nature didn't attract mass crowds - in 2021 it was fewer than 1000, hampered by social distancing rules. The event was dropped in 2022 due to a lack of funding.

The Kings Jam festival, with music of black origin and culture, started in 2016 and aimed to diversify audiences and showcase local talent. Organised by Malaki Patterson of The Music Works, it began in Kings Square but moved to Gloucester Park in 2021 when the Square was being redeveloped, attracting an audience of around 1300. The 2023 event was cancelled due to lack of funds, but it hoped to return in 2024.

The 'Bright Nights' Festival was introduced in 2020 as a winter festival of spectacular light installations across the city, including at locations such as Llanthony Priory, Robinswood Hill, Kings Square and Blackfriars Priory. Other features have included illuminated windows hanging across Westgate Street, an illuminated inflatable creature outside the Cathedral, lamp posts which record and play back people's shadows and an illuminated swim at GL1 Leisure Centre.

These events all have their merits, but a tension exists between putting on mainstream events to attract footfall – something which is more important now given the diminished attraction of physical retail – and putting on events to broaden the cultural horizons of the population. It's a fine balance between the two.

Graffiti depicting Heston Blumenthal on a building near Gloucester Park following his record attempt to make the world's biggest ice cream.

16. SACRED SPACE AND COMMON GROUND

Gloucester Cathedral is without doubt the city's finest building. It is widely-believed to be the best example of Norman Gothic architecture in Europe. As Anthony Hodge, the City Council's former Head of Regeneration, often said, it is our 'anchor tenant'. It has always been a special place for me and has played a big part in my life. It's where I was married, where my two children were baptised and where I've spent more time than at any other church. As a councillor, particularly as Leader of the Council and as Sheriff of Gloucester, I attended numerous Civic Services, Remembrance Day Services, Christmas Carol Concerts and many more besides.

It's where the city comes together – and not only for Christians. When there was an attack on two mosques in Christchurch, New Zealand in March 2019, Hash Norat (a local Muslim and founder of the Gloucester Feed The Hungry organisation) came to me to ask where we could all gather to show our solidarity, the Cathedral grounds seemed the obvious place and The Dean didn't hesitate to agree.

A gated community?

Until fairly recent times, there was a feeling that the Cathedral had somehow failed to fulfil its potential, both as a visitor attraction and as a focal point for the city. To many, it felt remote, perhaps a bit stuffy and detached. That may be unfair but it's how many people looked upon it. When Stephen Lake, who became Dean of the Cathedral in 2011, took a taxi from the railway station to his interview, he asked the driver, "What do you think of the Cathedral?" The driver replied, "Brilliant". Stephen asked him if he ever went there. The driver answered, "No, why would I go there?"

It wasn't always the Cathedral which was resistant to change. In July 1995, there was a planning application to relocate the SPCK Christian bookshop from Southgate Street to 4 College Green, in the Cathedral precincts. It might sound harmless enough, but Conservative Group Leader Mike Pullon objected strongly, saying, "This is an area of the city which for centuries has been guarded to keep it safe from change. The thought of turning it into a bookshop appals me." He added, "There will be blasted placards in the window and signs all over it". His deputy Andrew Gravells disagreed and commented, "We are talking about a small, harmless bookshop selling Christian literature." David Bennett of Churches Together in Gloucester said it was an ideal place and the City Council "needs to wake up". It was allowed by a majority of one.

To be fair to the Cathedral authorities, they were willing to listen to criticism. A report on the marketing and development of the Cathedral in 2008, written by the Destination Management Group (DMG) – whose offices were within the Cathedral precincts and whose Director Philip Cooke was a former City Council Chief Leisure and Tourism Officer – pulled no punches.

It noted that the Cathedral was "taken for granted by the city" and, for its part, was "not proactive". It said that a 'Cathedral/Business partnership' was needed. From a marketing perspective, its observation included that there was "no visitor orientation or information inside the Cathedral"; "signage in the city is poor"; "marketing resources are inadequate at all levels. The basic business plan for most Cathedral operations seems to be doing everything on the cheap."

The Cathedral even seemed to be falling short in its core purpose as a place of worship, with DMG noting that "attendance at services is generally poor" – something it attributed to a "lack of information, weak invitation and relative isolation of Cathedral from daily life of the city."

The report added that the Cathedral "does not appear to be fulfilling its potential as a performance venue", branding its flagship Three Choirs Festival "disruptive as well as elitist" for shutting out tourists during the peak August period. Its withering conclusion was that "the Cathedral is caught in a downward spiral. Lack of investment has resulted in poor facilities. Therefore, hire charges and activity levels are much lower than they could and should be." In a nutshell, it concluded that the "Cathedral looks and feels like a closed community."

The setting for the city's finest building on its main approach was a tarmac car park. Many visitors, as well as heritage experts, couldn't understand why this was the case. To most in the city, it was what they had always known. As long ago as the late 1980s, there were moves to change this. A report on the Cathedral's 900 Year Fund presented to the City Council's Lotteries Sub-Committee in June 1989 recorded that the "Dean & Chapter have commissioned a complete redevelopment which will transform College Green into an inner city oasis", noting that "the main approach to the Cathedral looks more like a public car park than the setting for one of the World's architectural treasures." It noted that "the cost, including placing an impressive set of gates across College Street, will be £500,000."

The gates were installed in 1992, according to the plaque next to them, "through the generosity of the Gloucester City Council and of Nuclear Electric plc" but the car park remained. The gates were controversial – they looked impressive and made traffic control easier but reinforced the sense of separation between Cathedral and city. The DMG report noted that the "College Street gates cut the Cathedral off from the city. The Cathedral became more closed and peripheral to the city on the day the gates went up." In an article in Cotswold Style magazine in April 2011, I wrote: "The addition of iron gates at the College Street entrance has only served to cut the Cathedral off from the rest of the city centre." The gates broke just before Stephen Lake took up his position as Dean and were left permanently open. Despite the protestations of some residents of the Cathedral Close, he refused to get them fixed, telling them pointedly, "We are not a gated community." It was a symbolic move.

Gloucester Cathedral before work on Project Pilgrim started. Credit: Gloucester Cathedral

Improving the Cathedral's setting

The DMG report also restated the need to improve the setting of the Cathedral, commenting that the "car park at the front of the Cathedral is unattractive" and recommending "if possible, and ideally, the car park at the front of the Cathedral should be removed and the area suitably landscaped." In a 2011 *Cotswold Style* article,

I noted that "many would like to see the gates removed and the parking relocated as a way of bringing the two (Cathedral and city centre) together."

Chris Oldershaw, Chief Executive of the Gloucester Heritage Urban Regeneration Company, had already recognised the need and the potential impact it would have. Inspired by the setting of Exeter Cathedral, he had held discussions with Dean Nicholas Bury and Bishop Michael Perham, who sat on the GHURC Board, and had earmarked £500,000 in a list of 'reserve schemes' to be funded by the South West Regional Development Agency. Like a number of other schemes, it was shelved when SWRDA turned off the taps in the years following the financial crisis of 2008, when the 'Sword of Damocles' hung over it ahead of the 2010 general election.

More than just a place of worship

The Dean of the Cathedral's role is not just to provide spiritual leadership – it is, effectively, to be the Cathedral's Chief Executive. Under Nicholas Bury's stewardship, the Cathedral became more adventurous with the activities taking place within the building and grounds at the same time as resisting any move to introduce entrance charges – something which his successor, Stephen Lake, continued. To put this into context, at the time of writing, Westminster Abbey charges £27 for adults, York Minster £16 and Salisbury Cathedral £11.

The filming of Harry Potter and the Philosopher's Stone in 2001, the Chamber of Secrets in 2002 and the Half Blood Prince at the Cathedral in January 2008 were particularly significant, giving the Cathedral something else that could attract visitors from across the world. The Warner Bros filming entourage filled up the whole of the King's School car park off Gouda Way to create short, but nonetheless important, parts of the films. There is speculation that because JK Rowling grew up in Gloucestershire she might have visited Gloucester Cathedral and taken inspiration from the Cloisters for the Hogwarts School. Various cosmetic changes had to be made to transform the Cathedral Cloisters into the corridors of Hogwarts for the filming, including covering electric switches with timber painted to look like stone. One of the wooden covers still remains and will forever be known as the 'Harry Potter Box'!

Locals were reportedly excited to see movie stars Daniel Radcliffe (Harry Potter), Kenneth Branagh (Gilderoy Lockhart) and Rupert Grint (Ron Weasley) in the city when the Chamber of Secrets was filmed in January 2002. But not everyone was pleased with the Harry Potter connection. In February 2001, Pastor Peter Kelly from the City Gates evangelical church wrote to Dean Nicholas Bury, on behalf of his 80 worshippers, objecting to the use of the cloisters for filming because of the association with witchcraft. Dean Nicholas responded that he recognised there were "great dangers" in modern witchcraft, but that "modern witches do not fly about on broomsticks".

The first high profile filming at the Cathedral was a BBC adaptation of Joanna Trollope's novel 'The Choir' in 1995. The Harry Potter connection raised the Cathedral's profile and standing as a filming location to a new level and various other productions followed including Wolf Hall in 2014, Henry IV & V (starring Jeremy Irons and Tom Hiddlestone), Mary Queen of Scots and the Spanish Princess. The Doctor Who Christmas Special was filmed at the Cathedral and surrounding streets in 2008 when David Tennant was The Doctor and the show returned in 2019, with Jodie Whitaker in the title role, when it made use of the new landscaping in the Cathedral Close.

More varied events took place, notably The Crucible sculpture exhibition in 2010. The 70 works on display included sculptures by Sir Eduardo Palozzi, Lynn Chadwick, Antony Gormley and Damien Hirst. It stayed open an extra week by popular demand, attracting 136,000 visitors and giving an estimated £4 million economic boost to city centre traders, particularly those in Westgate Street. It returned as 'Crucible II' in 2014 with 100 works and attracted 140,000 visitors.

Other events included a football tournament, the G15 school sports tournament, rock concerts not just classical, rugby and other dinners, a circus and art installations, including Luke Jerram's 'Museum of the Moon' and 'Gaia' – huge 3D replicas of the Moon and the Earth in the Nave in 2019 and 2020. Christmas activities also saw new innovations, including 'Carols on the Hour' and a Christmas market in the cloisters.

The roots of Project Pilgrim

Project Pilgrim was conceived as a result of the Cathedral's quinquennial (five-yearly) inspection in 2009 which identified conservation, access and environmental issues that needed to be addressed. Stephen Lake's appointment as Dean was announced in January 2011. Citizen Editor Ian Mean interviewed the new Dean, describing him as having the 'X-Factor'. Friends of his predecessor, the popular but slightly more traditionalist Nicholas Bury, saw this as a slight to their man and wrote to the newspaper's letters column to protest.

Part of Stephen Lake's brief in 2011 from the Honours and Appointments Secretariat at 10 Downing Street, who play a key role in the recruitment for what is a Crown Appointment, was to strengthen the Cathedral's connections to the city. It was felt that the Cathedral was inward looking. Indeed, at the time I wrote that "one of his many challenges will be to ensure the Cathedral remains relevant and becomes an even more important part of city life." It was felt that The Crucible exhibition had gone fairly well and showed that people would come if you put on these events. When I interviewed him for this book, Stephen Lake joked he was "brought in to lower the tone" and had succeeded! He wanted Gloucester to become the Cathedral that likes to say 'Yes' rather than 'Computer Says No'.

Project Pilgrim was unveiled in July 2012. Stephen Lake said, "Every generation seeks to enhance the Cathedral and its environment and we should be no different. Project Pilgrim seeks to work out in practical terms what it means to be in tune with heaven and in touch with daily life."

A new five-year vision for the Cathedral was published in September 2013. Entitled 'In Tune with Heaven, In Touch with Daily Life', which by that time had become a familiar phrase, the 31-page document sought to do more to connect with people in the city and improve its infrastructure to support the Cathedral's growing ambitions. The document said the Cathedral's weaknesses included being perceived as "diffident" and that its user base was "largely white and middle class".

Stephen Lake was quoted at the time saying: "I think it is about being bold. The particular challenge in this city is that there can sometimes be a lack of confidence - when we have got so much to be proud of here. I think the Cathedral can play a vital role in encouraging that sense of confidence. We can make sure that people feel welcome. We can make sure that people feel this belongs to them - we talk about 'your cathedral' and that breaks down barriers."

The appointment of Rachel Treweek as Bishop of Gloucester, England's first woman Diocesan Bishop who was installed in September 2015, also served to make the Cathedral feel more inclusive.

The external works to replace the tarmac car park with an attractive, landscaped public space were the most high-profile element of Phase I of Project Pilgrim but in truth it was about much more than that. In Stephen Lake's words, it was a "commitment to making the whole site more physically, spiritually and intellectually accessible". Project Pilgrim needed to create a narrative to join the inside and outside.

In June 2014, a Stage One grant (to work up a detailed project) of £320,000 from the Heritage Lottery Fund was announced. Nerys

Watts from the Heritage Lottery Fund said, "We were impressed with these ambitious plans, phased over a decade, to conserve the site and make it a much more open and welcoming place. Our country's cathedrals are extraordinary feats of architectural genius and skilled craftsmanship and Gloucester is no different." In response, I commented, "I want Gloucester to be at the top end of the Premier League of Cathedral cities and these plans will help us to achieve just that."

The funding was used to develop the project in more detail, working up the design of the scheme, gaining the necessary permissions and taking the planning to the point of asking for a full grant from the Heritage Lottery Fund. A small project team, made up of a Project Manager, Project Assistant and Community Engagement Manager, was appointed, which oversaw this work.

World Heritage Status

One idea which came from 'left field', which could have proved a major distraction from delivering Project Pilgrim, was the suggestion, made in a motion to the City Council from Liberal Democrat Group Leader Jeremy Hilton in January 2014, that the Cathedral should apply for 'World Heritage Status' – an accolade given only to places of 'Outstanding Universal Value to Humanity'. This idea didn't have the Cathedral's backing and they hadn't been consulted before the motion was tabled. There are 16 world heritage sites in England, including Canterbury Cathedral and Westminster Abbey. Cllr Hilton said it would be "a prestigious designation and it would help create a sense of pride for everyone who lives in Gloucester." He acknowledged it would be a "marathon" and admitted it would need "a lot of hard work to get to the point where you can first get on the government's shortlist and get the government to propose the site to UNESCO." UNESCO is the United Nations Educational, Scientific and Cultural Organization. It was estimated the process could take a decade.

At the time, I commented, "Gaining World Heritage status is an expensive, resource intensive and lengthy process and before embarking on it we need to be sure that it is the right course of action."

As a means of getting the Administration's budget through in 2014, when we didn't have a majority in the Chamber, I agreed to allocate £10,000 to support the Cathedral, including for a study into the idea's feasibility to be undertaken by the University of Gloucestershire. A cross-party working group of councillors was established to oversee the study and, in February 2016, a 94-page report was issued by Dr Richard Harper and John Humphreys, Senior

Lecturers in Heritage Management and Tourism in what was then the University's Department of Leisure and Performing Arts.

It concluded that World Heritage Status for the Cathedral "may not be possible or even desirable". The nomination process would cost in the region of £500,000 and there would be "ongoing administration, maintenance and research commitments". UNESCO was looking to create a 'balanced list' and Cathedrals and places of worship were already well-represented.

The Cathedral authorities were "sceptical of the additional benefits it might bring" and "did not want to divert its limited resources away from its current community project (Project Pilgrim) at the moment". The report acknowledged that there was "some division" within the City Council about the proposal and "some belief that resources could be better directed to supporting Project Pilgrim".

The report concluded that "ongoing programmes in the city could more efficiently and effectively realise the City Council's regeneration goals without going through the UNESCO nomination process." As is often the case, something announced with great fanfare was allowed to quietly fade from the public's consciousness.

Delivery of Project Pilgrim Phase One

Anne Cranston joined as Project Manager in October 2014. A Stage Two bid to the Heritage Lottery Fund was submitted before the end of 2015. Project Pilgrim was designed as a decade-long, three phase programme. Phase I included essential repairs to the building.

The 15th century Lady Chapel, described as "cold, damp and dirty" was at risk from damp, humidity and water penetration. New interpretation, which won national awards, told the history of the Cathedral in a much more coherent and compelling way. Measures to improve physical access were introduced, meaning the whole ground floor became accessible for all, unaccompanied, for the first time in its history. For example, the entrance to the Lady Chapel had a central stone pillar – meaning you couldn't get a wheelchair in there. It was thought that it supported the Great East Window. But someone found an old picture which showed it not being there and engineers confirmed it wasn't supporting anything. The South Porch, which was nicknamed 'the catflap', was replaced by a far more attractive glass entrance, to make it more welcoming.

Replacing the car parking with a new public space, although now accepted as the right thing to have done, was controversial with some at the time. Some contended, apparently without irony, that the car park "had always been there". Supporters of the project privately mocked the idea that "Jesus died that we should park." One armchair commentator suggested an underground car park was the answer. I imagine they hadn't thought through the cost, the impact on archaeology or the effect on the structural integrity of an 11th century building! Some detractors, believed to be those who lived in the Cathedral Close whose parking would be affected, unfairly labelled the endeavour 'Project Grim'. One resident who lived near to the Cathedral asked how she would get a fridge delivered! Some Cathedral supporters even threatened to take away donations.

Tim Hall, a retired surveyor, a Cathedral shop volunteer and member of a choir that met in the Chapter House, told The Church Times in June 2015: "Removing the Cathedral car park is most likely to decrease the Cathedral audience, participation, and economic sustainability - all of which the vision desires to increase."

He pointed to the Cathedral's own feedback survey, which showed that 44 per cent of the nearly 400 respondents wanted reassurance about parking. "My gut feeling is that Gloucester Cathedral will suffer more than it gains by removing its car park," he said. If it continued, it was "in danger of being out of touch with daily reality".

He accused the Dean and Chapter of forcing through the car-park removal on the back of the other much more popular aspects of Project Pilgrim. In an email to the Chapter, he wrote: "Rather than being a problem to be removed, convenient car parking is an asset to be cherished. Neighbouring streets are already clogged up by people attending Cathedral events and gatherings. Does the Cathedral really want to make this situation worse? I accept that, visually, it will look nicer, but any action has consequences, and I just see a lot of negative consequences."

The City Council assisted by relocating volunteer parking temporarily to the Barbican car park in Ladybellegate Street (now developed as student accommodation).

Groundworks took more time and effort than anticipated. Digging almost anywhere in Gloucester city centre risks uncovering archaeology. Doing it on the doorstep of the Cathedral makes it pretty much a certainty. Phase One of Project Pilgrim was designed, following archaeological investigations, to minimise the need for any further archaeology. Cathedral bosses knew there were two former burial sites in the areas where work was taking place.

In May 2015, excavations uncovered a 1000-year-old monastic graveyard near the Cathedral's West End, which was part of the former Minster's cemetery. Two Anglo-Saxon burials were uncovered, one of which had to be lifted – a man in his 50s, who was almost certainly a monk. The body was buried with charcoal to combat the smell and absorb the moisture, which indicated it was a monk or nobleman. The full extent of the cemetery isn't known, but it would have been disused after the Norman Conquest.

Most of the building work took place to the south of the Cathedral in what was the lay cemetery of St Peter's Abbey – which would have been in use from the 12th to the 18th century and would have been the main burial plot for the town during the medieval period. It was necessary to remove around 250 bodies from near the Cathedral's south aisle. They were reinterred on-site once construction was finished. Other finds included a section of wall or monument, believed to be part of a 17th or 18th Century graveyard.

In November 2015, a seventeenth-century family burial vault was discovered under the floor of the Cathedral's north transept when archaeologists lifted a nearby ledger stone in preparation for the installation of a lift. The vault contains the remains of the wealthy Hyett family of Painswick, including an infant, who had been buried in well-preserved coffins.

Archaeologist Richard Morriss said there was always a "high possibility" of unearthing burials. "We had always believed it was a 1,000-year-old cemetery," he added. "But the most exciting finds are connected with how the lives of those buried were commemorated and memorialised. The family ledger slab is remarkably well-preserved from the 1690s and in giving us the names of a local family, it shows the connection the Cathedral has always had in the lives of Gloucester residents." All discoveries were carefully recorded and the trenches back-filled to ensure they were not disturbed.[269]

During the row over the removal of parking, one disgruntled person said, "What next? Solar panels on the roof?" It was ironic that they should say that! An important part of the project's aims was to improve the Cathedral's sustainability. This led to the idea of installing solar panels on the south side of the Nave roof. According to the Cathedral's website, "It was the need to rectify a defect at the ridge of the lead roofing, where the metal was beginning to crack, which provided the impetus for the project to go ahead. The new ridge detail is a perfect securing point for the metal frame which, resting on soft pads against the lead, supports the solar panels."

A consultation of 400 local residents carried out by staff working on Project Pilgrim found that 87% of them supported installing solar PV on the roof, while 66 residents said they would be prepared to sponsor a solar panel at a cost of £500. In the end, over 120 individuals donated to the project by 'sponsoring' a solar panel, covering over half of the £100,000 cost.

The Cathedral obtained permission from Cathedrals Fabric Commission for England and planning consent from the City Council. Stephen Lake told me, "When we discovered we could do it, we decided we should do it." However, the planning documents lodged with the City Council noted the expectation that the installation would "not be without potential controversy" and that it does "not intend to set a precedent". However, the Nave roof is 30 metres above ground, making the panels virtually invisible from the surrounding area and the roof itself was only about 50 years old.

Dean of Gloucester Stephen Lake blesses solar panels fitted to the roof of Gloucester Cathedral. Credit: Gloucester Cathedral

Installed in November 2016 by local renewable energy firm Mypower, the 150 panels generate about 29,000 kW of energy each year or over a quarter of the Cathedral's electricity needs. This initiative made Gloucester the first ancient cathedral, the oldest building in the country and the oldest cathedral in the world to have solar panels fitted. Bradford Cathedral had some on a small roof and Salisbury has copied the idea on its cloisters.

Never one to miss a PR opportunity, The Dean blessed the panels, wearing full robes, on the regional television news. The Cathedral's famous tower was illuminated green in celebration.

The Heritage Lottery Fund, who had been such tremendous supporters of our efforts in Gloucester, awarded Project Pilgrim £4.16 million, with an announcement made in March 2016. Other funding included £1.58 million raised from Friends of Gloucester Cathedral, the City and County Councils and charitable trusts like the Summerfield Trust, the Gloucestershire Environmental Trust and the Garfield Weston Foundation. Volunteer hours were estimated to be worth over £180,000. Stephen Lake described it at the time as "a once-in-a-generation opportunity for the Cathedral to play an even greater role in the lives of local people and in the regeneration of the city," adding that "There are further challenges ahead but this achievement signifies a huge step towards realising our aspiration to ensure that Gloucester Cathedral remains open, accessible and free to all."

The City Council contributed £150,000 in three tranches of £50,000 from its Regeneration Account, which was made up of income from former Regional Development Agency properties and is ringfenced for regeneration purposes. The first grant was agreed by the Council's Cabinet in October 2014. I commented in the press release to say, "It is right that our most important building should play a central role in Gloucester's regeneration. I have no doubt that Project Pilgrim will help the Cathedral to strengthen its position at the heart of the city's life and I am delighted that the City Council has been able to contribute to this project financially and practically. I am grateful to the Heritage Lottery Fund for their continued generous support for heritage projects in the city and to everyone else who has worked so hard to make this application a success." Another £50,000 was agreed in March 2017. The final £50,000 was agreed in October 2018, meaning the City Council was both the first organisation and the last to contribute to Phase I. Anthony Hodge said he called Stephen Lake 'The £50,000 Man' as every time he saw him, he asked for another £50,000! The Council also gave a more modest £12,680 for security lighting.

The major landscaping work for the scheme got underway in January 2017. The former Bishop of Gloucester Michael Perham died in April 2017 and his funeral took place while the Cathedral grounds were still a building site. The Heras fencing protecting the site was covered in coloured cloth for the occasion. The landscaping work was completed in June 2018, with stonemasonry for the Lady Chapel completed in November of that year.

Gloucester Cathedral during the Project Pilgrim works. Credit: Gloucester Cathedral

A celebration event for those involved took place in Summer 2018, attended by the great and the good, including a representative of the Heritage Lottery Fund. I commented on how many people had claimed to be responsible for the idea of removing the car park and replacing it with a landscaped area. "Success has many fathers," I quipped, before acknowledging that it was "perhaps not the right thing to say in a place where there is only one Father".

Visitor numbers dropped by almost a quarter, from 484,618 to 380,627 between 2016 and 2017 as a result of the building works taking place, before recovering to 411,837 in 2018. Numbers fell to 165,564 in 2020 when the Covid pandemic hit, closing the Cathedral for the first time in 800 years. Numbers grew again after Covid restrictions were lifted and, at the time of writing, seem on course to return to pre-pandemic levels. According to figures published in a City Council report in November 2019, Phase I of Project Pilgrim had led to 120,000 more visitors and 120 new volunteers.

Strengthening links with the city

Stephen Lake's appointment as Chair of the City's Regeneration Advisory Board helped to strengthen the link between the Cathedral and the city, to the benefit of Project Pilgrim and other regeneration schemes.

In his introduction to the City Council's Regeneration Strategy in 2016, Stephen Lake wrote: "The Cathedral is at the heart of the city and tells its most enduring story. The vision of those who built this icon was greater than anything we hope for today but we should tune into that commitment and sacrificial example in order to achieve a future for all that lasts and has a deep-rooted integrity. We can do this and we should do this as a kind of 'coalition of the committed' to Gloucester."

The enhanced sense of partnership was underlined by the introduction of a ceremony to install the Mayor into their special stall in Quire – something which signifies how the Corporation saved the Cathedral from demolition in the days of Oliver Cromwell.

A benefit of the close relationship was that we could make things happen at short notice. It was perhaps fitting that the last VIP visitor I received in Gloucester before I stood down as Leader should be at the Cathedral. One Sunday I was watching the US Ambassador to the UK at the time, Robert 'Woody' Johnson, being interviewed on the Andrew Marr show. He described how he liked to get out and about and meet 'real people'. Given the strong US connections to Gloucester (John Stafford Smith, Button Gwinnett, George Whitefield etc) and the fact that people in the city are some of the most 'real' you can meet, I wrote to the Ambassador to invite him to Gloucester. I didn't hear back, so sent a follow up email which was acknowledged and kept chasing every so often to see how the scheduling of his diary was progressing. In November 2019 when I was working away for a few days in Woking, I had an email from the US Embassy asking me to give them a call. They told me that they had found a slot in the Ambassador's diary to visit Gloucester. When I asked when it was, they told me: "next Wednesday". I sent a text to Stephen Lake asking him for an urgent call.

In a few days we pulled together a good programme for him. Before inviting Ambassador Johnson, I hadn't really researched who he was but I did before he visited. Whereas UK Ambassadors tend to be career diplomats, US Ambassadors – particularly to key allies like the UK – are more likely to be the President's friends. Woody Johnson is a billionaire businessman from the Johnson & Johnson toiletries empire. He owns the New York Jets American Football team, estimated to be worth a cool $3.2 billion in September 2019. The programme was meticulously planned including a walk through with his security officer a couple of days before. The Mayor of Gloucester Colin Organ, the High Sheriff Charles Berkeley, Ben Hau from Marketing Gloucester, local historian Phil Moss (who the Ambassador took a real shine to) and Liz Jack, a distant descendant of Button Gwinnett, joined us.

I was tipped off that the Ambassador was a big fan of bells, so we arranged for him to climb to the organ loft, which he did effortlessly for a 72-year-old with a dodgy leg! In fact, he went right to the top of the Cathedral Tower. He also heard American organ scholar Mary Tan play the Star-Spangled Banner on the Cathedral organ. In a lovely coincidence that you just couldn't choreograph, two US citizens who were visiting the Cathedral at the time walked past just as it was being played, stopped and put their hands on their hearts.

The Ambassador also visited St Michael's Tower to see one of the famous Rudhall bells, St Mary De Crypt and the Soldiers of Gloucestershire Museum where he spent a long time talking to Korean War veterans Tommy Clough and Brian Hamblett. In 2020, after he had finished as Ambassador, Johnson sent at my request (and within 24 hours) a video message to congratulate Tommy Clough on reaching his 90th birthday. The video was played on regional television.

Working towards Phase Two

At my last Cabinet meeting as Leader in November 2019, we also agreed funding of £150,000 over three years towards Phase Two of Project Pilgrim which was to use the Cathedral's heritage, plus its partnerships and platform, to showcase the potential within all cathedrals. The work, for which £8 million overall is needed, will involve structural improvements in the Chapter House, the Garth and the Cloister exterior walls, the north Nave, the Parliament Rooms and the café. At the same time the Cathedral was also embarking on a £1.5 million fundraising project to refurbish the organ (which has since become the £3 million 'In Tune' organ and music campaign) and needed another £500,000 for the long-term conservation of the Great Cloister.

The Cathedral received a hugely generous donation in September 2022 of £550,000 from Julia and Hans Rausing, part of the family behind the Tetrapak empire, who live near Tetbury in Gloucestershire. At the time, the Rausings commented, "No one who walks through the Cloister at Gloucester Cathedral can fail to be struck by its overwhelming beauty. The intricate design of the stonemasonry, particularly the fan vaulted ceiling, is remarkable and its visual impact touches the many thousands of visitors to the Cathedral each year. We are delighted to help ensure that this magnificent feat of medieval architecture is preserved so that visitors and worshippers can continue to enjoy it for hundreds of years to come."

The Expression of Interest to the National Lottery Heritage Fund for Project Pilgrim Phase 2 was approved in Spring 2022. This meant the Cathedral could submit a full Round One application, but still needed to consult widely, work up detailed costs and budgets, raise match funds and create detailed delivery plans.[270] Work on Phase Two was paused in August 2022 due to the loss of key personnel and having a number of other projects on the go, such as refurbishment of the organ and conservation work on the Cloisters. Stephen Lake left to become Bishop of Salisbury in April 2022. His immediate successor as Interim Dean, Canon Andrew Braddock, became Dean of Norwich in January 2023, with new Dean of Gloucester Andrew Zihni taking up the role in April 2023. Project Manager Anne Cranston and Chief Operating Officer Emily Mackenzie both also moved to new roles. The Cathedral confirmed it is "committed to recommencing Phase Two when it is less likely to be negatively impacted by construction industry inflation, the cost-of-living crisis and a challenging fundraising landscape".[271]

Looking Forward

Gloucester Cathedral plays a huge part in the life of the city, spiritually, cultural and economically. It is important that it is seen to be connected, both physically and emotionally, to the city centre and the wider city. Phase I of Project Pilgrim has been seen to be a huge success in improving the setting and the accessibility of the Cathedral and Phase II is awaited with anticipation.

17. RUGBY AND REGENERATION

Rugby and Gloucester Rugby Club has long been a big part of life in the city and it's been a big part of my life too. My late Grandfather was born in Deans Way, in the shadow of the Kingsholm Stadium, and supported the Club throughout his life. I started going to matches with him when I was about 10. The first match I went to was against Waterloo. It wasn't a great match, but I remember sitting on the steps underneath the clock on the Shed side to watch it. With the size of the crowds these days, you couldn't do that now! We used to park in St Mark Street, outside my Great Aunty Edna's house and call round to see her for tea and biscuits afterwards – a far cry from the rather boozy affair it tends to be today.

For 17 years, I lived in a flat right opposite the stadium in a building called Pitch View, although since the building of the new East Stand (the Buildbase as most people still know it), there hasn't been a view of the pitch! Although I moved to Longlevens in 2010, I'm still a season ticket holder, making me a regular at Kingsholm for almost 40 years. Even my election to the City Council, which initially was for the Kingsholm ward, may have owed something to the Rugby Club. A matter of days before polling day in 1996, one of the Liberal Democrat councillors for Kingsholm (David Evans, a retired planning officer) suggested moving the stadium to a site outside the city. Although match-day parking has long been an issue, most residents put up with it for a few hours 15 or so times a year without complaint, because they recognise what the Club does for the city. I opposed the move, which probably gained me quite a few votes, contributing to my 279-vote majority on a day when Pam Tracey and I were the only Conservative candidates to be elected.

Professionalism and a new investor

When I started attending, Gloucester Rugby Football Club was run by a committee of stalwarts – the likes of Peter Ford, Doug Wadley, Terry Tandy, Alan Brinn and my one-time teacher at The Crypt, Terry Close.

Most of these had been players at one point and many were successful businessmen. Peter Ford ran a wholesale fruit and vegetable business based at the Cattle Market and employed Tandy and Wadley. Alan Brinn, one of my constituents in Longlevens, ran a small sports shop in Eastgate Street where you could buy a Gloucester Rugby Club season ticket. I remember buying one as a 'Junior', for the princely sum of £12.

I was pleased to be able to name new streets after Doug Wadley, as well as fellow club stalwart Arthur Hudson and former captain Mike Nicholls, at the Civil Service Club development off Estcourt Road/Denmark Road in 2019. The players, too, had other jobs. Richard Mogg, the long-serving winger/centre, famously used to spend Saturday mornings digging up the road for Severn Trent before donning his Cherry & White shirt to run at the opposition in the afternoon.

But the sport was changing. Clubs were turning professional and if Gloucester wanted to stay in the top flight, they needed to find a backer wealthy and generous enough to put some serious money in. Following a declaration by the International Rugby Board in August 1995, English Rugby's first season as a professional sport was in 1996/7. In July 1996, Gloucester Rugby Football Club Ltd became an entity and in March 1997 the Directors were given permission to find an investor.

The following month, 800 members packed into the Birds Eye Walls Social Club at Barnwood. Chairman David Foyle, a local auctioneer, explained that there was a forecast £360,000 loss in the current year and a predicted loss of £1 million for the following year, if the Director of Rugby was given the budget he had requested. Foyle announced that the club had secured an investor.

The Citizen speculated that the new owner was Virgin boss Richard Branson (presumably because he was rich and famous, not because he was particularly interested in rugby) or the Cheltenham and Gloucester Building Society. There were rumours that Branson's helicopter had been spotted landing in the car park at Kingsholm. The C&G were generous sponsors and had diversified into selling houses by acquiring a number of local estate agents (a move they later reversed) but owning a professional sports club seemed like a stretch. On 29th April 1997, the new majority owner of the Club was revealed as Formula One tycoon Tom Walkinshaw, a rugby fan who lived in Oxfordshire.

An Extraordinary General Meeting was held to increase the share capital of GRFC Ltd. The shares were transferred to Cherry White Ltd, later Try Investments Ltd – Walkinshaw's company set up for this purpose. Walkinshaw paid £50,000 plus £2.5 million through a sponsorship agreement for his stake.

The move to professionalism has been documented more comprehensively elsewhere but, in short, it meant the players became full-time, so were able to spend more hours in training, making them stronger and faster. They became more disciplined (in most cases) with their diet. They were also coached by a full-time professional, with back-up from strength and conditioning experts and specialists in attack and defence. Former Bath and England scrum-half Richard Hill (pronounced 'Richer Dill' by many of the fans) was the first professional head coach.

The Club had to be run more like a business. The old committee had brought in former Gloucester, England and British Lions prop Mike Burton to generate income through sponsorship. Burton had a successful and growing sports travel business in the city, initially based at Bastion House in Brunswick Road. He was a larger-than-life character in every sense. A brilliant raconteur - he had so many stories - I recall going into his office and coming out tired, but thoroughly entertained, after listening to them for what must have been a couple of hours. Gullivers Chilcott, run by former Bath prop Gareth Chilcott, leased the hospitality space in the new boxes at the 'Tump' end nearest Deans Walk. Local businessmen, like commercial property agent Tim Heal of Alder King, Mike Warner of local car dealers, the Warner Group and Gary Jones of Glevum Windows, were brought in to give the benefit of their advice and contacts.

Walkinshaw raised the commercial side to another level, understandably bringing in his own people. Hamish Brown, a former TWR (Tom Walkinshaw Racing) Executive, became Chief Executive. Pete Darnbrough, also from TWR, was made Finance Director. In 1999, Walkinshaw brought in Ken Nottage, a former basketball international, from Newcastle Sporting Club. Nottage was nicknamed 'Basil', because of his likeness to John Cleese's character Basil Fawlty of Fawlty Towers fame. Whereas Walkinshaw could be difficult to work with, Nottage had the patience of a saint. Where Tom might upset people, Ken would smooth things over.

After the move to professionalism, rather than being a team made up of locals, Gloucester became a cosmopolitan side with a new 'Foreign Legion' of players. One wag of a sports journalist commented that former French captain Philippe St André, who would go on to become the Club's head coach, was now considered a local! One of the imports was the Samoan centre Terry Fanolua, who made over 200 appearances between 1997-2006. He became a favourite with the crowd who would chant his name. I was honoured to make a presentation on behalf of the city to Tezza at his leaving dinner in 2006 before he departed to play at French club Brive. The Club was also at the forefront of signing code-switching players from rugby league, with Henry Paul joining in 2001 and Lesley Vainikolo in 2007, both from Bradford Bulls. Both players made it into the English national side, but neither reached the heights of their rugby league careers.

Redeveloping Kingsholm

The facilities at Kingsholm would be massively improved under its new ownership, but it would take several attempts before a redevelopment of the ground would actually take place. The Club did look at options to relocate from Kingsholm. In April 2002, *The Citizen* reported that the King's School's playing field at Archdeacon Meadow was the Club's preferred option. Headmaster of the King's School, Peter Lacey, commented that "everyone could be a winner", but Gloucester Rugby's MD, Ken Nottage, said that it was "one of many options we are looking at."

In October 2003, Gloucester Rugby launched 'Project Kingsholm'. A fans' organisation, 'Kingsholm Supporters Mutual' (KSM), chaired by Bob Rumble, was set up by the Club, to help fundraise towards the redevelopment of the Kingsholm Stadium, including through a supporters' share issue. Despite KSM meeting the fundraising targets, the Club abandoned the plan.

A planning application for a major redevelopment was submitted in November 2003, based on three phases. The planned first phase was the main grandstand, phase two was The Shed and the final phase would be the Kingsholm Road stand. The application was scaled back to include just a new 7000-seat grandstand and a demountable hospitality stand and was approved by the Council's Planning Committee in December 2004, although formal planning consent wasn't issued until April 2006.

In the meantime, planning consent was granted for a new 3000-seat Kingsholm Road stand in September 2004 and was built in 2005.

In April 2005, Tom Walkinshaw went onto the pitch before the game against Leeds Tykes. Microphone in hand, he faced The Shed and famously said in his deep Scottish tones, "Take a look at that stand behind you. That's going to go." He pledged that an £8 million development of a 7500 all-seater replacement grandstand would start in weeks. It would take the stadium's capacity from 13,000 to 17,500 and included a bar, club shop, conference facilities and corporate boxes.[272]

He told the crowd, "I'm delighted to be able to confirm that it will now go ahead this summer, in time for the new season. We have been working non-stop in the last few days to get to the stage where we can press the green button." It would be the "biggest solo club rugby union ground in the premiership" and an "all-year round business". Walkinshaw added, "You've all told us how much you want the ground to develop, and now it's going to happen."

Demolition was planned to start after the last home match of the season against Saracens on 14th May 2005. Ominously, Gloucester lost to Leeds Tykes 33-15 in a display Walkinshaw described as "absolute rubbish". One fan was reported to have handed what remained of his season ticket to Director of Rugby, Nigel Melville.

Bob Rumble, Chairman of Kingsholm Supporters Mutual, said, "A development which keeps the club at Kingsholm gets our vote." The plans were shelved a few weeks later due to 'technical issues'.

In November 2005, *The Citizen* reported, under the headline of 'My Kingsholm Dream', how the plans were now for a 20,000-capacity stadium. Walkinshaw explained, "Rugby's getting more and more popular, so the size of the stadium you have has to be continually upgraded."[273]

In February 2006, *The Citizen* reported that Tom Walkinshaw had put the plans on ice as the idea for a new stadium at the Railway Triangle was evaluated. Ken Nottage was quoted as saying, "At this point, we are holding back on pressing the button at Kingsholm until we know for sure whether the Railway Triangle is a doable site. Discussions have opened but we are a million miles away from concluding them."[274]

These various changes in circumstances led to a number of planning applications with different designs. There were competing factors with the design and a compromise had to be reached between the position of the hospitality boxes (wanting them to be close to the pitch), maximising the seat capacity and inserting pillars. Ultimately it would be Tom Walkinshaw who made the final decision as to what would go ahead.

A second planning consent for the main grandstand was granted in August 2006 with an increased capacity of 7488 due to the removal of the first-floor function room and hospitality boxes. The Planning Committee "regretted" the omission of the function room. The original grandstand design avoided columns which would interfere with the spectators' view, using a suspended roof system with a row of stanchions (vertical bars) on the roof. The later designs went back to using a traditional steel frame with columns.

A third application went to the Planning Committee in December 2006, which reintroduced hospitality suites. The capacity was 7244 supporters including those in the hospitality boxes. Ken Nottage addressed the Planning Committee. He "thanked (Council Planning) Officers for their assistance with the application and declared he was a little embarrassed at the third application within a year, but promised that the building would go ahead this time." He added it wouldn't prohibit the club taking part in a new stadium at Railway Triangle "at some time in the future".

Work had been due to start in July 2006, but Walkinshaw announced it had been delayed until 2007 to avoid the need for temporary seats, which would reduce capacity and deprive some fans of their favourite place to watch the game. He said work would now start in March 2007 and be completed in time for the 2007/8 season, adding, "We are still determined that the development will go ahead. If people want a top-flight rugby club, there has to be change, which means bigger and better facilities."[275]

A new £8.9 million stand, built in modular construction was created, housing new hospitality boxes, banqueting space, offices for the Club's staff, a camera gantry, ticket office and club shop as well as bars and changing rooms. The boxes and hospitality spaces were turned over to conferencing and banqueting on non-match days, giving the city facilities it hadn't previously enjoyed. The demolition of the old stand started in April 2007, with the construction of the new one following straight after, completing in September 2007.

In the Chapter on 'The GHURC Years', I tell the story of the aborted plans in 2007 to move the Kingsholm Stadium to a new ground shared with Gloucester City Football Club. I had my doubts as to whether this would happen and, in hindsight, it was probably a good thing that it didn't. The Kingsholm atmosphere would be hard to recreate elsewhere and the economic benefits of having a ground within easy walking distance of the city centre are enormous.

In January 2007, the club announced plans to redevelop The Shed terracing to become seating. A 'Save Our Shed' or 'SOS' campaign was initiated by KSM, who warned Walkinshaw that the majority of fans would not support his plans. The campaign was also backed by *The Citizen* newspaper. In September 2008, Tom Walkinshaw confirmed there were plans for the Shed to be redeveloped and it would remain as a terrace with hospitality units above it – although the planners had concerns about the impact of this on the houses in St Mark Street.

I remember sitting in a meeting where Walkinshaw threatened to move the Club out of the city into Oxfordshire if he didn't get his way with a planning application for The Shed. I was fairly sure he wouldn't do it. Sources told me that plans were drawn up to relocate the stadium to a greenfield site near Witney, where his TWR Group's HQ was based. To be fair to Tom, I'm told the plans were promoted by others, but Tom realised many Gloucestershire-based supporters just wouldn't make the trip up the A40. The proposals to redevelop The Shed have never been pursued and it seems unlikely they will be revisited any time soon.

Success in the professional era

The 2002-3 season saw arguably the finest Gloucester team ever. Gloucester had started to gel spectacularly at the end of the 2001-2 season, beating bitter rivals Bath 68-12 and winning the Zurich Championship Final (a play-off between the top 8 teams) against Bristol at Twickenham. I had the honour of representing the city as Sheriff and watching from the Royal Box.

Gloucester beat all-comers during the 2002-3 season. I was proud to witness a winning Gloucester team at Twickenham again, with them beating Northampton in the Powergen Cup in April 2003. A few days later I joined the squad on a celebratory open-top bus tour from Kingsholm, ending up in Northgate Street at the New Inn, where they were mobbed by fans.

They also dominated the Premiership. I recall being at the New Inn while a Leicester fan was checking in and he said to the receptionist, "I think we're going to get a thrashing this afternoon!" That didn't happen very often! The team ended the season 15 points clear, but had to play the winner of a 2nd versus 3rd play-off, which saw them pitted against Wasps in the final. This meant an enforced lay-off while the play-off took place, putting them at a disadvantage. In the meantime, we held a Civic Reception for them and in my speech, I said we were proud of them and would still be proud of them whatever happened in the final. That was probably the wrong message! I was watching again from the Royal Box as Sheriff when an early Fraser Waters score indicated that the afternoon may not be plain sailing. It ended 39-3 to Lawrence Dallaglio's side, leaving Cherry & White fans disappointed. The Mail on Sunday's back page the next day carried a photo of Wasps celebrating, with the headline 'Call Yourselves Champions?' But Gloucester had signed up to the format of the competition at the start of the season, so couldn't really complain.

That year was also England's triumph in the Rugby World Cup, with Gloucester players Phil Vickery, Trevor Woodman and Andy Gomarsall all members of the victorious squad. Woodman and Vickery played in the final. The City Council decided to grant them Freedom of the City in recognition of their success, with a Council meeting taking place on the pitch at Kingsholm – probably the only time that has ever happened!

Gloucester tasted cup success in 2006 in the European second-string competition at Harlequins ground, The Stoop, beating London Irish with a late James Forrester try. I travelled up with Mayor Lise Noakes and Sheriff Bob Gardiner, but didn't join them in hospitality. Surreally, when we got back to Gloucester, we met actors Sean Bean and Danny Dyer, who had been shooting scenes for the film 'Outlaw" in a white transit van in the Land Registry car park off

Bruton Way. The photo we took with them was Lise's Facebook wallpaper right until her tragic death in May 2019. They also won the same competition again at The Stoop in May 2015, beating Edinburgh 19-13 with tries from Charlie Sharples and Billy Meakes. That weekend, Chief Executive Stephen Vaughan's wife gave birth to twins, meaning he had a double reason to celebrate. Gloucester also won the LV Cup in 2011, beating Newcastle 34-7 at Northampton's Franklin's Gardens stadium. The Club have failed to win at Twickenham since the Powergen final, losing the Premiership Final to Leicester 44-16 at the end of the 2006-7 season and losing out to Cardiff 50-12 in the EDF Energy Cup Final in 2009. They also topped the Premiership table at the end of the 2007-8 season but lost their home semi-final to Leicester by a single point.

Life after Walkinshaw

Tom Walkinshaw died in December 2010 after a short illness. A memorial service was held at Gloucester Cathedral in February 2011 and was attended by leading figures from rugby and motorsport. At the reception in the Chapter House following the service, I turned around and Eddie Jordan, owner of the Jordan Grand Prix Formula One team, was next to me.

Shortly after, Gloucester MP Richard Graham praised Tom Walkinshaw at Prime Minister's Question Time in the House of Commons, saying: "Last week, there was a memorial service in Gloucester Cathedral for Tom Walkinshaw, a constituent of the Prime Minister and a legend in my city for all he did to revive Gloucester Rugby. Does the Prime Minister agree that Tom, and many others like him who have invested so much of their own money in our great sports, have done a lot to increase self-belief and pride in our cities?"

Prime Minister David Cameron, in whose West Oxfordshire constituency Walkinshaw lived, responded by saying, "My hon. Friend speaks very well of someone who lived in my constituency and invested not only in rugby, but in Formula 1, which has been an absolutely world-beating industry for our country. We should celebrate that, particularly in my region, where so many people are employed in this incredibly high-tech endeavour."

Players' agent David McKnight (who had represented Henry Paul, amongst others) became non-executive Chairman of the Board, on a caretaker basis, in January 2011 while Tom's son Ryan learnt the ropes. Ryan took over as Executive Chairman in June 2012. The Club was put up for sale in April 2015 for £25 million following a review by Cavendish Commercial Finance. The price tag of £25 million was optimistic and was an exercise in seeing whether there was a buyer out there prepared to pay a premium to acquire the Club. There wasn't and the Walkinshaw family shares were sold to Martin St Quinton in February 2016, giving him complete control of Gloucester Rugby.

In 2017, there was someone willing to pay a premium for a stake in the Club – a French-Syrian scaffolding magnate Mohed Altrad, who had offered to invest £10 million for a 45% share. He has a fascinating backstory, having been born in the desert to a young mother. His father gave him away to his grandparents at age four following his mother's death. He is unsure of his date of birth, so he "picked a date from a hat" in order to celebrate one. The only problem with the takeover plan was that he already owned French club Montpellier. For that reason, Premiership bosses vetoed the deal and full ownership remained with St Quinton.

Rugby World Cup 2015

In May 2012, I received a call from Ken Nottage saying that someone from England Rugby wanted to talk to the Council about potentially holding Rugby World Cup matches in Gloucester and would we be interested. I said that we absolutely would be interested and we arranged to meet Mick Hogan, England Rugby's City & Regional Operations Manager, who would go on to be MD of Newcastle Falcons. England had successfully bid to the International Rugby Board (IRB) to be the host nation and had received the thumbs-up in July 2009. Kingsholm was mentioned in the bid document but this didn't guarantee the stadium would host any matches.

The Club had a recent track record of successfully hosting big matches, both domestic and international, including The Barbarians – thanks to Mike Burton's connections with the side. This gave us a head start. Although we don't know it for sure, I suspect Mike Burton's influence with the rugby powers-that-be may have played a helpful role in our successful bid.

It became clear from the meeting with Hogan that this would be about much more than just staging some matches at Kingsholm. It involved 'City Dressing' (flags and banners), Commercial Rights Protection (making sure the interests of the sponsors were looked after – although the Council had no legal powers to enforce this) and creating a 'Fanzone' for the duration of the knockout stages. I secured support from both other political group leaders, who either lived in or represented Kingsholm but weren't exactly rugby fans. We initially agreed a budget of £275,000 which was later revised upwards to £350,000. We set about putting together our bid, with Vicki Rowan (the Council's Head of Cultural Services). Vicki wasn't a rugby fan either, although I did persuade her to go to a match. She went about the task with enthusiasm and learnt very quickly, finding out with some help from me which countries we could demonstrate a connection with, rugby or otherwise. Gloucester's 'Foreign Legion' of players proved very useful here! We also gathered letters of support from key partners and some of our local rugby legends like Messrs Burton, Teague, Vickery and Tindall, City MP Richard Graham and Lord Lieutenant Janet Trotter. We finalised the bid on the morning before I flew off on holiday in September 2012. I made sure the bid was finished before I started packing my case!

Mick Hogan visited the city to see how we put on a big event. We took him to the Gloucester Quays Food Festival to watch Phil Vickery and his sidekick, fellow Gloucester Rugby legend Andy Deacon. Phil told Mick Hogan afterwards that "I'll come and find you" if Gloucester doesn't get awarded host city status. I think he was joking, but it probably had the desired effect!

We heard the result in May 2013 and it was announced at a press conference I fronted up with Sheriff of Gloucester Phil McLellan (who was a Kingsholm season ticket holder himself), Gloucester Head Coach Nigel Davies and world cup winners, England's Mike Tindall and All Black Jimmy Cowan from the current Gloucester squad. Gloucester was one of only two club rugby grounds included – the other was Sandy Park, Exeter.

Paul James with rugby star Mike Tindall after the announcement that Gloucester had been awarded Host City status for the 2015 Rugby World Cup.

Ken Nottage left in August 2012 to become Chief Executive of the Three Counties Agricultural Society (one suspects for a quieter life!) after a marathon stint as the Club's MD. He sadly passed away in November 2023 at the age of 64. He was replaced in the interim by Finance Director Chris Ferguson before the appointment of Stephen Vaughan as Gloucester's permanent Chief Executive Officer in December 2012. Steve was a high flyer – he was only 37 when he was appointed and had been a professional football player for Walsall and MD of Club 18-30 before working on the London 2012 Olympics for Thomas Cook. Some of the people working on London 2012 would also later be part of the team for the Rugby World Cup, including England 2015 Chief Executive Debbie Jevans.

Vaughan was an entertaining speaker and presented to the Council's staff awards event in the Cathedral, showing a set of slides, including one of an old 18-30 advert saying, 'Be Up at The Crack of Dawn – or Lisa or Julie'. I thought he was at risk of getting struck down showing that in the Cathedral and goodness knows what the council employees with those names (and there were some) made of it! But it certainly got a laugh!

The closure of Kingsholm Road needed for the Rugby World Cup had already been used when Gloucester faced Munster in the Quarter Final of the Heineken Cup in April 2008. Any encounter between these two clubs is special, with a warm bond between the two sets of fans. But a European Quarter Final made it even more so. Kingsholm Road was closed before, during and after the match and street entertainment was laid on. Tickets were in hot demand, but a special screening of the match at GL1 bombed when, as legend has it, some Gloucester fans sold their tickets at inflated prices to their Munster counterparts. That didn't stop, so the story goes, the local B&Q store selling out of ladders as fans without a ticket found other ways to get into the stadium! Munster won 16-3 after Gloucester full-back, the Scottish international Chris Paterson (one of world rugby's most reliable goal-kickers), missed three early penalties which could have given Gloucester momentum.

There were 54 separate projects at Kingsholm to get the stadium ready for the tournament – from altering the pitch size to new wi-fi, medical facilities and stronger bulbs in the floodlights.

Former Gloucester Rugby captain Adam Balding was recruited as the city's Rugby World Cup Co-ordinator in August 2013. He was a top bloke, a great ambassador and, after 15 years of playing professional rugby for a number of different clubs, had plenty of contacts. But it's fair to say that working for a local authority is very different from being a professional rugby player and it took some adjustment. Adam was well-supported though by other council officers, including Directors Martin Shields and Ross Cook, and other key partners including Marketing Gloucester and Gloucestershire Highways.

In July 2013, *The Citizen* reported that GFirst, who at the time had responsibility for tourism marketing for Gloucestershire, and VisitEngland wanted to market the Rugby World Cup as being in the Cotswolds. It's true that the Cotswolds is a stronger national and international tourist brand, but fans, including me, were adamant it must be Gloucester. Dave Smith from Whitminster said, "I thought it took the biscuit when I heard about Cotswold Rugby. Now Gloucester has got the Rugby World Cup coming to town they were suddenly interested. You don't see the tourist people sniffing around Gloucester at most other times, so why start now?"

One of the requirements of the bid was to create a fanzone with a big screen to show the main matches on i.e. the England matches and those being staged at Kingsholm. The fanzone needed to sell food and drink and have a place for Rugby World Cup merchandise to be sold. We considered the options. Kings Square, being in the city centre and close to the Kingsholm Stadium, seemed the obvious choice but it wasn't exactly the most attractive and we genuinely believed that by September 2015 it would be a building site. So, we settled for Orchard Square at the Docks as the next best site, with probably the best possible backdrop. The fanzone requirement was a 5000 capacity. Orchard Square could only take 3500, but Mariners Square in the Docks (adjacent to the Mariners' Church) was used as an 'activation zone' of rugby-related activities, so that made up the 1500 difference. Within the fanzone, as well as screening the matches, there was entertainment such as flash mobs, bands and walkabout performers (including those dressed as heavily-muddied rugby players!).

As it turned out, Kings Square wasn't a building site in September 2015 and wouldn't be for four more years after that. In hindsight, I wish we'd gone for Kings Square. Having the Fanzone at the Docks added to the narrative that the Docks 'gets everything' at the expense of the city centre. The Fanzone was successful – so much so that it drew criticism from city centre publicans that it pulled away their customers, although people did disperse in all directions once the matches had finished. The pubs did okay from the Rugby World Cup though. I did a quick tour of the city centre pubs before matches were on at Kingsholm (it's a tough job but someone's got to do it!) and those that had made an effort were healthily busy. Those that hadn't were less so, but that's life.

There was some pressure to extend the fanzone's operation into the knockout stages, but I resisted it because a) England had already been eliminated b) it would have cost an extra £90,000 which we hadn't budgeted for and c) I thought it was only fair to give the city's pubs a free run for the rest of the tournament. Gloucester Rugby set up a fanzone of sorts at Kingsholm but take-up was limited.

The Rugby World Cup Fanzone at Gloucester Docks. Credit: Mhairi Smith

Gloucester Rugby opened a shop in the Gloucester Quays Outlet Centre, initially on a temporary basis primarily to serve the fanzone, but it was such a success that they wished to continue operating it beyond the end of the temporary consent. It was a sensitive issue and the Council didn't really want to be seen taking enforcement action against the city's leading sporting club. In the end, the issue was resolved by the Club and its clothing provider offering a discount range to fit in with the Outlet Centre's planning conditions. The shop continues to operate today.

In September 2013, we installed a number of sets of rugby posts in parks across the city to encourage participation, including one in Gloucester Park. For a publicity shot, I was asked to kick for goal. Fortunately, my kick just crept over the posts.

In March 2014, we put out a call for volunteers for the tournament for what would be called 'The Pack'. There was no shortage of interest, with 600 people queuing at an event at GL1 in September 2014 to sign up.[276] It was always my hope that an increase in volunteering on an ongoing basis would be a legacy of the tournament for Gloucester.

The USA qualified for the tournament in April 2014. There was speculation that President Barack Obama could visit Kingsholm. There was a cherry and white connection as former Gloucester coach Nigel Melville was the USA's Director of Rugby. Prime Minister David Cameron said he would try to get Obama to come to Gloucester, saying, "Whether I can get him to come to Gloucester and whether I can convince him he is a Shedhead might be more challenging".[277]

Mayor of London, Boris Johnson, visited Gloucester in May 2014 to give his advice on how major sporting events can help regeneration, using his experience of the 2012 Olympics. He said, "We saw in London that if you hold a big sporting event, you get big rewards. People will see it on the television, they will see the atmosphere, they will want a piece of Gloucester."[278] After visiting the Kingsholm Stadium, he went on a walkabout in the city centre. He got a hugely warm reception with dozens of people coming up and taking selfies with him. I don't know whether he'd get quite the same treatment today.

We got a taste of how popular the international matches were likely to be in November 2014 when Tonga and the USA, two of the teams we would host, met at Kingsholm. Tonga ran out winners by 40 points to 12 in front of a near 9000 crowd.

Tickets for the Rugby World Cup went on sale in Spring 2015 and Kingsholm was soon sold out. There was less capacity for the Rugby World Cup than the usual Gloucester matches due to different standards for crowds – largely due to a reduced density in The Shed. England Rugby 2015 hired Kingsholm in its entirety for a total of 37 days.

I was determined that Gloucester wouldn't just meet the requirements of being a host city, we'd go over and above it. And we did. One of my favourite memories was the 'ball pass' in September 2015, where a rugby ball would be passed from person to person, starting at St Mary de Crypt Church in Southgate Street and ending up at the Cathedral. There, the ball would be kicked through a set of rugby posts on the Cathedral Green and caught before being taken on to Kingsholm where Japan were playing Georgia in a warm-up match. I'd read in *The Citizen* that I'd be catching the ball, which made me slightly nervous! On the day, hundreds of people took part in the ball pass, which had a real community feel. When we got to the Cathedral, City MP Richard Graham (wearing a suit and smart shoes) offered to take the kick at the posts. I spread out some young helpers behind the posts ready to catch in case RG's kick should go astray. I needn't have bothered. To my surprise, his left-footed shot came straight into my arms. We hadn't practised it and it probably wouldn't have gone so well if we had!

My sure-footed catch gave me a false sense of security. When a ball went into touch, heading towards me, during the Japan/Georgia match, I thought it would be easy for me to pluck it out of the sky. It's more difficult than it looks! I slightly misjudged it and instead of falling gracefully into my arms, it whacked me on the face. I hoped that in a less-than-capacity Kingsholm nobody had noticed – until Mark Cummings asked me about it live on his Radio Gloucestershire Breakfast Show!

There was also a museum exhibition of rugby memorabilia called 'Wow! Rugby' including items donated by the likes of Messrs Burton, Teague and Vickery. Phil lent his 2003 World Cup Winner's medal and Mike Teague lent us his British Lions 'Player of the Series' trophy. Hartpury College's Danielle Waterman lent her Women's Rugby World Cup final shirt from England's victory in 2014. There were paintings of Gloucester players past and present by local artist Russell Haines.

Each host city held a Welcome Ceremony for one of the teams. We were fortunate to be allocated Scotland. They were playing against Japan at Kingsholm and had their training base at nearby Hartpury College, which was also Gloucester's training ground. We decided to host the event at the Cathedral – which wasn't a difficult decision. The purpose of the event was, as the name suggests, to welcome the squad and hand out their international caps. There was an opportunity for someone to make a speech on behalf of the host city. You could make the case that it should have been the Mayor, but I decided I wasn't going to give this one up!

We invited anyone with a Scottish connection we could think of – including former Gloucester players who were Scottish internationals like Ian Smith and Peter Jones, John Simonett (who had captained the Scotland Under-19 side), Regional Director of BT (sponsors of the Scottish team) Paul Coles and Norman Douse of the Gloucester Scottish Society. There was a suggestion that Scottish First Minister Nicola Sturgeon would attend, but on checking with her office that proved not to be the case, although she did send her best wishes for the event. Television presenter Jill Douglas, a Scot herself and partner of Gloucester coach Carl Hogg, hosted the ceremony without charging her usual fee.

In my speech, I made reference to Gloucester Cathedral being the burial place of Edward II, who was defeated by Robert the Bruce at the Battle of Bannockburn – which was the inspiration for the Scottish National Anthem "Flower of Scotland". I added that the highest-ranking casualty of that battle was Gilbert de Clare, the 8th Earl of Gloucester, whose family coat of arms still forms part of the city crest today. I spoke about each of the Scottish internationals who had played for Gloucester – from Ruari Maclean (my form teacher at The Crypt) to Rory Lawson (grandson of revered commentator Bill McLaren), Scott Lawson, Big Jim Hamilton to Chris Paterson (the country's record points scorer who spent a season at Kingsholm) and current squad members Alasdair Strokosch and Alasdair Dickinson. Thanks to Malc King from the Gloucester Rugby Heritage Project, I was also able to talk about Donald Crichton-Miller who played for Scotland in 1931 – the first Gloucester player to receive international honours for a country other than England. I somehow neglected to mention another Scot whose efforts had been key to Gloucester hosting RWC matches – former owner Tom Walkinshaw. I hope a mention here goes a small way towards putting right that omission.

Holding Scotland's Welcome Ceremony was particularly appropriate, I remarked, as their captain Greg Laidlaw was "one of our own". At the end of my speech, Greg and I exchanged gifts. I gave him a 'Scrumpty' painted in Scotland colours, which made its way to Murrayfield, and he presented me with a 'quaich' – a two-handled Scottish drinking cup which is now in the glass cabinet outside the Council Chamber at North Warehouse.

A number of different towns and cities had introduced Sculpture Trails to encourage footfall and movement around their centres. Bristol had the Gromit Trail, Norwich had Gorillas and more locally Cirencester and the wider Cotswolds had the March Hare Trail. So what should Gloucester do? We had the chance to be part of the Shaun the Sheep Trail for the Rugby World Cup, but I wanted something of our own. We looked at various options from Tailor of Gloucester mice to Old Spot pigs and seagulls (but I reckoned the city had enough of those already)! Don't ask me how, but I noticed that Humpty Dumpty was a similar shape to a rugby ball. As Humpty Dumpty was said by some to be based on a Civil War Siege Engine used in Gloucester, I thought we could combine these. 'Scrumpty' seemed like the obvious name! My early attempts to show others my idea didn't hit the spot, but I persisted and designers from Amalgam, who had worked on the Bristol sculpture trail, came up with a cute-looking design.

In November 2014, Scrumpty was unveiled. I commented, "The enormous success of sculpture trails such as Gromit in Bristol and Hares in Cirencester convinced us that this would be a fantastic thing to bring to the city. Next year is our big year in Gloucester and we are sure the sculpture trail will mirror the successes in other cities and bring real benefits to the local economy by increasing visitors to the city, as well as being a fun activity for all the people of Gloucester."[279]

Artists came up with nearly 30 different designs from the Tailor of Gloucester mouse (which went outside the Cathedral) to a monk (which went outside Blackfriars), an egg and spoon (positioned on The Cross) and a pirate (at the Docks). Local businesses, including estate agents Naylor Powell and plant hire company Keyway, were signed up to sponsor each sculpture and hundreds of thousands of trail maps were given out. The trail was the most popular hit on the Visit England website relating to the Rugby World Cup. The trail launched just as my daughter Eirys was born. I joked on social media that they were both my creations, but I'd "only been involved in the fun bits, with other people doing the hard work."

The sculptures suffered some minor vandalism - the ear was ripped off the Tailor of Gloucester mouse (sponsored by Naylor Powell) outside the Cathedral and the spoon from the Egg & Spoon Scrumpty on The Cross (sponsored by Café Rene) suffered the same fate.[280] Apart from these isolated incidents the sculptures were treated respectfully.

Scrumpty had his own lapel badges, key rings, tea towels and even his own beer, Scrumpty Gold by the Butcombe Brewery. He was even nominated for the Ambassador of the Year at the Believe in Gloucester Awards in 2015! We had a special Scrumpty costume made so he could make guest appearances at events and lots of people wanted their photo taken with him. Several Scrumpties are still on show around the city, including one by Stroud-based artist Swarez outside Dr Foster's pub at the Docks and a soldier outside the Soldiers of Gloucestershire Museum. Schools took part with designs for 'mini-Scrumpties' and a number of those are still around too. I had hoped that, given his popularity, Gloucester Rugby might adopt Scrumpty as their mascot, but I couldn't persuade them to. I live in hope though!

We tried to make the city look and feel its best for the tournament. We introduced free wifi in the city centre. New 'Welcome to Gloucester' signs were installed on the gateways to the city, featuring images of the Cathedral, the Docks and, of course, the Kingsholm Stadium.[281] In the Kingsholm area, rugby-themed street art was added to the railway arches in Hare Lane, to the Coach & Horses pub and to bins just by the ground. Our colleagues at the County Council resurfaced Kingsholm Road (which really did need it). I was keen to have a permanent Rugby World Cup feature in the city and Pascal Mychalysin, the master mason at the Cathedral, designed a splendid Rugby World Cup-themed stone bench with the badge of each visiting nation, which we installed in Kings Square. Individuals and businesses were given the opportunity to contribute towards this by buying a brick paviour with their name engraved on it to be laid next to the bench. I readily signed up as did others, but it was harder work to attract contributions towards it than I thought it would be.

Kingsholm set the stage (almost literally!) for the tournament by hosting concerts by Elton John and Madness in the summer of 2015.

The Rugby World Cup could be looked upon as the start of Gloucester's cultural renaissance. Marketing Gloucester successfully applied to the Arts Council for £85,000 to put on a cultural programme, based on the nations playing in Gloucester. We had the 'Ensemble Rustavi' Georgian choir in the Cathedral, the 'Red Hot Chilli Pipers' with their brand of 'bagrock' (bagpipes with attitude), American Lindy Hop dancing and Japanese Taiko drummers performing in Kings Square and an Argentinian Tango flash mob in the gate streets. Scouts from Simon Cowell's 'Britain's Got Talent' came to a 'Show and Prove' dance battle in Kings Square, described as 'hip-hop in its rawest form' and hosted by Avant Garde Dance, on the lookout for star performers. The Georgian Ambassador, Revaz Gachechiladze, became a great friend of Gloucester and I was honoured to attend his leaving party at the St John's Hyde Park church in London. I was a proud Gloucestrian when I saw a Barnwood Shopfitting van parked outside!

The matches at Kingsholm went well and there was a tremendous atmosphere in the city on those days. The first match in the city was Tonga v Georgia on 19th September – the second match of the tournament. Georgia won 17-10. My tweets about the match were picked up by a Tongan government official, the exotically-named Elsie Fukofuka.

I enjoyed having photos taken with visiting fans, particularly the Japanese. Scotland v Japan on 23rd September was a highlight, attended by Princess Anne as Patron of the Scottish RFU and Sir Bill Beaumont as English RFU President. Japan, coached by Eddie Jones, had beaten South Africa in the shock of the tournament, but couldn't repeat their giant-killing exploits and went down by 45-10. Gloucester players Greg Laidlaw and Alasdair Dickinson featured for Scotland.

A beautiful sunset over Kingsholm Stadium for the final Rugby World Cup match to be held there in 2015. Credit: Hayley Mortimer

Argentinian fans descended on the city in great numbers on 25th September, turning it into a mini-Buenos Aires. They beat Georgia

54-9. The final pool match of the tournament, the USA v Japan, on 11th October took place at Kingsholm under a beautiful red sky (captured by Citizen journalist Hayley Mortimer and retweeted over 700 times!). The Cathedral was also lit up in blue and pink for the occasion, with USA v JPN beamed onto the tower. Japan ran out victors 28-18.

The Citizen's headline that US President Barack Obama could be attending didn't turn out to be the case, but a number of officials from the Embassy did come for the match. They visited the Gwinnett family tomb at Down Hatherley (where the parents of Button Gwinnett, second signatory to the US Declaration of Independence are buried) and watched a re-enactment of George Whitefield's first sermon at St Mary de Crypt.

Japan coach Eddie Jones, who was recruited by England after the World Cup, said, "It was interesting coming on the bus here (Kingsholm), we were driving in and the fans on the side of the road with Japanese flags – most of them didn't look Japanese. What a wonderful thing for the team to achieve that."[282]

I was privileged to attend a number of Rugby World Cup receptions during the course of the tournament and the run-up to it. At one, held at the House of Commons, I asked Laurence Dallaglio if he remembered being turned inside out by James Simpson-Daniel at Kingsholm before he offloaded to James Bailey for a famous try. He did. He asked me if I remembered Wasps beating Gloucester 39-3 at Twickenham. Unfortunately, I did. Touché!

Another reception was held at the Foreign Office in Whitehall. Prince Harry and Prime Minister David Cameron attended. Cameron gave a passionate speech about the tournament, without notes, although some people remarked that he could have done the same if he was talking about table tennis. I took the opportunity to take a few items in a carrier bag to be signed by any big names there, for the Mayor's charity. Luckily, I was able to grab Jonny Wilkinson, who was happy to oblige, and Dallaglio. I also met Mr Yoshiro Mori, former Prime Minister of Japan and the then President of the Japan RFU. I gave him a Scrumpty tea towel, which I'm sure he treasures to this day!

The other time I was able to get things signed to sell off for charities happened by chance. I was on holiday in the Algarve and was wandering around Vilamoura marina. Someone walked by with their family and I thought they looked familiar. I then realised it was Francois Pienaar, the South African world cup-winning captain. I said this to my girlfriend (now wife), but she was more worried about running out of time on our parking – otherwise I would have said hello to him. When our holiday was over, I did some detective work and managed to get an email address for him. I dropped him a line to check it was him and, to his credit, he replied straight away to say it was. I tried to get him to come to Gloucester when he was in the UK as a RWC television pundit but unfortunately none of his matches were near here. I did, however, get him to agree to sign some specially made copies of Gloucester poet William Henley's poem 'Invictus'. This was the title of a film telling the story of the 1995 South African victory in the Rugby World Cup, in which Pienaar was played by Matt Damon. Nelson Mandela read the poem Invictus, which describes the struggle against adversity, every day when he was imprisoned on Robben Island. These were auctioned for local charities, raising over £1000.

At the end of the pool stages, there was a reception at Buckingham Palace for the host cities and competing nations. I knew I wouldn't get away with a carrier bag of goodies at the Palace, but I put a few specially-created cards in my inside pocket that I could get anyone famous to sign, again for the civic charities. On the way in, I bumped into South Africa speedster Bryan Habana. Inside, I chatted to Wales captain Sam Warburton and his forlorn-looking English counterpart Chris Robshaw (whose team didn't progress beyond the pool stages) and had a bear hug from Samoa's Alesana Tuilagi.

The Queen, Prince Philip and Prince Harry (Patron of England Rugby 2015) all attended, with Harry giving a speech. In March 2016, when ITV broadcasted 'The Queen at 90', I was amazed when they showed a clip of me swigging a glass of champagne at the reception, just as Her Majesty was about to walk in. I didn't even know the cameras were there!

Gloucester was given plaudits as the place with the best atmosphere after Twickenham. It was announced that over 100,000 rugby fans had been welcomed to the city, including 57,327 to Kingsholm and 55,000 to the fanzone. Accountants and business advisers EY (formerly Ernst & Young) estimated that the economic benefit to the local economy of Gloucester being a host city was £48 million. Most importantly, we'd shown that we could deliver a major event when the eyes of the world were upon us.

Paul James with Japanese rugby fans in Gloucester city centre.

Some of the Scottish rugby squad with the Tailor of Gloucester Scrumpty outside the Cathedral.

Strengthening links between Club and City

During the amateur days, Gloucester's rugby players trained on a pitch at the former Oxstalls School, a short distance from the Kingsholm ground. A £3 million plan to upgrade facilities as part of a wider development of Oxstalls was included in the 1999/2000 budget, to be funded by the Club and the County Council. The plans didn't progress but Oxstalls continued to be used for several years as facilities were developed elsewhere. In 1999, a plan was put together for training facilities at the rapidly-expanding Hartpury College, a few miles to the west of Gloucester. Apparently, the Club also considered the Imjin Barracks at Innsworth, home to NATO's Allied Rapid Reaction Corps with whom the Club retains close links but the MoD was apparently unwilling to commit to a long-term deal, which the Club thought necessary.

The facilities at Hartpury served the Club well until 2021, by which time both the Club and the College had grown to the extent that there wasn't room for both of them. After looking at a number of options, the Club chose to move its training facility to a vacant warehouse formerly occupied by SLG Beauty (and before that Arjo and its predecessor Mecanaids) which was next door to the Kingsholm Stadium. It was a popular move, bringing the players into the heart of the city.

In my view, it was a shame that the link between the two was weakened when, in 2005, the Club stopped using the City Crest as its badge. It did so because it wanted a logo which it could own and for which it could protect the intellectual property rights. The Club came up with a slightly different crest, which was never hugely popular, and was dropped in favour of the current lion design in May 2018. The shirt for the 2021-22 season and others since have featured the chevrons and roundels from the city crest, but it wasn't the same.

Not every senior executive at Kingsholm has understood the importance of the link between the Club and the City. Indeed, one (who will remain nameless) told me that they would never open a Gloucester Rugby shop in the city centre because it "didn't fit with their brand". Lance Bradley, the former boss of Mitsubishi Motors UK, who was appointed Chief Executive in September 2019 and served until July 2023, certainly did get it and wanted to see the Club and City working closely together. George Skivington, who came in as Head Coach in June 2020, took the players on walkabouts around the city centre as a way of connecting them with the place.

Rugby and regeneration really did come together on 30th April 2022 – when the official opening of the newly-revamped Kings Square took place in the morning and Gloucester beat fierce rivals Bath 64-0 at Kingsholm in the afternoon. As I tweeted at the time, that was a good day for the city!

Again, this may feel like a slightly random collection of stories, so how do they fit with the regeneration theme? In short, having a successful professional sports club has a huge economic benefit for the city – both directly in terms of spend and through 'putting Gloucester on the map', as Boris Johnson pointed out on his visit in 2014. As one of Gloucester's greatest assets, the rugby club's strengths must continue to be harnessed for the wider benefit of the city.

18. FOOTBALL'S COMING HOME

Whether or not Gloucester is a 'rugby city' is a vexed question and one which stimulates much debate amongst local fans of the two sports on social media. It's true that Gloucester's rugby side plays at a higher level and attracts a much bigger crowd than their footballing counterparts. Despite that, I've always recognised the importance of football too. Many hundreds of young people play football in the city and having a good side is important to give them local sporting idols to look up to and for civic pride generally. Just as Gloucester had for many years been one of few cities of its size not to have a university, it is also one of a handful of English cities never to have had a Football League club. Gloucester City Football Club has a similar length heritage to Gloucester Rugby, having been founded in 1883 and with 2000 players donning the shirt since that time.

I played football for the school team at Calton Road Juniors and, although in my day The Crypt only played rugby in PE lessons, at break time we played football. But, as I recount in the chapter about rugby, when my grandfather took me to watch a match at Kingsholm, my passion for rugby was ignited and my interest in football waned. Some Gloucester City fans claimed that because I was a rugby supporter, I wasn't interested in helping the Football Club in my role as Leader of the Council. This wasn't true and nor was it, in my view, borne out by the facts.

Gloucester City had led something of a nomadic existence even before the events of recent years. The Club's Stadium was in Longlevens from 1935, near the Greyhound track (now the Greyhound Gardens housing estate). It moved in 1964 to a new stadium in Horton Road by the gas holder station, which apparently was big enough to hold 30,000 spectators! The Club chairman in the 1980s was Geoff Hester, the boss of Westbury Homes – a Cheltenham-based housebuilder which grew massively in the 1980s and 1990s before being acquired by Persimmon. He later set up Clifton Homes. It was because of Westbury's sponsorship that

Gloucester City played for many years in their corporate colours of yellow and black. Given these connections, it was perhaps not surprising that City's ground was developed for housing. They moved to a new stadium at Meadow Park, Hempsted in 1986. The roads on the Horton Road housing estate, known as Swallow Park, are named after some of Gloucester City's most prominent footballers, (Stan) Myers Road, (Dicky) Etheridge Place and (Ron) Coltman Close amongst others.

The Club has also undergone a succession of owners over the years, with some coming in and splashing the cash on players with relatively high wages and leaving the Club with financial troubles when they lost interest or ran out of money and others who followed them to steady the ship. Previous owners/chairmen include Les Alderman, a Bath-based businessman who bankrolled the Club's success for the 1990/91 campaign but left suddenly the following season. It was believed that he had sold his businesses but deposited the cash in the BCCI bank, which then collapsed. He was followed by George Irvine, who ran the Roaduser car parts chain, who saw the Club through the next few seasons.

Then came Keith Gardner, a flamboyant Rolls-Royce-driving owner of the 'Video Nest' video library chain, when such things were in vogue. Gardner had plans for an all-seater stadium, all-weather pitch, leisure centre and ice rink – none of which, ultimately, came to pass. During Keith Gardner's tenure, the Club acquired the adjacent Fieldings Social Club and, as well as using Gardner's own cash, took on debt in order to do so. This put the Club under financial pressure.

Eamonn McGurk had joined as a sponsor, director and minority shareholder in the 1995/96 season. As a youngster, Eamonn played football for Gloucester Schools. Living in Widden Street, he walked past City's Horton Road stadium on the way to St Peter's Junior School every day before moving to Elmbridge Road. When City had moved to Meadow Park, Eamonn was in business in Hempsted, adjacent to Llanthony Priory. As the Club was short of money, Eamonn bought a 10% share off owner Keith Gardner, then bought a strip of land from him. When another financial crisis hit at the end of the season, Eamonn bailed the Club out and Gardner handed over his shares.

After majority ownership passed to Eamonn McGurk, the first

chairman was Rob Thomas, boss of Renault dealer Hartland Motors, who took over in August 1997. The Club stood on the brink of bankruptcy. In January 1998, Thomas launched a 'Save The Tigers' campaign after discovering an unpaid 1996/7 tax bill. The Club had paid £82,000 but still had to find £8000 a month. The campaign was backed by *The Citizen* newspaper. Local companies, including Birds Eye Walls, raised £22,000 in nine days to help meet the tax bill. Many local people also chipped in to help. Local Conservatives held a skittles night at The Avenue pub, raising £500. City Council Leader at the time, Jon Holmes, had been a Director of the Football Club a few years before. At that point, directors paid £5000 a year for the privilege and most were local businessmen, like estate agents Michael Tuck, John Beacham and Darryl Cox. The Council lent the Club £20,000 to stave off the Inland Revenue. It was reported that, in December 1999, the Club was believed to have debts of around £500,000 and there were 12 different mortgage charges on the Meadow Park ground.

Rob Thomas resigned in July 1999 and was succeeded by Tracey Newport, a solicitor for the local firm of Eggletons and a former Gloucester City player. Newport was a controversial figure, who hit the headlines in October 2001, when he was dismissed from Eggletons following a dispute with the firm. Colin Gardner (no relation to Keith), who ran burglar alarm business Gardner Security, was a respected figure who took over as chairman in November 2001 and stayed until the end of the 2003-4 season, later becoming chairman of Forest Green Rovers.

Gloucester City FC has had significant financial support from Eamonn McGurk during the quarter of a century of his ownership. Many would argue it owes its continued existence to him. Gloucester-born but of Irish descent, Eamonn sometimes gets a hard time from some City fans, but it is, in my view, unfair. He is a very private individual, who doesn't own a football club for the glory. Over the years he has put in a very substantial seven figure sum to the Club with very little to show for it. He certainly doesn't brag about it. In fact, he is slightly embarrassed by it. He sees it as one way in which he can give back to the community – and he gives in lots of other ways besides.

For most of the time that Eamonn has been the Club's major

shareholder, others have been the Club's chairman, including Chris Hill, Dave Phillips, Nigel Hughes, Stuart Pike (who owned the Burger Star takeaway in Westgate Street), Mike Dunstan and Rod Jenner (of Dowdeswell Estates – see section on The Fleece Hotel in the 'Unfinished Business' chapter).

A History of Flooding

Meadow Park is in the floodplain and had suffered severe flooding on a number of occasions – in 1990, 2000 and, most recently, in 2007. In 2000, the Club was insured by Independent Insurance who went bust and didn't pay out the claim – leaving the Club to foot the bill for £80,000 of damage. It also meant they could only get insurance with a flood exclusion thereafter. Club photographer Neil Phelps captured each of the flood events. He told me how in 1990 you could see Minsterworth Church in the distance. In 2000 you couldn't – something he puts down to the build-up of the adjacent landfill site, which he feels was a contributory factor to the severity of the 2007 flood.

Eamonn McGurk told me that in 2007 the Club was in a good place with a well-maintained stadium. The floods in July that year changed all that. On Sunday 22nd July Meadow Park was hit, with the floodwaters almost reaching the crossbar – something which became one of the iconic images of that event. Club photographer Neil Phelps gained access to the Club on Monday 23rd July to capture the image. He went straight after work still dressed as a postman with his camera in his pouch, meaning he got through unchallenged.

The floods meant the Club could no longer get insurance – one of the conditions of operating a league ground. Once the waters had receded, attention started to turn to what the Club could do. After being hit time and time again, the Club was worried it would continue to be a recurring problem. Indeed, issues around flooding were some of the most complex and expensive to resolve as it sought, eventually, to return to Meadow Park.

The goalposts at Gloucester City's Meadow Park stadium under water – an iconic image of the 2007 floods. Credit: Neil Phelps.

Searching for Alternatives

On 16th August 2007, *The Citizen* urged, "Let's find a new home for City". Manager Tim Harris said that it would be "ludicrous" for the Club to go back to Meadow Park with the risk of flooding. The Railway Triangle, which was undeveloped at that time, was suggested as a possible new home.

The City Council and the Club set up the 'Football Task & Finish Group'. I attended the first meeting and nominated the then Cabinet Member for Culture & Leisure Martyn White to chair it. The opposition nominated Liberal Democrat Leader Jeremy Hilton and they had the numbers to win the vote.

The Group looked at a huge number of options – from the Railway Triangle to the Winget Ground in Tuffley Avenue, Coney Hill Rugby Club, St Peter's High School, Tuffley Rovers, Marconi Drive at Waterwells, Javelin Park near Junction 12 of the M5, Saintbridge Rugby Club, Blackbridge at Podsmead, land at the rear of the Walls factory in Barnwood, land south of Grange Road, and land at Hempsted Lane. The Club wanted to stay within the city boundary. In October 2007, news broke of a possible deal with Quedgeley

Wanderers for their site at Waterwells, but within a month those talks had broken down and it was back to the drawing board.

In November 2008, City MP Parmjit Dhanda secured an adjournment debate on the future of the Football Club and, at the time, was promoting land at Blackbridge in Podsmead as his favoured solution. Parliamentary Under-Secretary for Culture, Media and Sport, Barbara Follett MP (wife of the author Ken Follett) responded for the Government, but effectively said it was a matter for the local councils to sort out.

In December 2008, it was reported that Gloucestershire County Council had agreed in principle to make land available at Blackbridge playing fields for a new stadium. Cabinet Member, Councillor Ray Theodolou said that "positive discussions have taken place between the Club and council officers". The idea didn't progress, apparently because of concerns about poor access roads and a spate of vandalism that was taking place in the area at the time.

Secretary of State for the Department of the Environment, Food and Rural Affairs, Hilary Benn MP, came to Gloucester in May 2009 at the invitation of City MP Parmjit Dhanda, to meet officials from the Club and the Environment Agency, along with City Planners, and visited the Meadow Park ground.

The Football Task and Finish Group was wound up in May 2010. By this time the Club had gone full circle and decided to work towards a return to Meadow Park which, despite its obvious problems, had the advantage of being owned by Club majority shareholder Eamonn McGurk.

When progress with Meadow Park stalled, some fans promoted the idea of a groundshare with Gloucester Rugby. Chief Executive of the Rugby Club, Stephen Vaughan, did look at the idea, but the costs of opening even parts of the ground would swallow up the ticket revenue (based on crowd numbers at the time). In addition, there were concerns about scheduling of matches and whether the pitch, which at the time was grass, could withstand two lots of matches.

Redrow Homes had acquired the former Civil Service Club site in between Estcourt Road and Denmark Road. In 2013, they looked at whether the site could accommodate a stadium for Gloucester City alongside their housing development. It always felt rather cramped and there were concerns about potentially having the city's two main sports stadia so close together, which could have caused issues if their fixtures coincided. So Meadow Park remained the preferred option.

A Nomadic Existence

In the meantime, City led a rather Nomadic existence – sharing grounds with Forest Green Rovers at Nailsworth for one season, Cirencester (two seasons), Cheltenham Town (seven seasons) and then outside the county at Evesham (three seasons). A hardcore of fans continued to follow the Club around from ground to ground, but whereas one FA Cup match against Leyton Orient at Cheltenham attracted a crowd of 1381, the final match played at Evesham saw just 161 fans attend. Those involved with the Club tell me that the extended period away from Gloucester led to a "lost generation of fans".

The team performed remarkably well on the pitch given their lack of a genuine home ground, winning promotion in the 2008/9 season. Rather perversely they were promoted from the BGB Premier League to the Blue Square Conference North rather than South, meaning some long round trips to away fixtures of over 500 miles. Oddly, Worcester played in the Conference South! Despite a campaign by *The Citizen* and an Early Day Motion in Parliament (effectively a Parliamentary petition) the decision was not changed. The Club was granted a Civic Reception by the Mayor of Gloucester in recognition of their achievement.

City's groundshare deal with Cheltenham Town started in 2010. In 2013, the BBC reported that the rent was £40,000 a season – something which Cheltenham Town Chairman Paul Baker described as "a good commercial arrangement". The rent wasn't always paid on time, due to City's hand-to-mouth existence, and extensions to the arrangement weren't agreed until debts had been cleared, but Cheltenham chairman Paul Baker was described by City sources as "a gentleman" to deal with. In March 2010, the City Council agreed to contribute £20,000 towards the cost of rent and assisted with smaller amounts for a number of other seasons. The groundshare wasn't popular with Cheltenham fans, both because of the late payments and because having two Clubs holding matches at the stadium led to the condition of the pitch deteriorating. It wasn't that popular with City fans either. At one match I attended, I heard the chant (to the tune of 'Sloop John B' by the Beach Boys) of "We want to go home. We want to go home. Cheltenham's a s***hole. We want to go home."

In a letter in support of the Meadow Park planning application, Supporters Trust Chairman Phil Warren set out the sequence of events, saying: "The Club became a tenant of Forest Green FC, a very hasty arrangement forced on the Club just weeks before the start of the 2007-8 season. No-one at the Club bleated about it. Circumstances determined a subsequent move to Cirencester Town, the Club got on with it accepting philosophically that we were inevitably going to be itinerants for a while. Success on the pitch meant a promotion to the Conference Football League for which facilities at Cirencester weren't sufficient. The Club moved to groundshare with Cheltenham Town. Supporters were feeling like vagabonds and longed for the time when they might return home."

I was very clear that the extended period of time that our Football Club was playing out of the city was "an embarrassment". Fans were extremely patient, feeling that a carrot was forever being dangled in front of them, but at times their frustration boiled over. Occasionally, open meetings for supporters were held. One such meeting was held in March 2013, when it was revealed that Eamonn McGurk had spent £250,000 on fees relating to the stadium plans to date. The final figure was higher, at well over £300,000.

People said to me that I wouldn't have let it happen to the Rugby Club. The reality is that if something similar had happened to the Rugby Club, they would have had the resources to do whatever was necessary very quickly. This was a theme picked up by Timothy Clark, the Club statistician, in his submission to the planning application. He insisted he was "not rugby bashing" but said, "There is no doubt in my mind that had this been Gloucester Rugby Club in the same predicament a swifter return would have been accommodated." He added that the Club was leading a "frustrating nomadic existence", noting that "the area has now become sexy with the surrounding developments changing it beyond recognition. Indeed, there is now a bridge in St Ann Way which was not there in 2007 to add to the extra and easy accessibility to the new Meadow Park."

In January 2014, an advert for insurance giant Aviva claimed Gloucester had no football club and only played rugby and skittles! After an outcry they withdrew the advert and donated a football shirt from Norwich City (who they sponsored) to the Club. The Club also received celebrity support from Gloucester-born singer Nathan Sykes of 'The Wanted' who in March 2013 urged his legion of Twitter followers to get behind the Football Club, using the hashtag #saveourcity.

A Bold New Vision

The initial vision for a new Meadow Park after the floods was for a 4000-spectator stadium with scope to increase to 5000. The old ground could hold 4000 with crowds reaching 1500 in 1990s, which had dwindled to a few hundred before the floods.

The stadium would be sited to "exploit the key vista from the South West Bypass". To help finance the new stadium there was a proposal to develop 2.2 hectares of employment land alongside it, as well as 177 car parking spaces for the stadium, 6 coach parking and 20 cycle spaces.

A planning application was lodged in 2011. Another application was submitted that year to store empty waste bins at the stadium, which was largely made up of green garden waste bins no longer wanted by residents after the City Council started to charge for collections. That also perhaps became an iconic image of the Club's wilderness years.

The application was originally reported to the Planning Committee in September 2012. They welcomed the proposal and offered in principle support subject to further flood modelling and certainty on flood risk and highways issues. They noted that the employment development was to help make the project financially viable. The proposed flood works included upgrading 120m of existing flood defences along the Severn, the construction of an additional 640m long earth embankment across the floodplain and raising the site by 3m. The works would also improve access to the nearby Household Recycling Centre during a flood event. The complication was that the flood alleviation works would be on land owned by third parties and would need the permission of those landowners. One Council Officer described to me how various pieces of land in Hempsted are owned by people who have known each other since childhood and don't like each other – so the chances of securing agreement were slim.

The committee was told that raising the site would have involved importing 80,000m3 of material, which would have taken 18-24 months and involve almost 500 lorry movements a month. This led to claims that the "Football Club (was being) used as a smokescreen for industrial development and tipping", although there was no evidence that this was the case – and the amount of money to be made from tipping was a drop in the ocean compared with the cost of a new stadium.

The Environment Agency, who have responsibility for flood-related matters, advised that development should not start until the flood defences were constructed and operational.

There were 128 letters of support, a 1651-signature petition in favour and 16 objections. Football veteran Colin Peake addressed the committee in support of the application. The Environment Agency's Anthony Perry said that the flood assessment was based upon one dimensional flood modelling. Planning officers advised that "employment development (was) inappropriate for a flood risk area".

The Club's agent proposed a resolution to grant permission subject to flood modelling, but the Council Solicitor advised that Council could be open to judicial review if it made a decision based on current information, so the application was deferred for further work to be undertaken on flooding and highways issues. Agent Paul Duncliffe said, "It has not been possible to positively conclude a number of matters raised by the Planning Committee, although it is not for the want of trying".

The Planning Committee also resolved that the Club "should make every attempt to secure the land needed for an alternative access" rather than rely on the existing narrow Sudmeadow Road access. This is a story in itself. When the Spinnaker Park industrial estate was granted planning consent in 1993, the legal agreement included an obligation to provide a new access to the Football Club. A small area of land between the new road and the Football Club is, apparently, in third party ownership and despite a number of High Court cases brought by the City Council the access has never been completed.

The application returned to the committee in August 2013. Malcolm Prince of Ashleworth spoke against the application because of the loss of floodplain. Councillors Lewis, McLellan, Hobbs and Smith all expressed their sadness and disappointment but concluded they had no choice but to refuse it.

The lack of progress was having an effect on those in leading positions at the Club. Chairman Nigel Hughes told the BBC in November 2013, "I used to have dark hair when I started. Now it's grey and falling out."

A new outline application was submitted in June 2014 for a 4000-capacity stadium, with a 1000-seater stand. Club Chairman at the time Mike Dunstan commented, "It's fantastic to take this significant step towards a return to our city, and I hope fans are as thrilled with the scale and ambition of the plans as we are." The Club's Planning Consultant Paul Duncliffe commented at the time, "The current planning application has addressed the fundamental flooding issues that have persisted for several years and we are pleased to report that the Environment Agency has no objections to the new stadium." To achieve this the Club had agreed to contribute £75,000 to flood improvement works in the Hempsted area and at The Rea. The application was given the thumbs-up unanimously by the Planning Committee in October 2014, subject to 45 planning conditions. Dunstan commented, "It will spring the Club into life again and give everyone the boost they need because it's been a long wait and many of us are tired." After all the legal paperwork was agreed and completed, planning consent was finally issued in September 2015.

In August 2015, it was reported that the Tigers faced another year away from Meadow Park. An article in *The Citizen* advised that the Club planned a two-phase application but the planners wanted a whole scheme put forward. In October 2015, the Club marked 3000 days away from Meadow Park and pledged that a planning application would be submitted soon.

Despite Eamonn McGurk's financial support, the Club lived a fairly hand to mouth existence and finding the money to progress the Stadium project wasn't easy for them. I announced in my budget speech in February 2016 that we would make available £100,000 from the Council's Regeneration Account to support them in moving the project forward. This would pay for fees etc – not players' wages.

Mostly it went down well and my Twitter post confirming it was one of my most viewed ever, but the occasional person stopped their car and wound down their window to tell me how disgusting it was. You can't please all the people all the time! I commented at the time, "This is ring-fenced money. It is not available to support day to day services. I look at regeneration in a very broad sense and I see the Club coming back to Gloucester as regeneration."[283]

The Football Club didn't even have a project manager for what was a very big undertaking. I was able, in my mind, to justify the £100,000 support to the Football Club on the basis that the Council had spent £350,000 on the Rugby World Cup in 2015 (although that money didn't go to the Rugby Club itself).

In May 2016, a new planning application was submitted to allow development to take place on a phased basis to meet minimum requirements for National Ground Grading Category – enabling them to play in National League North. The capacity for the latest iteration of the stadium was 3068.

There was an objection from the Police "based on inappropriate location of stadium, unsuitable access and parking, and layout of building. Suitability of site access for construction and matchday traffic and emergency vehicles." There was also concern about alcohol consumption, noting that the "city and Quays has changed considerably since the stadium was built". The Police recommended that "the use of the site should be objectively considered as it appears unfit for purpose." They were rather late in voicing these opinions as the principle of a new stadium on the site had been established with the 2014 application.

Police and Crime Commissioner Martin Surl intervened after meeting Club Chairman Mike Dunstan and issued a pun-filled press release, describing the Police's comments as an "own goal" and describing how he'd "come off the bench" to put it in the "back of the net". He was quoted as saying, "Technically speaking, the police make some valid and useful points. Perhaps, unfortunately for Gloucester, officers are working to specified criteria which relate to much bigger grounds than the Chairman tells me they want to build.

"As I understand it, many Football League and Premiership grounds are in challenging locations but they have history on their side. Gloucester's crowds are much more modest by comparison but I am assured by the Chairman that the club has an excellent relationship with the police and would coordinate closely for any major fixture so I'm sure there is room for compromise that will enable the development to go ahead."

Concerns about tipping were again expressed in some of the comments on the application. One claimed, "If you let the land be tipped without a contract let for a replacement stadium there will never be a new stadium," while another commented that "The tipping is the golden egg for the land".

The application went to the Planning Committee in October 2016. Jeremy Chamberlayne from Maisemore addressed the committee regarding flooding. He stated that he was not objecting but simply raising issues. There were 59 letters of support, 1 objection and 1 comment. The Committee approved the plans.

One of the remarks in the report to the Planning Committee was that the application had been submitted with yellow/buff bricks which weren't acceptable and the Club had been persuaded to change them to red/orange. This led to the memorable Citizen front page headline of "Yellow Brick 'No'". Eamonn McGurk was quoted as saying, "I don't care as long as we get planning permission" and *The Citizen*'s own Comment column stated that it "should not be seen as a dealbreaker." It was probably just as well that the yellow bricks weren't used as the Club changed back to their original red strip, with a new badge representing the city which was made up of the Cathedral, Docks and a tall ship, in the 2019/20 season.

Scaled Back Ambitions

Despite achieving planning consent, the Club felt the scheme was not feasible due to time and financial constraints. Revised plans were released in October 2018, with Chairman Rod Jenner commenting, "The original plan for the £4 million build, whilst it would have been brilliant, was overly ambitious." In early 2019, a new full planning application was submitted for the retention and refurbishment of the existing clubhouse (including a new raised terrace area), two covered seating stands, a club shop, toilet blocks, turnstiles, dugouts, one covered standing terrace, one uncovered standing terrace, fencing and floodlights. The covered standing terrace would be known as the Tom Webb T End (after the Club's record appearance holder) and the open standing terrace would be known as the Evesham Stand.

Once again there was a Police objection. The Constabulary claimed that "the road system (is) so restricted that it would impede emergency vehicles attending any occurrences. Police attending a serious incident would be hindered and obstructed by vehicles and people leaving." Again, they were rather late in making these comments as the principle of the stadium had already been established by previous applications. Once again Police and Crime Commissioner Martin Surl stepped in. He wrote on Twitter on 24th April 2019 that his office had been working with the Constabulary to overcome their concerns and that he was "hopeful a solution will be found before the deadline". He told the Club, "The sooner you're home the better."

The committee was advised that demolition would take 8-10 weeks. It would take a further 42 weeks to import the 40,350 cubic metres of material needed to raise the pitch by the 4m required. Construction would last another 52 weeks. So although planning consent was granted in May 2019 it would still be more than a year before the Club would be home.

There would still be one more planning application. In 2020, the Club applied to change the surface of the pitch from grass to a 4G artificial surface.

The Club applied to the Football Stadium Improvement Fund once the planning application was approved, in May 2019, and I sent a letter of support. I was delighted when they agreed to award the Club £500,000. In fact, I was at an event in London with Eamonn McGurk when the news came through that the bid had been successful.

The team off the pitch

The Football Club's Board had seen a fair number of people come and go. Earlier in this chapter, I mentioned how the Chairmanship of the Board had passed through several different sets of hands during my time as Leader. Some changes also took place to the Club's shareholders.

Chris Gabb, boss of Barnwood Construction & Shopfitting, acquired a stake in the Club and put his hand in his pocket to help keep the Club going through the years of exile. He wasn't necessarily a big football fan, but got involved for family reasons - his wife Sue's parents were involved in the Club and were stewards when the Club was in Longlevens. It was where Chris needed to go to win his lady! Chris took on the stadium project and certainly had the skills and drive to make it happen. His closest friend was Jeff Roberts of Roberts Limbrick Architects, whose firm worked on the project. Chris sadly died in 2019 without seeing the stadium rebuilt

But it was the introduction of Alex Petheram, boss of Soldi Construction, in the 2017/18 season, which gave the project real momentum. He became Co-Chairman along with Eamonn McGurk when Rod Jenner stepped down. Petheram is a friend of McGurk through business and comes from a footballing family – his uncle played with George Best. Born in Gloucester, he moved away to pursue his business career but his Dad still lives here. McGurk invited him to a match against Bath, then he agreed to a sponsorship deal and later he agreed to buy into the Club – and, as they say, the rest is history.

A crunch point came when City's temporary home at Evesham failed its ground grading for the following season. The League said City needed a sensible long-term option or they could face relegation. The Club considered yet another ground share and even spending money on Evesham's ground, but the best option was to speed up the return to Meadow Park.

As a Chartered Quantity Surveyor, Petheram looked at the existing plans and ripped them up, saying they were "unfundable and affordable". Planning consultant Rob Ellis, a local lad who had returned to the city after a spell working away, joined the Gloucester City AFC Board and piloted the revised planning application through the system. There was, perhaps unusually, praise for the city's planners who turned round the application quickly. Petheram seized the Stadium project and got moving on it, with him and McGurk each putting in what was described as a seven-figure sum in cash.

Before work could begin in earnest there was the not-so-small matter of relocating a 20m tall telephone mast which stood in the way of the pitch. Planning consent for its location was granted in September 2016 and it was moved in September 2018 – shortly after city marked 4000 days away from Meadow Park. When the mast came down, the Club evoked Shakespeare's Hamlet and tweeted

'Goodnight sweet prince'.

Petheram's business also supplied labour for the project free of charge and McGurk's plant hire company provided the kit at his cost. Patrick McGurk was often found operating the digger.

Alex Petheram and Eamonn McGurk worked on the drainage for the pitch together and worked throughout the project without ever falling out. The two were very different characters. Whereas McGurk preferred to stay in the background, Petheram was happier to be front and centre both in terms of the media and interacting with fans and players, whom he would greet with a fistbump! Malvern Tyres boss Rob Freeman, who grew up with Eamonn, became a director of the Club in 2019. The two of them would sit in the corner of the ground drinking beer every Friday while the project was underway and, without fail, would phone Petheram to joke that his "blokes are digging too deep" or some other wind-up. Rob Freeman sadly passed away in May 2021 after a short illness.

Help came in from across the football community. The plastic seats coming from China got caught up in the pandemic, so were instead supplied by a company in Derby who had provided them for the Plymouth Argyle stadium, which Alex's company had worked on. Plymouth's groundsman helped design the pitch, with the size and markings coming from Tottenham Hotspur's new £1 billion stadium. Bath City offered Gloucester a groundshare, on the basis of a handshake, in case the project wasn't finished in time. In the end, that wasn't needed. Representatives from Gloucester visited the ground of Marc White's Dorking Wanderers, who also have a 3G synthetic pitch. 46 shipping containers forming the stand around the pitch were ordered from Cleveland Containers. The playing surface was supplied by Tiger Turf, who announced a stadium sponsorship deal in March 2022.

Petheram's regular blogs on the project kept fans and other interested parties informed. His other main sporting interest was basketball, becoming co-owner of the City Knights team in 2021. There was even talk of building a new arena for them at Meadow Park. Jointly with McGurk, he created 'Gloucester Sport' to be the 'team behind the team', bringing in former professional basketball player Jay Marriott as Chief Executive.

It was a regret of mine that I wasn't able to watch Gloucester City

Football Club play in the city during my time as Leader. But I was able to stand down in the knowledge that the project was underway and it would happen. The 'New Meadow Park' stadium was completed in 2020, with the first game played in September (an FA Youth Cup under 18s match against Cirencester Town). In a cruel twist of fate, the first team's first competitive outing at the Stadium, against Kettering, had to be played behind closed doors because of pandemic-related restrictions. City ran out 3-1 winners. In a demonstration of how topsy-turvy the world had become, Gloucester City topped their league when the season was abandoned because of the pandemic while Gloucester Rugby were languishing at the bottom of the Premiership.

In December 2022, it was announced that McGurk and Petheram were standing down as co-chairmen, although they would retain ownership of the Club and Meadow Park ground. In January 2023, it was announced that Patrick Chambers, up to this point the Chairman of Hungerford Town, would take over as Chairman. His wife Nicky became Operations Director, but both left their positions in November 2023 following a poor start to the season by City.

19. PUTTING GLOUCESTER ON THE MAP

One of my frustrations when I took up office as Cabinet Member for Regeneration was the lack of joined-up efforts to promote the city. It's not that nobody was trying, but it just wasn't coherent or consistent and there wasn't a clear brand for the city.

Early efforts to create a strategy

There had been various efforts over the years to come up with one. Prior to me being elected as a councillor, in 1994, there was a fairly forgettable attempt to run a 'Go Gloucestering' campaign, which was run in newspapers across the Midlands and, according to reports at the time, caused the phones in the Tourism Office to ring off the hook. After that, it sank without trace. In the early 2000s, there was a more successful 'Gloucester's Great for …' campaign which gained some traction but it didn't amount to a proper strategy.

In 1998, the Council appointed Philip Cooke (formerly the Chief Leisure and Tourism Officer) as Director of Marketing and he produced a marketing strategy. But that was as much about improving the product as it was promoting it – and it never had the resources or focus to do either.

Philip Cooke's marketing strategy was honest about where the city found itself. It acknowledged that Gloucester "starts from a weak position" and that "existing marketing activity is poorly resourced, has no organisational focal point, weight or direction and there is very little material to work with". It recognised that "shops & hotels (are) poor, festivals and events weak, presentation of historic sites mixed". Interim targets included attracting new hotels and improving the bus station. Amongst the longer-term objectives were developing Gloucester as a destination shopping centre, building on the tourist potential of the Docks and establishing a public/private marketing partnership.

Philip left in 1999 and was replaced by a Head of Communications and Marketing for the Council, whose role it was to promote (and defend) the council rather than the city as a whole. The role was dubbed a "civic spin doctor" by the Western Daily Press. I commented at the time, "A marketing strategy has been written but no-one has the job of implementing it. It's likely now to just gather dust in a filing cabinet." And that's exactly what did happen.[284]

Pulling it all together

When we became the Administration in 2004, the elements of what was required were there but it all needed pulling together. Looking after the city centre was the Central Gloucester Initiative (CGI), run by City Centre Manager Richard Dennery. He was a charismatic American who sported a trademark bow tie. A recognisable figure, many people had heard of him but few seemed to understand what he did. I joked, perhaps unfairly, in a speech following the re-enactment of Dick Whittington's walk from Pauntley to London (in which he took part) that Dennery was like Whittington, saying that "most people didn't realise he existed and simply thought he was a mythical character." The CGI organised a successful annual Medieval Festival in Westgate Street and a legal conference bringing in a few dozen Americans to the University of Gloucestershire, but it didn't add up to a coherent programme for the city.

The Council's Tourism Team produced some great material and the Tourist Information Centre provided a first-class, and later multi-award winning, service. The small Economic Development Team put together an Economic Development and Tourism Strategy, but its scope was limited to the area for which they were responsible. The council also had a talented events team based at the Guildhall putting on some good community (but not really brand-building) events, but they too operated to a degree in isolation.

The Urban Regeneration Company recognised that effective marketing of the city was vital for Gloucester's regeneration programme to be delivered and, together with the City Council and the CGI, it commissioned consultants DTW to undertake a review in December 2005. At the time, Citizen Editor and URC Vice Chairman Ian Mean commented, "We feel strongly that the regeneration of Gloucester must go hand in glove with a coordinated marketing strategy to promote the city throughout the UK."[285]

Inevitably, comparisons were drawn with Cheltenham and DTW noted that "the city lags behind its more glamorous neighbours and major competitors". It added that the city's "potential outweighs the current offer and few people will travel to look at potential." Residents they spoke to commented that Gloucester was "a giant about to awake", "a city with huge potential but one which has lacked vision and has been hampered by negativity and division" and, cruelly, "like a neglected northern town with absolutely no status".

The consultants commented that "people of Gloucester are not taking enough pride in their city. It is imperative that levels of pride are improved" and noted that "eyesore buildings are in competition with iconic buildings like the Cathedral". They did compliment the Civic Trust, saying it was "a unique group which should be capitalised upon".

They recommended bringing the tourism, events and city centre management functions together but also made clear that the product needed to be improved before large-scale national promotion would be worthwhile – otherwise there would be the risk of people visiting, being disappointed and, like Dr Foster, not coming back again. They believed the proposed development at Gloucester Quays would both improve the city's offer and also bring resources, believed to be around £1 million a year, to promote it as a destination.

DTW's report stated that "only with true leadership and financial commitment will the results come through". They recommended the City Council chaired the board of the new organisation (although the Council's lawyers would later advise me the opposite!) and that a new post of Marketing Director should be created at a salary of approximately £50,000 a year. They were clear that to "do nothing is not an option". GHURC backed the Marketing Alliance with a commitment of £25,000 a year.[286]

The rationale for creating a new organisation wasn't just about better coordination. An arms-length company would be able to bring in funding not available to the Council, would be able to leverage the collective marketing strength of key attractions in the city like the Cathedral, Gloucester Rugby and Gloucester Quays and it could move more quickly without having to go through the Council's inevitably bureaucratic decision-making processes.

A new organisation

The Council's Tourism Manager Vicki Rowan, who tragically died from cancer some years later at the age of 40, was seconded to create a new organisation bringing together all of these activities. And so Marketing Gloucester Ltd (MGL) was born. It set about recruiting a Chief Executive on a £65,000 a year salary. There were around 100 applicants. It was announced in August 2008 that the successful applicant was Graham Walker, who had previously been Chief Executive of Sale Sharks and created the Rose Bowl stadium brand when at Hampshire County Cricket Club. His CV also included managing a £21 million debenture issue for Cardiff's Millennium Stadium and generating £25 million in sponsorship for the Football League. Although I wasn't involved in the recruitment process, it seemed like a good appointment and hopes were high that he would be able to work his magic in Gloucester.

Mark Owen, Chairman of the local branch of the Federation of Small Businesses and owner of a successful local agency, Moose Marketing and PR, agreed to join the board and was elected its first Chairman in 2008. The Board was made up of some good people – like Paul Chalmers, Manager of Kings Walk shopping centre, Neil Draper, his opposite number at Eastgate, GHURC's Chris Oldershaw, Anne-Marie Delrosa of train operator First Great Western, Franco Muccini from Gloucester Quays, Pete Grzonka of Gloucester Rugby and Paul Drake from the University of Gloucestershire.

The company set up offices in the Alexandra Warehouse at Gloucester Docks. The staff who moved over from the City Council – the likes of Dom Stevens, Lucy Wright, Sheila McDaid, Mhairi Smith and Kelly Gingell – were highly-regarded. Andrew Mitchell-Stead, who had done a great job programming acts at the Guildhall, joined a year later. Over the years, by and large, the company recruited well and had a team of very talented and committed people who went over and above what was required of them.

When the company was established, the country was going through a long and deep recession following the credit crunch, the task of getting private sector sponsorship (which was seen as one of the benefits of creating an arms-length company) was made far more difficult. One of the company's early pieces of work was to come up with a new branding for the city, 'Your Gloucester'- based on Marks & Spencer's 'Your M&S'. It was quite safe and did the job, but didn't strike me as particularly distinctive or exciting.

The difficult economic climate made it tough on the high street too and Gloucester suffered from an increased number of empty shops. Councillor Pam Tracey, in her unique direct style, collared Graham Walker at a Chamber of Trade dinner in 2009 and asked him what he was going to do about it. He said he had an idea. What he had in mind addressed the symptoms rather than the underlying cause. The company created a set of vinyls to put in vacant shop windows showing Gloucester Rugby players Iain Balshaw and Anthony Allen (who both left the Club before the vinyls came to the end of their life) dressed as Roman soldiers in the city's Eastgate Chamber. This got the city some excellent publicity, including at national level, although it did draw attention to our empty shops, but the cost was fairly substantial.

Financial Troubles - Part One

Due to the difficult economic climate as a result of the global financial crisis, some unexpected costs and the fact the company was set up without any reserves, Marketing Gloucester struggled financially. In particular, some events like the 2009 Tall Ships Festival – which was otherwise extremely successful (see chapter on Events) – cost more than anticipated. The full-year loss for its first year of trading turned out to be £165,000, as shown in the 2010 accounts lodged at Companies House.

In September 2010, word got out that the company was in trouble and the City Council set about bailing it out. Christmas activities that year were slashed and the Council pulled out of jointly funding the Victorian Christmas Market with Gloucester Quays. A number of staff were made redundant. The City Centre Management function transferred back to the City Council. Graham Walker left in October that year. The outstanding debt to the Council was converted to a loan which sat on the company's balance sheet. A number of directors stood down – all of whom worried, understandably, about the impact on their professional lives. I took over as Chair on what was meant to be a temporary basis. It wasn't ideal, as I had a potential conflict of interest - meaning I couldn't take part in decisions on council funding for MGL. But I took the view that this was manageable and, for most of the time at least, what was good for MGL should be good for the council and the city as a whole. I also couldn't devote huge amounts of time to it - outside of board meetings and major events, I could only give it, literally, an hour or two a week.

Chris Oldershaw had sat on the Board to represent the Gloucester Heritage Urban Regeneration Company, who continued to put money into Marketing Gloucester. He was persuaded, although he wasn't a marketeer, to become Chief Executive of MGL as well as GHURC. He was a steady pair of hands and would ensure the figures came in on budget and reports to the Board were comprehensive. The company even made modest surpluses which were used to repay some of the City Council loan. When GHURC was finally wound up, Chris decided not to apply for the permanent position of Chief Executive and left the company in the summer of 2013.

A new Chief Executive

The company advertised for a new Chief Executive, based on the two days a week that Chris worked. The interview panel was Citizen Editor Ian Mean (by now an MGL director), fellow director Nick Bishop (an accountant and partner with Pitt, Godden & Taylor) and me. I was supported by City Council officers through the process. We had a good range of candidates to choose from, including an internal one and the head of a destination marketing organisation from elsewhere. We chose Jason Smith, a marketing professional with a business background who grew up in Gloucester, based on his business experience and his clear enthusiasm for the city and the role. His maternal grandfather John Rigby ran the fish stall in the Eastgate Market and was President of the Chamber of Trade. Ian Mean later wrote in an article, "We spent a day interviewing eight very good candidates for the job and Jason clearly showed us he has the skills and experience needed for this important role."

Jason Smith took up his position in January 2014. He was full of energy and you couldn't doubt his passion for Gloucester. He got on well with, and had the support of, lots of people, but there were others with whom his relationship wasn't so positive - including, later, some senior officers at the City Council. I did my best to smooth things over, but as is often the way, these relationships were difficult to manage.

Solid Achievement

The next couple of years would be a period of solid achievement. The events programme, including the Tall Ships Festival, grew in quality and impact. The preparations for the Rugby World Cup, including securing funding for a cultural programme and sponsorship for the Scrumpty sculpture trail (see the chapter on Rugby and Regeneration) were one example. MGL sorted out sponsorship for roundabouts in the city, which council officers had been trying to do for years, giving the council an ongoing income. The 'Believe in Gloucester' campaign was another achievement. It was based on Peel boss John Whittaker commenting, when announcing another chunk of investment at Gloucester Quays, that he "believed in Gloucester". The campaign was launched in 2012 by rugby star Phil Vickery and struck a chord. In July 2013, Gloucestershire Media launched the 'Believe in Gloucester' awards, with MGL as a key partner. The sponsorship opportunities and tickets for the event, held at Kingsholm, soon sold out. The event became one of the highlights of the year. I was gutted to miss the first event in November 2013 as I was working away – especially an impassioned acceptance speech by Paul Soden, owner of Café Rene, (who sadly passed away in 2022) who may have been speaking with the aid of some Dutch courage! I was sad to see that the event didn't return after the pandemic, until it was brought back by the Gloucester BID in 2024, and I was proud to have won the 'Lifetime Achievement Award' at the ceremony in 2019.

In 2015, Gloucester overtook Cheltenham in terms of the number of day visitors and the total spend of visitors. By 2018, visitor spend in the city had reached £212 million - a 68% increase on 2010. Marketing Gloucester was innovative and creative in how it put Gloucester on the map. The re-enactment of the Coronation of Henry III in Gloucester Cathedral in 2016, to mark its 800th anniversary, gained national and international publicity, including in Italy and China. We badged 2015, with the Rugby World Cup and the Tall Ships Festival, as 'Our BiG Year' (for 'Believe in Gloucester'). The branding for this was widely-used on everything from lapel badges to the back of Stagecoach buses to bags from Hudson's sports shop and this was perhaps the most successful attempt at branding for the city.

Marketing Gloucester also transformed Gloucester's digital promotion. MGL's social media channels and website built up a good reach – even to this day the Visit Gloucester Twitter account has more followers than Visit Cheltenham, due largely to the work put in by the MGL team.

Funding reductions

MGL continued to make modest surpluses up to and including the year ending 31st March 2016, which chipped away at the deficit sitting on the balance sheet. The City Council was still facing severe financial challenges, which had been ongoing since 2011 when the Coalition Government started to cut local government funding as it battled to get the country's books back to balance. The Council had so far protected MGL's funding, rightly in my view, as growing the visitor economy was seen as a priority. But questions were being asked why that had gone on for so long when others, particularly the voluntary sector (the likes of the Law Centre and Citizens Advice Bureau), had seen their funding sliced year on year. I could understand that. Because of my position as Chair of the Board I was excluded from any Cabinet discussion about MGL's funding and Cabinet Members were very sensitive about even the suggestion of me lobbying privately about it, so I didn't. I had to leave that to other board members.

Funding was cut by £100,000 in 2016/17 and by another £100,000 the year after. This was around half of the company's overall funding from the council and about two thirds of the funding towards core running costs as the £160,000 events budget was effectively ringfenced. In reality the events cost far more than the grant given, but that extra cost got lost in the core funding part of the grant. It's true that MGL had income from other sources, particularly sponsorship, but those tended to relate to a particular event or activity rather than pay towards running costs. Some years, mainly when the Tall Ships Festival was held, MGL's turnover was close to £1 million – more than double its grant from the council.

Plans were put forward to make up the shortfall, but they were never agreed by the council. The issue just drifted and the funding cut was imposed. The problem was that those involved liked the work the company was doing and didn't want it to stop, but wanted it to be done with a lot less funding – which proved impossible. The company made efforts to cut costs, including moving offices, cutting staff costs and looking to bring in new sources of income.

The company lost £50,000 in 2016/17 (compared with a £100,000 cut in funding) and £100,000 in each of 2017/18 and 2018/19 (compared with a £200,000 cut in funding in each of those years) – so it had delivered half of its savings target without stopping doing anything, which in itself was quite an achievement, but it just wasn't enough. The losses weren't a secret - the accounts were published online by Companies House and the Council had to sign them off each year to confirm they still supported the company financially so the auditors could say the company was a 'going concern'.

A BID for Gloucester

The City Council had been trying for some time to bring forward a Business Improvement District (BID) for the city centre. This is where a small levy is added to the business rates bill and the funding is used for activities to support the businesses in that area – by implementing priorities that they have helped to formulate. The proposal needs to be approved by eligible businesses in a ballot. When the City Council's Economic Development Team was leading the process, it was struggling to get any momentum. Jason Smith and the MGL team picked this up and ran with it, achieving an 83% approval vote in the ballot in July 2017. Nick Brookes, who ran the Knobbly Cobb sandwich bar in Westgate Street and was the Chair of the BID steering group, said, "I'm delighted by this amazing result which provides us with a strong and clear mandate to deliver on behalf of the businesses in the BID area. I'm confident the BID will have a huge positive impact on the city." The agreed priorities were more events, marketing and the introduction of 'City Protection Officers' to deal with low level crime and anti-social behaviour and provide a reassuring presence. These were co-funded by the City Council and the Police & Crime Commissioner.

Jason Smith and MGL managed the BID and organised events to drive footfall for them for an agreed fee, including the Folk Trail, the Country Music Festival and Civil War re-enactments in Gloucester Park (which brought 1000 thirsty re-enactors to stay in the city, camping at Westgate Park). This was another example of the efforts

MGL made to bring in income from other sources. In the end, the BID outlasted MGL and former Marketing Gloucester employee Emily Gibbon was appointed manager of the BID in November 2020. I was delighted when the BID secured a second five-year term in its renewal ballot in June 2022, with over 70% of businesses voting in favour.

The UK Digital Retail Innovation Centre

Marketing Gloucester had an aim in its 2016-21 Business Plan to put Gloucester at the forefront of the digital high street revolution and to be a testbed for new technologies. In 2016, there was an opportunity to apply for £400,000 in funding from the GFirst Local Enterprise Partnership for a project known as 'Retail Lab'. This was about encouraging entrepreneurs to try out their retail ideas without the big commitment of taking on premises etc. Initially the LEP were keen to locate this at Gloucester Quays, but this didn't fit comfortably with their Outlet Centre planning status (which required the sale of discounted goods) or our desire to support the city centre. It looked at one point as though it might go to Cheltenham. Jason Smith saw the opportunity and put together an application for the funding. I was happy to support it as it was a good thing for the city. Senior City Council officers were aware of the project, with one including it in a presentation to an outside organisation of all the good things happening in the city. Marketing Gloucester was required to ask the council for formal approval to enter into transactions over £100,000. In this case it didn't, which was a management failing. But the council did know about the project and didn't ask the company to request a formal consent.

The funding bid was approved in January 2018 and what would become known as the UK Digital Retail Innovation Centre (UKDRIC) was established on the first floor of the Eastgate Shopping Centre, transforming the former Food Court area which had sat empty for many years. LEP Chair Diane Savory OBE said, "This is an exciting opportunity as it further demonstrates that our urban areas are proving to be leaders in the development of innovation of digital retail solutions."

Jason Smith was quoted saying, "This is a huge opportunity for Gloucester to progress our ambition to be a showcase and testbed for digital technologies. There are huge challenges facing the UK retail sector and the UKDRIC has the potential to be a gamechanger which could have a far-reaching impact."

The City Council owned the freehold of the centre and would later buy in the long lease, giving it full control of the centre – so ultimately the project enhanced its asset. The works were carried out by local company Barnwood Shopfitting. The centre opened in May 2019 with a formal ceremony with the then Digital Minister Margot James MP and LEP Chair Diane Savory.

The ultimate demise of MGL forced the closure of the UKDRIC in February 2020. This was a great shame, given that the physical work had been done to create it. The centre would have been of huge value during the pandemic, when online sales rocketed, and in a post-Covid world where a digital presence remains of huge importance to retailers.

Financial Troubles - Part Two

There weren't many things which kept me awake at night, but MGL's financial position did. The reasons for this were numerous. The principal factor was the reduction in funding from the council, which amounted to £500,000 over three years, but there were others. The Tall Ships Festival in May 2017 took place the weekend after the bombing of an Ariana Grande concert in Manchester, which affected attendance and therefore income. Having police wandering around with machine guns and strategically parked cars to block vehicle-based terrorist attacks was a little unsettling. This gave the company another financial hit.

There was also disagreement as to whether the 2017/18 events programme could be delivered within the budget available, including a disputed invoice for the 'Kings Jam' event (a grime music festival in Kings Square) which was never paid.

MGL tried other ways to generate extra funds, including offering to promote the Council's car parks to earn income for both parties, but this particular idea wasn't adopted despite many months of negotiation. The company had hoped that the 2019 Tall Ships Festival would return a healthy surplus to bolster its finances, but in the end the profit was fairly modest.

I had offered on a number of occasions to stand aside as chair of the company, but there were no takers – perhaps unsurprisingly given the challenges it faced, particularly financially. I did enjoy the role and the ability of the company to get things done, but I couldn't give it the time it really needed. In May 2019, my deputy Jennie Watkins offered to replace me. It didn't resolve the issue around conflicts of interest, but having someone new I felt was a good thing, so I stood down as chair and from the board entirely.

In summer 2019, it emerged that the company needed an injection of cash in order to stay afloat. This came as a shock to many of us, but perhaps shouldn't have done given the years of accumulated losses. The council's solution was to lend the company £240,000. The Liberal Democrats, predictably, 'called in' the decision which meant it had to go to a special meeting of the council's Overview & Scrutiny Committee. I didn't have to appear in front of the committee at this stage, although I would later appear twice (in December 2019 and March 2020, spending several hours answering questions in public). It divided on party political lines and the decision was confirmed. This meant the funding could be released to the company and they could pay the bills. But from then on things unravelled at an increasing pace.

Liquidation and the end of MGL

In February 2020, the MGL Board decided to put the company into liquidation. The directors' statement said that the company's deficit was just under £1 million – a headline figure which was widely reported in the media. The £1 million figure included the £400,000 grant from the Local Enterprise Partnership for the UKDRIC, which theoretically was repayable if the centre ceased to operate – but the LEP's Chief Executive had gone on record to say they were satisfied the funding had been spent in the way that was intended. The list of creditors was long – from well-known businesses in the city to the man who put up the Christmas lights. It saddened me that local businesses were losing out and I couldn't understand how the finances had suddenly got so bad. It had been the board's belief that the City Council was underwriting the company's finances, but the council disputed this and the legal documents relating to this point were ambiguous. Staff were made redundant, although a few were taken on by the City Council on short-term contracts to continue to deliver marketing activity for the city.

The company's liquidators, Bishop Fleming, confirmed to me in October 2020 that the "reality is rather different". The company's 'debt' was not £1 million at all but just over £420,000[287], offset by £30,000 the company had in the bank. £340,000 of the 'debt' was to the City Council, so the true figure was about £50,000 of non-council creditors - although that number may be slightly understated because some creditors decided not to lodge a claim with the liquidator. That's nothing to be proud of, but a far cry from the £1 million figure quoted in the media. It also needs to be seen in the context of the £500,000 reduction in City Council funding and the historic debt which had sat on the company's balance sheet since 2010.

In September 2020, a story appeared in the media of how allegations about the management of Marketing Gloucester and Gloucester BID had been referred to the Police, after they had been raised in a Full Council meeting. The Police confirmed in writing to me in August 2021 that they had found nothing that was worthy of investigation (let alone charging anyone!) and had referred the matter to the City of London Police for a second opinion, who had reached the same conclusion. The City Council was informed of the outcome in March 2021

The City Council bought all of MGL's assets from the liquidator, including the UKDRIC, for a token £2,000. In the financial year 2020/21, when MGL's functions were brought back in-house, despite activity being curtailed by the pandemic the City Council spent £140,000 more on events and destination marketing than it gave Marketing Gloucester the previous year. In the financial year 2021/22, the council budgeted £200,000 more than the grant given to MGL. This gave credence to those who believed the council had been asking the impossible of MGL and an admission that the council couldn't itself deliver what it was asking of MGL within the budget it had granted the company.

The Covid-19 pandemic hit in March 2020, meaning the media focus was, quite rightly, elsewhere from then onwards, and the outcomes of allegations which had previously appeared were never reported.

I stood down from the City Council at the end of June 2020. My departure had been delayed by the postponement of the City

Council elections in May 2020, due to the Coronavirus pandemic. I worried that the momentum that MGL had helped to create over the last decade would be lost with the company's demise. I wasn't the only person to have that concern. In their 48th Annual Report, in April 2020, Gloucester Civic Trust chairman, Robin Morris, said, "The promotion of Gloucester under the stewardship of Jason Smith at Marketing Gloucester has been an outstanding success. This is in comparison with the previous feeble achievements of earlier efforts where there were no tangible results. One suspects that any successor organisation will revert to form."

The pandemic has made it difficult to judge what effect it has had. The value of Gloucester's visitor spend tumbled from £221 million in 2019 to just £99 million in 2020 and had only recovered to £160 million in 2021 - the last set of figures available.[288] Many comment that the city has lost some of its 'buzz' since the energetic and creative team at MGL was disbanded and the function went back 'in-house' to the City Council. Some others will, no doubt, take a different view. Only time will tell who is right.

20. A BALANCED APPROACH

Regeneration shouldn't just be about buildings. Physical change is important in terms of creating a better environment and engendering civic pride. But on its own it isn't enough. After all, government, both national and local, should be about improving the lives of people. The example of London's Canary Wharf was often quoted, where billions of pounds went into regenerating the area and creating plush and iconic new office buildings, but local people – many of whom lived in poverty – saw no benefit from it. I was determined this wouldn't happen in Gloucester, but delivering that in practice was difficult.

Tackling Deprivation

Areas of the city were, and still are, in the top 10% most deprived in the country. These include parts of Westgate, Podsmead, Matson and Barton & Tredworth wards. How to tackle this was something we wrestled with. In the early days particularly, it was hard enough to get investor and developer interest and to get development schemes to stack up commercially, without adding additional costs in terms of local labour clauses or social value requirements.

So, our approach was to try and bring in extra resources from the public sector and other sources. One example was when I was told that the Big Local (which was announced by the Big Lottery Fund, funded through the National Lottery, in July 2010) were looking for an area of the city to invest in. I recommended Podsmead for funding of £1 million over 10 years. I was delighted when that proposal was accepted. The announcement was made in February 2012. The Big Local works in 150 different local areas across the country, supported by a national organisation called Local Trust.

In Podsmead, the money has been used so far to provide a new play area and to introduce accessible play equipment at another; to improve public open spaces by clearing areas overgrown with brambles, plant flower meadows and lay new paths and to support community organisations. Events, like picnics in the park, have been put on to bring the community together. Local residents were involved in making the funding decisions. Podsmead's Big Local also took a lead supporting the community during the pandemic. They have worked closely with the team behind plans for a new sports hub at Blackbridge in Podsmead, particularly on the community aspect of the project. The Blackbridge Charitable Community Benefit Society will be the legacy organisation for the Big Local when it comes to an end in 2026.

Addressing Unemployment

Unemployment in Gloucester has been consistently the highest in the County, although not particularly high by national standards. It has been stubbornly high in the wards where deprivation is most acute. We sought to tackle this with the City Employment and Skills Programme, otherwise known as 'Gloucester Works'. This was financed by £6 million from the European Social Fund and other partners and was designed to give unemployed people in these areas the skills needed to match the vacancies that businesses struggled to fill.

The Director of the programme was my old Crypt School contemporary Ahmed Goga who went on to hold senior positions with Oxfordshire's Local Enterprise Partnership and the CBI. Ahmed told me he had a meeting in 2007 with City Council Chief Executive Julian Wain and Marinos Paphitis, Area Director of the Learning and Skills Council and older brother of Dragons Den star Theo Paphitis, to come up with the concept. They put together the business case with Ian Knight of the Regional Development Agency and commissioned consultants Shared Intelligence to undertake statistical and labour market work. The partners were the City Council, the County Council, Jobcentre Plus, the Urban Regeneration Company, Gloucestershire First, the Learning and Skills Council, NHS Gloucestershire and the Regional Development Agency. Preparatory work got underway in October 2007 with the programme formally commencing in August 2008 and running until June 2011.

The programme ran from Neighbourhood Job Hubs, including the

Trust Centre in Barton and Gloucester Library in the city centre, alongside a dedicated hub on Bristol Road run by Prospect Training. It worked in Podsmead, Matson, White City, Coney Hill, Moreland and Kingsholm as well as in Barton & Tredworth and Westgate (principally the city centre). The programme gave help to jobseekers through help with CV writing, job searching and referral to one of the 20 training providers involved. On the employer side, there was an 'integrated offer' with aftercare and a single point of contact.

An Employer Development Programme ran in Gloucester Quays and the city centre, designed to ensure local people benefited from the jobs being created by the city's regeneration programme. In total, over 300 employers were engaged with. A training review was undertaken with each company, with the aim of upskilling people within the business.

In a report to the City Council's Overview & Scrutiny Committee in February 2010, Ahmed Goga reported that by the end of 2009 the programme had helped 400 people back into work and assisted just under 3000 people in some form or other. The figure had risen to over 600 people back into work by October 2010. This was despite the difficult economic climate at the time following the financial crash of 2008. In particular, Rank Xerox at Mitcheldean had made a large number of redundancies and those who had lost their jobs and were more 'work ready' were competing with the people who Gloucester Works were trying to help, even if it was only until a better job came along. According to an evaluation report in September 2011, by the end of the programme 870 businesses had been assisted, over 4200 people had been helped to develop their skills and over 1100 people had been moved off benefits and into employment.

When the programme ended, sadly nothing took its place – at least not on the scale that Gloucester Works was able to achieve with its multi-million-pound funding. Despite the best efforts of those working in this sphere, those areas of stubbornly high unemployment still exist today, showing that this is an issue that you can never declare has been tackled for good.

Culture

Culture is important too. In many ways Gloucester is rich in culture, with a diverse population and, according to some, over 200 languages spoken in the Barton & Tredworth area alone. But in other ways it has been considered a 'cultural desert'. The Guildhall is the city's biggest dedicated venue but can only seat 250 in its biggest space, limiting the range of performances it can put on. Theatre provision too is constrained. The Kings Theatre in Kingsbarton Street is run by volunteers but has a capacity of around 100. The Olympus Theatre in Barton Street, where I shared the part of Alderman Fitzwarren with Mark Hawthorne in the Dick Whittington pantomime in 2005, was sold by the Gloucester Operatic and Dramatic Society in 2007. Since then, it has only been open sporadically, but, in more recent times, a project led by Phil McCormick, boss of Nicks Timber and a stalwart of the city's arts scene, sought to reopen it as a community theatre, but ultimately those plans didn't come off. Neither venue has the scale or funding of Cheltenham's Everyman Theatre.

In July 2007, the City Council adopted a document by ABL Cultural Consulting called 'Towards a Cultural Strategy', which had been commissioned jointly with the County Council and the Urban Regeneration Company. It sought to reposition Gloucester as "the South West's most happening place to live, work and play" that was "not an average Cathedral city". It noted that the city suffered from low aspiration, low participation and poor self-image in cultural terms and suggested the city's residents should have a "cultural entitlement".

It recommended seven "action areas", including "making sense of the city centre" (i.e. better signage, public art and even a "heritage orientation centre"), "raising the stakes for creativity", "broadening excellence in sport", "enjoying and supporting diversity" and "planning for a transformational project". Part of what was recommended around creativity included making provision for growth in the creative industries. In later years, incubator hubs were established at the Alexandra Warehouse in the Docks and the former Blackfriars Inn in Commercial Road, before the JOLT facility was opened at Kings House. The report also recommended a "music and media hub", which you could argue was what The Music Works delivered at Kings House over a decade later. In terms of the "transformational project", ABL suggested it could be a "living heritage attraction" based on historic shipbuilding with an adjacent film centre.

The ABL report was the framework for a cultural strategy rather than the whole picture, but it was adopted as the strategy anyway. Shortly after it was adopted the lead officer who was dealing with it left, austerity hit and it wasn't fully progressed in the way that was intended. Update reports were given to Cabinet regularly but these tended to be lists of cultural activity which probably would have happened anyway.

The ABL document was a 10-year strategy and it was updated ahead of time in March 2016 when a new Cultural Strategy for the city was adopted. The strategy had the strapline of "Putting Culture at the Heart of Gloucester for the Good of All" – something which Dean of Gloucester Stephen Lake had come up with. The strategy envisaged that "Gloucester would be known for its distinctive culture" which would be "innovative and excellent, quirky and edgy, diverse and community-based, with a strong focus on young people". Its objectives included developing artists and arts organisations, broadening the cultural offer, developing audiences, putting Gloucester on the map (including evaluating a potential bid to be City of Culture) and setting up a Culture Board (which evolved into a Culture Trust).

In the introduction, Councillor Lise Noakes, who I brought into the Cabinet to focus on Culture and Leisure, noted that Gloucester still had "a long way to go to have the cultural offering residents deserve". Phil Gibby, the Arts Council's Area Director for the South West, added that culture "creates jobs and economic growth and builds strong communities".

The Arts Council had not provided any substantial funding to the city for some time, but the £80,000 awarded for the cultural programme which ran alongside the 2015 Rugby World Cup seemed to prise that door open again. The creation of the Gloucester Culture Board, which later became the Gloucester Culture Trust, pushed it wide open. The Board had a wealth of good quality members such as University Vice Chancellor Stephen Marston and Anne Cranston, who had been heading up the Cathedral's Project Pilgrim. Hollie Smith-Charles, who had worked at Cheltenham Festivals, was recruited as the Trust's Director. In March 2017, the Trust was successful in applying for £1.5 million of funding from the 'Great Places' fund from the Arts Council and Heritage Lottery Fund, which was matched by £1.6 million of funding from a variety of partners including the Paul Hamlyn Foundation. The funding was used to support a variety of different organisations to develop talent and enable more people in the city to get creative.

Many people felt that Gloucester needed a larger performance venue to attract bigger acts to the city and stop people having to go to larger cities like Bristol and Birmingham for their entertainment. Marketing Gloucester took up this issue, with Chief Executive Jason Smith saying, "The research we have done is that a multi-use venue with a capacity of between 1300 and 1800, coupled with a four-star hotel, would be ideal for Gloucester. It would be the place which would have concerts, touring West End shows, conferences and banquets."[289]

In November 2018, the Culture Trust, using funding from the Great Places programme, commissioned AEA Consulting to look into the feasibility of a performance venue of around 1000 seats. Their report said that embarking on a new venue at this point would be "premature" and it would only work in Gloucester if there was "concerted investment in growing audiences and getting people involved as volunteers, performers and back stage."[290] At the time, Adrian Ellis of AEA said, "We looked at a number of different arts venues around the country; some flourishing, others less so. A new arts centre is an exciting prospect for any county and can be a fantastic asset, but a lot of work needs to be done beforehand, usually over several years, if it is to thrive. Successful venues have a clear mission, strong leadership, active audiences, robust partnerships, and reliable funding. All of these things need to be in place if a venue is to prosper."

I responded, saying, "I know that many people in the city are keen for us to have a new and larger performance venue, but it is important that we don't create a 'white elephant' or risk public money, which we know is in short supply. This is a comprehensive and well researched report. It provides a clear way forward towards achieving our ambition to deliver a commercially sustainable new venue in Gloucester for performance, events and conferences. By working together, I am confident we can put in place the conditions we need to ensure the success of a new venue for the city." The demise of Marketing Gloucester, the pandemic and economic uncertainty all conspired to push this issue firmly onto the backburner.

There was talk of a City of Culture bid during my time as Leader, but no firm decision was made as there seemed no likelihood of a cross-party consensus, which I felt was needed. However, the City Council announced in June 2021 that it would be bidding for City of Culture 2025, saying it was a "serious contender" and winning would put the city and county on the map.

In a rapid about-turn, the bid was abandoned just a few weeks later, in July 2021. The Council said it would not submit an expression of interest as the bid needed "significant resources" and it wanted to focus on the city's recovery from the pandemic instead. Gloucester Culture Trust said it was disappointed as it "wholeheartedly believed" it would have been chosen. Opposition groups were worried that a bid would have been "all-consuming" and several key stakeholders were believed not to have been consulted before the announcement was made.

Good news on the cultural front came in November 2022 when both Gloucester Guildhall and Gloucester Culture Trust were announced as part of Arts Council England's National Portfolio, meaning a three-year funding deal. The Guildhall was awarded £250,000 a year. The funding allows the venue to offer workshops and programmes that enable communities from across the city to develop and showcase new skills in dance, circus, live music and performance. Gloucester Culture Trust secured £150,000 a year to support others in developing the cultural offer.

They joined Strike A Light, a drama and dance organisation based in the city, who became National Portfolio Organisation in 2018, initially gaining £85,000 a year, which rose to almost £250,000 a year for the 2023-26 period. Strike A Light have been involved in a range of events across the city over a number of years, including the Rooftop Festival, Bright Nights and the launch of the new Kings Square.

Housing

Poor housing is one of the greatest contributors to the deprivation indicators and, more importantly, to people's life chances and their health. In the early 2000s, Gloucester's 4500 council houses and flats were generally in a fairly poor state and the way they were managed was rated poor by the Audit Commission. An options appraisal was undertaken in 2003 to assess how the Council would find the £40 million shortfall to meet the Government's 'Decent Homes Standard' by 2010 (later extended to 2012). In 2005 Gloucester City Homes (GCH) was set up as an 'Arms-Length Management Organisation' (ALMO), a move which was supported by 73% of tenants. As the name suggests, this took it one step away from the Council and gave it the freedom to change the way it worked. The project to establish GCH was headed up by Ashley Green, a Gloucester boy who had worked his way up to be the Head of Revenues at the City Council and went on to be GCH's Chief Executive.

Ashley stepped in after the previous Head of Housing Management left in controversial circumstances, with a pay-off financed from tenants' rents, which later became public. Ashley led the Housing Management service as well as keeping his previous role as Head of Revenues and Benefits for a year, before heading up the new project. The Government decided that funding for the Decent Homes programme wouldn't be given to Councils – only ALMOs. GCH initially moved out of the council offices to Southgate House in Southgate Street before later moving to Railway House on Bruton Way.

GCH had to improve the customer service for tenants. In the summer of 2005, the Council's housing department received a zero-star (poor) rating and GCH had to be awarded a two-star (good) rating to unlock £38.6 million of Government funding – something it achieved in 2007. In addition, the City Council contributed around £15 million. Getting two stars was in Ashley's contract and failure would have resulted in his dismissal. Cabinet Member for Housing and Health, Andrew Gravells, was concerned about the consequences, particularly for tenants, of falling short. GCH went on to be awarded the top rating of three stars (excellent service) in November 2010.

I was proud to be Leader when the Council's housing stock was brought up to 'Decent Homes Standard'. In fact, GCH had developed a 'Gloucester Standard' set by GCH tenants, which exceeded the Government's guidelines. In real terms, this meant double glazing, new electrics, new bathrooms and kitchens and new heating systems. The programme was completed in 2012. To give credit where it is due, GCH was set up under a previous administration and the approval for the Decent Homes programme, which was paid for by borrowing, was given by the Labour Government.

It bought us some time, but wasn't the complete answer as the projections for future years showed that the Council would struggle to find the money it needed to maintain the housing stock to an acceptable level. The borrowing for the Decent Homes programme pushed the Council's Housing Revenue Account (which, by law, was separate from its non-housing budget) towards its borrowing cap. The challenges included the age of the stock and the fact that 33% of it was of non-traditional construction (i.e. not brick). GCH were also keen to build new affordable housing and didn't want to let the hard-won gains of the Decent Homes programme slip back.

In 2010-11, a 'Housing Options Appraisal' was undertaken, working with tenants and across all political parties, and the best way forward was seen as transferring the stock to Gloucester City Homes, who would be set free of constraints imposed on councils by becoming a housing association. Transferring the housing stock was a sensitive issue in Gloucester. In the late 1980s, there was a proposal to sell the City's Council homes to North Housing – a Newcastle-based housing association. This was hugely controversial at the time and is a story in itself. Indeed, a book has been written on this subject. Such was the controversy that the police had to attend council meetings to ensure the safety of councillors and the protests turned into some of the bitterest and most personal ever seen in the history of local government in Gloucester.

The issue contributed to the Conservatives losing control of the City Council at a by-election following the death of Westgate councillor Len Journeaux. The proposal was abandoned by the new Labour/Liberal administration before it got to a vote of the tenants. The Conservatives would be out of power in Gloucester for the next 15 years but, in a twist of irony, Andrew Gravells who was Chairman of the Housing Committee when the North Housing proposal was put forward was the Cabinet Member for Housing when the GCH transfer was being progressed. In the end, he left the Cabinet to take up a County Council role and Colin Organ was the Cabinet Member who finally got it over the line.

In October 2013, there was some media reporting that a "decision to sell off 5500 homes" was approved by the Cabinet in just 13 minutes. In reality, the debate had taken place and the work had been done long before it came to Cabinet. And, ultimately, it wasn't our decision, but the tenants'.

Whereas some councils have become cash-rich by selling off their housing stock, Gloucester wasn't in that position. The figures would only work if the Government was persuaded to write off a huge chunk of housing debt – over £50 million. City MP Richard Graham lobbied the Government hard on this and I was personally handed a letter by Housing Minister Kris Hopkins confirming the write-off on a visit to Gloucester in April 2014. He told me he'd signed it in the pub the night before. I didn't know if he was joking and I didn't care. (He later confirmed to me that was true!) It was the most valuable piece of paper from the whole of my time as council leader. The transfer was approved by tenants in a ballot in September 2014 with an overwhelming 89% voting in favour on a 64% turnout.

In March 2015, GCH became an independent housing association, taking ownership of the stock. The final document was signed at 8pm on Tuesday 16th March 2015 after three sets of lawyers, some of whom camped out in my office, hammered out the final details. So intense was the final legal work that the lawyers racked up £48,000 in fees in a single day!

Chancellor George Osborne announced a 1% rent reduction just two months later, which reduced the valuation of the housing stock by £30 million, meaning the Council should have paid GCH £9 million to take the properties off its hands!

Since becoming a housing association, GCH has brought over £100 million of investment to the city and delivered more than 500 new homes, with plans for another 500 by 2030. It spends £5 million a year maintaining the stock and employs 170 staff.

The stock transfer didn't solve the problem completely as large parts of the housing stock needed major regeneration in the long-term, particularly Matson and Podsmead. Both had poor quality tower blocks, prefab bungalows and the condition of housing

21. LEADERSHIP AND DELIVERY

Regeneration is a team game. No one person can deliver it on their own. When you have long-term projects, they are likely to last beyond the electoral lifetime of what legendary Question Time host, and former Crypt School pupil, Sir Robin Day described as "here today, gone tomorrow politicians". Some in the business say that "regeneration is a marathon, not a sprint". Even my sixteen years at the forefront of the city's regeneration efforts weren't long enough to see the job through fully. In some ways, regeneration is like painting the Forth Bridge – once you think you've finished it, it's time to start at the beginning again.

One advantage of being in a small city like Gloucester is that everyone knows each other. One key figure in the Urban Regeneration Company said to me that, because of this, if an issue arose on a Friday people would talk to each other over the weekend and everything would be sorted by Monday.

Because regeneration doesn't work neatly within electoral cycles – because things like land acquisition, planning, legal work, archaeology and utility diversions all take time before anything comes out of the ground – it's important to have cross-party consensus where possible, so developers can take long-term investment decisions knowing that a change in the political leadership isn't going to throw it all up in the air.

Regeneration takes a mix of skills and there are a whole range of people in the background working away on the essential detail of any scheme. But it needs leadership. Someone has to have the vision, the determination, the persistence and the patience (as Peel's John Whittaker put it) to see it through. Someone has to lead from the front, to give direction and be prepared to put themselves in the firing line – because, as I very quickly learnt, you can't please all of the people all of the time. Part of the criticism of politicians is that they are taking the credit for other people's work. That is, to some degree, fair because we don't directly deliver the regeneration but on the flip-side we also get the criticism when things go wrong which we weren't directly responsible for either – but that's what leadership is all about.

The aim of this chapter is to identify some of the key people involved in the city's regeneration and to give credit where it is due. It won't be possible to name everyone, just because of the sheer numbers involved. Many of those who are due credit will not be familiar names to everyone as they have worked behind the scenes and never sought the limelight. But let's deal with the politicians first.

It is only in relatively recent times that political parties and candidates in Gloucester have felt the need to show their regeneration credentials. Only in the last twenty years have the City's successive Members of Parliament become involved in regeneration, both as the need for it has increased and the expectations of what they should do locally have grown. You can argue that during Sally Oppenheim's tenure from 1970-87, the city didn't really need regeneration as it had only just been through a development boom. Douglas French served from 1987-97 but was more focused on other constituency issues. I'm not sure Tess Kingham ever became involved with regeneration during her brief stint as City MP from 1997-2001, although she did rail against (pun intended) the state of the subway from the station to Great Western Road and vowed to sort it out – something we now have £6 million of funding to address a quarter of a century on.

Parmjit Dhanda, who served for two terms between 2001-2010, deserves credit on a number of fronts. It was his question at Prime Minister's Question Time that sparked the creation of the Urban Regeneration Company. His lobbying and his willingness to use Parliamentary devices to highlight the needs of the constituency brought in funding for the South West bypass and the Docks linkages, amongst other things. He also brokered the meeting that unlocked the building of the new Gloucestershire College campus at Llanthony, freeing up the Brunswick Road sites for housing development.

Richard Graham has taken a similarly energetic approach to his role in regeneration, campaigning before his election in 2010 that it should be "across the city, not just at the Docks". He deserves credit for championing the regeneration of the Railway Triangle, despite protests that it should be the site of a new railway station. His support for the bids for Government funding for the bus station/transport hub, Blackfriars, railway station/subway improvements and more recently for £20 million from the Levelling Up Fund to support the University of Gloucestershire's City Campus and The Forge at Kings Quarter and £11 million for the Greyfriars Quarter has also been crucial. He was tenacious, using a variety of Parliamentary methods, in unlocking a deal for a new railway station car park on Great Western Road.

Turning to local government leaders, Labour's Kevin Stephens deserves credit for having ambition and for trying. He had two stints as Leader between 1989-95 and 1999-2003. As I have covered in detail elsewhere in this book, his efforts to bring about the regeneration of the Blackfriars area and to build a new hotel and conference centre on the site of the Westgate Street car park didn't end well. As Kevin himself acknowledges, he will forever be associated, unfairly or not, with these failures. But to be fair to him, he was also involved in the early days of both St Oswald's Park and Gloucester Quays, although both started on site after Labour had lost control of the City Council and Kevin wasn't a councillor. He also played a role in the rebuilding of the Leisure Centre and the creation of the new university campus at Oxstalls.

Mark Hawthorne was Leader of the City Council between 2004-7 and created the Regeneration cabinet portfolio which I held until February 2020 when it was broken up. Prior to 2004 regeneration was within the 'Sustainable Development' portfolio which at that time also included roads – before the highways function went back to the County Council – and planning. So, it tended to get lost amongst complaints about potholes and requests for zebra crossings. When Mark was Leader he held responsibility for Council-owned assets within his own Corporate Performance portfolio – including Kings Quarter and the Eastgate Shopping Centre. Mark piloted the Gloucester Quays planning application through Full Council, got the St Oswalds Park scheme on site and was the driving force behind the interim works in Kings Square as described in Chapter 11. He also delivered a £2.5 million programme funded from the Government's Liveability Fund for various improvements around the city, including a £1.2 million revamp of Gloucester Park – although it should be acknowledged that the bid was put in by the previous Labour/Lib-Dem administration. Mark has remained a committed supporter of the city's regeneration during his long spell as Leader of the County Council (from 2010 onwards), particularly with the refurbishment of Shire Hall and the development at Quayside, which is covered in the chapter on Blackfriars.

After my marathon 12 years as Leader, my successor Richard Cook largely continued with the regeneration programme I had set out, particularly with Kings Square and Kings Quarter. His Administration secured £20 million from the Government's Levelling Up Fund for several city centre regeneration projects as mentioned above. He also committed the Council to financing the £107 million cost of the Kings Quarter development – a bold and brave move for a small council, but one which had cross-party support.

I have described in other chapters the role of some of the developers involved in the city's regeneration – Jason Pullen of Peel, Nick Alford of Grantchester and then LXB, Terry Webster of High Star, Adrian Goodall of Rokeby and Stewart Deering of Reef Group to name a few. I have also given space to the key role of the former Dean of Gloucester (now the Bishop of Salisbury) Stephen Lake, both as Chair of the Regeneration Advisory Board and in having the vision for Project Pilgrim and the determination to deliver it, and the University of Gloucestershire Vice Chancellor Stephen Marston. The chapter on the Urban Regeneration Company recognises the contribution of Chief Executive Chris Oldershaw, Chair Greg Smith and Vice Chair Ian Mean.

But I want to highlight the roles of a number of other people who have stayed out of the public eye. Chief Executives of the City Council clearly have played a role, but it isn't possible to name them all. Graham Garbutt, who held the role for just over a decade until 2001, was a visionary who was never short of big ideas – some of which didn't happen like the National Youth Centre for Performing Arts and others that did – like the Western Waterfront, running from St Oswalds through the Docks to Gloucester Quays, including a new college campus. As I mentioned earlier in this book, Jerry Spencer, as Head of Planning at the time, and his team deserve credit for setting out the ambition in the 2001 Urban Design Strategy for Gloucester.

Phil Staddon was appointed the City Council's first Director of Regeneration in 2008. I worked closely with Phil as my right-hand man while he was in this role. After learning the planning trade at Derby City Council, he joined Gloucester City Council in 1999 as the Development Control Manager with the task of sorting out the Council's Planning function which at that time was considered something of a basket case. He did a remarkable job of this and it was transformed to one of the best-performing in the country, by introducing a performance culture and customer focus, implementing new IT systems and setting up a scheme of delegation so uncontentious applications could be decided without going in front of the Planning Committee. Known for his pinstripe suits, which weren't quite a match for Ian Mean's but almost, Phil was the go-to man for developers and personally saw through the St Oswalds Park and Gloucester Quays planning applications. He left the Council in 2013, set up his own very successful planning consultancy and still lives in Gloucester.

When Phil left the Council, it created a vacuum. An interim director, Ged Lucas, was appointed and Chief Executive Julian Wain also dabbled in regeneration, but it wasn't the same. After a gap of about a year, Anthony Hodge was appointed in a narrower (or you could say more focused) role of Head of Regeneration and Economic Development. Anthony grew into the role and was supremely loyal, tenacious and enthusiastic. He deserves huge credit for delivering phase one of Bakers Quay and being an important part of the team which delivered the bus station/transport hub. He was also instrumental in securing the £4.13 million of funding to help bring about the regeneration of the Blackfriars area. I was disappointed when he told me he was leaving the Council to take up a new job at Staffordshire County Council. Anthony was based in Manchester but lived locally in the week. He really took the city to heart and his passion shone through. He said of Gloucester, "I've never known a city try so hard to improve itself."

Anthony worked closely with the City Council's Regeneration Consultant Philip Ardley. Philip joined the Council in May 2007 and at the time of writing was still working as hard as ever. He was previously Regional Managing Partner of GVA, covering the

South West and Wales from offices in Bristol and Cardiff, so had an amazing range of contacts and had "been there and done that" before. He retired from GVA at the end of 2006 and had four months of 'retirement' before joining the City Council on a 'temporary' six-month contract. Earlier in his career, he had worked on the planning of Hong Kong's mass transit system in the 1970s. He didn't work for the money but did it because he enjoyed it. A brilliant negotiator, he struck deals to buy land off Aviva which was necessary to deliver the bus station and Kings Quarter schemes. He negotiated the deal with Reef Group to enable the acquisition of Kings Walk. He oversaw the management of the Docks estate and project managed the construction of the bus station/transport hub. He also negotiated the £54 million acquisition of the St Oswald's Retail Park from Hammerson and the £11.5 million purchase of the Eastgate Shopping Centre for the council. There are various other projects he has worked on and he doesn't even work full-time for the Council! The people of Gloucester as a whole may not know it but their city's regeneration owes a great deal to Philip Ardley.

The other council officer who has made a major contribution but stays even more in the shadows is Adam Smith. His role as Principal Planner for major applications was created by Phil Staddon and means he has dealt with most of the planning applications at Gloucester Quays, the Docks, Bakers Quay, the University's new Business School, Blackfriars, the Prison and Kings Quarter. He does so always in a calm and considered way and has the respect of all parties involved.

In the early days, when the Urban Regeneration Company was formed, Colin Molton of the South West Regional Development Agency was instrumental in using his no-nonsense approach to get it up and running. On the abolition of the RDAs, he went on to be the Deputy Chief Executive of the Homes and Communities Agency (later Homes England) and caused some controversy in Bristol when it was revealed he was being paid £263,000 a year in his role as interim Executive Director of Growth and Regeneration, between 2017 and 2021.

His colleague Ian Knight is another who is unknown to the vast majority of people in Gloucester but who had a disproportionately large impact and deserves a good deal of credit. In their heyday, the Regional Development Agencies had £1.2 billion a year to spend and SWRDA's share was £160 million. Gloucester had its fair share of that (some would say more than its fair share) with investment in the Docks and the South West bypass in particular. Knight as Area Director for Gloucestershire had control of the purse strings (sometimes needing the approval of the RDA Board), so his support was crucial. Like so many former RDA officers, Knight moved on to the Homes and Communities Agency when the RDA was wound up.

Another former SWRDA surveyor who followed that path was Esther Croft. Esther was involved with the acquisition of The Fleece and land at Blackfriars which ultimately enabled the development of the student accommodation. Esther also led on the building of the Language Immersion Centre at Blackfriars and the transfer of SWRDA assets to the City Council when the agency was wound up. After going to the Homes and Communities Agency, she joined LDA Design – who came up with the Docks linkages scheme. Esther became involved with Kings Quarter when the scheme was repurposed away from being retail-led and the City Council parted company with Stanhope. LDA and Jones Lang LaSalle were appointed to work up a business plan and planning application with Esther leading the team. She was headhunted by Reef Group in 2018 but continued to work on the project until leaving the company at the end of September 2023. Full of energy and a keen hockey player, Esther combines living in deepest rural Somerset with working on urban regeneration schemes.

David Warburton, as Area Director for Southern England for English Partnerships (the Government's national regeneration agency which then became the Homes and Communities Agency), sat on the GHURC Board. He led on the acquisition of the GlosCAT Greyfriars site and supported the College in its move to the new Llanthony campus. He was also a key player in delivering the High Orchard Bridge over the canal, which was crucial in enabling the Gloucester Quays development to take place, as well as providing the funding to unlock the Bakers Quay land acquisition.

Jeremy Williamson, or Jem as he is known, was for some years the Vice Principal of Gloucestershire College, responsible for managing its estate. He delivered a new campus in Princess Elizabeth Way in Cheltenham and repeated the process in Gloucester with the new

Llanthony Campus. Through this connection he became Chair of the Llanthony Secunda Priory Trust, overseeing and indeed driving its restoration. He was appointed Managing Director of the Cheltenham Task Force – becoming one of the few people to successfully bridge the gap between town and city, simultaneously contributing to the regeneration of both.

Also at the sharp end of delivery of some of the key projects were Anne Cranston, Project Manager for the Cathedral's Project Pilgrim, Edwina Bell, who performed a similar role at Llanthony Priory, and Nicola Dyer, who was seconded by the Prince's Foundation to manage the Discover DeCrypt project. Claire Dovey-Evans managed both the Southgate Street Townscape Heritage Initiative and then the Cathedral Quarter High Street Heritage Action Zone, helping restore dozens of historic buildings, from February 2015 until the time of writing.

What this chapter is designed to show is that you need people around you with specialist knowledge and skills to deliver regeneration. Anyone who says they have regenerated a place of any size on their own is most likely deluded. It is the combined efforts of a whole range of people, far too numerous to mention, which has moved forward Gloucester's regeneration over the last 25 years or so. No doubt many more will be involved, in one way or another, in completing the remaining projects.

22. UNFINISHED BUSINESS

Turning round a city, even a relatively small one like Gloucester, is a long-term undertaking. The Gloucester Heritage Urban Regeneration Company (GHURC) when it was set up had a ten-year life expectancy, although it only lasted seven. Part of that time was marred by the financial crisis of 2008 and the recession that followed, the effects of which carried on into the period when the City Council 'took back control' of regeneration. At its inception, GHURC set itself a target of £1 billion of investment. A decade and £1 billion was felt to be the length of time and amount of money needed to make a significant difference, but even that wasn't enough to finish the job.

You can probably trace back the roots of the city's current programme of regeneration to the St Oswald's Park development which started on site in 2004, but was conceived in the late 1990s. So, at the time of writing, the journey has taken over twenty years and there is still plenty to go at. I have mentioned elsewhere in this book the efforts to deliver the Kings Quarter development, which after many years of work is only now on-site and due to be completed in 2024. The conversion of the former City Council offices at the Docks still needs to be delivered, as does the regeneration of the remaining land at St Oswalds Park which I wrote about in Chapter 6. Still in the Docks, the Southgate Moorings car park remains a development site in the longer-term. The development of the remainder of the County Council's land at Quayside and what, if anything, happens to the NCP car park in Ladybellegate Street are as yet uncompleted elements of the Blackfriars regeneration.

In this chapter, I want to concentrate on a number of other projects which, at the time of writing, remain on the 'to do list'. Let's start with the former Fleece Hotel site.

The Fleece

The Fleece hotel opened in 1497 as one of the three 'Great Inns' built by the Abbey of St Peter (now the Cathedral) to cater for pilgrims who came to Gloucester to visit the tomb of King Edward II after his grisly murder in Berkeley Castle. There is a medieval undercroft beneath the Fleece Hotel which once traded as the Monk's Retreat. It was a unique bar, part of a 12th century Benedictine Monastery, and it was once described as 'the most curious bar in England'. It was used as an air raid shelter during the war. For a time in the 1960's, the Monk's Retreat was converted into a pseudo-German bierkeller with beer served in lidded steins. The hotel had 40 bedrooms.

It is a place which holds a lot of sentimental memories for people in Gloucester and beyond. Many met there for their first date, held their wedding receptions there or just remember great nights out having a few drinks in the Monk's Retreat.

Over the years, it has had its fair share of famous visitors. Margaret Thatcher attended a Conservative Ladies' lunch meeting there. Actress Gracie Fields, Poet John Betjeman, former Chancellor and Foreign Secretary Geoffrey Howe and cricketers David Gower and Ray Illingworth were all guests at one point or another. The Rotary Club of Gloucester held their meetings at The Fleece and the Old Cryptians' Club would hold their meals there after the Crypt School Founders' Day Service at the Cathedral. The spy Kim Philby, who was revealed as a double agent for the Soviet Union, stayed there for a number of days, leading to the hotel's owner Cyril Rich being interviewed by MI5 when Philby ran off to Russia!

The site also included a Gentleman's Club which could be joined by invitation only. It had its own squash courts, washrooms and saloon areas for food. Staff lived on-site upstairs.

When Gloucester really was the 'crossroads of England', the hotel was a thriving business. The building of the Severn Bridge (which opened in 1966) took some trade away, but the pedestrianisation of Westgate Street in the 1980s had a bigger impact. The hotel changed from being on the side of a busy road to having its entrance in a narrow one-way lane.

The proposed Blackfriars development in the 1980s and 1990s cast a shadow of uncertainty over it, meaning that the owners couldn't make long-term investment decisions. Parts of The Fleece had been included in the Compulsory Purchase Order for Blackfriars, but that was never enforced following the collapse of the scheme at the end of

2001.

It closed in 2002 when electrical works estimated at £150,000 were required. This was too much for the owners, the Rich family (but unfortunately not that rich!) who had owned it for over 90 years. Cedric Rich and his wife Barbara had run it for the last 29 years. The Rich family had bought the hotel when Samuel Rich had moved to the city from Okehampton in 1908. His son Cyril and then grandson Cedric had taken on the mantle.

The Citizen announced in August 2002 that the hotel was to close. Cedric Rich was quoted as saying, "It is very sad, because we had hoped to make it to 100 years, but it was not to be. The last straw was the latest electrical inspection which would have meant completely rewiring the hotel. That is an investment we could not make with the threat of redevelopment hanging over us.

"We have had 12 years of uncertainty caused by the Blackfriars scheme. It has been on, then off. We have had Compulsory Purchase Orders and public inquiries but still nothing has happened. We are going to close the hotel and sit tight. This is my home as well as the family business."[291]

Chris Witts, then acting Leader of the City Council, said, "I am deeply saddened. The Fleece is an institution in Gloucester and I have many happy memories of it. Let's hope that revised redevelopment proposals for the area are made as soon as possible. The problems with the new hotel (the ill-fated Westgate car park scheme) mean we need all the hotel rooms we can muster in the city centre."

Just before it closed, I had a pint (a rather cloudy one as I recall) with Cedric Rich and wished him well in the next chapter of his life. I tried to persuade the Chapman Group, then owners of the New Inn, to buy it as I thought the two could be run together, but that wasn't to be. In the end it was acquired by the Regional Development Agency in April 2003 with the intention of forming part of a future Blackfriars regeneration scheme.

I wrote to the RDA's Ian Knight in October 2003 saying, "It should be brought back into use as soon as possible – both because such a historic building should be open for the public (and tourists) but also because Gloucester desperately needs more city centre hotel accommodation. Being back in use would of course be the best way to ensure a full and much-needed refurbishment of the building –

both inside and out."[292] I commented to *The Citizen*, "The RDA is a Government agency and the concern is they may do what Government departments do sometimes – take a long time to make a decision."[293] I warned that "I will be putting pressure on them if they seem to be letting the situation drag on at all."[294]

The RDA replied to me saying, "Whilst elements of the building are of great heritage significance, large sections of the overall holding comprise modern structures of mediocre quality. An important element of the building assessment will include working with city council planners, English Heritage etc to agree exactly what is to be preserved and what can be redeveloped."

The RDA did undertake work to make the property wind and watertight, commissioned architectural and historical assessments and painted the black and white Westgate Street frontage. The RDA did some great work in the city, particularly in the Docks, but their stewardship of The Fleece was not their finest hour. I was very critical of their lack of action, but the City Council has now owned The Fleece for longer than the RDA did and I better appreciate what a huge challenge its regeneration represents.

The Citizen reported in July 2010 that The Fleece was on English Heritage's 'At Risk' register. The RDA's Esther Croft is quoted as saying, "Our aim is to secure a developer to progress this project".[295] SWRDA appointed King Sturge to market The Fleece, with potential uses including a hotel, housing, retail, bars and restaurants.[296] No buyer was found though.

When the RDA was wound up in 2011, The Fleece was part of the package of their assets acquired from the Government by the City Council. In fact, The Fleece was in such poor condition that it was attributed a negative value, meaning the City Council picked up a huge chunk of real estate that SWRDA had built up over the years for a very modest price (around £250,000).

As soon as the City Council completed the purchase, it undertook urgent stabilisation works to the tune of £350,000. The buildings had wet rot, dry rot, cracked timbers, stolen lead and water ingress, to name but a few of the problems. Food was still in the freezer and some parts of the building had not seen daylight since 2002. Work started in September 2011. At the time I commented that the "condition is every bit as bad as I expected it to be".[297] Surveyor

Hayley Taylor led this work on behalf of the Council.

Soon after the Council took on ownership of the complex, the Diocese of Gloucester started to look at relocating their offices to the site. This seemed highly fortuitous, but I soon picked up that they were cooling on the idea. By the time I was able to secure a slot in Bishop Michael Perham's diary, it was too late and they had already decided against the move.

The City Council tried to market the site in September 2013. There was interest from the YMCA, who wanted to develop hostel-style accommodation and from Verve, a London-based developer specialising in unusual buildings who had regenerated the Paintworks in Bristol. *The Citizen* reported in April 2014 that the YMCA had a £12 million plan. I commented saying, "I know some people are a bit sniffy about the YMCA but it has changed a lot over the last 30 years and some places are very smart." Unfortunately, although the YMCA had a £12 million plan, they didn't have the £12 million needed to implement it.

Both interests petered out, so the Council decided to carry out further de-risking works before going to the market again.

The City Council's bid for funding to regenerate Blackfriars (see Chapter 5), which was awarded in January 2015, included £200,000 for The Fleece. This was used for intrusive site investigations, including a 3D laser survey of the 12th century undercroft, and archaeological excavations. City Council Surveyor Iona Lennon, who was passionate about the buildings, led the project.

In November 2016, an archaeological dig found a large amount of medieval pottery, a tankard, three onion bottles (used for wine) and smoking pipes from the 17th and 18th century - what City Archaeologist Andrew Armstrong called "medieval pub waste". The excavation also found a row of footings for late medieval timber framed buildings fronting onto Cross Keys Lane – just 20cm below ground level.[298]

In July 2017, a fire started in the Edwardian block. The block was designed and built by the Rich family with the help of architects. Fortunately, thanks to the efforts of firefighters, the blaze was contained. Jamie Hiam, 29, of Priory House, Greyfriars was jailed for three and a half years for arson relating to The Fleece and another fire at the former Brunswick pub in Park Road. Some council officers privately lamented the fact that the damage was not serious enough to justify demolition of the block, which would have made development of the site easier. Instead, insurance monies paid for the damage to be put right including a new roof on the building.

Gloucester Culture Trust showed some interest in the buildings and a businessman from Cheltenham drew up plans for the site and held several meetings with the Council, but did not want to go through a competitive process and, again, both of these interests withered. By this time, Westgate councillor Dawn Melvin had been elected and became a driving force behind the plans to regenerate the site.

In December 2017, the City Council's Cabinet considered a report on the future of The Fleece. Officers were instructed to prepare a development brief. I commented, "The Fleece has a place in the hearts of many local people, who will have fond memories of time spent there. It has been empty for far longer than we would have liked but we are now in a strong position to secure investment for its future."

The Council decided to go out to a 'Competitive Dialogue' procurement process to find a developer partner for The Fleece. This process allowed the Council to talk to the various bidders as they went through the different stages of the process. The shortlist of four included some good quality names and ultimately it was Dowdeswell Estates who were chosen. Dowdeswell were connected with SuperDry founder Julian Dunkerton and had undertaken several ultra-high-quality restorations for his Lucky Onion Group of hotels in Cheltenham and elsewhere in the county. Dowdeswell Estates MD, Rod Jenner said his involvement with Gloucester City Football Club alerted him to the opportunity.

Jenner said, "I could see the enormous potential of the site. We firmly believe that the quality of both our concept and the projects we have a track record of delivering will see the finished Fleece Hotel become a catalyst for the regeneration of the rest of the city and raise the bar in terms of the development of Gloucester city centre."[299]

I added, "The Fleece is an enormously complex site, which has been difficult to find a solution for, but I am confident we are now going to achieve this. This is a game changer for the whole city."

The Council had also taken the decision to include the crumbling

Longsmith Street multi-storey car park in the scheme. Dowdeswell's proposals included a boutique hotel, a diverse food and beverage offer at the back of the Fleece site and residential on the car park site with a conference centre above. When I spoke at a business event with Dowdeswell's Rod Jenner in 2019, he said he saw it as a five-year project. With the intervention of the Covid pandemic, it's probably still a five-year project at the time of writing.

The project received a boost in October 2021 when the City Council's Levelling Up Fund bid to the Government was approved. Of the £20 million bid, it was believed that £6.3 million was earmarked for The Fleece, although it was revealed in January 2024 that the funding has been diverted to other projects due to the lack of progress.

In March 2022, initial work got underway to remove modern material and expose more of the medieval timber framework so that it can be properly recorded and understood prior to conservation work and refurbishment of the building. The start of this work was hailed as an "important milestone" for the project. The investigations uncovered 15th century timber with original carpenters' marks, helping to understand the original size of the buildings on site. A wallpaper expert was brought in and identified a range of medieval wallpapers dating from 1740 until the late 19th century. Activity paused in July 2022 due to health and safety fears about bird droppings.

At the time of writing, the future of the site was unclear as the Dowdeswell Estate Building Company Limited had gone into liquidation in May 2022 following a court battle with shareholder and Superdry boss Julian Dunkerton, which was reported in the Daily Mail but not locally. The Council insisted its relationship was with Dowdeswell Group (a company incorporated in November 2019) rather than Dowdeswell Estates, but the Council later confirmed that Dowdeswell's interest had "fallen away". In February 2024, it was reported that there was another interest, from the Phoenix Village Project, to use The Fleece (including the Longsmith Street multi-storey car park) as a "state-of-the-art community hub" to "teach, train and mentor disenfranchised young adults."

Eddie Rich, Cedric and Barbara Rich's son, told me what it was like growing up in the hotel, where regular customers were "like Aunts and Uncles". He saw his family as custodians of the heritage and looks back with some sadness that the place he called home has been closed up and becoming increasingly derelict for over twenty years. He worries that his children will never see the beauty of the Westgate Room, the Marmion Room and the Monks Retreat. Indeed, there is now a whole generation who have never known it open and many don't know it exists. Let's hope that situation doesn't continue for too much longer.

The former Fleece Hotel site, still awaiting regeneration at the time of writing.

The Prison

HM Prison Gloucester closed in March 2013. I was surprised by the announcement as I had only been chatting to its Governor a matter of days before, who was a glamorous lady called Chantel King - not your typical Prison Governor!

It shouldn't perhaps have been such a surprise that it was earmarked for closure. Its facilities had been criticised over the years and the Victorian buildings were no longer fit for purpose. In June 2007, the Independent Monitoring Board criticised Gloucester Prison for its overcrowding, poor dining provision and cramped cells.

In August 2007, the prison was criticised by Her Majesty's Chief Inspector of Prisons after an inspection report found the levels of organised activities for inmates at Gloucester (such as training and education) were "woeful". The report also stated that one wing of the prison should be refurbished. However, the prison was described as "very positive" overall because of good management.

Some people, like GHURC Chief Executive Chris Oldershaw and Citizen Editor Ian Mean, had identified the closure of the prison as a potential positive for the city as it made the site available for redevelopment but when I was asked for my reaction to the closure, I made clear that my first thoughts were with the staff who would either be relocated or would lose their jobs. City MP Richard Graham, who told me he took a call from Justice Secretary Chris Grayling while he was in Jakarta to inform him of the proposed closure, said, "In the short term, the closure is sad. In the medium term it is an opportunity."[300] As the next few years would demonstrate, redeveloping the prison site would not prove straightforward.

In 2013, local historian Phil Moss estimated that there could be up to 122 executed criminals buried in unmarked graves at the prison. The Ministry of Justice (MoJ) said it was aware of 17 burials there between 1874 and 1939. Trevor Osbourne, who developed Oxford Prison, said any developer of the Gloucester jail would need to take into account the cost of excavating any remains. "Clearly there's a great deal of records for Gloucester but you don't always know how complete those records are," he said, "Therefore it's important you embark on a project like this by doing as much investigation as possible. He added that, "At Oxford we thought it would be about £250,000. It turned out to be more than double that because we kept finding more and more bodies. We found 76 in the end. "You can't be sure how long it will take or how much it will cost."[301]

Jones Lang LaSalle's Bristol office was appointed by the Ministry of Justice to market the site and it went up for sale in February 2014, as a package with prisons at Portsmouth, Dorchester and Shepton Mallet. In fact, none of the prison sites would prove particularly straightforward to develop.

Paul Baker, a well-known figure in the regional property industry, led the marketing exercise. The City Council had written to the Secretary of State for Justice asking that the Government's Homes and Communities Agency take on the site to deliver it for housing – something which City MP Richard Graham had not approved. Looking back, it may not have been such a bad thing.

When asked for my thoughts on possible uses for the site, I said, "I'd like to see mixed use there – there is no reason why you cannot get residential, a heritage use and a hotel there". *The Citizen* speculated that the price for the Gloucester site was £3 million. My sources tell me there was a 'job lot' price, but offers would also be entertained for the individual sites and the offers for Gloucester alone were much less than £3 million.

There was pressure locally for the site to be turned into a visitor attraction. I asked Juliana Delaney, Chief Executive of Continuum Group (operators of some of the UK's most popular heritage attractions) to visit. Her view was that the site was too big and the story connected with it wasn't strong enough for it to work. It was the site of Gloucester Castle, where Royals including King Henry III stayed and was where Dinah Riddiford, Kylie and Dannii Minogue's great, great, great, great, great grandmother, was hanged. Along with her son Luke, she had taken two sides of bacon, two pigs' cheeks, a piece of tongue and a pat of butter, together with a copper tea kettle. Luke was spared and sent to an Australian penal colony, but his mother was put to death at a grim event nicknamed 'the granny hanging'. So there were certainly stories, but I took her point.

I regularly pressed Paul Baker for news of any buyer. There was speculation in the local media that the site would be turned into a "swanky" Malmaison hotel along the lines of the former prison at Oxford Castle, following a suggestion by local architect Jeff Roberts.[302] Interest was limited, not only because few developers like taking on a collection of heritage buildings but also because the MoJ was insisting on an 'unconditional' sale (i.e. not subject to planning permission) in order to lose the substantial costs of holding the property.

There was concern in some quarters locally when Andy Jones, who runs the rather macabre 'Crime Through Time' museum at Littledean Jail, expressed an interest in taking on the prison site.

In March 2014, it was reported that there were 30 expressions of interest. The deadline for bids was the end of April. At the end of October, it was reported that a 'mystery bidder' was in talks.

Eventually, Paul Baker told me that the City Council would be very pleased with the outcome. It was then revealed that the buyer was City & Country Residential – a high-quality specialist heritage developer who had developed some impressive schemes elsewhere in the country – who were chosen by the MoJ largely because of their track record. At the time they were working on the conversion of the former Bristol General Hospital into 200 apartments and had bought Factory No 1, Bedminster, again for conversion to apartments.

City & Country hosted three briefing sessions for councillors and the wider public to talk through their ideas, at different stages of the process, assisted by architects from top firm Feilden Clegg Bradley. Principally it was for new apartments – a mix of conversion and new build – apart from some small-scale commercial uses such as a cafe in the gatehouse. I'm told they did consider other uses, such as hotel and offices, early on but, guided by the financial viability, it was always likely to be a residential-led scheme. The issue was the extent of the commercial elements.

The developers undertook archaeological excavations, finding the old castle walls and keep – something which wasn't a surprise to many of us. *The Citizen* excitedly reported this with the front-page headline "Revealed – Norman Castle the size of Tower of London unearthed under Gloucester Prison for first time."[303] City Archaeologist Andrew Armstrong said he was surprised it was in such good condition. Cotswold Archaeology Chief Executive Neil Holbrook added, "I knew there was a castle but I had expected more of it to be destroyed." He described the castle as "a powerful symbol of Norman architecture, representative of how powerful the city was in Norman Britain."

The castle was the first in Gloucester to be built of stone and housed three chapels, two drawbridges and a royal chamber for the King and Queen. Mr Holbrook said the design was thought to have resembled Canterbury Cathedral and the Tower of London. The keep walls were just 60mm under the Prison's basketball court area. The walls were 12 ft wide and the keep is estimated to have been 30m long and 20m across.

City & Country's archaeologists dug further trial trenches during the course of the planning application. They found what they had anticipated, which gave them certainty for the design of the foundations. The proposed design worked around the archaeology – moving the buildings to the edge of the site and incorporating the castle keep into a viewing chamber as part of a landscape scheme. They did look at doing something more widely with the remains, but the archaeologists' view was that it wouldn't have looked good and wouldn't have helped the preservation of the remains.

Planning permission was granted in May 2018, for a total of 202 apartments. Most of them were in the new build element, on the side nearest The Quay. There was some concern about the height of these new blocks, which were up to six storeys, but the Planning Committee took the view that the regeneration benefits outweighed any harm to the heritage and granted consent. That, as so often is the case, wasn't the end of the matter. City & Country, to be fair to them, had made clear that overall the scheme lost money. The company and the Council's advisers had an arm wrestle to agree exactly how much they believed it would lose, as part of assessing what 'planning gain' contributions the development would make to things like affordable housing. They agreed on a notional loss of £7.7 million and no affordable housing.

When I had a 'what happens next?' phone call with bosses from City & Country, they assured me that they would be working hard to find ways to close the gap – including finding a site for 'enabling development', meaning building somewhere else and using the profits to subsidise the prison scheme. This seemed unlikely to me – if it was that easy, the chances are someone would have done it already.

The prison, particularly the main Victorian block, was a very popular building for the public. When City MP Richard Graham first offered tours as part of Heritage Weekend in September 2013, his office couldn't cope with the number of calls they got – over 600 in 24 hours.[304] Mr Graham persuaded Justice Minister Jeremy Wright to allow another weekend of tours – the only heritage prison to be given the opportunity – meaning over 1000 people got to see inside the prison. Mr Graham commented, "It is a sombre place to visit and those expecting to see how cushy life in our prisons is will be disappointed."

Such was the demand that a company, Jailhouse Tours, were appointed to run the site in the interim. They carried on until October 2018, when another company, Cracking Day Ltd run by Andy

Stevens, took it on to run as an airsoft shooting game venue. He continued with tours on Bank Holidays. I took my wife on a tour as a punter. We enjoyed it, but it did strike me that converting the Victorian block to apartments was awkward, to put it mildly. The cells, by their very nature, were shallow, had small windows and had very thick walls! It would also mean a lot of wasted space in the central area. I came back and looked at the plans, which showed that the apartments were created by knocking 7 or 8 cells together, which struck me as being very awkward and would involve a lot of intervention in the heritage. An interesting feature is that above the cell doors are serpents (representing evil) and lions' claws (representing the good suppressing the evil).

My preference would be to see the Victorian block used as an events space, which would mean less intervention in the heritage and would maintain public access. I also saw it as a way of getting the development to work as I couldn't see the point in City & Country losing millions by converting the buildings to apartments. Instead, I thought, it could be transferred to a charitable trust (along the lines of Llanthony Priory) who would be able to lever in other funds – from the Heritage Lottery Fund for example – to bring about its restoration.

City & Country started to market the front side of the site alongside The Quay, with consent to build 150 new apartments, through Jones Lang LaSalle in 2019. They submitted an application to vary or delete a lot of the conditions associated with their planning application, the most crucial one relating to phasing. Their original consent required them to convert the listed buildings (which would lose money) first, but they wanted to be able to do the new build elements first – which would enable them to sell off this part of the site. It meant, however, that the future of the heritage buildings was still uncertain. This application was approved, perhaps surprisingly, by the planners under 'delegated powers' despite an objection from the Council's Conservation Officer but without any word from the likes of the Civic Trust and with very little media coverage or scrutiny.

There was believed to be a buyer for the new-build element, but they didn't proceed in wake of the pandemic. City & Country undertook some demolition on site to keep the planning consent alive.

The other former prisons in the package acquired by City & Country also proved difficult. The developer secured planning consents for all of the sites. In Portsmouth they sold the site on – the new build element to a housing association and the conversion of existing buildings to a developer. In Dorchester, the site was put up for sale in 2020 for £10 million with planning permission for nearly 200 homes. At the time of writing, the site hadn't been sold and continues to be operated for events, experiences and filming by the same company as Gloucester Prison. In Shepton Mallet, City & Country started to implement the planning consent to keep it alive, but the site is being run as an attraction by the company Jailhouse Tours.

The Eastgate Shopping Centre and Indoor Market

Work started on building the Eastgate Shopping Centre in February 1967 as part of the city's major development at that time. It was financed by Electricity Supply Nominees (ESN), the pension fund for the electricity industry. The Eastgate Indoor Market was moved from being directly on Eastgate Street to the South Eastern side of the shopping centre – some would say it was 'tucked away'. The market was opened 31st October 1968 by the Duke of Beaufort. The Eastgate Market stone portico which was the entrance to the market was moved along Eastgate Street and now forms the Eastgate entrance to the shopping centre. The shopping centre opened on 2nd July 1973.

Over the years, the shopping centre was owned and managed by a variety of organisations. Scottish Widows owned it for a number of years until the early 2000s, buying in the 25,000 sq ft former C&A store in 2001. Capital & Regional bought the centre from Catalyst Capital for £43 million in 2004 and rebranded it as 'The Mall' with garish pink lettering. People still called it the Eastgate Shopping Centre. They sold it in 2010 to the US fund Rockspring, who had teamed up with John Wood's Other Retail Group, as part of a £136 million deal involving a number of shopping centres. Wood had previously been involved with Eastgate when he worked for Capital & Regional. Rockspring sold it to the Lone Star fund in 2014, forming what was known as the Tiger Portfolio - a collection of five UK shopping centres. With the rise of online retail, the shopping centre struggled – as did many others – and some units stayed vacant for long periods.

One of my more bizarre duties as Council Leader was in March 2011 when I cut the ribbon at a 'fish foot spa' called Funky Fish in the Eastgate Shopping Centre. They were something of a fad at the time. The idea was that Garruta fish would nibble the dead skin on your feet leaving them lovely and smooth. I performed the duty with a Harry Hill lookalike who owned the business. The novelty didn't last and the store closed in October 2011.

I also officially opened new lifts at the centre in September 2013, which were part of a £2 million package of investment in the centre, but the overall impact was minor. The centre certainly has a dated look about it. The last time it had a major refurbishment was a £5.5 million contract let by Scottish Widows in December 1993 and completed in late 1994, involving new flooring, lighting, lifts and the installation of the Tailor of Gloucester clock.

The Tailor of Gloucester clock by the entrance to the Indoor Market, which was a popular feature, was removed in 2013 when the cost of its frequent breakdowns became too much for the centre management and its removal is still much lamented. It was given to the Pied Piper Appeal with the idea of installing it at the Children's Hospital at Gloucestershire Royal. Despite years of negotiations, agreement couldn't be reached with the NHS and the clock was broken up, with the various characters refurbished by Severn Signs of Innsworth and given to various special schools around the county, including Milestone School in Longlevens, in 2021. At the time of its removal, Centre Manager Jason Robinson said the space it created would be used as a gallery for sculpture by students at Gloucestershire College, but for most of the time the space has remained empty.

The rooftop car park had an £800,000 council-funded makeover in 2016 but that only made a marginal impact in terms of the centre's environment.

In March 2019, it was reported that Lone Star had ceded control of the portfolio due to the falling values of the assets with its main lender, Austrian bank BAWAG, taking on the shopping centres. It is believed that Lone Star were trying to sell Eastgate and the other four centres but were unable to before BAWAG stepped in. There wasn't exactly a rush of buyers, with the City Council eventually picking it up for £11.5 million in December 2019. The City Council's rationale for buying it was not that it wanted to own another shopping centre – it had already taken on Kings Walk in 2017. But it had an onerous lease on the rooftop car park and a potentially big dilapidations bill (believed to be £1 million) on the Market Hall, which a new owner could enforce. Ownership also gave it greater control over the future direction of the city centre.

I said at the time, "This is another exciting acquisition for the Council that demonstrates our commitment to the city centre and gives us greater ability to shape its future. Town and city centres are evolving but still have a vitally important role to play and it is important that local councils show leadership by investing in them and helping to ensure they can survive and thrive into the future. The Council already has a number of financial interests in The Eastgate and it makes good long-term commercial sense to control it in its entirety. It also enables us to resolve the future of the Indoor Market and give traders the certainty they have been seeking."[305]

There are huge, unused spaces that could be brought back into income-generating use such as the former Laser Tag area overlooking Greyfriars and Addison House (also on the Greyfriars site). Addison House, or Addison's Folly, was built in 1864 as a memorial to Robert Raikes by Thomas Fenn Addison who lived in nearby Bell Lane. The tower was built high enough to give him a view of Hempsted Church where his wife was buried.

The Indoor Market had thrived for a lot of its time in its new location. But by the 1990s it was starting to look tired and vacant stalls started to creep in. In the early days it made the ratepayer substantial surpluses, but by the early 2000s it was actually starting to cost the taxpayer money. The number of vacant stalls was rising and concessionary terms were introduced to attract new traders, but weaning them off these 'soft deals' proved difficult leading to a confusing and unfair range of rents being paid. In November 2005, then Council Leader Mark Hawthorne proposed moving the Indoor Market to make way for an extension to the shopping centre, bringing in a new retail 'anchor' to the centre, with speculation that it could be Primark or TK Maxx. It was part of a wider plan for the area, including turning what was then the music library in Greyfriars House into a coffee shop. The grassed area would be brought alive with street entertainment. Addison House would have been used as the entrance for a hotel and town houses would have been built on the former bowling green along Constitution Walk.

A 10,000-signature petition to 'Save Our Market' was collected. All parties unanimously backed the market moving, but Labour said it must not be sidelined.[306] Ideas for where it could move to included the former Argos (now Sports Direct) in Northgate Street, the former BeWise store in Southgate Street and the former MVC unit in Kings Walk (originally Gordon Thoday Fabrics). Following protests, the plan was dropped. It was revisited in 2014, with a proposal to move the Indoor Market to the first floor of the shopping centre, which had been vacant since the closure of the Food Court area some years earlier and which would eventually be converted to form the UK Digital Retail Innovation Centre (see Chapter 19). This plan didn't progress either after objections from traders. Some feared the market would be hidden away upstairs. Others were close to retirement and just didn't want the upheaval of moving. TK Maxx eventually moved into the former Marks & Spencer store in Northgate Street.

A new indoor market hall was mooted as part of the revised Kings Quarter plan but with the scheme moving further away from being retail-focused and preferences from traders to stay at Eastgate, that changed to a plan to stay somewhere within the Eastgate Shopping Centre and investment of £1 million was promised, but never actually budgeted for.

The Council's purchase of the Eastgate Shopping Centre would enable it to solve the market problem, but it remained a regret of mine that I hadn't been able to do more to provide traders with a better environment during my time in office.

In August 2022, it was announced that the Council was submitting a second bid to the Government's Levelling Up Fund for £12.5 million to create a 'Garden Quarter' at Greyfriars. The market hall would be relocated to another part of the Eastgate Shopping Centre, with a contemporary new design that would see it open up onto a landscaped courtyard garden.

The existing market hall would be revamped to house a multi-purpose performance space for dance, music, fitness, cinema, community and leisure events. It would be linked to a unique covered outdoor space with an orangery and outdoor dining area within the remains of the Greyfriars friary. The plan also included serviced apartments in Addison House and flexible workspaces within Greyfriars House.

In February 2023, it was announced that the bid to the Levelling Up Fund had not been successful. The Council said that "options for short and long-term opportunities" were being reviewed. However, in November 2023, the Government announced £11 million of funding for the project from Round Three of the Levelling Up Fund.

Railway Station

The subway connecting the Gloucester Central railway station and Great Western Road has been pretty grim for as long as I remember. It is one of those places, like Kings Square, that people in Gloucester felt would never get sorted out.

Tess Kingham, who served as the city's Labour MP from 1997-2001, 'railed against' its condition in a campaigning newspaper before she was elected, but didn't stay in office long enough to see it through. The report of English Heritage's Urban Panel following their visit in 2003 said the railway station seemed "forbidding, inadequate and doomed".

In July 2010, the County Council had a £750,000 budget to refurbish the subway but it was cut by £330,000 as part of the council's budget savings package. The graffiti-covered walk-through had been scheduled to undergo a radical makeover for some time but a dispute between the County Council and Network Rail over insurance stalled the work.

Jeremy Hilton, then leader of the city and county council's Liberal Democrat groups, said: "I am hopping mad about this announcement. That money has been sitting in an account for five years and it hasn't been used. That subway is the first thing a lot of visitors see when they come to our city and it just isn't up to scratch. It's grotty and horrible. It needs a total refurbishment, not what the county council is now proposing."

The council was instead proposing to install a CCTV camera, new lighting and a new coat of paint over the graffiti. Previously it had been hoped that the project would include new walls and graffiti-proof tiles.

Councillor Stan Waddington, the Council's cabinet member for transport, said: "Because the coalition government has decided to cut the council's budget, we have to make savings in the areas they have identified. With regard to the station subway, although we have reduced the cost of the scheme, we will still be painting it with vandal-proof paint and installing CCTV. In these difficult times we simply cannot justify the extra expense of building brand new walls. We still expect the end result to be a substantial improvement than now and will represent value for money."

In recent years, a number of incremental improvements to the Station have taken place, largely after campaigning by Richard Graham MP. In 2013, Network Rail invested £2.9 million to make access easier for passengers, with a new footbridge and lifts providing step-free access from street level to all platforms for the first time. A new booking office with ticket gates was built to replace the former ticket office, as well as new passenger shelters on platforms 3 and 4 and a renovated canopy on platform 4.

In February 2014, *The Citizen* reported that the Station was "set for a £2 million revamp". In response to a letter from me, Network Rail Chief Executive, David Higgins, said, "We are pleased to confirm we are already in discussions regarding proposals for improvements. I understand that both Network Rail and First Great Western have committed some support." I commented at the time that "although we have had some improvements to the railway station in the last couple of years, it still doesn't give the impression we want it to give." It would still be some time before those improvements were delivered.

In March 2017, work started on a new 245-space car park to serve the station on Great Western Road. Richard Graham had been campaigning for a number of years to bring an unused, derelict former car park on Great Western Road back into use. It was owned by HM Courts & Tribunals Service, an agency of the Ministry of Justice, but had lay unused for almost a decade after plans for a new court building were abandoned. Richard Graham lobbied Ministers and secured Parliamentary debates to press the case. He said, "I proposed this idea to GWR, the Ministry of Justice, Transport Secretary and the City Council in 2013. It has taken more meetings with Ministers, Parliamentary questions, a dedicated debate and paperwork between all parties than any other car park in history." In a debate in December 2015, Justice Minister Shailesh Vara responded to Richard Graham to say agreement in principle had been reached but there were still details to iron out. The land would be sold to the City Council, who would grant a lease to GWR. The back-to-back arrangement would be at no cost to the council taxpayer. In all, it represented a £2.7 million investment by GWR. The first phase of 208 spaces opened in April 2018, with the remaining 35 spaces being completed that summer.

I commented, "It's taken a lot of effort from all sides to get to this stage and it's a good example of local government and central government and the private sector all working together."

In 2017, two bids for £4.8m and £9.5m were submitted to the GFirst Local Enterprise Partnership for improvement to the railway station, with the more expensive one including an iconic footbridge to connect the railway station to the Kings Quarter development, crossing over Bruton Way. I explained at the time, "The footbridge was added on the advice of the LEP to make the scheme stand out. Some people liked the idea and others didn't." It was later removed from the bid. The Council's Head of Regeneration, Anthony Hodge, told me that it was difficult to fit it in the space available and the designers struggled to get the 'landings' right.[307] In any case, the bid wasn't successful.

In February 2018, a second bid for funding for Railway Station improvements was launched, this time for £4.3 million. I told the *Gloucester Review*, "This isn't just about improving the station environment, important though that is, but improving connections between the city centre and Great Western Road to bring more footfall and help the development sites on the other side of the track come forward."[308]

The project included straightening out the subway at the Great Western Road end, using land the City Council owned on the adjacent Wessex House site (the former Edmundson Electrical building which had been derelict for a number of years). This was felt necessary because the kink in the subway on the Great Western Road side meant you couldn't see the full length of the subway – which made it feel unsafe in case anyone was hiding at the other end. Running under the railway lines, such changes were a complex engineering project and thus very expensive! New lighting and CCTV would be added. The scheme was also designed to improve access to the subway for pushchairs and wheelchairs which the steps at the railway station end made either difficult or impossible. Changes to the station forecourt were planned to reduce the conflict between pedestrians and vehicles and take traffic away from the busy Bruton Way crossroads with a new access onto Metz Way. Recladding the station building was also part of the scheme as a 'nice to have', but would later be removed as the budget wouldn't stretch that far.

We had to make our case, which had to be rooted in economic benefit rather than just cosmetic improvement, in front of members of the LEP Board and their advisers. The team presenting were myself, City Council Managing Director Jon McGinty and David Roberts of Jones Lang LaSalle (who was working with us on Kings Quarter), who was brought in to add a private sector perspective. The project also had the support of Gloucestershire County Council, train operator GWR and Network Rail.

We pointed to the thousands of people who work at Gloucestershire Royal Hospital and believed that a more attractive route would encourage more of them to come into the city centre. It would also help connect the development sites, such as Wessex House and the former Railway Sidings.

In February 2018, it was announced that we were to be awarded £3.7 million. It was less than we had hoped for, but still a welcome boost for the city. It meant we would either need to make up the shortfall from another source or 'value engineer' the plans to fit the budget.

GFirst LEP Chief Executive, David Owen, said; 'The investment will not only create a much better environment for passengers but will provide more attractive, safer and inclusive access. It will also improve the connectivity of the city.'

I added, "Working with GWR, Network Rail and Gloucestershire County Council, the investment at the Railway Station will not only create a much better environment for passengers but will also provide a safer, more attractive access and improve the connectivity of the city. I'd like to thank GFirst LEP for supporting this project and sharing our vision for the future of Gloucester."

Work had originally been planned to start in Spring 2020, but soon fell behind the original schedule. Such complex engineering projects are prone to slippage and Network Rail aren't renowned for being the fastest organisation to work with.

The LEP funding was later increased to £4.3 million and in September 2020, the Department for Transport announced another £1.7 million of funding for the project, making the overall total £6 million. This came from the Railway Station Improvement Fund and City MP Richard Graham tells me he put the bid together with GWR, writing to the then Rail Minister Chris Heaton-Harris. The new access onto Metz Way was officially opened in December 2021.

As the planning for the works advanced, it became apparent that the ceiling of the subway was suffering from corrosion. Works to the Bruton Way junction, including wider pavements and upgraded traffic lights, started after Easter 2022 and were completed by October 2022. The subway closed and construction work started in March 2023 but was delayed by issues relating to the electricity supply, with a new substation unexpectedly needing to be built. The subway wasn't expected to re-open until Summer 2024 at the earliest.

Westgate Street, the 'Cathedral Quarter'

In November 2019, the City Council successfully secured £1.9m of funding from Historic England to invest in Westgate Street.

In May 2019, Historic England had launched a £95 million High Streets Heritage Action Zones fund to revive historic high streets through the scheme. Gloucester was one of 68 towns and cities across England selected to receive a share of the funding.

The decision to focus our bid on Westgate Street was a fairly straightforward one as it has some fantastic buildings and is the most complete of our gate streets, but evidently needed a boost. It was decided to badge the bid as the 'Cathedral Quarter'. I was keen that our bid captured some of Westgate's great stories – like the Tailor of Gloucester, Colonel Massey and Jemmy Wood to name a few.

The Historic England website sets out the rationale behind the project, saying, "One of four original Roman routes, Westgate links the spectacular medieval cathedral to the rest of the city. Its array of stunning historic buildings includes the 15th century timber-framed Fleece Inn and Judges' Lodgings, both of which are on Historic

England's Heritage at Risk register. Despite its strong historic character, proximity to the cathedral and good location, Westgate Street is underperforming.

"Westgate's retail environment has changed dramatically in recent years. It once had a strong mix of independent businesses whose owners embraced the street's historic buildings, but many have moved on and prospective new owners feel the properties are expensive to run and difficult to convert. The street scene is tired, with poor paving, inconsistent signage, and general clutter. Many retail units stand vacant. Locals perceive the area in a negative light and of the thousands of visitors to the cathedral, few are attracted into Westgate Street.

"The Heritage Action Zone will capitalise on Westgate's untapped potential and boost the number of people living, working and taking pride in the area. The award of up to £1.9 million to Gloucester City Council will invest in Westgate Street's beautiful historic buildings, repairing buildings and historic shopfronts and converting vacant upper floors for new uses. There will be advice and support for businesses in historic properties, and the streetscape will be improved with new signage and branding. The area will be vibrant with cultural activities, from community archaeology to performing arts, and will become known for its attractive evening and night-time offer. The Heritage Action Zone will help Westgate thrive again by bringing a modern business approach to an outstanding historic environment."

The award was one of the last announcements to be made before I stood down as Leader of the Council. It came after our bid to the Government's Future High Streets Fund, for a much larger amount, was unsuccessful.

At the time, I commented: "This is fantastic news for Westgate Street and the city centre as a whole. Westgate Street is our most complete historic street, with the Cathedral, The Fleece and a host of other heritage buildings. It does need some help to make it the jewel we know that it can be and I'm delighted we have been awarded this grant funding to help it reach its full potential. The award also includes funding for The Fleece, which will boost the efforts we are already making to regenerate this important site."

At the time of writing, work had taken place to strip back buildings as part of The Fleece complex in order to reveal historic features and on the former Meek's shoe shop at number 14 Westgate Street. This is a Grade II*-listed building with a fine plasterwork ceiling dating from the 17th century. The funding is being used to convert the upper floors of the property into flats and to conserve and restore the plasterwork. Work has also taken place to secure the facade at St Nicholas House (the Dick Whittington pub) and repurpose the upper floors as function rooms. 39 and 41 Westgate Street, two long-term problematic buildings, also received attention. The yellow ochre-finished timber-framed exterior of number 41, a 500-year-old Grade II listed property which had been on the 'at risk' list for a number of years, was unveiled in August 2023. A grant is also being used to repair the roof and undertake an options appraisal for the former Poundstretcher building, which was once the Theatre Royal. An additional floor is being added to 88 Westgate Street (on the corner of Three Cocks Lane) on what was an incongruous single-storey building. As discussed in Chapter 12, the former Folk Museum (now named The Folk of Gloucester and run by the Civic Trust) had works undertaken to repair and restore its $16^{th}/17^{th}$ century façade and limewash it in the bright colours that would have been used at the time.

The scheme is due to run until the end of March 2024.

23. A TALE OF TWO CITIES

Since Gloucester Quays has been built, it has become almost fashionable to say that all of the investment in Gloucester has gone into the Docks and Quays and the city centre has been neglected. Former Citizen editor Jenny Eastwood used the phrase "A Tale of Two Cities", after the title of the Charles Dickens novel, to describe the situation, whereas my ambition was for Gloucester to be a "single, cohesive destination". But which is the reality?

It's true that, as things stand, the quality of the two environments is out of kilter and the long-term impact of the pandemic has been much more obvious for the city centre than for Gloucester Quays. Locations by water have a head start anyway, but the quality of the public realm in the Docks and Quays area is much higher than the rather tired state of the city centre gate streets, particularly Eastgate and Westgate, which were pedestrianised in the 1980s and early 1990s and have seen little investment since. The buildings too are more generally attractive, with the Docks and Quays having avoided any large-scale 1960s and 70s brutalist interventions of the kind that have scarred the city centre. It's also true that the management and maintenance of the Docks and Quays, funded through occupier and resident service charges, is better than can be afforded by council taxpayers in the city centre.

Since the development of the leisure quarter at Gloucester Quays, anchored by a relocated cinema, the balance of the city's evening economy has shifted. Gloucester Quays, and to a lesser extent the Docks, has become the go-to place for dining. It's true that the development here has stopped the leakage of a lot of night-time spend to other places, particularly Cheltenham. The city centre's night-time economy is now concentrated on the clubbers' strip in Eastgate Street, with a few heritage pubs like Café Rene, The Old Bell, The New Inn and The Fountain and a handful of independent restaurants.

Footfall levels in the city centre and at Gloucester Quays were poles apart a decade or more ago, but are now closer – although different counting systems make direct comparisons difficult. In its first year (2009/10), Gloucester Quays barely managed 1.5 million visitors whereas Kings Walk was believed to have recorded around 10 million. It's a busy route from the bus and railway stations to the rest of the city centre, so not all were shoppers but the difference was stark. As Gloucester Quays has become established, its footfall grew steadily to 8 million a year in 2019. There was, obviously, a decline in visitor numbers during the pandemic but both footfall and spend have seen year on year growth since restrictions were lifted. Kings Walk had seen its footfall gradually decline over the years, in common with many other city centres, and it nosedived during the pandemic, but is now seeing steady growth again.

Being in a single ownership, albeit after many years of patient land assembly, makes life much easier in terms of decision-making at the Quays than it is in the city centre with its fragmented ownership, often made up of absentee landlords. The same is largely true of the Docks, where the Canal and River Trust (formerly British Waterways) retains the freehold and the head leasehold covering much of the site is now in the hands of the City Council following the abolition of the South West Regional Development Agency. The City Council also owns the freehold of North Warehouse and the adjacent North Quay, as well as the long lease of its former offices at the Herbert, Kimberley and Phillpotts warehouses.

The South West Regional Development Agency (SWRDA) invested in the Docks, buying the headlease from developer Crest Nicholson and working in partnership with them to convert the warehouses, and later to transform the public realm from a sea of tarmac car parking to quality paving and public art. SWRDA also invested in the South West bypass, which was vital to enable Gloucester Quays to go ahead and financed the pedestrian linkages project connecting the Quays, Docks and city centre. English Partnerships paid for the new bridge over the canal next to the Peel Centre to connect to the bypass.

So, the public sector did invest many millions of pounds into the Docks and Quays but, aside from relocating its own offices to the Docks in the 1980s, none of that came from the City Council. The one exception was the assistance, by way of a loan, that the Council gave to Rokeby Merchant to acquire Bakers Quay, but even then the funding came from Homes England, channelled through the City Council. It certainly wasn't true that the Council owned Gloucester Quays as some claimed or that it had a vested interest in the decline of the city centre. In fact, the opposite was the case.

The City Council has a big financial interest in the city centre, firstly from running the car parks which have provided well over £2 million a year of income. For many years it has owned the freehold of the Kings Walk and Eastgate shopping centres, with others holding the long lease, but in more recent years it has joined in a partnership with Reef Group to take on the lease for Kings Walk in 2017 and buying in the lease of The Eastgate at the end of 2019.

The Council also committed £2 million, from the sale of land at St Oswalds to Tesco, to city centre projects as well as spending £7 million on land acquisition for the Kings Quarter scheme and approving a spend of £5 million for the long-awaited refurbishment of Kings Square. The deal with Reef for Kings Walk had led to a £1 million refurbishment of the Kings Walk car park, a redevelopment of the former BHS unit to house an upsized Primark store, new public toilets including the city centre's first Changing Places facility (just off Clarence Street) and a refurbishment of the Kings Walk mall. The Council also spent £700,000 refurbishing the Eastgate rooftop car park in 2016 and was awarded £11 million through the Levelling Up Fund in November 2023 to create a new garden quarter in the Greyfriars area, including improvements to the Eastgate Shopping Centre, in particular a new indoor market hall.

Upon acquiring The Fleece hotel site from SWRDA, the Council immediately spent £350,000 on emergency repairs, although none of this has been visible, with the doors of the former Inn remaining firmly closed. Further works were carried out to The Fleece as part of the Cathedral Quarter project, for which the City Council successfully secured £1.9 million of funding from Historic England. It also led to the restoration of a number of prominent buildings in Westgate Street.

Let's not forget the £8.7 million of public money (mostly Government grant) used to build the new bus station/transport hub, which opened in 2018. By far the biggest investment the City Council has made (in its entire history) is the £107 million commitment to building 'The Forum' at Kings Quarter, which was agreed in January

2021. For a council with an annual budget of around £14 million, this represents a brave, bold move.

The paving in the gate streets is, strictly speaking, the responsibility of the County Council as the highway authority. But, in reality, any major scheme to revamp it would have to be financed by the City Council as the County's finances are stretched with an ever-growing burden of Adult Social Care and Children's Services. I regret not being able to get this done, but at some point it will need to be addressed – although quite how the multi-million pound cost will be met is far from clear.

So although the City Council has put its own money into the city centre, the private sector hasn't invested in the centre in the same way as Peel had in the Quays. Peel's business model is different to that of many developers. It develops and holds its assets for the long-term, whereas most developers look for a quick return by developing and then selling the asset onto a financial institution. By contrast, financial appraisals for Kings Quarter under the Stanhope retail-led proposals never reached the required 15% profit margin and that's why it didn't go ahead.

Prior to their acquisition by the City Council, the owners of Kings Walk (Aviva) and Eastgate (which seemed to change every few years) hadn't invested in the assets and seemed to be content to sit back and collect the rent. In the short term that may have seemed an attractive proposition but in the longer term it was a flawed strategy. The failure of retail-led regeneration schemes firstly at Blackfriars and then at Kings Quarter, it could be argued, led retailers and landlords to hold off from major investments while they waited to see what happened. The lack of a major city centre regeneration scheme wasn't for the want of trying, but its consequences, both directly and indirectly, were profound.

There were some honourable exceptions, like the new M&S store in the former Woolworth store and TK Maxx opening in its former Northgate Street premises, but these didn't add up to anything comprehensive. The Linden Homes scheme at Greyfriars, supported by Homes England, the student accommodation at Blackfriars (aided by £4 million of Government grant) and the Rooftop housing scheme at Black Dog Way contributed to the long-term repopulating of the city centre, as did many other smaller schemes, but these were slightly away from the main historic core of the city centre.

The third sector played its part too, with Project Pilgrim at the Cathedral, Discover DeCrypt at St Mary de Crypt in Southgate Street and the Civic Trust's restoration of St Michael's Tower, all of which are set out in more detail elsewhere in this book.

Plenty of effort has gone into trying to regenerate the city centre over the years, some of it successful, other parts of it less so. In reality, it is complex in a historic city centre and difficult to make commercially viable where property prices and rents are low and costs, such as archaeology, are high. This means public sector intervention is needed to make things happen. As discussed earlier, the Regional Development Agency was abolished in 2011. English Partnerships (the Government's former regeneration agency) was replaced by the Homes and Communities Agency (later renamed Homes England), with a mission to deliver new housing rather than fulfil a broader regeneration role. This meant the role of leading regeneration fell squarely to the City Council, often bidding to the Local Enterprise Partnership (GFirst) for government funds.

There are only so many projects a small district council like Gloucester City can take on at once. At the time of writing, the Council is juggling Kings Quarter/The Forum, Kings Walk, the Eastgate Shopping Centre, The Fleece, Bakers Quay phase II, the former offices at the Docks, the Cathedral Quarter and St Oswalds Park. Major financial interventions are possible when interest rates are low, but can be difficult to make viable when rates are just a few per cent higher.

So what is the future for the city centre? There have been plenty of reports on the future of town and city centres over the years. There was the Mary Portas review and the subsequent 'Portas pilots' – which seemed more about creating a television series than effecting lasting change and seemed to sink without trace. Then there was the Timpson report by Sir John Timpson of the shoe repair chain and the Grimsey review by former Iceland boss Bill Grimsey.

All recognised that the amount of retail space needed in future would be reduced, due to the rise of internet shopping (which has been accelerated by the Coronavirus pandemic) as well as the expansion of supermarkets. Town centres would need to be about more than just retail and would need to offer a variety of experiences.

As Grimsey put it, they would need to be "community hubs not retail hubs".

I travelled to Roeselare in Belgium with Grimsey and other council leaders in July 2019. Roeselare, led by Mayor Kris Declercq, is held up as an example of a place which has successfully implemented the Grimsey recommendations. A phrase of Declercq's which stuck with me is "back to the Agora" – with the Agora being the Ancient Greek gathering place for civic, cultural, business and political life. Grimsey recommended setting up a 'Town Centre Commission' to oversee a 20-year plan for the centre. I made this recommendation in a report I put together after my trip to Roeselare and the city established its own commission in summer 2020 to replace the Regeneration Advisory Board.

Gloucester certainly needs more people living in the city centre and this is an objective the City Council has had for a number of years, with some success. There is more which can be done to repurpose vacant buildings in and around the city centre for residential. But on its own this is not enough – particularly if those people disappear out of the centre to go to work during the day. We need more people working in the city centre. This is unlikely to come in the form of traditional offices in the wake of Coronavirus, but more probably as flexible workspaces. The digital and technology campus being built at The Forum at Kings Quarter will be an important part of this, as is 'Jolt', the 'cultural entrepreneurs' hub' already established by the Gloucester Culture Trust at Kings House, overlooking Kings Square.

The refurbishment of Kings Square will only be a success if the space is animated with events and activities. Let's hope that is the case. Gloucester had built up a strong programme of events, but the pandemic and the demise of Marketing Gloucester took away that momentum. A strong events programme must be built now that life has returned to somewhere near normal.

Other cultural activity and making the most of our heritage will be vital as well. I genuinely hope the Museum of Gloucester will get the full revamp it deserves to make it a museum worthy of a city with the rich and proud history of Gloucester. I am confident that, under the Civic Trust's stewardship, The Folk of Gloucester in Westgate Street will become a thriving heritage resource for the city.

The demise of Debenhams is sad, particularly given its local heritage as the Bon Marche, but it also offers an opportunity. The building is around 230,000 sq ft. Back in 2017, Debenhams told me they only needed 70,000 sq ft. It's hard to believe that as the retailer's demise edged closer, there were some councillors saying it should remain as a department store at all costs. The plans by the University of Gloucestershire for a new City Campus, bringing in 4000 students to the city centre, are the best outcome Gloucester could have hoped for and will bring vibrancy to Kings Square in particular and the city centre in general. It's not the only large space in the city centre that will need to be repurposed. The closure of the Sainsburys supermarket and the collapse of Wilko have left two big holes in Northgate Street that will need to be filled.

In 2023, the City Council published a 5-year vision for the city centre drawn up by the City Centre Commission with the help of the University of Gloucestershire on which the public were consulted. As visions go, it's not a bad effort. It proposes bringing new uses into the city centre, more greenery, engaging the public with the city's history and celebrating its cultural identity, amongst a long wish-list of improvements. What is unclear at this point is how it will be made a reality.

So, to answer the question posed at the start of this chapter, the city centre hasn't received the same levels of overall investment as the Docks and Quays over the last 20 years or so but has, quite rightly, taken a greater proportion of the City Council's attention and resources. Just as Peel has taken a long-term view of Gloucester Quays, someone (and it is only likely to be the City Council) has to take a long-term view of the city centre. I believe it can have a bright future but that will take a clear vision, dedicated resources, ongoing investment and the political will to see it through. Only when the historic core of the city centre is regenerated, when locals feel proud of it and talk of 'A Tale of Two Cities' is no more, will people in Gloucester believe that the regeneration of the city is anywhere near complete.

24. PERSONAL REFLECTIONS

This book is intended to be, primarily, about the regeneration of Gloucester. I have taken a broad view of the events and issues which have shaped that regeneration over two decades or more but they cannot be wholly separated from the local, and to some degree national, politics which influences them.

Let me say at the outset that being Leader of Gloucester City Council for over 12 years, and a councillor for 24 years, was an enormous privilege. I've been places, met people and had experiences that I never would have done otherwise. But I never sought to be Leader. My first stint as Leader of the Conservative Group (in opposition) came when I was first elected in 1996 at the low point of the John Major Government, when Pam Tracey and I made up the entirety of the Conservative Group. Pam didn't want to be Leader and, as I recalled at our charity anniversary dinner in 2017, "I later discovered she didn't want to be led either." At that time, we were up against 25 Labour councillors and 8 Liberal Democrats. I stayed as Group Leader until 2002 when I stood down to become Sheriff of Gloucester.

My first regeneration role was the following year when I became Chair of the Regeneration Scrutiny Committee which had been formed in response to the collapse of the Blackfriars development. That wasn't supposed to happen. The Lib-Lab administration at the time had lined up Labour councillor Mark Hobbs for the role and it was only because Barnwood Liberal Democrat councillor Ken Mitchell, who was a character I got on well with, broke ranks and supported me.

When the Conservative Group formed a minority administration in 2004, I slotted easily into the new regeneration portfolio. At the same time, I was preparing to fight my second Parliamentary election in Gloucester. I stood in 2001, when Tony Blair secured his second landslide victory, halving the Labour majority. My 'twinned' candidate in that election (where a 'safe' seat is paired with a marginal one) was one David Cameron who had just been selected for the Witney constituency. He came to canvass in Gloucester and was sent down Tweenbrook Avenue, but nobody at that time would have recognised him. To his credit, even when he was Prime Minister, he never forgot me. In the 2005 election, despite a huge effort, I was unable to dent the Labour majority any further. Parmjit Dhanda, who had been elected in 2001, had been a very energetic MP in his first term, had barely put a foot wrong and received acres of positive coverage in *The Citizen*. Despite fighting two bruising election campaigns against each other, Parmjit and I always got on well and I am grateful to him for his help with this book.

When Mark Hawthorne unexpectedly decidedly to stand down as City Council Leader – and from the Council entirely – in 2007 I had to be persuaded to take over and only did so on my own terms. I didn't want to be Leader of the Opposition again. I'd done that for long enough already. So, my appointment wasn't confirmed until after that year's elections.

Mark had cut the Leader's role from the full-time position established by Kevin Stephens to one based on two days a week. I followed that pattern for a couple of years but increased it initially by half a day and then a full day to three days a week. This came at a personal financial cost to me, so it was pretty galling when there was a front-page headline in *The Citizen* when the Independent Remuneration Panel recommended a £2000 pay rise for me. There was even a picture of a pig's snout on the same front page, which may have been coincidental but it seemed too much of a coincidence to me. To be fair, in Editor Ian Mean's comment column he did balance it by describing me as a "true servant of our city" and acknowledging that I'd "sacrificed greater rewards in the private sector."

That brings me on neatly to talk about pay. Being Leader for such a long time did come at a financial cost. If I had put as much time and effort into my career, I would have earned far more money than I did as Council Leader. But that was my choice. As Council Leader, I earnt more than a lot of people, but less than a lot of people too. I remember a senior military figure from the Allied Rapid Reaction Corps at Innsworth asking me, "What's the difference between the Leader and the Chief Executive?". "About £90,000 a year," I replied. (At the time, the Leader's allowance was about £25,000 a year and the Chief Executive's salary around £115,000). The Leader's role doesn't come with a pension and you don't get a fixed number of days holiday. I took very few and some of my days off from my 'other job' were taken up with council business. There wasn't any job security either. When elections were held in three years out of four, my job was in the hands of Gloucester's voters on an almost annual basis. In total, I fought seven elections as Leader as well as the one as 'Leader-in-waiting' in 2007. When the Council switched to all-out elections in 2016, it gave greater certainty but I still needed to be elected by my own Group each year. That I never faced a leadership challenge was probably due to the fact that nobody wanted the job!

In reality, I had only intended to serve for five years maximum and had tried on a number of occasions to pass the baton on, but had been persuaded to continue. When I told my Group in May 2019 that I would stand down later that year it forced the issue.

Being Council Leader in a small city like Gloucester means you are more well-known and accessible than you are in a large, rural area. Being a place with challenges and where there is a lot going on adds another layer of pressure. It was almost impossible to walk down the street without seeing someone I knew or a resident saying, "Oh Mr James, could I just have a word?" I enjoyed being recognised but it did have its downsides too. I could be having a pint with a friend in the pub and somebody would come up and complain about their bin not being emptied or a parking ticket they felt they'd been given unfairly. Once I was out running and someone started running alongside me to lobby me on some issue or other. Obviously, they couldn't keep up for very long!

I worked long hours too. I would often be the first in the office and had a good relationship with the cleaners, Sandy and Esther. I could have up to a dozen appointments a day, as well as numerous letters, calls and texts, over 100 emails a day and, in more recent years, comments on social media to deal with. Most evenings and weekends I would have something on, whether it was a Council meeting or an event I'd been invited to attend. I often wouldn't get home until 9 or 10 at night. It didn't matter when I was young and single and I thrived on the adrenalin. I ran or went to the gym several times a week early in the morning and being physically fit was vital to keep pace with my schedule and stay mentally sharp.

When my eldest daughter Eirys was born in 2015, I knew I couldn't keep this up. Having reduced the size of the Cabinet from six to five and taken on extra responsibilities myself as a cost-saving measure, I reversed that decision and appointed Lise Noakes to the newly-created Culture and Leisure portfolio, despite some noise from the Opposition about the £9000 a year cost. I delegated parts of what was an enormous portfolio to hold in addition to the Leadership. Lise was able to give more time and attention to cultural issues and we reaped benefits from this, particularly in terms of Arts Council funding. On my non-council days, I would work for a few hours at home early in the morning before going into my job at estate agents Naylor Powell rather than going into the council offices. I tried to limit my evening and weekend commitment to the ones that really mattered so I could spend more time at home. I felt that I managed it fairly well, but it still seemed to me that I was being pulled in different directions.

It's worth pointing out that being invited to attend events, which

I readily accept is a privilege, still felt like work and even if I didn't have an official role like making a speech, I would still be lobbied about one issue or another and would end up with a list of things to follow up afterwards. I was conscientious in declaring any hospitality received. In fact, for years I thought the value threshold for declaration was £25 rather than the £100 it really was and I ended up declaring many invitations I didn't need to. In 2019, Private Eye, based on the declarations I'd made, accused me of "ligging" at Gloucester Rugby. I had to look up what it meant, which is "to attend a function in order to take advantage of free entertainment and refreshments". I did get invited to hospitality several times a season by different friends, businesses or the Club itself and I enjoyed it. I've had a season ticket at Kingsholm for almost 40 years (which, to the surprise of some people, didn't come as a perk of the job) and, while hospitality is nice from time to time, I probably enjoy the rugby most of all when I'm in my own seat watching the match and having a pint with no distractions at all.

Being a Council Leader is also a unique management challenge. You have to manage your own group of councillors, who can often be complex and unusual characters, who are there because they volunteered and were elected rather than being chosen by you. You have to be careful about upsetting them because you rely on them to re-elect you to your position each year. You have to invest time in the 'pastoral' side of management to keep your own side on board. You have to manage relationships with the Opposition Groups, particularly if you have a small majority or, as was often the case, no majority at all. And you have to manage relationships with Council Officers, although as a Council Leader you don't line manage anyone other than the Chief Executive and aren't allowed to directly instruct anyone more junior. Michael Gove famously referred to 'The Blob' in the Civil Service as being a blockage to making things happen. The same can be true of Council Officers. Have them on your side and they can help you to achieve results. Without them you can't really do anything. I've worked with all kinds during my time – from those who are supremely motivated to get things done and who go the extra mile, to those who do as little as possible and can find a reason for not doing anything. You have to invest time too in external relationships, whether that is with key partners like the County Council, the Local Enterprise Partnership, the University, the Police or the Cathedral or, from a regeneration perspective, investors and developers.

Most councillors are in it for the right reasons – to do their best for their community. But even local politics can be a brutal business. I am grateful to many of my former councillor colleagues for their loyalty and support over the years. On the whole, we were a pretty united band. But, as I learnt, you can't always rely on people who you have supported, promoted and dug out of holes on many occasions to return the favour when you need it. That's just life, I guess.

To end on a positive note, it's often said that being a Council Leader is a thankless task. It isn't. As well as the brickbats that get thrown, the criticism for things that aren't even in your control and the abuse on social media, you do get plenty of thanks too – when you can achieve positive outcomes for individuals and when things go right for the city as a whole.

I remember being out in Hampden Way clearing litter as part of one of our community clean-up days. Someone approached me and said, "I just want to say that I know that sometimes it must feel like a crap job, but I just want you to know that we appreciate it." I wasn't sure if she recognised me or thought I was a street cleaner, but the principle is the same and it's comments like this that make it all worthwhile.

Did I enjoy my time as Leader? Yes, without doubt. Did I get everything right? Of course not. Do I wish I had done some things differently? With hindsight - yes, absolutely. My motivation has only ever been to help the city I was born and brought up in and what was most important to me was being able to go to sleep at night in the knowledge I had done my best. During my time in office, together (and that's the most important word) we achieved a lot. There's plenty still left to work on and my greatest wish is that the regeneration of this wonderful city, which so many people have worked so hard and so long to achieve, is completed and Gloucester fulfils the enormous potential we all know it has.

25. GLOUCESTER'S REGENERATION – A TIMELINE

March 1985
Council moves out of the ground floor of The Guildhall.
July 1986
Refurbished North Warehouse handed over to the City Council.
November 1986
Official opening of The Guildhall as an arts centre.
July 1987
Pearce Developments granted outline planning consent for mixed-use development of The Docks.
May 1987
Official opening of North Warehouse.
April 1988
National Waterways Museum opened.
April 1989
Outline planning consent granted for new magistrates' court at Blackfriars.
November 1990
City Council goes out to procurement to find developer partner for Blackfriars scheme.
April 1992
John Major's Conservative Government unexpectedly re-elected with a small majority.
Secretary of State 'calls in' planning application for magistrates' court at Blackfriars.
June 1992
City Council agrees to investigate creating a University for Gloucester.
Action Group established to fight Tesco supermarket proposal at Oxstalls.
July 1992
Public inquiry into magistrates' court proposals. The application is rejected.
May 1993
Planning appeal for Oxstalls supermarket dismissed.
July 1993
Oxstalls Campus closed.
August 1993
Outline planning consent granted for supermarket at Cattle Market site.
July 1994
Local Plan inspector rules that new supermarket should be at the Cattle Market not Oxstalls.
Planning consent granted for magistrates' court designed by Quinlan Terry.

April 1995
Arrowcroft chosen as developer for Blackfriars scheme.

October 1995
Consultants Strategic Leisure told to press ahead with Lottery bid for Leisure Centre.

Government issues moratorium on the building of new courts, scuppering plans for a new magistrates' court at Blackfriars.

November 1995
Planning application for Blackfriars submitted.

December 1996
Detailed planning consent issued for Tesco supermarket at the Cattle Market.

March 1997
City Council 'minded to grant' planning consent for Blackfriars development.

April 1997
Tom Walkinshaw buys majority stake in Gloucester Rugby Club.

May 1997
Tony Blair's Labour Government elected by a landslide.

February 1998
New Inn closed after being put up for sale by owners Greene King.

April 1998
City Council approves funding for Leisure Centre rebuild. Provisional award of Sports Lottery funding of £10.453 million.

June 1998
Planning application approved for Leisure Centre rebuild.

July 1998
Gloucester Leisure Centre closes ahead of a rebuild. Lottery funding confirmed.

August 1998
Council issues development brief for St Oswalds to shortlist of developers.

September 1998
Crest Nicholson submits a planning application for a new Leisure Quarter including a multiplex cinema at Gloucester Docks.

October 1998
Councillors choose Grantchester as developer for St Oswalds.

January 1999
Arrowcroft submits a planning application for the first phase of the Blackfriars development including a multiplex cinema and multi-storey car park. M&S pull out of Blackfriars development.

May 1999
Phase I of Leisure Centre works completed.

Compulsory Purchase Order issued for land at Blackfriars including BT's car park.

June 1999
Beatties department store signs up as 'anchor tenant' for Blackfriars. Land at Blackfriars sold by the County Council to the City Council for £1.1 million.

July 1999

Work starts on the Llanthony to Hempsted Bridge section of the South West Bypass.

Cinema schemes for the Docks and Blackfriars considered by Full Council.

February 2000

Outline planning consent granted on appeal for Docks cinema.

March 2000

City Council decides that a livestock market will no longer be part of plans for St Oswalds site.

April 2000

Planning application for St Oswalds development submitted.

July 2000

Hempsted section of South West Bypass completed.

August 2000

City Council's attempt to overturn decision on Docks cinema dismissed. Second Blackfriars Compulsory Purchase Order issued.

October 2000

City Council issues planning consent for Blackfriars cinema

November 2000

Demolition starts at Oxstalls Campus.

December 2000

Planning Inspector grants consent for hotel at Barnwood.

January 2001

City Council publishes an Urban Design Strategy for Gloucester.

February 2001

Docks cinema building design approved on appeal.

March 2001

City Council 'minded to grant' planning permission for Westgate Street hotel.

April 2001

Planning consent issued for comprehensive redevelopment at Blackfriars. Blackfriars Compulsory Purchase Order inquiry opens.

May 2001

BT lodges judicial review of the City Council's decision to issue planning permission for Blackfriars redevelopment.

June 2001

Parmjit Dhanda elected as Labour MP for Gloucester. Tony Blair's Labour Government elected by another landslide.

July 2001

City Council transfers Westgate Street car park to Selsdon Group to build new four-star hotel.

August 2001

City Council approves planning application for St Oswalds development.

September 2001

The Livestock Market which had been closed due to Foot & Mouth Disease will not reopen.

October 2001

Cheltenham and Gloucester College of Higher Education granted university title to become the University of Gloucestershire.

November 2001
Judge quashes planning consent for Blackfriars development, causing the Compulsory Purchase Order inquiry (and the development) to collapse.
January 2002
Council Leader Kevin Stephens declares Blackfriars scheme "Dead in the water".
March 2002
Gloucester Quays planning application submitted.
June 2002
St Oswalds Park planning decision 'called in' by the Government Office for the South West.
July 2002
City MP Parmjit Dhanda asks PM Tony Blair if he will approve an Urban Regeneration Company for Gloucester.
Concerns raised about possible fraud in relation to Westgate Hotel proposals.
August 2002
Kwik Save supermarket in Northgate Street closes.
New Leisure Centre GL1 opens to the public.
October 2002
New Oxstalls Campus officially opened by Parmjit Dhanda MP.
Fleece Hotel in Westgate Street closes.
October/November 2002
St Oswalds development planning Public Inquiry held.
February 2003
St Oswald's planning inspector's report sent to Deputy PM John Prescott.
April 2003
Fleece Hotel bought by SW Regional Development Agency.
Work starts on the Castlemeads section of the South West Bypass.
May 2003
Submission made to the Office of the Deputy Prime Minister requesting approval for an Urban Regeneration Company for Gloucester.
June 2003
City Council recovers land at Westgate Street car park after court case.
October 2003
John Prescott gives go-ahead for St Oswalds Park.
February 2004
Approval given by Government to set up Gloucester Heritage Urban Regeneration Company (GHURC).
March 2004
GHURC first board meeting following Government approval.
April 2004
English Partnerships, the Government's regeneration agency, buys the GlosCAT Brunswick Campus.
June 2004
Conservatives form a minority administration on the City Council under Mark Hawthorne's leadership.
The Learning & Skills Council agree £15 million towards the new GlosCAT Campus.

July 2004
Plans for £1.1 million revamp of Gloucester Park published.
September 2004
First meeting of the GHURC Board under the chairmanship of Greg Smith.
Work starts on St Oswalds Park development.
Designs for new Barge Arm and Barge Arm East buildings in the Docks revealed.
October 2004
Plans revealed by Highland Developments for 84 apartments on the old Kwik Save site.
November 2004
Announcement that the Debenhams building has been acquired by Morley Fund Management (part of Norwich Union).
Gloucester Quays development given the thumbs-up by the City Council after a marathon 5-hour meeting.
January 2005
Speculation that Costco could be coming to the Railway Triangle.
February 2005
Castlemeads section of South West Bypass opens to traffic.
April 2005
County Council Cabinet instructs contractor Norwest Holst to start work on the final (Netheridge) section of the South West Bypass.
Crest Nicholson completes the refurbishment of the Vinings and Double Reynolds warehouses at the Docks.
Tom Walkinshaw pledges to redevelop main grandstand at Kingsholm.
May 2005
Parmjit Dhanda re-elected as MP for Gloucester as Tony Blair wins a third general election for Labour.
Chris Oldershaw appointed Chief Executive of GHURC.
Bishop Michael Perham joins the Board of GHURC.
June 2005
Deputy PM John Prescott orders a public inquiry into the Gloucester Quays development.
July 2005
Comet sign up for a unit at St Oswalds Park.
August 2005
Gloucester Antiques Centre in the Docks put up for sale with a price tag of £1 million.
The House of the Tailor of Gloucester, the Beatrix Potter Museum and Shop in College Court, closes.
September 2005
The old B&Q closes.
October 2005
New B&Q at St Oswalds Park opens.
Laing Homes complete their development at West Quay in the Docks.
Work starts on new GlosCAT campus at Llanthony.
November 2005

Share appeal launched to buy the House of the Tailor of Gloucester.
Gloucester Quays planning inquiry starts.
December 2005
Consultants DTW appointed to come up with a Marketing Strategy for the city.
February 2006
Compulsory Purchase Order for residential elements of St Oswalds Park confirmed.
March 2006
£160,000 target to buy the House of the Tailor of Gloucester reached.
April 2006
Westbury Homes' plan for 450 homes at St Oswalds approved.
Plans for a new bridge over the canal to connect the 'road to nowhere' to the South West Bypass are revealed.
June 2006
South West Regional Development Agency completes the Mariners Square public realm works at the Docks.
Gloucester Quays development approved by Secretary of State Ruth Kelly.
Plans for a new 7500-seater stand at the Kingsholm Stadium are submitted to the City Council.
July 2006
Regeneration Framework approved by GHURC Board.
August 2006
Nightclub Jumpin' Jaks in Brunswick Road closes its doors for the last time.
September 2006
GHURC appoints Donaldsons to undertake a feasibility study for a community stadium at the Railway Triangle.
Keys for former Teapots building, in Westgate Street, handed over to Swan Developments.
October 2006
Crest Nicholson completes the construction of new apartments, commercial units and multi-storey car park at the Barge Arm at the Docks.
Plans revealed by Gloucester Civic Trust to rejuvenate St Michael's Tower as a Heritage Centre.
GHURC Regeneration Framework launched at Gloucester Cathedral and the Houses of Parliament.
Lock Warehouse 'believed to be' sold to developer Evan Maindonald.
Pizza Piazza and Maddison's Café at Merchants Quay in the Docks close.
November 2006
Gloucester holds its Christmas lights switch-on event – with no lights!
December 2006
Biddle & Shipton Warehouses at the Docks converted into apartments.
Edinburgh Woollen Mill at Merchants Quay closes.
January 2007
City Council & Norwich Union sign the Kings Quarter Co-operation Agreement. Thornfield Properties appointed as development consultants by Norwich Union.
February 2007

English Partnerships award the contract to construct the St Ann Way bridge.

March 2007

City Council Cabinet approves the lease of St Michael's Tower to Gloucester Civic Trust.

English Partnerships select Edward Ware Homes as their preferred development partner for the Greyfriars development.

April 2007

Gloucester Rugby decide to stay at Kingsholm, their 'spiritual home', prompting a rethink of the Railway Triangle proposals.

Vinings Restaurant opens at Gloucester Docks.

Planning application for Contract Chemicals site in Bristol Road submitted by Commercial Estates Group.

May 2007

Paul James elected Leader of Gloucester City Council.

£90 million Bakers Quay plan by Broadway Malyan architects unveiled by the Bishop family and presented to the GHURC Board.

Urban Initiatives appointed to produce Kings Quarter masterplan.

Final stretch of the South West Bypass opens.

Borders bookstore at St Oswalds Park approved by Planning Committee.

June 2007

Construction work starts on the St Ann Way bridge.

Construction work on Gloucestershire College's new Llanthony Campus is completed.

Construction work starts on Gloucester Quays outlet centre.

Clothing giant Next quits its city centre store.

Gordon Brown succeeds Tony Blair as Prime Minister.

July 2007

Gloucester hit by severe flooding, affecting hundreds of homes and Gloucester City's football stadium. The water supply is lost for 17 days.

August 2007

Sainsbury's confirm they are opening an 84,000 sq ft store at Gloucester Quays.

Borders bookstore pulls out of its plan to open at St Oswalds Park.

September 2007

The new Gloucestershire College at Llanthony opens.

New grandstand at Kingsholm completed.

October 2007

Inaugural Gloucester Tall Ships Festival held.

November 2007

Kings Square International Design Competition launched by GHURC.

January 2008

Plans revealed to relocate the University of Gloucestershire's Arts, Media and Communications faculty to Blackfriars.

Planning application for new Sainsbury's supermarket at Gloucester Quays lodged.

February 2008

LDA Design and other specialists appointed to work on Docks linkages project.

Plans for 417 homes at Bakers Quay revealed.
GVA Grimley appointed to work on Railway Triangle masterplan.
March 2008
Sainsbury's granted detailed planning consent for new superstore at Monk Meadow as part of Gloucester Quays development.
Retail scheme for the former B&Q site on Trier Way involving Next and TK Maxx set to be turned down.
March 2008
Mark Owen elected as Chairman of Marketing Gloucester and £65,000 a year Chief Executive job advertised.
April 2008
'Gloucester Through The Ages' event held in the city.
HeadKandy Hairdressing opens in the Barge Arm East at Gloucester Docks.
May 2008
Persimmon Homes pauses work on speculative developments including The Marketplace at St Oswalds Park.
English Partnerships re-tenders Greyfriars scheme following unsatisfactory progress with the Edward Ware Homes proposals.
'Topping out' ceremony at Gloucester Quays.
HomeSense opens at St Oswalds Park.
June 2008
Shock as The New County Hotel in Southgate Street closes.
July 2008
Niall McLaughlin Architects and Churchman Landscape Architects appointed to design new Kings Square.
South West Regional Development Agency completes Shipton Square public realm works.
Marks & Spencer signs up as one of the anchor stores at Gloucester Quays.
Purpose-built 199-pitch market site at Hempsted Meadows opens.
August 2008
Graham Walker appointed Chief Executive of Marketing Gloucester.
Plans unveiled for a £9 million investment to refurbish and extend the cinema at the Peel Centre and add four new restaurant units.
City Employment and Skills Programme formally launched with Ahmed Goga as its Director.
September 2008
Ecclesiastical Insurance announces plans to build a new multi-million-pound headquarters on the Southgate Moorings car park at Gloucester Docks.
The New County Hotel could be turned into 10 apartments with a restaurant on the ground floor.
The collapse of US bank Lehman Brothers prompts a worldwide financial crisis.
October 2008
Plans for a 120-room Ramada Encore hotel next to Llanthony Priory are submitted.
Businessman Martin St Quinton buys 25% of Gloucester Rugby from Tom

Walkinshaw.
Pirates Weekend held at Gloucester Docks.

November 2008
The St Ann Way bridge, now renamed High Orchard Bridge, is opened to traffic.
Public art within the Docks commissioned from Wolfgang Buttress and Katayoun Dowlatshahi.
Construction of new Sainsbury's superstore at Gloucester Quays commences.
£21 million 169-home development by Rooftop Housing and ExtraCare Living gets underway at St Oswalds Park.
The Robert Raikes' House pub in Southgate Street opens after a £4.5 million refurbishment.

December 2008
Marketing Gloucester goes live.
Bakers Quay plan "put on hold for two years".

January 2009
Woolworths closes its Eastgate Street store with M&S tipped to take it over.
Envy & Lansons nightclub (formerly KCs) closes.
Linden Homes confirmed as development partner for English Partnerships at Greyfriars.
Commercial Estates Group obtains planning permission for the former Contract Chemicals site on Bristol Road.

February 2009
Planning consent granted for residential development on the former Monk Meadow Trading Estate.
City Council starts process of finding a developer partner for Kings Quarter.

March 2009
Regional Development Agency announces budget cuts running into tens of millions, with concerns for the Quays linkages scheme.
Work starts on £300,000 facelift of St Michael's Tower.

April 2009
Idea of a statue of Colonel Edward Massey, to be installed in the city centre, floated by the Civic Trust.

May 2009
Parmjit Dhanda MP secures an Adjournment Debate on funding for the Quays/city centre linkages.
75,000 people visit the second Tall Ships Festival on the same weekend as the Gloucester Quays Outlet Centre opens.
Crest Nicholson lodges planning application to demolish Merchants Quay.
Caffé Tucci to open within a month at the Barge Arm East in the Docks.

June 2009
106-bedroom Travelodge and Sainsbury's supermarket at Gloucester Quays opens.
Plans revealed for a 23-metre tall piece of public art at The Docks.
Gloucester Antiques Centre moves to new premises at Gloucester Quays.

July 2009

Kings Square interim works unveiled.
City Council puts Greyfriars land deal for proposed Four Gates Centre on hold following withdrawal of SWRDA funding.
Moving City Council offices to Blackfriars dismissed as "unrealistic and prohibitively expensive".
City MP Parmjit Dhanda tells a Westminster debate that the Docks linkages scheme is "absolutely crucial".
England win rights to host Rugby World Cup 2015. Kingsholm is named in bid document but this doesn't mean it will necessarily host matches.

August 2009
Replacement Merchants Quay building goes to City Council planning committee.
Consultation launched on latest Blackfriars masterplan.
National Waterways Museum could close by the end of September unless volunteers found to run it.

September 2009
St Michael's Tower opens with a dedication service from Bishop Michael Perham.
Pizza Express to open at Gloucester Quays.
Nandos to open at Gloucester Quays before Christmas.
Planning committee rejects proposal for a 'Swingers' Club at the New County Hotel. It opens anyway a short time after.

October 2009
University of Gloucestershire pulls out of Blackfriars plans.
County Council secures £5 million from Department for Schools, Children and Families for the construction of a Language Immersion Centre.
New plan for Kwik Save site goes public.
Bandstand demolished at Gloucester Park.
Government gives go-ahead for £7.4 million of funding for Docks linkages scheme.

November 2009
Contract for 'Route 1' of the Docks linkages along the Victoria Basin, including Back Badge Square, awarded to Britannia Construction.

December 2009
'Club Mystique' opens at the former New County Hotel.

January 2010
Planning committee considers Victorian-style replacement bandstand.

February 2010
Planning permission granted for phase one of Bishop family's proposed development at Bakers Quay.
Balfour Beatty start work on Southgate Street section of linkages project.

March 2010
Spartans RFC and Kingsholm & Wotton Neighbourhood Partnership move into former YMCA building in Sebert Street.
Artist Tom Price selected to develop public art in new Kimbrose Square.
Kings Quarter developer Thornfield Properties goes into administration.

April 2010
City Council approaches St Oswalds developer Hammerson to take on Kings

Quarter project.
<u>May 2010</u>
Richard Graham defeats Parmjit Dhanda to become Conservative MP for Gloucester. Conservatives and Liberal Democrats form coalition government with David Cameron as Prime Minister.
'Club Mystique' at the New County closes.
Former British Legion buildings and BT car park at Blackfriars acquired by City Council for a total of £1.2 million with SWRDA funding.
Demolition of Merchants Quay gets underway.
<u>June 2010</u>
City Council agrees to bid to English Heritage to run Blackfriars Priory as an events venue.
New bandstand now in place in Gloucester Park.
Funding agreed for Horsbere Brook flood alleviation scheme.
Hammerson say a viable development of Kings Quarter is not deliverable.
SWRDA and Ecclesiastical Insurance agree terms for a new office HQ at Southgate Moorings in Gloucester Docks.
<u>July 2010</u>
County Council grants planning permission for the Language Immersion Centre on the former Clutch Clinic site at Blackfriars.
Fleece Hotel is placed on the English Heritage 'at risk' register.
£700,000 RDA investment into Blackfriars Priory agreed.
Plans for Victorian Market at Gloucester Docks announced.
<u>August 2010</u>
Railway Triangle masterplan published.
'The Candle' at The Docks is installed. Planning permission is granted for St Kyneburgh's Tower and the Art Wall at Kimbrose Triangle.
Eastgate Shopping Centre bought by investment fund Rockspring as part of a package of shopping centres.
City Council set to move out of North Warehouse.
<u>September 2010</u>
News breaks that Marketing Gloucester is in financial trouble.
Domino's Pizza to open at St Oswalds Park.
Discover DeCrypt project launched.
<u>October 2010</u>
St Oswalds ExtraCare Village opens.
GHURC to be slimmed down and transferred to the City Council.
<u>November 2010</u>
EG Carter start construction of Language Immersion Centre.
Fears of 'fire sale' of RDA assets in the city.
Tewkesbury Borough Council approves Horsbere flood alleviation scheme.
<u>December 2010</u>
Phase II of public realm works in the Docks, from Albion Square to Back Badge Square, completed.
Demolition of BT Repeater Station and E & J Printers building at Blackfriars approved.
Demolition of GlosCAT Tower approved by Planning Committee.

January 2011
City Council enters into 'exclusivity agreement' with Stanhope for Kings Quarter.
Works underway on £2.1 million Back Badge Square at the Docks.
Stephen Lake named as the new Dean of Gloucester Cathedral.
Planning application for Greyfriars submitted by Linden Homes.

February 2011
Work on Horsbere flood scheme about to start.
Application lodged to demolish Pulp record store, underground 'bear pit' toilets and former Golden Egg restaurant in Kings Square.

March 2011
Southgate Street and Kimbrose Triangle elements of Quays to city centre linkages work completed.

April 2011
GlosCAT Tower demolished.
North and East Ranges of Blackfriars Priory opened for public use.
Demolition of the Golden Egg approved.
Former SWRDA assets to be transferred to the City Council.
Debenhams to get multi-million-pound refurbishment.

May 2011
M&S to move to former Woolworths store in Eastgate Street.
Ecclesiastical Insurance sign deal with SWRDA to move to new HQ in the Docks.
Bakers Quay up for sale.
New £25 million Tesco to be built at St Oswalds.

June 2011
City Council Cabinet approves disposal of North Warehouse.

July 2011
Developer LXB exchange contracts with Network Rail and sign up Morrisons supermarket for the Railway Triangle.

August 2011
Work set to start in Kings Square to demolish Pulp record store and demolish underground 'bear pit' toilets.
Railway Triangle planning application submitted.
'Disturbances' in the city centre and Barton & Tredworth.
Gloucester Tall Ships Festival takes place.

September 2011
Urgent works start on The Fleece.
£60 million leisure quarter on the way at Gloucester Quays.

October 2011
Work starts on the conversion of Lock Warehouse at the Docks.
Museum dedicated to the Korean War could be opening at the Docks.

November 2011
Planning application submitted for new cinema and restaurants at Gloucester Quays.
Planning committee approve Greyfriars planning application for 257 residential units and associated commercial units.

December 2011
Supermarket proposals for Tesco at St Oswalds and Morrisons at the Railway Triangle approved by Planning Committee.
£200,000 Eastgate Viewing Chamber replacement set to start next month.
January 2012
£2 million pledged for the city centre from Tesco land sale.
Heads of Terms agreed with Stanhope for Kings Quarter.
February 2012
Crest Nicholson completes development at Merchants Quay in the Docks.
Frustration as Aviva says it will refurbish rather than demolish the Golden Egg.
March 2012
Rugby star Phil Vickery launches the Believe in Gloucester campaign.
Speculation that a new IKEA store could be coming to the Peel Centre.
May 2012
Opening of Language Immersion Centre at Blackfriars.
First stage approval given for £1.2 million Southgate Street Townscape Heritage Initiative.
June 2012
Keys to Blackfriars Priory handed over by English Heritage Commissioner Sir Tim Laurence to the City Council to run as an events venue.
July 2012
Project Pilgrim at Gloucester Cathedral unveiled.
New M&S opens in Eastgate Street.
September 2012
Work starts on new cinema at Gloucester Quays.
Smiths Demolition start work on the Railway Triangle.
Kings Quarter development agreement with Stanhope signed.
TK Maxx coming to former M&S in Northgate Street. B&M to take Southgate Street store.
Gloucester City Football Club application goes to planning committee, but no decision is made as further work is needed, particularly on flooding and highways.
October 2012
Gloucester in the running to be Rugby World Cup host city.
Barnwood Construction wins contract to build Railway Triangle supermarket for Morrisons.
November 2012
Lock Warehouse showhome opened by Richard Graham MP.
December 2012
Work underway at North Warehouse in the Docks to convert it to a Regus Business Centre.
January 2013
Closure of HM Prison Gloucester announced by Ministry of Justice.
Rokeby Developments present development proposals for Bakers Quay to the GHURC Board.
Planning Committee approve 50% reduction in affordable housing at

Greyfriars following fears about viability.
Barnwood Construction start on site to build the new Morrisons Supermarket at the Railway Triangle.

February 2013
City Council allocates £100,000 for Kings Quarter design work.
Ecclesiastical pull out of Docks HQ move.

March 2013
Commencement of demolition at GlosCAT media site.
Premier Inn hotel, Brewers Fayre restaurant and Costa Coffee drive thru announced for Bakers Quay.
Planning application for 80-bed care home on Southgate Street site submitted by Markey Developments.
Wren Kitchens to open at St Oswald's Park.
£493,000 Heritage Lottery award for the Soldiers of Gloucestershire Museum.
Meadow Park still the preferred option for Gloucester City FC but the former Civil Service Club site also being considered.
GHURC is wound up with a new Regeneration Advisory Board taking its place.

April 2013
TK Maxx pulls out of deal to occupy the former M&S Northgate Street store.

May 2013
Formal announcement that Gloucester will be a Rugby World Cup host city.
Gloucester Tall Ships Festival takes place.
Former GHURC Chair and Vice Chair Greg Smith and Ian Mean granted Freedom of the City.

June 2013
Stanhope says it has an anchor tenant for Kings Quarter but won't be submitting a planning application just yet.

July 2013
Believe in Gloucester awards launched.
City Council agrees £350,000 budget for Rugby World Cup.
Bid for cash for new bus station to Gloucestershire Local Transport Board unsuccessful.

August 2013
Staff at Gloucester Antiques Centre turn up to find the doors locked at Gloucester Quays premises.
Gloucester City Football Club stadium planning application refused.

September 2013
The Fleece Hotel goes on the market.
Liberal Democrats 'call-in' Llanthony Priory decision.
Southgate Street Townscape Heritage Initiative and Discover DeCrypt both have first stage Heritage Lottery grants approved.

October 2013
Planning permission granted for new hotel in Clarence Street.

November 2013
Morrisons supermarket opens at the Railway Triangle.

Demolition order slapped on the Golden Egg.
Llanthony Secunda Priory awarded first stage lottery grant of £311,400.
December 2013
The Golden Egg is going at last – work to start in the New Year.
2000 sign petition against moving the Indoor Market.
January 2014
Competition launched to find members of the public to 'take a crack' at the Golden Egg.
Appointment of Jason Smith to be Chief Executive of Marketing Gloucester announced.
Former M&S in Northgate Street, The Fleece and the former furniture shop in Kings Walk all possible sites to relocate the Indoor Market.
February 2014
Home Bargains application to open store at the Peel Centre refused.
Gloucester Prison put up for sale.
£2 million revamp on the cards for Gloucester Railway Station.
TGI Friday's set to come to Gloucester Quays and plans for new 'Market Square' at Gloucester Docks revealed.
March 2014
30 expressions of interest received for former Prison site.
Dobbies Garden Centre could open at Tesco St Oswald's site.
Richard III exhibition, including reconstructed head, on display at City Museum.
Stanhope's Martyn Chase says the Kings Quarter development will be completed by the end of 2018.
April 2014
Artist's impression of reclad Eastgate Street car park frontage revealed.
USA qualify for Rugby World Cup leading to speculation that Barack Obama could visit Kingsholm.
New 'Welcome to Gloucester' signs put in place in time for Rugby World Cup.
YMCA's £12 million plan for The Fleece goes public.
External works start on St Michael's Tower.
City MP Richard Graham tells Parliament of his vision for the Blackfriars area.
Local Transport Body approves £2.2 million for bus station.
Dick Bishop promises an announcement on Bakers Quay in 3-4 weeks.
Deadline for bids for Gloucester Prison.
May 2014
Fewer retail units and more residential now planned for Kings Quarter.
Mayor of London, Boris Johnson, visits Gloucester.
Agreement signed between City and County Councils to develop Blackfriars masterplan.
Archaeological dig in Kings Square.
June 2014
£320,000 award from Heritage Lottery Fund for Project Pilgrim at Gloucester Cathedral.
Eastgate Indoor Market to stay put.

Gloucester City Football Club submits detailed planning application.
Archaeological dig at the bus station.
August 2014
'Alice Through the Looking Glass' filmed at Gloucester Docks.
September 2014
TK Maxx renews interest in the city.
Planning inquiry into Home Bargains Peel Centre application.
City MP Richard Graham and City Council Leader Paul James launch regeneration hitlist.
Eastgate Shopping Centre put up for sale by Rockspring.
600 people queue at GL1 Leisure Centre to be Rugby World Cup volunteers.
October 2014
Gloucester City Football Club stadium application goes to Planning Committee.
City Council Cabinet agrees £50,000 grant for Cathedral's Project Pilgrim.
Home Bargains planning appeal for new store at the Peel Centre allowed.
'Mystery bidder' in talks over Prison.
November 2014
'Scrumpty' figure for sculpture trail unveiled.
Landmark deal for Kings Quarter land acquisition agreed.
December 2014
Bill's Restaurant to come to Gloucester Quays.
Claims that the city will be pleased with the identity of the buyer of Gloucester Prison.
January 2015
Tesco scraps its plans for a new store at St Oswalds.
Former M&S in Northgate Street to be filled by discount store Pure Bargains.
City Council debates a Compulsory Purchase Order for Bakers Quay.
Transport Secretary Patrick McLoughlin visits Gloucester to announce £4.13 million of Government Growth Deal funding for Blackfriars.
February 2015
Stanhope's promise to deliver Kings Quarter by December 2018 branded a "Christmas Miracle" by *The Citizen*.
City Council Leader Paul James announces exchange of contracts on the sale of Bakers Quay at a Full Council meeting.
March 2015
Blackfriars joint City/County Council masterplan launched.
Deal signed to transfer the City Council's 4442 units of housing stock to Gloucester City Homes.
Plans to relocate the University of Gloucestershire's Business School from Cheltenham to Oxstalls unveiled.
May 2015
Artist's impression of new bus station revealed.
Richard Graham re-elected as MP for Gloucester and Conservatives win overall majority in Parliament under David Cameron. Gains help Conservatives to win an overall majority on the City Council.
Long-term vacant building at 27-29 Commercial Road put on the market to

find a developer.
Bakers Quay images revealed.
Former Jumpin' Jaks building in Brunswick Road sold and plans revealed to open it as an over 25s venue.
Planning committee approves the conversion of Albion House in Southgate Street to apartments, with a terrace of four houses to the rear and a new apartment building adjacent to it.
Gloucester Tall Ships Festival takes place.
Trial archaeological trenches dug at Gloucester Cathedral to inform Project Pilgrim.

June 2015
Carluccio's restaurant coming to Gloucester Quays.

July 2015
Wetherspoons pub, The Lord High Constable of England, opens at the Docks.
Cladding of ugly buildings won't be done in time for the Rugby World Cup.
The Citizen reports that discussions are taking place between Stanhope and the City Council on a 'Plan B' for Kings Quarter.
Brewhouse & Kitchen to open at Gloucester Quays.

August 2015
Gloucester Quays visitor numbers reach 5 million a year.
The Citizen reports that the City Council has spent £7 million on the Kings Quarter project.

September 2015
Bakers Quay planning application submitted.
New restaurants planned for 27-29 Commercial Road.
Rachel Treweek inaugurated as the Bishop of Gloucester – the country's first female Diocesan Bishop.
Planning consent granted for new stadium for Gloucester City Football Club.

September/October 2015
Rugby World Cup matches played in Gloucester.

October 2015
Gloucester City Football Club mark 3000 days away from Meadow Park.
Fire at Provender Mill building at Bakers Quay.

November 2015
Archaeologists uncover an incredible tomb full of coffins while digging at Gloucester Cathedral.
Kwik Save site to come forward with an as yet un-named housing association.
Work starts on 26 Westgate Street to prepare for the new Gloucester Antiques Centre to move in.

December 2015
Norman castle walls and keep found at former Prison site.
New Gloucester Antiques Centre opened in Westgate Street.
Planning permission for new bus station granted.

January 2016
Former M&S store in Northgate Street sold to Northgate No 1 Securities Ltd.
City Council debates whether Gloucester should petition for Royal City status.

Sydney Opera House-style performance venue building suggested for Gloucester Docks.

Work starts on Rygor Mercedes-Benz commercial dealership at the Railway Triangle.

February 2016

It is reported that the City Council could leave the Docks.

Demolition work starts on new bus station site.

Image of new Provender Mill released.

University Business School plans recommended for approval.

Council budget includes £100,000 to help Gloucester City Football Club return to Meadow Park.

Martin St Quinton buys the Walkinshaw family stake in Gloucester Rugby.

It is announced that Gloucester's magistrates court is to close.

City Council approves reduction in Marketing Gloucester's funding of £200,000 a year over two years.

March 2016

Labour and Liberal Democrat Group Leaders say it is time to 'scrap Kings Quarter'.

Kings Quarter mixed-use 'Plan B' revealed.

Deal agreed between City Council, GWR and Ministry of Justice for new railway station car park.

£4.8 million land acquisition loan agreed by City Council for Bakers Quay.

New planning application submitted by Gloucester City Football Club for phased stadium development.

£7 million Heritage Lottery Fund grant agreed for two city heritage sites – Gloucester Cathedral and Llanthony Priory.

April 2016

City Council buys freehold of 23-25 & 27-29 Commercial Road.

May 2016

All-out elections held for the City Council. Conservatives win 22 out of 39 seats.

Kier Construction appointed to build new bus station.

June 2016

Barnwood Construction appointed to build phase one of Bakers Quay.

Demolition at old bus station complete.

Announcement that Kings Walk shopping centre has been 'sold' to Vixcroft for £20 million.

EU referendum held. Britain votes to leave. Prime Minister David Cameron quits.

Consultation on revised Kings Quarter plans.

July 2016

Archaeological dig at bus station site begins.

Theresa May becomes Prime Minister.

4 options unveiled for Kings Quarter.

August 2016

Brexit threatens £20 million Kings Walk sell-off as financial backer pulls out.

Archaeologists discover Roman flood defences at bus station site.

September 2016

Vixcroft working to find alternative backer for Kings Walk.

Coronation of Henry III re-enacted at Gloucester Cathedral to mark its 800th anniversary.

HRH The Duke of Gloucester buries a time capsule at the bus station site.

Home Bargains set to open before Christmas at the Peel Centre.

October 2016

Gloucester City Football Club stadium planning application approved.

Second archaeological survey work begins at Gloucester Cathedral for Project Pilgrim.

November 2016

Local Development Order submitted for Blackfriars.

Jones Lang LaSalle and LDA Design appointed to work up Kings Quarter planning application.

First apartments at Albion House, Southgate Street go on show.

Archaeological dig takes place at The Fleece.

December 2016

Work at Bakers Quay has started.

Stage Two Heritage Lottery grant for Discover DeCrypt approved with an award of £1.36 million.

January 2017

City Council turns down investment in Kings Walk with Vixcroft.

Work starts on former Kwik Save site.

Third consultation event for Gloucester Prison site.

Landscaping works begin at Gloucester Cathedral for Project Pilgrim.

February 2017

Planning consent granted for first phase of student accommodation at Blackfriars.

March 2017

TK Maxx opens in Northgate Street.

Work starts on highway changes for new bus station.

£50,000 contribution for Project Pilgrim announced by City Council.

May 2017

Communities Secretary Sajid Javid approves Blackfriars Local Development Order.

Tall Ships Festival takes place with launch of Henson Pig trail.

June 2017

General election held. Conservatives, under Theresa May, lose overall majority in Parliament.

Bids for £4.8m and £9.5m for Railway Station improvements submitted.

£700,000 investment in 'grand staircase' and performance area at Docks approved.

Announcement that City Council could move to Shire Hall.

July 2017

City Centre Business Improvement District (BID) approved in ballot with 83% voting in favour.

Partnership deal between City Council and Reef Group for Kings Walk approved.

Bus station plans "scaled back" – by 1 metre!

10th anniversary service for the 2007 Floods held at Cathedral.

Arson attack at The Fleece.

August 2017
Consultation on Royal City status for Gloucester starts.

September 2017
Kings Quarter will be split into four plots and work could start in 12 months.

October 2017
City Council decides against pursuing Royal City status for Gloucester.

Council offices at the Docks could become a hotel.

November 2017
Plans for a Tom Denny stained-glass window at Gloucester's new bus station revealed.

'Secret talks' over St Oswalds land.

December 2017
City Council Cabinet agrees to draw up a development brief for The Fleece and to test the market with potential developers.

January 2018
Primark deny they have any plans to relocate their Gloucester store.

UK Digital Retail Innovation Centre planned for the first floor of the Eastgate Shopping Centre is awarded £400,000 of funding.

February 2018
Bruton Way car park and Bentinck House to be demolished next year.

Second bid for Railway Station funding of £4.3 million.

March 2018
Reef Group consult on improvements to Kings Walk.

April 2018
Foundation stone laid on stone-built section of new bus station.

First phase of new railway station car park complete.

'Topping out' ceremony at new bus station.

June 2018
Work gets underway to create new public space now known as Orchard Square at The Docks.

Construction work finishes at Gloucester Cathedral for Project Pilgrim.

August 2018
Council office move plans 'don't add up' say Liberal Democrats.

Grand re-opening of Llanthony Priory marked with Stone Carving Festival.

September 2018
Latest proposals unveiled for Kings Quarter.

New Business School opens at the Oxstalls Campus.

Student accommodation at Blackfriars completed.

October 2018
City Council debates return of Gloucester City Football Club.

New bus station (Gloucester Transport Hub) opens.

November 2018
50th anniversary of Eastgate Indoor Market (in current location).

Ecclesiastical Insurance announce they are to leave their city centre offices.

Phase Two of Blackfriars student accommodation approved by Planning Committee.

Stonemasonry works to the Lady Chapel finish at Gloucester Cathedral as part of Project Pilgrim.

December 2018

Planning application submitted for Kings Quarter.

City needs 1000 capacity venue according to Marketing Gloucester Chief Executive Jason Smith.

January 2019

Planning application submitted for scaled back stadium for Gloucester City Football Club.

February 2019

Archaeologists are hoping to uncover Whitefriars Friary.

April 2019

Report into new performance venue for Gloucester published by AEA Consulting.

May 2019

Tall Ships Festival held.

Planning consent issued for scaled back Gloucester City Football Club stadium.

Paul James steps down as Chair of Marketing Gloucester.

July 2019

City Council deal with Reef for Kings Walk wins MJ (Municipal Journal) Award.

Boris Johnson becomes Prime Minister following Theresa May's resignation.

September 2019

Dowdeswell Estates announced as preferred bidder for The Fleece.

City Council approves £240,000 loan to Marketing Gloucester.

November 2019

£1.9 million awarded to make Westgate Street a High Street Heritage Action Zone.

New images of Kings Square revealed.

Paul James stands down as Leader of Gloucester City Council and is replaced by Richard Cook.

City Council Cabinet agrees to contribute £150,000 over three years to Phase II of the Cathedral's Project Pilgrim.

December 2019

Part of Prison site put up for sale.

Conservatives win 80-seat majority in snap general election called by Prime Minister Boris Johnson.

City Council confirms £54 million purchase of St Oswalds Retail Park.

January 2020

Midas appointed contractor for Kings Square.

City Council confirms purchase of the Eastgate Shopping Centre.

February 2020

Marketing Gloucester put into liquidation.

March 2020

City Council grants planning consent for Kings Quarter/Kings Square.

Demolition of unsafe elements of Downings Malthouse at Bakers Quay takes place.
First Covid-19 lockdown.

September 2020
Extra funding granted for improvements to Gloucester Railway Station.
First match played at Gloucester City Football Club 'New Meadow Park' stadium.

October 2020
Announcement that the 'long lost' Whitefriars Friary has been found.

November 2020
Work re-starts in Kings Square with local firm EG Carter as contractor.

January 2021
City Council approves £107 million investment in Kings Quarter with Reef Group.
City Council grants detailed planning consent for Plot 3a at Kings Quarter – a ground floor retail unit for Tesco with apartments above.

March 2021
The University of Gloucestershire announces it has purchased the Debenhams building in Kings Square to create a new City Campus.

May 2021
Conservatives secure a big majority on the City Council in the postponed elections, winning 26 out of 39 seats.
Contractors EG Carter start work on new Tesco Express store with 19 apartments above on Market Parade as part of Kings Quarter.
The Debenhams store in Gloucester shuts its doors for the last time.

June 2021
Peel announce that the Gloucester Quays Outlet Centre and Leisure Quarter is up for sale for £105 million.

September 2021
The JOLT creative workspace and Music Works studios open on the upper floors of Kings House, overlooking Kings Square.

October 2021
Gloucester is awarded £20 million from the Government's Levelling Up Fund towards the University of Gloucestershire's new City Campus in the former Debenhams, The Fleece and The Forge at Kings Quarter.
Peel sell Madleaze Trading Estate on Bristol Road to Picton Property for £13 million.

December 2021
Project by the City Council and Rooftop Housing Group to develop housing on the remaining land at St Oswald's Park awarded £2.2 million from the Government's Brownfield Land Release Fund.

February 2022
Kier Construction appointed contractor for Phase Two of Kings Quarter/The Forum with work due to start in March 2022.
Final Covid restrictions lifted.

March 2022
First tenants for Gloucester Food Dock revealed.

Planning consent granted for the conversion of the former Debenhams building to the University of Gloucestershire's City Campus.

April 2022

The 'new' Kings Square officially opened.

May 2022

Gloucester Tall Ships Festival takes place, having been delayed for a year by the pandemic.

November 2022

Reports that plans for four-star hotel at former council offices at the Docks are 'set to fail'.

December 2022

Phase Two of the Blackfriars student accommodation is completed.

February 2023

A £12.5 million bid to the Government's Levelling Up Fund for a new 'garden quarter', based around Greyfriars and the Eastgate Shopping Centre, is rejected.

Plans for over 300 homes on disused railway land in Great Western Road approved by the Planning Committee.

March 2023

Hotel Indigo sign up to be operator of the hotel at The Forum at Kings Quarter.

April 2023

Plans for the 'Downings Tower' at Bakers Quay approved by the Planning Committee – on the Chair's casting vote.

July 2023

Contracts exchanged for the sale of land at St Oswald's Park to Rooftop Housing Group to deliver 300 homes.

Announcement that Costco are to build a new store on the former Interbrew site on Eastern Avenue.

October 2023

The City Council secures £477,903 from the Government's Brownfield Land Fund to unlock development of 32 more apartments at The Forum.

The City Council selects a new preferred developer for the Herbert, Kimberley and Phillpotts Warehouses at the Docks.

November 2023

Reports that Gloucester Quays is being marketed for sale by agents Cushman & Wakefield for £85 million.

Government announces £11 million for Greyfriars 'garden quarter' project from Round Three of the Levelling Up Fund.

January 2024

It is revealed that the City Council has diverted £6.3 million of Levelling Up Fund money from The Fleece project to the University of Gloucestershire's City Campus and The Forum.

February 2024

New interest in The Fleece revealed from the Phoenix Village Project to create a "state-of-the-art community hub".

NOTES

[1] https://www.city-journal.org/html/horror-story-12312.html
[2] *The Citizen* 28/5/01
[3] GHURC submission May 2003
[4] *The Citizen* 10/12/84
[5] *The Citizen* 2/7/86
[6] *The Citizen* 2/11/92
[7] *The Citizen* 1/5/90
[8] *The Citizen* 28/9/90
[9] *The Citizen* 20/9/00
[10] *The Citizen* 4/10/00
[11] *The Citizen* 13/2/01
[12] *The Citizen* 31/3/95
[13] *The Citizen* 24/6/95
[14] City Council Higher Education sub-committee March 1996
[15] Hugh Worsnip column, *The Citizen* 13/12/96
[16] Higher Education sub-committee February 1997
[17] City Council Highways & Planning Committee June 1997
[18] Higher Education sub-committee February 1999
[19] *The Citizen* 2/10/97
[20] *The Citizen* 2/1/98
[21] City Council Directors Board & Chamber of Commerce meeting 2/2/99 & Higher Education sub-committee February 99
[22] *The Citizen* 10/10/98
[23] *The Citizen* 15/7/96
[24] *The Citizen* 19/5/98
[25] Planning permission ref 01/758/COU & listed building consent ref 01/741/LBC granted for a variation of consent ref 99/673/COU & 99/674/LBC.
[26] GHURC final report
[27] *The Citizen* 16/1/16
[28] *The Citizen* 10/1/11
[29] *The Citizen* 23/6/17
[30] *The Citizen* 27/10/11
[31] *The Citizen* 8/5/15
[32] *The Citizen* 13/2/16
[33] GHURC annual report 2008/9
[34] GHURC Regeneration News

[35] *The Citizen* 26/5/11
[36] *The Citizen* 26/2/13
[37] City Council planning committee report
[38] Letter from Janet Trotter 3/8/92
[39] *The Citizen* 3/7/93
[40] *The Citizen* 19/5/93
[41] *The Citizen* 11/7/94
[42] *The Citizen* 27/7/94
[43] *The Citizen* 27/5/93
[44] *The Citizen* 12/7/94
[45] *The Citizen* 28/1/95
[46] *The Citizen* 20/6/96
[47] *The Citizen* 19/8/96
[48] *The Citizen* 16/12/96
[49] *The Citizen* 17/12/96
[50] *The Citizen* 22/7/98
[51] *The Citizen* 26/8/98
[52] *The Citizen* 22/10/99
[53] City Council Members Information Sheet 5/7/00
[54] *The Citizen* 28/9/00
[55] GHURC Network News February 2008
[56] *The Citizen* 30/1/08
[57] *The Citizen* 14/6/89
[58] *The Citizen* 28/7/89
[59] Blackfriars judgement 2001
[60] *The Citizen* 12/11/90
[61] *The Citizen* 3/8/93
[62] *The Citizen* 13/7/94
[63] *The Citizen* 14/9/94
[64] *The Citizen* 26/3/96
[65] *The Citizen* 7/4/95
[66] *The Citizen* 18/4/95
[67] *The Citizen* 8/11/95
[68] *The Citizen* 19/12/95
[69] *The Citizen* 26/3/96
[70] City Council Planning sub-committee 18/3/97
[71] *The Citizen* 9/6/98
[72] *The Citizen* 29/1/99
[73] City Council report July 1999
[74] City Council report July 1999

[75] *The Citizen* 12/5/99
[76] *The Citizen* 29/1/99
[77] *The Citizen* 21/6/99
[78] *The Citizen* 16/7/99
[79] Planning application ref 44668/01/OUT granted 27.4.89
[80] *Gloucester News* 23/3/89
[81] *The Citizen* 28/4/89
[82] *Gloucester News* 4/10/90
[83] *Gloucester News* 8/11/90
[84] *The Citizen* 23/5/91
[85] *The Citizen* 5/8/93
[86] *The Citizen* 30/7/93
[87] *The Independent* 24/8/93 (https://www.independent.co.uk/arts-entertainment/art/news/architecture-update-courthouse-row-1463304.html).
[88] Planning application ref 44688/06/FUL 12/7/94
[89] *The Citizen* 14/7/94
[90] *The Citizen* 13/7/94
[91] *The Citizen* 5/4/95
[92] *The Citizen* 26/10/95
[93] *The Citizen* 11/8/97
[94] Memorandum 21/10/98
[95] *The Citizen* 4/8/99
[96] *The Citizen* 12/4/01
[97] C Mallard letter to G Seaman BT 7/12/98 offering to buy BT land
[98] *The Citizen* 10/12/01
[99] *The Citizen* 12/12/01
[100] *The Citizen* 24/1/02
[101] Gloucester Civic Trust 30th Annual Report 2001
[102] *The Citizen* 26/3/02
[103] *The Citizen* 18/10/03
[104] *The Citizen* 11/7/06
[105] *The Citizen* 29/8/07
[106] *The Citizen* 17/7/09
[107] *The Citizen* 7/8/09
[108] http://urbed.coop/projects/blackfriars-project-creative-quarter-gloucester
[109] City Council Asset Management Strategy 2012
[110] *The Citizen* 15/11/93
[111] https://vhh.co.uk/project/gloucester-blackfriars/

[112] *The Citizen* 1/10/03
[113] GHURC Regeneration News November 2010
[114] BBC website
[115] *The Citizen* 17/5/10
[116] *The Citizen* 11/4/14
[117] Hansard 10/4/14
[118] *The Citizen* 16/5/14
[119] Hansard 9/9/14
[120] *The Citizen* 30/1/15
[121] *The Citizen* 7/3/15
[122] *The Citizen* 16/10/96
[123] *The Citizen* 5/7/96
[124] *The Citizen* 21/3/97
[125] *The Citizen* 21/11/98
[126] *The Citizen* 20/3/00
[127] *The Citizen* 17/3/00
[128] *The Citizen* 8/9/00
[129] *The Citizen* 21/10/00
[130] *The Citizen* 22/9/01
[131] *The Citizen* 26/8/03
[132] *The Citizen* 26/8/03
[133] *The Citizen* 16/10/03
[134] *The Citizen* 15/9/04
[135] *The Citizen* 29/11/94
[136] *The Citizen* 1/5/08
[137] *The Citizen* 22/11/08
[138] *The Citizen* 15/10/10
[139] *The Citizen* 26/1/21
[140] *The Citizen* 16/11/17
[141] Report to City Council Scrutiny Committee October 2002
[142] *Gloucester Voice* magazine Summer 1999
[143] *The Citizen* 23/3/00
[144] *The Citizen* 16/1/99
[145] *The Citizen* 30/6/99
[146] *The Citizen* 16/1/02
[147] *The Citizen* 20/2/02
[148] Report to City Council Scrutiny Committee October 2002
[149] *The Citizen* 18/2/98
[150] *The Citizen* 19/2/98
[151] *The Citizen* 19/5/98

[152] *The Citizen* 5/4/96
[153] *The Citizen* 22/9/94
[154] *The Citizen* 18/4/00
[155] *The Citizen* 14/9/00
[156] Gloucester City Council Members' Information Sheet February 2004
[157] City Council Members' Information Sheet February 2004
[158] City Council Cabinet report Jan 2006
[159] *The Citizen* 6/9/00
[160] GHURC final report
[161] *The Citizen* 8/1/04
[162] *Western Daily Press* 3/3/04
[163] GHURC final report
[164] *The Citizen* 29/10/04
[165] *The Citizen* 24/10/06
[166] GHURC final report
[167] *The Citizen* 2/6/09
[168] *The Citizen* 16/2/11
[169] *The Citizen* 4/6/11
[170] City Council Planning Committee report November 2011
[171] *The Citizen* 11/9/06
[172] GHURC Network News September 2007
[173] GHURC annual report 2008/9
[174] Parmjit Dhanda MP Parliamentary News 2008
[175] *The Citizen* 15/2/16
[176] *The Citizen* 27/9/07
[177] GHURC annual report
[178] *The Citizen* 6/8/10
[179] *The Citizen* 7/7/11
[180] GHURC final report
[181] *The Citizen* 30/1/01
[182] *The Citizen* 31/1/01
[183] *The Citizen* 10/6/04
[184] *The Citizen* 16/8/04
[185] *The Citizen* 18/8/04
[186] *The Citizen* 22/11/04
[187] *The Citizen* 22/11/04
[188] *Western Daily Press* 24/11/04
[189] *The Citizen* 27/9/11
[190] *The Citizen* 26/2/14
[191] *GloucestershireLive* 12/6/21
[192] Network News April 2007 & January 2008 and Broadway Malyan masterplan

[193] *The Citizen* 7/2/08
[194] GHURC Business Plan 9/7/08
[195] *The Citizen* 11/12/08
[196] Planning applications ref 09/00346/LBC & 09/01096/REM
[197] *The Citizen* 30/5/11
[198] *The Citizen* 2/3/13
[199] *The Citizen* 25/3/16
[200] Gloucester City Council minutes 19/7/01
[201] *The Citizen* 26/10/95
[202] *The Citizen* 9/9/04
[203] *The Citizen* 18/3/06
[204] *The Citizen* 1/4/06
[205] *The Citizen* 3/6/13
[206] *The Citizen* 7/12/13
[207] *The Citizen* 17/2/09
[208] *The Citizen* 26/6/11
[209] *The Citizen* 7/4/11
[210] *The Citizen* 28/9/12
[211] *The Citizen* 22/6/13
[212] *The Citizen* 29/5/14
[213] *The Citizen* 9/2/15
[214] *The Citizen* 15/2/16
[215] *Gloucester Review* 10/11/17
[216] *Gloucester Review* 18/3/16
[217] *The Citizen* 21/3/16
[218] *The Citizen* 9/9/17
[219] *The Citizen* 15/9/17
[220] *The Citizen* 2/10/17
[221] *The Citizen* 27/12/18
[222] *The Citizen* 22/11/04
[223] *GloucestershireLive* 26/8/23
[224] *The Citizen* 25/9/13
[225] *The Citizen* 13/11/13
[226] *The Citizen* 1/4/16
[227] *The Citizen* 31/8/18
[228] *The Citizen* 3/2/09
[229] *The Citizen* 8/3/07
[230] *The Citizen* 23/12/11
[231] BBC website 14/3/12
[232] *The Citizen* 16/5/05
[233] *The Citizen* 19/8/16

[234] *The Citizen* 30/5/05
[235] *The Citizen* 21/3/97
[236] *The Citizen* 11/9/08
[237] *The Citizen* 1/6/09
[238] *The Citizen* 25/11/16
[239] *The Citizen* 12/3/13
[240] *The Citizen* 9/10/04
[241] *The Citizen* 13/11/15
[242] *The Citizen* 22/3/10
[243] *The Citizen* 4/4/13
[244] *The Citizen* 12/11/13
[245] *The Citizen* 17/12/13
[246] *The Citizen* 25/1/14
[247] *The Citizen* 12/6/14
[248] *The Citizen* 16/6/14
[249] *The Citizen* 4/9/14
[250] *The Citizen* 4/3/15
[251] *The Citizen* 13/7/15
[252] *The Citizen* 17/7/15
[253] *The Citizen* 5/1/16
[254] *The Citizen* 20/1/09
[255] The Pitt Report
[256] Chief Constable's report to the Police Authority
[257] Chief Constable's report to the Police Authority
[258] Chief Constable's report to the Police Authority
[259] *The Citizen* 19/11/05
[260] *The Citizen* 8/12/05
[261] *The Citizen* 23/11/06
[262] *The Citizen* 16/11/07
[263] https://www.bbc.co.uk/news/uk-england-gloucestershire-19107992
[264] https://www.gloucestershirelive.co.uk/news/gloucester-news/former-mayor-gloucester-help-bring-2906917
[265] *The Citizen* 29/9/11
[266] *The Citizen* 2/9/04
[267] *The Citizen* 1/12/03
[268] *The Citizen* 7/9/04
[269] https://www.bbc.co.uk/news/uk-england-gloucestershire-32843365
[270] Friends of Gloucester Cathedral Annual Report 2022
[271] Friends of Gloucester Cathedral Annual Report 2023
[272] *The Citizen* 11/4/05
[273] *The Citizen* 29/11/05

[274] *The Citizen* 15/2/06
[275] https://www.epcrugby.com/2006/07/13/kingsholm-development-update/
[276] *The Citizen* 26/9/14
[277] *The Citizen* 10/5/14
[278] *The Citizen* 14/5/14
[279] *The Citizen* 18/11/14
[280] *The Citizen* 4/8/15 & 8/8/15
[281] *The Citizen* 4/4/14
[282] *The Citizen* review of the year 2015
[283] *The Citizen* 27/2/16
[284] *Western Daily Press* 22/11/99
[285] *The Citizen* 19/12/05
[286] GHURC *Network News* June 2007
[287] This figure increased by nearly £50,000 in the liquidators' report published in May 2023, as a result of additional claims by HM Revenue & Customs and the City Council, although at the time of writing it is not known if these claims were accepted.
[288] South West Research Company
[289] *The Citizen* 27/12/18
[290] *The Citizen* 4/4/19
[291] *The Citizen* 7/8/02
[292] *The Citizen* 31/10/03
[293] *The Citizen* 31/10/03
[294] *The Citizen* 24/11/03
[295] *The Citizen* 9/7/10
[296] GHURC *Regeneration News* November 2010
[297] *The Citizen* 6/9/11
[298] *The Citizen* 26/11/16
[299] *The Citizen* 19/9/19
[300] GHURC final report
[301] BBC website 22 February 2013
[302] *The Citizen* 12/1/13
[303] *The Citizen* 8/12/15
[304] https://www.bbc.co.uk/news/uk-england-gloucestershire-24061262
[305] *The Citizen* 16/1/20
[306] *The Citizen* 20/9/05
[307] *The Citizen* 21/6/17
[308] *Gloucester Review* 2/3/18

Printed in Great Britain
by Amazon